MW01707332

Foundations

Readings in Pre-Confederation Canadian History

Margaret Conrad
University of New Brunswick

Alvin Finkel
Athabasca University

PEARSON
Longman
Toronto

National Library of Canada Cataloguing in Publication

Foundations : readings in pre-Confederation Canadian history / edited by Margaret Conrad and Alvin Finkel.

Includes bibliographical references and index.
ISBN 0-201-74378-7

1. Canada—History—To 1763 (New France) 2. Canada—History—1763–1867. I. Conrad, Margaret II. Finkel, Alvin, 1947–

FC161.F66 2004 971 C2002-906019-2
F1032.F68 2004

ISBN 0-201-74378-7

Vice President, Editorial Director: Michael J. Young
Acquisitions Editor: Christine Cozens
Marketing Manager: Ryan St. Peters
Developmental Editor: Adrienne Shiffman
Production Editor: Richard di Santo
Copy Editor: David Handelsman
Production Coordinator: Patricia Ciardullo
Page Layout: Heidi Palfrey
Literary Research: Lisa Brant
Photo Research: Amanda McCormick
Art Director: Mary Opper
Cover Design and Interior Design: Michelle Bellemare
Cover Images: Top-left: National Archives of Canada/C40162; top-centre: Jeffreys, Charles William/National Archives of Canada/C-010687, reproduced with permission of C.W. Jeffreys Estate, Toronto; middle-left: Institut und Sammlung für Völkerkunde der Universität Göttingen; botom-left: courtesy of Alberta Community Development, Alberta Provincial Archives; background: National Archives of Canada/MIKAN 99947

5 08 07 06 05

Printed and bound in Canada.

PEARSON
Longman

Contents

List of Sources

PART I

Ken S. Coates and William R. Morrison, "Winter and the Shaping of Northern History: Reflections from the Canadian North," in Kerry Abel and Ken S. Coates, eds., *Northern Visions: New Perspectives on the North in Canadian History* (Peterborough, ON: Broadview Press, 2001), 23–35.

"Constitution of the Iroquois Nations," www.constitution.org/cons/iroquois.htm

Ramsay Cook, "1492 and All That: Making a Garden out of a Wilderness," in Ramsay Cook, *Canada, Quebec, and the Uses of Nationalism* (Toronto: McClelland and Stewart, 1995), 51–72.

Alan Gordon, "Heroes, History, and Two Nationalisms: Jacques Cartier," *Journal of the Canadian Historical Association*, New Series, 10 (1999): 81–102.

James P. Ronda, "'We Are Well As We Are': An Indian Critique of Seventeenth-Century Christian Missions," *William and Mary Quarterly*, 3rd ser., 34, 1 (1977): 66–82.

Karen Anderson, "Commodity Exchange and Subordination: Montagnais-Naskapi and Huron Women, 1600–1650," *Signs* 11, 1 (Autumn 1985): 48–62.

PART II

R. Cole Harris, "The Seigneurial System in Canada during the French Regime," in *The Seigneurial System in Early Canada: A Geographical Study*, 2nd ed. (Madison, WI: University of Wisconsin Press, 1984), 193–198.

Fernand Ouellet, "Free or Exploited? The Peasant Before 1850," in Fernand Ouellet, *Economy, Class, and Nation in Quebec: Interpretive Essays*, edited and translated by Jacques A. Barbier (Toronto: Pearson Education Canada, 1991), 40–60.

Colin M. Coates, "Images of Heroism and Nationalism: The Canadian Joan of Arc," in Colin M. Coates and Cecilia Morgan, *Heroines and History: Representations of Madeleine de Verchères and Laura Secord* (Toronto: University of Toronto Press, 2002), 41–67.

Christopher Moore, "Charles Renaut's Letter," in *Louisbourg Portraits: Life in an Eighteenth-Century Garrison Town* (Toronto: Macmillan, 1982), 118–145.

Peter Kalm, excerpts from *Travels in North America* (New York: Dover Publications, 1964), vol. 2: 415–447.

Naomi E.S. Griffiths, "1755–1784: Exile Surmounted," in *The Contexts of Acadian History, 1686–1784* (Montreal: McGill-Queen's University Press, 1992), 95–127.

PART III

Peter Moogk, "'The Apples Do Not Fall Far from the Tree': The Legacy of New France in Modern Canada," in *La Nouvelle France: The Making of French Canada—A Cultural History* (East Lansing: Michigan State University Press, 2000), 265–281.

Norman Knowles, "'Chiefly Landholders, Farmers, and Others': The Loyalist Reality," Chapter 1 of *Inventing the Loyalists: The Ontario Loyalist Tradition and the Creation of Usable Pasts* (Toronto: University of Toronto Press, 1997), 14–25.

Ann Gorman Condon, "The Family in Exile: Loyalist Social Values after the Revolution," in Margaret Conrad, ed., *Intimate Relations: Family and Community in Planter Nova Scotia* (Fredericton: Acadiensis Press, 1995), 42–53.

George Sheppard, "'Cool Calculators': Brock's Militia," in *Plunder, Profit, and Paroles: A Social History of the War of 1812 in Upper Canada* (Montreal: McGill-Queen's University Press, 1994), 40–67.

Carolyn Podruchny, "Unfair Masters and Rascally Servants? Labour Relations among Bourgeois, Clerks and Voyageurs in the Montréal Fur Trade, 1780–1821," *Labour/Le Travail* 43 (Spring 1999): 43–70.

Lyle Dick, "The Seven Oaks Incident and the Construction of a Historical Tradition, 1816 to 1970," *Journal of the Canadian Historical Association* (1991): 91–113.

PART IV

Ian Ross Robertson, "Reform, Literacy, and the Lease: The Prince Edward Island Free Education Act of 1852," *Acadiensis* 20, 1 (Autumn 1990): 52–71.

Gail Campbell, "The Most Restrictive Franchise in British North America? A Case Study," *Canadian Historical Review* 71, 2 (June 1990): 159–188.

Jerry Bannister, "The Campaign for Representative Government in Newfoundland," *Journal of the Canadian Historical Association*, New Series, 5 (1994): 19–40.

Ralph Pastore, "The Collapse of the Beothuk World," *Acadiensis* 19, 1 (Autumn 1989): 52–71.

Marjorie Griffin Cohen, "Division of Labour in a Staple-Exporting Economy," in *Women's Work, Markets, and Economic Development in Nineteenth-Century Ontario* (Toronto: University of Toronto Press, 1988), 29–58.

Allan Greer, "Parish Republics," in *The Patriots and the People* (Toronto: University of Toronto Press, 1993), 219–257.

William Lyon Mackenzie's Draft Constitution, 15 November 1837 (See Cornelius J. Jaenen and Cecilia Morgan, *Material Memory: Documents in Pre-Confederation History*, Vol. 1 (Toronto: Addison Wesley Longman, 1998) 238–241.

Sylvia Van Kirk, "The Role of Native Women in the Creation of Fur Trade Society in Western Canada, 1670–1830," in S. Armitage and E. Jameson, eds., *The Women's West* (Norman: University of Oklahoma Press, 1988), 53–62.

Adele Perry, "Hardy Backwoodsmen, Wholesome Women, and Steady Families: Immigration and the Construction of a White Society in Colonial British Columbia, 1849–1871," *Histoire sociale/Social History* Vol. 33, no. 66 (November 2000): 343–360.

PART V

Claudette Knight, "Black Parents Speak: Education in Mid-Nineteenth-Century Canada West," *Ontario History* 89, 4 (December 1997): 269–284.

Brian McKillop, "Education and Authority," in *Matters of the Mind: The University in Ontario, 1791–1951* (Toronto: University of Toronto Press, 1994), 3–25.

Paul Craven and Tom Traves, "Dimensions of Paternalism: Discipline and Culture in Canadian Railway Operations in the 1850s," in Craig Heron and Robert Storey, eds., *On the Job: Confronting the Labour Process in Canada* (Montreal: McGill-Queen's University Press, 1986), 47–74.

Jan Noel, "French Canada Awakens" and "Patriotism and Sackcloth," in *Canada Dry: Temperance Crusades before Confederation* (Toronto: University of Toronto Press, 1995), 153–182.

Ged Martin, "The Case Against Canadian Confederation, 1864–1867," in Ged Martin, ed., *The Causes of Canadian Confederation* (Fredericton: Acadiensis Press, 1990), 19–49.

British North America Act, 1867, http://canada.justice.gc.ca/loireg/rapport/en/p1t1-1.html

Preface

Foundations: Readings in Pre-Confederation Canadian History offers students a sample of some of the best of recent scholarship on the history of Canada before Confederation. Although designed to accompany our two-volume *History of the Canadian Peoples* and our one-volume synthesis, *Canada: A National History,* this book can supplement any survey of Canadian history or serve as a stand-alone text. The readings are grouped in overlapping time periods that have become more-or-less conventional for the study of pre-Confederation history: Beginnings to 1663; France in America, 1663–1756; The Origins of British North America, 1749–1821; Maturing Colonial Societies, 1815–1867; and Industrializing Canada, 1840–1867.

Our main goal in selecting which articles to publish was to ensure a balance of social, political, and economic topics as well as a balanced coverage of Canadian regions. Given the size of Canada and the explosion of historical research in recent years, this proved to be a difficult task. We also wanted to make the selections as accessible to the general reader as possible. To best achieve our several goals, we have abridged some of the articles published here. Notes documenting where the article was originally published will enable students to consult the full version should they wish to do so.

The scholarly articles in this book are what historians call *secondary* documents. They offer a historian's interpretation of events in the past. To enable students to experience some of the excitement of coming face-to-face with the raw material of historical inquiry, we have also included in this reader a few *primary* documents. We hope that such classic documents as the Constitution of the Iroquois Nations, Peter Kalm's account of his travels in New France in 1750, William Lyon Mackenzie's Draft Constitution, and the British North America Act, 1867, will whet the reader's appetite for more. Students who find that they enjoy working with primary documents are encouraged to consult Cornelius Jaenen and Cecilia Morgan, *Material Memory: Documents in Pre-Confederation History* (Toronto: Pearson Education Canada, 1998).

Many of the articles published here are less concerned with what happened in the past than with the different perspectives that historians bring to the study of history. Thus, for example, Alan Gordon argues, after looking at the available evidence, that "Jacques Cartier is really a nineteenth-century figure." By this he means that a sixteenth-century explorer was "invented" as a hero in the nineteenth century by French Canadians inspired by visions of national achievements. The study of how history has been written and its changing interpretations over time is called *historiography.*

In recent years, the lines between history—what happened in the past—and historiography—the study of how history has been written—have blurred somewhat. Most professional historians recognize that their interpretations, like those of their predecessors, are shaped by present biases and interests. As a result, they are more modest in their claims to objectivity and, instead, strive to examine their own motivations and explore a variety of perspectives on the topics they analyze.

The bias of this reader is toward articles in social history, a field of study that gained prominence in the 1960s. As a result, many of the readings in this text deal with issues of class, culture, gender, and region—the mantra of social historians—categories of analysis that have changed the way Canadian history has been written. Articles such as the one by Karen Anderson on Native women in the early seventeenth century and Christopher Moore on the life of a Louisbourg fisherman have benefited greatly from the work of social historians, who have developed new avenues of inquiry. Social history has also changed the way older fields, such as economic history, have been understood. For instance, feminist approaches to the past have enabled Marjorie Cohen in her article published here to explore how the gendered division of labour operated on nineteenth-century Ontario farms. Even political history has been transformed by social history approaches, as the article by Allan Greer on the Lower Canada Rebellion of 1837 attests.

In approaching secondary historical sources, students will need to apply their own critical reading skills. Some readings are more accessible than others, and a few can be downright challenging, even to the experienced professional historian. Whatever the style of historical writing, students must engage the material. It is often best to read quickly, jotting down arguments and themes that seem most apparent. In particular, it is important to establish the thesis, or the controlling argument, of the reading. Ideally, the thesis will be stated in a sentence or two. In a well-written essay, the thesis is usually clearly stated at the beginning and elaborated upon throughout the rest of the piece.

Once the arguments and themes have been determined, it is important to evaluate them. Are the arguments sound and well supported? One way of making such an assessment is to check the endnotes to see if the author has consulted primary and secondary sources relevant to the topic. Evaluating sources is a fundamental exercise for students of history. Another approach is to consult additional publications on the topic to see if they corroborate the author's claims or at least do not contradict them.

It is also important to evaluate the author's point of view, which often has an impact on how source materials are selected and interpreted. All of the articles in this reader have been written by trained historians so it can be assumed that they know the nuts and bolts of their craft. Nevertheless, we must also remember that they write in a context that may slant their interpretations. For example, a historian may be eager to prove that a political policy has been damaging to a particular group and offer only evidence to support such a claim, ignoring all counter-evidence. Students often have not read broadly enough to detect such bias, but there are shortcuts to help them in their efforts. By finding out what else the author has published, it may be possible to discover that the article has been written by someone who has produced one or more books on the topic that have been reviewed by other scholars. These reviews usually highlight the positive and negative aspects of the author's approach.

The tone of the article also reveals something about the author. While some historians strive for a detached, impersonal style, others bring passion and political commitment to the work; still others may be ironic or even sarcastic. History is written by people with their own special character traits and it is useful to reflect on how these find expression in their publications.

While it is often easier to detect bias in primary sources than in secondary ones, the same basic rules of assessment apply to both. It is important when reading primary sources to establish the credibility of the author(s) of the document and the context in which it was written. In addition, it is useful to consider how assumptions, based on conditions at the beginning of the twenty-first century, shape our judgment of the sources. For example, the Fathers of Confederation produced the British North America Act in a particular political and social context. Although the document has stood the test of time remarkably well, there may be clauses that have a different meaning today. Concepts such as provincial rights and social services, for instance, have changed dramatically since 1867. It is the job of a good historian to show not only how the past shapes current conditions but also how the past differs from the present.

We hope that students will find these readings both challenging and enlightening. By helping students understand that the past as represented in textbooks is constructed from sources such as the ones published here, we hope to open a window not only on developments in Canada's past but also on the discipline of history, which is ever evolving.

We would like to thank the following people who were instrumental in the production of this volume: Adrienne Shiffman, Lori Will, and Richard di Santo from Pearson Canada; our copy editor, David Handelsman; and Michael Dale (Conestoga College), Robert A. Campbell (Capilano College), and Ruth Compton Brouwer (King's College), who reviewed this project during development.

PART I

Beginnings to 1663

Courtesy of Manitoba Culture, Heritage and Tourism, Historic Resources Branch

The human history of today's Canada traces back many millennia. Before Europeans began to fish, trade furs, and finally settle in the lands of the First Nations in the 1500s and 1600s, Natives had created a variety of societies that were adapted to the environmental conditions of the various regions of Canada. The European newcomers, having their own cultural inheritance, tended to dismiss the achievements of the First Nations even as they depended upon them to make the fur trade profitable.

Our readings in Part 1 explore the environment in which first the Natives and then the Europeans built their societies. We examine the social values of the First Nations, and then proceed to discuss the justifications that the Europeans used in their efforts to impose their own social values on the long-established inhabitants of North America. We also explore the ways that Natives resisted efforts to change them into Europeans.

The first reading, "Winter and the Shaping of Northern History: Reflections from the Canadian North," provides an overview of the history of human habitation in Canada's northernmost regions. Ken S. Coates and William R. Morrison emphasize the key role of geography in defining challenges that faced those who made the North a permanent or even temporary home: "From the seasonal movements of Inuit hunters to the attempts of British explorers to survive in a land they did not understand, from the springtime arrival and fall departure of tourists, geological teams, scientists, construction workers and others, winter has remained a prominent, indeed the dominant, factor in the evolution and development of northern society."

The authors contrast the cultural adaptations of First Nations and Europeans to the North. For the Inuit and the Dene, "a minimalist adaptation that stripped life to its essentials" was the key to a culturally rich life of relative ease. Europeans, by contrast, have only gradually come to find the North a more hospitable place, and then only because of the application of elaborate technologies meant to limit the impact on their lives of a harsh climate.

Just as the Northern indigenous peoples learned to harmonize their lives with their environments, First Nations in the Great Lakes region produced societies that reflected the resource potential of their region. Their populations expanded due in large measure to an abundance of game and wild berries. When they began to plant crops in the fertile soil of the area, further population gains followed. With population growth came increased hostilities and warfare among tribes, and a perceived need to codify social rules. "The Constitution of the Iroquois Nations" is a remarkable "document" from the period before European contact that survived through the oral history practices of the Five Nations. According to Native tradition, Dekanawidah, a Huron from today's southeastern Ontario who lived his adult life among the Seneca of today's New York, organized a congress of Iroquoian groups on the south shore of Lake Erie and Lake Ontario. The Five Nations concluded the details for a constitution that provided for a system of loose collective governance, but as importantly, underlined the solidarity among the peoples who smoked the peace pipe together to signify their allegiance to the provisions of the constitution. These elaborate provisions reveal much about the social values of the Five Nations in the precontact period: their emphasis on consensus, their view that everyone had a right to participate in governance, and their inclusion of both men and women in decision making.

The ideas embodied in the Five Nations constitution would later play a role in the thinking of the American revolutionaries of the 1770s. But, on the whole, the Europeans who came to the Americas from the 1500s onwards dismissed Native attitudes and behaviours as "savage." They regarded the New World through lenses shaped by their experiences in Europe rather than through Native eyes. While First Nations religious beliefs emphasized harmony among all elements of nature, including humans, Christian Europeans believed fervently that humans were God's special creation, and that the natural world must be subordinated to humans' needs. Ramsay Cook's article, "1492 and All That: Making a Garden Out of Wilderness," assesses critically the language that Europeans used to describe both the state of the Americas and their intentions to transform its character.

As Cook observes, the European conquerors not only aimed to transform the natural environment of the Americas, but also wished to dispossess the original inhabitants. Their insistence that Natives had left their lands in a "wilderness" state, failing to establish either European-model agriculture or European-style social relations, provided, they argued, a moral justification for ignoring the rights of indigenous peoples to the enjoyment of their territories. The lands collectively shared by various First Nations groups were parcelled out as "property" for Europeans, who intended to use them in ways reminiscent of Old-Country practices.

The attitudes of the European explorers, traders, settlers, and missionaries coloured historical accounts of the "discovery" of Canada for centuries. Relying on documents left by the European "founders of Canada," and sharing many of the social values of these early Euro-Canadians, historians did not, until relatively recently, question the biases inherent in the record left by the so-called founders. As Alan Gordon's article demonstrates, members of elites who built memorials to the founders went further, not only celebrating uncritically the contributions of early Euro-Canadians in Canada but associating them with achievements that they could hardly have envisioned, much less accomplished. "Heroes, History, and Two Nationalisms: Jacques Cartier" explores how the memory of past events is "socially constructed" to serve present-day goals. In the case of Jacques Cartier, the explorer's erecting a cross to claim territory for France was taken out of its political context by elites with political agendas that Cartier could not have predicted. The unveiling of a monument to Cartier in 1889 improbably linked him with the Jesuit role in New France beginning almost a century after his explorations, so as to enlist Cartier's name in a battle of Quebec's Catholic elite for fair compensation for Jesuit properties seized by the British after the Conquest of Quebec. The commemoration in 1934 of Cartier's supposed role in founding Canada provided a venue for both English-Canadian and French-Canadian nationalists to link the ancient explorer with the nationalisms present in Canada 400 years later.

All of this celebration of European conquest of the Americas begs the question of how the original inhabitants of the continent viewed the newcomers and their efforts to intervene in Natives' lives. James P. Ronda, relying mainly on a close reading of the *Jesuit Relations,* the detailed account that the Jesuits provided of their daily dealings with both Natives and French in Canada, reveals much of the skepticism of the First Nations regarding the applicability of Christianity to their lives. Ronda's article, " 'We Are Well As We Are': An Indian Critique of Seventeenth-Century Christian Missions," shows that Natives defended their own spiritual views against the claims of Christianity, and challenged the missionaries' view that Christ's message was universal.

Karen Anderson's article, "Commodity Exchange and Subordination: Montagnais-Naskapi and Huron Women, 1600–1650," studies Native women's efforts to resist missionaries' attempts to impose women's subordination to men. Anderson challenges earlier works that suggest that whenever "commodity exchange" between Europeans and Natives became entrenched, women lost their former social status as their husbands became property owners. Instead, she suggests that women attempted to maintain traditional gender-based kinship relations that guaranteed every member of society access to the means of production. In Huronia, for example, despite the missionaries' best efforts, kinship groups maintained their former power and women's subordination to men did not occur. By contrast, the Montagnais-Naskapi who moved to the Jesuit-run community of Sillery to escape Iroquois incursions proved unable to resist Jesuit efforts to weaken community relations, and women's power and influence was a key casualty.

Winter and the Shaping of Northern History: Reflections from the Canadian North

KEN S. COATES AND WILLIAM R. MORRISON

Early in this century,[1] the American author Jack London, who had travelled in northern Canada during the Klondike gold rush, wrote a story called "To Build a Fire." A man travelling alone in the North during the winter falls through the ice of a sub-Arctic creek. Wet and freezing, he knows he must get warm and dry, or die. His fingers numb, he struggles to build a fire, using his dwindling supply of matches. On the last match, a small pile of twigs catches fire, and soon he has a roaring blaze. Steam begins to rise from his clothes; soon he will be dry and safe. Unfortunately, however, he is not a very experienced northerner, and has built his fire under a tree whose branches are heavily laden with snow. Without warning, the snow above him gives way and falls on the fire, instantly smothering it. He is doomed; a simple but fatal error in dealing with the North has killed him.[2]

Taking the average temperatures in the country as a whole, Canada is the coldest country in the world, and particularly in the northern part of the country, winter is the dominant season. Since the earliest days of human habitation in the North, the dark and cold months of winter have influenced social and economic life, shaped the response of outsiders to the region, and have forced newcomers to adapt to the realities of Arctic and sub-Arctic living. From the seasonal movements of Inuit hunters to the attempts of British explorers to survive in a land they did not understand, from the springtime arrival and fall departure of tourists, geological teams, scientists, construction workers and others, winter has remained a prominent, indeed the dominant, factor in the evolution and development of northern society.

"Winter" and "northern" tend to be synonymous in Canada, for although it is not always winter in the North, it is for a great deal of the time, and it is winter that in large part makes the North northern. Without winter, the North is only a direction, not a place; the two are thus inseparable. In the nineteenth century, Canadian nationalists, looking for something to distinguish this country from others (particularly the United States), hit upon the North as a foundation of our national identity. As the historian Carl Berger observed,

> The adjective "northern" came to symbolize energy, strength, self-reliance, health, and purity, and its opposite "southern," was equated with decay and effeminacy, even libertinism, and disease. A lengthy catalogue of desirable national attributes resulting from the climate was compiled. No other weather was so conducive to maintaining health and stimulating

> robustness.... Compared even to the "warm, moisture-laden atmosphere of the British isles," the sharp clear air of northern America was calculated to make perception more clear and more penetrating. "The Canadian is super-eminently quick-witted," wrote one observer, because the very air of the country has "tonic properties."[3]

To speak of winter in Canada is to speak of the obvious. No Canadian can be blind to the realities of the coldest season or to its impact on the people, society, and economy of the North. Those who write on purely northern subjects—Arctic exploration, for example—have outlined in great detail the ravages and hardships of the winter months, particularly as they have affected inexperienced Europeans who have ventured into the region. Those who have written on gold rushes, mining exploration, and construction projects both civil and military know well the influence of seasonal rhythms on history. But as is sometimes the case with historical analysis, the prominent and obvious features exist without systematic commentary or detailed consideration. Here we propose to provide a preliminary outline of the impact of winter on human life in northern Canada and, in doing so, to begin a discussion of the broader role that winter has played in the shaping of northern history.

In recent years, a number of scholars have begun to examine the role of winter in history. Blake McKelvey's *Snow in the Cities: A History of America's Urban Response,*[4] Bernard Mergen's *Snow in America,*[5] and Ruth Kirk's more general work, *Snow,*[6] provide a promising start to this field of inquiry. Their studies have focused on more southerly regions, but they have provided a good framework for the pursuit of the subject in regions where winter is more severe, and where the impact of the season on human activity is more pronounced. Their studies have already drawn important conclusions: that winter worsened the gap between the rich and the poor, that it established a seasonal economic cycle that determined the nature of business and labour, that it shaped attitudes toward charity, and that it shaped the attitudes of urban government toward seasonal adaptation. Winter, these authors contend, conditioned national and regional attitudes, reinforcing the North American self-image of hardiness, determination, and adaptability.

Coming to terms with winter has presented a series of technological challenges in transportation, communications, construction of homes and other buildings, urban design, and snow removal. The ability, or lack thereof, to respond to these challenges has played an important role in the history of North American society. This is particularly true in the Canadian Arctic and sub-Arctic regions, where human society has been compelled to cope with extreme cold, long periods of darkness, and many months of winter. The struggle with winter in these regions has largely been unexamined by scholars, perhaps because it is so much a part of Canadian life that it has seemed unremarkable, and has been dealt with implicitly rather than explicitly. In this chapter we hope to move winter from the background—a mere stage-setting for historical events—to the foreground where it belongs. Our contention is that the main determining factor in the development of human societies in the Canadian North is the reality of winter, and that the season has thus played a fundamental role in determining the nature, the extent, and the character of northern Canadian life.

Nowhere is this more true, of course, than in the history of Canada's indigenous peoples. Indigenous cultures have been, in ways that newcomer societies have never been, attuned not only to the perils, but also to the opportunities of winter. For winter was not simply a time of hardship and peril; it could also be a time of ease and opportunity. First Nations people in Canada adapted to their environment in many ways, reflecting the impact of winter in everything from their seasonal movements to their methods of transportation, from their clothing to their housing. The Inuit were, much to the wonder of Europeans, perfectly adapted to their seemingly perilous environment. To the Inuit, winter was not the most difficult season; spring and fall were more so. Winter was the main season, the one which was incorporated as the centrepiece of their way of life, when travelling was easy and dwellings could be made on the spot with a cutting instrument and a supply of suitable snow. The Inuit developed exceptional techniques for making clothing, winter shelters, sleds, hunting implements, and the other necessities of life. Newcomers to the region, struggling to deal with northern winter, and with their own entrenched attitudes of colonial superiority to indigenous people, nevertheless marvelled at the ability of the Inuit to survive and even flourish in the winter months.

The Dene, living in the sub-Arctic regions to the south of the Inuit, made much less of an impression on the early Europeans, for their adaptations to winter seemed much easier. Living in the forests as they did, they had adequate supplies of heat and shelter, and their adaptations to winter were thus less dramatic. While Europeans were always fascinated by igloos, the Inuit snow houses, they rarely commented on what they considered to be the primitive tents or shelters of the First Nations of the boreal forest. These dwellings, they believed, were much inferior to the ingenious igloos, as simply inferior versions of European dwellings. The fact that both kinds of dwellings served their residents well was less important than the exoticism of the igloo.

It is one of the great clichés of northern history that the indigenous people adapted well to their surroundings and developed economic and social systems that were perfectly in tune with it. Winter is the great proof of this assertion, for it was this season that tested the ingenuity of indigenous societies in many different ways. Long periods of extreme cold required the development of harvesting techniques that were unique in the world. The danger of blizzards during periods of travel affected their lives. Winter's impact on the movements of animals and birds, and on accessibility to fish and marine life, exerted an exceptional influence on the lives and the life patterns of northern indigenous peoples.

Nearly thirty years ago, the anthropologist Marshal Sahlins, in his book *Stone Age Economics,* spoke of the Dene as "the original affluent society."[7] His thesis was that these northern dwellers, far from being a starving, destitute people who spent every waking hour searching for a meagre food supply, had more leisure time than Europeans did during the contact period, and more time in fact for cultural and other leisure activities than our society today. The reason for this paradox was simple enough: the Dene were not a materialist society; they needed only food, shelter, the means to make fire, and the material for clothing. All these wants were satisfied by a work week which consumed perhaps 15 hours. Because their survival depended on a high degree of mobility, they did not accumulate possessions that they could not easily carry; their very survival depended on a simple, direct way of life. It is, in a way, ironic: whereas our modern adaptation to the North involves a tremendous amount of technology (special clothing, elaborate and expensive equipment, and a complicated support infrastructure), the Dene adaptation was exactly the opposite: a minimalist adaptation that stripped life to its essentials. It seems a simple idea once someone points it out, but it speaks to the vast gulf between European culture and that of the first peoples of northern Canada. Of course, this minimalist way of life owed nothing to genetics, and everything to environment; Aboriginal peoples who lived in more benign parts of the Western Hemisphere indulged in prodigies of monument-building and accumulation of material wealth that rivalled those of the Roman Empire.

First peoples in northern Canada adapted to their environment, therefore, not because of any inherent racial virtue, but simply because they had to in order to survive. In contrast, newcomers to the region brought much less refined adaptive skills. For Europeans, the rapid and easy conquest of the more southerly parts of North America engendered a contempt for "natives" and a confidence, bordering on arrogance, that nature was easily conquered, and that the natives knew nothing that a European needed to learn. Not all felt this way, of course, for the fur trade in particular was based on indigenous technology, and it was hard to ignore the superiority of, for instance, the canoe as a means of transport. But the North seemed so bleak and empty to the Europeans, and its inhabitants so primitive, that it was difficult for Europeans to believe that they had anything to learn from them. For too long, for instance, the British spurned Inuit footgear, made of caribou skin, light, warm, and easily dried, in favour of clumsy leather boots in which their feet froze. Eventually Europeans learned lessons from the Inuit, but these lessons were hard, painful, and a long time coming.

The best example of this hard lesson is the career of Sir John Franklin (1786–1847). Interestingly, this unlucky explorer is the most famous in the long history of European exploration of the Canadian North, not because of his accomplishments, though his life was not without these, but because of the manner of his death. Since it is not known exactly where, when, or how he died, his fate is one of those "mysteries" that continues to attract popular interest, and expeditions are still sent north to find the exact location of his doomed ships and to find other traces of his last expedition. Franklin had a long and mostly successful career. He joined the Royal Navy at the age of 14, and served honourably in battles from Copenhagen (1801) to New Orleans (1815). In 1818, 1819, and 1825 he participated in and then led expeditions to the Northwest Passage, Hudson Bay, and the Mackenzie Delta, and then served a term as governor of Van Diemen's Land.

The disaster that overtook Franklin and his crew in the expedition of 1845 was perhaps inevitable. It was not that it was badly planned or badly led, for despite Franklin's defects as a commander, he was experienced in Northern exploration, brave, and conscientious. It was simply that the whole concept was wrong. Its very size—around 130 men—made it terribly vulnerable. Franklin's two ships brought with them everything that the men could possibly need, but when the ships became trapped by ice, the supplies were bound to run out, and then the men were doomed, for a crew of that size could not possibly live off the land. It is true that the British contempt for indigenous technology led them to spurn skin clothing and the use of dogs for transportation, an attitude which helped to kill Robert Scott sixty years later. It is also true that the Franklin expedition seemed to go out of its way to show this contempt by bringing European trinkets with them. In a truly bizarre episode, the members of the expedition who were still alive in the spring of 1848, three years after the expedition had been launched, tried to trek south to the nearest fur-trade post, inexplicably dragging with them a whaleboat containing silverware and Delftware tea cups, until they died. But as Vilhjalmur Stefansson liked to point out—and as his own career proved—a small group of men living off the land was the only sure recipe for success in the North, and even then (something he tended to downplay) there was always an element of luck. In order for a large group of people to live in the North in European style, one needed ships and airplanes to bring in southern supplies and comforts.

It was with good reason, therefore, that Europeans came to the Canadian North with some apprehension. They knew enough about winter in the southern parts of the country, where it is bitter in comparison with more salubrious zones, to be wary of the far northern regions. Once the fantasies of open polar seas had been laid to rest, the prevailing attitude developed that the northern regions were virtually uninhabitable, an attitude which the sparseness of the population only reinforced. The explorers themselves added strength to this view. At times it benefitted them to exaggerate the harshness of their northern experience, since in doing so their accomplishments seemed more impressive. Artists and writers in the nineteenth century in particular emphasized the grandeur and the terrors of nature in the North, establishing a conceptual foundation for understanding the region that lingers to the present. Theirs was a North of extremes: brilliant summer nights, depressingly dark winter days, dangerous rivers, massive icebergs, endless herds of caribou, ferocious polar bears, and the like. Men such as Franklin, Mackenzie, and Rae created evocative word pictures designed to portray an impressive landscape to their readers. Sometimes they (or their editors) altered their diaries for publication to make the land seem more forbidding than it actually was.

These descriptions—powerful, dramatic, exaggerated, and focused on northern exceptionalism (that which made the North different from other regions)—entrenched the image of the North as an inhospitable and dangerous, albeit dramatically beautiful, land. More to the point, they created the impression—one which is not totally inaccurate—of the Arctic and sub-Arctic regions as lands of perpetual winter. Douglas Owram, in his excellent study of the intellectual history of the prairie West, argued that John Franklin's published account of his 1819–21 expedition (a travelogue full of accounts of inconceivable hardship and winter suffering) helped solidify the impression that all of the Canadian Northwest, from the Great Lakes to the Arctic, was a winter wasteland. Over the following generations, writers found that there was a market for thrilling tales from high latitudes, and the image established by the early explorers was reinforced. Writers wrote about the physical beauty of the North, but they also always wrote about its dangers and limitations.[8]

The basic attributes of the northern climate, cold and snow, are partly a test of technology—the capacity to provide enough shelter, food, and clothing to sustain life. But they are also a test of humanity, and it was here, in the sphere of human adaptation to winter, that the season exacted its most dramatic toll on the newcomers. The indigenous people of the North had found mechanisms for coping with winter. The value attached to communal life and to storytelling, for instance, provided them with the social outlets necessary to deal with the long, though familiar, winter season. Newcomers, however, had few or no such mechanisms. For them, the onset of winter (and some Arctic expeditions remained locked in ice for two or more winters) presented a difficult challenge. The season forced Europeans into tightly confined social spaces. Sailors, for instance, were trapped below decks with each other, cold, cramped, and often unhealthy or half-starved. With no women or children, and often without much recreation or diversion, their winters were miserable tests of endurance.

Winter created a uniquely northern social world, one marked by isolation and loneliness, by a struggle to survive and hang on until spring, by a fear of cold and snow, and by outbursts of what writers called "cabin fever."[9] Expedition commanders who were aware of this problem arranged activities for their crews: plays, lessons of various kinds, and busy-work around the ship were offered as an antidote to the mind-numbing boredom of winter captivity. In the scattered settlements, the presence of fur traders, missionaries, and Mounted Police officers provided a wider social sphere, though one which was closed to indigenous people.

Along the gold-bearing creeks of the Yukon, where miners lived uncomfortable lives searching for the strike that would bring both wealth and escape from the North, men lived alone or in pairs, working so hard that they rarely took time to protect themselves socially from the dreariness of winter.

Some newcomers did adapt to winter, adopting indigenous clothing and learning to adjust to the seasonal rhythms. But for the most part, people who lived in the North did so only temporarily, so few felt the need to make the necessary adaptations. Most who came to the North brought southern things with them, so that in Canada some northern towns look like transplanted southern towns (especially the ones built for non-Native rather than indigenous people), the houses, community plans, and public buildings just like those of southern communities. Few newcomers opted to live with the indigenous people, or to live as they lived, nor was there much effort expended to develop housing or other technologies that were specifically meant for northern settings. The goal of newcomers was not to adapt to the North, but by the use of technological superiority or the expenditure of a great deal of money, to *conquer* the North and make it irrelevant to them. However, as many found out, it was possible to keep winter outside the house, but it was not possible to escape it.

The main impact of winter on the non-indigenous society of the Canadian North was the creation of a seasonal order, a way of life geared to seasonal dictates in a manner that did not exist in the south. The North had its seasonal rituals: freeze-up in the fall, the spring break-up, the preparation of stacks of firewood and supplies of food for the long cold season. Until the advent of bush planes in the 1930s, northern transportation was locked into the dictates of winter. In the spring, rivers opened, bringing food, supplies, and workers to northern communities. Along the Arctic coast, the movement of ice made ocean navigation possible, or, if it failed to move, impossible. In some sectors, particularly the mining industry in the Yukon, winter imposed limits on work, since it was impossible to carry out dredging and hydraulic operations in the winter.

Winter therefore created a seasonally transient society in parts of the Canadian North. Workers in several industrial sectors came north only for the summer, and left again in the fall. This was particularly true of the Yukon gold sector, but it was also true of the men who operated the river steamboat service. Even the Yukon's two judges took turns living "outside" in the winter, and eventually they came north only in the summertime; trials waited until the ice left the river. Fur traders, missionaries, and police officers were compelled by the nature of their work to spend the whole year in the North, and some truly came to appreciate the region. A few fell in love with the North, and spent the rest of their lives there. Others, particularly Roman Catholic priests, were assigned to northern missionary work, learned the indigenous language, and spent decades working with the First Nations. The missionaries belonging to other denominations, however, often served in the North with one ear cocked for a call to a church in kinder climates, and some stayed barely long enough to learn a few words of the unfamiliar languages. For many northerners, northern work was not a permanent choice, and they left for the south after a year or two. These two forms of transiency—seasonal movements between north and south to capitalize on summer work or business opportunities, and the mobility of short-time northern residents—became the dominant features of non-indigenous life in the North, and they remain so to this day.

Winter, then, created social instability and flux, with all of the political, cultural, social, and economic implications associated with movement of this type. Many people who were assumed to be long-term northerners spent a good part of each year—half or more—in the South, and organized their lives so as to avoid most of the northern winter. When in October 1918 the Canadian Pacific steamer *Princess Sophia* sank near Juneau, Alaska, killing all 354 people on board, the subsequent class action suit (which was ultimately unsuccessful) against the company required that a biography of each victim be drawn up. It was discovered that many long-term residents of the North, people who had considered themselves northerners for up to twenty years, had spent every June but few or no Januarys in the region, preferring to winter in Victoria or Seattle.[10]

Northern Canada until quite recently attracted only a few permanent non-indigenous settlers, and of those a good number married into the indigenous population. The result was that the majority non-indigenous population had little vision of the future of the region and little commitment to building a permanent society, and indeed lived in a society which had little stability. In contrast, the indigenous people retained their commitment to the region, providing much of what continuity it possessed. It was in this way that winter set the parameters for northern society; its non-indigenous population was characterized by seasonality, impermanence, and a lack of commitment to the region. The pattern, established in the early days, of "making a killing, not a living" became a hallmark of the regional order.

To be sure, there were always visionaries and northern promoters who saw through the ice and cold, believing that the North had a grand future as the source of Canada's future prosperity, and indeed the wellspring of the country's identity. One such man, both visionary and promoter, was Vilhjalmur Stefansson (1879–1962), the Canadian-born Arctic explorer and entrepreneur. Stefansson embraced the North with a passion, falling in love with it on his first trip there as a member of a 1906 expedition to the Beaufort Sea. Stefansson's fame rested on his accomplishments as an explorer and also on his genius for publicity and self-promotion. Those who came to the North in his era and later seem to have regarded it either as a horrible place to flee from at the first opportunity or to endure as a martyrdom, or else they found it the best place in the world. Stefansson was in the latter category, though his enthusiasm sometimes led him astray. At one point after his second (1908) expedition, he announced that he had found the Inuit of Victoria Island to have lighter complexions and hair than other Inuit, and speculated that they might be descendants of the lost Norse of Greenland. The press announced that Canada had a race of "blond Eskimos," a story which Stefansson never lived down, and which brought him a good deal of animosity from academic anthropologists, who resented his brashness and envied his fame. One of his books, *The Friendly Arctic, the story of five years in Polar regions,*[11] painted a picture of a benign, accessible land, posing no danger to the hardy and the intelligent.

Many ridiculed Stefansson's vision, and it is true that he was lucky as well as determined, and that some of his wilder schemes for the North—a commercial reindeer herd, and the acquisition of Wrangel Island, north of Siberia, for Canada—were abject failures. He was in fact morally responsible for the deaths of a number of men who participated in his Wrangel Island scheme. Still, he did find a receptive audience, though more in the United States than in Canada. His most visionary book, *The Northward Course of Empire,*[12] offered a dream of the peopling and development of the Arctic and sub-Arctic, presenting this idea as not only practical, but inevitable. Stefansson rejoiced in the North, and in winter. The region and its climate provided him with a career, with professional and personal fulfilment. After the Canadian Arctic Expedition of 1913–18, which was the high point of his career, he spent the rest of his long life as an advisor to government, not to the Canadian authorities, who shunned him, but to the US army. He ended his days as resident sage at Dartmouth College in New Hampshire, where he taught undergraduates how to make igloos on the campus. But few Canadians shared his vision of the North as a "Polar Mediterranean," to quote one of his more imaginative slogans. Winter in southern Canada was enough for them, and most recoiled at the thought of living in the frozen reaches of the true North.

The past half-century has witnessed some dramatic changes in northern living. Affluence and technological innovation rather than changing attitudes have provided the means of combatting the most severe disadvantages of northern life. Improvements in transportation technology, particularly air travel and coastal shipping, have made it possible to move more goods into the Canadian North, and at a faster rate. Scheduled air service has made it easy to go north, and also to flee the region, at will; no longer do people stand on the river banks watching the last ship depart for the south, as they did in the central Yukon until 1940, knowing that they were imprisoned in the North for the next six months. Improved housing design, including the development of effective insulation, triple-paned windows, more efficient furnaces, and the like, have made northern housing more comfortable, though housing still mirrors southern designs. Modern affluence has resulted in the provision of much better facilities, including schools, stores, and recreational complexes, that have significantly reduced the difference between northern and southern living. Many northerners and other Canadians are wealthy enough to repeat the historical migrations, but now do so as "snowbirds," travelling on holiday or even for most of the winter in southern climates. The Canadian Snowbirds Association claims that there are 800,000 Canadians who spend at least one month of every winter in the southern United States. It is clear then that one popular method of adaptation to winter is simply to flee from it. New communications technologies have tied the North into the national and international worlds: the satellite telephones that Inuit carry with them when they take their snowmobiles out on the land, the television networks that bring fifty channels into some of the most remote communities in the world. The isolation of the North is no more.

In the present day, substantial strides have been taken toward defeating winter in the Canadian North, or at least in taming it. Northern non-indigenous residents earn wages that are higher than the national average, and enjoy, for the most part, a prosperous lifestyle. If their reason for living in the North ends, as for instance with the closure of a mine, they usually leave. It is money and job opportunities that draw most people to the North, not the lure of the region itself, though for a significant minority the opposite is true. For those who remain in the North throughout the winter—and, as in the past, not all do—technology has created a southern world in an Arctic and sub-Arctic setting. The residents of the new North are better positioned to enjoy the beauty of the land and the opportunities for recreation and outdoor activity, knowing that they can retreat to the comfort of an artificial environment.

It is too much to say that winter has been totally defeated; in fact one might claim that it is in many ways as challenging as ever. Occasional storms, such as the ice storm that devastated Eastern Canada in January 1998, remind us that all of Canada, not just the North, is a northern country where winter can kill. Winter still shapes economic activity, determines the movements of much of the population, and thus influences the core of our society. The contrast with the northern experience of the nineteenth century, however, is striking. Northerners then were constantly at the mercy of the elements, dependent on indigenous technology for survival, if they had the sense to adopt it. Now they do not need it, in fact, and increasingly the indigenous population has become dependent on the introduced technology.

Where then does winter fit in the history and the future of the Canadian North? Canadians tend to be an anxious people, lacking in self-confidence, and have long debated the nature and meaning of being a Canadian, striving earnestly, and perhaps tiresomely, to discover the "Canadian identity." For some, the North and winter have held the key to the Canadian character, either because they see it shaping the very fabric of our life, or because our rejection of the North and winter is a classic indication of our national inability to develop that which is most important to our past and future. It is clear that winter has played a major role in shaping human society in the Canadian North, and by extension, in all of Canada. In the broadest of senses, winter was a dominant limiting factor, along with distance, isolation, and the absence of agriculture, in the development of the North. But what is lacking here is an understanding of the nuances, the exceptions, and the specific patterns relating to human adaptation to winter.

Historians will learn more when they begin to explore the individual response to winter, to consider the reaction to winter within the various segments of northern culture—fur traders, whalers, police, missionaries, miners, government officials, transportation workers—and to examine how technological and social change affected the ability of indigenous people to cope with winter. The historical experience of other northern countries, where indigenous and non-indigenous people mingled over time, will provide a vital comparative dimension to this question, and will provide an opportunity to consider the degree to which the Canadian pattern of northern and winter activities is unique to this country.

The writing of northern history, as with many other fields of inquiry, remains wedded to notions of national exceptionalism. We seek to describe what is Canadian about the Canadian North, rather than trying to describe what is northern about most of Canada. Historians of the Arctic and sub-Arctic around the world work in areas that share a common element: the experience of winter and the reality of the northern environment. The comparative study of winter provides a unique and important opportunity for northern scholars to consider one of the key elements in the shaping of northern society while at the same time examining the degree to which national and regional adaptations stand apart from a more general pattern of the southern occupation of the North.

Winter has shaped and influenced northern societies throughout history. Canadian artists and writers have played with the love/hate dichotomy that has long characterized national attempts to understand the North. But the basic facts have not changed. Despite technology, mid-winter temperatures are just as cold, the blizzards just as dangerous, the aurora borealis just as beautiful, and the season just as long as when the ancestors of the Inuit first set foot on this land. The ability to escape winter by fleeing inward to modern buildings or by flying to Hawaii has changed but not eliminated the effect of winter on northern life. As we continue the task of exploring the historical reality of winter in the Canadian and Circumpolar world, we may hope to come closer to understanding the social adaptations to environment that stand at the centre of northern experience. In the process, and by highlighting the role of winter in the history of the North, we can capture the reality of the harshest season and better explain the significance of winter in the shaping of northern history.

Notes

1 The twentieth century—*eds.*

2 Jack London, "To Build a Fire," originally published in *The Youth's Companion* 76/22 (May 29, 1902), 275. Now available in dozens of editions, including on the Internet. See, for example, Jack London, *To Build a Fire and Other Stories,* Bantam Classics, 1990.

3 Carl Berger, *The Sense of Power: Studies in the Ideas of Canadian Imperialism, 1867–1914* (Toronto: University of Toronto Press, 1970), 129–30.

4 Rochester, NY: University of Rochester Press, 1995.

5 Washington, DC: Smithsonian Institution Press, 1997.

6 New York: Morrow, 1977.

7 Chicago: Aldine-Atherton, [1972].

8 Douglas Owram, *Promise of Eden: The Canadian Expansionist Movement and the Idea of the West, 1856–1900* (Toronto: University of Toronto Press, 1980).

9 Recently, medicine has given a scientific name to one of the scourges of winter. What once was called "cabin fever" is now labelled "seasonal affective disorder," and is ascribed to light deprivation. The cure is, not surprisingly, more light, and seriously affected people are placed in front of a strong artificial light source, a remedy which apparently does work. Other studies have also shown a correlation between latitude and the consumption of alcohol, and between northernness and suicide, although of course other social and cultural factors influence both of these problems. Historians have not yet looked to see if these patterns developed in the early northern settler societies.

10 K. Coates and W. Morrison, *The Sinking of The Princess Sophia: Taking the North Down With Her* (Toronto: Oxford University Press, 1990).

11 New York: Macmillan, 1921.

12 New York: Macmillan, 1924.

Constitution of the Iroquois Nations: The Great Binding Law, Gayanashagowa

1. I am Dekanawidah and with the Five Nations' Confederate Lords I plant the Tree of Great Peace. I plant it in your territory, Adodarhoh, and the Onondaga Nation, in the territory of you who are Firekeepers.

   I name the tree the Tree of the Great Long Leaves. Under the shade of this Tree of the Great Peace we spread the soft white feathery down of the globe thistle as seats for you, Adodarhoh, and your cousin Lords.

   We place you upon those seats, spread soft with the feathery down of the globe thistle, there beneath the shade of the spreading branches of the Tree of Peace. There shall you sit and watch the Council Fire of the Confederacy of the Five Nations, and all the affairs of the Five Nations shall be transacted at this place before you, Adodarhoh, and your cousin Lords, by the Confederate Lords of the Five Nations.

2. Roots have spread out from the Tree of the Great Peace, one to the north, one to the east, one to the south and one to the west. The name of these roots is The Great White Roots and their nature is Peace and Strength.

   If any man or any nation outside the Five Nations shall obey the laws of the Great Peace and make known their disposition to the Lords of the Confederacy, they may trace the Roots to the Tree and if their minds are clean and they are obedient and promise to obey the wishes of the Confederate Council, they shall be welcomed to take shelter beneath the Tree of the Long Leaves.

   We place at the top of the Tree of the Long Leaves an Eagle who is able to see afar. If he sees in the distance any evil approaching or any danger threatening he will at once warn the people of the Confederacy.

3. To you Adodarhoh, the Onondaga cousin Lords, I and the other Confederate Lords have entrusted the caretaking and the watching of the Five Nations Council Fire.

   When there is any business to be transacted and the Confederate Council is not in session, a messenger shall be dispatched either to Adodarhoh, Hononwirehtonh or Skanawatih, Fire Keepers, or to their War Chiefs with a full statement of the case desired to be considered. Then shall Adodarhoh call his cousin (associate) Lords together and consider whether or not the case is of sufficient importance to demand the attention of the Confederate Council. If so, Adodarhoh shall dispatch messengers to summon all the Confederate Lords to assemble beneath the Tree of the Long Leaves.

   When the Lords are assembled the Council Fire shall be kindled, but not with chestnut wood,[1] and Adodarhoh shall formally open the Council.

"Constitution of the Iroquois Nations," www.constitution.org/cons/iroquois.htm. Reprinted courtesy of the National Public Telecomputing Network, the Constitution Society, Gerald Murphy and Jon Roland.

Then shall Adodarhoh and his cousin Lords, the Fire Keepers, announce the subject for discussion.

The Smoke of the Confederate Council Fire shall ever ascend and pierce the sky so that other nations who may be allies may see the Council Fire of the Great Peace.

Adodarhoh and his cousin Lords are entrusted with the Keeping of the Council Fire.

4. You, Adodarhoh, and your thirteen cousin Lords, shall faithfully keep the space about the Council Fire clean and you shall allow neither dust nor dirt to accumulate. I lay a Long Wing before you as a broom. As a weapon against a crawling creature I lay a staff with you so that you may thrust it away from the Council Fire. If you fail to cast it out then call the rest of the United Lords to your aid.

5. The Council of the Mohawk shall be divided into three parties as follows: Tekarihoken, Ayonhwhathah and Shadekariwade are the first party; Sharenhowaneh, Deyoenhegwenh and Oghrenghrehgowah are the second party, and Dehennakrineh, Aghstawenserenthah and Shoskoharowaneh are the third party. The third party is to listen only to the discussion of the first and second parties and if an error is made or the proceeding is irregular they are to call attention to it, and when the case is right and properly decided by the two parties they shall confirm the decision of the two parties and refer the case to the Seneca Lords for their decision. When the Seneca Lords have decided in accord with the Mohawk Lords, the case or question shall be referred to the Cayuga and Oneida Lords on the opposite side of the house.

6. I, Dekanawidah, appoint the Mohawk Lords the heads and the leaders of the Five Nations Confederacy. The Mohawk Lords are the foundation of the Great Peace and it shall, therefore, be against the Great Binding Law to pass measures in the Confederate Council after the Mohawk Lords have protested against them.

   No council of the Confederate Lords shall be legal unless all the Mohawk Lords are present.

7. Whenever the Confederate Lords shall assemble for the purpose of holding a council, the Onondaga Lords shall open it by expressing their gratitude to their cousin Lords and greeting them, and they shall make an address and offer thanks to the earth where men dwell, to the streams of water, the pools, the springs and the lakes, to the maize and the fruits, to the medicinal herbs and trees, to the forest trees for their usefulness, to the animals that serve as food and give their pelts for clothing, to the great winds and the lesser winds, to the Thunderers, to the Sun, the mighty warrior, to the moon, to the messengers of the Creator who reveal his wishes and to the Great Creator who dwells in the heavens above, who gives all the things useful to men, and who is the source and the ruler of health and life.

   Then shall the Onondaga Lords declare the council open.

   The council shall not sit after darkness has set in.

8. The Firekeepers shall formally open and close all councils of the Confederate Lords, and they shall pass upon all matters deliberated upon by the two sides and render their decision.

   Every Onondaga Lord (or his deputy) must be present at every Confederate Council and must agree with the majority without unwarrantable dissent, so that a unanimous decision may be rendered.

   If Adodarhoh or any of his cousin Lords are absent from a Confederate Council, any other Firekeeper may open and close the

Council, but the Firekeepers present may not give any decisions, unless the matter is of small importance.

9. All the business of the Five Nations Confederate Council shall be conducted by the two combined bodies of Confederate Lords. First the question shall be passed upon by the Mohawk and Seneca Lords, then it shall be discussed and passed by the Oneida and Cayuga Lords. Their decisions shall then be referred to the Onondaga Lords (Fire Keepers) for final judgement.

   The same process shall obtain when a question is brought before the council by an individual or a War Chief.

10. In all cases the procedure must be as follows: when the Mohawk and Seneca Lords have unanimously agreed upon a question, they shall report their decision to the Cayuga and Oneida Lords who shall deliberate upon the question and report a unanimous decision to the Mohawk Lords. The Mohawk Lords will then report the standing of the case to the Firekeepers, who shall render a decision as they see fit in case of a disagreement by the two bodies, or confirm the decisions of the two bodies if they are identical. The Fire Keepers shall then report their decision to the Mohawk Lords who shall announce it to the open council.

11. If through any misunderstanding or obstinacy on the part of the Fire Keepers, they render a decision at variance with that of the Two Sides, the Two Sides shall reconsider the matter and if their decisions are jointly the same as before they shall report to the Fire Keepers who are then compelled to confirm their joint decision.

12. When a case comes before the Onondaga Lords (Fire Keepers) for discussion and decision, Adodarho shall introduce the matter to his comrade Lords who shall then discuss it in their two bodies. Every Onondaga Lord except Hononwiretonh shall deliberate and he shall listen only. When a unanimous decision shall have been reached by the two bodies of Fire Keepers, Adodarho shall notify Hononwiretonh of the fact when he shall confirm it. He shall refuse to confirm a decision if it is not unanimously agreed upon by both sides of the Fire Keepers.

13. No Lord shall ask a question of the body of Confederate Lords when they are discussing a case, question or proposition. He may only deliberate in a low tone with the separate body of which he is a member.

14. When the Council of the Five Nation Lords shall convene they shall appoint a speaker for the day. He shall be a Lord of either the Mohawk, Onondaga or Seneca Nation.

   The next day the Council shall appoint another speaker, but the first speaker may be reappointed if there is no objection, but a speaker's term shall not be regarded more than for the day.

15. No individual or foreign nation interested in a case, question or proposition shall have any voice in the Confederate Council except to answer a question put to him or them by the speaker for the Lords.

16. If the conditions which shall arise at any future time call for an addition to or change of this law, the case shall be carefully considered and if a new beam seems necessary or beneficial, the proposed change shall be voted upon and if adopted it shall be called, "Added to the Rafters."

Rights, Duties and Qualifications of Lords

17. A bunch of a certain number of shell (wampum) strings each two spans in length shall be given to each of the female families

in which the Lordship titles are vested. The right of bestowing the title shall be hereditary in the family of the females legally possessing the bunch of shell strings and the strings shall be the token that the females of the family have the proprietary right to the Lordship title for all time to come, subject to certain restrictions hereinafter mentioned.

18. If any Confederate Lord neglects or refuses to attend the Confederate Council, the other Lords of the Nation of which he is a member shall require their War Chief to request the female sponsors of the Lord so guilty of defection to demand his attendance of the Council. If he refuses, the women holding the title shall immediately select another candidate for the title.

    No Lord shall be asked more than once to attend the Confederate Council.

19. If at any time it shall be manifest that a Confederate Lord has not in mind the welfare of the people or disobeys the rules of this Great Law, the men or women of the Confederacy, or both jointly, shall come to the Council and upbraid the erring Lord through his War Chief. If the complaint of the people through the War Chief is not heeded the first time it shall be uttered again and then if no attention is given a third complaint and warning shall be given. If the Lord is contumacious the matter shall go to the council of War Chiefs. The War Chiefs shall then divest the erring Lord of his title by order of the women in whom the titleship is vested. When the Lord is deposed the women shall notify the Confederate Lords through their War Chief, and the Confederate Lords shall sanction the act. The women will then select another of their sons as a candidate and the Lords shall elect him. Then shall the chosen one be installed by the Installation Ceremony.

When a Lord is to be deposed, his War Chief shall address him as follows:

> So you, __________, disregard and set at naught the warnings of your women relatives. So you fling the warnings over your shoulder to cast them behind you. "Behold the brightness of the Sun and in the brightness of the Sun's light I depose you of your title and remove the sacred emblem of your Lordship title. I remove from your brow the deer's antlers, which was the emblem of your position and token of your nobility. I now depose you and return the antlers to the women whose heritage they are.

The War Chief shall now address the women of the deposed Lord and say:

> Mothers, as I have now deposed your Lord, I now return to you the emblem and the title of Lordship, therefore repossess them.

Again addressing himself to the deposed Lord he shall say:

> As I have now deposed and discharged you so you are now no longer Lord. You shall now go your way alone, the rest of the people of the Confederacy will not go with you, for we know not the kind of mind that possesses you. As the Creator has nothing to do with wrong so he will not come to rescue you from the precipice of destruction in which you have cast yourself. You shall never be restored to the position which you once occupied.

Then shall the War Chief address himself to the Lords of the Nation to which the deposed Lord belongs and say:

> Know you, my Lords, that I have taken the deer's antlers from the brow of the emblem of his position and token of his greatness.

The Lords of the Confederacy shall then have no other alternative than to sanction the discharge of the offending Lord.

20. If a Lord of the Confederacy of the Five Nations should commit murder the other Lords of the Nation shall assemble at the place where the corpse lies and prepare to depose the criminal Lord. If it is impossible to meet at the scene of the crime the Lords shall discuss the matter at the next Council of their Nation and request their War Chief to depose the Lord guilty of crime, to "bury" his women relatives and to transfer the Lordship title to a sister family.

    The War Chief shall address the Lord guilty of murder and say:

    > So you, __________ (giving his name) did kill __________ (naming the slain man). with your own hands! You have committed a grave sin in the eyes of the Creator. Behold the bright light of the Sun, and in the brightness of the Sun's light I depose you of your title and remove the horns, the sacred emblems of your Lordship title. I remove from your brow the deer's antlers, which was the emblem of your position and token of your nobility. I now depose you and expel you and you shall depart at once from the territory of the Five Nations Confederacy and nevermore return again. We, the Five Nations Confederacy, moreover, bury your women relatives because the ancient Lordship title was never intended to have any union with bloodshed. Henceforth it shall not be their heritage. By the evil deed that you have done they have forfeited it forever.

    The War Chief shall then hand the title to a sister family and he shall address it and say:

    > Our mothers, __________, listen attentively while I address you on a solemn and important subject. I hereby transfer to you an ancient Lordship title for a great calamity has befallen it in the hands of the family of a former Lord. We trust that you, our mothers, will always guard it, and that you will warn your Lord always to be dutiful and to advise his people to ever live in love, peace and harmony that a great calamity may never happen again.

21. Certain physical defects in a Confederate Lord make him ineligible to sit in the Confederate Council. Such defects are infancy, idiocy, blindness, deafness, dumbness and impotency. When a Confederate Lord is restricted by any of these conditions, a deputy shall be appointed by his sponsors to act for him, but in case of extreme necessity the restricted Lord may exercise his rights.

22. If a Confederate Lord desires to resign his title he shall notify the Lords of the Nation of which he is a member of his intention. If his coactive Lords refuse to accept his resignation he may not resign his title.

    A Lord in proposing to resign may recommend any proper candidate which recommendation shall be received by the Lords, but unless confirmed and nominated by the women who hold the title the candidate so named shall not be considered.

23. Any Lord of the Five Nations Confederacy may construct shell strings (or wampum belts) of any size or length as pledges or records of matters of national or international importance.

    When it is necessary to dispatch a shell string by a War Chief or other messenger as the token of a summons, the messenger shall recite the contents of the string to the party to whom it is sent. That party shall repeat the message and return the shell string and if there has been a summons he shall make ready for the journey.

    Any of the people of the Five Nations may use shells (or wampum) as the record of a pledge, contract or an agreement entered into and the same shall be binding as soon as shell strings shall have been exchanged by both parties.

24. The Lords of the Confederacy of the Five Nations shall be mentors of the people for all time. The thickness of their skin shall be seven spans — which is to say that they shall be proof against anger, offensive actions and criticism. Their hearts shall be full of peace and good will and their minds filled with a yearning for the welfare of the people of the Confederacy. With endless patience they shall carry out their duty and their firmness shall be tempered with a tenderness for their people. Neither anger nor fury shall find lodgement in their minds and all their words and actions shall be marked by calm deliberation.

25. If a Lord of the Confederacy should seek to establish any authority independent of the jurisdiction of the Confederacy of the Great Peace, which is the Five Nations, he shall be warned three times in open council, first by the women relatives, second by the men relatives and finally by the Lords of the Confederacy of the Nation to which he belongs. If the offending Lord is still obdurate he shall be dismissed by the War Chief of his nation for refusing to conform to the laws of the Great Peace. His nation shall then install the candidate nominated by the female name holders of his family.

26. It shall be the duty of all of the Five Nations Confederate Lords, from time to time as occasion demands, to act as mentors and spiritual guides of their people and remind them of their Creator's will and words. They shall say:

> Hearken, that peace may continue unto future days!
>
> Always listen to the words of the Great Creator, for he has spoken.
>
> United people, let not evil find lodging in your minds.
>
> For the Great Creator has spoken and the cause of Peace shall not become old.
>
> The cause of peace shall not die if you remember the Great Creator.

Every Confederate Lord shall speak words such as these to promote peace.

27. All Lords of the Five Nations Confederacy must be honest in all things. They must not idle or gossip, but be men possessing those honorable qualities that make true royaneh. It shall be a serious wrong for anyone to lead a Lord into trivial affairs, for the people must ever hold their Lords high in estimation out of respect to their honorable positions.

28. When a candidate Lord is to be installed he shall furnish four strings of shells (or wampum) one span in length bound together at one end. Such will constitute the evidence of his pledge to the Confederate Lords that he will live according to the constitution of the Great Peace and exercise justice in all affairs.

When the pledge is furnished the Speaker of the Council must hold the shell strings in his hand and address the opposite side of the Council Fire and he shall commence his address saying: "Now behold him. He has now become a Confederate Lord. See how splendid he looks." An address may then follow. At the end of it he shall send the bunch of shell strings to the opposite side and they shall be received as evidence of the pledge. Then shall the opposite side say:

> We now do crown you with the sacred emblem of the deer's antlers, the emblem of your Lordship. You shall now become a mentor of the people of the Five Nations. The thickness of your skin shall be seven spans—which is to say that you shall be proof against anger, offensive actions and

criticism. Your heart shall be filled with peace and good will and your mind filled with a yearning for the welfare of the people of the Confederacy. With endless patience you shall carry out your duty and your firmness shall be tempered with tenderness for your people. Neither anger nor fury shall find lodgement in your mind and all your words and actions shall be marked with calm deliberation. In all of your deliberations in the Confederate Council, in your efforts at law making, in all your official acts, self interest shall be cast into oblivion. Cast not over your shoulder behind you the warnings of the nephews and nieces should they chide you for any error or wrong you may do, but return to the way of the Great Law which is just and right. Look and listen for the welfare of the whole people and have always in view not only the present but also the coming generations, even those whose faces are yet beneath the surface of the ground—the unborn of the future Nation.

29. When a Lordship title is to be conferred, the candidate Lord shall furnish the cooked venison, the corn bread and the corn soup, together with other necessary things and the labor for the Conferring of Titles Festival.
30. The Lords of the Confederacy may confer the Lordship title upon a candidate whenever the Great Law is recited, if there be a candidate, for the Great Law speaks all the rules.
31. If a Lord of the Confederacy should become seriously ill and be thought near death, the women who are heirs of his title shall go to his house and lift his crown of deer antlers, the emblem of his Lordship, and place them at one side. If the Creator spares him and he rises from his bed of sickness he may rise with the antlers on his brow.

    The following words shall be used to temporarily remove the antlers:

    Now our comrade Lord (or our relative Lord) the time has come when we must approach you in your illness. We remove for a time the deer's antlers from your brow, we remove the emblem of your Lordship title. The Great Law has decreed that no Lord should end his life with the antlers on his brow. We therefore lay them aside in the room. If the Creator spares you and you recover from your illness you shall rise from your bed with the antlers on your brow as before and you shall resume your duties as Lord of the Confederacy and you may labor again for the Confederate people.

32. If a Lord of the Confederacy should die while the Council of the Five Nations is in session the Council shall adjourn for ten days. No Confederate Council shall sit within ten days of the death of a Lord of the Confederacy.

    If the Three Brothers (the Mohawk, the Onondaga and the Seneca) should lose one of their Lords by death, the Younger Brothers (the Oneida and the Cayuga) shall come to the surviving Lords of the Three Brothers on the tenth day and console them. If the Younger Brothers lose one of their Lords then the Three Brothers shall come to them and console them. And the consolation shall be the reading of the contents of the thirteen shell (wampum) strings of Ayonhwhathah. At the termination of this rite a successor shall be appointed, to be appointed by the women heirs of the Lordship title. If the women are not yet ready to place their nominee before the Lords the Speaker shall say, "Come let us go out." All shall leave the Council or the place of gathering. The installation shall then wait until such a time as the women are ready. The Speaker shall lead the way from the house by saying, "Let us depart to the edge of the woods and lie in waiting on our bellies."

When the women title holders shall have chosen one of their sons the Confederate Lords will assemble in two places, the Younger Brothers in one place and the Three Older Brothers in another. The Lords who are to console the mourning Lords shall choose one of their number to sing the Pacification Hymn as they journey to the sorrowing Lords. The singer shall lead the way and the Lords and the people shall follow. When they reach the sorrowing Lords they shall hail the candidate Lord and perform the rite of Conferring the Lordship Title.

33. When a Confederate Lord dies, the surviving relatives shall immediately dispatch a messenger, a member of another clan, to the Lords in another locality. When the runner comes within hailing distance of the locality he shall utter a sad wail, thus: "Kwa-ah, Kwa-ah, Kwa-ah!" The sound shall be repeated three times and then again and again at intervals as many times as the distance may require. When the runner arrives at the settlement the people shall assemble and one must ask him the nature of his sad message. He shall then say, "Let us consider." Then he shall tell them of the death of the Lord. He shall deliver to them a string of shells (wampum) and say, "Here is the testimony, you have heard the message." He may then return home.

It now becomes the duty of the Lords of the locality to send runners to other localities and each locality shall send other messengers until all Lords are notified. Runners shall travel day and night.

34. If a Lord dies and there is no candidate qualified for the office in the family of the women title holders, the Lords of the Nation shall give the title into the hands of a sister family in the clan until such a time as the original family produces a candidate, when the title shall be restored to the rightful owners.

No Lordship title may be carried into the grave. The Lords of the Confederacy may dispossess a dead Lord of his title even at the grave.

Election of Pine Tree Chiefs

35. Should any man of the Nation assist with special ability or show great interest in the affairs of the Nation, if he proves himself wise, honest and worthy of confidence, the Confederate Lords may elect him to a seat with them and he may sit in the Confederate Council. He shall be proclaimed a 'Pine Tree sprung up for the Nation' and shall be installed as such at the next assembly for the installation of Lords. Should he ever do anything contrary to the rules of the Great Peace, he may not be deposed from office — no one shall cut him down — but thereafter everyone shall be deaf to his voice and his advice. Should he resign his seat and title no one shall prevent him. A Pine Tree chief has no authority to name a successor nor is his title hereditary.

Names, Duties and Rights of War Chiefs

36. The title names of the Chief Confederate Lords' War Chiefs shall be:

Ayonwaehs, War Chief under Lord Takarihoken (Mohawk)

Kahonwahdironh, War Chief under Lord Odatshedeh (Oneida)

Ayendes, War Chief under Lord Adodarhoh (Onondaga)

Wenenhs, War Chief under Lord Dekaenyonh (Cayuga)

Shoneradowaneh, War Chief under Lord Skanyadariyo (Seneca)

The women heirs of each head Lord's title shall be the heirs of the War Chief's title of their respective Lord.

The War Chiefs shall be selected from the eligible sons of the female families holding the head Lordship titles.

37. There shall be one War Chief for each Nation and their duties shall be to carry messages for their Lords and to take up the arms of war in case of emergency. They shall not participate in the proceedings of the Confederate Council but shall watch its progress and in case of an erroneous action by a Lord they shall receive the complaints of the people and convey the warnings of the women to him. The people who wish to convey messages to the Lords in the Confederate Council shall do so through the War Chief of their Nation. It shall ever be his duty to lay the cases, questions and propositions of the people before the Confederate Council.
38. When a War Chief dies another shall be installed by the same rite as that by which a Lord is installed.
39. If a War Chief acts contrary to instructions or against the provisions of the Laws of the Great Peace, doing so in the capacity of his office, he shall be deposed by his women relatives and by his men relatives. Either the women or the men alone or jointly may act in such a case. The women title holders shall then choose another candidate.
40. When the Lords of the Confederacy take occasion to dispatch a messenger in behalf of the Confederate Council, they shall wrap up any matter they may send and instruct the messenger to remember his errand, to turn not aside but to proceed faithfully to his destination and deliver his message according to every instruction.
41. If a message borne by a runner is the warning of an invasion he shall whoop, "Kwa-ah, Kwa-ah," twice and repeat at short intervals; then again at a longer interval.

    If a human being is found dead, the finder shall not touch the body but return home immediately shouting at short intervals, "Koo-weh!"

Clans and Consanguinity

42. Among the Five Nations and their posterity there shall be the following original clans: Great Name Bearer, Ancient Name Bearer, Great Bear, Ancient Bear, Turtle, Painted Turtle, Standing Rock, Large Plover, Deer, Pigeon Hawk, Eel, Ball, Opposite-Side-of-the-Hand, and Wild Potatoes. These clans distributed through their respective Nations, shall be the sole owners and holders of the soil of the country and in them is it vested as a birthright.
43. People of the Five Nations members of a certain clan shall recognize every other member of that clan, irrespective of the Nation, as relatives. Men and women, therefore, members of the same clan are forbidden to marry.
44. The lineal descent of the people of the Five Nations shall run in the female line. Women shall be considered the progenitors of the Nation. They shall own the land and the soil. Men and women shall follow the status of the mother.
45. The women heirs of the Confederated Lordship titles shall be called Royaneh (Noble) for all time to come.
46. The women of the Forty Eight (now fifty) Royaneh families shall be the heirs of the Authorized Names for all time to come.

    When an infant of the Five Nations is given an Authorized Name at the Midwinter Festival or at the Ripe Corn Festival, one in the cousinhood of which the infant is a member shall be appointed a speaker. He shall then announce to the opposite cousinhood the names of the father and the mother of the child together with the clan of the mother. Then the speaker shall announce the child's name twice. The uncle of the child shall then take the child in his arms and walking up and down the room shall sing: "My head is firm, I am of the Confederacy." As he sings the opposite cousinhood shall respond by chanting, "Hyenh, Hyenh, Hyenh, Hyenh," until the song is ended.

47. If the female heirs of a Confederate Lord's title become extinct, the title right shall be given by the Lords of the Confederacy to the sister family whom they shall elect and that family shall hold the name and transmit it to their (female) heirs, but they shall not appoint any of their sons as a candidate for a title until all the eligible men of the former family shall have died or otherwise have become ineligible.

48. If all the heirs of a Lordship title become extinct, and all the families in the clan, then the title shall be given by the Lords of the Confederacy to the family in a sister clan whom they shall elect.

49. If any of the Royaneh women, heirs of a titleship, shall wilfully withhold a Lordship or other title and refuse to bestow it, or if such heirs abandon, forsake or despise their heritage, then shall such women be deemed buried and their family extinct. The titleship shall then revert to a sister family or clan upon application and complaint. The Lords of the Confederacy shall elect the family or clan which shall in future hold the title.

50. The Royaneh women of the Confederacy heirs of the Lordship titles shall elect two women of their family as cooks for the Lord when the people shall assemble at his house for business or other purposes.

    It is not good nor honorable for a Confederate Lord to allow his people whom he has called to go hungry.

51. When a Lord holds a conference in his home, his wife, if she wishes, may prepare the food for the Union Lords who assemble with him. This is an honorable right which she may exercise and an expression of her esteem.

52. The Royaneh women, heirs of the Lordship titles, shall, should it be necessary, correct and admonish the holders of their titles. Those only who attend the Council may do this and those who do not shall not object to what has been said nor strive to undo the action.

53. When the Royaneh women, holders of a Lordship title, select one of their sons as a candidate, they shall select one who is trustworthy, of good character, of honest disposition, one who manages his own affairs, supports his own family, if any, and who has proven a faithful man to his Nation.

54. When a Lordship title becomes vacant through death or other cause, the Royaneh women of the clan in which the title is hereditary shall hold a council and shall choose one from among their sons to fill the office made vacant. Such a candidate shall not be the father of any Confederate Lord. If the choice is unanimous the name is referred to the men relatives of the clan. If they should disapprove it shall be their duty to select a candidate from among their own number. If then the men and women are unable to decide which of the two candidates shall be named, then the matter shall be referred to the Confederate Lords in the Clan. They shall decide which candidate shall be named. If the men and the women agree to a candidate his name shall be referred to the sister clans for confirmation. If the sister clans confirm the choice, they shall refer their action to their Confederate Lords who shall ratify the choice and present it to their cousin Lords, and if the cousin Lords confirm the name then the candidate

shall be installed by the proper ceremony for the conferring of Lordship titles.

Official Symbolism

55. A large bunch of shell strings, in the making of which the Five Nations Confederate Lords have equally contributed, shall symbolize the completeness of the union and certify the pledge of the nations represented by the Confederate Lords of the Mohawk, the Oneida, the Onondaga, the Cayuga and the Seneca, that all are united and formed into one body or union called the Union of the Great Law, which they have established.

A bunch of shell strings is to be the symbol of the council fire of the Five Nations Confederacy. And the Lord whom the council of Fire Keepers shall appoint to speak for them in opening the council shall hold the strands of shells in his hands when speaking. When he finishes speaking he shall deposit the strings on an elevated place (or pole) so that all the assembled Lords and the people may see it and know that the council is open and in progress.

When the council adjourns the Lord who has been appointed by his comrade Lords to close it shall take the strands of shells in his hands and address the assembled Lords. Thus will the council adjourn until such time and place as appointed by the council. Then shall the shell strings be placed in a place for safekeeping.

Every five years the Five Nations Confederate Lords and the people shall assemble together and shall ask one another if their minds are still in the same spirit of unity for the Great Binding Law and if any of the Five Nations shall not pledge continuance and steadfastness to the pledge of unity then the Great Binding Law shall dissolve.

56. Five strings of shell tied together as one shall represent the Five Nations. Each string shall represent one territory and the whole a completely united territory known as the Five Nations Confederate territory.

57. Five arrows shall be bound together very strong and each arrow shall represent one nation. As the five arrows are strongly bound this shall symbolize the complete union of the nations. Thus are the Five Nations united completely and enfolded together, united into one head, one body and one mind. Therefore they shall labor, legislate and council together for the interest of future generations.

The Lords of the Confederacy shall eat together from one bowl the feast of cooked beaver's tail. While they are eating they are to use no sharp utensils for if they should they might accidentally cut one another and bloodshed would follow. All measures must be taken to prevent the spilling of blood in any way.

58. There are now the Five Nations Confederate Lords standing with joined hands in a circle. This signifies and provides that should any one of the Confederate Lords leave the council and this Confederacy his crown of deer's horns, the emblem of his Lordship title, together with his birthright, shall lodge on the arms of the Union Lords whose hands are so joined. He forfeits his title and the crown falls from his brow but it shall remain in the Confederacy.

A further meaning of this is that if any time any one of the Confederate Lords choose to submit to the law of a foreign people he is no longer in but out of the Confederacy, and persons of this class shall be called "They have alienated themselves." Likewise such persons who submit to laws of foreign nations shall forfeit all birthrights and claims on the Five Nations Confederacy and territory.

You, the Five Nations Confederate Lords, be firm so that if a tree falls on your joined arms it shall not separate or weaken your hold. So shall the strength of the union be preserved.

59. A bunch of wampum shells on strings, three spans of the hand in length, the upper half of the bunch being white and the lower half black, and formed from equal contributions of the men of the Five Nations, shall be a token that the men have combined themselves into one head, one body and one thought, and it shall also symbolize their ratification of the peace pact of the Confederacy, whereby the Lords of the Five Nations have established the Great Peace.

The white portion of the shell strings represent the women and the black portion the men. The black portion, furthermore, is a token of power and authority vested in the men of the Five Nations.

This string of wampum vests the people with the right to correct their erring Lords. In case a part or all the Lords pursue a course not vouched for by the people and heed not the third warning of their women relatives, then the matter shall be taken to the General Council of the women of the Five Nations. If the Lords notified and warned three times fail to heed, then the case falls into the hands of the men of the Five Nations. The War Chiefs shall then, by right of such power and authority, enter the open council to warn the Lord or Lords to return from the wrong course. If the Lords heed the warning they shall say, "we will reply tomorrow." If then an answer is returned in favor of justice and in accord with this Great Law, then the Lords shall individually pledge themselves again by again furnishing the necessary shells for the pledge. Then shall the War Chief or Chiefs exhort the Lords urging them to be just and true.

Should it happen that the Lords refuse to heed the third warning, then two courses are open: either the men may decide in their council to depose the Lord or Lords or to club them to death with war clubs. Should they in their council decide to take the first course the War Chief shall address the Lord or Lords, saying: "Since you the Lords of the Five Nations have refused to return to the procedure of the Constitution, we now declare your seats vacant, we take off your horns, the token of your Lordship, and others shall be chosen and installed in your seats, therefore vacate your seats."

Should the men in their council adopt the second course, the War Chief shall order his men to enter the council, to take positions beside the Lords, sitting between them wherever possible. When this is accomplished the War Chief holding in his outstretched hand a bunch of black wampum strings shall say to the erring Lords: "So now, Lords of the Five United Nations, harken to these last words from your men. You have not heeded the warnings of the women relatives, you have not heeded the warnings of the General Council of women and you have not heeded the warnings of the men of the nations, all urging you to return to the right course of action. Since you are determined to resist and to withhold justice from your people there is only one course for us to adopt." At this point the War Chief shall let drop the bunch of black wampum and the men shall spring to their feet and club the erring Lords to death. Any erring Lord may submit before the War Chief lets fall the black wampum. Then his execution is withheld.

The black wampum here used symbolizes that the power to execute is buried but that it may be raised up again by the men. It is buried but when occasion arises they may pull it up and derive their power and authority to act as here described.

60. A broad dark belt of wampum of thirty-eight rows, having a white heart in the center, on either side of which are two white squares all connected with the heart by white rows of beads shall be the emblem of the unity of the Five Nations.[2]

The first of the squares on the left represents the Mohawk nation and its territory; the second square on the left and the one near the heart, represents the Oneida nation and its territory; the white heart in the middle represents the Onondaga nation and its territory, and it also means that the heart of the Five Nations is single in its loyalty to the Great Peace, that the Great Peace is lodged in the heart (meaning the Onondaga Lords), and that the Council Fire is to burn there for the Five Nations, and further, it means that the authority is given to advance the cause of peace whereby hostile nations out of the Confederacy shall cease warfare; the white square to the right of the heart represents the Cayuga nation and its territory and the fourth and last white square represents the Seneca nation and its territory.

White shall here symbolize that no evil or jealous thoughts shall creep into the minds of the Lords while in Council under the Great Peace. White, the emblem of peace, love, charity and equity surrounds and guards the Five Nations.

61. Should a great calamity threaten the generations rising and living of the Five United Nations, then he who is able to climb to the top of the Tree of the Great Long Leaves may do so. When, then, he reaches the top of the tree he shall look about in all directions, and, should he see that evil things indeed are approaching, then he shall call to the people of the Five United Nations assembled beneath the Tree of the Great Long Leaves and say: "A calamity threatens your happiness."

Then shall the Lords convene in council and discuss the impending evil.

When all the truths relating to the trouble shall be fully known and found to be truths, then shall the people seek out a Tree of Ka-hon-ka-ah-go-nah,[3] and when they shall find it they shall assemble their heads together and lodge for a time between its roots. Then, their labors being finished, they may hope for happiness for many days after.

62. When the Confederate Council of the Five Nations declares for a reading of the belts of shell calling to mind these laws, they shall provide for the reader a specially made mat woven of the fibers of wild hemp. The mat shall not be used again, for such formality is called the honoring of the importance of the law.

63. Should two sons of opposite sides of the council fire agree in a desire to hear the reciting of the laws of the Great Peace and so refresh their memories in the way ordained by the founder of the Confederacy, they shall notify Adodarho. He then shall consult with five of his coactive Lords and they in turn shall consult with their eight brethren. Then should they decide to accede to the request of the two sons from opposite sides of the Council Fire, Adodarho shall send messengers to notify the Chief Lords of each of the Five Nations. Then they shall despatch their War Chiefs to notify their brother and cousin Lords of the meeting and its time and place.

When all have come and have assembled, Adodarhoh, in conjunction with his cousin Lords, shall appoint one Lord who shall repeat the laws of the Great Peace. Then shall they announce who they have chosen to repeat the laws of the Great Peace to the two sons. Then shall the chosen one repeat the laws of the Great Peace.

64. At the ceremony of the installation of Lords if there is only one expert speaker and singer of the law and the Pacification Hymn to stand at the council fire, then when this speaker and singer has finished addressing one side of the fire he shall go to the opposite side and reply to his own speech and song. He shall thus act for both sides of the fire until the entire ceremony has been completed. Such a speaker and singer shall be termed the "Two Faced" because he speaks and sings for both sides of the fire.

65. I, Dekanawida, and the Union Lords, now uproot the tallest pine tree and into the cavity thereby made we cast all weapons of war. Into the depths of the earth, down into the deep underearth currents of water flowing to unknown regions we cast all the weapons of strife. We bury them from sight and we plant again the tree. Thus shall the Great Peace be established and hostilities shall no longer be known between the Five Nations but peace to the United People.

Laws of Adoption

66. The father of a child of great comeliness, learning, ability or specially loved because of some circumstance may, at the will of the child's clan, select a name from his own (the father's) clan and bestow it by ceremony, such as is provided. This naming shall be only temporary and shall be called, "A name hung about the neck."

67. Should any person, a member of the Five Nations' Confederacy, specially esteem a man or woman of another clan or of a foreign nation, he may choose a name and bestow it upon that person so esteemed. The naming shall be in accord with the ceremony of bestowing names. Such a name is only a temporary one and shall be called "A name hung about the neck." A short string of shells shall be delivered with the name as a record and a pledge.

68. Should any member of the Five Nations, a family or person belonging to a foreign nation submit a proposal for adoption into a clan of one of the Five Nations, he or they shall furnish a string of shells, a span in length, as a pledge to the clan into which he or they wish to be adopted. The Lords of the nation shall then consider the proposal and submit a decision.

69. Any member of the Five Nations who through esteem or other feeling wishes to adopt an individual, a family or number of families may offer adoption to him or them and if accepted the matter shall be brought to the attention of the Lords for confirmation and the Lords must confirm adoption.

70. When the adoption of anyone shall have been confirmed by the Lords of the Nation, the Lords shall address the people of their nation and say: "Now you of our nation, be informed that such a person, such a family or such families have ceased forever to bear their birth nation's name and have buried it in the depths of the earth. Henceforth let no one of our nation ever mention the original name or nation of their birth. To do so will be to hasten the end of our peace."

Laws of Emigration

71. When any person or family belonging to the Five Nations desires to abandon their birth nation and the territory of the Five Nations, they shall inform the Lords of their nation and the Confederate Council of the Five Nations shall take cognizance of it.

72. When any person or any of the people of the Five Nations emigrate and reside in a region distant from the territory of the Five Nations Confederacy, the Lords of the Five Nations

at will may send a messenger carrying a broad belt of black shells and when the messenger arrives he shall call the people together or address them personally displaying the belt of shells and they shall know that this is an order for them to return to their original homes and to their council fires.

Rights of Foreign Nations

73. The soil of the earth from one end of the land to the other is the property of the people who inhabit it. By birthright the Ongwehonweh (Original beings) are the owners of the soil which they own and occupy and none other may hold it. The same law has been held from the oldest times.

    The Great Creator has made us of the one blood and of the same soil he made us and as only different tongues constitute different nations he established different hunting grounds and territories and made boundary lines between them.

74. When any alien nation or individual is admitted into the Five Nations the admission shall be understood only to be a temporary one. Should the person or nation create loss, do wrong or cause suffering of any kind to endanger the peace of the Confederacy, the Confederate Lords shall order one of their war chiefs to reprimand him or them and if a similar offence is again committed the offending party or parties shall be expelled from the territory of the Five United Nations.

75. When a member of an alien nation comes to the territory of the Five Nations and seeks refuge and permanent residence, the Lords of the Nation to which he comes shall extend hospitality and make him a member of the nation. Then shall he be accorded equal rights and privileges in all matters except as after mentioned.

76. No body of alien people who have been adopted temporarily shall have a vote in the council of the Lords of the Confederacy, for only they who have been invested with Lordship titles may vote in the Council. Aliens have nothing by blood to make claim to a vote and should they have it, not knowing all the traditions of the Confederacy, might go against its Great Peace. In this manner the Great Peace would be endangered and perhaps be destroyed.

77. When the Lords of the Confederacy decide to admit a foreign nation and an adoption is made, the Lords shall inform the adopted nation that its admission is only temporary. They shall also say to the nation that it must never try to control, to interfere with or to injure the Five Nations nor disregard the Great Peace or any of its rules or customs. That in no way should they cause disturbance or injury. Then should the adopted nation disregard these injunctions, their adoption shall be annulled and they shall be expelled.

    The expulsion shall be in the following manner: The council shall appoint one of their War Chiefs to convey the message of annulment and he shall say, "You (naming the nation) listen to me while I speak. I am here to inform you again of the will of the Five Nations' Council. It was clearly made known to you at a former time. Now the Lords of the Five Nations have decided to expel you and cast you out. We disown you now and annul your adoption. Therefore you must look for a path in which to go and lead away all your people. It was you, not we, who committed wrong and caused this sentence of annulment. So then go your way and depart from the territory of the Five Nations and from the Confederacy."

78. Whenever a foreign nation enters the Confederacy or accepts the Great Peace,

the Five Nations and the foreign nation shall enter into an agreement and compact by which the foreign nation shall endeavor to persuade other nations to accept the Great Peace.

Rights and Powers of War

79. Skanawatih shall be vested with a double office, duty and with double authority. One-half of his being shall hold the Lordship title and the other half shall hold the title of War Chief. In the event of war he shall notify the five War Chiefs of the Confederacy and command them to prepare for war and have their men ready at the appointed time and place for engagement with the enemy of the Great Peace.

80. When the Confederate Council of the Five Nations has for its object the establishment of the Great Peace among the people of an outside nation and that nation refuses to accept the Great Peace, then by such refusal they bring a declaration of war upon themselves from the Five Nations. Then shall the Five Nations seek to establish the Great Peace by a conquest of the rebellious nation.

81. When the men of the Five Nations, now called forth to become warriors, are ready for battle with an obstinate opposing nation that has refused to accept the Great Peace, then one of the five War Chiefs shall be chosen by the warriors of the Five Nations to lead the army into battle. It shall be the duty of the War Chief so chosen to come before his warriors and address them. His aim shall be to impress upon them the necessity of good behavior and strict obedience to all the commands of the War Chiefs. He shall deliver an oration exhorting them with great zeal to be brave and courageous and never to be guilty of cowardice. At the conclusion of his oration he shall march forward and commence the War Song and he shall sing:

    Now I am greatly surprised
    And, therefore I shall use it —
    The power of my War Song.
    I am of the Five Nations
    And I shall make supplication
    To the Almighty Creator.
    He has furnished this army.
    My warriors shall be mighty
    In the strength of the Creator.
    Between him and my song they are
    For it was he who gave the song
    This war song that I sing!

82. When the warriors of the Five Nations are on an expedition against an enemy, the War Chief shall sing the War Song as he approaches the country of the enemy and not cease until his scouts have reported that the army is near the enemies' lines when the War Chief shall approach with great caution and prepare for the attack.

83. When peace shall have been established by the termination of the war against a foreign nation, then the War Chief shall cause all the weapons of war to be taken from the nation. Then shall the Great Peace be established and that nation shall observe all the rules of the Great Peace for all time to come.

84. Whenever a foreign nation is conquered or has by their own will accepted the Great Peace their own system of internal government may continue, but they must cease all warfare against other nations.

85. Whenever a war against a foreign nation is pushed until that nation is about exterminated because of its refusal to accept the Great Peace and if that nation shall by its obstinacy become exterminated, all their rights, property and territory shall become the property of the Five Nations.

86. Whenever a foreign nation is conquered and the survivors are brought into the territory of the Five Nations' Confederacy and placed under the Great Peace the two shall be known as the Conqueror and the Conquered. A symbolic relationship shall be devised and be placed in some symbolic position. The conquered nation shall have no voice in the councils of the Confederacy in the body of the Lords.

87. When the War of the Five Nations on a foreign rebellious nation is ended, peace shall be restored to that nation by a withdrawal of all their weapons of war by the War Chief of the Five Nations. When all the terms of peace shall have been agreed upon a state of friendship shall be established.

88. When the proposition to establish the Great Peace is made to a foreign nation it shall be done in mutual council. The foreign nation is to be persuaded by reason and urged to come into the Great Peace. If the Five Nations fail to obtain the consent of the nation at the first council a second council shall be held and upon a second failure a third council shall be held and this third council shall end the peaceful methods of persuasion. At the third council the War Chief of the Five Nations shall address the Chief of the foreign nation and request him three times to accept the Great Peace. If refusal steadfastly follows the War Chief shall let the bunch of white lake shells drop from his outstretched hand to the ground and shall bound quickly forward and club the offending chief to death. War shall thereby be declared and the War Chief shall have his warriors at his back to meet any emergency. War must continue until the contest is won by the Five Nations.

89. When the Lords of the Five Nations propose to meet in conference with a foreign nation with proposals for an acceptance of the Great Peace, a large band of warriors shall conceal themselves in a secure place safe from the espionage of the foreign nation but as near at hand as possible. Two warriors shall accompany the Union Lord who carries the proposals and these warriors shall be especially cunning. Should the Lord be attacked, these warriors shall hasten back to the army of warriors with the news of the calamity which fell through the treachery of the foreign nation.

90. When the Five Nations' Council declares war any Lord of the Confederacy may enlist with the warriors by temporarily renouncing his sacred Lordship title which he holds through the election of his women relatives. The title then reverts to them and they may bestow it upon another temporarily until the war is over when the Lord, if living, may resume his title and seat in the Council.

91. A certain wampum belt of black beads shall be the emblem of the authority of the Five War Chiefs to take up the weapons of war and with their men to resist invasion. This shall be called a war in defense of the territory.

Treason or Secession of a Nation

92. If a nation, part of a nation, or more than one nation within the Five Nations should in any way endeavor to destroy the Great Peace by neglect or violating its laws and resolve to dissolve the Confederacy, such a nation or such nations shall be deemed guilty of treason and called enemies of the Confederacy and the Great Peace.

It shall then be the duty of the Lords of the Confederacy who remain faithful to resolve to warn the offending people. They shall be warned once and if a second warning is necessary they shall be driven from the territory of the Confederacy by the War Chiefs and his men.

Rights of the People of the Five Nations

93. Whenever a specially important matter or a great emergency is presented before the Confederate Council and the nature of the matter affects the entire body of the Five Nations, threatening their utter ruin, then the Lords of the Confederacy must submit the matter to the decision of their people and the decision of the people shall affect the decision of the Confederate Council. This decision shall be a confirmation of the voice of the people.

94. The men of every clan of the Five Nations shall have a Council Fire ever burning in readiness for a council of the clan. When it seems necessary for a council to be held to discuss the welfare of the clans, then the men may gather about the fire. This council shall have the same rights as the council of the women.

95. The women of every clan of the Five Nations shall have a Council Fire ever burning in readiness for a council of the clan. When in their opinion it seems necessary for the interest of the people they shall hold a council and their decisions and recommendations shall be introduced before the Council of the Lords by the War Chief for its consideration.

96. All the Clan council fires of a nation or of the Five Nations may unite into one general council fire, or delegates from all the council fires may be appointed to unite in a general council for discussing the interests of the people. The people shall have the right to make appointments and to delegate their power to others of their number. When their council shall have come to a conclusion on any matter, their decision shall be reported to the Council of the Nation or to the Confederate Council (as the case may require) by the War Chief or the War Chiefs.

97. Before the real people united their nations, each nation had its council fires. Before the Great Peace their councils were held. The five Council Fires shall continue to burn as before and they are not quenched. The Lords of each nation in future shall settle their nation's affairs at this council fire governed always by the laws and rules of the council of the Confederacy and by the Great Peace.

98. If either a nephew or a niece see an irregularity in the performance of the functions of the Great Peace and its laws, in the Confederate Council or in the conferring of Lordship titles in an improper way, through their War Chief they may demand that such actions become subject to correction and that the matter conform to the ways prescribed by the laws of the Great Peace.

Religious Ceremonies Protected

99. The rites and festivals of each nation shall remain undisturbed and shall continue as before because they were given by the people of old times as useful and necessary for the good of men.

100. It shall be the duty of the Lords of each brotherhood to confer at the approach of the time of the Midwinter Thanksgiving and to notify their people of the approaching festival. They shall hold a council over the matter and arrange its details and begin the Thanksgiving five days after the moon of Dis-ko-nah is new. The people shall assemble at the appointed place and the nephews shall notify the people of the time and place. From the beginning to the end the Lords shall preside over the

Thanksgiving and address the people from time to time.

101. It shall be the duty of the appointed managers of the Thanksgiving festivals to do all that is needed for carrying out the duties of the occasions.

The recognized festivals of Thanksgiving shall be the Midwinter Thanksgiving, the Maple or Sugar-making Thanksgiving, the Raspberry Thanksgiving, the Strawberry Thanksgiving, the Cornplanting Thanksgiving, the Corn Hoeing Thanksgiving, the Little Festival of Green Corn, the Great Festival of Ripe Corn and the complete Thanksgiving for the Harvest.

Each nation's festivals shall be held in their Long Houses.

102. When the Thanksgiving for the Green Corn comes the special managers, both the men and women, shall give it careful attention and do their duties properly.

103. When the Ripe Corn Thanksgiving is celebrated the Lords of the Nation must give it the same attention as they give to the Midwinter Thanksgiving.

104. Whenever any man proves himself by his good life and his knowledge of good things, naturally fitted as a teacher of good things, he shall be recognized by the Lords as a teacher of peace and religion and the people shall hear him.

The Installation Song

105. The song used in installing the new Lord of the Confederacy shall be sung by Adodarhoh and it shall be:

Haii,	haii	Agwah wi-yoh
"	"	A-kon-he-watha
"	"	Ska-we-ye-se-go-wah
"	"	Yon-gwa-wih
"	"	Ya-kon-he-wa-tha

Haii,	haii	It is good indeed
"	"	(That) a broom, —
"	"	A great wing,
"	"	It is given me
"	"	For a sweeping instrument.

106. Whenever a person properly entitled desires to learn the Pacification Song he is privileged to do so but he must prepare a feast at which his teachers may sit with him and sing. The feast is provided that no misfortune may befall them for singing the song on an occasion when no chief is installed.

Protection of the House

107. A certain sign shall be known to all the people of the Five Nations which shall denote that the owner or occupant of a house is absent. A stick or pole in a slanting or leaning position shall indicate this and be the sign. Every person not entitled to enter the house by right of living within it upon seeing such a sign shall not approach the house either by day or by night but shall keep as far away as his business will permit.

Funeral Addresses

108. At the funeral of a Lord of the Confederacy, say:

> Now we become reconciled as you start away. You were once a Lord of the Five Nations' Confederacy and the United People trusted you. Now we release you for it is true that it is no longer possible for us to walk about together on the earth. Now, therefore, we lay it (the body) here. Here we lay it away. Now then we say to you, 'Persevere onward to the place where the Creator dwells in peace. Let not the things of the earth hinder you. Let nothing that transpired while yet you lived hinder you.

In hunting you once took delight; in the game of Lacrosse you once took delight and in the feasts and pleasant occasions your mind was amused, but now do not allow thoughts of these things to give you trouble. Let not your relatives hinder you and also let not your friends and associates trouble your mind. Regard none of these things.'

Now then, in turn, you here present who were related to this man and you who were his friends and associates, behold the path that is yours also! Soon we ourselves will be left in that place. For this reason hold yourselves in restraint as you go from place to place. In your actions and in your conversation do no idle thing. Speak not idle talk neither gossip. Be careful of this and speak not and do not give way to evil behavior. One year is the time that you must abstain from unseemly levity but if you can not do this for ceremony, ten days is the time to regard these things for respect.

109. At the funeral of a War Chief, say:

Now we become reconciled as you start away. You were once a War Chief of the Five Nations' Confederacy and the United People trusted you as their guard from the enemy. (The remainder is the same as the address at the funeral of a Lord).

110. At the funeral of a Warrior, say:

Now we become reconciled as you start away. Once you were a devoted provider and protector of your family and you were ever ready to take part in battles for the Five Nations' Confederacy. The United People trusted you. (The remainder is the same as the address at the funeral of a Lord).

111. At the funeral of a young man, say:

Now we become reconciled as you start away. In the beginning of your career you are taken away and the flower of your life is withered away. (The remainder is the same as the address at the funeral of a Lord).

112. At the funeral of a chief woman, say:

Now we become reconciled as you start away. You were once a chief woman in the Five Nations' Confederacy. You once were a mother of the nations. Now we release you for it is true that it is no longer possible for us to walk about together on the earth. Now, therefore, we lay it (the body) here. Here we lay it away. Now then we say to you, 'Persevere onward to the place where the Creator dwells in peace. Let not the things of the earth hinder you. Let nothing that transpired while you lived hinder you. Looking after your family was a sacred duty and you were faithful. You were one of the many joint heirs of the Lordship titles. Feastings were yours and you had pleasant occasions...' (The remainder is the same as the address at the funeral of a Lord).

113. At the funeral of a woman of the people, say:

Now we become reconciled as you start away. You were once a woman in the flower of life and the bloom is now withered away. You once held a sacred position as a mother of the nation. (Etc.) Looking after your family was a sacred duty and you were faithful. Feastings... (etc.) (The remainder is the same as the address at the funeral of a Lord).

114. At the funeral of an infant or young woman, say:

Now we become reconciled as you start away. You were a tender bud and gladdened our hearts for only a few days. Now the bloom has withered away... (etc.) Let none of the things that transpired on earth hinder you. Let nothing that happened while you lived hinder you. (The remainder is the same as the address at the funeral of a Lord).[4]

115. When an infant dies within three days, mourning shall continue only five days. Then shall you gather the little boys and girls at the house of mourning and at the funeral feast a speaker shall address the children and bid them be happy once more, though by a death, gloom has been cast over them. Then shall the black clouds roll away and the sky shall show blue once more. Then shall the children be again in sunshine.

116. When a dead person is brought to the burial place, the speaker on the opposite side of the Council Fire shall bid the bereaved family cheer their minds once again and rekindle their hearth fires in peace, to put their house in order and once again be in brightness for darkness has covered them. He shall say that the black clouds shall roll away and that the bright blue sky is visible once more. Therefore shall they be in peace in the sunshine again.

117. Three strings of shell one span in length shall be employed in addressing the assemblage at the burial of the dead. The speaker shall say:

> Hearken you who are here, this body is to be covered. Assemble in this place again ten days hence for it is the decree of the Creator that mourning shall cease when ten days have expired. Then shall a feast be made.

Then at the expiration of ten days the speaker shall say:

> Continue to listen you who are here. The ten days of mourning have expired and your minds must now be freed of sorrow as before the loss of a relative. The relatives have decided to make a little compensation to those who have assisted at the funeral. It is a mere expression of thanks. This is to the one who did the cooking while the body was lying in the house. Let her come forward and receive this gift and be dismissed from the task.

In substance this shall be repeated for every one who assisted in any way until all have been remembered.

Editor's Notes:

1 Chestnut wood throws out sparks in burning, thereby creating a disturbance in the council.

2 This is the Hiawatha Belt, now in the Congressional Library.

3 A great swamp Elm.

4 The above ellipses and 'etc.' remarks are transcribed directly from the text I (Gerald Murphy) copied.

1492 and All That: Making a Garden out of a Wilderness

Ramsay Cook

"The Land is a Garden of Eden before them, and behind them a desolate wilderness."

Joel 2:3

"Is not America," Fernand Braudel asks in *The Perspective of the World,* the third volume of his magisterial *Civilization and Capitalism,* "perhaps the true explanation of Europe's greatness? Did not Europe discover or indeed 'invent' America, and has Europe not always celebrated Columbus's voyages as the greatest event in history 'since the creation?'" And then the great French historian concludes that "America was...the achievement by which Europe most truly revealed her own nature."[1] Braudel wrote without any intended irony, but that final remark about Europe truly revealing "her own nature" is perhaps what is really at issue in the current reassessment of the implications of Columbus's landfall at Guanahari, or San Salvador, as he named it in his first act of semiotic imperialism. ("Each received a new name from me,"[2] he recorded.)

That "nature" is captured by Marc Lescarbot in a sentence from his remarkable *History of New France,* published in 1609, which goes right to the heart of what we have apparently decided to call the "encounter" between the Old World and the New that Columbus symbolizes. Acadia, he wrote, "having two kinds of soil that God has given unto man as his possession, who can doubt that when it shall be cultivated it will be a land of promise?"[3] I hardly need to explain why I think that sentence is so revealing of the European "nature," but I will. It forthrightly articulates the renaissance European's conviction that man was chosen by the Creator to possess and dominate the rest of creation. And it further assumes that, for the land to be fully possessed, it must be cultivated: tilled, improved, developed. The result: a promised land, a paradise, a garden of delights. Lescarbot's observations seemed so axiomatic then, and for nearly five centuries afterward, that almost no one questioned his vision of a promised land—at least almost no European. But that has begun to change. Contemporary Europe, as much in its western as in its eastern portions, struggles to redefine itself. Consequently Europe overseas, as J.G.A. Pocock recently argued in a brilliant essay,[4] is being forced to look again at the meaning of what Gómara in his *General History of the Indies* (1552) called "the greatest event since the creation of the world"[5]—the meaning of the "discovery of America." [...]

The process whereby a way of life—the European one—triumphed over the Amerindian one was fairly rapid in New England, being virtually completed by 1800. Since the colonization of Acadia, a vast area that included present-day Nova Scotia, New Brunswick, Prince Edward Island, part of Quebec (Gaspesia), and a portion of Maine, advanced at a slower pace, the two ways

Excerpt from Ramsay Cook, "1492 and All That: Making a Garden Out of Wilderness," from Ramsay Cook, *Canada, Quebec and the Uses of Nationalism,* Second Edition (Toronto: McClelland and Stewart, 1995), 51–72, 259–262. Used by permission, McClelland & Stewart Ltd. The Canadian Publishers.

of life existed side by side, interacting with one another, for a longer period of time. Leslie Upton's study, *Micmacs and Colonists,* noted that at the beginning of this period, the Treaty of Utrecht of 1713, the number of Micmac people of Acadia still roughly equalled European settlers even though the Native population had declined drastically. In the seventeenth century Acadia had been the scene of imperial competition and war between France and Britain and that had hardly been conducive to extensive settlement. By 1650 there were some fifty households at Port Royal and Le Have; that population had grown to about 900 souls by the 1680s. So, too, population was spreading from Port Royal to the Minas Basin, to Beaubassin and scattered along the north shore of the Bay of Fundy. "When the British took control for the third and last time," Upton writes, "capturing Port Royal in 1710, there were just over 1,500 native born Acadians with roots going back from two to four generations. The Micmac population stood at about the same number having declined from 3,000 or so at the beginning of the seventeenth century. In one hundred years the French had been able to establish a white population only half the size of the Micmacs' at their first arrival."[6] It is the very slowness of the process, and the richness of the documentation for the seventeenth century, that makes the study of the ecology of contact in Acadia so fascinating.

Between 1604 and 1708 six major writers—of varied background—composed accounts of what Nicolas Denys called "the natural history" of Acadia (and this leaves out Jacques Cartier's sixteenth-century account). Now I think it is highly significant that Denys believed that "natural history" included not just geography, geology, climate, and the flora and fauna, but also the inhabitants of the new land. The model, of course, was Pliny's *Natural History,* a work that played such a large part in determining what was discovered in America that the Roman almost deserves to be ranked with Columbus.[7] Nor was Denys in anyway unique: Champlain, Lescarbot, Biard, Le Clercq, and Dièreville, the authors of the other five major contemporary accounts of seventeenth-century Acadia, all followed a similar recipe though varying the amounts of the ingredients somewhat. Each of these writers approached Acadia from an ecological perspective, setting people squarely in their environment and noting the contrast between European and Amerindian ways of living in, and belonging to, their environment.

Each of these seventeenth-century writers devoted a substantial portion of his book to descriptions of the natural world. There was a certain awesomeness about this wilderness and its abundance of birds, beasts, fish, and flowers. In 1604, at Seal Island, Champlain's keen eye identified firs, pines, larches, and poplars, and more than a dozen species of birds, not all of which he recognized. At nearly every landing he made similar observations.[8] He identified the skimmer with its extended lower bill, while Denys described the majestic bald eagle carrying off a rabbit in its talons. Marc Lescarbot provided comparable descriptions. His famous poem "Adieu à la Nouvelle France" is a versified catalogue of the environment, including that indigenous marvel, "*un oiselet semblable au papillon,*" the hummingbird. This ornithological marvel, sometimes called the Bird of Heaven, provided the same sense of admiration in early visitors to North America that the flamboyant parrot produced in explorers of South America, beginning with Columbus. The parrot, captured and transported, quickly became the symbol of America in post-Columbian art. The hummingbird, impossible to rear in captivity, remained in the Americas. Among insects the firefly was highly appealing, the mosquito detested.[9]

Of the creatures of the animal world none attracted more curiosity than the beaver. It became an animal more marvellous in the Plinean imaginations of Le Clercq and Denys than in reality. It performed as architect, mason, carpenter, even hod carrier, walking upright with a load of mud piled on its broad tail. A natural rear end loader! "Its flesh is delicate," Father Le Clercq reported, "and very much like that of mutton. The kidneys are sought by apothecaries, and are used with effect in easing women in childbirth, and in mitigating hysterics."[10] The value of beaver pelts hardly needed comment.

Then there was the moose that cured itself of epilepsy by scratching its ear with its own cloven hoof. At least the flying squirrel was the real thing. Denys's description of the cod fishery, not surprisingly since he was a merchant, was accurate and detailed. On the southeast coast of St. Mary's Bay, when the tide dropped, Champlain found mussels, clams, and sea snails, while elsewhere oysters abounded. The swarms of fish that swam in the waterways filled these men with excitement. On the Miramichi, Denys claimed that he had been kept awake all night by the loud sounds of salmon splashing. The fertility and agricultural potential of the new land were naturally a constant preoccupation. "The entire country is covered with very dense forests," Champlain wrote of the site that would become Annapolis Royal, "...except a point a league and a half up the river, where there are some oaks which are very scattered and a number of wild vines. These could be easily cleared and the place brought under cultivation." Nor did Champlain miss the minerals and metals—silver at Mink Cove, iron further north on Digby Neck.[11]

Moreover, it is from these writers that at least a partial sketch of the lives and customs of the Northeastern Algonquian peoples can be reconstructed. Champlain recorded the practice of swidden agriculture among the Abenaki—corn, beans, and squash—and even noted the use of horseshoe crab shells, probably as fertilizer.[12] Hunting and fishing methods were remarked upon, though the lack of details is somewhat surprising, particularly when contrasted with the lengthy accounts of religious beliefs—or supposed lack of them—of the various inhabitants of Acadia. "Jugglery," or shamanism, and also medical practices were of particular interest—indeed, Dièreville even convinced himself of the efficacy of some shamanistic cures. So, too, dress, hairstyles, courtship and marriage customs, and ceremonies surrounding childbirth and death were carefully recorded and sometimes compared to classical and contemporary European practices. Lescarbot, for example, concluded that the Jesuits were quite mistaken in attempting to force Christian monogamy on the Micmacs, arguing that indigenous marriage customs would best be "left in the state in which they were found." In contrast to some Jesuit writers—and Brian Moore—Lescarbot judged the Aboriginal people very modest in sexual matters. This he attributed partly to their familiarity with nakedness but chiefly "to their keeping bared the head, where lies the fountain of the spirits which excite to procreation, partly to the lack of salt, of hot spices, of wine, of meats which provoke desire, and partly to their frequent use of tobacco, the smoke of which dulls the senses, and mounting up to the brain hinders the functions of Venus." On the other hand, he believed that one romantic innovation introduced by the French actually contributed to the improvement of Aboriginal life: the kiss. Though Professor Karen Anderson has followed up Lescarbot's insight about the impact of the missionaries on marriage among the Native people of New France, no one, as far as I know, has advanced our knowledge of the relationship between civilization and osculation.[13]

Virtually all male European visitors to Acadia were struck by the division of labour in Aboriginal communities. Women, it was agreed, "work harder than the men, who play the gentleman, and care only for hunting or for war." Despite this, Lescarbot wrote approvingly, "they love their husbands more than women of our parts." It is interesting that in his discussion of the ease with which Micmac marriages could be dissolved, Father Le Clercq remained detached and uncensorious. "In a word," he remarked laconically, "they hold it as a maxim that each one is free; that one can do whatever he wishes: and that it is not sensible to put constraint upon men." And the priest understood that the maxim applied to both men and women.[14]

Games and the Native peoples' apparent penchant for gambling were described though not always understood. Then there were science and technology. Father Le Clercq, perhaps the most ethnologically astute of seventeenth-century observers, provided an intriguing account of the ways the Gaspesians read the natural world: their interpretation of the stars and the winds, how they reckoned distance and recognized the changing seasons. The usefulness and limitations of indigenous technology were also commented upon. The efficiency of the birchbark canoe won widespread admiration. "The Savages of Port Royal can go to Kebec in ten or twelve days by means of the rivers which they navigate almost up to their sources," Lescarbot discovered, "and thence carrying their little bark canoes through the woods they reach another stream which flows into the river of Canada and thus greatly expedite their long voyages." While household utensils, manufactured from bark, roots, and stumps, were ingenious, the French realized that the Aboriginals were happy to replace them with metal wares. War and its weaponry drew the somewhat surprised comment that "neither profit nor the desire to extend boundaries, but rather vengeance, caused fairly frequent hostilities between native groups." Torture was graphically described, and condemned, though it was recognized—and judged a sign of savagery—that "to die in this manner is, among the savages, to die as a great captain and as a man of great courage."[15]

Much else also caught the attention of these ethnologists: the commonality of property, the importance of gift exchange, the practice of setting aside weapons before entering into discussions with strangers, and the expectation that strangers should do the same. And even though the Natives were "crafty, thievish and treacherous," Lescarbot admitted somewhat superciliously that "they do not lack wit, and might come to something if they were civilized, and knew the various trades."[16]

Though observations and judgements were made with great confidence, indeed, often rather cavalierly, these Europeans were aware that there often existed an unbridgeable communications chasm between the observers and the observed. Like every explorer before them, the French in Acadia attempted to resolve the problem in two ways. The first was to take young Natives back to France for an immersion course in French. ("We had on board a savage," Lescarbot noted in 1608, "who was much astonished to see the buildings, spires and windmills of France, but more the women, whom he had never seen dressed after our manner.") While these interpreters were doubtless helpful in breaking down the "effect of the confusion of Babel," it was hardly a permanent resolution to what Father Biard realized was a fundamental problem. Yet for the French to learn the local languages was time-consuming and the results often frustrating. Learning words was not the same as learning to communicate. "As these Savages have no formulated Religion, government, towns, nor trade," Biard recorded in exasperation, "so the words and proper phrases for all of these things are lacking." The confusion of words with things, of the sign with the referent, was, as Todorov has brilliantly shown, endemic to the European attempt to comprehend America. Acadia was no exception, though I have, unfortunately, not found any example quite so delicious as the linguistic dilemma encountered by Protestant missionaries in Hawaii. There the Islanders reportedly practised some twenty forms of sexual activity judged illicit—perhaps better, non-missionary. Each had a separate name in the native language, thus making translation of the Seventh Commandment virtually impossible without condoning the other nineteen forms of the joy of sex! The Native peoples of Acadia were apparently much less resourceful—or the celibate Jesuits less well trained as participant-observers.[17]

The natural, ethnographic, and linguistic accounts were not, of course, the work of biological scientists or cultural anthropologists—even taking into account our contemporary scepticism about the objectivity of anthropologists. Rather, they were the observations of seventeenth-century Frenchmen taking inventory of a new land they intended to explore, settle, develop, and Christianize—in brief, to colonize. It is in their works that much of what Braudel called Europe's "own nature" is "most truly revealed." In differing ways it is made emphatically plain by each of these authors that the French objective in Acadia, in the words of Father Biard, was "to make a Garden out of the wilderness." Nor should this be read narrowly as simply meaning the evangelization of the people who lived in Acadia.[18]

In the revealing introduction to his rich and thoughtful *Relation* of 1616, Biard wrote: "For verily all of this region, though capable of the same prosperity as ours, nevertheless through Satan's malevolence, which reigns there, is a horrible wilderness, scarcely less miserable on account of the scarcity of bodily comforts than for that which renders man absolutely miserable, the complete lack of the ornaments and riches of the soul." The missionary continues, offering his scientific conviction that "neither the sun, nor malice of the soil, neither the air nor the water, neither the men nor their caprices, are to be blamed for this. We are all created by and dependent upon the same principles: We breathe under the same sky; the same constellations influence us; and I do not believe that the land, which produces trees as tall and beautiful as ours, will not produce as fine harvests, *if it be cultivated.*" Wilderness the expanses of Acadia might be, but a garden it could become, if cultivated. For Father Biard and his contemporaries, "subjugating Satanic monsters" and establishing "the order and discipline of heaven upon earth"[19] combined spiritual and worldly dimensions. Champlain, for whom the Devil and his agents were as real as for Biard, expressed the same objective in a more secular way when he told the local people he met in the region of the Penobscot River that the French "desired to settle in their country and show them how to cultivate it, in order that they might no longer live so miserable an existence as they are doing." The comment is made the more striking when we remember that Champlain knew that some of the inhabitants of Acadia did practise agriculture—though he never suggested that they "cultivated" the land.[20]

It is perhaps not too much to suggest that "cultivation" was a distinctly European concept. "For before everything else," Marc Lescarbot maintained, "one must set before oneself the tillage of the soil." At the first French settlement in Ste. Croix gardens were sown and some wheat "came up very fine and ripened." The poor quality of the soil was one reason for the move across the Bay of Fundy to establish Port Royal, "where the soil was ample to produce the necessities of life." But there was more to cultivation than the production of simple foodstuffs. For Lescarbot, at least, the powerful symbolism of planting a European garden in what had been a wilderness was manifest. He wrote on his departure from Port Royal to return to France in July, 1607:

> I have cause to rejoice that I was one of the party, and among the first tillers of this land. And herein I took the more pleasure in that I put before my eyes our ancient Father Noah, a great king, a great priest and a great prophet whose vocation was the plough and the vineyard; and the old Roman captain Serranus, who was found sowing his field when he was sent to lead the Roman army, and Quintus Cinncinnatus, who, all crowned with dust, bareheaded and ungirt, was ploughing four acres of land when the herald of the Senate brought him the letters of dictatorship.... Inasmuch as I took pleasure in this work, God

> blessed my poor labour, and I had in my garden as good wheat as could be grown in France.

While Lescarbot might be dismissed as suffering from an overdose of renaissance humanism, it seems more sensible to take him seriously. His florid rhetoric should be seen for what it really was: the ideology of what Alfred J. Crosby has called "ecological imperialism"—the biological expansion of Europe. What Lescarbot, and less literary Europeans, brought to bear on the Acadian landscape was the heavy freight of the European agricultural tradition with its long-established distinction between garden and wilderness. In that tradition God's "garden of delight" contrasted with the "desolate wilderness" of Satan. Though the concept of "garden" varies widely, as Hugh Johnson notes in his *Principles of Gardening,* "control of nature by man" is the single common denominator.[21]

The transformation of the wilderness into a garden is a constant theme in the early writings about Acadia. Father Biard had brought European seeds with him when he arrived in 1611 and at St. Saveur "in the middle of June, we planted some grains [wheat and barley], fruit, seeds, peas, beans and all kinds of garden plants." On Miscou Island (Shippegan Island) Denys discovered that although the soil was sandy, herbs of all sorts as well as "Peaches, Nectarines, Clingstones" and what the French always called "the Vine"—grapes—could be grown. But, as so often is the case, Lescarbot provides the most striking account of what gardening meant. At Port Royal, he "took pleasure in laying out and cultivating my gardens, in enclosing them to keep out the pigs, in making flower beds, staking out alleys, building summer houses, sowing wheat, rye, barley, oats, beans, peas and garden plants, and in watering them." European seeds, domestic animals—chickens and pigeons, too—fences—mine and thine.[22]

Of course, before a garden could be planted, the land had to be cleared. Denys described the work—and its by-product: squared oak timber that could fill the holds of vessels that would otherwise have returned empty to France. If clearing the land did not produce enough space for the garden, then the sea could be tamed, too. In the Minas Basin, where the settlers apparently found cultivating the land too difficult, Dièreville recounted the construction of a remarkable piece of European technology:

> Five or six rows of large logs are driven whole into the ground at the points where the Tide enters the Marsh, & between each row, other logs are laid, one on top of the other, & all the spaces between them are so carefully filled with well pounded clay, that the water can no longer get through. In the centre of this construction a Sluice is contrived in such a manner that the water on the Marshes flows out of its own accord, while that of the Sea is prevented from coming in.

Thus the tidal marshes were dyked for cultivation.[23]

Pushing back the forest, holding back the water, fencing a garden in the wilderness. The rewards would be great—"better worth than the treasures of Atahulpa [sic]," Lescarbot claimed. Was the symbolism intentional? Atahualpa, the defeated ruler of Peru, offered his Spanish captors led by Francisco Pizarro a room full of gold and silver in return for his freedom. The Spaniards accepted a ransom and then garrotted the Inca. Hardly a scene from a garden of delights.[24]

The French in Acadia were certainly not the Spanish in Peru. Still, the garden they planned was intended to produce a greater harvest than just sustenance for anticipated settlers. It was to be a garden for the civilization of the indigenous peoples. "In the course of time," Champlain observed on his initial meeting with the people he called Etechemins (Maliseet), "we hope to pacify them, and put an end to the wars which they wage against each other, in order that in the future we might derive service from them, and convert them to the Christian faith." The words were almost exactly those attributed to Columbus at his first sighting of the people of the "Indies": "they would be good servants... [and] would easily be made Christians." Even the most sympathetic observers of the Native peoples of Acadia were appalled by their apparent failure to make for themselves a better life, a failing that was often attributed to their unwillingness to plan for the future. For Father Biard, Christianity and husbandry obviously went hand in hand. Living the nomadic life of hunters, fishers, and gatherers resulted in permanent material and spiritual backwardness. "For in truth, this people," he claimed, "who, through the progress and experience of centuries, ought to have come to some perfections in the arts, sciences and philosophy, is like a great field of stunted and ill-begotten wild plants...[they] ought to be already prepared for the completeness of the Holy Gospel...Yet beholden [them] wretched and dispersed, given up to ravens, owls and infernal cuckoos, and to be the cursed prey of spiritual foxes, bears, boars and dragons." In Father Le Clercq's view the "wandering and vagabond life" had to be ended and a place "suitable for the cultivation of the soil" found so that he could "render the savages sedentary, settle them down, and civilize them among us." Though Lescarbot's outlook was more secular, he shared these sentiments completely and expressed them in verse:

> This people are neither brutal, barbarous
>   nor savage,
> If you do not describe men of old that way,
> His is subtle, capable, and full of good sense,
> And not known to lack judgement,
> All he asks is a father to teach him
> To cultivate the earth, to work the grape vines,
> And to live by laws, to be thrifty,
> And under the sturdy roofs hereafter to shelter.

The leitmotif of the rhetoric is obvious: the images of the Christian garden and the satanic wilderness, summed up in the verse from the Book of Joel, quoted by Father Biard: "The Land is a Garden of Eden before them, and behind them a desolate wilderness."[25]

Yet it would be quite wrong to assume that these seventeenth-century French visitors to the New World were blind to the potential costs of gardening in the Acadian wilderness. Indeed, there is considerable evidence of nagging suspicions that the very abundance of nature provoked reckless exploitation. Denys witnessed an assault on a bird colony that is reminiscent of the profligacy of Cartier's crew among the birds at Funk Island in 1534. Denys's men "clubbed so great a number, as well of young as of their fathers and mothers... that we were unable to carry them all away." And Dièreville captured all too accurately the spirit of the uncontrolled hunt when he wrote that:

> ..., Wild Geese
> And Cormorants, aroused in me
> The wish to war on them....

He used the same militant language in his admiring account of the "Bloody Deeds" of the seal hunt, and also provided a sketch of another common pursuit: the theft of massive quantities of birds' eggs. "They collect all they can find," he remarked, "fill their canoes & take them away." Scenes like these presaged the fate of the Great Auk, the passenger pigeon, and many other species.[26]

These were the actions of men whose attitude toward the bounty of nature contrasted markedly with that of the indigenous inhabitants of North America. In Europe the slaughter of birds and animals was commonplace, indeed it was often encouraged by law. As Keith Thomas remarks in his study of *Man in the Natural World*—which is largely restricted to Great Britain—"It is easy to forget just how much human effort went into warring against species which competed with man for the earth's resources." Without succumbing to the temptation to romanticize the attitude of North American Native people toward their environment—they hunted, they fished, some practised slash and burn agriculture—there is no doubt that their sense of the natural world was based on a distinctive set of beliefs, a cosmology that placed them in nature rather than dominant over it. Animistic religion—"everything is animated," Father Le Clercq discovered—a simple technology, a relatively small population, and what Marshall Sahlins has termed "stone age economics" made "war" on nature unnecessary, even unacceptable. "They did not lack animals," Nicolas Denys noted, "which they killed only in proportion as they had need of them." By contrast, the Europeans who arrived in Acadia at the beginning of the seventeenth century belonged to a culture where, in Clarence Glacken's words, "roughly from the end of the fifteenth to the end of the seventeenth century one sees ideas of men as controllers of nature beginning to crystalize." Or, as Marc Lescarbot put it, articulating as he so often did the unstated assumptions of his fellow Frenchmen, "Man was placed in this world to command all that's here below."[27]

The distinction between the "wilderness" and the "garden," between "savagery" and "civilization," between "wandering about" and commanding "all that is here below," is more than a philosophical one, important as that is. It is also, both implicitly and explicitly, a question of ownership and possession. In what has been called "enlightenment anthropology"—though I think that places the development too late—the function of the term "savage" was to assert the existence of a state of nature where neither "heavy-plough agriculture nor monetarized exchange" was practised and from which, therefore, civil government was absent. Moreover, civil government, agriculture, and commerce were assumed to exist only where land had been appropriated, where "possessive individualism" had taken root. Thus the wilderness was inhabited by nomadic savages, without agriculture or laws, where the land had never been appropriated. Consequently, when Europeans set about transforming the wilderness into a garden, they were engaged in taking possession of the land. "The ideology of agriculture and savagery," in the words of J.G.A. Pocock, "was formed to justify this expropriation."[28]

As European gardeners began slowly to transform the wilderness of Acadia, so, too, as was their intent, they began the remaking of its indigenous inhabitants. And once again, though they rarely expressed doubts about the ultimate value of the enterprise, some Europeans did recognize that a price was being exacted. First there was the puzzling evidence of population decline. In a letter to his superior in Paris in 1611, Father Biard wrote that the Micmac leader Membertou (who himself claimed to be old enough to remember Cartier's 1534 visit) had informed him that in his youth people were "as thickly planted there as the hairs upon his head." The priest continued, making a remarkably revealing comparison:

> It is maintained that they have thus diminished since the French have begun to frequent their country; for, since they do nothing all summer but eat; and the result is that, adopting an entirely different custom and thus breeding new diseases, they pay for their indulgence during the autumn and winter by pleurisy, quinsy and dysentery which kills them off. During this year alone sixty have died at Cape de la Hève, which is the greater part of those who lived there; yet not one of all of M. de Poutrincourt's little colony has ever been sick, notwithstanding all the privations they have suffered; which has caused the Savages to apprehend that God protects and defends us as his favorite and well-beloved people.[29]

The reality, of course, was more complex than this assertion that God was on the side of the immunized. Though the French were unaware of it, Acadia, like the rest of the Americas, was a "virgin land" for European pathogens. Denys hinted at this when he wrote that "in old times...they [the Natives] were not subject to diseases, and knew nothing of fevers." Certainly they had not been exposed to the common European maladies—measles, chickenpox, influenza, tuberculosis, and, worst of all, smallpox. (The "pox"—syphilis—Lescarbot believed was God's punishment of European men for their promiscuous sexual behaviour in the Indies.) The immune systems of the indigenous peoples of Acadia were unprepared for the introduction of these new diseases, which were consequently lethal in their impact. Father Le Clercq, at the end of the century, reported that "the gaspesian nation...has been wholly destroyed...in three or four visitations" of unidentified "Maladies." Marc Lescarbot probably identified one important carrier of European infections when he stated that "the savages had no knowledge of [rats] before our coming; but in our time they have been beset by them, since from our fort they went over to their lodges."[30]

Disease, radical alternations in diet—the substitution of dried peas and beans and hardtack for moosemeat and other country foods—and perhaps even the replacement of polygamy by monogamy with a consequent reduction in the birth rate all contributed to population decline. Then there was the debilitating scourge of alcohol, another European import for which Native people had little, if any, tolerance. Just as they sometimes gorged themselves during "eat all" feasts, so they seemed to drink like undergraduates with the simple goal of getting drunk. Even discounting Father Le Clercq's pious outlook, his description of the impact of brandy on the Gaspesians was probably not exaggerated. The fur traders, he charged, "make them drunk quite on purpose, in order to deprive these poor barbarians of the use of reason." That meant quick profits for the merchants, debauchery, destruction, murder, and, eventually, addiction for the Amerindians. Though less censorious, or less concerned, than the priest, Dièreville remarked that the Micmacs "drank Brandy with relish & less moderation than we do; they have a craving for it."[31]

Estimating population declines among Native peoples is at best controversial, at worst impossible. Nevertheless, there seems no reason to doubt that Acadia, like the rest of the Americas, underwent substantial reduction in numbers of inhabitants as a result of European contact. Jacques Cartier and his successors, who fished and traded along the coasts of Acadia, likely introduced many of the influences that undermined the health of the local people. Therefore Pierre Biard's 1616 estimate of a population of about 3,500 Micmacs is doubtless well below pre-contact numbers, as Membertou claimed. Since it has been estimated that neighbouring Maliseet, Pasamaquoddy, and Abenaki communities experienced reductions ranging from 67 to 98 per cent during the epidemics of 1616 and 1633 alone, Virginia Miller's calculation that the pre-contact Micmac population stood somewhere between 26,000 and 35,000 seems reasonable.[32] That was one of the costs of transforming the wilderness into a garden.

If the effects of disease and alcohol were apparent, though misunderstood, then another aspect of the civilizing process was more subtle. That process combined Christian proselytizing, which eroded traditional beliefs, with the fur trade, which undermined many aspects of the Native peoples' way of life. There is among contemporary historians of European-Amerindian relations a tendency to view the trading relationship, which was so central to the early years of contact, as almost benign, a relation between equals. Missionaries, politicians, and land-hungry settlers are credited with upsetting the balance that once existed between "Natives and newcomers" in the fur trade. There can be no doubt that recent scholarship has demonstrated that the Natives were certainly not passive participants in the trade. Far from being naive innocents who gave up valuable furs for a few baubles, they traded shrewdly and demanded good measure.[33]

Nevertheless, it is impossible to read seventeenth-century accounts of the trade and still accept the whole of this revisionist account. These were eyewitness testimonies to the devastating impact of alcohol on the Native traders and their families: murder of fellow Natives, maiming of women and abuse of children, the destruction of canoes and household goods. Beyond this, brandy, often adulterated with water, was used by Europeans "in order to abuse the savage women, who yield themselves readily during drunkenness to all kinds of indecency, although at other times...they would be more like to give a box on the ears rather than a kiss to whomsoever wished to engage them in evil, if they were in their right minds." The words come from the priest, Father Le Clercq, but the merchant, Nicolas Denys, concurred. That, too, was part of the fur trade.[34]

Moreover, the trade cannot be separated from other aspects of contact that contributed to the weakening of Micmac culture. Fur traders carrying disease and trade goods unintentionally contributed to the decline of both traditional skills and indigenous religious belief. Nicolas Denys's discussion of Micmac burial customs illustrates this point neatly. Like other Native people, the Micmacs buried many personal articles in graves so that the deceased would have use of them when they disembarked in the Land of the Dead. The French judged this practice both superstitious and wasteful—especially when the burial goods included thousands of pounds of valuable furs. They attempted to disabuse the Native of the efficacy of this practice by demonstrating that the goods did not leave the grave but rather remained in the ground, rotting. To this the Natives replied that it was the "souls" of these goods that accompanied the "souls" of the dead, not the material goods themselves. Despite this failure Denys was able to report that the practice was in decline. The reason is significant and it was only marginally the result of conversion to Christianity. As trade between the French and the Micmacs developed, European goods—metal pots, knives, axes, firearms—gradually replaced traditional utensils and weapons that had once been included in burial pits. The use of European commodities as burial goods proved prohibitively expensive. Denys wrote that "since they cannot obtain from us with such ease as they had in retaining robes of Marten, of Otter, of Beaver, [or] bows and arrows, and since they have realized that guns and other things were not found in their woods or their rivers, *they have become less devout.*" Technological change brought religious change. It also led to dependence.[35]

No doubt the exchange of light, transportable copper pots for awkward, stationary wooden pots was a convenient, even revolutionary change in the lives of Micmacs. But convenience was purchased at a price, and the Native people knew it. Father Le Clercq was vastly amused when an old man told him that "the Beaver does everything to perfection. He makes us kettles, axes, swords, knives and gives us drink and food without the trouble of cultivating the ground." It was no laughing matter. If, at the outset of European contact, the Native people of Acadia had adapted to the trade with Europeans rather successfully, they gradually lost ground, their role of middlemen undermined by overseas traders who came to stay. While Nicolas Denys deplored the destructive impact of itinerant traders and fishermen on the Native people, his only solution was to advocate European settlement and the enforcement of French authority. "Above all," he concluded his assessment of the changes that had taken place in Native society during his time, "I hope that God may inspire in those who have part in the government of the State, all the discretion which can lead them to the consummation of an enterprise as glorious for the King as it can be useful and advantageous to those who will take interest therein." In that scheme, when it eventually came to pass, the Micmacs and their neighbours found themselves on the margin.[36]

To these signs that the work of cultivation produced ugly, unanticipated side effects must be added the evidence of near crop failure in the spiritual garden of Acadia. In 1613 a disgusted Father Biard reported meeting a St. John River sagamore (Cacagous) who, despite being "baptized in Bayonne," France, remained a "shrewd and cunning" polygamist. "There is scarcely any change in them after baptism," he admitted. Their traditional "vices" had not been replaced by Christian "virtues." Even Membertou, often held up as the exemplary convert, had difficulty grasping the subtleties of the new religion. He surely revealed something more than a quick wit in an exchange that amused the Jesuit. Attempting to teach him the Pater Noster, Biard asked Membertou to repeat in his own language, "Give us this day our daily bread." The old sagamore replied: "If I did not ask him for anything but bread, I would be without moose-meat or fish." Near the end of the century, Father Le Clercq's reflections on the results of his Gaspé mission were no more optimistic. Only a small number of the people lived like Christians; most "fell back into the irregularities of a brutal and wild life." Such, the somewhat depressed Recollet missionary concluded, was the meagre harvest among "the most docile of all the Savages of New France...the most susceptible to the instruction of Christianity."[37]

It was not just these weeds—disease, alcohol, dependence, and spiritual backsliding—in the European garden in Acadia that occasionally led the gardeners to pause and reflect. Possibly there was a more basic question: was the wilderness truly the Devil's domain? The Northeastern Algonquian people were admittedly "superstitious," even "barbarian," but certainly not the "wild men" of medieval imaginings, indistinguishable from the beasts. If they enjoyed "neither faith, nor king, nor laws," living out "their unhappy Destiny," there was something distinctly noble about them, too. Despite the steady, evangelical light that burned in Biard's soul, he could not help wondering if the Micmac resistance to the proffered European garden of delights was not without foundation. "If we come to sum up the whole and compare their good and ill with ours," he mused briefly in the middle of his *Relation* of 1616, "I do not know but that they, in truth, have some reason to prefer (as they do) their own kind of happiness to ours, at least if we speak of the temporal happiness, which the rich and worldly seek in this life." Of course, these doubts quickly passed as he turned to consider "the means available to aid these nations to their eternal salvation."

Marc Lescarbot, for whom classicism and Christianity seemed to have reached their apogee in the France of his day, and whose fervour for cultivating the wilderness was unlimited, found much to admire in the peoples of Acadia. They lived "after the ancient fashion, without display": uncompetitive, unimpressed by material goods, temperate, free of corruption and of lawyers! "They have not that ambition, which in these parts gnaws men's minds, and fills them with cares, bringing blinded men to the grave in the very flower of their age and sometimes to the shameful spectacle of a public death." Here surely was "the noble savage," a Frenchman without warts—"a European dream," as J.H. Elliott remarks of the humanists' image of the New World, "which had little to do with American reality."[38]

There was yet another reason for self-doubts about the superiority of European ways over Amerindian ways; the Native people struggled to preserve their wilderness, refusing the supposed superiority of the garden. Even those who had become "philosophers and pretty good theologians," one missionary concluded, preferred "on the basis of foolish reasoning, the savage to the French life." And Father Le Clercq found that some of the people of Gaspesia stubbornly preferred their movable wigwams to stationary European houses. And that was not all. "Thou reproachest us, very inappropriately," their leader told a group of visiting Frenchmen, "that our country is a very little hell in contrast with France, which thou comparest to a terrestrial paradise, inasmuch as it yields thee, so thou sayest, every provision in abundance...I beg thee to believe, all miserable as we may seem in thine eyes, we consider ourselves nevertheless much happier than thou in this, that we are contented with the little that we have." Thus having demonstrated, 300 years before its discovery by modern anthropology, that having only a few possessions is not the same as being poor, the Algonquian leader then posed a devastating question: "If France, as thou sayest, is a little terrestrial paradise, are thou sensible to leave it?" No reply is recorded.[39]

It is simple enough to imagine one. Even those who could describe as "truly noble" the Aboriginal people of Acadia remained convinced that civilization meant cultivation. "In New France," Lescarbot proclaimed, "the golden age must be brought in again, the ancient crowns of ears of corn must be renewed, and the highest glory made that which the ancient Romans called *gloria adorea,* a glory of wheat, in order to invite everyone to till well his field, seeing that the land presents itself liberally to them that have none." The state of nature, a Hobbesian state of nature without laws or kings or religion, would be tamed, "civilized," when men "formed commonwealths to live under certain laws, rule, and police." Here, in Braudel's phrase, Europe's "own nature" was revealed.[40]

Perhaps such thoughts as these filled the heads of the Frenchmen who, according to Micmac tradition, gathered to enjoy one of the "curious adventures" of Silmoodawa, an Aboriginal hunter carried off to France "as a curiosity" by Champlain or some other "discoverer." On this occasion the Micmac was to give a command performance of hunting and curing techniques. The "savage" was placed in a ring with "a fat ox or deer...brought in from a beautiful park." (One definition of "paradise," the *OED* reports, is "an Oriental park or pleasure ground, especially one enclosing wild beasts for the chase.") The story, collected in 1870 by the Reverend Silas Tertius Rand, a Baptist missionary and amateur ethnologist, continues: "He shot the animal with a bow, bled him, skinned and dressed him, sliced up the meat and spread it out on flakes to dry; he then cooked a portion and ate it, and in order to exhibit the whole process, and to take a mischievous revenge upon them for making an exhibition of him, he went into a corner of the yard and eased himself before them all."[41]

If, as Lescarbot's contemporaries believed, the wilderness could be made into a garden, then the unscripted denouncement of Silmoodawa's performance revealed that a garden could also become a wilderness. Or was he acting out the Micmac version of Michel de Montaigne's often quoted remark about barbarians: we all call wilderness anything that is not *our* idea of a garden?

Notes

1 Fernand Braudel, *The Perspective of the World* (London, 1985), pp. 387, 388.

2 Cecil Jane, ed., *The Journal of Christopher Columbus* (New York, 1989), p. 191; Patricia Seed, "Taking Possession and Reading Texts: Establishing the Authority of Overseas Empires," *William and Mary Quarterly*, XLIX, 2 (April, 1992), p. 199.

3 Marc Lescarbot, *History of New France* (Toronto, 1914), III, p. 246. The theme of my lecture might have benefited had I been able to substantiate the claim, sometimes made, that "Acadie" is a corruption of "Arcadie"—an ideal, rural paradise. Unfortunately the claim, sometimes made on the basis of Verrazzano's 1524 voyage when he described the coast of present-day Virginia as "Arcadie," is unfounded. "Acadie" likely is derived from the Micmac word "Quoddy" or "Cadie," meaning a piece of land. The French version became "la Cadie" or "l'Acadie," even though the French sometimes thought of the area as a potential "Arcadie." See Andrew Hill Clark, *Acadia: The Geography of Early Nova Scotia* (Madison, Wisconsin, 1968), p. 71.

4 J.G.A. Pocock, "Deconstructing Europe," *London Review of Books*, 19 December 1991, pp. 6–10.

5 J.H. Elliott, *The Old World and the New, 1492–1650* (Cambridge, 1989), p. 10.

6 Leslie Upton, *Micmacs and Colonists: Indian-White Relations in the Maritimes, 1713–1867* (Vancouver, 1979), p. 25.

7 Peter Mason, *Deconstructing America: Representations of the Other* (London, 1990); Antonello Gerbi, *Nature in the New World* (Pittsburgh, 1985).

8 *The Works of Samuel D. Champlain* (Toronto, 1922), I, p. 243 (hereafter Champlain).

9 Lescarbot, III, pp. 484–85; Nicolas Denys, *Description and Natural History of the Coasts of North America (Acadia)* (Toronto, 1908), pp. 393, 390; Hugh Honour, *The New Golden Land: European Images of America from the Discovery to the Present Time* (New York, 1975), pp. 36–37.

10 Denys, pp. 362–69; Le Clercq, *New Relations of Gaspesia* (Toronto, 1910), p. 279.

11 Le Clercq, p. 275; Denys, pp. 257–340; Champlain, pp. 368, 247; Denys, p. 199.

12 Champlain, p. 327. For a discussion of the distribution of Native peoples, see Bruce J. Bourque, "Ethnicity in the Maritime Peninsula, 1600–1759," *Ethnohistory*, 36 (1989), pp. 257–84.

13 Sieur de Dièreville, *Relation of the Voyage to Port Royal in Acadia* (Toronto, 1933), pp. 130–41; Lescarbot, III, pp. 54, 205, 164; Karen Anderson, *Chain Her by One Foot* (London, 1990).

14 Lescarbot, III, pp. 200–02; Le Clercq, p. 243.

15 Le Clercq, pp. 135–39; Denys, p. 420; Marc Lescarbot, *The Conversion of the Savages*, in Reuben Gold Thwaites, ed., *The Jesuit Relations and Allied Documents* (New York, 1959), I, p. 101; *Jesuit Relations*, III, p. 83; Le Clercq, pp. 265, 273.

16 Le Clercq, p. 243; Lescarbot, III, p. 333.

17 Lescarbot, III, pp. 365, 27, 113; *Jesuit Relations*, III, p. 21; Todorov, *Conquest*, pp. 27–33; Marshall Sahlins, *Islands of History* (Chicago, 1985), p. 10.

18 *Jesuit Relations*, III, pp. 33–35.

19 *Ibid.*, p. 33.

20 Champlain, p. 295.

21 Clarence J. Glacken, "Changing Ideas of the Habitable World," in William L. Thomas, ed., *Man's Role in Changing the Face of the Earth* (Chicago, 1956), pp. 70–92; Lescarbot, III, pp. 241, 351, 363–64; Alfred W. Crosby, Jr., *Ecological Imperialism: The Biological Expansion of Europe, 900–1900* (Cambridge, 1986); A. Barlett Giamatti, *The Early Paradise of the Renaissance Epic* (Princeton, N.J., 1969); Hugh Johnson, *The Principles of Gardening* (London, 1979), p. 8.

22 *Jesuit Relations*, III, p. 63; Denys, p. 303; Lescarbot, I, p. xii.

23 Denys, pp. 149–50; Dièreville, pp. 94–95. See Clark, *Acadia*, pp. 24–31.

24 Lescarbot, II, p. 317; John Hemming, *The Conquest of the Incas* (London, 1983), pp. 77–88.

25 Champlain, p. 272; Jane, ed., *Columbus*, p. 24; Le Clercq, p. 115; *Jesuit Relations*, III, p. III; Le Clercq, p. 205; Lescarbot, III, p. 487.

26 Denys, p. 156; Dièreville, pp. 75–77, 102, 122–23.

27 William M. Denevan, "The Pristine Myth: the Landscape of the Americas in 1492," *Annals of the Association of American Geographers*, 82, 3 (1992), pp. 369–85; Keith Thomas, *Man and the Natural World* (New York, 1983), p. 274; Le Clercq, p. 331; Marshall Sahlins, *Stone Age Economics* (Chicago, 1972); Denys, p. 403; Clarence J. Glacken, *Traces on the Rhodian Shore: Nature and Culture in Western Thought from Ancient Times until the End of the Eighteenth Century* (Berkeley, 1967), p. 494;

Lescarbot, III, p. 137. See also Richard White, "Native Americans and the Environment," in W.E. Swagerty, ed., *Scholars and the Indian Experience* (Bloomington, Indiana, 1984), pp. 179–204; Lescarbot, III, p. 137.

28 Lescarbot, III, pp. 94, 127; J.G.A. Pocock, "Tangata Whenua and Enlightenment Anthropology," *New Zealand Journal of History,* 26, I (April, 1992), pp. 35, 36, 41. Pocock bases much of his intricate argument on late seventeenth-century and eighteenth-century sources, yet Marc Lescarbot's *History of New France,* first published in 1609, already articulates and assumes, though in a somewhat unsystematic way, a fairly full-blown version of the theory. See also John Locke's chapter "Of Property" in his *Essay Concerning the True Original Extent of Civil Government* (1640).

29 Lescarbot, III, p. 254; *Jesuit Relations,* I, p. 177.

30 Denys, p. 415; Lescarbot, III, p. 163; Le Clercq, p. 151; Lescarbot, III, p. 227. Professor John Marshall has pointed to the importance of domestic animal imports as disease carriers by drawing my attention to Jared Diamond, "The Arrow of Disease," *Discover* (October, 1992), pp. 64–73.

31 Le Clercq, pp. 254–55; Dièreville, p. 77.

32 Dean R. Snow and Kim M. Lamphear, "European Contact and Indian Depopulation in the Northeast," *Ethnohistory,* 35 (1988), pp. 15–33; Virginia P. Miller, "Aboriginal Micmac Population: A Review of Evidence," *Ethnohistory,* 23 (1976), pp. 117–27, and "The Decline of Nova Scotia Micmac Population, A.D. 1600–1850," *Culture,* 3 (1982), pp. 107–20; John D. Daniels, "The Indian Population of North America in 1492," *William and Mary Quarterly,* XLIX, 2 (April, 1991), pp. 298–320.

33 Bruce G. Trigger, *Natives and Newcomers* (Montreal, 1985), pp. 183–94.

34 Le Clercq, p. 255; Denys, pp. 449–50.

35 Denys, p. 442.

36 Calvin Martin, "Four Lives of a Micmac Copper Pot," *Ethnohistory,* 22 (1975), pp. 111–33; Le Clercq, p. 277; Denys, p. 452. See also Wilson D. Wallis and Ruth S. Wallis, *The Micmac Indians of Eastern Canada* (Minneapolis, 1945); Bruce J. Bourque and Ruth Holmes Whitehead, "Tarrentines and the Introduction of European Trade Goods in the Gulf of Maine," *Ethnohistory,* 32 (1985), pp. 327–41.

37 *Jesuit Relations,* I, pp. 166–67; Le Clercq, pp. 193–94.

38 Denys, p. 437; *Jesuit Relations,* III, p. 135; Lescarbot, III, p. 189; Elliott, *The Old World,* p. 27.

39 Le Clercq, pp. 125, 104.

40 Lescarbot, III, pp. 256–57, 229.

41 Rev. Silas Tertius Rand, *Legends of the Micmacs* (London, 1894), 279.

Heroes, History, and Two Nationalisms: Jacques Cartier

ALAN GORDON

Jacques Cartier is really a nineteenth-century figure. Although he lived and flourished in the sixteenth century, he was virtually unknown before the 1830s. Thus, the "Discoverer of Canada" is a product of nineteenth-century scholarship, attitudes, and biases. At the end of the seventeenth century his exploits had been reduced to little more than a sentence or two in most authors' accounts of French expansion in the New World. As Jacques Mathieu has noted, Cartier simply did not exist in the minds of French Canadians until well into the British regime.[1] But this began to change in the 1830s as French Canadians discovered their own distinct history. The first monument to commemorate Cartier's "discoveries" was inaugurated on 14 September 1835 in Quebec City's Lower Town, near the Hôpital de la Marine. It was a simple wooden cross bearing an inscription announcing its intent to "marquer l'endroit ou Jacques Cartier, le célèbre navigateur qui a decouvert Québec, a passé l'hiver de 1535–1536."[2] It was a plan engineered by J.-B. Faribault, then an ambitious civil servant in the Lower Canadian Assembly, but soon to be renowned for his efforts to strengthen Canada's archival holdings. Faribault wanted to replace this temporary wooden marker with a more permanent and elegant monument paid for by public subscription. But despite holding a contest to design it, Faribault's monument was never built. A depressed economy and the well-known events of the latter 1830s interfered with his plans.

Nonetheless, Cartier's second odyssey, his rise from obscurity to historical herodom, began in the decade following the 300th anniversary of his arrival in the New World. In 1843, Faribault published the first new edition of Cartier's *Relations* since Richard Hakluyt had released an English translation of an Italian version in 1598. A few years later, a young artist named Théophile Hamel painted a copy of a French portrait of Cartier, which was then lithographed for wide distribution. Suddenly the memory of Jacques Cartier was evoked in everything from city squares and postage stamps to labour unions and schools.[3] A veritable "Cartiermania" swept French Canada in the 1850s and 1860s that lasted at least until the end of the century. It became nearly impossible for an official nationalist ceremony to omit the memory of Jacques Cartier. This much has been well documented by scholars. This paper will not take a contrary stance to the works that precede it. Instead it will attempt to show how historical heroes are used for specific political ends. That is, partisan groups seize broader "national" heroes to legitimise or universalise their much narrower policy objectives.

Alan Gordon, "Heroes, History, and Two Nationalisms: Jacques Cartier," in *Journal of the Canadian Historical Association*, New Series, 10 (1999): 81–102. Reprinted by permission of Alan Gordon.

However, this process reveals a deeper function of historical heroes. Heroes unite people in a political community, but they do so in ways that sometimes eschew cold reason. The bond of the imagined community is an emotive, noumenal bond. It is noumenal in Immanuel Kant's negative sense that it is profound knowledge that cannot possess empirical or phenomenal reality. Bill Butler notes that heroes, historical, political, or mythical, are marshalled to support social order. But the desire to exalt a hero, one of humanity's most common symbols, represents more than straightforward social control. Heroes personify our desirable characteristics and reflect an ideal conception of social behaviour.[4] In 1840,Thomas Carlyle proposed his theory of the hero as a means to see history as a series of biographies of great men. Heroic acts are not part of everyday experience, but the existence of the hero implies their genuine reality.[5] Political communities such as nations, then, seek to find their "genuine" past in the deeds of historical heroes. At a level deeper still, heroes can help structure our shared memories of the communal past. Although he has passed into the mists of history, communities imagine their identity with the hero.[6] The hero is a figure that supports the shared hopes, dreams, meanings, and especially memories of a society.

I

Although many authors argue that French-Canadian nationalism in the post-Rebellion years rejected the liberal-national project generally attributed to the *Parti patriote*—there has been a tendency to conflate all French-Canadian nationalist ideas into a single, clerical vision—a liberal nationalist tradition persisted.[7] Despite this apparent triumph of conservatism, French-Canadian liberalism survived. In the first nine provincial elections following Confederation, Liberals attracted an average of 45 percent of ballots in Quebec, though this generally did not translate to an equivalent number of seats.[8] Moreover, liberal-minded people continued to support nationalist policies through the 1840s, 1850s, and 1860s. *Rouge* papers, such as *L'Avenir* and *Le Pays,* often made use of nationalist rhetoric to promote their visions. In arguing for repeal of the Union in 1848, *L'Avenir* stood on the "natural" division of Canada into its French- and English-speaking halves, never mind the large anglophone population living in the "French" half. Nationality was thus the guiding political principle and the Union was "un act contre nature," because different nations cannot coexist in a unitary political formation. Louis-Antoine Dessaulles, likewise, felt that the Union was unnatural because it infringed on this principle of nationality. And these liberals often pointed to historical heroes to personify their ideals, the most notable being the *patriote* "martyrs" of the Rebellions, Pierre Bédard, or Vaudreuil. But Jacques Cartier was not at first a major hero in the liberal pantheon. The earliest authors to write on Jacques Cartier were almost all conservatives. Faribault, for instance, began his career under the protection of the Dalhousie administration, and remained connected to conservatives. Before becoming the first *Bleu* premier of Québec, Pierre-J.-O. Chauveau wrote a poem called "Donaconna," in which the Canadian chief accepts the Catholic faith Cartier had brought and voluntarily exiles himself to France. Paul des Cazes, who delivered papers on Cartier to the Royal Society in the 1880s, had been a friend of Honoré Mercier in his youth, but remained a staunch enemy of the *rouges.* Indeed, of some 15 essays, plays, and poems written in French about Cartier before 1890, at least 12 were written by conservative partisans.

Cartier was, especially at first, a figure who justified the conservative vision of the French-Canadian nation. It might seem obvious that an old-regime figure would more easily justify an ideological position that, its opponents believed, wanted to return French Canada to the eighteenth century. But not all old-regime figures can be so easily characterised. Colbert and Jean Talon found favour among liberals for their "modernising" initiatives and status, however questionable, as "new men." Garneau wrote approvingly of Talon's struggles against the authority of the Jesuits and of "la plus grande liberté qui venait d'être accordé au commerce" during his Intendancy.[9] By contrast, ultramontanes saw Cartier as the founder of Catholicism in the New World. For instance, the abbé Ferland's *Cours d'histoire du Canada* insisted that Cartier was deeply religious and undertook his second voyage in order to convert the natives.[10] Among the most explicit efforts was George-Etienne Cartier's comparison of the explorer to John the Baptist, claiming that both prophesied the coming of the true faith to North America. Mgr. Laflèche, the Bishop of Trois-Rivières, took the hyperbole further. He compared the explorer to Abraham, the biblical father of the faithful. To this conservative, Catholic mind, Cartier represented the founding of French Canada's religious vocation, its divine mission to defend the Catholic faith in the New World. Thus, for conservative thinkers, Jacques Cartier embodied the link between their French ethnic roots and their religious origins. He represented a particular view of the French-Canadian nation that supported conservative politics. This connection between memories of Cartier and conservatism meant that the image of the explorer commonly appeared at political celebrations.

The ubiquitousness of the image and memory of Jacques Cartier produced the first French-Canadian "national" historical hero. As the nineteenth century reached its final decades, Cartier had been established as the leading figure in the national pantheon of heroes. In part, this was because control of the "official" pantheon rested in the hands of conservative thinkers, especially the priests in control of the educational system and the lay leaders of French Canada's national societies, the *Associations Saint-Jean-Baptiste.* Cartier routinely appeared at Saint-Jean-Baptiste Day celebrations on floats, in medallions and, at least in Montreal, in the live representation of a boy dressed as the sixteenth-century explorer accompanying another child dressed as John the Baptist at the end of the national parade.[11] Cartier, then, had taken on a universalising function in harmony with the social order espoused by clerical and political leaders. And this harmony reached a crescendo at the Saint-Jean-Baptiste Day unveiling of a new Cartier monument in Quebec City's Lower Town. In the 1880s, the *Cercle catholique de Québec,* a sectarian literary and historical society, initiated a drive to replace the long-disappeared cross at the site of Cartier's first winter in Canada. *Cercle* membership was very conservative. Members included the lay leaders of the ultramontanes: Jules-Paul Tardivel and Senator F.-X. Trudel, as well as Narcisse-Eutrope Dionne, briefly the editor of the *Courrier du Canada.*[12] Lay ultramontanes styled themselves *Castors* after 1882. They emerged, initially, as a segment of Quebec's *Bleu* party that opposed its leader J.-A. Chapleau and his questionable associations with the ex-Liberal politician and financier L.-A. Sénécal. When Chapleau quit provincial politics for Ottawa, the *Castors,* and especially the *Cercle catholique,* turned their attacks on his friend and successor J.-A. Mousseau. They never had control of their party, but the *Castors* influenced a number of ministers and policies. Still, many abandoned the *Bleus* and rallied to Honoré Mercier's call for a national front to defend French Catholic interests against anglo-protestant attacks following the Riel Affair of 1885. Many ultramontanes initially opposed Mercier's use of the Riel Affair to form a new political movement, his *Parti national.* Mercier, after all, was a liberal.

Bishop Laflèche insisted that Mercier's agitation was "evil," but differences between the ecclesiastical hierarchy and the lay *Castors* divided conservatives in Quebec. Certainly Mercier exploited this division further as *Castor* support helped bring his *Parti national* to power.

In the midst of this manoeuvring, the *Cercle catholique* decided to pay double homage to Cartier and the Jesuit missionaries of New France. Although the Jesuit Order was founded in Cartier's lifetime, there is really very little historical connection between the two. Thus, a full understanding of this plan requires a slightly longer sojourn through the nineteenth-century politics of religion and education in Quebec. The Jesuits first came to Canada with Samuel de Champlain in the third decade of the seventeenth century. Very quickly they established themselves as the dominant missionary and educational order in New France, as they had in Europe. Protestant Great Britain would have probably preferred to eliminate all vestiges of Catholicism in Canada following the Conquest, but its tenuous hold over the French population necessitated a lenient stance. However, the hated Society of Jesus did not benefit from the full leniency of the Treaty of Paris. The Jesuits had been founded in 1542 as a missionary society by a former soldier, Ignatius Loyola, and organised along quasi-military lines. In and of itself, the Jesuit system of organisation was not particularly offensive, but Jesuit efficiency and success had brought down considerable Protestant hatred. Moreover, the Jesuit emphasis on practicality exposed the order to accusations of Machiavellianism. To be fair, even Catholic countries had grown leery of Jesuit influence in their courts and pressure from France's House of Bourbon convinced the Pope to abolish the order in 1773. Thus Jesuit property was, by Church law, to revert to the diocese. But in Canada there were complications. The 34 Jesuits in the colony had been permitted to stay and hold on to their properties, but no new Jesuits could replace them. Slowly their numbers dwindled until the last Jesuit, Père Casot, died in 1800. In accordance with civil law, the property formerly owned by the order reverted to the Crown. Neither the Crown nor the Catholic Church would fully accept the legitimacy of the other's claims, and another claim by the estate of Jeffrey Amherst further complicated the mess.

Although successive efforts to settle the issue failed, by 1831 the Colonial Office had restricted use of the Estates to education. At Confederation this restriction, coupled with the division of powers of the *British North America Act,* passed control of the Estates to the new Government of Quebec. However, the educational restriction meant that interest in the Estates pitted the Archbishop of Quebec, head of the Church in Canada, against a Society of Jesus reconvened by the Pope in 1814. In 1849, the Jesuits founded the Collège Sainte-Marie in Montreal and set up a rivalry with the Seminary of Quebec (which became Laval University in 1853). Rivalry between the Archbishop and the Jesuits, backed by the ultramontane Bishop of Montreal, was intense, particularly over issues of the control of education. The Bishop of Montreal desperately wanted a degree-granting university of his own and the Archbishop of Quebec desperately defended the monopoly of Laval University. These issues wound their way into public policy in the late 1880s. When Mercier manoeuvred the *Parti national* into power in early 1887, the Jesuits, at least, had reason to cheer. The new premier had been a student at the Collège Sainte-Marie and he had retained close ties with his former instructors. Mercier did not disappoint them. He granted the Society of Jesus provincial incorporation and thus the right to own property. This first step aroused little controversy, but when Mercier began negotiating compensation for the Jesuits' Estates with the Holy See, he stepped into a seething cauldron of sectarian and intra-faith distrust and hatred. Negotiating compensation for what was, in legal title, Crown land was bad enough, but Mercier's solution enraged many Protestants. Mercier set the value of the estates at $400,000, which he agreed to divide between the Jesuits and other teaching orders. However, in order to prevent accusations of funding Catholic education with state money, he granted an additional $60,000 to Protestant schools. The result was exactly the opposite of the intent. The Protestant gift seemed a pittance in comparison, and provoked cries of "Popery" and discrimination.[13]

At the height of this dispute, the *Cercle catholique* sent out a circular soliciting donations to its monument fund. Twenty-three people promptly pledged a total of $1,030, which encouraged the committee to reissue the form an additional 14 times. Over three years, and 15 calls for subscriptions, some 528 people offered a total of just over $5,000 towards the construction of the Cartier monument. A breakdown of these pledges indicates that the appeal of the plan was not likely tightly restricted along class lines. Pledges ranged from a high of two hundred dollars to a low of 25¢. Although the majority of the money came from large donations of $20, $50, or $100, the majority of subscribers pledged modest sums of a few dollars. Assuming that the average income for a Quebec industrial worker of about $260 per year remained true for this cohort, the average donation of $9.48 would have represented about two weeks' pay.[14] However, this figure is a little misleading. The average is skewed by the large contributions of such notables as Lord Lansdowne ($100), the Mayor of Saint-Malo, France ($200), Sir Donald Smith ($50), and Lord Stanley of Preston ($100).[15] Almost half of the total, 223 donations, were no more than two dollars. Even if not truly "popular" in composition, the lists of subscribers point to a broad support for the project from local small businesses, professionals, priests, and otherwise undistinguished men. A full analysis of who gave and why is impossible. For similar reasons we cannot "know" how spectators of monument unveilings reacted to and used the speeches and spectacles they witnessed.[16] Audience agency, the audience's active participation in shaping the meaning of performances, leaves behind little historical documentation. It can be found, but with great difficulty. Leaving behind this caveat that it is dangerous to take official memory at face value, the planned ceremonies offer a revealing glimpse into one political use of a national hero.

The unveiling ceremonies were an interesting mix of military and religious elements, but the spiritual side predominated. On Sunday, 24 June 1889, Quebec City celebrated French Canada's *fête national.* The day's festivities opened with the 65th Battalion of Montreal and the 9th Voltigeurs of Quebec marching to the Basilica for mass. Later, the same battalions lent a martial air to the monument unveilings, standing as honour guard and firing a thunderous cannon salute to greet the arrival of Lieutenant-Governor A.-R. Angers at the site. Angers's presence was particularly symbolic. The *Cercle catholique* program noted that he was a French-Canadian governor of Quebec, thus putting him in a line of succession that included other historical heroes such as Frontenac, Vaudreuil, and La Galissonière. Despite the institutional rupture between colonial New France and Quebec as a province in the young Dominion, Angers served as another means to tie the glorious past to the present as a continuity of French ethnicity. But the ceremony was more religious than military. Following Angers, the Archbishop of Quebec and the President of the *Société Saint-Jean-Baptiste de Québec* took their places at the head of an assembly of perhaps 100,000 people gathered for the celebration of mass.

The official speakers made a great deal of the importance of place in the past. The monuments offered a dual celebration of both Jacques Cartier and the Jesuit missionaries. The site, near Cartier's fort of 1535–36, and the cross erected in 1835, was also the location of the first Jesuit property in the New World. In 1626, Père Brébeuf took possession of the land in the name of his order. The Cartier-Brébeuf monument announced these facts in its inscription. On one face, it read:

> Jacques Cartier et ses hardis compagnons les marins de la Grande Hermine, la Petite Hermine et de l'Émerillon passèrent ici l'hiver de 1535–36.
>
> Le 3 mai 1536 Jacques Cartier fit planter, à l'endroit où il venait de passer l'hiver, une croix de 35 pieds de hauteur portant l'écusson fleurdelisé et l'inscription franciscus primus dei gratia rex regnat.

These two sentences explained the nearby cross, but on another face the inscription added another interpretation:

> Le 23 septembre 1625 les pères Jean de Brébeuf, Ennemond Massé et Charles Lallemant prirent solennellement possession du terrain appelé Fort-Jacques-Cartier situé au confluent des Rivières St-Charles et Lairet pour y ériger la première résidence des missionaires jésuites à Québec.

Thus it presented a vision of the past that connected the Jesuit claims of possession to Jacques Cartier's original claim of possession in the name of the King of France. And as Cartier represented to many the first "French Canadian," this connection helped legitimise Jesuit claims.

The connection between Cartier and the Jesuits was not at all rational. It was not really intended to be rational. Historical heroes do not assume their place of importance by the strength of rational discourse, but by the power of emotion and symbolism. This case was deliberately emotional. Pierre J.-O. Chauveau, former premier of Quebec, closed the ceremonies with a speech and a passionate reading of his widely read, romantic poem "Donaconna." The poem opens with the Stadaconan chief brooding in his forest kingdom:

> Stadacona dormait sur son fier prommontoire:
> Ormes et pins, forêt silencieuse et noire

The presence of Cartier, and the God he represents, troubles the old king. He considers sending his warriors to kill the French interlopers, but "inutile espoir! Leur magic est plus forte." Eventually he succumbs to the lure of the Christian God and consents to return with Cartier to France as Chauveau recounts the passing of time:

> Douzes lunes et vignt, et bien plus se passèrent
> Cinq hivers, cinq étés lentement s'écoulèrent
> Le chef ne revint pas

Donaconna had passed away during the long years in France, though Cartier did not admit it on his third voyage. But Chauveau's account draws upon a sublime connection between old, disappeared Stadacona and nineteenth-century Quebec City:

> Vieille Stadacona ! Sur son fier prommontoire
> II n'est plus de forêt silencieuse et noire:
> Le fer a tout détruit.
> Mais sur les hauts clochers, sur les blanches
> murailles,
> Sur le roc escarpé, témoin de cents batailles
> Plane une ombre la nuit.

And as the poem closes, Chauveau invokes the mysterious echo of the past that haunts Quebec's mountains, forests, and plains. Then, suitably prepared to feel the sublime significance of the past, each national or trade society filed past the Cartier-Brébeuf monument in turn. Each saluted the memory of Jacques Cartier, the silent hero of Chauveau's "Donaconna," before joining an immense triumphal procession through the Faubourg St.-Roch to the Marché Jacques-Cartier. The procession filed beneath flags and ornaments, as well as the watchful eyes of young women in the windows above the streets of St.-Roch, for over three hours before dispersing. But not everyone went straight home. The crowd had dwindled to about half its former size that evening when the lighting of the bonfire, at the Glacis cliff overlooking the monument, signalled the last hours of the festival.

Saint-Jean-Baptiste Day was itself an emotional holiday that united French Canadians through the dual pillars of nationality and faith. Passion was the link that united the people, and tied them to the historical interpretation offered by the monument. Of course, this interpretation ignores the fact that the land had long been used by Amerindians before and after Cartier's pronouncement. It also ignores industrial activity beginning in 1688 (shipyards and pottery works). And it curiously ignored the farm that, even in the 1880s, continued to occupy a portion of the surrounding land.[17] In other words, it was a selective choice of the past that not only affirmed a specific national vision, but also affirmed a specific political policy. The Cartier-Brébeuf monument announced French Canadians' dual identity, which in turn defended the *Jesuits' Estates Act* and Mercier's *Parti national.* That evening Mercier delivered his famous speech that urged French Canadians to quit their "fratricidal strife" and unite under his brand of unified nationalism:

> Quand nous disparaîtrons, nous dirons à la génération appelée à nous succéder: Nous sommes catholiques et françaises, et quand vous, nos successeurs disparaîtrez à votre tour, vous devrez dire à la génération qui vous remplacera: Nous mourons catholiques et françaises! Ce sera notre testament et le leur; dernières volontés suprêmes d'un peuple héroïque, transmises de père en fils, de génération en génération, jusqu'à la consommation des siècles. Pour obtenir ce grand résultat et consolider ainsi nos destinées, nous avons un devoir impérieux, urgent, solonnel, à remplir.

And he finished with this memorable cry: "Cessons nos luttes fratricides; unissons-nous!"[18] This was perhaps Mercier's greatest speech.[19] For Mercier, the message brought past, present, and now future together; in honouring the historical hero, French Canadians honoured their unity.

II

The Cartier-Brébeuf unveiling represents a sort of dual apogee. It was, as political historians have concurred, the apogee of Mercier's career. But it was also the last great French-Canadian commemoration of Jacques Cartier. It was not the last Cartier celebration. Only a few years later, the Montreal suburb of Saint-Henri inaugurated its own Cartier monument, a monstrous, wrought-iron, Victorian fountain with a statue of the explorer at the top.[20] And in 1905, Cartier's home-town erected another monument honouring his birth.[21] But these events paled in comparison with the national celebration of the founder-hero in Quebec City's Lower Town. Nonetheless, this apogee of a form of French-Canadian nationalism helped establish interest in Jacques Cartier among English-speaking Canadians. Until the 1890s, few anglophones had paid much attention to Jacques Cartier. Francis Parkman, the famous American historian, had praised some of Cartier's exploits in the 1850s. And in 1860 Morgan's *Sketches of Famous Canadians* proclaimed Cartier the father of Canada. But not until 1887 did an English-speaking author publish specifically on Jacques Cartier.[22] An essay contest promoted by the *Cercle catholique* in conjunction with the Cartier-Brébeuf celebrations produced the first book-length studies of Cartier in English. Hiram

Stephens, a Montreal journalist, and Joseph Pope, the personal secretary of John A. Macdonald, each won a prize for their accounts of Cartier's life.[23] Although these books are fairly unremarkable in themselves, each little more than a rewording of Cartier's *Relations,* Pope's in particular became the main reference for anglophones slowly discovering the French-regime past of Canada at the turn of the century. Indeed, little by little, English-speaking Canadians began to recognise Cartier as the discoverer of their country as well.[24] However, for English-speaking Canadians, Cartier could not be used to legitimate a French and Catholic nationalism. Cartier had to be remade to suit a different nationalism. Stephens, tellingly, compared Cartier to Columbus to set up a discovery myth parallel to, but distinct from, the American one.

As early as 1921, an American museum curator, John M. Clarke, urged the erection of a monument to commemorate Cartier's landing and taking possession of Canada in the name of the King of France. Clarke's interest in Cartier stemmed from his frequent summer stays in the Gaspé region of the province. There, in 1908, he had discovered a hidden wooden medallion that, for no good reason, he believed depicted Jacques Cartier.[25] Clarke's pleas went unanswered, but in 1930 more powerful voices likewise urged building a monument to celebrate the coming 400th anniversary of the discovery of Canada. Rodolphe Lemieux, Speaker of the House of Commons and MP for Gaspé, took up the cause in 1929. At the same time, the Bishop of Gaspé, Mgr. F.-X. Ross, organised a committee in his diocese with the plan of raising a monument and building a commemorative cathedral in time for the 400th anniversary.[26] The committee was chaired by Quebec's well-known conservative historian Thomas Chapais.[27] That same year, the abbé Groulx took a public stance on the issue in the pages of *Le Devoir.* Groulx proclaimed that this monument should not be simply a local initiative, but "il faut que ce monument soit l'ouvre véritable d'une souscription nationale, comme il faut un grand act de foi et de gratitude national." Groulx's position was twofold. First, Cartier represented the opening of Canadian history, the first official contact between Canada and Europe and the moment at which Canada became a French country. This national affirmation was crucial because it would help assure French Canada's traditional rights:

> Notre pays est envahi par toutes les races du monde, lesquelles n'ayant pas toujours le temps d'apprendre notre histoire, n'ont que trop d'inclination à meconnaitre ou à sousestimer notre passé, nos privilèges et nos droits. Encore qu'aux nouveaux venus, et en dépit des penibles expériences, il ne faille pas négliger de faire savoir nos droits constitutionels et politiques...[28]

While Groulx played to the political and constitutional significance of Cartier, he did not ignore the traditionally held religious significance of the arrival of "un thaumaturge fameux." Lemieux likewise insisted that the celebration should be religious as, borrowing from nineteenth-century misconceptions, Cartier was the first herald of the teachings of Christianity in Canada. Moreover, Cartier's own narrative provides "ample evidence of his profound spirituality and his earnest desire to convert the pagan Indians."[29] Into the twentieth century Cartier remained a symbol of the French and Catholic identity of his imagined progeny. But obviously such an emphasis could not unite all Canadians. Nonetheless, interest was not confined to Quebec. Local newspapers across Canada commented on the plans. The Brockville *Recorder and Times* erroneously informed its readers that the province of Quebec planned to celebrate the 400th anniversary of the first attempt to colonise Canada. Agreeing with the *Brantford Expositor,* the *Recorder and Times* asserted that Cartier should not be dismissed as a French-Canadian figure, but embraced as the father of "our" country.[30] But once again the depths of the economic recession quickly put an end to these ambitious plans.

While all this was going on, the federal government, through the offices of its Historic Sites and Monuments Board, was also examining the possibility of putting a monument somewhere as a commemoration of the discovery of Canada. The HSMB had been established in 1919 to take control of federal commemorations of Canada's history. The Board consisted of a committee of respected historians and the commissioner of the Parks Branch of the Ministry of the Interior, J.B. Harkin. Its activities consisted of identifying sites of "national historical importance" and placing explanatory plaques at them. The Board, typically slow moving and poorly informed about local initiatives, had actually determined to raise such a monument as early as 1927, three years prior to the public efforts of Ross, Lemieux, and Groulx. Moreover, it had already decided to raise a cross, deviating considerably from its normal monument form of a stone cairn with a bronze plaque. Does this apparent conformity of plans suggest a broad consensus on the significance of Cartier in Canadian history? Evidence suggests otherwise. The Board chose a cross primarily because it had already raised a cross in honour of Cartier's less historically important visit to Isle-aux-Coudres in the St. Lawrence River, some 60 miles east of Quebec. That plan was initiated by the curé of the Parish of Isle-aux-Coudres, the abbé Paul Lavoie, and especially a Quebec City lawyer named Georges Bellerive. Their effort to attract the Board's attention began early in the 1920s. Bellerive prodded Aegidius Fauteux, then the Quebec representative on the Board and, following his resignation, pressured his successor, Pamphile Demers.[31] The idea of erecting a cross was Bellerive's initiative. Thus, the cruciform commemoration of Cartier, the mimicry of Cartier's own acts, emerged from the francophone community of Quebec. Indeed, Groulx did not rest with a proposal for one Cartier cross. He imagined the province as a vast sea of Cartier crosses, symbolically united in cruciform commemoration of its French and Catholic roots. At a congress of school inspectors for the provincial Department of Public Instruction, he urged every school to erect a commemorative cross. The Department promptly distributed plans as well as explanations of the symbols involved and estimated costs at $30 per cross.[32] Although the ambition had been to erect one cross for every village in Quebec, few were ever raised. Local residents no doubt preferred the spontaneity of their own wayside crosses and one scholar suggests that the few that were raised were in towns that did not already have a wayside cross.[33]

The HSMB took the different approach of concentrating on a single site. Its first task was to find an appropriate spot for the monument. The Board tended to prefer situating its monuments on, or as close to, the "exact" location of the event it wished to commemorate. Early on in its history, this objective had created problems. But the difficulty was especially profound in the case of Cartier's voyages, not simply because Cartier left few clues in his *Relations,* but because a considerable debate had already sprung up on the subject by the 1930s. This debate extended back to the eighteenth-century Jesuit explorer Charlevoix, who attempted to fix the key stops of his various predecessors in the actual terrain of New France. However, its modern guise really began with William Francis Ganong's paper read before the annual meeting of the Royal Society of Canada in 1887. And, although a Newfoundland Anglican bishop wrote the "final word" on the subject ten years later, such well-known historians as H.P. Biggar continued to search for the locations. By the fourth decade of the twentieth century, the Board was faced with at least five potential sites, all in or around the entrance to Gaspé harbour: Arnold's Bluff, O'Hara's Point, York Beach,

Sandy Beach, and the Gaspé Peninsula, as well as a last minute suggestion of Jacques Cartier Point.[34] The Board dispatched its Quebec representative, Edouard Surveyer, to Gaspé to inspect the options and report back. Despite having to endure the hardship of a train with no buffet car, Surveyer pressed on to the tiny village where he agreed with the defunct local committee on O'Hara's Point, conveniently next to the parish church. This claim rested on F.J. Richmond's presentation to the 1922 annual meeting of the Canadian Historical Association. Richmond's claim to expertise stemmed mostly from being among the oldest inhabitants of the village, and he founded his research on J.M. Clarke's interviews with a local sea captain. In other words, it was almost pure speculation.[35] However, the site was well served by a good road and owned by Bishop Ross, who was favourably disposed to leasing a plot for a federal monument.

Even as Surveyer and various Parks Branch technicians searched the relevant literature for an exact spot, another dispute welled up within the Board's ranks. This dispute, over the historical meaning of Cartier's cross, provides greater insight into the thinking of non-Quebecers on the question of Jacques Cartier. The Board had decided on a simple inscription at its annual meeting in 1933: "In commemoration of the Four hundredth Anniversary of the landing of Jacques Cartier at the entrance to this harbour on 24th July, 1534." However, unhappy with this sterile interpretation of the discovery of Canada, Surveyer asked Thomas Chapais to draft an alternative inscription. Chapais added the key phrase "and of his taking possession of Canada." Almost immediately, two Board members registered their displeasure. D.C. Harvey and J.C. Webster protested that Cartier himself had made no such claims, but had explained away his cross as a navigational beacon. The inclusion of the phrase, "Vive le roi," they insisted, cannot be taken as an indication of taking possession.[36] E.A. Cruickshank felt this protest was ludicrous because even the "untutored Indian" Donnacona knew Cartier's intent. However, he also felt that the whole affair embarrassed the Board and could not be resolved without initiating a new dispute.[37] Cruickshank's premonition proved accurate.

Working alongside the federal Board was a political committee headed by Senators C.P. Beaubien and Raoul Dandurand. This committee met irregularly and, at least as far as the HSMB could tell, appeared to do very little. However, from a larger perspective, this National Committee (or sometimes styled Quebec Committee by its detractors) served as a liaison between the Canadian planners and the French *Comité France-Amérique,* a quasi-governmental goodwill committee that promoted French cultural ties with Canada. In the fall of 1933, Dandurand travelled to France where he met many of the French dignitaries planning to come to Canada the following summer. Convinced that this occasion could easily become an important international event, he returned to Canada and immediately urged the federal government to build a more "worthy" monument.[38] The HSMB had already designed a 15-foot cross, but Dandurand wanted to double its height. And he continued to agitate for it over the winter, meeting with federal ministers, civil servants, newspaper reporters, and especially pressuring the Quebec member of the HSMB, Montreal's Judge Surveyer. Surveyer's correspondence with the Parks Branch commissioner became increasingly tense in the new year. On 4 January 1934, he wrote Harkin to complain that the 30-foot cross would be too large for the selected site, although Dandurand had criticised that choice as well. Moreover, as plans were already made and the land had been deeded, nothing could be changed.[39] A flurry of mail flew back and forth between the various members of the Board. Could anything be done? The answer, it seemed, was no. The smaller cross was already under construction, the site had been chosen, and there just was not enough money to start over again. Then, suddenly, the Montreal *Gazette* reported that Dandurand had won an additional $5,000 from the federal government. The *Gazette* article was premature, but Harkin later learned that the Minister of the Interior had agreed that the cross was too small and approved spending additional money on a larger one.[40]

Suddenly, with only a few months to go before the planned ceremonies, the Board had to abandon its already-built cross and start over with a larger one. Money was no longer a problem, but time was. First the Prime Minister himself phoned Harkin to suggest that the model then in use—incredibly it was a Celtic cross—was inaccurate. Cartier had built with timber, and therefore would not have been able to make a circle. The board redrafted its plan in response.[41] However, the next proposal, a 30-foot cross cut from a single block of stone, posed its own problems. It would obviously be time-consuming to manufacture. But D.C. Harvey had some more biting concerns:

> In regard to Québec's passion for identical measurements of Cartier's cross, I am wondering if historical exactitude would not suggest a pole instead of a granite shaft, particularly in view of the difficulty of having such huge arms of granite suspended as a perpetual warning to tourists not to walk beneath them.[42]

Nonetheless, the Prime Minister wanted a 30-foot, single-piece, granite cross, and that was that. But the 46-ton cross cost $6,935, nearly $2,000 over budget. And, it could not be transported from Quebec City to Gaspé by train because the local railway bridges could never handle its weight. It had to be floated by barge, further slowing the project. Still, the cross was standing in place by 15 August, nine days before the big event.[43]

This was only one major headache for Harkin. About the time that Dandurand began to pester Surveyer and Harkin over the height of the Gaspé cross, another Board member began to feel pressure from his part of the country. Harvey came under increasing pressure to take up the cause of commemorating Cartier's landing somewhere on Prince Edward Island at the beginning of June 1534. The idea appealed especially to another Maritimer, J.C. Webster, who saw no good reason why "all the honours should go to Quebec." Indeed, he felt that Cartier's real "discovery of Canada" had actually occurred at P.E.I. as it was there that he first landed on what would become Canadian soil.[44] H.R. Stewart, the province's deputy secretary, concurred. For him, it was crucial to have a ceremony when the French delegation sailed past the island because it was there that Cartier made the "true discovery" of Canada.[45] The Board seemed to have found a place for its extra cross. Although Harvey felt that the island had "no claim" for a cross, Harkin promptly offered the original 15 footer to the Premier of Prince Edward Island. The offer was flatly rejected.[46] The main reason for the province rejecting the cross was that, as Harvey pointed out, Cartier had not raised one himself when he landed briefly on the island. Therefore, it was historically inaccurate. But, more importantly, the Island Committee (as Webster, Harvey, and the local authorities came to be known) felt they were staking a claim of priority over Quebec. A smaller cross would imply inferiority. Their claim to priority was evident in their enthusiasm for pointing out that Cartier had visited the Northumberland Strait before heading up to Gaspé. They backed their claim using, not a modern translation of Cartier, but the Englishman Richard Hakluyt's 1598 translation of the text on the explanatory plaque. Hakluyt, in some way, lent historical authenticity to the claim. After all, Faribault had simply retranslated his English version back to French when he published a French edition in 1843. It served to emphasise that French ignorance of Cartier had been overcome by English scholarship. Webster complained that the Quebec Committee—especially Senators Dandurand and Beaubien—routinely slighted the Island Committee and the historical importance of Prince Edward Island.

Thus, this commemoration was contested to a much greater degree than the Cartier-Brébeuf celebrations. Part of the reason is that in 1889 the commemoration was of Cartier's discovery of Quebec City; in 1934 it was of his discovery of Canada. In addition, rather than a fairly homogeneous group of French-Canadian backers, the later project drew in planners from across Canada: English, French, Catholic, and Protestant. Another complicating factor at the 1934 celebrations was the importance placed on attracting tourists. Indeed, some predicted the celebrations at Gaspé could surpass even the 1908 Tercentenary of Quebec City festivities. Tourism was, indeed, a major concern in the 1930s. In 1929 tourism added some $300,000,000 to Canada's Gross National Product, but that figure had slumped to a mere $117,000,000 at the depths of the Great Depression in 1933. In response, the Senate launched a special committee to look into what could be done to promote visits to Canada. Chaired by Senator W.H. Dennis of Nova Scotia, the committee recommended a massive and aggressive promotional campaign to draw attention to Canada's numerous attractions.[47] Although the committee met in May 1934, when plans for the Cartier 400th were already advanced, the prospects of using such events to "pep up" Canada's image abroad figured prominently in the committee's vision. The testimony of the assistant to the Director of Publicity of the federal Department of Trade and Commerce, W.H. Van Allen, produced an exchange between Ontario's Senator Hocken and Senator MacArthur of P.E.I. MacArthur suggested that, while the Chicago World's Fair would likely keep many Americans in the U.S., the Cartier celebrations could be expected to showcase Gaspé and thus draw many from Great Britain and France to come for a tour and take advantage of the Depression's low steamship rates. Hocken, picking up the possibility of using Cartier as an advertisement, suggested striking a deal with the Radio Commission for a live broadcast for the thousands outside Quebec who might have an interest in it. To this, MacArthur hastened to add that the "French of Louisiana" might also pay attention.[48] The following week, Hocken pursued his radio idea with Theodore Morgan of the Canadian Association of Tourist Bureaus. "Would you focus on this summer's Cartier celebrations?" he asked, when Morgan suggested the government launch an advertising campaign, only to be disappointed with Morgan's dismissive reply. Federal advertising should not focus on such "passing events," concluded Morgan.[49] Nonetheless, tourist advertising was a concern during the planning and unveiling of the Cartier monuments of 1934. H.R. Stewart had insisted that P.E.I.'s monument be at Charlottetown, miles from any probable historical landing, because it had to be close to tourist traffic. Another argument in favour of the Hakluyt translation was that "the quaintness of the wording will catch the interest of visitors."[50] And, indeed, the unveiling ceremonies were enormously popular with the travelling public. Gaspé was expected to be mobbed, as newspapers reported heavy ship, rail, and road traffic and it was virtually impossible to find lodgings in Charlottetown by August 1934.[51]

III

On 24 August, the packet boat *Champlain* landed at Charlottetown where a distinguished French delegation was greeted by Senator Beaubien and ushered to Province House for the unveiling of the cairn bearing the Board's plaque recounting Cartier's arrival at P.E.I. The unveiling showcased the rhetoric of racial fusion that

Cartier represented in official Canadian programmes. Ottawa's finance minister E.N. Rhodes and Premier MacMillan emphasised the lessons of Canada's past: that two peoples had come together to work in peace to build a new nation. But, speaking for the French delegation, Henry Bordeaux of the *Académie française* hinted that France saw a broader diplomatic meaning behind the summer's commemorations:

> Nous nous trouvons...sur le sol canadien mais ce n'est pas de fait un sol étranger....nous avons trouvé des descendents de nombreuses anciennes familles d'Europe dont plusieurs françaises.

Not only did these old families speak French, "the language of liberty," but Bordeaux pointed out that the deeper ties of blood between France and Canada were remembered in Canadian war graves on the battlefields of the Western Front.[52] Following Bordeaux's speech, the Lieutenant-Governor of P.E.I. unveiled the cairn and the band played "God Save the King" and "La Marseillaise." There was a pattern to the island ceremony that repeated itself the next day in Gaspé. For the HSMB, Cartier represented European discovery of Canada. For many French Canadians, he represented the founding of their people. One newspaper proclaimed that "l'hommage à Cartier fut aussi un homage au Canada français."[53] For some Canadians, both English- and French-speaking, Cartier represented the fusion of Canada's people. But for the French dignitaries, and possibly for some astute Canadian politicians, Cartier symbolised Anglo-French alliance. The French delegation had requested that the Charlottetown cairn be draped in the Union Jack and *Tricouleur,* much to the dismay of the historically minded HSMB.[54] The Cartier celebrations, then, were part of a line of commemorations in Canada and Europe, including the Vimy Ridge memorial, Montreal's statue of Jean Vauquelin, and a Nova Scotian commemoration of the Duc d'Anville, that diplomats used to keep these two major European powers on friendly terms.[55]

Charlottetown was but a prelude to the main festival at Gaspé on 25 August. The *Champlain* arrived in the harbour amidst a wondrous salute of 70 fishing boats decked out in flags bearing Breton and Norman arms from the sixteenth century. These little vessels had come from far and wide, and at their own expense, to salute the dignitaries and no doubt their crews helped swell the five thousand that gathered that sunny Saturday afternoon on a hill overlooking the harbour. The town was suitably decorated with triumphal arches and flowers, creating a celebratory landscape that confronted the senses. The evening held the prospect of fireworks over the bay, building illuminations, concerts, and feasts. But the focus of the day was the stone cross high above the waterfront. The unveiling ceremony was a thing of legend before it had even begun. As a fitting tribute, the newspapers reported, the 30-foot cross was cut from stone sent to Canada from Saint-Malo, Cartier's birthplace. The rumour was untrue, but this bit of popular myth-making was an appropriate opening to the quest for symbolism that appeared in the dignitaries' speeches.[56] Quebec's Lieutenant-Governor, E.-L. Patenaude, opened the discourse. He spoke of how the French and English peoples had come together in Canada through discovery and battle to commerce and art. Speaking directly to the visitors from England, France, and the United States, he reminded them that alongside their people, Canadians had sacrificed their young men and resources on the battlefields of Europe. Canada's peaceful development had been interrupted by the Old World, and so it was fitting that the representatives of the Old come together to pay homage to the man who had founded this New World of peace. Next Prime Minister Bennett took the podium and, in English noted *La Presse,* repeated the familiar story of Canada's two founding peoples learning to honour their combined past. The Sulpician priest, Pierre Boissard, echoed the rhetoric of racial fusion:

> Le sacrifice de Cartier a donc été fecond par l'apport des deux grands peuples, qui a fondé et fait grandir une race puissante a qui nous resterons toujours unis, la nation canadienne, qui demeure l'un des boulevards les plus solides de la civilisation chrétienne.

Meanwhile the leader of the French delegation, Pierre-Etienne Flandin, reminded everyone that Cartier symbolised the common past, and especially common sacrifices. Thus, as at Charlottetown, official memories stressed the fusion of Canada's two peoples and tried to turn the Cartier cross into a surrogate war memorial. It was a compelling message, especially as France nervously eyed events unfolding in Germany.

However, an older interpretation crept into the Gaspé celebrations. Cardinal J.-M.-R. Villeneuve, the Archbishop of Quebec, followed the Prime Minister to the podium. Villeneuve was, at the time, active in the same nationalist circles as Lionel Groulx and his address returned to a semblance of the nineteenth-century religious Cartier:

> Mais est-il dans les fastes de l'histoire humaine un tableau plus grand et une figure plus saisissante que ce Jacques Cartier "dont le geste immortel hante notre mémoire." Les siècles ont passé mais son oeuvre demure.... Vous ne vous étonnez point, messieurs, que ce quatrième centennaire soit célébré à Gaspé sous l'égide de l'Église, en même temps que l'État, qu'a côté d'une croix souvenir s'élève un temple votif de granit...[57]

Villeneuve's "granite temple" was, of course, Bishop Ross's memorial cathedral plan ambitiously revived four years after its first failure. The next day was Sunday and Villeneuve had come to Gaspé with a papal delegation to bless the basilica's corner stone and celebrate a pontifical mass on its site. This was a message the French delegation wanted to ignore. The *Champlain* was scheduled to depart for the St. Lawrence River Saturday night amidst a triumphant send off of fireworks and ship horns, but public pressure forced a last minute change. The ship would sail after mass.

Sunday morning beneath an outdoor altar and a canopy of maple branches and garlands, Villeneuve celebrated mass. Camille Roy, the Rector of the Seminary of Quebec, pronounced the sermon. Roy opened with a passage from the Good Friday liturgy: "Voici que par ce bois une grande joie s'est répandue dans le monde." His sermon was an effort to remind French Canadians of the other element of their dual origins. Cartier had chosen Christ's cross as the sign of his "conquest" of the New World, and this symbol united French Canadians much as Groulx had ambitiously planned:

> Et les croix, qu'au voyage de 1535, Jacques Cartier va éléver sur d'autres rivages, qu'il découvre en remontant notre grand fleuve, témoignent encore de son dessein d'unir toujours dans sa pensée, et les ambitions légitimes de son roi, et le conquête spirituelle des âmes.

Following Roy's sermon, the papal delegate, Mgr Cassulo, blessed the corner stone of the memorial basilica. With the close of the ceremony, the crowd dispersed, leaving the village of Gaspé, this centre of a nation's origins, an isolated and quiet outpost.

Once again, the memorial cathedral proved too ambitious a project and it was never built. The *Champlain* and its distinguished passengers left Gaspé on Sunday afternoon. They sailed on to Quebec, Trois-Rivières, and Montreal, attending Cartier ceremonies at each stop. But no other occasion rivalled the seriousness of the Gaspé cross unveiling. Of course, even in Gaspé not everyone was that serious. Not long after the dignitaries had left the little village, and life had returned to its anonymous normalcy, local children discovered that the Cartier cross was an excellent subject for target practice, and took to throwing stones at it from the road below as they walked to and from school.[58] However, official memory returned to the war. Four years later, following the unveiling of the Vimy Ridge Memorial, Maréchal Pétain made a curious request. During the ceremony he handed some grains of wheat from Vimy to Canadian Legion officials and asked that they be planted at the Gaspé cross. The Canadians, through the HSMB and the Gaspé site caretaker, obliged by sowing the wheat in a little plot behind the cross. Each year, they replanted it along with a plot of poppies, turning the Cartier cross into a surrogate war memorial. It was a curious decision, as the cross stands within a hundred yards of the village war memorial.[59]

Thus, as with the *Cercle catholique*'s use of Cartier to help legitimise the *Jesuits' Estates Act,* twentieth-century thinkers tried to connect Cartier to a fairly specific political position. Cartier represented, loosely, fraternity and the common struggle of French and English. But more specifically, he promoted a war effort. Although some French Canadians resisted this interpretation in the 1930s, it resonated with English Canadians, the British, and the French. Historical heroes are thus themselves historical constructs. Cartier's meaning shifted over the course of some four decades from a religio-national affirmation to a symbol of cultural ties. Similarly, his historical context shifted; Jacques Cartier is not fixed in historical memory. In 1835, and again in 1889, Cartier was portrayed as the discoverer of Quebec, and in particular of Quebec City. By the 1930s, his significance had broadened to the discovery of Canada, with differing interpretations as to what that meant. The argument, in each case, was more emotional than rational. Cartier, obviously, could not have foreseen the rise of New France, its Conquest, and the eventual peaceful cohabitation of French and English any more than he tried to convert the "Canadian" natives. Historical heroes are not rooted in reason, but in lived experience, or more precisely, in lived noumenal experience. The examples cited here suggest that they help add legitimacy—or "genuineness"—to the shifting aspirations and self-images of imagined communities.

Notes

1 Jacques Mathieu, *Les mémoires québécoises* (Sainte-Foy, 1991), 318–20. Michel Bideaux makes a similar point in his "Introduction," *Jacques Cartier Relations* (Montreal, 1986), 9.

2 Archives du Séminaire de Québec, polygraphie 6, no 81; *Le Canadien,* 28 septembre 1835. This story can be followed in J. Robert, "L'invention d'un héros," in *Le Monde de Jacques Cartier,* F. Braudel, ed. (Montréal, 1984), 295.

3 Hamel's portrait toured Canada East in 1847. That year Montreal changed the name of the New Market to Place Jacques-Cartier and Quebec City opened its Marché Jacques Cartier. In 1858, the Government of the United Canadas issued a Jacques Cartier postage stamp denominated at 20 pence. In 1857, the newly established French-language teacher training college in Montréal was christened the École normale Jacques-Cartier. The Union typographique Jacques-Cartier was likely local 145 of the ITU.

4 Bill Butler, *The Myth of the Hero* (London, 1979); JC. Henderson, "Ancient Myths and Modern Man," in *Man and His Symbols.* C Jung, ed., (London, 1964), 110. See also, Bruno Hébert, *Monuments et patrie* (Jolliette, 1980), 269–75.

5 BH. Lehmon, *Carlyle's Theory of the Hero* (New York, 1966), 41–88.

6 The choice of masculine pronouns is primarily a stylistic device intended to focus attention on Jacques Cartier, the subject of this paper. French

Canada's heroes are primarily male, but there are also significant female heroes, such as Jeanne Mance and Madeleine de Verchères.

7 See, as an example, Fernand Ouellet, "Nationalisme canadien-française et laïcisme au XIXe siècle," *Recherches sociographiques* (janvier–avril 1963), 47–70.

8 Calculated from figures given in Paul-André Linteau, *Histoire du Québec contemporain,* 2 vols (Montreal, 1981), 1: 271.

9 F-X. Garneau, *Histoire du Canada,* 5th edition (Paris, 1913), 256.

10 J-B.-A. Ferland, *Cours d'histoire du Canada* (Quebec, 1861, 1969), 20–21.

11 Alan Gordon, "Inventing Tradition: Montreal's Saint-Jean-Baptiste Day Re-Examined," Unpublished paper presented to the Canadian Historical Association Annual Meeting, St. Catharines, Ontario, June 1996.

12 Constitution du Cercle Catholique de Québec (Quebec, 1878). On the *Courrier du Canada* and its politics see André Beaulieu and Jean Hamelin, *La press québécoise des origines à nos jours* (Quebec, 1973), 1: 203–206.

13 A full treatment of this issue can be found in J.R. Miller, *Equal Rights: The Jesuits Estates Act Controversy* (Montreal, 1979).

14 This figure is a crude estimate based on the 1891 Census (Tableau II) which notes total wages of $30,699,115 paid to 117,389 men, women, and children at 23,037 Quebec industrial establishments.

15 Figures compiled from *Premier bulletin du Comité littéraire et historique du Cercle Catholique de Québec: Ouevre du monument Jacques-Cartier* (Quebec, 1888), 6–14 and *Deuxième bulletin du Comité littéraire et historique du Cercle Catholique de Québec: Ouevre du monument Jacques-Cartier* (Quebec, 1890).

16 There is, however, some evidence that in social environments, people rely on the lead of their "betters" in recalling stories. See Mary Susan Weldon, "Collective Memory: Collaborative and Individual Processes in Remembering," *Journal of Experimental Psychology: Learning, Memory, and Cognition* (September, 1997): 1160–75.

17 Canadian Heritage, Research Bulletin no. 312, *Cartier-Brébeuf National Historic Site: In Search of Jacques Cartier* (Ottawa, 1994).

18 Quoted in Robert Rumilly, *Honoré Mercier et son temps,* 2 vols (Montreal, 1975), 2: 94–95.

19 On this, see Gérard Bergeron, *Révolutions tranquilles à la fin du XIXe siècle* (Montreal, 1997), 49–50; and Gilles Gallichan, *Honoré Mercier: La politique et la culture* (Sillery, 1994), 52–53. It should be noted that Robert Rumilly counted 16 speakers at the evening's banquet, including Wilfrid Laurier, who spoke for a different brand of nationalism.

20 See Archives de la Ville de Montréal, P23, fonds de la municipalité de la cité de Saint-Henri.

21 Royal Society of Canada, *Proceedings* (1906), xix. A copy of this monument was erected in Quebec City in 1971. Rodolphe Fournier, *Lieux et monuments historique de Québec et environs* (Quebec, 1976), 9.

22 Morgan, *Sketches of Famous Canadians and Persons Related to Canada* (Québec, 1862), 1; W.F. Ganong, "Jacques Cartier's First Voyage," Royal Society of Canada *Transactions* (1887).

23 Joseph Pope, *Jacques Cartier: His Life and Voyages* (Ottawa, 1890); and H.B. Stephens, *Jacques Cartier and His Four Voyages to Canada* (Toronto, 1890).

24 The anthropologist Peter Pope alleges that anglophone Canadians promoted John Cabot as Canada's discoverer in order to diminish Cartier's claim. See his *The Many Landfalls of John Cabot* (Toronto, 1997). Pope's assertions are somewhat overstated. Although Samuel Dawson insisted that Cabot landed at Cape Breton, his was never close to a majority position. Moreover, even Dawson hedged his argument by admitting that Cartier opened Canada for exploration, whereas Cabot merely visited in 1497. Nonetheless, there was a Cabot lobby which promoted the Italian's claim to the discovery of Canada and the erection of a Cabot monument in Montreal in 1933 provoked a considerable controversy. See, for example, *Le Devoir,* 6 octobre 1933 and *Le Canada,* 6 octobre 1933.

25 See John M. Clarke to C.C. Ballantyne, 3 May 1921. Reprinted in *Bulletin de la Société de Géographie de Québec* 15, 4: 195–97; see also Clarke's "Un médaillon de Jacques Cartier," *Revue canadienne* 5 (janvier–juin, 1910), 6–15.

26 Lionel Groulx, *Mes mémoires,* X vols (Montréal, 1972), 3: 48.

27 NA, RG 84, vol 1250, F-X. Ross to J.B. Harkin, 16 March 1933. Chapais had succeeded Narcisse Dionne as editor of the *Courrier du Canada* in 1884.

28 *Le Devoir,* 22 octobre 1930.

29 Rodolphe Lemieux, "Canada's Quadcentenary, 1934," *Canadian Geographical Journal* 1 (November 1930): 556–73.

30 Brockville *Recorder and Times,* 31 October 1930.

31 NA, RG 84, vol. 1277, Pamphile Demers to J.B. Harkin, 15 June 1927.

32 "L'enseignment primaire," *Education-Instruction* (septembre, 1934).

33 Paul Carpentier, *Les Croix de Chemin: Au-dela du signe* (Ottawa, 1981), 63.

34 NA, RG 84, vol. 1250, JA. Bastien to G.W. Bryan, 1 May 1933; E.-F. Surveyer to J.B. Harkin, 3 April 1934; *L'Evenement,* 29 mars 1934. It was really only five sites as it was later determined that Jacques Cartier Point was an obscure local name for Arnold's Bluff. NA, RG 84, vol. 1250, E.-F. Surveyer to J.B. Harkin, 9 May 1934.

35 NA, RG 84, vol. 1250, GW. Bryan to J.B. Harkin, 1 September 1933. F.J. Richmond, "The Landing Place of Jacques Cartier at Gaspé in 1534," CHA *Annual Report* (1922), 38–46.

36 NA, RG 84, vol. 1250, J.B. Harkin to E.-F. Surveyer, 27 July 1933; J.C. Webster to J.B. Harkin, 1 August 1933.

37 Ibid., EA. Cruickshank to J.B. Harkin, 7 August 1933.

38 Ibid., Raoul Dandurand to J.B. Harkin, 29 November 1933; 16 December 1933.

39 Ibid., E.-F. Surveyer to J.B. Harkin, 4 January 1934.

40 Montréal *Gazette,* 5 February 1934; NA, RG 84 vol. 1250, H.H. Rowatt to J.B. Harkin, 29 March 1934.

41 NA, RG 84 vol. 1250, J.B. Harkin to H.H. Rowatt, 9 April 1934.

42 NA, RG 84, vol. 1213, D.C. Harvey to J.B. Harkin, 10 April 1934.

43 NA, RG 84, vol. 1250, R.A. Gibson to J.B. Harkin, 30 May 1934: T.S. Mills to J.B. Harkin, 24 August 1934.

44 NA, RG 84, vol. 1213, J.C. Webster to J.B. Harkin, 4 March 1934; 8 March 1934.

45 Ibid., H.R. Stewart to J.C. Webster, 9 April 1934.

46 Ibid., D.C. Harvey to J.B. Harkin, 10 April 1934: J.C. Webster to J.B. Harken, 10 May 1934.

47 Canada Parliament. Senate, *Report and Proceedings of the Special Committee on Tourist Traffic* (Ottawa, 1934), ix–xiv.

48 Ibid., 19.

49 Ibid., 57–58.

50 NA, RG 84, vol. 1213, H.R. Stewart to J.C. Webster, 9 April 1934; Fred Landon to J.B. Harkin, 26 April 1934.

51 See Halifax *Chronicle,* 19 July 1934; *Le Soleil,* 27 août 1934.

52 *Le Soleil,* 25 août 1934.

53 *La Presse,* 27 août 1934.

54 NA, RG 84, vol. 1213, A.G. Doughty to J.B. Harkin, 13 July 1934.

55 See Alan Gordon, "Contested Terrain: The Politics of Public Memory in Montréal, 1891–1930," PhD thesis, Queen's University, 1997, 200–203.

56 See, especially, Ottawa *Citizen* 30 March 1934 and 27 August 1934. The second *Citizen* headline read: "Great Cross of St. Malo Quarry Stone Unveiled."

57 Cited in *La Presse,* 27 août 1934.

58 NA, RG 84, vol. 1250, J.B. Harkin to S.R. Sams, 18 May 1936.

59 Ibid., M.F. Gregg to F.H.H. Williamson, 12 April 1937. The wheat and poppies were still growing into the 1940s when an American tourist complained to the Parks Branch that, compared to the immaculate war memorial nearby, the cross site was deplorably maintained and covered with weeds and "hay." Ibid., B.R. Thompson to "The Department," 11 July 1941.

"We Are Well As We Are": An Indian Critique of Seventeenth-Century Christian Missions

James P. Ronda*

Historians' interpretations of Christian missions to the Indians in seventeenth-century North America have changed dramatically in the past decade. It had long been traditional historical wisdom to hold that missionaries played an essentially benevolent role in culture contact and change. Merchants, traders, and politicians were usually identified as the agents of change in native American life, while missionaries were associated with otherworldly concerns. Because missionaries were dedicated, self-sacrificing people who truly believed in their task, historians have tended to see them as they saw themselves: as humble servants, saving souls from savagery and damnation, all for the greater glory of God.[1] Several scholars have recently challenged this view. Francis Jennings, Robert Berkhofer, Jr., Neal Salisbury, and James Axtell have demonstrated that the Christian mission to native Americans was neither an attempt to save them from land-hungry settlers nor a guileless exercise in soul-winning.[2] These historians view it as a revolutionary enterprise, designed to bring about a radical transformation of Indian culture. Native Americans were required to become like Europeans in all aspects of life—in matters of sex, marriage, economy, and government, as well as religion. The Indian who embraced Christianity was compelled, in effect, to commit cultural suicide. He was required to renounce not only his own personal past, but that of his forefathers as well, forsaking—and despising—all traditional beliefs and practices. Because missionaries demanded no less than "cultural revolution,"[3] their attacks on Indian religions "cannot be regarded simply as a matter of criticism of some abstract philosophical hypothesis."[4] These attacks posed a threat to the very survival of native American society.

The new interpretations recognize the importance of that threat but still tend to emphasize only one side of the issue. They continue to concentrate upon the words and actions of missionaries to the neglect of Indian responses and initiatives. Native Americans reacted to missionary activity in a wide variety of ways, each of which deserves our attention if we are to understand the role of the mission in culture contact and change. Some Indians accepted the new religion and the new life-patterns it commanded. Others incorporated certain Christian elements into their lives while rejecting the essence of the white man's message. Most native Americans reaffirmed their traditional beliefs and strenuously resisted Christianity. But what-

James P. Ronda, "'We are Well as We Are': An Indian Critique of Seventeenth-Century Missions," *William and Mary Quarterly*, 3rd series, 34, 1 (1977): 66–82.

*Mr. Ronda is a member of the Department of History at Youngstown State University. This essay is part of a larger investigation of Indian–mission relations in early America. The author wishes to thank James Axtell, Jeanne Ronda, and Mary Young for their criticisms and suggestions, and the National Endowment for the Humanities for its support.

ever their responses, Indian peoples did demonstrate that their traditions were dynamic intellectual systems, capable of change. The fact that most native Americans chose to retain their beliefs does not mean that Indian societies could not change; the evaluation and reaffirmation of accepted belief constitute in themselves a kind of transformation.

Failing to note this kind of change, historians have tended to view mission history as a one-sided struggle between ossified Indian traditions and a vital European Christianity.[5] As a result, important Indian comments have been ignored or dismissed as the mere rantings of jealous Indian leaders. To restore the Indian critique of mission work to its proper place in the study of culture contact, historians must find and verify those crucial observations. This is often a complicated matter. Indian speeches were filtered through white interpreters, recorded by white secretaries, and ultimately arranged in the memoirs of white missionaries. Historians searching for Indian perspectives must read such accounts with caution. We must be sensitive to the circumstances surrounding each recorded speech or dialogue if we are to hear those Indian voices so long ignored.[6]

Some of the most compelling voices were those of Huron and Montagnais Indians in New France. The Massachuset, Wampanoag, and Nipmuc tribes of southern New England also produced thoughtful critics who tried to construct sensible replies to the missionary assault on their cultures. These men and women reacted emphatically against the Christian theological ideas of sin, guilt, heaven, hell, and baptism. A reconstruction of the native American critique of the mission must begin with their responses to those ideas.[7]

Sin and guilt were central themes in Christian dogma. From apostolic times missionaries knew that unless potential converts understood and accepted them, the mission would have little chance to win genuine believers. Many native American religions did not contain the idea of sin as either a primordial fault or a moral transgression against the will of God. These religions recognized personal wrongdoing but did not assign it any cosmic significance. Huron religion, for example, emphasized instead the presence of certain evil forces and the dangerous consequences that might result from failing to do proper service to a particular deity. Indians found the Christian view of sin and guilt both incomprehensible and useless. When a Jesuit urged a Huron to acknowledge her sins and be baptized, she and her friends protested that she had always lived in innocence and without sin. The woman clearly rejected the Christian insistence that a person who lived a moral life might also be a great sinner.[8] *"May a good man sin sometimes?"* wondered one of John Eliot's New England converts. *"If a man be almost a good man and dyeth; whither goeth his soule?"* asked another.[9] Eliot was closely questioned by an Indian who was interested in the origin of good and evil ideas. *"Do all evill thoughts come from the Devill,"* he asked, *"and all good ones from God?"*[10] Most Indians simply dismissed the concept of personal sin and guilt. "It would be useless," insisted one Huron, "for me to repent of having sinned, seeing that I never have sinned."[11]

Hurons, both converts and traditionalists, found the doctrines of sin and guilt confusing. "How...do we sin?" asked one man. "As for me, I do not recognize any sins."[12] When the missionaries attempted to explain how one could sin even in one's thoughts, they often encountered utter disbelief. "As for me, I do not know what it is to have bad thoughts," replied one old man. "Our usual thoughts are, 'that is where I shall go,' and 'Now that we are going to trade, I sometimes think that they would do me a great favor when I go down to Kebec, by giving me a fine large kettle for a robe that I have.'"[13] Even among converts the missionaries met considerable resistance to the ideas of sin and guilt. When a recently converted Huron came to confess, the missionaries rejoiced: "He was about to accuse himself," they thought, "of having violated what the Father had taught." They were soon disappointed, however, for the convert came rather to accuse another Indian of stealing his cap. He had assumed that this "confession" would win him another cap from the Jesuits.[14]

Indians tended to view the conceptions of heaven and hell with even less regard. The Huron, Montagnais, and New England native Americans all anticipated an afterlife but assumed that it would be spent in morally neutral surroundings, not in a place of heavenly reward or hellish punishment. The Hurons spoke of a "village of souls" populated by the spirits of the dead. Life in those villages was believed to resemble life on earth with its daily round of eating, hunting, farming, and war-making. Missionary efforts to impress Indians with the delights of heaven met with disbelief and derision. Because the Jesuits described heaven in European material terms, the Hurons concluded that heaven was only for the French. When one Huron was asked why she refused to accept the offer of eternal life, she characteristically replied, "I have no acquaintances there, and the French who are there would not care to give me anything to eat."[15] The father of a recently deceased convert child urged the missionaries to dress her in French garments for burial so that she would be recognized as a European and permitted entrance into heaven.[16] Most native Americans rejected the European heaven, desiring to go where their ancestors were. The mission compounded this rejection by telling potential converts that heaven contained neither grain fields nor trading places, neither tobacco nor sexual activity—surely a dreary prospect. Some Indians resented the notion that one had to die in order to enjoy the blessings of conversion, while others observed that an everlasting life without marriage or labor was a highly undesirable fate.[17]

Missionaries provoked an even stronger negative response when they preached about everlasting punishment in a fiery hell. The hell the Jesuits described must have profoundly affected their Indian listeners, for the Huron and Montagnais were no strangers to the horrors it was said to contain. The torture by fire of captured warriors was a customary part of Iroquoian warfare, and Huron and Montagnais men knew that such would be their fate if they fell into enemy hands. They themselves practiced torture rituals on their own captives, applying burning brands and glowing coals to the bodies of the condemned before execution. Men and women who had participated in such events must have responded emphatically to the idea of hell. But the evidence suggests that most responded in disbelief. Though the torments of hell were all too imaginable, they were rejected because they seemed to serve no useful purpose. In fact, the most common objection to the Christian hell was that it only lessened the delights of earthly life. "If thou wishest to speak to me of Hell, go out of my Cabin at once," exclaimed one Huron. "Such thoughts disturb my rest, and cause me uneasiness amid my pleasures." Hurons resented what seemed to them a Christian obsession with death and punishment. This resentment may have sprung from Huron anxiety about death and about the uneasy relationship between the living and the spirits of the dead.[18] Whether or not disturbed by this prospect, one Huron spoke for many when he said simply, "I am content to be damned."[19]

Other native Americans went beyond rejecting hell as an unpleasant place to question the basic Christian assumptions about postmortem punishment. "We have no such apprehension as you have," said a Huron, "of a good and bad Mansion after this life, provided for the good and bad Souls; for we cannot tell whether every thing that appears faulty to Men, is so in the Eyes of God."[20] Other Hurons found sinister political motives behind the preaching of hell; they contended that hell was a weapon of intimidation used by the missionaries to force acceptance of French social and political domination.[21] When Eliot attempted to preach the doctrine of hell to the Massachuset Indians, he encountered similar reasoned resistance. Perceiving the connection between Eliot's mission and the political goals of Massachusetts Bay, one sachem charged that the concept of punishment in hell was designed by Englishmen "to scare us out of our old Customs, and bring us to stand in awe of them."[22] Another Indian, disturbed by the apparent contradiction of a loving God who decreed everlasting torments, demanded to know *"Why doth God punish in hell for ever? man doth not so, but after a time lets them out of prison again. And if they repent in hell, why will not God let them out again?"*[23]Many of Eliot's questioners were clearly thoughtful and thorough people who tried to reconcile the idea of hell with other Christian doctrines. One alert Massachuset noted that *"God made hell in one of the six dayes. Why,"* he implored, *"did God make Hell before Adam sinned?"*[24]

To silence the skeptics the Jesuits in New France resorted to the use of highly colored pictures that depicted the torments of hell in gruesome detail. Indian critics soon turned the images against the missionaries. When the pictures were shown, Huron religious leaders proclaimed that those writhing in the flames were not the unbelievers but the converts. If hell existed at all, they seemed to be saying, it would surely be reserved for those traitors who have abandoned the way of their fathers.[25] Most native Americans found the concept of hell a meaningless fiction. Even when presented with imagery bound to strike fear in their hearts, they concluded that the ideas of sin, heaven, and hell were just "so many Fabulous and romantick Stories."[26]

Indians and missionaries might have debated endlessly the merits of those stories, but one Christian doctrine presented native Americans with a more immediate dilemma. The question of baptism and its consequences brought the confrontation to a matter of human survival. Jesuit policy was to withhold baptism from a potential convert until that person was at the moment of death or the missionaries were sure that he or she would not apostatize. Thus in the first years of the mission in New France most Indians who received the sacrament were soon dead. The critique of baptism developed by the Hurons grew slowly until by the late 1630s it consisted of several related arguments all devastating in their impact on the mission effort. At first, Hurons believed that baptism might restore health; they were inclined to view the sacrament as one more of the many healing ceremonies common to Huron life.[27] Father Paul Le Jeune, superior of the Huron mission, was shocked to discover some who believed that the more water was used in baptism, the more healthful would be the consequences.[28] This positive view quickly changed when smallpox swept the Huron villages. Since the Jesuits baptized only those on the verge of death, many Hurons concluded that the rite was the immediate cause of death. Charles Meiachkawat, a recent convert, was assailed by his wife who cried, "Dost thou not see that we are all dying since they told us to pray to God? Where are thy relatives, where are mine? the most of them are dead; it is no longer a time to believe."[29]

Huron and Montagnais religious leaders employed the fear of baptism to diminish missionary influence. Huron shamans argued persuasively that missionaries "had a secret understanding with the disease" and used baptism to spread it. This belief became so widespread among the Hurons that by 1639 many political leaders, as well as ordinary people, were calling for the execution of the Jesuits as an act of self-preservation.[30] By connecting baptism with the spread of smallpox, native Americans mounted a compelling indictment of the mission and its methods. The disease served as an ever-present warning that to abandon the traditional ways was to court death. Even the zealous mission worker Jerome Lalemant was forced to admit that "no doubt we carried the trouble with us, since, wherever we set foot, either death or disease followed us."[31]

Indian critics found even greater fault with the missionary effort to discredit traditional healing ceremonies. Among the native Americans of southern New England the powwow was a rite that had both medical and religious significance. The Hurons held similar annual gatherings called *ononharoia.* In addition, Hurons when ill might employ the services of various curing societies. Missionaries who observed such healing rituals uniformly condemned them. Such condemnation was usually motivated by the desire to weaken the power of traditional religious leaders. Eliot bitterly attacked the healers as "great witches having fellowship with the old Serpent, to whom they pray."[32] He described all Indian healing efforts as "sinfull and diabolicall."[33] Jesuits also condemned the ceremonies. Healers were branded as "imps of satan" whose "art was founded upon falsehood."[34]

Both Protestant and Catholic missionaries forbade their converts to take part in the ancient healing acts. This ban, coming as it did at the very moment when native Americans were suffering the effects of European diseases, provoked a torrent of angry criticism from both converts and traditionalists. The dilemma faced by converts was especially agonizing. They were required to abandon traditional sources of medicine and solace while watching members of their families die of strange and dread diseases. One powwow leader in Martha's Vineyard expressed astonishment that any Indian would turn away from the customary means of healing. He warned one convert of the recklessness of his stand. "I wonder that you that are a young Man," he chided, "and have a Wife and two Children, should love the *English* and their Ways, and forsake the *Pawwaws;* what would you do if any of you were sick? whither would you go for Help? If I were in your Case, there should be nothing to draw me from our *Gods* and *Pawwaws.*"[35] As disease stalked the Hurons, similar pleas were made to those now derisively called "the Believers." "My nephew," entreated one Huron captain, "make a truce for one day with the Faith. Our Country is going to ruin; the sick are dying. Whither can we flee to avoid death? Why do you keep away from our dances? Why do you refuse to do this act of kindness to the People? It is the Christians who kill us, since they will not help us. Come and dance today, my nephew, and to-morrow thou shalt resume the practice of Faith."[36]

Huron traditionalists strongly assailed the missionary campaign against the accepted healing rites. They argued that unless proper services and acts of worship such as dances and feasts were performed, smallpox epidemics would continue to rage. Failure to participate was interpreted as both disloyal and suicidal. "There is nothing we would not do to preserve our lives," explained one Huron, "and if it be necessary to dance night and day to drive away the disease, all decrepit as I am, I will begin first, in order to save the lives of my children."[37]

Angered at missionary attacks on customary healing rites and fearful of baptism as a carrier of disease, Indians in New France extended their criticism of the mission to an assault on the physical symbols of European Christianity. Before the smallpox epidemics began, Hurons and other Indians had found French material culture interesting and often amusing. Window glass, clocks, weather vanes, writing, and even doors were regarded with curiosity.[38] But as disease and crop failures began to ravage Huronia, curiosity turned to suspicion. When a severe drought brought widespread crop damage in the summer of 1635, Huron religious leaders charged that the presence of Jesuit crosses had driven away the rain. Tehorenhaegnon, a prominent shaman, insisted that unless the crosses were removed and the missionaries expelled, no rain would fall.[39] Even after rain did come, the fear of the Christian cross persisted. That fear was fueled in later years by the relentless smallpox. As the disease spread, Hurons became increasingly critical of other Christian symbols and images. Their criticism was based on the belief that all symbols possessed independent life and could be a source of grave personal danger. In the Huron mind the Christian cross was the living presence of an alien deity—a deity bent on destroying Hurons by unknown diseases. Similarly, instead of inspiring a fear of hell, the Jesuits' explicit pictures provoked a fear of all images. Even serene representations were considered hazardous. One missionary reported that many Hurons were convinced that "tainted influences issue... down into the chests of those who look" at images of Christ and the Holy Family.[40] By 1640 all mission property, whether or not religious, had become suspect. The Jesuits' inkstands, books, and letters, as well as their sacred objects, were viewed with suspicion as potential hiding places for disease-bearing demons.[41] The Indian assault on Christian symbols was motivated by neither simple iconoclasm nor fear alone. It was predicated on the premise that such symbols were deeply repugnant to true religion. This idea was prominent in the theologies of both the Indians and the missionaries. Both agreed that grave consequences would result if the offending emblems—the signs of the others' faith—were not removed.

Indians and missionaries shared another basic belief in their assessment of one another. Missionaries saw Indian religious leaders as devils, demons, sorcerers, and witches. Indian priests and shamans viewed their Christian counterparts in the same light. The Jesuits "are not men," contended one group of Huron leaders; "they are demons."[42] Others believed that the missionaries were sorcerers with vast evil powers. It was rumored that the Jesuits were either raising or hiding evil charms in mission cabins. These charms were said to take the form of domestic animals or serpents and were thought to spread disease. One shaman, who had evidently heard something about the Eucharist, accused the Jesuits of bringing a corpse from France to infect Hurons with a terrible plague. Other charges ranged from consorting with strange spirits to infanticide.[43] Huron and Montagnais religious leaders largely succeeded in depicting missionaries as disease-bearing sorcerers who possessed horrible charms and displayed a sinister obsession with guilt, death, and punishment.[44]

In the eyes of Indian political leaders, the missionary-sorcerers were conniving imperialists as well—the advance guard of European political domination. Sachems, village elders, and band chiefs were intensely aware of the missions' attack on their sovereignty. Their resistance to Christianity was noted by nearly every missionary in early America. One New England sachem graphically explained what conversion would mean to his own political power. "If I be a praying Sachem, I shall be a poor and weak one, and easily be trod upon by others, who are like to be more potent and numerous; and by this means my Tribute will be small, and my people few, and I shall be a great loser by praying to God." The same sachem denounced Christianity and its political implications as "a bitter Pill, too hard for me to get down and swalow."[45] An Algonquian politician named Agwachimagan spoke for many native Americans when he offered his assessment of missionary imperialism: "I have been among the French at Quebec and at the Three Rivers. They have taught me the very substance of their doctrine. I know everything about matters of the Faith. But, the more I fathomed their mysteries, the less clearly did I see. They are fables, invented to inspire us with real fear of an imaginary fire; and, in the false hope of good that can never come to us, we involve ourselves in inevitable dangers." Those dangers included death by European diseases and eventual French political control. Agwachimagan returned again and again to the theme of the loss of autonomy. His oration concluded with a call for renewed Indian self-determination. "Since those who refuse to worship him [the Christian God] are happier than those who are his subjects, if you, my brothers, like me, have any feeling and love for yourselves, for your children, and for your country, choose with me to consider him rather as an enemy than as a friend."[46]

These were powerful responses. Agwachimagan and many other thoughtful Indian critics like him identified the "enemy" only after weighing the evidence. They carefully considered their positions before answering the missionaries. Scholars have tended to ignore the fact that the exchanges between Indians and missionaries constituted genuine theological debates, in which both parties represented well-reasoned religious systems. To fully appreciate the scope and intensity of those debates we must move beyond the discussion of specific doctrinal ideas to glimpse some of the encounters in context. Both Le Jeune and Eliot participated in lively exchanges that may well typify native American responses to Christianity.

For Le Jeune the contest began shortly after his arrival in Quebec. During the winter of 1633–1634 he joined the roving hunt of a Montagnais band. Mixing language training with evangelism, he attached himself to the household of Carigonan, a noted holy man. The days were spent in grueling pursuit of moose and other game, but at night Le Jeune and Carigonan embarked on a quest of another kind. Inside dark, smoky bark cabins the French priest and the Montagnais shaman matched wits and challenged each other's theology. Their first major discussion contained all the elements of later ones. Predictably, Le Jeune began by asking Carigonan what he believed about life after death. All souls travel on foot to a great village beyond the western edge of the world, Carigonan replied. When the Jesuit ridiculed this interpretation, Carigonan snapped back, "Thou art mistaken... either the lands are united in some places, or there is some passage which is fordable over which our souls pass." Carigonan found it incomprehensible that Le Jeune would prefer to believe that souls float upward to a village in the sky. Le Jeune demanded to know what souls ate on their long trip, and was promptly told that they "eat bark... and old wood which they find in the forest." Le Jeune retorted that it was little wonder the Montagnais feared death, if that was what they would have to eat on such a tiresome journey. Undaunted, the Indian theologian described in more detail the activities of souls after death: they eat, hunt, and sleep as they had in life. Le Jeune scoffed, adding that Carigonan's idea of heaven was preposterous. Turning practical for the sake of argument, the Jesuit noted that Indians believed that all beings had souls and that no heaven could be large enough to contain them all. Carigonan was appalled by Le Jeune's apparent ignorance. "Thou art an ignoramus, thou has no sense," he declared. "Souls are not like us, they do not see at all during the day, and see very clearly at night; their day is in the darkness of the night, and their night in the light of the day." When Le Jeune protested that Carigonan had hardly answered the question, the shaman cut him short. "Be silent," he commanded. "Thou askest things which thou dost not know thyself; if I had ever been in yonder country, I would answer thee."[47]

Despite their many differences, Le Jeune and Carigonan shared more than they realized. Each embraced a religious system that emphasized the supernatural and its interaction with man. The Jesuit believed that human beings could be affected for good or ill by the actions of spirits and demons; Carigonan acknowledged the existence of equally influential beings called *khichikouai.* Both theologians accepted the dichotomy of soul and body as well. It was in the realm of religious practice—the manipulation of the sacred—that the differences between their theologies became most apparent. Le Jeune did not claim to have any personal supernatural powers, but Carigonan claimed direct communication with and control over supernatural forces. He believed himself capable of healing the sick, insuring good hunts, and killing distant enemies. He told Le Jeune that his soul could leave his body at will. Claims such as these reinforced Le Jeune's conviction that Carigonan was indeed a sorcerer and a formidable enemy of the faith. Le Jeune was further outraged by the rituals of the Montagnais. He witnessed dances, "eat-all" feasts, the ritual treatment of beaver and moose bones, and extended trances. His suspicions were heightened by the fact that shamans conducted some sacred ceremonies in secret.

Because neither Le Jeune nor Carigonan distinguished between belief and practice, their encounters continued to emphasize these differences. The severity of the early debates did not subside in subsequent meetings; the combatants argued, cajoled, and threatened well into the night each time. Each held his own. Le Jeune, a gifted professor of rhetoric, found Carigonan a worthy opponent. Carigonan demonstrated that Montagnais religion was as reasoned and systematic as Christianity. Several times in 1634 the shaman sought out Le Jeune to discuss troublesome points of doctrine in more detail. The evidence suggests that Carigonan's thought matured as a result of the debates. When Le Jeune's journey with the Montagnais was over, the Jesuit was grudgingly forced to admit that the Montagnais held to their faith as tenaciously as did any pious Christian.[48]

John Eliot's exchanges with Indian theologians were undoubtedly as fascinating as Le Jeune's, but Eliot and his coworkers did not leave records as detailed as the *Jesuit Relations.* Today's scholars must content themselves with a tantalizingly brief glimpse of the encounters. Eliot compiled lists of questions posed by Indians and included them—without answers or comment—in his mission reports. The lists allow us to reconstruct, in part, discussions that were surely as searching as those between Le Jeune and Carigonan.

The most extensive list survives in a letter written by Eliot in November 1648. This list is especially important because it was compiled early in the period of mission contact and reflects the beliefs of traditional coastal Algonquians. Eliot's questioners were evidently concerned about a wide range of subjects. The sixty-question list encompasses matters of natural history, ethics, and biblical interpretation. Some Indians were clearly disturbed by the hypocrisy of the English settlers. They questioned Eliot about the relationship between Christian commitment and the sharp business dealings they had observed. *"Doe not Englishmen spoile their soules to say a thing cost them more than it did? and is it not all one as to steale?"* asked one native American. Others were apprehensive about the Christian concepts of the soul, punishment for sin, and life after death. They pressed Eliot for more details. *"When the soule goes to heaven, what doth it say when it comes there,"* asked one Indian, *"And what doth a wicked Soule say when it commeth into Hell?"* Many new converts inquired about the kind of justice they would receive from Eliot's god. Their concern betrays the anguish of men and women cut off from traditional beliefs. *"If I doe that which is a sinne,"* asked one man, *"and do not know it is a sin, what will God say to that?"*[49]

When confronted with Christian doctrines, symbols, and ceremonies, Indians asked searching questions. A few accepted the answers of the missionaries and were converted; others rejected what they saw as an alien ideology and reaffirmed their traditional beliefs. But native Americans did not respond to missionary activity solely by accepting or rejecting Christianity. So long as political autonomy was not totally compromised, Indians were able to produce positive religious movements to counter Christianity.[50] Anthropologists have labeled these movements revitalization religions. Syncretistic in nature, revitalization religions often blended Indian and Christian theological elements around the central figure of an Indian prophet or savior. These movements were distinct from the kind of accommodation that seems to have occurred in many Indian convert congregations. The phenomenon was not limited to any one place or time. Revitalization prophets may be discerned throughout the Americas. From the Aztec Huichilobos to Handsome Lake and Wovoka, they represent a major and often neglected aspect of the native American response to Christianity.[51]

As early as 1639, revitalization movements began to appear among the Hurons. A woman, deathly ill with smallpox, reported that she had seen a vision of an Indian savior while passing from life through death and back to life. This savior urged her to dress in red garments and studiously perform all the old rituals. Welcomed by Huron leaders as a sign of deliverance from the disease, the vision resulted in widespread feasting and public processions. The Jesuits angrily reported that the vision and the renewed zeal it inspired had cost the mission dearly.[52] In the following year another exemplary episode of revitalization took place. A young Huron fisherman reported that a spirit had appeared to him and revealed his hopes for Huron regeneration. "I am Iouskeha," declared the spirit, "I am the one whom the French wrongly call Jesus, but they do not know me. I have pity on your country, which I have taken under my protection." Iouskeha, already known to the Hurons as the Master of the Earth, charged that the Jesuit mission was spreading death among the Huron people. "You can prevent this misfortune," insisted the spirit. "Drive out of your village the two black gowns who are there." Iouskeha instructed the young man to reinstitute traditional healing ceremonies and religious observances.[53] Well into the 1640s visions of Huron prophets were regularly recounted by both laymen and religious leaders. Each visionary denounced Christianity as a dangerous, alien ideology, and stressed the value of Huron cultural unity.[54] In New England the evidence for revitalization movements is lacking. The mission records of Eliot and others make no mention of Indian prophets or visionaries. It can be argued, however, that some Indians quietly embraced a kind of revitalization religion while accepting the outward forms of Christianity. Neal Salisbury has suggested that active Indian participation in congregational singing and church discipline invested "the imposed religion with traditional meaning."[55] Demonstrating the continuing vigor of tradition, the revitalization movements offered both sharp criticism of the mission and an alternative for those unwilling to accept Christian conversion.[56]

Native American responses to the Christian mission effort indicate that Indians were quick to recognize the deep philosophical difference between their religions and Christianity. Native Americans observed that Europeans practiced a rigid, exclusivist religion. Both the message and the tactics of the missionaries reflected the dictum of Christ: "I am the way, and the truth, and the life; no man cometh unto the Father, but by me" (John 14:6). Indians knew that they would be required to worship the Christian god alone—and in conformity with European customs—if they converted. In contrast, Indian religions were inclusive. They permitted their adherents to hold a wide variety of beliefs simultaneously. Although these religions were as culture-bound as Christianity, they were remarkably flexible. Traditional rites and ceremonies were scrupulously performed year after year, but new elements and experiences found their way into the rituals. Christian elements were even incorporated on occasion, but Indians strenuously resisted the notion that indigenous beliefs and practices must be set aside to make way for them. Clearly, Indian religions did not contain any missionary impulse.[57] Native Americans understood the intense evangelistic drive of the missionaries but were unimpressed by it. They preferred to practice what might be called a kind of pragmatic cultural relativism. Each people possessed unique social and intellectual traits, they argued—traits that should not be imposed upon others. An Iroquois might be "converted" to a Huron, but that conversion or adoption was radically different from the Christian conception. The idea of a single religion shared by all peoples seemed to the Indian an absurdity. In their perspective, religious affiliation was determined by tribal birth, not by rebirth in Christ. Most Indians endorsed a philosophy that can best be described as a "two roads" or "two ways" approach. A Huron explained it to Jesuit Jean Brébeuf in this way: "Do you not see that, as we inhabit a world so different from yours, there must be another heaven for us, and another road to reach it?"[58] When Jesuits pressed the Hurons and Montagnais to give up their ways, they consistently received the same answers: "such is the custom of our country," or "such is not our custom; your world is different from ours; the God who created yours did not create ours."[59] When Christian Indians from the praying town of Natick attempted to convert their traditionalist kinsmen, they encountered similar arguments. "Our forefathers were (many of them) wise men, and we have many wise men now living, they all delight in these our Delights: they have taught us nothing about our Soul, and God, and Heaven, and Hell, and Joy, and Torment in the life to come.... We are well as we are, and desire not to be troubled with these new wise sayings."[60]

Indian politicians added their own perspective to the two-roads analogy. In 1637 elders in the Huron village of Wenrio met with the Jesuits to consider the impact the mission might have upon their town. Aenons, a prominent politician, listened carefully to the missionaries' demands for culture change and then responded, "we have our own ways of doing things and you yours, as well as other nations. When you speak to us of obeying and acknowledging as our master him whom you say has made Heaven and earth, I imagine you are talking of overthrowing the country. Your ancestors assembled in earlier times, and held a council, where they resolved to take as their God him whom you honor, and ordained all the ceremonies that you observe; as for us, we have learned others from our own Fathers."[61]

Aenons did not overdramatize his case when he suggested that the Jesuits spoke of "overthrowing the country." His analysis, like that of many New England sachems, rightly acknowledged the revolutionary character of the mission. Native Americans understood all too well the goals of the mission and its profoundly disturbing impact on their life. Critics like Aenons, whether openly rejecting the mission or blending the concept of a savior into a revitalization movement, recognized both the ethnocentrism and the imperialism of the missionaries. They saw what the dedicated missionaries could not see—the cruel irony in the mission enterprise. Missionaries promised heaven, but brought devastation. "You tell us that God is full of goodness," lamented one Huron, "and then, when we give ourselves up to him, he massacres us. The Iroquois, our mortal enemies, do not believe in God, they do not love the prayers, they are more wicked than the Demons—and yet they prosper; and since we have forsaken the usages of our ancestors, they kill us, they massacre us, they burn us—they exterminate us, root and branch. What profit can there come to us from lending ear to the Gospel, since death and the faith nearly always march in company?"[62]

Notes

1 Alden T. Vaughan, *New England Frontier: Puritans and Indians, 1620–1675* (Boston, 1965), 235–308; Ola Elizabeth Winslow, *John Eliot: "Apostle to the Indians"* (Boston, 1968); Stephen Neill, *A History of Christian Missions* (Grand Rapids, Mich., 1965); William V. Bangert, *A History of the Society of Jesus* (St. Louis, 1972), 265.

2 Francis Jennings, *The Invasion of America: Indians, Colonialism, and the Cant of Conquest* (Chapel Hill, N.C., 1975), 43–57, 228–253; Robert F. Berkhofer, Jr., *Salvation and the Savage: An Analysis of Protestant Missions and American Indian Response, 1787–1862* (Lexington, Ky., 1965); Neil Salisbury, "Red Puritans: The 'Praying Indians' of Massachusetts Bay and John Eliot," *William and Mary Quarterly,* 3d Ser., XXXI (1974), 27–54; James Axtell, "The European Failure to Convert the Indians: An Autopsy," Proceedings of the Sixth Algonquin Conference, National Museum of Man, *Mercury Series* (Ottawa, 1975).

3 James P. Ronda and Jeanne Ronda, "The Missionary as Cultural Revolutionary: Two Seventeenth-Century Examples," presented at the Great Lakes Regional History Conference, May 1975.

4 Cara E. Richards, *Man in Perspective: An Introduction to Cultural Anthropology* (New York, 1972), 278–279.

5 Clifford Geertz, *The Interpretation of Cultures: Selected Essays* (New York, 1973), 170: "Our view of Asian and African religions as such is oddly static. We expect them to prosper or decline; we do not expect them to change."

6 This new direction is explored in Cornelius J. Jaenen, "Amerindian Views of French Culture in the Seventeenth Century," *Canadian Historical Review,* LV (1974), 261–291. Historians of African missions are far ahead in this enterprise. For examples see T. O. Beidelman, "Social Theory and the Study of Christian Missions in Africa," *Africa,* XLIV (1974), 235–249; H. W. Mobley, *The Ghanaian's Image of the Missionary* (Leiden, 1970); and Matthew Schoffeleers and Ian Linden, "The Resistance of the Nyau Societies to the Roman Catholic Mission in Colonial Malawi," In T. O. Ranger and I. N. Kimambo, eds., *The Historical Study of African Religions* (Berkeley and Los Angeles, 1972), 252–273. These perspectives can be given theoretical focus by applying the concepts developed in Wilhelm Dupré, *Religion in Primitive Cultures: A Study in Ethnophilosophy* (The Hague, 1975).

7 Because ethnographic material on Indian religions so pervades this essay, I have chosen to list all major sources in one note: T.J.C. Brasser, "The Coastal Algonkians: People of the First Frontiers," in Eleanor Burke Leacock and Nancy Oestreich Lurie, eds., *North American Indians in Historical Perspective* (New York, 1971), 64–91; Harold E. Driver, *Indians of North America* (Chicago, 1961); Dupré, *Religion in Primitive Cultures,* 99–112; William W. Newcomb, Jr., *North American Indians: An Anthropological Perspective* (Pacific Palisades, Calif., 1974); Robert F. Spencer *et al., The Native Americans: Prehistory and Ethnology of the North American Indian* (New York, 1965); and Bruce G. Trigger, *The Huron Farmers of the North* (New York, 1969). The concepts of tradition, religion, and social change employed in this essay are drawn from the following: Robert A. Nisbet, *The Social Bond: An Introduction to the Study of Society* (New York, 1970), 301–394; Edward Shils, "Tradition," *Comparative Studies in Society and History,* XIII (1971), 122–159; Keith Thomas, *Religion and the Decline of Magic* (New York, 1971), 151–173; and Anthony F. C. Wallace, *Religion: An Anthropological View* (New York, 1966).

8 Reuben Gold Thwaites, ed., *The Jesuit Relations and Allied Documents: Travels and Explorations of the Jesuit Missionaries in New France, 1610–1791...* (Cleveland, Ohio, 1896–1901), XIII, 201, hereafter cited *as Jesuit Relations.*

9 Edward Winslow, "The Glorious Progress of the Gospel amongst the Indians in New England..." (1649), Massachusetts Historical Society, *Collections,* 3d Ser., IV (1834), 84–85.

10 Henry Whitfield, "The Light appearing more and more towards the perfect Day..." (1651), *ibid.,* 129.

11 *Jesuit Relations,* XIII, 211.

12 *Ibid.,* XXIII, 111.

13 *Ibid.,* XIV, 91.

14 *Ibid.,* 81–83.

15 *Ibid.,* XIII, 127.

16 *Ibid.,* 31.

17 *Ibid.,* 179.

18 Trigger, *Huron Farmers,* 102.

19 *Jesuit Relations,* XXIII, 189.

20 Baron [Louis Armand de Lom d'Arce] Lahontan, *New Voyages to North-America,* II: *Giving a full Account of the Customs, Commerce, Religion, and strange Opinions of Savages of that Country* (London, 1703), 92.

21 *Jesuit Relations,* XXIII, 189.

22 John Eliot, *Indian Dialogues, for Their Instruction in that great Service of Christ...* (Cambridge, Mass., 1671), 7.

23 Winslow, "Glorious Progress," Mass. Hist. Soc., *Colls.,* 3d Ser., IV (1834), 91.

24 *Ibid.,* 85.

25 *Jesuit Relations,* XI, 97–99, XIV, 103–105. For a recent study of the graphic arts in the Jesuit missions see François-Marc Gagnon, *La Conversion par l'Image* (Montreal, 1975), esp. plates 11, 12, 23, and 24.

26 Lahontan, *New Voyages,* II, 91.

27 *Jesuit Relations,* X, 13.

28 *Ibid.,* XII, 229.

29 *Ibid.,* XX, 197.

30 *Ibid.,* XIX, 91–93.

31 *Ibid.,* 93.

32 [John Eliot], "The Day-Breaking, if not The Sun-Rising of the Gospell With the Indians in New-England" (1647), Mass Hist. Soc., *Colls.,* 3d Ser., IV (1834), 20. In a letter dated Sept. 24, 1647, written to Thomas Shepard, Eliot revealed the strategy he would use to discredit the powwows. He suggested that some praying Indians be trained in European medicine at English expense. "By this meanes," wrote Eliot, "wee should traine up these poore *Indians* in that skill which would confound and root out their *Powwaws,* and then would they be farre more easily inclined to leave those wayes, and pray unto God." Thomas Shepard, "The Clear Sun-shine of the Gospel Breaking Forth upon the Indians in New-England..." (1648), *ibid.,* 57. Eliot's attack on the powwows can be placed in perspective by consulting Thomas, *Religion and the Decline of Magic,* 51–77.

33 Winslow, "Glorious Progress," Mass. Hist. Soc., *Colls.,* 3d Ser., IV (1834), 84. For similar uses of sacramental healing magic in England see Thomas, *Religion and the Decline of Magic,* 177–211.

34 *Jesuit Relations,* XIX, 83, XVI, 149.

35 Experience Mayhew, *Indian Converts: Or, some Account of the Lives and Dying Speeches of a considerable Number of the Christianized Indians of Martha's Vineyard, in New England...* (London, 1727), 4.

36 *Jesuit Relations,* XXIII, 49.

37 *Ibid.,* XIII, 235.

38 *Ibid.,* VIII, 109–113.

39 *Ibid.,* X, 37.

40 *Ibid.,* XIV, 51–55, XV. 19, XIX, 115–117.

41 *Ibid.,* XVIII, 41.

42 *Ibid.,* XIII, 165.

43 *Ibid.,* XIV, 103–105, XV, 31–35, XIX, 97.

44 *Ibid.,* XV, 69.

45 Eliot, *Indian Dialogues,* 46, 50. For corroborating evidence see Whitfield, "Light Appearing," Mass. Hist. Soc., *Colls.,* 3d Ser., IV (1834), 139.

46 *Jesuit Relations,* XXVI, 301–305. Anthony J. Dachs, "Missionary Imperialism: The Case of Bechuanaland," *Journal of African History,* XIII (1972), 647–658, suggests some important African similarities.

47 *Jesuit Relations,* VI, 177–181. For other meetings between Le Jeune and Carigonan see *ibid.,* VII, 99–103, 187–191. Le Jeune had a similar set of exchanges with another Montagnais theologian named Makheabichtichiou in 1637. *Ibid.,* XI, 239–269. The problem of interpreting non-Christian theologies is treated by Dupre, *Religion in Primitive Cultures,* 1–15, 117–149 and Peter Winch, "Understanding a Primitive Society," in D. Z. Phillips, ed., *Religion and Understanding* (New York, 1967), 9–42. Vine Deloria, Jr., *God is Red* (New York, 1973), offers some very perceptive observations on the differences between Christian and native American theologies.

48 *Jesuit Relations,* VI, 163–171, 193–201.

49 Winslow, "Glorious Progress," Mass. Hist. Soc., *Colls.,* 3d Ser., IV (1834), 84–86. For similar lists see *ibid.,* 91–92; Shepard, "Clear Sun-shine," *ibid.,* 46–47; and John Eliot, "A Late and Further Manifestation of the Progress of the Gospel amongst the Indians in New-England..." (1655), *ibid.,* 277–278.

50 The relationship between the loss of political autonomy and Indian responses has caused considerable controversy among historians. In *Salvation and the Savage* Berkhofer argues that once autonomy was lost, Indian responses to mission challenges were very limited. This view has been sharply criticized by those who have examined mission history in a global perspective. Cf. T. O. Ranger, "Indian and African Responses to Christianity: A Critique of *Salvation and the Savage,*" UCLA Seminar on the Interactions of Indian and African Historiography, Winter 1971.

51 Vittorio Lanternari, "Nativistic and Socio-religious Movements: A Reconsideration," *Comp. Studies in Soc. and Hist.,* XVI (1974), 483–503; J. D. Y. Peel, "Syncretism and Religious Change," *ibid.,* X (1968), 121–141; Margaret Sanford, "Revitalization Movements as Indicators of Completed

Acculturation," *ibid.* XVI (1974), 504–518; Anthony F. C. Wallace, "Revitalization Movements: Some Theoretical Considerations for Their Comparative Study," *American Anthropologist,* LVIII (1956), 264–281.

52 *Jesuit Relations,* XVII, 165–179.

53 *Ibid.,* XX, 27–31.

54 *Ibid.,* XXX, 25, 27–33.

55 Salisbury, "Red Puritans," *WMQ,* 3d Ser., XXXI (1974), 51.

56 Richard O. Clemmer, "Resistance and the Revitalization of Anthropologists: A New Perspective on Cultural Change and Resistance," in Dell Hymes, ed., *Reinventing Anthropology* (New York, 1969), 213–247.

57 This important distinction between exclusive-evangelizing religions and inclusive-tribal ones is drawn from Richards, *Man in Perspective,* 263–264, and Murray Wax, "Religion and Magic," in James Clifton, ed., *Introduction to Cultural Anthropology* (Boston, 1968), 224–242.

58 P. F. X. de Charlevoix, *History and General Description of New France,* ed. and trans. John Gilmary Shea, II (New York, 1870), 7–9.

59 *Jesuit Relations,* X, 19, XI, 7–9.

60 Eliot, *Indian Dialogues,* 7, 9.

61 *Jesuit Relations,* XIII, 169–175.

62 *Ibid.,* XXV, 35–37.

Commodity Exchange and Subordination: Montagnais-Naskapi and Huron Women, 1600–1650*

Karen Anderson

In recent years, scholars have debated two questions with increasing frequency: Under what conditions do women and men occupy egalitarian positions in society? and, Under what conditions do men come to dominate women? Although some theorists are convinced that egalitarian relations between women and men are impossible,[1] a growing number point to historical and contemporary data that document the existence of these relations under certain conditions. However, those who agree that women's subordination to men is not a universal phenomenon do not agree on the circumstances that bring about male domination.

Certainly, Friedrich Engels's work has influenced this debate. In *The Origin of the Family, Private Property, and the State,* he argued that introducing commodity production and exchange into primitive societies inevitably resulted in women's economic, social, and sexual subordination to men. Commodity exchange, he said, disrupted "the collectivity of production and appropriation" by laying the groundwork for the notion of private property and creating the nuclear family as a property-owning and inheriting unit. Through various mechanisms, property came under the exclusive control of male household heads, while women became their economic wards and sexual chattels.[2]

Several contemporary writers, including Mona Etienne and Eleanor Leacock, repeat Engels's theme. Summarizing the findings of essays in their edited volume *Women and Colonization,* Etienne and Leacock note that, as precapitalist societies began to produce commodities for exchange with Europe, the sexual division of labor developed to the extent that adult men and women produced or procured "significant quantities of different things (rather than virtually the same things) creat[ing] the possibility for ties of economic dependence that had not previously existed." This, in turn, laid "the basis for inequalities both among women and men and between women and men."[3]

Women and Colonization presents a number of historical and contemporary examples that strongly suggest two conclusions: women and men in certain noncapitalist societies occupy "egalitarian" (but not equal) statuses, and a direct causal link exists between the introduction of commodity production and exchange and the deterioration of women's position.

Karen Anderson, "Commodity Exchange and Subordination: Montagnais-Naskapi and Huron Women, 1600–1650," *Signs* 11, 1 (Autumn 1985): 48–62.

*An earlier draft of this paper benefited from the comments of Wallace Clement, Richard Lee, and Meg Luxton.

Indeed, some of the evidence is so compelling that one hesitates to question this connection between commodity production and women's subordination. The case of the seventeenth-century Huron, however, counters those described in the Etienne and Leacock collection.

The Huron were a group of Iroquoian-speaking horticulturalists who lived on the shores of the Georgian Bay of Lake Huron at the time of contact with the French. Both they and the Montagnais-Naskapi, a group of Algonkian-speaking hunter-gatherers who summered on the shores of the St. Lawrence River, were intermediaries in the French fur trade network and were proselytized by Jesuit missionaries. Despite these similarities, the records left by French explorers and missionaries for the period 1600–1650 make it clear that Huron women were much more successful than their Montagnais-Naskapi counterparts in resisting male domination. While there is ample evidence of the declining position of Montagnais-Naskapi women under the pressures of the fur traders and Jesuit missionaries, nothing indicates that Huron women experienced the same fate.

Although Leacock has suggested that participation in the fur trade and exposure to proselytization enabled male domination among the Montagnais-Naskapi, the case of the seventeenth-century Huron suggests the need for another explanation. This article argues that the fur trade and Jesuit activity played an important role in the subordination of Montagnais-Naskapi women only when traditional kinship structures and gender-based social relations of production were destroyed. Differences between Montagnais-Naskapi and Huron women can be attributed to variations in the extent to which French traders, missionaries, and state officials were able to undermine existing kin- and gender-based social relations and to institute new forms of social relations modeled after the seventeenth-century French peasantry. Only when the traditional basis of male-female relations had been undermined could private property, in the hands of men, have any negative implications for the status of women.

Social, Economic, and Political Organization of the Montagnais-Naskapi and the Huron

The Montagnais-Naskapi were one of the many groups of hunter-gatherers who summered on the shores of the St. Lawrence River and who wintered along its tributaries. Their economy followed a seasonal cycle. In the summer and fall, they lived by fishing, gathering, and trapping small game. Then they broke up into ten- to twenty-member bands made up of several nuclear families who lived together for the entire winter in a conical lodge that served as a base camp from which the men left to hunt. Residence rules were most likely flexible, and people moved according to personal choice and the need to balance the working group between young and old, men and women. Ideally, though, a man resided with his wife's kin after marriage.[4]

The Montagnais-Naskapi social division of labor assigned men and women different economic tasks. Men hunted and waged war. Women transported the game men killed, gathered wood, made household articles, skinned and prepared hides, caught fish and even hunted small game, made canoes, and set up tents. Marriages were sometimes polygamous, and leaders often had more than one wife to help with the extra tasks their role entailed.[5]

Although the Jesuits identified certain Montagnais-Naskapi men as chiefs, their accounts verify that chiefs had little authority. Decisions about group life were made by all adults in the group. This situation led Jesuit observers to comment, "The Savages cannot endure in the least those who seem desirous of assuming superiority over the others: they place all virtue in a certain gentleness or apathy." The Montagnais-Naskapi "have neither political organization, nor office, nor dignities, nor any authority, for they only obey their chief through goodwill toward him."[6]

Unlike the Montagnais-Naskapi, the Huron were semisedentary horticulturalists who lived on a strip of land about thirty-five miles long and twenty miles wide, bounded on the west by Georgian Bay and on the east by Lake Simcoe. The population of this confederacy of five tribes stood at about 21,000 when they were first encountered by the French and at about 9,000 after the epidemics of the 1630s.[7] From 1609 to 1649, when they were effectively dispersed by the Iroquois, the Huron were distributed among eighteen to twenty-five villages ranging in size from about 300 to 1,600 persons.[8]

The economy of the Huron centered on relatively few activities: slash-and-burn horticulture, fishing, hunting and gathering, and barter. Labor was also devoted to offensive and defensive warring, construction of longhouses and palisades, domestic manufacture, and ritual life. The tribes raised corn as their major food staple, which supplied about two-thirds of their diet along with beans, squash, and pumpkin.[9] Among the Huron and other Iroquoian peoples of southern Ontario and northwestern New York State, the basic unit of production, consumption, and residence was the longhouse, composed of three to six related "households" or nuclear family units. Several longhouses together made up a village.

Like the Montagnais-Naskapi, the Huron based their social division of labor on gender. Women were responsible for supplying virtually all horticultural labor, as well as for providing firewood to heat the longhouses during the winter, a formidable task. Women also performed domestic work such as child care; made household goods, clothing, and pottery; and prepared food for storage and consumption. Huron men were responsible for clearing new land, fishing, hunting, trading, and warfare. Women often accompanied men on fishing and hunting trips to prepare the catch and transport it back to the village.

The Huron's political organization at the village, tribal, and pantribal levels was much more elaborate than that of the Montagnais-Naskapi. The tribes were composed of eight matrilineal clans, and members of each clan were represented in most Huron villages.[10] Clan membership was the organizational basis for village and tribal political life as well as an important factor in the distribution of material goods, the operation of social support systems, and the selection of marriage partners.

Chiefs, drawn from all the clans and organized in village councils, were assigned the role of managing public affairs and administering public policy. Their task was to persuade their clan members to carry out decisions made in council meetings. Often they had great difficulties in controlling their clan members' actions, which made their chieftainship largely honorific. As the Jesuits observed, "These positions are servitudes more than anything else." A clan chief, they reported, was always responsible for attending assemblies, which often took place in other villages, and for publicizing council decisions. Yet, at the same time, he exercised "small authority over his subjects" and was unable to govern by command or with absolute power, having "no force at hand to compel [his people] to their duty."[11]

Clearly, the Huron, as settled horticulturalists, had a more highly developed social, economic, and political organization than did the Montagnais-Naskapi. First, the Huron's use of corn as a major foodstuff allowed them both a semisedentary way of life and the possibility of much larger concentrations of population. Second, their division of labor, which was essentially gender-based like the Montagnais-Naskapi's, had a greater elaboration of roles for men; some specialized as traders, others as warriors or hunters.[12] Finally, the Huron's political organization was more extensive than the

Montagnais-Naskapi's. Decision making was carried out on many levels, and even in the villages councils represented the various clans of the residents.[13] Decision making among the Montagnais-Naskapi, on the other hand, involved the entire adult membership.

Despite these differences, the two groups shared very important characteristics. First, both the Montagnais-Naskapi and the Huron were divided into two mutually exclusive groups—males and females—and gender determined all economic and social activities: a woman's tools, activities, and life experiences were not a man's. What gender divided, however, kin relations united. Production and reproduction in both Huron and Montagnais-Naskapi social formations depended on kin relations, which organized men and women into viable units of production and distribution that could live and work together on a daily basis. Although kin ties were more elaborately defined and employed among the Huron, their strength was no less impressive among the Montagnais-Naskapi.

A look at any aspect of Huron or Montagnais-Naskapi life reveals some form of gender-based kinship organization—whether real or adoptive—that guaranteed all members of society access to the means of production and to the products of social labor. Moreover, kinship provided each individual with a set of mutually interdependent relations that defined units of production, consumption, and residence as well as political representation and emotional support. A woman or man without real or adoptive kin, whether Huron or Montagnais-Naskapi, remained outside society and was likely to face death from neglect or starvation. Because the specific content of kin ties as social relations of production was gender-based, the reproduction of both Huron and Montagnais-Naskapi societies depended on the existence of both males and females. But since neither gender occupied a position that allowed control of the means of production or the products of social labor, neither could use such control to claim special status.

There is a second similarity that makes a comparison between the two social formations compelling: both were exposed to the French fur trade and to Jesuit proselytization. The Jesuits' presence in New France was closely tied to the fur trade and to colonization, even though fur traders, missionaries, and state authorities occasionally pursued contradictory policies.[14] Despite temporary differences, state, trade, and church in New France were in general harmony concerning Indian policy. The first governors of New France, Samuel de Champlain and his successor Charles Huault de Montmagny, supported the Jesuits' missions to the Huron and the Montagnais-Naskapi by providing military aid and by granting Christianized Indians preferred trading rights. Both acts were intended to tie the fur trade to the Indians' acceptance of the Jesuits and Christianity; Christianized Indians would, the governors hoped, become loyal subjects willing to fight for the interest of French sovereignty in New France.

Given this very powerful support for their missions, the Jesuits went to live among the Huron and the Montagnais-Naskapi with the express objective of transforming both societies. In the process they observed and wrote about many aspects of Montagnais-Naskapi and Huron life. Most often they wrote disapprovingly, especially of the liberties afforded women in the areas of marriage, divorce, and sexuality. Women, they noted, were under no obligation to respect, obey, or remain with their husbands unless they so chose. One of the Jesuit missionaries' main goals became the solemnization of marriages between practicing Christians in order to bring Huron and Montagnais-Naskapi women under the control of their male relatives and to bring both men and women under the control of the Catholic church and the French state.

The Effects of French Contact on Women's Status

THE MONTAGNAIS-NASKAPI

The Montagnais-Naskapi household was that group's most important unit of social organization, the focal point for economic, social, political, and residential functions. Marriage, divorce, procreation, and the disposal of the product of labor were all expressions of the nature of relations between men and women and were carried out within or between households. In such a society, changes in women's social, economic, and political roles occur first in the realm of domestic relations and indicate a transformation in women's status vis-à-vis men.

In the early years of their contact with the Jesuits, Montagnais-Naskapi men and women were reported to have had an equal right to free choice in marriage and divorce and to initiate sex or to reject a suitor. Both men and women controlled their own work, and the Jesuits remarked that both knew just what they were supposed to do: "Neither meddles with the other." Women decided when to move camps. "The choice of plans, of undertakings of journeys, of winterings," the Jesuit missionary Paul Le Jeune reported, "lies in nearly every instance in the hands of the housewife." Men left the arrangements of household affairs to the women, who distributed both their own and their husbands' produce without any interference. "I have never seen my host," Le Jeune commented, "ask a giddy young woman that he had with him what became of the provisions, although they were disappearing very fast." "Women," he further remarked, "have great power.... A man may promise you something and if he does not keep his promise, he thinks he is sufficiently excused when he tells you that his wife did not wish him to do it."[15]

All this was soon to change with the Jesuits' plan to convert the Montagnais-Naskapi to Christianity and to turn them into settled agriculturalists and, ultimately, French citizens.[16] To do this they were determined to institute Christian marriages, subordinate women and children to husbands and fathers, and, finally, to subject all Montagnais-Naskapi to the authority of the church and the French state.

This goal was not easily accomplished. In his annual report of 1633 to his superior in Rome, Le Jeune commented that men who were accustomed to "a life of idleness," would have "difficulty in embracing one of hard work such as cultivating the soil." Again in 1635 he reported to his superior in Paris that because "these poor barbarians have been for a long time accustomed to be idlers, it is hard for them to locate and cultivate the soil unless they are assisted." He added that if they could be made "docile and sedentary...they will not die of hunger so often as we will be able to instruct them easily." Finally, he noted that "the bond, so strong, which holds man and wife under the same yoke, will be very hard to fasten upon the savages."[17]

But certain events were working in the Jesuits' favor. By the 1630s the Montagnais-Naskapi were feeling the effects of Iroquois raids. As governor of New France, Champlain promised to help the Montagnais-Naskapi construct a protected village and to clear land if they agreed to convert to Christianity and to approve Jesuit education for their children. This offer met with some success, and by the late 1630s the Jesuits were in charge of four households of Montagnais-Naskapi settled at Sillery, about six miles above Quebec.

In 1640 Le Jeune happily reported to his superior that "the Gentlemen of the Company of New France, in order to induce the savages to settle, have granted the same favour in their store to the sedentary Christians as to the French." These same "Gentlemen" had some cultivated land given as a dowry to young Christianized Montagnais-Naskapi girls in order to induce their new husbands to settle and stay with one wife. Help like this was only a beginning. Le Jeune, through the *Jesuit Relations,* appealed to potential benefactors in France, reporting that the Indians' life would be so much easier if they could become sedentary, but that the difficulty of clearing the land made it almost impossible to encourage them to do so. They preferred, he said, "to live in repose and in the idleness of animals to enjoying the fruits of labour." He added, however, that some of the Indians were asking for assistance from the French in clearing land, especially since game was becoming scarce; according to his estimate, a ten or twelve *ecu* donation from a benefactor would "ensure" that a marriage was properly started.[18]

Le Jeune's appeals succeeded in attracting some money from Monsieur Sillery, a member of the court of Louis XIII, who paid for French workers to build four houses "in the French style" and to clear land for a settlement bearing his name.[19] On the basis of this donation the Jesuits were able to attract thirty-five or forty families to Sillery. Those Montagnais-Naskapi men who, in the Jesuits' opinion, had become loyal, practicing Christians were given cleared land as private property.

Once settled at Sillery with their husbands and fathers controlling landed property, Montagnais-Naskapi women experienced a rapid and drastic change in status. They were humiliated and forced to make public declarations of obedience to their husbands. The following account of the church marriage between a male convert whom the Jesuits recognized as a "captain" and the woman to whom he was already married according to Montagnais-Naskapi custom is revealing:

> They both agreed to [a church marriage] and proceeded to the Church to receive the Blessings of the Priest, who first asked Charles [the name the Jesuits had given to this "captain"] if he took such a one for his wife. "Wait a little," answered Charles; and, turning to his wife, he said: "But thou, wilt thou continue to be proud, disobedient, and ill-tempered, as in the past? Answer me; for if thou wilt not behave better, I will not take thee for my wife,—I shall easily find another." She was quite abashed, and replied that she would conduct herself better in the future. "Speak louder," said Charles: "we do not hear thee. When thou art angry, thou screamest like a mad woman; and now thou wilt not open thy mouth." The poor woman had to shout aloud, and protest publicly that she would be obedient to her husband, and live with him in gentleness and in the utmost humility. "That is right," said Charles, "provided thou doest as thou sayest, otherwise, thou wilt cause me to be angry; and if I get angry, I shall go to Hell, and so wilt thou." Then speaking to the Father, "Go on," he said, "I am satisfied. I will always love her as my only and my lawful wife."

Le Jeune concluded, "God has visibly blessed this marriage, and we have never seen a greater change than in this woman, who has now become truly a lamb, and has very deep and affectionate feelings of devotion."[20]

The willingness of newly converted Montagnais-Naskapi men to subordinate women did not stop with the public humiliation of recalcitrant wives. Women who left their husbands were beaten and thrown in jail. Although there are several such examples in the *Jesuit Relations,* the following illustrates the extent to which women were subdued: "[The Captains instigated a search for] a young woman [who had] fled...into the woods, not wishing to obey her husband,...and [they] came to ask us [the Jesuits] if, having found her, it would not be well to chain her by one foot; and if it would be enough to make her pass four days and four nights without eating as penance for her fault."[21]

Moreover, women began to police their own behavior. An older woman took to locking up the younger girls inside a house at night to prevent clandestine meetings with young men. Even young women themselves came to the Jesuits to ask for nighttime protection against young men. The Jesuits were so successful in instilling an aversion to extramarital sexual activity that Le Jeune was able to file this report: "All the converts show great solicitude to avoid the sins they have abandoned, especially the licentious acts and speech so prevalent among their countrymen; and the girls drive away their pagan suitors with firebrands."[22]

By 1640 the women at Sillery were well under the control of both their male relatives and the church. They had lost their right to self-determination, to free choice in marriage and divorce, to independence from oppressive authority. They had been subjected to male scorn, beatings, imprisonment, food deprivation, and public humiliation. Once proud and free-willed, women became, in the Jesuits' words, "as docile as little lambs."[23] How could this have come about? Leacock suggests that the Montagnais-Naskapi were ready to accept the Jesuits' teachings because a century of participation in the fur trade had already undercut "the economic basis for unquestioned cooperation, reciprocity, and respect for individual autonomy."[24] The contrasting experiences of the Huron under similar conditions, however, demand an alternative explanation.

THE HURON

Like the Montagnais-Naskapi, the Huron were involved in the fur trade as intermediaries to the French and by 1630 were providing up to half of the fur exported from New France.[25] The Huron were likewise offered inducements to convert to Christianity: French protection from their enemies, better treatment by French traders, assistance from French benefactors. Yet the Jesuits had little success in establishing Christianity among the Huron. They had even less success in instilling women's subordination to their husbands or in ending male and female rights to divorce and remarriage. Even in the later years of the Jesuits' mission to the Huron, the *Jesuit Relations* report that both men and women exercised autonomy in marriage and divorce and were free to enter and conclude marriages at will. At a time when the Montagnais-Naskapi women were requesting aid from the Jesuits against the sexual advances of men, Huron women were exercising a "sexual licence" that the Jesuits deemed detrimental to the instituting of Christian marriages.

Throughout the entire period of their mission to Huronia from 1633 to 1649, the Jesuits recorded again and again that Huron women refused to convert to Christianity either because they could not bind themselves to "marital fidelity" or because they could not promise to live with only one man for the rest of their lives. One Jesuit observer commenting on the Huron practice of "licence in marriage" noted that the freedom to leave a spouse on the slightest "pretext" was fundamental. The church, he lamented, "cannot hold the women to the marriages." Marriage was nothing more than a "conditional promise to live together so long as each shall continue to render the service that they mutually expect from each other."[26]

Huron women were still able to decide to leave their husbands even in the latter decades of the Jesuit missions, a fact made clear in a discussion that the Jesuits recorded between two Huron seminarians at Quebec. "If we take a wife," one of them reportedly said, "at the first whim that seizes her she will at once leave us, and then we are reduced to a wretched life, seeing that it is the women in our country who sow, plant and cultivate the land and prepare the food for their husbands." The rate of marriage, divorce, and remarriage among the Huron provoked one Jesuit to comment that it was "the ordinary practice of the savages...to change wives at almost every season of the year."[27]

Personal autonomy in marriage and divorce extended to the right of both men and women to exercise decisions about the deployment of sexuality. The Recollet lay brother Gabriel Sagard, Champlain, and the Jesuits all noted—with a sense of shock and outrage appropriate to their social class and time—that Huron women were willing not only to engage in sexual relations with men outside of marriage but to initiate the contact. Young girls, Sagard reports, vied with one another for the greatest number of lovers. Each village, he added, had its "procurers" whose occupation was to bring men and women together for intercourse.[28]

Champlain, who mirrored Sagard's sexual attitudes in his own writings, reports that he was taken aback when, on leaving his cabin to escape the fleas, he was followed and propositioned by a woman.[29] Three decades later the Jesuit Charles Lalemant commented on the same issue, mentioning that "assignations" in the woods between men and women were common and that women could initiate them just as easily as men. The Jesuits further remarked about the "libertinage to which the girls and women here abandon themselves."[30]

There are many indications that both Huron women and men had individual autonomy in conducting their daily lives and in making decisions about important social, economic, and ideological matters. Nowhere is this more evident in the historical record than in the Jesuits' reports on the conflicts that arose between husbands and wives over the question of baptism and conversion to Christianity. Conversion to Christianity was an important issue for Huron men involved in the fur trade, for the French gave Christians better protection from the Iroquois and better terms of trade. Despite these obvious advantages to traders, Huron men who converted to Christianity were far from able to force their female relatives to convert along with them. In fact, the Jesuits indicate that Huron men were in a much more vulnerable position than Huron women, susceptible to coercion by their wives and, more often, by their mothers-in-law.

Because Huron men usually resided in their wives' longhouses after marriage, any man who displeased his mother-in-law ran the risk of expulsion from his home. It is clear from the *Jesuit Relations* that some Huron matrons were in a position to threaten husbands or sons-in-law with ostracism or expulsion to force them to behave. This power is clearly illustrated in references to the misfortune of men whose female relatives opposed their conversion to Christianity. Male converts often experienced the severest kind of rejection, not only from members of their wives' longhouses, but often from their own clan members as well. The Jesuits report, for example, on the "plight of a poor man, the only Christian in all his family" who refused to renounce his "faith" despite all efforts to make him do so. According to the Jesuits:

> They drove him away from their cabins, and refused to give him anything to eat; they reproached him with the death of one of his nieces, who had been baptized. He was left without means of support, and was compelled to do what is usually the work of women. He was mocked at, and spurned from every company: and quarrels were picked with him. If at any time he was invited to a feast, some insolent persons present would call out that he should not have been invited, because he was a Christian, and because he brought misfortune where ever he went; that he might certainly make up his mind to die sooner than he expected; and that he would be clubbed to death as a Sorcerer.[31]

In a similar vein, the Jesuits reported the case of a "Christian man" who was about to be abandoned by his wife and children "in consequence of the persecutions of his mother-in-law, who could not bear to have him in her house when she found that he was a Christian."[32] The husband and wife had lived together for fifteen or sixteen years and had five children, yet on the insistence of her mother, his wife intended to leave him.

These examples are interesting for two reasons. First, they illustrate the structural position of men and women in the exercise of authority: matriarchs exercised personal authority over their daughters and had enough influence to compel sons-in-law to obey. Second, they exemplify the coercive, rather than absolute, nature of power. Even chiefs were not immune from their female relatives' anger when they made unpopular decisions, and in some instances they renounced their offices in favor of conversion to Christianity. One such chief who renounced his position found "his mother, his wife, his relatives and all his village leagued against him, but nothing of this [shook] him. 'Poverty...will not frighten me. God shall take the place of my relatives and of my mother, and he alone shall be my support. Let my wife leave me and deprive me of my children.' "[33]

Conclusion

The Jesuits expended a great deal of effort in proselytizing both the Montagnais-Naskapi and the Huron, although the historic record indicates very different results. While the *Jesuit Relations* report progress in the conversion of the Montagnais-Naskapi, the Huron continued to disappoint the missionaries. Clearly, Jesuit success among the Montagnais-Naskapi cannot simply be attributed to effects of the fur trade, as Leacock has suggested; similar economic conditions prevailed among the Huron without the same decline in the position of women. But if the subordination of Montagnais-Naskapi women was not caused by the fur trade alone, how do we explain the decline in their position relative to that of Huron women? The answer, I suggest, lies in the presence of the French state and the Catholic church, together with a set of conditions that made French charity and protection attractive as well as a legitimized and effective system for punishing those who resisted French influence. The suppression of women was only part of a much larger program to bring men, women, and children under the control of the church and the state.

The Montagnais-Naskapi's inducement to settle at Sillery is clear. Iroquois were raiding on the St. Lawrence, and a life on the land, distant from others who might give succor against murderous enemies, was not nearly as appealing as residence in a palisaded village protected by French soldiers. Game, too, was becoming scarce, and French offers of cleared land and housing understandably drew a number of Montagnais-Naskapi families to Sillery. Once there, it must have been quickly apparent that the most zealous Christians got the most favorable treatment by the French: cleared land, dowries, elaborate marriages, gifts, better trading rights, and, possibly, French housing. The Jesuits also made the most devoted male converts "captains" and gave them the means to hand out charity to other villagers. Speaking of one of the best converts, Le Jeune wrote, "That excellent neophyte knows how to dispense the goods that God and men have given him to the poor Christians who he considers as his children. He succors the old women, the poor widows, the orphans—giving them bread, peas, Indian corn, eels and even robes."[34]

At Sillery, the Jesuits succeeded in reassigning the traditional redistributive role of "giddy young women" to sober Christian men. Familial ties and gender arrangements were undermined as men gained control over not only the means of production but also the very conditions of existence. The means of production and of subsistence were no longer made available through the mutual sets of rights and obligations among male and female kin; they were now distributed by Christianized men whom the Jesuits thought to be ideologically reliable and willing to conform to the authority of the Catholic church and the French state. Jesuit-appointed "captains" soon became very powerful in the village, carrying out the wishes of church and state officials with a vigor that sometimes took the Jesuits themselves aback. "The savages," Le Jeune happily summarized, "know very well that [Sillery] is not a place that is open to apostates from the faith or to those who live scandalously in sin.... Their captain gave them clearly to understand that the walls which have been built were not for the purpose of sheltering vice, but of preventing it from entering."[35]

Despite their success among the Montagnais-Naskapi at Sillery, the Jesuits could never gain control over the Huron's means of subsistence or the distribution of goods necessary to life. They were never able, therefore, to undermine the organization of Huron domestic units and the authority that women had in them. While the Jesuits did persuade a few Huron women to convert to Christianity and to obey their male relatives, the missionaries never possessed the means whereby they could forcibly deny women right of access to the means of production and the social production of labor and compel them to rely solely on their fathers or husbands for survival.

The fur trade was only one of the ways in which the Huron reproduced themselves. Subsistence production, the distribution of trade goods, and the distribution of all means of livelihood remained organized on kin lines; no one individual or group of individuals possessed the authority or power to make access dependent on submission to church and state authority. It was for these reasons that the Huron women, but not the Montagnais-Naskapi women, were able to retain their relatively undominated status even in the face of commodity production and exchange.

The key to understanding the relationship between the subordination of women and commodity production and exchange lies not in the advent of commodity production but in the effect of this change on a society's unit of production and reproduction. The fabric of Huron society was certainly damaged by the fur trade and Jesuit proselytizing, but it was not torn apart. Social relations continued to be gender-specific as well as kin-based and sanctioned. The survival of the longhouse organization ensured that old symbols and emotions concerning the proper nature of male-female relations could be evoked and reinforced. Not so among the Montagnais-Naskapi settled at Sillery, where property, production, and redistribution were reorganized along lines that diverged greatly from native tradition. New forms of social control took the place of older ones: the church, the French military, and the system of Jesuit-appointed "captains." What made the subordination of Montagnais-Naskapi women a reality, therefore, was not simply the introduction of the fur trade but the efforts of French church and state to create and enforce systems of private property and charity in a way that nullified the gender-specific rights and obligations formerly guaranteed under traditional social arrangements.

By seizing control of the economic base of those Montagnais-Naskapi settled at Sillery, the Jesuits were able to change the very foundation of the society and thereby to undermine the basis of egalitarian relations between women and men. Montagnais-Naskapi women, formerly guaranteed their status in society by right of access to meaningful productive activity and to control of the products of their labor, were now dependent on their male relatives, who, in turn, gained their access to the material means of existence by submitting to Jesuit and state authority.

Among the Huron, however, kin-based social relations of production continued to guarantee women, as well as men, the right of unmediated access to the necessities of life. As a result men gained little leverage over women's social, economic, or political activities. At the same time, both Huron women and men, unlike the Montagnais-Naskapi, were able to escape the far-reaching control of the French state and the Catholic church.

Notes

1 Maurice Godelier, "The Origins of Male Dominance," *New Left Review* 127 (May/ June 1981): 3–14.

2 Friedrich Engels, *The Origin of the Family, Private Property, and the State* (New York: International Publishers, 1972), p. 233.

3 Mona Etienne and Eleanor Leacock, eds., *Women and Colonization* (New York: Praeger Publishers, 1980), p. 13. Although Maurice Godelier agrees with the editors on this point, he differs with them on the inevitability of women's subordination to men: "It seems at the moment reasonable to suppose that men so far dominate power in the last analysis" (p. 10). Etienne and Leacock, by contrast, observe that "the implicit or explicit belief in the universal subordination of women, if not in its inevitability," continues to obstruct efforts to understand both other societies and our own" (p. 2).

4 Eleanor Leacock, *Myths of Male Dominance* (New York: Monthly Review Press, 1981), p. 48.

5 Ruben G. Thwaites, ed., *The Jesuit Relations and Allied Documents*, 73 vols. (Cleveland: Burrows Brothers, 1896–1901), 31:169, 5:101.

6 Ibid., 16:165, 6:231.

7 For a discussion of Huron history as well as political, economic, and social organization, see Conrad Heidenreich, *Huronia: A History and Geography of the Huron Indians, 1600–1650* (Toronto: McClelland & Stewart, 1971); and Bruce Trigger, *The Children of Aataentsic,* 2 vols. (Montreal: McGill-Queen's University Press, 1976), esp. 1:27, 2:500–602.

8 See Heidenreich, pp. 125–34, for a discussion of Huron village size. The maximum figure of 1,600, based on a computer simulation, is below Trigger's estimate of 2,000 persons (2:752) and Heidenreich's estimate of 2,400 persons (p. 102). For a full account of the application of this simulation, see Karen Anderson, "Huron Women and Huron Men: The Effects of Demography, Kinship, and the Social Division of Labour on Male/Female Relations among the Seventeenth-Century Huron" (Ph.D. diss., University of Toronto, 1982). See also H. P. Biggar, ed., *The Works of Samuel de Champlain,* 6 vols. (Toronto: Champlain Society, 1922–36); G. M. Wrong, ed., *The Long Journey to the Country of the Hurons* (Toronto: Champlain Society, 1939); and Thwaites, ed., 8:155, 10:314, 19:25–27.

9 Biggar, ed., 3:123; Wrong, ed., pp. 96–109; Heidenreich (n. 7 above), pp. 159–61.

10 See Heidenreich (n. 7 above), p. 78. At the village level, these localized clan segments were important for the organization of relations between members of different longhouses. See also Thwaites, ed., 33:243, 33:247, 38:283.

11 Thwaites, ed., 10:233.

12 Anderson, p. 172.

13 Heidenreich, p. 78.

14 For example, the Jesuits' attempts to settle hunter-gatherers found disfavor among fur traders, who wanted to see as many Indians as possible trapping.

15 Thwaites, ed. (n. 5 above), 5:111, 13:6, 5:133, 7:175, 6:233, 5:179.

16 Leacock (n. 4 above), p. 26.

17 Thwaites, ed. (n. 5 above), 12:151, 13:57, 14:261.

18 Ibid., 16:33, 6:143.

19 The *Jesuit Relations* were written, in part, to encourage wealthy patrons to contribute financially to the conversion of Indians in New France. See Thwaites, ed. (n. 5 above), 23:307.

20 Ibid., 25:175–77.

21 Ibid., 18:107.

22 Ibid., 15:17, 18:5.

23 Ibid., 20:267.

24 Eleanor Leacock, "Montagnais Women and the Jesuit Program for Colonization," in Etienne and Leacock, eds. (n. 3 above), p. 38.

25 For a discussion of the Huron's role in the fur trade, see Heidenreich (n. 7 above); Anderson (n. 8 above).

26 Thwaites, ed. (n. 5 above), 20:225, 24:187, 28:54, 21:135.

27 Ibid., 14:5, 15:77.

28 Wrong, ed. (n. 8 above), pp. 133–34.

29 Biggar, ed. (n. 8 above), 3:138.

30 Thwaites, ed. (n. 5 above), 26:229, 38:253.

31 Ibid., 23:67.

32 Ibid., p. 127.

33 Ibid., 26:271.

34 Ibid., 39:153.

35 Ibid., 36:193.

PART II

France in America 1663–1756

Jeffreys, Charles William/National Archives of Canada/C-010687. Reproduced with permission of C.W. Jeffreys Estate, Toronto

In 1661 Louis XIV, king of France (1643–1715), decided to assert personal control over the affairs of state. One of his main goals was to establish a French overseas empire that would reflect positively on his wealth and power. As a result, New France became the focus of an intense, if brief, period of colony building. The French empire in North America at its height in the early eighteenth century included Newfoundland and Acadia, extended along the St. Lawrence and Great Lakes (the region called Canada), into the Prairies, and down the Mississippi. Though valued for the primary resources (mostly fish and fur), military potential, and prestige that they brought to the Crown, France's North American colonies never attracted many settlers and were ceded to Great Britain in the treaties ending the War of the Spanish Succession (1702–1713) and the Seven Years' War (1756–1763). Nevertheless, the legacy of French settlement in North America endures and prompts historians to continue to explore the characteristics of societies that proved so durable and adaptable.

The readings in this section reflect the rich historiography that has developed around questions relating to colonial societies in New France. For many historians, the French regime in North America offers clues to Quebec's distinctiveness as a province of Canada—though historians have rarely been in agreement about the nature of that distinctiveness. The jury is still out, for example, on whether the average Canadian peasant was liberated by the fur trade frontier and its Native inhabitants or increasingly shaped by institutions and values imposed by France. What is clear is that New France represented a way of life that has been greatly transformed since the eighteenth century by the institutions and values associated with the Industrial Revolution and the information age. The extraordinary documentary legacy of New France thus offers a splendid opportunity to evoke a time when people did things differently than they do today. Change and continuity are major preoccupations of historians and those who are drawn to the history of New France are rewarded with a sense of the significance of historical developments and the tenacity of cultural practices over the *longue durée*.

In this section the first two readings focus on seigneurialism, the system by which land was administered in the colony of Canada. Seigneurs were granted large tracts of land by the Crown as a means of establishing their elite status in the colony. In return, they were required to develop the land with the help of tenant farmers called *censitaires,* a term derived from the annual fees—*cens et rentes*—paid to the seigneur. Seigneurialism reflected feudal class structures and landholding traditions in Europe that were beginning to crumble in France at the time when the colonies were established. While there is little doubt that seigneurialism left its mark on the St. Lawrence landscape in the form of narrow strip farms, historians have begun to question its role as a social and economic institution in New France. Seigneurialism failed to take firm root in Acadia, was abandoned by French authorities entirely in Île Royale and Louisiana and, as R. C. Harris argues here, "remained in the background of Canadian life" during the French regime. Only in the post-conquest period, he suggests, did seigneurialism become "the social and economic framework of life in rural Canada."

Fernand Ouellet takes this argument further, concluding that the exploitative character of the seigneurial system became far more evident at the beginning of the nineteenth century with the commercialization of agriculture. As colonial elites tried to bolster their own wealth by pressing their rights to the limit, tenant farmers were forced to take jobs off their farms, often in the forest industry, to survive. Poverty and lack of land, Ouellet maintains, not notions of freedom and independence derived from an open frontier, were the determining factors in the rebellions of 1837 and 1838 and also in the outmigration from Lower Canada/Canada East to the United States in the mid-nineteenth century.

By this time, Canadiens and Acadians had begun to look to the past for inspiration in their attempts to maintain a sense of their distinct identity in North America. While the Acadians took up the fictional character of Longfellow's *Evangeline* as the symbol of their struggle to survive against difficult odds, Quebec nationalists idealized ordinary individuals who seemingly showed great heroism in defending their besieged homeland. Adam Dollard des Ormeaux, the soldier and fur trader who died in his efforts to lead an ambush against the Iroquois at Long Sault in 1660, was one such individual singled out for heroic interpretation. Another was Madeleine de Verchères. In his article, Colin Coates shows how francophone historians in the second half of the nineteenth century rediscovered the "Canadian Joan of Arc," attaching a variety of nationalistic concerns to the slim thread of evidence available on her efforts to resist an Iroquois attack on her family farm in 1692.

Coates's article contributes to the growing literature on historical memory. Focusing on the ways that people create mythologies concerning the past, this literature analyzes the concerns and values of the myth-makers rather than investigating the events or individuals being commemorated. Just as Alan Gordon's article in Part 1 highlights both elite and popular understandings of Jacques Cartier through the ages, Coates' focuses less on retrieving the actual experiences of Madeleine de Verchères than on recovering the meanings attached to her at a later period.

Life for the ordinary people of New France, few of whom left behind written records, is often difficult for historians to fully grasp. Although considerable effort has been made to understand the experience of fur traders during the French regime, less attention has been paid to the much larger number of men from France who engaged in the fisheries, the resource that initially attracted Europeans to northern North America. We publish here one of the most engaging efforts to fill this gap. By painstakingly piecing together the context of a rare surviving letter written in 1731, Christopher Moore offers a complex picture of what life was like for the men from France whose lives revolved around the fisheries off the coast of Île Royale (Cape Breton).

Historical sources vary but one of the most informative accounts of life in New France was penned by Peter Kalm, a Swedish scientist who visited North America in 1749–50. A skilled observer, he kept detailed notes on everything from the flora and fauna he encountered, to the crops grown in Canadian gardens and the length of women's skirts. A Protestant, Kalm was particularly intrigued by the religious orders in the colony and described their activities in minute detail. Like later historians, Kalm was also interested in the cultural differences he perceived among the North American colonies. He was impressed by the sophistication of the administrators in New France and the liveliness of the peasants but noted the lack of a printing press. This excerpt from the English version of his published account includes his observations as he journeyed by boat from Montreal to Quebec and his first impressions of the capital of New France.

The deportation of the Acadian population from the British colony of Nova Scotia in 1755, and later from Île Saint-Jean (Prince Edward Island) and Île Royale, is covered in most textbooks. What happened to the Acadians after they arrived at their initial destinations is rarely mentioned and, until recently, not well researched. Naomi Griffiths tackles this difficult topic in "Exile Surmounted." From the fragments of information on the Acadian diaspora that she has been able to glean, Griffiths concludes that the strong ties of family and community developed in Acadie/Nova Scotia served the Acadians well during their difficult ordeal. The deportation, she argues, "destroyed Acadian power but not Acadian identity." That identity continues to thrive today in the Atlantic Provinces of Canada, Louisiana, and many other areas of the world where people can trace their genealogy back to "le grand dérangement."

The Seigneurial System in Canada during the French Regime

R. Cole Harris

With long, thin fields stretching away from the St. Lawrence and straggling rows of farmhouses along either bank of the river for two hundred miles and more, the landscape of rural Canada towards the end of the French regime presented a unique face. Visitors commented on its distinctive charm, and scholars since have assumed that its distinctiveness reflected the influence of the seigneurial system. Yet, the seigneurial system was largely irrelevant to the early geography of Canada. The pattern of rotures was an important part of the geography of the colony, and the imprint of these early concessions is still preserved in the landscape of rural Quebec, although these patterns, the possible by-products of many methods of land-granting, were not in themselves the seigneurial system or even a reflection of it. Neither settlement patterns nor those of social and economic activity reflected the influence of the seigneurs. Seigneuries were indefinite units on the land, and seigneurial boundaries neither enclosed nor altered any of the principal patterns of human activity in the colony.

The seigneurial system could have shaped much of the geography of early Canada only if it had provided a mold first for settlement and then for social and economic development of the colony, but there is little indication that during the French regime the system was ever such a mold. Few seigneurs profited from their concessions in a colony where seigneuries were often divided among many coseigneurs, where seigneurial dues were low and, above all, where settlers were few and far between. In the seventeenth century, when there was only a handful of censitaires in their seigneuries and the land was a potential expense rather than a source of revenue, the seigneurs often neglected their holdings for years. Their censitaires often paid no dues, and may have forgotten their seigneurs' names. The censitaires, who often came to Canada with vivid memories of a seigneur's social and economic role in France and who quickly decided that illegal participation in the fur trade was the easiest road to wealth in the colony, sought to avoid most contacts with their seigneur. Their uneasiness about the seigneurs waned in the eighteenth century, to be replaced largely by indifference, and they settled into a way of life which was little influenced by him one way or the other. To be sure, in the last decades of the French regime land was becoming scarce in some seigneuries near Quebec, and the population in a number of seigneuries near either Quebec or Montreal had risen to the point where seigneurial revenues were substantial. Seigneurs took a more active interest in their concessions; without cheap land

Richard Colebrook Harris, "The Seigneurial System in Canada during the French Regime," in *The Seigneurial System in Early Canada: A Geographical Study*, Second Edition (Madison WI: University of Wisconsin Press, 1984), 193–198, 228.

nearby, censitaires were increasingly tied to their own rotures. But Canadian seigneurs, always closely supervised by royal officials, found it difficult if not impossible to extend their influence over their censitaires, and even in these later years the seigneurial system remained in the background of Canadian life.

Certainly some seigneurs may have thought of their titles as status symbols even when the seigneuries which they controlled were wilderness tracts. Some may have viewed their titles as entrées for themselves or their sons to appointments in the army or civil service. These are matters on which the geographical evidence sheds no light, but which cannot alter the conclusion that the seigneurial system was largely irrelevant to the general social and economic development of the colony.

In the years before the English conquest a French way of life had been recast in Canada. Canada and France were 3,000 miles apart, and the connection between them was a precarious voyage of several months' duration. Royal officials brought the king's authority to Canada and administered his laws as carefully as they could when the king's wishes were known often only after long delay, and often did not apply well to a Canadian situation. Frenchmen trickled across the Atlantic to settle in Canada, but the flow was so small that French ideas and customs were not replenished through immigration. The few who did come found a vastly different land. The colony was a ribbon of settlement in a wilderness of trees, rock, and water. Land was everywhere, and it was free. The fur trade was open to all able-bodied men and offered, in addition to the revenue from beaver pelts, complete independence from the traditional channels of authority. In these circumstances a French way of life had been transformed.

The principal change in Canada was towards more individual independence. Royal officials in Quebec and Montreal could regulate the commercial life of the towns and supervise the exports and imports which passed through Quebec, but exerted relatively little control over habitants who were spread out for more than two hundred miles along the banks of the St. Lawrence, and who could vanish into the interior to escape any unwelcome pressure. The seigneurs found control expensive, and equally difficult to administer. The Church may have become the strongest of the traditional sources of authority, although its influence on the habitants is extremely difficult to assess. Certainly the habitants never quarreled with its dogmas, but its controls and interdictions may have sat lightly on them. In later years an aged Philippe de Gaspé described the Canadian habitant as "l'homme le plus indépendant du monde,"[1] and if this was an exaggeration, there is no doubt that his independence was such that the seigneurial system, one of the sources of control in France, quickly disintegrated in Canada.

When Frederick Jackson Turner's frontier thesis was first vigorously challenged, ripples of the debate reached back to New France, and Turner himself wrote a short defense of the relevance of his ideas to an understanding of the French colony.[2] Turner knew little enough about New France, and his critics probably knew even less. Although the evidence in this study suggests that Turner was closer to the truth than were his critics, no one would want to reopen the argument along the earlier lines. There can be little doubt that in 1760 Canada was not an enclave of French civilization. Ideas and institutions, the way of life, had changed, and if it is helpful to consider a colony which had not moved westward in a hundred years a frontier, then the frontier was a seat of change, albeit one without a cutting edge where the metamorphic force of the wilderness reshaped European ways with particular alacrity.

Turner's contention that the change was related to the availability of free land to the west, to isolation, and to the safety valve is both shrewd and misleading when applied to

Canada. Settlement in early Canada filled in a line between Quebec and Montreal; it did not expand westward. The fact that free land within seigneuries along the lower St. Lawrence was more important than free land to the west meant that those aspects of a legal system which were designed to protect scarce land, and of the social hierarchy which were based on the control of scarce land were superfluous. It also led to the development of a much more extensive agricultural system than was characteristic in northwestern France. In the sense that a French king and his ministers kept an interested if often poorly informed watch on Canada, and that his representatives in the colony maintained a closer vigilance, the colony was not isolated from France. And yet the very closeness of this contact inadvertently reinforced the collapse of a French institution; it must not be forgotten that the seigneurial system disintegrated in Canada in part because a French king reduced the prerogatives and the dues to which his Canadian seigneurs were entitled. When the conquest broke this French connection, seigneurial dues and seigneurial influence probably began to increase, and they might have done so long before if the seigneurs had been more isolated from French authority. There would not have been an explosion had safety valves in the direction of the Great Lakes or the American colonies not existed, but the alternative to farming and the ready escape from authority which they provided were fundamental ingredients in the Canadian situation.

And yet, Canada bore little resemblance to the unruly American settlements in the Appalachian valleys in the middle of the eighteenth century and, in the nineteenth century, in some areas farther west which had been settled before law and order were established. There were royal courts in Quebec, Trois-Rivières, and Montreal, as well as the intendant and Conseil Supérieur in Quebec, and the censitaire could appeal for justice to any one of them. When Canada was organized into parishes, a curé was seldom more than a few miles from any farm in his parish. Although a seigneur or coseigneur was usually no farther away, the censitaire needed little from him. However, he went to mass, and may have taken many problems to his curé. The records of all the colony's courts attest to the use the censitaire made of them. The machinery of control had come to Canada but its oppressive features were mitigated or atrophied from disuse because control was possible only to the degree that the censitaires would cooperate.

That the seigneurial system was not a way of life in Canada during the French regime is certain beyond reasonable doubt, but that much of it remained as a legal system is equally definite. Some French laws had been modified and new laws introduced, but on the whole Canadian law at the end of the French regime was little different from that at the beginning. Parts of this legal framework, as has been shown, came to have a substantial influence on the geography of Canada. Even the laws which treated the relationship between a seigneur and his vassals were often observed, although the original justification for them had long since vanished. In 1732 the seigneur of an arrière-fief in Lachenaie paid *foi et hommage* to his seigneur, who did not maintain a manor in the seigneurie, by knocking on the door of the miller's hut on three separate days, and crying to the surrounding wilderness: "Monsieur de Repentigny I bring and offer to you the *foi et hommage* that I am obliged to bring and offer to you by virtue of my fief located and situated in the said seigneurie of Lachenaie...."[3] When this statement was drawn up by a notary and witnessed by the miller it constituted a legal title which was proof of ownership, and it had been made for this reason. The statement took the legal form of earlier French feudalism, and is but an extreme example of the decay of feudalism in all but legal form which had taken place in Canada.

Most of whatever flesh was added to these legal bones must have appeared after the conquest. Then the intendant was replaced by English officials who did not understand French civil law, and who relied on the seigneurs for interpretations of it. In this situation seigneurs may have begun to enlarge their influence by introducing new charges and by increasing the old. As the population grew, many seigneuries became profitable to their seigneurs for the first time. By the end of the eighteenth century, agricultural land had become scarce along the lower St. Lawrence, and expansion to the west was partially blocked by English settlement. The outlets to the fur trade could support only progressively smaller proportions of the total population. French Canada fell back upon the agricultural resources of the lower St. Lawrence, and as land became scarce a French social and economic system which was based in large part upon the organization and control of land was no longer completely incongruous. Moreover, some French Canadians may have seen the seigneurial system a potential bastion against English cultural encroachment, and have encouraged its consolidation in the years after the conquest. Thus it is entirely possible that in the late eighteenth and early nineteenth centuries the seigneurial system became the social and economic framework of life in rural Canada which it had never been before, and that the preconquest geography of the seigneurial system was significantly altered. Several descriptions of seigneurial life which date from this later period pictured respectful habitants, kindly seigneurs involved in the development and maintenance of their seigneuries, and, after the middle of the nineteenth century, parish priests leading their flocks from the overpopulated St. Lawrence lowland to new homes along the margin of the Shield. If these pictures were correct, much had changed since the days of the French regime.

Notes

1 Philippe A. de Gaspé, *Mémoires* (Quebec, 1885), p. 530.

2 F. J. Turner, "The Rise and Fall of New France," *Minnesota History*, XVIIII (Dec., 1937), 383–98.

3 "Monsieur de Repentigny je vous fais Et Portte La foy et homage que je suis tenue de vous faire Et Porter à cose de mon fief scise et Citué en lad[ite] Seigneurie de Lachainay...," Act de foy Et hommage à Monsieur de Repentigny par le Sr Pierre Martelle, June 14, 1732, in APQ, Pièce détachée, Lachenaie.

Free or Exploited? The Peasant Before 1850*

FERNAND OUELLET

The theme of the exploitation of the habitant by the francophone elite is almost entirely absent from French Canadian historiography. Since F.-X. Garneau and until recently, the glorification of institutions that have given shape to a homogeneous nation and an independent peasantry has dominated such writing.[1] Absolutism tempered by paternalism, the seigneurial regime cleansed of all feudal taint, a Catholic Church free of all traces of heresy—these were the elements that, as this historiography would have it, produced free peasants.

Lionel Groulx's thought at once synthesized these views, so often repeated since, and found an appropriate historical foundation for them in the very process of French colonization. Indeed, according to him, France's ancien régime institutions were universally purified before being implanted in New France. Seen from this angle, colonial society was the fruit of the best of France,[2] an adaption of the original more perfect than in any province of the metropolis. It could not help but give birth to a "sociological milieu characterized by a rare level of moral hygiene,"[3] with its "family and parish, profoundly impregnated with the Christian spirit," with its peasants and its "living Catholicism, brought forth by the best spring." This society had only one thorn in its side—the coureur de bois, this frequenter of natives.[4] "Who would dare," he asked, "drink with impunity the philtre of savagery?"

Obviously, given Groulx's predilections, the hierarchical ancien régime society had to be characterized by relatively trouble-free social mobility, one with "paliers franchissables," as he was to say.[5] For this reason, the seigneurs and censitaires were "two juxtaposed classes rather than being co-ordinated or hierarchized." Needless to say, because he saw the peasant as nearly equal to the seigneur,[6] Groulx judged relations between the peasantry and the clergy (whether seigneurs or curés) according to the same norms.

Groulx's nationalism and his interpretation of the past were not only the result of a powerful historiographical tradition faithfully assimilated. They were also the fruit of his reaction to the industrial revolution, which he saw as a second conquest more disastrous perhaps than that inflicted by the English.[7] For Groulx, the need for a victorious struggle against the consequences of both the Conquest and industrialization was based on the idea that Quebec had always enjoyed a classless society and homogeneous nationhood, both of which rested on a free peasantry. In short, the purification of French ancien régime institutions had eliminated the exploitative mechanisms that they had originally harboured.

Fernand Ouellet, "Free or Exploited? The Peasant Before 1850," in Fernand Ouellet, *Economy, Class, and Nation in Quebec: Interpretive Essays*, edited and translated by Jacques A. Barbier (Toronto: Pearson Education, 1991), 40–60.

*Originally published as "Libéré ou exploité! Le paysan québécois d'avant 1850," *Histoire sociale/Social History* 13, 26 (November 1980): 339–68. This paper was first presented at the annual Research Conference of the University of Ottawa, March 1980.

In his *Civilisation de la Nouvelle France* (1944), Guy Frégault remained faithful to this image of the nation, although he did not hesitate to define colonial society as feudal.[8] In the matter of the seigneurial regime, he repeated and insisted upon Groulx's interpretation. For him, the seigneurial regime was not meant to allow one class to live from the labour of another; it was merely meant to provide the colony with an appropriate economic organization.[9] To illustrate his point of view further, Frégault pointed out that around 1700, one-third of the seigneuries belonged to peasants and that in 1760, "most of the seigneurs [were] the sons of habitants." To be more convincing, he even recalled that the king of France had given one fief to the poor. He also pointed out, however, that its administration had been entrusted to the nuns of the Hôpital Général de Québec! All of this, of course, in order to assert that the St. Lawrence valley did not contain the slightest trace of exploitation, even though it had a stratified society based on the feudal model.

The nationalist model, as applied by the historians discussed here, does not completely avoid the idea of exploitation. Yet it only introduces it when dealing with the outside world or with foreigners. Thus peasants were free inside their own society but exploited from outside. In this regard, Maurice Séguin's thesis in *La nation canadienne et l'agriculture (1760–1850)* (1970) extended the thesis of Groulx and Frégault by making it more precise. Indeed, this Montreal historian mentioned the abuse of traditional practices by certain seigneurs, most particularly anglophone, but nonetheless concluded that, on the whole, the seigneurial system helped to absorb the shock of conquest.[10] It served as a scarecrow against the British,[11] who might otherwise have seized the Canadians' lands, and it helped to preserve the integrity of the conquered society by granting land to a poor peasantry on a cost-free basis. As Séguin writes, "The seigneurial regime... [was], with the Catholic religion, the French language and French civil law, one of the factors which was able to maintain the national distinctiveness of Canadians. Shield of the Canadian nation, it guaranteed to its people a homogeneous settlement of a perfectly delimited territory, an essential element for any group... [which aspires] to independence."[12]

Glorification of the old institutions, and particularly of the seigneurie (Groulx and Séguin even said that we should be grateful to the seigneurs[13]), was pushed much further by Jean-Pierre Wallot. "In Canada," he wrote, "the seigneurial regime, although colonizing and feudal by its very name and legal forms, in a larger sense and congruently with its objectives, worked in such a way as to benefit the peasants more than it did the bourgeois aristocrats. Two worlds, two mentalities, trade and peasantry, coexisted and were integrated in relative freedom."[14]

The essential elements of this tradition have recently been taken up once more, by Denis Monière. Although he used Marxist expressions, Monière still spoke of the peasants of New France in idyllic terms: owners of the means of production, the peasants were not compelled to sell their labour; freed from clerical influence and authority, rather libertine on the whole, they were subjected to a feudalism that was merely symbolic and to an absolutism more formal than real.[15]

In essence, proponents of this dominant intellectual current valued the concept of the independent peasant because they were fundamentally preoccupied either with the affirmation and survival of the nation and its institutions or with the promise of independence. In consequence, they did not wish to deal with the problem of internal exploitation because it would necessitate the assumption that the nation was heterogeneous, threaten the idea that established values were absolute, and ultimately might well have unleashed class struggle.

The strength of this historiographical tradition was such that it was very difficult even to try to see the question from a different angle and to research it from a rejuvenated perspective. My own work over the last twenty-five years,[16] that of Louise Dechêne,[17] and the writings of Gilles Bourque[18] represent this type of effort. The sociologist Bourque recently affirmed that "the peasants...[were] not independent small producers, whatever might be their individualism and their lack of submission. [T]hey were involved in exploitative relationships thanks to which a class absorbed a part of their production."[19]

I also believe that the ancien régime in its social manifestations rested on a systematic sharing of revenues drawn from the land, an arrangement that was favourable to the governing classes of clerics and nobles. The exaction of revenue from habitants took place because these groups were supposed to perform certain social functions over which they had a near monopoly.[20] Naturally, the state also benefited from a system of taxation in which seigneurial rights, tithes, tariffs, *quêtes* (collections), military service, and corvées channelled a part of peasant revenues towards classes that filled military, religious, educational, and charitable roles in an aristocratic society. A newspaper report of 1789, although exaggerated, expressed the significance of this mechanism quite well:

> The unfortunate peasant is always enveloped in hardship. Nothing can pluck him from indigence. The export of wheat enriches the state but does not bring plenty to the countryside; those who draw off its substance spread it in the cities, and in the country hardship remains. But, say those men who see things only from afar, with all the fields being tilled and the harvest increasing in price, the peasant at work must be growing rich. To that there is only one way to reply. Is it he who works the land who reaps? Has it not been shown that most of the land belongs to seigneurs, or to rich individuals who spend its revenue in the cities? When this is agreed, the conclusion is that the countryside is inhabited only by poor labourers, who reap no wheat at all or only what is necessary to feed their families, and who in consequence do not profit by the increase in price of a product which they consume; on the contrary, if they do not have enough of that product, they must buy it more dearly, and being paid no more for their days of work they grow still more impoverished. There will be found in the country no more than ten farmers in a condition to await those happy turns of trade which will enrich them. Pressed to repay the money they owe, they hasten to sell their wheat to the grasping merchant, who exports it or locks it away in storehouses which cannot be opened unless he be given a golden key.[21]

This document, in addition to raising the problem of the relations of the peasantry with the merchant bourgeoisie, incites us to look at its relations with the seigneurs (whether nobles, bourgeois, or ecclesiastics) and the state, and also implicitly suggests that we scrutinize its role as seasonal labour.

The Censitaire

The most widespread interpretation of St. Lawrence society, that of anglophone partisans of the frontier thesis[22] and of francophone nationalists, characterized the seigneur as a "mere agent of colonization": in a word, as a representative of the state in the distribution of the land to peasants. Richard Cole Harris even maintained that the seigneurial system—which lasted two centuries, whose abolition required fifty years of struggle, and which disappeared very slowly even after being legally abolished—"was irrelevant" to the St. Lawrence valley.[23] The seigneurs, according to this historian, could not play an economic or social role, and choosing them was therefore so unimportant that governors and intendants had freely distributed seigneuries without concerning themselves with the social origins of the recipients. Harris maintains that anyone in New France could become a seigneur.[24]

The "agent of colonization" thesis, once supported by Marcel Trudel, has been brought into question by his most recent work.[25] This shows not only that a nobility already existed in 1663, but that the nobles constituted the majority of seigneurs and held an even larger proportion of the seigneurial lands. Until 1763, this petty nobility continued to be the principal beneficiary of royal largess, as at least 66 percent of seigneuries granted up to that time were received by noble or ennobled individuals.[26] Only 30 percent of grants were awarded to non-nobles (*roturiers*), and the vast majority of these were bourgeois. Only a handful of peasants or artisans ever received a seigneurie. During the same period, the purchase and sale of seigneuries did not significantly alter the situation. In 1760, 53 percent of seigneurial lands was held by the military nobility, while the bourgeoisie and clergy held only 21 and 24 percent, respectively. It is difficult to believe that the king of France would have proceeded in this fashion if he had decided to limit the seigneurs to the role of "land agent," and if he had intended to prevent them from fully exercising their traditional social and economic functions.

The ownership of a seigneurie involved a number of legal obligations. The seigneur had to concede land on a no-cost basis to such censitaires as might request it and was not allowed to sell land on which some clearing had not been done. Historians, quite reasonably, have been impressed by the scope of this responsibility compared to that of seigneurs in France, where available land was extremely rare in this period. The fief-holder was not indefinitely confined to this legal role, however, and nor was the role unimportant. As long as lands were abundant and the population limited, the seigneurs in general respected their legal obligations over the free distribution of land, and in doing so played an important social and economic role. Once land values rose, however, and as available properties became more rare around 1800 because of continued population growth, the owners of seigneuries with vacant lots began to resist the demand for free distribution. Despite a spirited defence of the seigneurial conception of property, they used a number of subterfuges to increase their income. They conceded land to dependable people, who undertook to clear some of it and return all to the seigneurs so that they might legally sell it. Bribes were another device by which the zone gradually entered into a new regime, one in which even uncleared land might be sold just like any other form of property.

In Quebec, as in France and elsewhere, the seigneurial regime had particular economic and social functions. These were performed in a context that included the development of commercial capitalism (the fur trade and the commercialization of agriculture), led progressively to the rise of a capitalist conception of landed property, and thus paved the way to a conflict between seigneurialism and capitalism. Of course, the merchants were the first to question the seigneurial structure openly. Yet by their contradictory practices in matters of land grants, the seigneurs not only increased the scarcity of land and encouraged the proletarianization of farmers' children, but in doing so they became active participants in the emergence of such conflict themselves.

The *cens et rentes* constituted one of the oldest foundations of seigneurial revenues. The theoretically modest nature of these charges has led to assertions that there was a fixed and immutable rate for these exactions, which the intendants helped to maintain. Yet the tariff already varied in New France according to the quality of the soil, the proximity of cities, and the whim of the seigneur. After the Conquest—as agriculture became more commercialized, prices rose, and population increased—fief owners began to obtain more from granted lands. After 1800, and earlier in some regions, the onset of land scarcity allowed the seigneurs to maintain or increase these high levels, even as the peasants' living standards fell. The higher charges were maintained even after 1815, when the price level of agricultural commodities declined. The result was that the seigneurial system burdened the habitant more heavily than previously. Asking for their dues both in kind and in currency provided fief owners with a hedge against economic fluctuation. This habit was also an instrument for drawing more revenues from the peasants in times of bad harvests and prolonged decline in wheat production. No matter what happened the seigneurs won.

The seigneur was obliged to build a mill. As long as the population of the seigneurie was relatively limited, the fief owner often had to be coaxed into honouring an obligation that would yield them only one *minot* of wheat for every fourteen ground. It was only with the growth of population and production that seigneurs could derive a profit from the operation of a mill. Thus for a long time they were relatively uninterested in waterfalls and other sites appropriate for the construction of mills. The expansion of forestry production and other circumstances, however, eventually induced them to try to monopolize a variety of activities completely: to reserve for themselves marketable wood found on the lands of the censitaire; at times to exploit stone quarries and firewood; and to use the right of *retrait* to recuperate rights too easily relinquished in times past. All of this shows the degree to which the fief owners had become sensitive to the use and expansion of their rights, behaviour not characteristic of mere agents of colonization.

After the *cens et rentes* and mill charges, the *lods et ventes* were the third source of seigneurial revenues. As the entire system was aimed at guaranteeing the stability of landed property, the seigneur was awarded one-twelfth of the sale price of land, not only on the lot itself but also on the improvements that had been made. The productivity of this tax naturally depended on the degree of turnover of property, and consequently it varied considerably according to the location of the parish in relation to urban centres and to whether the lots were located in the countryside or the city. As capitalism increasingly penetrated the economic structure, if one makes allowances for economic cycles, the revenues from the *lods et ventes* increased continuously up to 1850.

In all areas where hunting and fishing were commercial activities, and perhaps even in places where they only had a role to play in the subsistence of peasants, the rights the seigneurs collected from these activities were never really merely honorific. The fief holders transformed them into onerous burdens. They also obtained revenues from the use of common lands and from seigneurial justice in those areas where they existed before 1760. In addition, the censitaires owed their lords a certain number of days of corvée labour, whether this obligation was contained in the original seigneurial title or simply imposed on the peasants by seigneurial contracts. There were also a number of honorific advantages accorded the seigneur: the seigneurial pew, the *pain bénit,* and so on. Finally, note that in principle only the seigneurs of non-noble origin were obliged to contribute to the road-building and maintenance corvées on the king's roads.

Keeping in mind that seigneurial rights were applied in a great variety of ways in seventeenth- and eighteenth-century France and that a similar diversity was growing in Canada, one can see that the Canadian seigneurie was not really different from its French counterpart. In both cases, censitaires were obliged to give part of their production to their seigneur. Some dues collected by Canadian seigneurs were lower than those imposed in the metropolis, while others were heavier. Overall, however, the Canadian and French seigneurie rested on the same mix of feudal and seigneurial rights. When conceived of in this fashion, the issue is not really the percentage of their production that peasants had to give to the seigneur or the equity of exchanges between the lord and the censitaires but the dependency of the censitaires on the lord, and the fact that the property rights of the former were limited in every regard. They were not really the owners of their means of production.

Nevertheless the percentages are important because they allow us to judge the *degree* of exploitation and clarify the reaction of the peasant to the seigneurial system. Historians who wrote about the seigneurie in the era of New France were right to maintain that, on the whole, the weight of seigneurial dues was not especially heavy. Between 1730 and 1739, per capita wheat production was 14.3 *minots*, which was about 100 *minots* of wheat for a family of seven or around 125 *minots* per farm.[27] The portion of the wheat held back as seed—calculated from average yields—was around 15 to 20 percent of the harvest (between 18 and 25 *minots*).[28] That dedicated to feeding the peasant family amounted to between 70 and 84 *minots* (between 10 and 13, and at times even 15, *minots* per person), while the tithe took up about 5 *minots* (1 out of 26) and the *banalité* almost 6 *minots* (1 out of 14), without taking into account other seigneurial and ecclesiastical charges. One obvious conclusion to be drawn from a rapid examination of these figures is that as long as the peasant could obtain revenues from the sale of a surplus, the most productive farms felt the weight of seigneurial and ecclesiastical exactions the least. Nonetheless, in this period, when the peasants who produced a surplus were certainly very numerous, there existed a substantial minority who produced too little for subsistence or seed. Their number increased suddenly in years of bad harvest and remained high in the years that followed. For these peasants, the burden imposed by seigneurs and curés was certainly heavy. A second conclusion asserts itself. In this period, wheat exports were not voluminous and came above all from the stocks of the seigneurs and curés. The direct participation of peasants in the export wheat market seems to have been relatively weak and the revenues they obtained from it rather inconsequential.

The relative weight of seigneurial dues was undoubtedly related to the attitudes of the seigneurs but depended mainly on the short-, medium-, and long-term trends in prices and production. During the second half of the eighteenth century, wheat production (which represented at least 70 percent of the harvest)[29] rose, on the whole, from one decade to the next as the overseas market increased in importance. According to my estimates, it reached an average of 180 *minots* per farm in 1802, which implies an increase in the proportion of surplus-producing peasants and an improvement in living standards. At the same time, seigneurial revenues rose with prices, albeit more slowly.

Of course, payments in kind faithfully followed the evolution of prices, but these were only part of the dues. In the eighteenth century, seigneurs received less from their dues than they might have because the part that was paid in cash lost value with the rise in grain prices. Although some tried to compensate, seigneurs were most often unable to demand that payment be made entirely in kind. Thus, from 1730 to 1802, the burden of seigneurial dues became less and less onerous for the majority of producers, who supplied an ever greater proportion of the exported grain. In 1802, when the per capita export of wheat rose to the level of 5.5 *minots*, around 15 percent of these exports came directly or indirectly from curés, 18 percent from seigneurs (thus, around one third between the two groups), and the rest from merchants who had acquired wheat from peasants.[30] This situation, however, did not last. By 1831, 66 percent of the wheat that Lower Canada exported abroad came from curés and seigneurs.

One can easily understand why the eighteenth-century peasant rarely expressed discontent with seigneurial dues. When resistance did arise it largely concerned those demands that tended to limit the amount of labour available for farming, and thus slowed the expansion of production: military service and state and seigneurial corvées. And as capitalism was slow to penetrate the economic system, the bourgeoisie for its part did not as yet really have an alternative to the seigneurial regime, although the majority of anglophone merchants were profoundly uncomfortable with it on ideological grounds.

From the start of the nineteenth century, however, the exploitative character of the seigneurial system became far more evident. The new practices of the seigneurs were certainly a fundamental reason for this change. Even prudent and moderate lords, such as the Séminaire de Québec, adopted them, to some degree. Although it grew slowly in the nineteenth century and experienced strong variations, the per capita yield of seigneurial rights was nevertheless 36 percent higher in 1831 than in 1790.[31] One should not conclude from these figures that the rising wealth of many seigneurs was simply a reflection of the prosperity of the censitaire. On the contrary, even in the difficult economic circumstances of the time, seigneurial revenues in many instances increased despite the declining standard of living of the majority of peasants. The average production of wheat per farm declined from the previously estimated 180 *minots* in 1802, to 60 *minots* in 1831. By the latter date, the per capita average wheat production, which had been 14.3 *minots* in 1734, had fallen to 6.6 *minots.*[32] This decline continued in the years following: in 1842, 92 percent of wheat producers harvested 50 *minots* per farm or less;[33] in 1844, the per capita production was down to 1.3 *minots.* Even if one assumes that the 1831 peasants had reduced their intake of bread to half of what they consumed in the eighteenth century—in other words, from 35 to 42 *minots* per year for a family of seven—they would have found it impossible to meet the seigneurs' financial demands without falling into debt. Because of declining yields, peasants now had to dedicate at least 37 percent of the harvest for seed, which contributed to making the impositions of the seigneurial class more and more intolerable.[34] In 1831, the vast majority of peasants suffered from a deficit in grain production and survived thanks only to the potato. Indeed, this relatively new crop was generally used for subsistence by francophones, as anglophones produced potatoes for the market much more often.[35]

The phenomenon of peasant indebtedness therefore tended to become universal. Under the circumstances, it is hardly surprising that there was rising discontent, first among peasants and later and more aggressively among the bourgeoisie, who were particularly bothered by the *lods et ventes.* The seigneurial question, like that of the tithe, was therefore destined to find a place among the forces that polarized public opinion and penetrated to the very heart of the revolutionary events of 1837–1838.

The nationalist ideology of the period was meant to counter the growth of popular discontent. In 1821, Louis-Joseph Papineau, the leader of the nationalist movement, accused the peasants of being as blinded by their immediate interests as other social classes, and added: "The payment of tithes and seigneurial dues begins to irk them, and they don't see that their jealousy for their superiors is the same as the jealousy of the landless for them."[36] This view of divergent interests could easily take the form of blackmail, designed to turn peasant proprietors against any concerted action against the seigneurs and the curés. To the peasants who complained about the abusive practices of their lords, Papineau and his followers explained that they were wrong to feel aggrieved: the seigneurial regime was not feudal and the seigneur was no more than an agent of colonization, albeit inadequately supervised since the disappearance of the intendants in 1760. In any event, they maintained, the seigneur was the father of the censitaire, and even the guardian of social equality. To these indebted and land-hungry peasants, the nationalists even went so far as to maintain that the seigneurie was a national institution protecting them from anglophone immigrants and speculators whose only wish was to dispossess them. The significance of this ideological discourse coming from people whose self-interest demanded that they defend the ancien régime society in its entirety is beyond doubt.

The Peasant and the Curé

The clergy's hold on the peasant's existence was exercised in a multitude of ways. In New France, only a single religion was allowed and the Catholic clergy, united to the state, assumed exclusive control of various areas of life: religion, teaching, health care, and charity. Because it took on these functions, the clergy not only benefited from royal gratuities but also received from the sovereign an immense and splendid urban and rural domain, spread over the entire colonial territory. These seigneuries were granted mainly in the seventeenth century. Grants subsequently ceased because the Crown feared that the clergy would become too powerful to be contained within the limits imposed by a Gallican and monarchical state. The seigneurial lands of the clergy were composed of some of the best-situated fiefs in the colony. Among other territories, the Sulpicians received the island of Montreal, of which they were also the curés.[37] The Séminaire de Québec became the proprietor of Ile Jésus and, to mention only the largest of the seigneuries, the Côte-de-Beaupré, whose frontage was forty-five miles long and fifteen miles deep. The Jesuits were equally well endowed, receiving Laprairie, Batiscan, Cap-de-la-Madeleine, Saint-Gabriel, Notre-Dame-des-Anges, Sillery, and so on. The female orders also received substantial blocks of land. These vast holdings continued to grow after 1760. The Church's landed property, which amounted to 24 percent of seigneurial territory at the Conquest, had grown to 27 percent by 1781. The discussion above about seigneurial exploitation also applies to ecclesiastical seigneurs and particularly to religious orders. It hardly applies to the parish clergy, however, which had its own sources of revenue: that which properly belonged to the curé, such as the tithe, and that which belonged partly to the curé and partly to the *fabrique* ("fabric"), parish revenues administered by the church wardens.

The personal income of the curés was based, first of all, on the tithe, which took one twenty-sixth of the peasants' harvest.[38] This was not a voluntary contribution, as the parishioner was not morally or legally free to refuse it. Abolished in 1763 by the British government but paid regardless by the habitants, the legal obligation to tithe was re-established in 1774 and has remained ever since. In principle, hay and potatoes, like other vegetables, escaped payment. Nonetheless, some priests, whose revenues were affected by the decline in wheat production after 1800, managed to obtain payment for these commodities from their parishioners. These are exceptions, I believe, but they tell a great deal about the care with which the curés managed their revenues. Even if they took only 4 percent of the harvest, through the tithe and other revenues owed to the fabric of the Church they manipulated considerable quantities of agricultural products which they released onto the market at advantageous times. On the other hand it must be admitted that during periods of bad harvest, the priests used the resources of the fabric on occasion to help their parishioners to plant seeds. On the basis of nine hundred estimates of the tithe that indicate the numbers of *minots* received—and this is based on figures sent by the priests to their bishop—I have attempted to give an idea of the living standard of the curés (Table 1).

It is obvious that the personal income of the

TABLE 1 | LEVEL OF TITHING ACCORDING TO THE REPORTS OF THE CURATES, 1784-1837

Grain received (in *minots*)	Number of reports	Percentage
500 or less	297	33
501–1000	349	39
1001–3000	254	28
Total	900	100

Sources: These reports are kept in the archives of the archdiocese of Quebec and Montreal. About one hundred can be found in Ivanhoé Caron, La colonisation de la province de Quebec, vol. 1 (Quebec, 1923), appendix, 275–80.

Quebec curé, judged only from tithe receipts, was higher than that of the average peasant and that the chasm separating them was very deep indeed. One cannot speak of lower clergy in an economic sense when one is dealing with curés who received more than five hundred *minots* of grain, particularly as they accounted for 67 percent of priests charged with parishes. The curés and the seigneurs, unlike the individual peasants, were in a strong position vis-à-vis grain exporters and local merchants, who accepted wheat in payment for store purchases. The curés' life style also brought them close to the bourgeoisie. (Lartigue, the first Bishop of Montreal, sometimes compared their presbytaries to seigneurial manors.) The recruitment of priests did alter in the nineteenth century, and it seems likely that they were increasingly drawn from social groups nearer to the rural population. Given their revenues, however, this may not have changed their habits. It is doubtful that they became the avant-garde of clerical democracy.[39]

In the eighteenth century, as agricultural production rose and the proportion of surplus-producing farmers increased, the burden of the tithe does not seem to have been very heavy for the majority of peasants. Later, as the number who ran a deficit rose to become a majority, that 4 percent of the harvest became as difficult to pay as the rest of the lay and clerical dues. For the indebted habitant, who was forced to dig deeper for the means of subsistence, the tithe could become oppressive. Overall, however, it seems that peasants did not really resist the pressure of their masters who insisted on being paid promptly and exactly. The tithe book of the curé of Yamachiche seems to confirm this impression.[40] Grain production in this parish, according to the census, amounted to 83 228 *minots* in 1831. Going through the tithe book, tithe payer by tithe payer, and multiplying the total by 26 yields a total theoretical production of 77 969 *minots*, a difference of only 6.3 percent from the census figure. It could be that the peasants were more fearful of the priests, armed as they were with the commandments of the Church, than of seigneurs and merchants. Towards the latter group, arrears seem to have been a more general response.[41]

Among the assessments in kind imposed by the priests for themselves or for the parish, the *quête de l'Enfant-Jésus* (also called the *quête des biens de la terre)* was second to the tithe in importance of value. Unlike the tithe, which was a legal obligation, the *quête* called upon the institutionalized generosity of the faithful. When it was to be collected, the visits of priests and church wardens were carefully prepared for on the previous Sunday by a well-chosen sermon which included warnings directed against those who might have a tendency towards avarice or niggardliness. In response, peasants offered a variety of products drawn from agriculture, fishing, and domestic industry. Although cash had a role to play in this process, most of what was given consisted of those products most in demand in local and foreign markets: wheat, lard, and tow (*filasse*). The distribution among the various products varied from one century to the next as agriculture changed. Compared to the quantity of wheat given for the tithe, that received by the *quête* was still substantial. In the parish of Varennes, the *quête* was between 7 and 13 percent of the tithe between 1774 and 1832.[42] As a part of the gross revenues of the parish, however, the *quête* lost importance from the eighteenth to the nineteenth century. In Longueuil and Sault-au-Récollet the *quête* amounted to about one third of parish revenues before 1800, but by 1822 this had fallen to 10 or 11 percent. (The tithe is not included in parish revenues for this calculation, as it was the personal income of the priest.) In addition, the decline in the quantity and value of wheat given to the *quête* shows the decline in peasant revenues, as is illustrated by the evolution of the per capita value of the *quête* in Varennes and Longueuil (Table 2).

The sources of revenue for the priests and the parishes were complex and some enjoyed a rather large measure of autonomy from economic forces. An historian would therefore be ill-advised to consider any increase in parish revenues as an indication of improvements in the living standards of peasants. An epidemic, for example, which would increase death rates dramatically and most often coincided with a bad harvest, produced a certain degree of increase in parish revenues. This was the case in Sault-au-Récollet, where burial income doubled during the smallpox and cholera epidemics in 1785 and 1834.[43] Generally, the *casuel* ("surplice fee") was among the revenues that remained somewhat independent of economic conditions.

Because the Catholic Church was not a voluntary association in New France or Lower Canada and the privileges that it had enjoyed under the French regime were preserved in their entirety under the British, its clergy was responsible for the maintenance of the civil register, just as its Anglican counterpart was. Unless they converted to Protestantism, francophones necessarily passed through the hands of the parish clergy to be baptized, confirmed by the bishop, married, and buried. In between, they confessed their sins, took communion, went to mass on Sundays and holy days, did their Easter duties, and took part in religious activities. Many of these acts involved either paying fees or making gifts to the Church. Among the factors influencing the evolution of these forms of revenue, the most important was undoubtedly demography. Indeed, the French Canadian population

TABLE 2 | PER CAPITA YIELD OF THE QUÊTE DE L'ENFANT-JÉSUS (IN SOLS)*

	Parish of Varennes	Parish of Longueuil
1784	11.82	11.73
1822	9.64	
1825	6.29	6.19
1831	4.13	4.99

*There are 20 *sols* in each *livre courante*.

Sources: Account books of the parishes. Data gathered by Richard Chabot.

was one of the most prolific extant; its rates of birth, marriage, and death since the start of the eighteenth century were around 50, 9, and 25 per 1000 inhabitants, respectively,[44] and the population doubled every 26 or 28 years. Thus demographic evolution could—insofar as it was somewhat autonomous—cushion the impact of economic fluctuations on curé and parish revenues. To understand the rhythm of this type of revenue, however, one cannot simply count up births, marriages, and burials; one must also pay attention to the development of fees and their variation according to individuals' circumstances, social standing, and desire to make a mark. Thus, at Sault-au-Récollet in 1830, the schedule of prices for burials ran as follows: burial in the Church plus religious service, 160 livres; *grande sépulture,* 8.7 livres; *petite sépulture,* 2 livres; *libera,* 1 livre; *grand-messe,* 6 livres; *messe d'action de grâce,* 6 livres; and *service anniversaire,* 19 livres. All of this communicates social inequalities and their impact on revenues rather well.

Most of the elements composing the so-called *casuel* were divided: the curés received 50 percent, the beadle or verger 30 percent, and the fabric 20 percent. The revenues from pews, however, belonged completely to the parish. Buying a pew was perhaps the most frequent means for individuals to differentiate themselves socially—from elites to the least well-off peasant—to the benefit of ecclesiastical revenues. The auction of pews, a practice that placed people in opposition to one another, easily allowed expenditure and prestige to be tied together and readily created an illusion of upward social mobility. From this flowed both the great inequalities between the various buyers and the significant number of those who, after having purchased a pew, were unable to meet their obligations (see Table 3).[45] The relative importance of the sale of pews increased considerably between 1784 and 1840. At Varennes and Longueuil, it finally amounted to over 50 percent of the revenues of the fabric (see Table 4). The per capita growth of this type of revenue was tied to its character, which allowed it to be relatively independent of economic conditions and thus capable of growth even in a period of economic crisis.

The extreme vulnerability of the peasant in the face of agricultural fluctuations is obvious from the foregoing. This contrasts markedly with the considerable flexibility of the revenues of the seigneurs and curés, who extracted a part of the peasant's production in a multitude of ways, however minimal these demands might have been in certain circumstances.

TABLE 3 | BUYERS OF PEWS IN THE PARISH OF SAULT-AU-RÉCOLLET

Price paid	Buyers in 1778		Buyers in 1804	
(in livres)	Number	Percentage	Number	Percentage
6–8	36	49	25	29
9–12	23	32	34	39
13–36	14	19	28	32
Total	73	100	87	100

* All further references to *livres* or to pounds are to French *livres courantes* or to English current pounds respectively, unless otherwise specified.

Source: Data collected from the account book of the parish, a copy of which was provided by Richard Chabot.

TABLE 4 | PER CAPITA YIELD OF THE RENTES DES BANCS (IN LIVRES)

	Parish of Longueuil	Parish of Sault-au-Récollet
1784	0.46	1.15
1825	1.67	1.28
1831	1.55	1.45

Sources: Account books of the parishes.

The Peasant and the State

Within the seigneuries, Quebec peasants were dominated by the lay and ecclesiastical seigneurs and within the parish by the curés. In addition, however, they also depended upon the state. The most popular thesis in this regard sees the habitants as having been exempt from the constraints of state fiscal impositions. It is often maintained that they had real power which originated within a quasi-indigenous institution, the militia captain. This point of view is a reflection of the desire to see colonization in terms of the purification of feudal institutions. Seen from this perspective, the militia captain is presented by most nationalist historians as the spearhead of peasant democracy. (The exception is Guy Frégault, who sees the captain as an agent of state centralization.)[46] It is true, of course, that the ancien régime society that flourished in New France had a markedly military character.[47] This was in fact normal, as the uncontested priority in the seventeenth century was defence of the colony from the Iroquois and English menace. Military danger continued past 1760, in an attenuated fashion to 1815. Although peasants were certainly continuously involved in the defence of the colonial territory, the principal responsibility belonged to the state and to the social group on which it depended most, the nobility.[48]

The petty nobility was the true governing class of New France. Its influence went beyond military and seigneurial spheres and infiltrated the fur trade in order to draw an income from the bourgeoisie, which actually managed the trade. There can be no doubt that the nobility also played a decisive political role. As long as the *troupes de la marine* did not become a permanent element in colonial life, members of the military nobility remained in the militia and dominated its corps of local officers.[49] The bourgeoisie, in particular those who had bought or obtained seigneuries and aspired to join the ranks of the nobility, were also part of the group of militia officers. In fact, the ennobled would constitute an important part of this land-holding and military nobility.

From the time that the *troupes de la marine* became an adequate milieu for the nobles, the ennobled, and their sons, the posts of militia officers passed into the hands of merchants and other bourgeois elements. Even after 1715, to use an arbitrary date, militia captains were not recruited from the average peasants, but from men of substance and influence in local communities.[50] In fact, even though the state appointed militia captains, they were so often chosen from among seigneurs, and particularly from those who were bourgeois, that one must ask if those who were not lords were not in most cases their creatures. Individuals' accumulation of seigneurial, military, administrative, and judicial functions had an authentically feudal character despite the efforts of the state to maintain necessary distinctions between different social functions.

All things considered, the peasant maintained his lowly place as the militiaman par excellence in both peace and war. Whatever the situation, it was always up to the military leaders, who were never peasants, to choose among the various options. Conscription, whether partial or general, was part of the peasants' universe and they could never avoid it. Nor could they avoid multiple corvées, either for building fortifications or for road-work.[51] Corvées were used to build the road between Quebec and Montreal for example, and constituted a system that was clearly a part of the fiscal exactions of the ancien régime. Some corvées were paid, but so badly that, as Louis XIV said, a paid corvée was a tax and an unpaid corvée a double tax.

As long as agriculture remained a subsistence-oriented activity, the peasant bore the corvées without great difficulty. The opening of external markets for Quebec wheat and the consequently limited commercialization of agriculture incited peasants to complain, however, and to resist the orders of the political leadership more and more. The establishment of the principle of voluntary participation after 1760 and the temporary abolition of the militia in 1765 reinforced this tendency.[52] Fundamentally, the development of the agricultural sector tended to undermine the foundations of the previously dominant military society. It created a conflict between individual self-interest and the traditional value of service to the king, reinforced the civil character of society, and forced the government to depend more on professional soldiers for the protection of colonial territory. This situation is perfectly illustrated by the contrasting behaviour in 1775 of a nobleman named De Lery and an anglophone merchant. The former, who bore the Croix de Saint-Louis, refused to serve against the Americans unless he was awarded a rank in the regular British army. The latter, however, gladly volunteered for the militia because it interfered with his business far less than if he had become a member of the regular military establishment.[53]

The peasantry felt the same way. It resisted British demands for mobilization because it desired to keep the family labour force on the farm. In fact, the peasantry did not believe that its vital interests were menaced by the foreign invasion. Although its fears of deportation and of being forced to serve outside the country (which was contrary to militia tradition) were genuine reasons for avoiding service, they were not the primary ones. In fact, the peasantry was responding to ongoing changes in agriculture. Peasant resistance reached significant levels at the time of the American Revolution, continued to the end of the century, and took aim not only at militia service but also at the other corvées of the state and the seigneurs.

Society gradually lost its military character, in part because peasants, impelled by the commercialization of agriculture, tried to control their own labour. Their effort coincided with the emergence of class consciousness in the mercantile bourgeoisie, who were responsible for agricultural commercialization at the market level. The gradual decline of the military nobility, whose role as land holders became more important after 1760, and the increasing interest of merchants in seigneurial properties after 1780,[54] widened the gap between the peasantry and the old elite families whose privileges were less and less justified by their military role. This reality was even more striking after the end of the Revolutionary and Napoleonic Wars, and after the end of the War of 1812.

The Peasant As Seasonal Labourer

The Quebec peasantry was not shaped in solitude, isolated in its countryside and cut off from the rest of the universe. One need only look at the curve of Quebec agricultural prices (particularly that of wheat) to understand the degree to which the economy reflected international events.[55] The connection between the peasantry and the rest of the world was not limited to the level of rural production, however, as the peasant economy also made a major contribution at the level of labour supply.

All non-agricultural economic activities in the St. Lawrence valley used two different types of workers. Naturally, there was a solid core of specialized workers or professionals (such as the coureurs de bois in the fur trade) but this was always seconded by a great mass of seasonal workers or hired hands (engagés), who were drawn almost entirely from the countryside.[56] Although the fisheries, forest industries, and naval construction of the eighteenth century were not dominant economic activities, they used the same form of labour recruitment. Even the Saint-Maurice Ironworks, which depended on a large contingent of specialized workers, used peasants to obtain the firewood and produce the charcoal necessary to the enterprise. It was the fur trade, however, that in its time raised this system to the height of perfection. According to my estimates, 35 million hides were exported to Europe between 1660 and 1815 and were all handled, at one time or another, by hired hands who were peasants or sons of peasants. The work force mobilized by this activity consisted of more than 1000 workers in 1720 and 3000 workers in 1783, but the reservoir of labour required to allow the system to function was at least twice that size.

This system, in fact, largely explains the ruralization of Quebec society from the seventeenth century to at least the middle of the nineteenth century. Given the inevitable subsistence orientation of agriculture in the early days of settlement, and the need to meet the demands of seigneurs and curés, some way of earning income had to be found to allow peasant society to take root. The fur trade filled the bill admirably. If peasant families continued both agricultural and fur trade activities once established on farms or after several generations of life in a particular zone, it was not mainly because they were attracted to the mirages of the West or because they liked to hunt. It was because agriculture as they practised it was apparently an inescapably subsistence-oriented activity. Under these circumstances, they could not have paid for imported products if they had devoted themselves to agriculture alone. In addition, as the peasant family was usually large, the family farm had an ample labour supply available for those activities whose seasonal rhythm did not conflict with agricultural pursuits.

The increasing commercialization of agriculture after 1730 saw, as a secondary effect, the reduction of the number of workers who could participate in both of these economic spheres. Peasants who produced large surpluses did not need the constant seasonal coming and going for their survival as they had in the past, yet although in decline, the percentage of those who remained tied to seasonal labour remained very substantial—about 25 to 30 percent around 1780. All farmers who ran a deficit or who had problems sending a surplus to market (because they needed seed, and had to satisfy the demands of the priest and seigneur) depended upon seasonal activities.

The incessant mobility of seasonal labour, which allowed peasants to periodically and temporarily escape the control of the seigneur, curé, and family, and to have the cash to pay off part of their debts to local merchants, was only apparently liberating. It did not imply a heightened level of economic freedom for the individual producer. In the seigneurial system, peasants were not really the owners of their means of production; in the fur trade, they were merely hired hands. It is true that the seasonal departures of the engagés and the prolonged absence of the coureurs de bois out of the countryside and towards Montreal and the West could have salutary effects. Nonetheless, the men who left remained absent for longer than expected and the women remained at home, compelled to assume a role that ran counter to the need for submission instilled by law and religious tradition.

This situation, perpetuated over several centuries and a source of dissatisfaction for all concerned, may also have contributed to the forging of a solid bond among women, religion, family, and priests. This phenomenon may be more fundamental to understanding the evolution of Quebec society than one might believe. In any event, it is certain that the continuous coming and going did not contribute to the creation of an independent peasant. On the contrary, it served as a safety valve, a kind of permanent shock-absorber for the internal social tensions of ancien régime society until the middle of the nineteenth century and beyond.[57] Eventually, emigration to the United States would serve the same function.

The peasantry's participation in a variety of economic worlds did not end with the decline of the fur trade at the start of the nineteenth century. The growing scarcity of land, accentuated by the restrictive practices of seigneurs in granting it, eventually produced a rural proletariat which was available for all sorts of employment. Around 1840, non-proprietors constituted about 38 percent of householders in the Montreal region, an area even more rural than the Quebec district in this period. The drastic fall in peasant living standards as a result of the collapse of wheat production was another event that cast into vivid relief the role of forest industries and naval construction as full-time and seasonal employment for the rural population. Under these disastrous circumstances, the massive arrival of British immigrants searching for land and jobs began after 1815.[58] The nationalist currents of the 1830s were in large part a concrete response to this context and paved the way for the insurrections of 1837–1838.

These events, of course, took place before the start of mass emigration of French Canadians to the United States. These emigrants left Quebec because they felt trapped by poverty and the lack of land, not because they had been made independent and free by the purification of ancien régime institutions, and not to seek the wide open opportunities of the frontier. The thesis of the independent, free peasant, which has been repeated by successive generations of historians since Garneau, is a myth devised by the French Canadian elite of the 1820s and 30s in its struggle to preserve the ancien régime institutions that served its interests.

Conclusion

While carrying out the research that was to bear fruit in his *Democracy in America,* Alexis de Tocqueville undertook a brief sojourn to Lower Canada in 1831. In Montreal he met Quiblier, the head of the Sulpicians, and asked him if the "feudal" system was still in force. "Yes," answered Quiblier, the seigneur of the island of Montreal, "but more in name than anything else." With respect to the tithe, Quiblier, whose Order was also responsible for the parish of Notre-Dame, responded that the peasants paid it "ungrudgingly and easily." The Mondelets, lawyers in Montreal, were also consulted and declared without hesitation that "generally speaking, our clergy is eminently national." Without consulting Montrealers, de Tocqueville's Quebec guides told him the same story as if they had learned it by heart:

> The French Canadian is deeply religious; he pays his tithe without reluctance.... The clergy here is just one compact body with the people.... Yes, [there are still some traces of feudalism here] but so slight that they are almost unnoticed.... [The lord is normally a farmer himself.... All the people have some property and are religious and order-loving; they made good choices.[59]

De Tocqueville was no doubt impressed by these unanimous and categorical affirmations but he was beset by doubt. On the 29th of August he wrote in his diary, "Today we went on horseback to visit the countryside without a guide." He profited from the opportunity by going to speak directly with the peasants, who did not seem as happy as he had been told:

> Their jealousy is acutely aroused by the daily arrival of newcomers from Europe.... One sees that all one says on this subject touches their feelings, but they do not see the remedy clearly.... We were able to notice in our talks with the people of this country, a basis of hatred and jealousy of the lords.... I found again at the bottom of the hearts of those peasants the political passions which brought about the Revolution.... We thought, too, that we noticed that the peasant did not see the clergy's right to levy the tithe without repugnance, and that he was not without envy in contemplating the wealth which this tax put into the hands of some ecclesiastics. If religion ever loses its sway in Canada, it will have been by that breach that the enemy has come in.[60]

So, at the time that de Toqueville was writing his *Democracy in America*—presenting the new continent as the natural habitat of democracy and equality of conditions—he discovered a population that was not only French-speaking but had also preserved most of the characteristics of the French ancien régime. While he anticipated the end of the feudal system and clerical power, de Toqueville could not have foreseen the great setback that francophones experienced with the extraordinary growth of clerical domination during the next century.

Notes

1 F-X. Garneau, *Histoire du Canada depuis sa découverte jusqu'à nos jours,* 1st ed. (Quebec, 1845), 1:12.

2 Lionel Groulx, *Histoire du Canada depuis la découverte* (Montreal, 1952), 2:12.

3 Ibid., 2:194.

4 Ibid., 2:193.

5 Ibid., 2:187.

6 Ibid., 2:82.

7 Groulx, *Histoire du Canada* (Montreal, 1953), 4:197.

8 Guy Frégault, *La civilisation de la Nouvelle-France* (Montreal, 1944), 182.

9 Ibid., 184.

10 Maurice Séguin, *La nation canadienne et l'agriculture (1760–1850). Essai d'histoire économique* (Trois-Rivières, 1970), 184.

11 Ibid., 169. See also 152 and 154.

12 Ibid., 171.

13 Groulx, *Histoire du Canada,* 2:182; Séguin, *La nation canadienne,* 171.

14 Jean-Pierre Wallot, *Un Québec qui bougeait* (Trois-Rivières, 1973), 235.

15 Denis Monière, *Le développement des idéologies au Québec des origines à nos jours* (Montreal, 1977), 60–61, 64, 66ff., 75.

16 Fernand Ouellet, "L'abolition du régime seigneurial et l'idée de propriété," *Hermès* 14 (1954): 22–37; "Le régime seigneurial dans le Québec, 1760–1854," in Fernand Ouellet, *Eléments d'histoire sociale du Bas-Canada* (Montreal, 1972), 91–113; *Economic and Social History of Quebec, 1760–1850* (Toronto, 1980), chap. 12, 14, 16; and *Lower Canada, 1791–1840: Social Change and Nationalism* (Toronto, 1980), chap. 5.

17 Louise Dechêne, "L'évolution du régime seigneurial au Canada," *RS* (1971): 143–83.

18 Gilles Bourque, *Classes sociales et question nationale au Québec, 1760–1840* (Montreal, [1970]), 15.

19 Ibid., 15.

20 Fernand Ouellet, "Propriété seigneuriale et groupes sociaux dans la vallée du Saint-Laurent (1663–1840)," in *Mélanges d'histoire du Canada français offerts au professeur Marcel Trudel* (Ottawa, 1978), 183.

21 Ouellet, *Lower Canada,* 124.

22 W.J. Eccles, "The Social, Economic and Political Significance of the Military Establishment in New France," *CHR* 52 (1971): 1–22.

23 Richard Cole Harris, *The Seigneurial System in Early Canada. A Geographical Study* (Quebec, 1966), 193–98.

24 Ibid., 44.

25 In Marcel Trudel, *Le régime seigneurial,* Canadian Historical Association booklet no. 6 (Ottawa, 1966), the author supports the thesis of the seigneur as an agent of colonization. His point of view subsequently changed. See *Les débuts du régime seigneurial* (Montreal, 1974), 50–78.

26 Ouellet, "Propriété seigneuriale," 188–94.

27 Statistics published in *Histoire du Québec,* ed. J. Hamelin (Saint-Hyacinthe, 1976), 196. My estimates are based upon these figures.

28 Harris, *The Seigneurial System,* 153.

29 Ouellet, *Economic and Social History of Quebec,* 84. It was around 65 to 75 percent during the first half of the eighteenth century.

30 Ouellet, *Lower Canada,* 350.

31 I have divided the revenues from the seigneuries of the Séminaire de Québec for 1790, 1825, and 1831 (see Ouellet, "Propriété seigneuriale") by the population of these fiefs at the same date (Ivanhoé Caron, *La colonisation de la province de Québec, 1760–1791* (Quebec, 1923), 272–74.

32 See the censuses of 1827 and 1831 in vol. 4 of the Census of 1871.

33 Ouellet, *Lower Canada,* 370.

34 I calculate the maximum yield at this date as being 2.7 *minots* for each one sown.

35 Ouellet, *Lower Canada,* 179–80.

36 Ibid., 187.

37 Ouellet, "Propriété seigneuriale," 194–95, 208–10.

38 Fernand Ouellet, "L'agriculture bas-canadienne vue à travers les dîmes et la rente en nature," *HS/SH* 8 (1971): 5–45.

39 Richard Chabot, *Le curé de campagne et la contestation locale au Québec (de 1791 aux troubles de 1837–1838)* (Montreal, 1975).

40 The tithe book, a copy of which was provided by R. Chabot, comes from the archives of the parish of Yamachiche.

41 In "Habitants of the Lower Richelieu: Rural Society in Three Quebec Parishes, 1740–1840" (Ph.D. diss., York University, 1980), published under the title *Peasant, Lord and Merchant: Rural Society in Three Quebec Parishes 1740–1840* (Toronto, 1985), Allan Greer has calculated that the indebtedness of the censitaires in the parishes of Sorel and Saint-Ours amounted to 163 158 *livres courantes françaises.* In 1803, 45 percent of the censitaires owed nothing, but by 1855, only 15 percent were in this category. In "Le rôle du seigneur dans le développement de la seigneurie de la Petite-Nation, 1800–1850" (M.A. thesis, University of Ottawa, 1980), Claude Baribeau calculates the total of the indebtedness of the peasants of the region at 100 000 *livres courantes.*

42 According to the account book of the parish (see Ouellet, *Lower Canada,* 183).

43 From 1782 to 1784, the average revenue for burials was 90 livres. It increased to 420 livres in 1785 and fell back to 229 the following year. The average was around 1078 livres from 1829 to 1831, but rose to 2260 in 1834. This information is drawn from the parish account book, a copy of which was provided by R. Chabot.

44 There are presently two series of rates, which differ one from another only because the base year is not the same: that of Jacques Henripin and Yves Péron, "La transition démographique de la province de Québec," in *La population de Québec: études rétrospectives,* ed. Hubert Charbonneau (Montreal, 1973), 43, which begins in 1711; and that of Ouellet, *Economic and Social History,* 660. The two series were constructed using the same procedures as described by Ouellet in "L'accroissement naturel de la population catholique québécoise avant 1850: aperçus historiographiques et quantitatifs," *Actualité économique* (hereinafter *AE*) 59 (1983): 402–22.

45 In "Habitants of the Lower Richelieu," Greer even suggests that the practice of auctioning off pews was established to stimulate revenue production (375). Fernand Ouellet, "Le mythe de l'habitant sensible au marché," *RS* 17 (1976): 115–32.

46 Frégault, *La civilisation,* 177.

47 Eccles, "The Social, Economic and Political Significance of the Military Establishment."

48 See chap. 4 in this text.

49 See chap. 3 and 4 in this text.

50 See chap. 4 in this text.

51 This fact is confirmed by the study of Yvon Desloges on the fortifications of Quebec in the eighteenth and nineteenth centuries: "La corvée militaire à Québec au XVIIIe siècle," *HS/SH* 15 (1982): 333–56. See also Roland Sanfaçon, "La construction du premier chemin, Québec-Montréal

et le problème des corvées (1706–1737)," RHAF 12 (1948): 3–29.

52 E.J. Chambers, *The Canadian Militia: A History of the Origin and Development of the Force* (Montreal, 1907).

53 National Archives of Canada (hereinafter NAC), Neilson Collection, miscellaneous, Masères to Camden, 22 June 1775.

54 See chap. 3 in this text.

55 Ouellet, *Economic and Social History of Quebec,* 663–45.

56 See chap. 6 in this text.

57 M. Trudel, "L'homme de ma génération, homme d'Ancien Régime," *Revue de l'Université d'Ottawa* (hereinafter *RUO*) 47 (1977): 251–69.

58 Ouellet, *Lower Canada,* 136–57, 177–82, 275–327.

59 Jacques Vallée, ed., *Tocqueville au Bas-Canada* (Montreal [1973]), 84–100. See J.P. Meyer, ed., *Alexis de Tocqueville: Journey to America* (New Haven, CT, 1960), 38–44.

60 Meyer, ed., *Alexis de Tocqueville,* 188–89.

Images of Heroism and Nationalism: The Canadian Joan of Arc

By Colin M. Coates

For over a century following her death in 1747, the story of Madeleine de Verchères almost disappeared. A handful of writers covered her exploit, usually in abbreviated fashion. Once her manuscript letters were rediscovered in the 1860s, she attracted much more attention. From the 1880s to the 1920s, she reappeared, not only as a historical figure, but also as a national icon, a heroic symbol of the "golden age" of French Canada. Her importance henceforth lay not merely in her act of heroism, but also in the larger meta-narrative that could be used to infuse the story with meaning and purpose. She was the principal lay heroine at a time of the growth of popular nationalist sentiment in French Canada, and the comparison to Joan of Arc allowed her to become a significant nationalist symbol. In order to use her as an appropriate emblem, writers and artists had to transform her from a woman warrior into a domesticated, if brave, young woman.

In one striking work, Frère Marie-Victorin, the renowned botanist and author, captured what Verchères came to signify for some three generations of French Canadians. In the midst of the conscription crisis that deepened the linguistic fault-line in Canada more than any previous issue had done, Frère Marie-Victorin's short play was first performed in January 1918. This play gives Madeleine de Verchères a major role in vindicating the worthiness of Quebec's past. The setting of *Peuple sans histoire* is in Quebec City shortly after the failed rebellion of 1837. Lord Durham resides in Haldimand's Castle while he writes his report on the causes of the rebellion. He pens his infamous phrase about French Canadians having "no history" and then falls asleep. His young servant Thérèse Bédard reads his report, and is appalled by the portentous words. She takes the page and writes in large letters, "THOU LIEST, DURHAM!" and signs the post-scriptum, "Madeleine de Verchères."

On awakening, Durham wishes to return to his important idea and is shocked to read the addition to his manuscript. When the servant returns, Durham asks her who was Madeleine de Verchères. After her rendition, he exclaims, "This story makes one think of a canto of the Iliad!... I did not know that this new country already had such glorious annals." Thérèse replies, "I was pleading a case in fact, your Excellency, that of my people, that of French heroism and its right to respect, to space, to survival, to liberty!" Having thus discovered the identity of the person who wrote on his report, Durham surrenders the page to Bédard, in recognition of the survival of the French in the New World: "I can see indeed that the fort of

Colin M. Coates, "Images of Heroism and Nationalism: The Canadian Joan of Arc" (re Madeleine Verchères) in Colin M. Coates and Cecilia Morgan, *Heroines and History: Representations of Madeleine de Verchères and Laura Secord* (Toronto: University of Toronto Press, 2002), 41–67. Reprinted with permission of the publisher.

Verchères is still French, and that, despite the passing of a hundred years, the shadow of the small Madeleine still returns sometimes during the night to the Castle to stand guard."[1] Frère Marie-Victorin's account is explicit, whereas many treatments of Verchères's heroism were merely implicit: the contribution of Madeleine de Verchères (along with other members of the French-Canadian pantheon of heroes and heroines) was to demonstrate that the history of the French colony was worthy and worth remembering. She provided a heroic substance to the past. The proud history of French Canadians justified their existence and their future.

Symbols of Nationhood

There can be little doubt of the importance of a shared history to the construction of national identity. Certain attributes are often considered to adhere to cultural or political nations. Taking a prime place among these attributes is the attitude towards the past. While nations are objectively very recent, they are considered by their inhabitants to be subjectively ancient. As a corollary, nations require heroes and heroines, emblems of a worthy history, so that the "people" can consider themselves full-fledged members of a distinct national entity. The appeal of national heroes, like nationalism in general, is at once specific and commonplace. Though eminently comparable to other locations, each national example must be *sui generis.* In the Canadian context, nationalism has often been experienced in contradistinction to other countries, and national heroes suffer and benefit from their comparison to other countries' figures.

In the late nineteenth and early twentieth century, there was a concerted effort to recognize the heroes and heroines of Canada's and Quebec's past. The great period of commemorative activity in both English and French Canada has been dated from the 1850s,[2] but Madeleine de Verchères did not fully enter the pantheon of heroes until the rediscovery and publication of her own narratives. French-Canadian historians had located Verchères's narratives by the 1860s, but their integral publication waited a number of decades. The national historian of French Canada, F.-X. Garneau, quoted from Verchères's second narrative in a 1864 companion volume to his earlier *Histoire du Canada.* In answer to his rhetorical request "Give an idea of the *military* courage of women in New France," he focused primarily on Madeleine de Verchères, citing her second account.[3] In 1869, Narcisse Faucher de Saint-Maurice wrote to a fellow historian to ask for a copy of the same letter.[4] When her accounts were published at the end of the century, editors announced them with a sense of breathless discovery. In 1897, Rodolphe Brunet reprinted both of Verchères's letters in *Le monde illustré,* claiming that they had only been discovered a few days previously. There was no doubt for Brunet that these letters constituted "[un] document très national."[5] Archivist Édouard Richard's publication of the documents in the annual report of the Public Archives of Canada waxed eloquent about the greater significance of Verchères's heroism:

> Tragic, and in a higher degree still, heroic deeds when invested with a national interest, are calculated to make a deep impression on our minds, and to strike the most sensitive chords of our nature. And should the object of our admiration be a woman, her name, borne on the wings of fame, is stamped in letters of gold upon the heart of the nation and becomes the object of a cultus at once tender and patriotic. The facts themselves, reproduced and magnified in romance and legend, those willing helpers of that craving for the marvellous, to which we are all in greater or less degree inclined, become glorified in our eyes, nourish patriotism, and impart to history the vivid light which fixes the mind and captivates the imagination. We are as yet but in the infancy of our career as a nation.[6]

Like Verchères, other figures of the French-Canadian nationalist pantheon were selected almost entirely from the period of New France. Governors and military figures like Count Louis de Buade de Frontenac and Pierre Le Moyne d'Iberville and explorers like René-Robert Cavalier de La Salle and Pierre Gaultier de La Vérendrye were celebrated alongside women like Marie de l'Incarnation, Jeanne Mance, Marguerite Bourgeoys, and Marguerite d'Youville.[7] No particularly memorable characters from the history of the post-Conquest period ever commanded the respect and admiration accorded to the figures of New France. Despite some attempts to elevate the military figure Charles-Michel Irumberry de Salaberry, victor of the Battle of Chateauguay during the War of 1812, few heroes emerged from the hundred years of British domination of the colony. The celebration of Salaberry had much to do with one particular fan, J.-O. Dion, who solicited funds for a statue to the military hero.[8] The rebels against British rule in 1837–8 also had some supporters, yet they presented clear difficulties as unifying icons. Such reminders of the armed uprising were difficult symbols of unity, and unlike the case of countries such as France, the overarching search for political and social unity generally prevailed over the desire to advance one group's political philosophy.

In contrast, the series of heroic figures from the period of French domination more easily affirmed the legitimacy and strength of both French-Canadian and pan-Canadian nationalist sentiment. French-Canadian nationalists drew on the historical figures in order to provide evidence of the longevity of the "national" struggle. English Canadians used the same figures in a similar fashion, though their use of the figures represented an attempt to appropriate the past of French Canada in order to provide a longer genealogy to the Canadian nation and to imply a continuous record of progress that linked French and English Canadians. In their reading, the history of the French colony was a prelude to British domination and Canada's evolution within the British Empire—a romantic preface, as it were, to the most significant part of the Canadian past from their perspective. The military antagonism between British and French that led to the conquest of New France could be subverted by the rather banal act of perceiving both sides as comprising "heroes" who laid the foundations for Canadian greatness. It is telling that the English-Canadian attempt to appropriate French-Canadian heroes did not occur in reverse. French-language school history textbooks provide little discussion of the standard heroes and heroines outside of French Canada. Knowledge of Laura Secord in Quebec, for instance, has always been mediated through the advertising of the candy company.

For French Canadians, the key icon was unquestionably Dollard des Ormeaux. As told by Lionel Groulx, the story achieved a canonical form in which Dollard's sacrificial military sortie at Carillon saved struggling Ville-Marie from a large-scale Iroquois attack. Like the Greek defence at Thermopylae, the sacrifice of the few protected the many. Dollard thus became a symbol of the French-Canadian nation in his bravery and daring, a literary flourish the more necessary in light of the accusations hurled at French Canadians during the debates over conscription in the First World War. The perception of a lower rate of enlistment in the armed services among French Canadians led to increasing antipathies between the two main linguistic groups. For their part, French-Canadian leaders proclaimed the willingness to fight, but only in the direct defence of their own country. Historical figures such as Dollard des Ormeaux and Madeleine de Verchères confirmed this rhetorical stance as they epitomized the courage French Canadians could reveal in the face of imminent danger. The reverberations of the split between English and French Canadians over the issue of conscription contributed to

Dollard's great popularity in the post-war years. The "rose de Dollard," a boutonnière which demonstrated the wearer's allegiance to the story and to French-Canadian nationalism, attained great popularity. Over one hundred thousand were sold in 1920 alone. Annual pilgrimages, beginning in 1919 and continuing through the 1920s, led hundreds of the faithful to the scene of his sacrifice.[9]

The larger cultural significance of Dollard's story placed it firmly in the mainstream of late nineteenth- and early twentieth-century French-Canadian nationalism. This nationalism focused on "la survivance": the survival of a small French-speaking and Catholic island in a wider English-speaking, Protestant, and increasingly materialistic sea. This survival was clearly against all the odds—a hostile British imperial government, the loss of a sustaining link to the mother country (not just because of change of empire, but because of the radical and republican changes in France itself in the nineteenth century), the examples of antagonism from Protestant compatriots, and so on. On the side of survival was the basic fact of demography. French-Canadian women still tended to bear large numbers of children, a fact that gave a large, if circumscribed, role to women in nationalist thought. Moreover, until the beginning of the twentieth century, Canada generally failed to attract and keep the immigrants who might have overwhelmed the French-Canadian position in the overall population. When net migration began to have a positive effect, concern grew over the increasing marginality of French Canadians. Much of the "survivance" nationalism which epitomized French-Canadian ideology during the late nineteenth and early twentieth centuries was specific to that part of the country, and the assumed audience remained within that linguistic group. The "nous" employed was an exclusive, not an inclusive, pronoun. Nonetheless, the same themes resonated strongly with English-Canadian elites, who also faced the daunting task of surviving in the face of external threats.[10]

Comparing Verchères

While there is no question that Madeleine de Verchères occupied an important place in the pantheon of historic figures, her appeal never approached that of Dollard des Ormeaux. But her sex established her as a key figure in French-Canadian and pan-Canadian nationalism. Other more influential women of the New France period were members of religious orders or had close ties with the Church. Their manifold virtues could not be summed up by a single heroic incident in the manner of Verchères. The hagiographers of these saintly women were often to be found within their own religious orders, and they provided the serious biographies—preludes often to petitions for canonization—of these key women.[11] The theme of sacrifice dominated their stories, as well. But they lacked the narrative panache of the defence of the family fort. Verchères, as a lay woman, had greater appeal to the public at large. A great part of her attraction was her comparability to other key heroines and figureheads from other countries.

Many countries have found a certain utility in having a woman fulfil the role of national figurehead. The image of Marianne in republican France, for instance, is a prime example, where the anonymous and mutable icon could serve as an emblem for the nation. However, through the nineteenth century, her figure did not inspire unanimity. As historian Maurice Agulhon concludes, "for some Marianne is a saint or a new goddess but for others she is the 'trollop.'" But because Marianne was an entirely invented symbol, she had no personal history for which to account.[12] In the United Kingdom, the anonymous icon of Britannia represented an analogous figure, a benevolent and mute symbol of imperialism and military might.

In the case of historical icons such as Joan of Arc, the personage became more of a symbol than a human being. French historian Jules Michelet penned an enduring portrayal of the heroine in 1841, in which she came to symbolize the nation: "My French compatriots, let us always remember that our homeland is born of a woman's heart, of her tenderness, of her tears, of the blood she shed for us."[13] The icon of Joan of Arc crossed many political chasms in France, appealing to political supporters of both the left and the right who struggled to appropriate her potent imagery. On the one hand, she defended her country's national and religious integrity, the eternal values of the French people, but she was also a woman "of the people" who revealed the weaknesses of the ruling classes.[14] At the end of the nineteenth century, the French minister of public instruction, Raymond Poincaré, called for a truce in the historiographical battle between right and left: "Joan can unite all the French people through all the fundamental values of patriotism, above party considerations, because she represents the passionate desire for the independence and greatness of the nation."[15] But such appeals for unity in commemoration did not mask the ideological interpretations, and the commemoration of Joan of Arc remained yet another field upon which French ideological battles were waged. Whatever the attempts to portray Joan of Arc as a symbol of national identity, as historian Michel Winock has shown, Joan's image often provided a staunchly Catholic cover for anti-Semitic sentiment. Most recently, Jean-Marie Le Pen's right-wing and anti-immigrant party Le Front National has tried to appropriate the symbol of the pure and patriotic Joan of Arc.[16]

In the late nineteenth and early twentieth centuries, Joan of Arc's popularity extended far beyond France. In Britain and the United States, as in her own country, her heroism appealed to feminists and socialists as much as to conservatives.[17] In Quebec, her cult also had resonances. Statues were raised to her memory, and streets and hospitals were named after her.[18] French-Canadian nationalists made pilgrimages to the sites associated with her heroism. In 1907, Lionel Groulx visited Orléans, a city "filled to overflowing with the memory of Joan of Arc."[19] French-Canadian Jesuit priest and nationalist activist Joseph-P. Archambault (Pierre Homier of the nationalist publication *L'Action française*) wrote to a friend in Montreal in 1913 on his pilgrimage to Joan of Arc's birthplace: "I prayed this morning to blessed and valiant Joan, for those in Canada who fight like her for French and Catholic traditions."[20]

Other countries boasted their own equivalent heroines. For the English, Boudicca, the rebel Iceni queen who fought against Roman invaders in A.D. 60–1, provided a counterpart to Joan of Arc. It is no coincidence that her Victorian-era statue was placed prominently on Westminster Bridge near the rebuilt Houses of Parliament. As one historian's analysis of the commemoration of Boudicca points out, "devoid of her sexual specificity, she has represented the more general and abstract ideas of Britain and national struggle." Nonetheless, in many accounts, especially those written by men, she emerges as a mother figure, a model for British womanhood.[21] The emphasis on "womanly" virtues rendered the image of the warrior queen much more palatable.

The persona of Madeleine de Verchères would also embody womanly attributes as she came to occupy the position of female figurehead in Quebec. There were different shades of opinion concerning her significance, as we shall see, but Verchères's image largely appealed to the nationalist right, if only because the left side of the political spectrum was relatively weak during this period in Quebec and was limited in its access to publication outlets. Although her similarities to Dollard des Ormeaux could also be used to accentuate her virtues, without question the key attraction of Madeleine de Verchères was the comparison one could make to Joan of Arc.

Both in their teens at the time of their famous exploits, the two women presented themselves as virgins, and cross-dressed to achieve their aims. But there were also some important differences between them. Unlike Verchères, Joan apparently never used her weapons. Unlike the exploits of Joan of Arc (and Dollard des Ormeaux), Verchères's actions were primarily defensive. Verchères led the defence of the family fort; she did not initiate the military confrontation.

Verchères's comparability to Joan and Dollard allowed her to assume an important place in the nationalist pantheon. As early as 1859, lawyer Maximilien Bibaud noted the comparison of Verchères to Joan of Arc.[22] In 1909, a writer in the popular magazine *Le monde illustré* called her "la Jeanne d'Arc du Canada."[23] Writing in the pages of the nationalist journal *L'Action française* in 1926, Marie-Louise d'Auteuil proposed a "Journée de Madeleine de Verchères" for schoolgirls, to accompany the increasingly popular Dollard Day, which was becoming the accepted name in Quebec for the holiday celebrated as Victoria Day elsewhere in Canada.[24] A few writers retelling Verchères's story preferred the comparison with Jeanne Hachette, defender of Beauvais. Given Hachette's successful rallying of her city's defenders in 1472, she offered a better analogy, even if it lacked some of the resonance of Joan of Arc.[25] The comparisons legitimized Verchères's heroism and, by extension, French-Canadian and Canadian history: "It was done," wrote journalist P. de la Chatre in a Trois-Rivières newspaper in 1929. "Canada had the right to compare itself to France in this way: it now had its own heroine."[26] Just as the 1867 and 1884 translations into French of Joan's trial contributed to her growing force as a heroine, so did the publication of Verchères's two narratives provide the authentic proof of her importance.

But authenticity was not always required of heroic national symbols. Evangeline, the semi-fictitious Acadian heroine, provides a further useful comparison, even if Verchères herself was never contrasted with this character. The creation of the American poet Henry Longfellow in 1847, she came to symbolize the sufferings of the Acadian people, deported from their homeland in the 1740s and scattered around the Atlantic world. Evangeline searched throughout North America for her deported fiancé, locating him only as he lay dying. Longfellow's poem was phenomenally popular in the English-speaking world and in Acadia, and it created a heroine who provided a romantic impulse for the surge of Acadian nationalism in the late nineteenth century. As French professor Ernest Martin wrote in 1936, her story inspired "the moral rehabilitation of an entire race, hope and pride brought back to the heart of a million people."[27] Although there was indeed a woman whose story can be said to resemble that of Evangeline, the problem with the character is her literary nature: useful for tourists as an attraction, she was nonetheless fictitious—not that she did not "exist," but that she did not have the ring of authenticity of flesh-and-blood heroines. Nonetheless, she came to represent the key motif in Acadian nationalist history, a figurehead for identity. Like Secord and Verchères, she too could become a focus for commercial advertising and tourist attractions both in Acadia and in Louisiana, an increasingly banal representation of national identity. Like them, she could also become the butt of ironic jokes: "Evangeline, the Acadian Queen," Acadian songwriter Angèle Arsenault sings—partly in English—with tongue in cheek.[28]

Where Verchères differed most strongly from Evangeline was the nature of her feat. Evangeline strove to find domestic bliss in her search for her true love. Verchères could not easily be cast as the romantic victim. She was a forceful protagonist, one whose very actions challenged strict gendered roles. Given the ideological constraints of the late nineteenth and early twentieth centuries, her heroism had to lead eventually, for narrative purposes, to domestic bliss.

Depicting Virtue

Between the 1860s and 1920s, dozens of published accounts commemorated Verchères's heroism. Writers dedicated poems, full narratives, or chapters in larger works to Madeleine's memory. Versions of Verchères's story cast her as a patriotic icon, with specific feminine attributes and virtues. While the emphasis varied to a small degree from author to author, the vast majority of the retellings of the tale of Madeleine de Verchères did not distinguish themselves by inventiveness. Most follow standard forms, with minor differences in wording and the choice of anecdotes, often depending on the ultimate source: one of the two narratives signed by Verchères, or the other accounts by Charlevoix or La Potherie. The attempts at commemoration feed upon each other, to the point of lacking originality. Very few of the accounts reflect in-depth research; this was not the strength of popular history. Rather, the defining trait of popular history seems to have been the retelling of a familiar story in a way that imbued it with moral values which surpassed the mere details of the narrative.[29] Protestants and Catholics, French Canadians and English Canadians, men and women, all placed their emphasis somewhat differently, although the versions generally had much in common with one another. The very familiarity of the story made it an appropriate inspiration for quick adaptations on a nationalist theme. Two participants in a 1918 literary contest run by the nationalist Société St-Jean-Baptiste de Montréal chose as their theme the story of the girl's heroism, even if the authors produced submissions strikingly similar to the usual accounts.[30]

In his 1877 volume on the history of New France, the American historian Francis Parkman introduced the term "Castle Dangerous" for the fort of Verchères, an exaggeration of the scale of the settlement, but one with a nice literary ring nonetheless.[31] There is otherwise little to distinguish his story from the many others. Still, it is a testimony to the influence of Parkman's work over many later popular historians that the phrase "Castle Dangerous" crops up so often in the accounts, particularly those destined for children. The inclusion of an excerpt from Parkman in the fourth reader for Ontario elementary school students meant that thousands of young English-speaking Canadians would be exposed to Verchères's story.

Many authors quote Verchères's own words for their resonance and authenticity. Both Catholic and Protestant authors laid emphasis on Verchères's religiosity, as did Verchères herself. Verchères's second letter recounts her prayers to the Virgin as she raced for the fort: "Holy Virgin, mother of my God, you know that I have always honoured and loved you like my dear mother; do not abandon me in the danger I am in! I would a thousand times more rather perish than fall into the hands of a people that does not know you."[32] Catholics were much more likely to include the prayer to the Virgin, but all were agreed that Verchères was a strong daughter of the Church. For Abbé F.-A. Baillairgé, the adult life of Verchères was that of a woman "strengthened by the Gospel."[33] A 1727 letter from the bishop indicating that Verchères later sponsored the construction of a new church in her seigneury served to prove her deep religiosity. For their part, Protestants acknowledged Verchères's deference to God, but they tended to bypass the saintly intermediary: for poet John Reade, "God gave courage to a maid to act the man."[34] Alan Sullivan agreed with Reade's emphasis: "the Lord is God of battle—He will help us to defend..."[35]

Writers also liked to quote Verchères's exhortation to her brothers: "Let us fight to the death. We are fighting for our fatherland [*patrie*] and for religion."[36] The fact that Verchères's concept of "patrie" had little relation to the recognizable boundaries of the late nineteenth and early twentieth centuries was of little import. As Diane Gervais and Serge Lusignan demonstrate, Verchères may have described her country (*pays*) as being "Canada," that is, the St Lawrence Valley settlements of New France, but her fatherland was France, a country of many regions. Her loyal actions, as she described them, only made sense within the context of her allegiance to the French king.[37] Nonetheless, both English- and French-language writers liked to interpret her heroism as an act of valiant nationalist defence against a foreign enemy. Her defence could serve as an example for contemporary readers.

In this fashion, a range of contemporary nationalistic concerns were grafted onto Verchères's narrative. In 1916, Dominion Archivist Arthur Doughty published his study of Verchères in order to raise money for the Imperial Order Daughters of the Empire, drawing a parallel between Iroquois and Germans that wartime readers could not miss: "Savage tribes who had lorded over the continent for centuries were challenging the advance of European civilization."[38] Verchères could also be cast as a defender of French language rights. Nationalist writer Pierre Homier applauded the French-Canadian youths who refused to answer a train conductor until he spoke to them in French. According to Homier, "it was their only response, but what a clear echo of the voice of the child of the fort of Verchères."[39] Albert Larrieu's patriotic song showed the contemporary lessons that the heroine proffered:

> Ton souvenir, Madelon de Verchères,
> Ne nous a pas quittés!
> La Canadienne, encor [*sic*] sous ta bannière,
> Sait comme il faut lutter!
> S'il fallait, pour defendre sa race,
> Et sa langue et sa foi,
> Sans hésiter, elle suivrait ta trace
> Et vaincrait comme toi![40]

> [Your memory, Madelon de Verchères
> Has not left us!
> Thc Canadian woman, still under your banner
> Knows how she must fight!
> If necessary, to defend her race,
> And her language and faith,
> Without hesitating, she would follow your path
> And would conquer as you did!]

Thus Verchères, like other heroic figures, fulfilled a mnemonic purpose: her image provided the means to remember and inculcate normative values. Verchères showed the way to defend specific attributes such as the French-Canadian language, or civilization in the case of the threat of wartime. The nation could be French Canada or it could be all of Canada.

One of the most successful treatments of the Madeleine de Verchères story was a short poem by William Henry Drummond. Irish-born Drummond had trained as a doctor in Canada, but he achieved international fame with his poetry. His earlier publication *The Habitant* had sold, one newspaper reported, over ten thousand copies. To sensibilities a hundred years later, the cloying rhymes of Drummond's poetry and the attempts to capture the French-Canadian accent in English do not stand up well. But Drummond was very popular in his own lifetime, achieving substantial critical acclaim and high honours.[41]

In 1898, Drummond published "Madeleine Verchères" in a chapbook with "Phil-o-Rum's Canoe."[42] "Madeleine Verchères" was recounted in orthodox English, although Drummond had attempted earlier versions in dialect, and the other poem in the chapbook attempted to capture French-Canadian English. One draft of "Madeleine Verchères" begins, "She has pass down by de reever / She has pass down by de shore."[43] Though the published version of the poem is in standard English, French words appear that make clear the provenance of the story. Drummond's poem is a tale told to a child:

I've told you many a tale, my child, of the old
heroic days
Of Indian wars and massacre, of villages ablaze
With savage torch, from Ville Marie to the
Mission of Trois Rivieres;
But never have I told you yet, of Madeleine
Vercheres.

Erupting into the bucolic setting of French-Canadian farmers working happily in their fields, the Iroquois attack the habitants. Verchères, like a mountain deer, escapes back to the fort and rallies her small garrison to the successful defence by blowing the war-bugle: "'T was a soldier of France's challenge, from the young Madeleine Vercheres!" Twice the poet reminds the readers that Verchères fought "for God and country." She awakened her compatriots' Norman blood, an important element in the attempt at the turn of the century to locate a pan-Canadian nationalism in the specious Norman origins of both English and French Canadians,[44] and they fought off the Iroquois foe. The weather reflects and punctuates the conflict: "And they say the black clouds gathered, and a tempest swept the sky, / And the roar of the thunder mingled with the forest tiger's cry, / But still the garrison fought on..." When De la Monnière (*sic*) arrives to relieve the fort, "he stood for a moment speechless, and marvelled at woman's ways." The poem ends with the poet's hope that no such frightful sights should ever be experienced again: "God grant that we in Canada may never see again / Such cruel wars and massacre..." In the context of the Indian wars in the United States and the rapid settlement of western Canada, such concerns represented a way of linking the contemporary national narrative of westward expansionism to historical struggles.[45]

Despite the standard English of this poem Drummond's effort was well received. His international reputation meant that his work was reviewed in a variety of American newspapers from Chicago to Pittsburgh. The *Chicago Chronicle* commented that "it is a thrilling, heroic story...and Dr. Drummond has embalmed it in swift, rhythmic, throbbing, heroic verse that will hardly fail to carry it far into the future."[46] Drummond sent a copy of his work to the governor general Lord Minto, whose secretary responded that His Excellency looked forward to learning about French Canada from the poems.[47] Fellow poet Louis Fréchette wrote to congratulate Drummond on his work, and to invite him to visit him in Varennes, whence they could make the short trip to Verchères.[48] With its forceful language and its ability to capture the contemporary narrative of national expansion, this "story of the maiden Madeleine" was one of the most successful English-language portrayals of the Verchères legend. It mixed patriotism, European expansionism, and a young woman's courage.

"Dangerous Women"

With the exception of the emphasis on her religious devotion, French and English Canadians tended to use Verchères as a symbol in similar ways. Unlike Joan of Arc, Madeleine de Verchères did not inspire writers to take widely divergent stances. It would be extremely difficult, for instance, to cast her as a woman of the "people" given the class background she claimed for herself. The principal divergences did not occur between English and French Canadians or between right and left, but between men and women.

Verchères's icon raised issues of gender, ethnicity, and religion that could be used to fend off modernity. It is ironic, but by no means contradictory, that Verchères's popularity peaked during a time when women were beginning to occupy new roles in Canadian society. This was a period when men and women were faced with challenges to gendered spheres of activity, as married and unmarried women participated in the paid workforce outside of the family home, and they increasingly demanded political recognition of their contributions to society. Such trends enhanced fears about the nature of gendered social roles.

The late nineteenth century was, in the major metropolises of the Western world, a period of gender anxiety and sexual experimentation.[49] While Montreal was not London or New York, and certainly provincial Quebec (or Canada, for that matter) was not in these same cultural networks, the influences were spreading. Important figures in this cultural ferment such as Sarah Bernhardt and Oscar Wilde visited Montreal. Bernhardt's tour created consternation among the Catholic clergy, while at the same time her performances enjoyed packed houses.[50] Alongside this cultural ferment, women's organizations were demanding new rights, in particular the vote, and this blurring of public space frightened many men.[51]

This fear of changes in women's roles was true of Quebec as much as elsewhere in Canada. Leading male social commentators of the time fulminated against this "problem." Influential nationalist writer Henri Bourassa, editor of *Le Devoir,* reprinted under the title *Femmes-hommes ou hommes et femmes?* a series of articles in which he attacked feminism. Describing the likely results of women's suffrage, he poured out his invective on "the woman-man, the hybrid and repugnant monster that will kill the woman-mother and the woman-*woman.*"[52]Bourassa was not alone in wishing to limit women's encroachments on the public sphere. As a quick illustration, we can take the views of two men who themselves played important roles in commemorating Madeleine de Verchères. In 1918, Liberal politician Rodolphe Lemieux rejected women's suffrage because elected female representatives would have to vote on military matters, an untenable position given his belief that "women...are unfitted for military service."[53] And Abbé F.-A. Baillairgé wrote a pamphlet in 1925 warning of the dangers of North American modernity, among which was the confusion that would result if women dressed as men: "The idea, for a woman, to become a man acts against nature.... Why make only one [sex], when God desires that there should be two?"[54] Gender anxiety had reached Quebec as well.

In such a context, one might have expected that a heroine who transgressed gender roles like Madeleine de Verchères would pose a problem for such men. Yet, as we have seen, even in the most conservative circles, another cross-dresser was having her second day in the sun. The image of Joan of Arc underwent a renaissance that culminated in her canonization in 1920 by the same Church that had burnt her at the stake.

Most authors and artists of this period chose not to emphasize the ways in which Verchères by her very actions tested gender boundaries. It was extremely rare for authors to acknowledge the "woman warrior" element in her depiction of herself. In a lengthy article in *Le Devoir,* Marc de Germiny returned to La Potherie's characterization as "a fourteen-year-old Amazon,"[55] a metaphor surprisingly missing in most of the early twentieth-century works on Verchères. Only one other author during this period of widespread popularity explicitly interpreted Madeleine de Verchères's story as the narrative of a woman warrior. Frédéric de Katner emphasized Verchères's noble lineage, an ancestry that the author was quick to point out he shared, and recognized Verchères as one in a line of "femmes guerrières." Indeed, he complained that most depictions portrayed her as too slight and wispish. He was clear, however, that she should not be seen as a burly, working-class woman.[56] His intervention is interesting, if only because it went unheeded by artists of the period. The pictorial images of Madeleine de Verchères emphasize her femininity, downplaying her military actions and presenting her as an innocent, young child. Gerald Hayward's 1912 illustration depicts her in a pink dress with her scarf intact, the fort of Verchères visible in the distance behind her. Artists like Louis-Philippe Hébert, who sculpted an image of Verchères in the first decades of the twentieth century, expressed his difficulty in executing her figure. His inspiration was suspended between the image of a young female hunter, weighed down by her oversized rifle, and that of a "virago." Both representations seemed inappropriate to him.[57] Given that no contemporary pictures of Verchères existed, artists could use their imagination to invent her as they wished.[58] The femininity of the illustrations is all the more striking.

Authors and artists, both men and women, suppressed or downplayed Verchères's challenge to normative gender roles. Though many mentioned that she took off her headdress and donned a hat, few accentuated the maleness of the apparel. Indeed, many did not suggest that Verchères changed her clothes, or indeed even fired any weapons. None of the visual imagery in the least disguised her femininity, as artists were always careful to show her long dress. Some authors and artists placed emphasis on Verchères's virginity, a fundamental element of the Joan of Arc figure. The scarf incident, with its virgin imagery, was often repeated, even though most writers relied on Verchères's second letter, which did not include this detail.

Images of Verchères's defence depicted particular moments in the episode: her flight to the fort, her grasp of the oversized rifle, or her firing of the cannon. The least awkward images emphasize Verchères's temerity—those which depict her in the midst of military action lack fluidity, as if the artist could not contain his difficulty with the concept of a woman's military prowess. One of the most prolific producers of historical images in this period, C.W. Jefferys, provided two images of Verchères, neither of which depicted her involved in military actions. None of the pictures created in the period up to the 1920s was designed by a female artist.

Even with the woman warrior imagery suppressed, Verchères represented a potentially unruly female figure, which male writers wished to tame. One way to do so was to associate her with the innocence and peacefulness of nature that existed before the Iroquois attack. Rev. Aen. McD. Dawson's poem situates her in the pastoral landscape to which she will eventually restore order:

> Where grandly flows St. Lawrence tide
> A maiden fair was seen to guide
> Her lonely steps. 'Mid sweetest flowers
> Her pleasure found and shady bowers.[59]

More directly, authors attributed specific feminine traits to Verchères. Abbé F.-A. Baillairgé assured the reader, "Yes, Madeleine, who was strong, was nonetheless soft and sensitive."[60] In a collection of stories of heroism in New France, Thomas Marquis was able to picture the young woman: "Her delicate, active figure, soft, *spirituelle* face—intelligent forehead, brilliant eyes and well-cut lips—all bespoke gentle breeding."[61] Whatever courage she may have shown, she did not lose any of her femininity.

Another way in which the narratives resolve the issue of the challenge to gender roles was to ensure closure, the return to the status quo. As her second narrative had done, they ended their story with Verchères surrendering arms to La Monnerie (or Crisafy). Lionel Groulx, after attributing to his niece the comment that "Madeleine was a little girl, and...a little girl is not a little boy," emphasized how Dollard's heroism surpassed that of Verchères. Women's active roles could only be fortuitous: "They must sometimes fill in for men, but they must render them the arms for the battles that are more appropriate to them."[62] Other male writers shifted the narrative to the soldiers' pursuit of the Iroquois and rescue of French prisoners.[63] Some added the apocryphal story, first raised by Abbé François Daniel, that Madeleine saved her future husband's life, and thus (illogically) "she became, in turn, the conquest of the man whose life she had saved."[64] And men and women emphasized that Verchères resumed her proper gender role following the incident. One journalist wrote in 1912 that "Magdelon was a perfect woman, as good a housekeeper as a mother."[65] For Raoul Renault, Verchères was "the perfect example of a model wife, of the true companion that God should give to all truly good and sincerely Christian men."[66] The editor of James LeMoine's version pointed out that the heroines of New France represented appropriate symbols for the youth of the day: "like so many stars, like so many beacons destined to lead us through the twisting paths of our existence, like so many patterns for our young French-Canadian women, like so many models of conjugal fidelity."[67] These designations rely on the story of Verchères's protection of her husband from the Abenaki attack, but they also represent appropriate completions to the story of her youthful heroism. How more appropriately could a woman have fulfilled the promise of her early bravery?

As a rule, authors felt constrained by Verchères's own words. One of the few exceptional treatments of her story, Rodolphe Girard's 1902 play *Madeleine de Verchères* or *Fleur de Lys,* turned it into a romance. Unlike the legion of historical enthusiasts and commemorators who were responsible for most of the versions of the heroine's story, the twenty-three-year-old Girard approached the narrative with a great deal of licence and situated the story far outside the boundaries of historical accuracy.

Girard introduces a romantic drama into the story: the Chevalier de Briac is in love with Verchères; Jeanne de Brémont competes for de Briac's attention; and the Baron de Meules, a cowardly traitor, wishes to dispose of de Briac. De Briac is condemned to die for the offence of having treacherously conspired with the Iroquois attackers, while he was really trying to chase after them. In good romantic style, as he faces the firing squad, de Briac states, "I die for having loved Madeleine de Verchères too much, she who loved me as well." Madeleine pleads for de Briac's life and throws herself in front of him: "If you fire, our two bodies will fall at the same time, our blood will mix together, we will be united in death and in eternity, since we have not been able to be so in life..."[68]

Verchères's defence of the fort is not the focus of the play. At one point, Verchères informs her mother that she had escaped some thirty Iroquois. "You know the rest," she adds laconically.[69] The play uses the Iroquois attack as a means of allowing the romantic machinations to take their course. Once de Meules's treachery is revealed, all ends well. The play finishes with Verchères's betrothal to the Chevalier de Briac, although Madeleine apparently has little to say in this development. Her father determines the end: "Forgive me, chevalier de Briac. I also must make reparation to you. Take my daughter, captain, take her, and may you have sons worthy of you and daughters worthy of her."[70]

One critic commented on Girard's use of the romantic genre, "the most popular genre today." Others mentioned their pleasure that the play adopted a Canadian theme. The play enjoyed a week's run at the Théâtre national in Montreal, after which the author expressed his pleasure at the public's response and the financial results of the presentations.[71] The play was sent to the United States to be translated and adapted to the American stage, but it does not appear that it was ever produced there.

Girard's play provides the main exception to the rule: the retellings of Madeleine de Verchères's story often remain strikingly standard, limited by the words (if not necessarily the meaning) of the heroine herself. While some introduce the romantic element through fictitious connections with her future husband, most accounts stem more from the gothic tradition of a damsel in distress finding the courage to save herself and her companions. For most audiences, at least, the apparent authenticity of Verchères's account explained its appeal. Even

Girard felt it useful to make the genealogical link between Verchères and contemporary society by dedicating his play to Charles Tarieu de Lanaudière, her direct descendant.

Women's Attitudes

Women as well as men commented on the closure to her story that Verchères's marriage to M. de La Pérade represented. In a period when maternal feminism was the dominant discourse of those in favour of women's rights, female writers wanted their subjects to fulfil the important aspects of the "standard" woman's biography, in which women, regardless of their desire to live differently, ultimately placed men at the centre of their lives.[72] Nonetheless, women's versions sometimes had a different purpose than those of men. They used the story to stake out a feminist claim on Canadian history, and in some cases to justify the contemporary shifts in gender roles.[73] Thus, Mary Sifton Pepper wrote in 1902, "Many of them [the women of New France] would even nowadays be looked upon as 'emancipated' and 'advanced.' "[74] Teresa Costigan Armstrong begins her account of Verchères's heroism by examining a number of heroic women: "The pioneer women of Canada have left behind them on the pages of history a long line of notable characters distinguished for their heroism, self-sacrifice and nobility of soul...[75]" In Marie-Claire Daveluy's short play, young girls at a convent school complain that "history is mostly for boys...because of battles and soldiers." An older girl rebukes them, saying, "And Madeleine de Verchères? She was not a boy.... And they talk about her in history."[76] Franco-American Corinne Rocheleau makes a similar point in her play illustrating the roles of women in New France: "It is said that happy people have no history. If this epigram applies to individuals, then the first French women settlers in America were happy women, because one never speaks about them...or so little that it is the same thing!"[77]

Members of women's historical societies were drawn to the biography of Madeleine de Verchères: Bellelle Guérin in Montreal, Emma Currie in St Catharines, Teresa Costigan-Armstrong in Ottawa. Asked to deliver an address to the Women's Historical Society of Montreal, Louyse de Bienville (Mme Donat Brodeur) declared that she had thought of talking about early Canadian heroes, but turned her attention to heroines: "Since I am a woman, my sympathy turns first to women."[78] Emma Currie, in a chapter of a book focusing on Laura Secord, discussed Verchères's exploits, regretting (incorrectly) that her heroism too had been unjustly ignored when it came to the request for a pension because she was "only a woman."[79]

Some women writers found it easier than their male colleagues to acknowledge the limitations on gender roles that Verchères had tested. Mary Sifton Pepper judged Verchères's actions in this way: "With a thoughtfulness that seems almost incredible in one so young, she tossed aside her woman's headgear and placed a man's hat upon her head, so that if the Indians saw her they would take her for a man and therefore a more formidable opponent."[80] Ethel Raymond supposed that Verchères "often wished that she had been born a boy..."[81] Mary Constance Du Bois, writing in the *St. Nicholas Magazine,* supplied Verchères's rallying words: "Do not lose sight of my soldier hat! You will always find it in the path of honor!"[82]

By expanding the scope of Canadian history to include women, it was not such a long step to desire to extend the purview beyond the history of elites. Robert Glasgow, publisher of the Chronicles of Canada series, commissioned Isabel Skelton before 1914 to write a book on Canadian heroines. Skelton wished to extend the range of the study to include ordinary women. Glasgow concurred in the modification of the early project to go beyond "the stereotyped heroines of the French period..."[83] In the end, Skelton's volume included sections on

Verchères, Marie Rollet, the first female settler in New France, and Marie de l'Incarnation. Skelton acknowledged the ways in which Verchères had tested the limits of women's actions and recognized her uniqueness: "Marie Madeleine confessed that she herself entertained sentiments which urged her on "to aspire to fame as eagerly as many men." Not to many girls or women has fortune been so kind in appeasing such a desire."[84] Skelton's study also covered the social history of early settlement in Upper Canada by looking at pioneer women. In the long run, the increasing interest in the social history of the common people would reduce the emphasis on the small number of heroes and heroines who occupied the historic pantheon.

Foreign Interest

While much of Verchères's appeal was specific to French Canada, other elements held more universal appeal. The reference to classical and literary traditions was important. John Reade wrote that "Grecian poet, had he seen her, would have deemed her race divine."[85] Mme Boissonault compared Verchères to the Greek hero Patrocles.[86] For Charles Colby, "she remains a bright, alluring figure, perennially young, like the maidens on Keats' Grecian Urn."[87] Despite her status as a national heroine, a general interest in heroic tales gave value to Verchères's virtues.

Beyond her nationalist appeal for French- and English-speaking Canadians, an interest that exemplifies the clash in the attempts to write the history of two nations, Verchères also attracted the interest of people from other countries. Initially the appeal of Verchères was as genealogical as it was in Canada, describing an ethnic nation that did not fit comfortably within state boundaries. Thus, a few Franco-Americans wrote stories about her, consciously attempting to transmit the values of French-Canadian culture. They reminded their audience of their ethnic allegiances at a time when American culture threatened to swamp the colonies of industrial workers in the New England states. The restrictions on educational freedom in the United States in the context of the Great War frightened many Franco-American elites. In 1918, Congress voted that only English be used in primary schools throughout the country. The application of the law varied from state to state, but the desire for Americanization represented a challenge to the survival of Franco-American distinctiveness.[88]

For different reasons, writers from France retold her story, sometimes from the perspective of genealogical connections between the old metropolis and the colony. The fact that her lineage apparently came from the Dauphiné district of France led a couple of authors to her story. For Marie X. Drevet, Verchères was following in the footsteps of her Dauphinois compatriot Philis de la Tour-du-Pin de La Charce: "Daughter of a Dauphinois man, the Canadian imitator of Philis merited this mention to our compatriots. Good blood never lies."[89] A correspondent of Abbé F.-A. Baillairgé commented on the interest that two of Verchères's distant relatives, the French Comtesse de Verchères and her sister the Countess of Madrid, showed towards her.[90] Thérèse de Ferron justified her interest by literary and patriotic reasons, and spoke of having encountered someone from the Verchères family in France. "We maintain, amongst our ancient French families, a very tender feeling and we are full of admiration towards our Canadian brothers who have remained so faithful to us..." Ferron was seemingly unaware of the deep chasms that had been driven into Canadian society by the experience of the Great War. She wished to re-establish ethnic ties that had lapsed over the decades.[91]

Other French authors have been attracted to the story for its sense of adventure and the possibility of presenting the heroism of a teenager for an adolescent audience. In his 1928 novel, Léon Ville laments the lost heroic values of the *ancien régime:* "Hum! I can barely imagine our young French girls today in such a situation."[92] French authors like Ville, Georges Cerbelaud-Salagnac, and, more recently, Nicole Vidal mention that the English were behind the actions of the Iroquois, implying that the Aboriginal people lacked the independence to pursue their own military strategies, and managing to score a point against the traditional antagonists of the French people.[93]

Likewise, a few Americans have also been interested in relating her tale, mostly from the perspective of young and adolescent readers. Perhaps the most intriguing of all the foreign contributions to the Verchères corpus is a series of three books aimed at adolescents by the Swedish author Helmer Linderholm. These books used the heroic story as a pretext for relatively standard Wild West novels in which the focus is more on the Aboriginal characters ("the warlike Iroquois") than on the young girl.[94]

This interest in a foreign national figure is in some ways surprising, yet the very specificity of Verchères also contributed to her universal character. Could she not be compared to heroines in other countries? Is not her fortitude in such adverse circumstances recognizable whatever the (Western) culture? Just as national figures are often in an odd way international in their appeal, so is nationalist sentiment an international belief, despite the specific culture to which it applies.

In this sense, the appeal of Madeleine de Verchères had much to do with the fact that she fit an international mould: she was the Canadian Joan of Arc, or the Canadian Jeanne Hachette. As such, she and Canadian or French-Canadian history, by extension, deserved respect and commemoration. For those reasons, when the list of historical figures was being drawn up for a historical procession to mark the 1908 Tercentenary Celebrations of Champlain's establishment of Quebec, there was no question but that Madeleine de Verchères would be invited. Beginning with François I and Marguerite d'Angoulême, a pageant of historical figures paraded through Quebec to demonstrate the compelling history of the colony. After the early explorers and the founders of the towns, "then followed Frontenac, whose striking personality dominates one of the best scenes in the Pageant. Then the female counterpart of him and Dollard, Mlle de Verchères, who held the Iroquois at bay with a courage as undaunted as that shown at Rorke's Drift against an equally pitiless foe."[95] As photographs of the procession show, she was placed along with her two brothers in front of Iroquois warriors. Verchères wore a man's hat, but her long dress reassured spectators that they had nothing to fear from the woman warrior.

Conclusion

In his long poem covering the heroic scope of the French-Canadian past, Louis Fréchette described the importance of the various heroes:

> Ô France, ces héros qui creusaient si profonde,
> Au prix de tant d'efforts, ta trace au nouveau
> monde,
> Ne méritaient-ils un peu mieux, réponds-moi,
> Qu'un crachat de Voltaire et le mépris d'un roi![96]
> [O France, these heroes that inscribed your
> trace so deeply,
> At such a high price, in the New World
> Did they not deserve a bit better, tell me,
> Than Voltaire's spit and the king's disdain!]

Much of the appeal of Madeleine de Verchères's story was wrapped up with the increase in Joan of Arc's popularity. Verchères became a national figure, primarily for French Canadians, but to a lesser degree for English Canadians as well. The ways in which the story was told reflected the particular class, religions, and gender politics of the artists. But the Canadian-ness of

Verchères's story was also inevitably caught up in its international comparability.

The key purpose of retelling Verchères's story was to provide a peg upon which to hang particular traits deemed useful for the population at large. In her own petitions, she provided some of the phrases that enhanced her appeal in the nationalistic period that lasted from the 1880s to the 1920s. But her strength also lay in the similarities between her story and Joan of Arc's. Canadian history was worthy precisely because it contained figures like Madeleine de Verchères. Still, specific elements of her narrative were not deemed useful by many in the same period: thus her challenge of gendered spheres was strongly downplayed. Nonetheless, she emerged as one of the key heroic figures from the past for French Canadians, and when English Canadians learned about the history of French Canada, its heroes and heroines were the embodiment of that story.

Yet despite the efforts of enthusiasts for a historiographical rapprochement between French and English Canadians, Verchères ultimately remained for most English Canadians a distant character. As prime minister and historian Lester B. Pearson recalled in his memoirs, his school-boy knowledge of Quebec was limited to a few key figures and events: "Quebec was virtually a foreign part which we read about in our school-books in terms of Madeleine de Verchères and the Battle of the Plains of Abraham."[97] For the francophile Canadian historian Arthur Lower, Verchères's heroism clearly proved the national mettle of French Canadians. Writing about the late seventeenth century, he commented: "It was the period of heroines like Madeleine de Verchères (1692), a period rich in the stuff of tradition, still vividly remembered by Canadians of French speech and the source of much of their spiritual strength today. English-speaking Canadians are the weaker for not possessing this trial-by-fire tradition."[98] As the major attempts to commemorate Verchères illustrate, she primarily became an emblem of French-Canadian national history.

Notes

1 "on croirait entendre un chant de l'Iliade!... J'ignorais que ce pays nouveau eût des annales déjà si glorieuses... Je plaidais une cause en effet, Excellence, celle des miens, celle de l'héroisme français et de son droit respect, à l'espace, à la survivance, à la liberté... Je vois en effet que le fort de Verchères est encore français, et que, malgré le siècle écoulé, l'ombre de la petite Madeleine revient parfois, la nuit, dans le Château, monter garde!" (Frère Marie-Victorin, *Peuple sans histoire: Fantaisie dramatique en acte et trois tableaux* [1937], 21–2).

2 Denis Martin, *Portraits des héros de la Nouvelle-France: Images d'un culte historique,* xiii; Norman Knowles, *Inventing the Loyalists,* 119.

3 "Donnez une idée du courage militaire de la femme dans la Nouvelle France" (F.-X. Garneau, *Additions à l'histoire du Canada de F.X. Garneau* [1864], 54–5).

4 Archives du Séminaire de Québec, Fonds Verreau, Faucher de Saint-Maurice to Rev. M. Verreault, 15 December 1869, 30, no. 15.

5 R. Brunet, "Chronique européenne," in *Le monde illustré* 14 (1897–8): 68–70. In 1888, J. Frémont had published Verchères's first narrative: "Notice sur Mademoiselle de Verchères," *Annuaire de l'Institut canadien de Québec* (1888), 69–72.

6 É. Richard, ed., *Supplement to Dr. Brymner's Report,* 5–6.

7 See Serge Gagnon, *Le Québec et ses historiens de 1840 à 1920,* chap. 1–2; Fernande Roy, "Une mise en scène de l'histoire: La fondation de Montré à travers les siècles," *RHAF* 46, no. 1 (Summer 1992): 22–30; Jacques Mathieu and Jacques Lacoursière, *Les mémoires québécoises,* 319–23.

8 Pierre-Georges Roy, *Les monuments commémoratifs de la Province de Québec,* vol. 2: 65–6.

9 Patrice Groulx, *Pièges de la mémoire,* 206–10; Susan Mann Trofimenkoff, *L'Action française: French Canadian nationalism in the twenties,* 43–4.

10 Jacques Chevalier, "Myth and Ideology in 'Traditional' French Canada: Dollard, the Martyred Warrior,"

Anthropologica n.s. 21, no. 2 (1979): 144; Ramsay Cook, *The Maple Leaf Forever: Essays on Nationalism and Politics in Canada,* chap. 8–9.

11 See Gagnon, *Le Québec et ses historiens,* chap. 1.

12 Maurice Agulhon, *Marianne into Battle: Republican Imagery and Symbolism in France, 1789–1880,* 3, 183.

13 "Souvenons-nous toujours, Français, que la patrie chez nous est née du coeur d'une femme, de sa tendresse, de ses larmes, du sang qu'elle a donné pour nous" (Michelet, quoted in Michel Winock, "Jeanne d'Arc," in Pierre Nora, ed., *Les lieux de la mémoire,* vol. 3. *Les France 3: De l'archive à l'emblème,* 701).

14 Eugene Weber, *Peasants into Frenchmen: The Modernization of Rural France, 1870–1914,* 111–12; Marina Warner, *Joan of Arc,* chap. 13: Martha Hanna, "Iconology and Ideology: Images of Joan of Arc in the Idiom of the *Action française,* 1908–1931," *French Historical Studies* 14, no. 2 (Fall 1985): 215–39.

15 Poincaré quoted in Gerd Krumeich, "Joan of Arc: Between Right and Left," in Robert Tombs, ed., *Nationhood and Nationalism in France: From Boulangism to the Great War, 1889–1918,* 71.

16 Winock, "Jeanne d'Arc," 710–14; Robert Gildea, *The Past in French History,* 164–5.

17 Martha Vicinus, *Independent Women: Work and Community for Single Women, 1850–1920,* 266; Elaine Showalter, *Sexual Anarchy: Gender and Culture at the fin de siècle,* 29; Judith Walkowitz, *City of Dreadful Delight: Narratives of Sexual Danger in Late-Victorian London,* 62.

18 On Joan of Arc's cult in Quebec, see *Nova Francia* 3 (1927–8): 381; and 4 (1929): 318.

19 "Pleine à déborder du souvenir de Jeanne d'Arc..." (Groulx, *Mes Mémoires,* vol. I: 128).

20 "J'ai prié ce matin Jeanne, la bienheureuse et la vaillante, pour ceux qui, au Canada, luttent comme elle au service des traditions françaises et catholiques" (Centre de recherche Lionel Groulx, Fonds Joseph Gauvreau, P39, Joseph-P. Archambault to Dr Gauvreau, 19 August 1913).

21 Sharon Macdonald, "Boadicea: Warrior, Mother and Myth," in Sharon Macdonald, Pat Holden, and Shirley Ardener, eds., *Images of Women in Peace and War: Cross-Cultural and Historical Perspectives,* 57; see also Antonia Fraser, *The Warrior Queens,* 299.

22 Maximilien Bibaud, *Les Machabées canadiens* (1859), 17.

23 L'Annaliste, "M. Rodolphe Girard: L'Homme du jour dans le domaine des lettres," *Le monde illustré* (7 March 1903): 1061. Frédéric de Kastner makes the same comparison in *Héros de la Nouvelle France* (1902), and Charles Colby pursues the allusion in a negative fashion by saying that "New France had no Maid of Orleans" *(Canadian Types of the Old Régime, 1608–1698* [1908], 338).

24 Marie-Louise d'Auteuil, "Vos Doctrines?" *L'Action française* 16, no. 6 (Dec. 1926): 381.

25 Louis Fréchette, *La légende d'un peuple* (1887); Jacques Cézembre, "Les romans de la vie: Madeleine de Verchères, la Jeanne Hachette canadienne," *Dimanche-illustré* (14 Sept. 1930): 5.

26 "C'en était fait: le Canada avait droit de se comparer à la France en ceci: il avait eu son héroïne" (P. de la Chatre, "L'Héroïne de Verchères," *Le Nouvelliste des Trois-Rivières* [8 Aug. 1929]).

27 Martin, quoted in Naomi Griffiths, "Longfellow's *Evangeline:* The Birth and Acceptance of a Legend," *Acadiensis* 11, no. 2 (Spring 1982): 36.

28 Ginette Pellerin, dir., *Evangeline's Quest* (National Film Board of Canada, 1996).

29 Cf. Roy, "Une mise en scène de l'histoire."

30 Bibliothèque municipale de Montréal, Salle Gagnon, Lot 10, C1, Concours littéraire Société St-Jean-Baptiste de Montréal, Valmoral, 7 November 1918, "Petite héroïne de quatorze ans"; F. Sophronius, 29 November 1918, "Une Héroïne de quatorze ans (Nouvelle historique)."

31 Francis Parkman, *Count Frontenac and New France under Louis XIV,* vol. II [1877]: 224.

32 "Vierge sainte, mere de mon Dieu, vous scavez que je vous ay toujours honorée et aimée comme ma chere mere, ne m'abbandonnez pas dans le danger ou je me trouve; j'aime mille fois mieux perir que de tomber entre les mains d'une nation qui ne vous connoit pas."

33 "forte de l'Évangile" (Baillairgé, *Marie-Madeleine de Verchères et les siens* [1913], 22).

34 John Reade, *Madeleine de Verchères* (1890).

35 Alan Sullivan, "Madeleine Verchères," in Ontario Women's Liberal Association, *Hearts of Gold: Being Chronicles of Heroism in Canadian History* (1915), 26.

36 "Battons-nous jusqu'à la mort. Nous combattons pour notre patrie et pour la religion."

37 Diane Gervais and Serge Lusignan, "De Jeanne d'Arc à Madeleine de Verchères," 178–9.

38 Arthur Doughty, *A Daughter of New France: Being a Story of the Life and Times of Magdeleine de Verchères, 1665–1692* (1916), 4.

39 "C'est leur seule réponse mats combien juste écho de la voix de l'enfant du fort de Verchères" (Pierre

Homier, "À travers la vie courante," *L'Action française* 3, no. 6 [June 1919]: 266).

40 Albert Larrieu, *Madeleine de Verchères.*

41 On Drummond's appeal, see Roy Daniells, "Minor Poets, 1880–1920," in Carl F. Klinck et al., eds., *Literary History of Canada: Canadian Literature in English,* 2nd ed., vol. 1: 438; Mary Jane Edwards, "Drummond, William Henry," in *DCB,* vol. XIII: 284–6.

42 William Henry Drummond, *Phil-o-rum's Canoe and Madeleine Verchères* (1898), 6–12.

43 McGill University, Osler Library of the History of Medicine, William Henry Drummond Fonds, P103, Box 2, 5.7, draft of "Madeleine Verchères," no date.

44 Carl Berger, "The True North Strong and Free," in J.M. Bumsted, ed., *Interpreting Canada's Past,* vol. 2, *After Confederation,* 164–5.

45 Daniel Francis, *The Imaginary Indian: The Image of the Indian in Canadian Culture,* chap. 4.

46 McGill University, Osler Library, Drummond Fonds, P103, Box 11, 32.3/6/3, clipping from the *Chicago Chronicle,* 30 Jan. 1899.

47 Ibid., Box 9, 17.2/35, Major L. G. Drummond, Governor General's Secretary to Drummond, 28 December 1898.

48 Ibid., Box 8, 17.3/77, Louis Fréchette to Drummond, 22 June 1898.

49 Showalter, *Sexual Anarchy;* Walkowitz, *City of Dreadful Delight.*

50 Ramon Hathorn, *Sarah Bernhardt's Canadian Visits.*

51 Susan Mann Trofimenkoff, "Henri Bourassa and 'the Woman Question'" in Trofimenkoff and Alison Prentice, eds, *The Neglected Majority: Essays in Canadian Women's History,* vol. II: 104–15; Trofimenkoff, *The Dream of Nation: A Social and Intellectual History of Quebec,* chap. 12; Andrée Lévesque, *La norme et les déviantes: Des femmes au Québec pendant l'entre-deux-guerres.*

52 "La femme-homme, le monstre hybride et répugnant qui tuera la femme-mère et la femme-*femme*" (Henri Bourassa, *Femmes-hommes ou hommes et femmes? Études à bâtons rompus sur le féminisme* [1925], 41 [article dated 28 March 1918]).

53 *House of Commons Debates,* Session 1918, vol. I: 655.

54 "L'idée, pour une femme, de se faire homme est contre nature... Pourquoi ne faire qu'un, là où Dieu veut qu'il y ait deux?" (F.-A. Baillairgé, *Jeunesse et folies* [1925], 40).

55 Marc de Germiny, "Une héroïne de quatorze ans: Marie-Magdeleine de Verchères," *Le Devoir* (31 Aug. 1912): 4.

56 Frédéric de Kastner, *Héros de la Nouvelle France* (1902), 82–91. Another aristocratic author emphasizing Verchères's social class was Thérèse de Ferron; see "Une héroïne de la Nouvelle-France: Marie-Madeleine de Verchères," *Revue hebdomadaire* (4 Oct. 1924): 89–102.

57 M. Hodent, "Philippe Hébert: Le maître de la sculpture canadienne," *La Canadienne* [Paris] 11, no. 9 (Sept. 1913): 164.

58 Martin, *Portraits des héros.*

59 Rev. Aen. McD. Dawson, "The Heroine of Verchères," *Canadian Antiquarian and Numismatic Journal* 6 (1878): 142–5. Poems by William Chapman ("L'Héroïne de Verchères," in *Les Quebecquoises* [1876], 150–6); Drummond *(Phil-o-rum's Canoe and Madeleine Verchères,* 6); and Sullivan ("Madeleine Verchères," 25) employ the same trope.

60 "Oui, Madeleine, qui était forte, n'en était pas moins douce et sensible" (Baillairgé, *Marie-Madeleine de Verchères et les siens,* 30).

61 Agnes Maule Machar and Thomas G. Marquis, *Stories of New France: Being Tales of Adventure and Heroism from the Early History of Canada* (1890), 216.

62 "Madeleine était une petite fille et...une petite fille n'est pas un petit garçon... On doit suppléer quelquefois les hommes, mais leur rendre les armes pour les batailles qui leur reviennent" (Lionel Groulx, *Notre maître, le passé,* 1st series [1924], 61–9).

63 Chapman, "L'Héroïne de Verchères"; J.M. LeMoine, *Les héroïnes de la Nouvelle-France* (1888), 16.

64 "elle devint à son tour, la conquête de celui dont elle avait sauvé les jours" (François Daniel, *Histoire des grandes familles françaises* [1867], 519).

65 "Magdelon fut une femme parfaite, aussi habile ménagère que bonne mère de famille" (T.G., "Magdelon la Canadienne," *Le Temps* [14 Aug. 1912]).

66 Raoult Renault, "Une héroïne canadienne," *La Revue canadienne* 31 (1895): 347.

67 "comme autant d'étoiles, de flambeaux conducteurs destinés à nous piloter à travers les sinueux sentiers de notre existence, comme autant de patrones [sic] pour nos jeunes canadiennes, comme autant de modèles de fidélité conjugale" (LeMoine, *Les héroïnes de la Nouvelle-France,* 23).

68 de Briac: "Je meurs pour avoir trop aimé Madeleine de Verchères, qui m'a aimé, elle aussi." Madeleine de Verchères: "Et si vous faites feu, eh bien! nos deux corps tomberont en même temps, notre sang se

mêlera, nous serons unis dans la mort et dans l'éternité, puisque nous n'aurons pu l'être dans la vie..." ("Fleur de lys: Page littéraire empruntée au drame de M. Rodolphe Girard," *Le monde illustré* [7 March 1903]: 1067). The play was published in thirteen parts in Ottawa's *Le Droit* newspaper from 19 February to 4 March 1936. The wording of the above extract was slightly different in the 1936 version.

69 "Madeleine de Verchères" (no. 9), *Le Droit,* 28 February 1936.

70 "Pardonnez-moi, chevalier de Briac. Moi aussi, j'ai une réparation à vous faire. Prenez ma fille, capitaine, prenez-la, et puissiez-vous avoir des fils dignes de vous et des filles dignes d'elle" (ibid., [no. 13], 4 March 1936).

71 "M. Girard a adopté le grand genre romantique, c'est-à-dire le genre le plus en vogue de nos jours" (L'Annaliste, "M. Rodolphe Girard," *Le monde illustré* [7 March 1903]: 1061; Madeleine Charlebois-Dirschauer, *Rodolphe Girard (1879–1956): Sa vie, son oeuvre*, 131, 29).

72 Carolyn Heilbrun, *Writing a Woman's Life.*

73 For similar projects by other English-Canadian women during this period, see the articles on Agnes Maule Machar (by Dianne M. Hallman), Sarah Anne Curzon (by Beverly Boutilier), and Isabel Skelton (by Terry Crowley) in Boutilier and Prentice, eds, *Creating Historical Memory.*

74 Mary Sifton Pepper, *Maids and Matrons of New France* (1902), 4.

75 Teresa Costigan Armstrong, "The Heroine of Verchères," *Women's Historical Society of Ottawa: Transactions* 5 (1912): 71.

76 "L'histoire, c'est fait surtout pour les garçons... à cause des batailles et des soldats... Et Madeleine de Verchères? Ce n'était pas un garçon... Et l'on en parle dans l'histoire" (Marie-Claire Daveluy, "Le cours improvisé" [1920], in *Aux feux de la rampe* [1927], 11–12).

77 "On dit que les peuples heureux n'ont pas d'histoire. Si cet épigramme s'applique aux individus, il faut croire que les premières Françaises établies en Amérique furent des femmes heureuses, car on n'en parle pas...ou si peu que c'est tout comme!" (Corinne Rocheleau, *Françaises d'Amérique: Esquisse historique* [1915], 3).

78 "Puisque je suis femme, ma sympathie doit d'abord se porter vers des femmes" (Madame Donat Brodeur, "Deux héroïnes de la Nouvelle-France," *Canadian Antiquarian* 3rd series, 5 [1908]: 65).

79 Emma A. Currie, *The Story of Laura Secord and Canadian Reminiscences* (1900), 83.

80 Pepper, *Maids and Matrons,* 228–9.

81 E[thel] T. Raymond, *Madeleine de Verchères* (1929), 8–9.

82 Mary Constance Du Bois, "Captain Madeleine (Wild Flower of Chivalry)," *St. Nicholas Magazine* (June 1928): 610.

83 Glasgow, quoted in Crowley, "Isabel Skelton: Precursor to Canadian Cultural History," in Boutilier and Prentice, eds, *Creating Historical Memory,* 173.

84 Isabel Skelton, *The Backwoodswoman* (1924), 77.

85 John Reade, *Madeleine de Verchères* (1890).

86 Mme Boissonault, "Magdelaine de Verchères," in *L'Huis du passé* (1924), 80.

87 Colby, *Canadian Types,* 343.

88 Yves Roby, *Les franco-américains de la Nouvelle-Angleterre, 1776–1930,* 290–300.

89 "L'émule canadienne de Philis méritait d'être signalée à nos compatriotes, étant fille d'un Dauphinois. Bon sang ne sait mentir" (Marie-X. Drevet, "Une héroïne de la Nouvelle-France: Marie-Madeleine de Verchères," *Le Dauphiné* [Grenoble] 3520 [19 Oct. 1924], 143–4). Likewise, Mlle Françoise Mournaud, *Les Allobroges au Canada (suivi de relation des faits historiques de Mlle Marie-Magdeleine de Verchère)* (1935).

90 Archives nationales du Québec à Trois-Rivières [hereafter ANQ-TR], Fonds de la famille Baillairgé, P29, Marie Antoinette Young to Abbé Baillairgé, n.d.

91 "Nous conservons, dans nos vieilles familles françaises, un sentiment très tendre et plein d'admiration envers nos frères du Canada qui n[ou]s sont demeurés si fidèles..." (ibid., de Ferron to Abbé Baillairgé, 30 Jan. 1923).

92 Léon Ville, *Madeleine de Verchères: Une héroïne canadienne* (1928), 70.

93 Ibid., 53; Georges Cerbelaud-Salagnac, *Mademoiselle de Verchères* (1958), 95; Nicole Vidal, *La nuit des Iroquois* (1983), 157.

94 *Riddarna och de röda. Madelon I* (1981); *I de rödas krig. Madelon II* (1982); *Fredens hemliga Stig. Madelon III* (1983). Lars Furuland et al., *Ungdomslitteraturen: Historik, kommentarer, texturval* (1994), 109–10.

95 Arthur Doughty and William Wood, *The King's Book of Quebec* (1911), 251.

96 Fréchette, *La légende d'un peuple,* 77.

97 Lester B. Pearson, *Mike: The Memoirs of the Right Honourable Lester B. Pearson, vol. I, 1897–1948,* 15. My thanks to Donald Wright for this reference.

98 Arthur R.M. Lower, *Colony to Nation: A History of Canada* (1946).

Charles Renaut's Letter

Christopher Moore

Charles Renaut's letter crossed the Atlantic in the spring of 1731, a single sheet of heavy parchment paper folded twice and sealed with a blob of wax. Across one side an address was inked in large and laboured characters: "to be given to Charles Renaut at the abitation of ian filepot at Scaterie on Cape Breton." It was another letter from his wife.

Writing late in April in their Norman fishing-village home, Marie-Joanne Renaut had sent off the letter as the annual migration of the fishermen was reaching its springtime peak, leaving towns like hers populated by women, children, and the old as the New World cod catch drew their men westward in thousands. From Basque seaports in southwestern France, from Brittany and the Channel ports of Normandy, flotillas of tiny fishing boats and larger merchantmen were sailing west, crammed with supplies for a season's work, crammed also with fishermen and shore labourers. Some would catch the cod of the open waters of the Grand Banks. Others would go to deserted shore-stations in Newfoundland or Labrador or on the Gaspé coast. Others sailed for Ile Royale, seeking shore space in one of the outport harbours or steering for Louisbourg, where the captain could trade his cargo while his passengers sought employment.

Charles Renaut's letter probably travelled on one of the Louisbourg-bound vessels, to come ashore amid a heap of other mail carried by the informal postal service of the transatlantic trading ships. Most of this far-flung correspondence was written by and for the businessmen of towns like Louisbourg, but whoever agreed to deliver Charles Renaut's letter would soon have headed out the Dauphin Gate in search of a fisherman's wharf and a shallop sailing up the coast to Scatary. Charles Renaut was rarely to be found in the bustling town. The fisherman's domain lay beyond the walls of Louisbourg.

Raised in a fisherman's town, Charles Renaut had found his career more by inheritance than by choice. The cod fishery that occupied his village was France's great economic interest in North America, more valuable than the fur trade, source of an important foodstuff, great employer of ships and men. It gave the nation an esteemed product to export and consume at home, and every naval strategist stressed its contribution to the training of seamen. In fishing ports like the one that raised Charles Renaut, the cod trade was the vital livelihood that sustained a way of life. For two hundred years—since time immemorial, Renaut would have said—his Norman forefathers had been sailing to the harbours and headlands of North American shores they lumped together as Terre-Neuve, the New World. The elders of the community could boast of forty or fifty voyages to Terre-Neuve, six to eight months of each year devoted to the catching and shipping of precious cod. Tradition was strong: addressing her letter in 1731, Renaut's wife disdained "Ile Royale" in favour of the centuries-old "Cap Breton," and she might easily have added "Terre-Neuve" as well.

A fisherman by his ancestry and heir to the tradition of his people, Charles Renaut took up

Christopher Moore, "Charles Renaut's Letter," in *Louisbourg Portraits: Life in an Eighteenth-Century Garrison Town* (Toronto: Macmillan, 1982), 118–145. Used by permission, McClelland & Stewart Ltd., The Canadian Publishers.

his community's seagoing vocation in his teens. Though he probably began in menial shore jobs, Renaut soon left these to inlanders. He graduated to small-boat fishing, the heart of the industry, where, by the mid 1720s, prowess proven in several seasons of work gave him a place among the veterans.

Thus established, Charles Renaut married and began a family—one he would leave behind to go with the fishing fleet each spring. Some years he sailed as early as February, for to be first on the fishing grounds was both a professional triumph and a commercial advantage. The fishing grounds kept him until September, and then the transatlantic migration began to reverse itself, to carry the summer's catch to market and take the migrant fishermen back to their families. Spring to fall at work in the New World, fall to spring at home in the old—like generations before him, Renaut was settling into the rhythms of the migratory fisherman, enduring half a year of privation to earn half a year in the security of his ancestral home.

In the fall of 1730 Renaut broke the pattern. Instead of sailing home after a summer in Ile Royale, he stayed on to take winter work. In the coldest months of the year, the fishermen who were settled in the colony extended their catches and revenues by sending boats out from November through January, pausing only when the ice drifting down from the north drove them ashore. One of those committed to this harsh winter fishery was Jean Phelipeaux, settler and fishery proprietor at the island outpost called Scatary, a few leagues east of Louisbourg. Catches had been good in the summer of 1730, and Phelipeaux wanted workers to expand his winter campaign. That fall he persuaded Charles Renaut and his brother Mathurin to winter in Ile Royale and work the second season with him. When the letter from France reached Jean Phelipeaux's fishing station at Scatary in the spring of 1731, the Renaut brothers' families had not seen them for a full year.

II

Close by the easternmost tip of Ile Royale the triangular island of Scatary lies cruelly exposed to the wild Atlantic, but the ecology that seemed so unwelcoming to human habitation drew schools of cod to the surrounding waters. Drawn in their turn by this rich resource, Renaut's forebears had noted the island's wood, fresh water, and snug harbours, and it was one of the first places settled when the colony took root. Seen from a shallop pitching in the Atlantic rollers, Scatary harbour in 1731 was little more than a series of wharves projecting from the rocky shore of a sheltering cove, with clusters of sheds and houses behind each wharf and the spruce woods closing the rear. Scatary existed only for the fishing, and only a mission priest and a surgeon lived there by other trades. The wives and daughters of a dozen proprietors were the community's only women. Migrant workers like the Renauts made up most of the population of about two hundred and fifty, and sea-links to Louisbourg provided most of their scant needs in exchange for fish. At Scatary Renaut and his fellows lived the plain life of hired fishermen through weeks and months dominated by the demands of their work.

For all the brevity of the fishing seasons, fishing businesses needed large catches to ensure their profits. The fishermen worked every day they could, and the church even spared them the obligation of observing holy days in the summer season. Every morning that weather permitted, in fog or rain or just in morning chill, Charles Renaut sailed from Phelipeaux's wharf with two companions. Their craft was an open boat called a shallop, a broad-beamed vessel perhaps thirty feet long and equipped with sails and oars. Before the dawn departure, someone had gone out to tend bait nets near the harbour. Now the shallop's bait barrels were packed with fresh herring or mackerel. Stashed near by were long, multi-hooked lines, a heap of weights, and a grapnel. A chart and compass, spare clothing, bread, a keg of spruce beer or watered wine—all the sundry supplies of a day's work—were stowed beneath the bows.

Each morning Renaut's shallop might run several miles under sail to a favoured fishing ground, and every trip tested the seamanship, skill, and endurance of the three-man crew. A misjudgment of weather or a trivial piloting error could be a death sentence to the men who faced the ocean in these heavy-laden open boats, so the shallopmaster needed sailing ability as well as the knack of finding where the cod would swarm. A crew reputed for finding cod would rarely be left alone on the sea, for Scatary outfitted dozens of shallops ready to follow the lead of a successful fisherman.

Come safely to their chosen spot, their shallop anchored or drifting over their prey in twenty fathoms or less, Renaut and his fellows baited and dropped as many multi-hooked lines as they could tend. If their choice of site was good, they would be busy all day, hauling in the heavy lines, dropping the fish into compartments in the floor of the shallop, then baiting and casting out their lines once more. The long day of labour and risk was an unremitting test of the boatman's endurance. They might pause to eat or drink, to hail their fellows or a passing ship, or even to hunt seals and seabirds, but pay as well as pride held them to their work, for hired fishermen were paid by what they caught.

The fisherman's work was gruelling even when warm sunshine lit an almost gentle ocean. More often weather exacted a further test of their hardiness, as squall lines and fast-moving fogs swept down upon the shallops. Even in high summer the intersection of warm land and cool ocean brought winds and damp fogs to chill them. The array of capes, caps, and gloves that every boat carried could never completely shelter the fishermen. In winter storm, frigid salt spray and ice-rimed gear were chronic hardships. It was a harsh career and a risky one. Each year storms and ice claimed a few shallops; each year collisions and accidents exacted their toll of lives and vessels.

If all went well, mid afternoon of the fishing day saw Renaut and his crew hauling in their lines to hoist sail and find their way back to Scatary, their shallop now laden down with several hundredweight of fish. At Jean Phelipeaux's wharf, a rustic structure of poles, planks, and heavy wharfing spikes, Renaut helped pitch his catch to the shore crews, who began to prepare the fresh fish for preservation. Catching the cod was only half the job; now a careful curing would ready it for transport and marketing.

The shoreworkers split, cleaned, and boned each newly landed fish, tossing livers to the oil press and dropping wastes between the wharf planks into the tide. The fresh, wet sides of fish went promptly into an immersion of salt or brine until they were salt-caked, and then they were carried from the wharf to the drying "flakes" behind.

There was an art to drying cod, slowly transforming perishable fillets of fresh fish into firm, dry slabs perfectly preserved for long storage and international export. Heat was not the vital agent here—too much sunshine would cook the outer layer of the drying fish, breaking down its proteins and spoiling its appearance. Instead, salt and the open air slowly drew the moisture out of the fish. Every boat from France brought a salt cargo from the tidal flats around La Rochelle, and a skilled shore crew would use just enough to draw out the fish's water content in the open air. To assist this work, the fishing property that stretched back from Phelipeaux's wharf and cleaning sheds was a broad expanse of "flakes," table-like platforms of raised branches and boughs where the slabs of fish dried for a month while free circulation of air produced a steady and even cure.

As Renaut and the boatmen continued their daily voyages to add to the supply of cod, the shore crews tended the drying catch, keeping pilferers and animals away, turning the exposed sides regularly, covering the flakes against rain, and monitoring the progress of the cure. All awaited the time when clients and creditors would come to haggle over the quality and price of the finished product. Premium cod, perfectly dried, would be rushed away to take top prices from choosy European buyers. Carefully assessed by experienced traders, the undersized, sunburnt, or oversalted fish would be marked down, cutting the income of both the proprietor and his men. Badly spoiled fish might only be fit for the West Indian market, where plantation slaves lacked the luxury of choice and masters appreciated a bargain.

The labour of men like Charles Renaut in the catching, curing, and selling of cod was the engine that drove the economy of Ile Royale. In Renaut's years there, his boat was only one among four hundred shallops gathering in the cod that teemed over the inshore banks, and the ports of Ile Royale also fitted out sixty or seventy ocean-going schooners to pursue the fish to banks as distant as Saint-Pierre and Sable Island. Several thousand fishermen and shoreworkers worked at the catch. Toward the end of summer there might be 150,000 hundredweights of dry cod ready for shipment along with 1,600 barrels of valuable cod-liver oil—enough to pay the wages of thousands of men, enough to meet all the debts incurred for mountains of supplies, enough to fill the holds of all the trading vessels crowding Louisbourg's broad harbour.

It was not just fishermen who cared about the catches of the little fishing ports up and down the coast of Ile Royale. Almost all the trades of Louisbourg and its colony fasted or grew fat according to the progress of the fishing industry. Cod paid for the goods that occupied merchants and shopkeepers and their clerks and employees. It hired the transport that employed boatmen and builders. It drew the trading vessels of distant seaports, and the ships made work for the sailors and warehousemen and brokers whose wages supported the inns, taverns, and shops of Louisbourg. Ultimately it was cod that generated the colonial revenues that justified the King's growing investment in the rising fortifications of Louisbourg. Though they might touch a perfumed hand-kerchief to their noses as the breeze carried the reek of the fishing stations across the town, even the most refined of Louisbourg's elite could not be too disdainful of the trade that sustained their community.

Indeed, Charles Renaut's humble product could claim global influence. He would return to Normandy with his pay, but his catch might be sold in the Caribbean, around the Mediterranean, or almost anywhere in northern Europe. Though Ile Royale's production was only part of France's cod catches, which competed in international markets against abundant British and American supplies of the same commodity, the little colony's cod still formed a significant portion of the world's cod supply, in turn an important contribution to the food resources of a burgeoning European population. A global economy that the nations often found worth warring over, the cod trade and the wealth it produced had fired the imagination of New World explorers, colony-builders, and naval theorists. It still depended on the daily labour of obscure fishermen like Charles Renaut.

Like nearly everyone in Ile Royale, Charles Renaut shouldered a working day that filled most of his waking hours. After spending the day in his shallop and part of the evening helping to clean the catch, he might still have boat-caulking or net-making duties to attend to. Even when such chores were not pressing, a man there only for the work lived austerely, his horizons circumscribed by Jean Phelipeaux's fishing station. Renaut lived close by the worksite, rarely escaping the sound and smell of the fishermen's labour. He slung a straw-filled *paillasse* and stowed a padlocked sea-chest in a bunkhouse provided by his employer, a simple structure adjacent to the work-sheds and flakes and perhaps roofed only with sailcloth.

Like most migrant workers, Renaut had brought few possessions with him beyond his changes of clothing. Besides his wearing apparel, Renaut possessed only a comb, some religious medallions, and a portfolio of papers and letters. Some of his fellows owned a knife or a gun, a sewing kit or some tools, but few owned more than would stow easily in a small trunk. Some must have been athletic, some able to play a flute or a fiddle, but on the whole the migrants left their valuables in France and carried only the most meagre assortment of essentials to their temporary homes on the fishing stations. There for the work, working most of the day, the hired man needed little for non-working hours.

Still, the fishermen did not work without cease. Merchant Bertrand Imbert of Louisbourg tells of walking out of the town to inspect a stock of cod in the middle of an August afternoon. The summer work should have been at its peak, yet after closing his deal, Imbert joined several unhurried fishermen for a drink at their quarters. Employers could tolerate occasional interruptions of this sort, for they were merchants to their men. Most employers sold liquor and other merchandise to their fishermen, deducting the price of all they sold from the employee's wages. In seasons when catches were small and profits smaller, some proprietors earned more from rum sales than from their fish. There were lurid tales of hired men tempted to drink away their earnings at their employers' gain, and the owners countered with diatribes against taverns that stole their workers' time and money. Renaut was more careful or abstemious than that, but eating and drinking were probably the major diversions with which he passed his scarce hours of leisure.

The hired men of the fishing industry lived communally, sharing quarters and possessions as they shared the risks and hardships of their profession. Together they ate the evening meal, either preparing their own bread, fish, and dried vegetables at the bunkhouse or being served by the employer's wife and servant in the big kitchen. After their meal, the hired men of a fishing station were likely to remain together, sociably drinking away what time remained before an early curfew. Their drink was often *sapinette,* brewed from an infusion of spruce boughs in water, molasses, and a little brandy. Served with the rations, spruce beer was potable a day after brewing, and its alcoholic content must have been negligible. Needing stronger drink, the men could mortgage their earnings to buy rum, brandy, or wine, sometimes mixing their liquor with *sapinette* in a hot beverage they called *ponche.*

Music and dance, contests and gambling could add to the group's entertainment, but simple talk was probably the major diversion of hard-labouring men completing long days of work. In the isolation of the worksite, common origins and outlooks sustained the bonds between the workers. There was nothing unusual in the partnership of brothers like Charles and Mathurin Renaut, and since Jean Phelipeaux's roots were Norman like theirs, many of his employees had probably travelled out together from the brothers' homeland. Renaut likely had friends and cousins near by, and such comradeship helped knit the fishing stations together.

In the fishermen's sociable conversation, the difficulties and embarrassments of employers would have been a common topic. Many of the small proprietors of Ile Royale had raised themselves from the status of hired hands; their successes and failures directly affected the men they employed. One year fishermen would have talked of Georges Desroches, who at twenty-eight had risen to master of a fishing business by an expedient marriage to his employer, a twice-widowed woman of sixty-nine. If it were the cynical marriage it seemed to be, it proved not much of a bargain for Desroches, for his aged wife lived another twenty years. Another year the butt of jokes would have been Henri Nadeau *dit* Lachapelle. Illiterate, indebted, and ambitious beyond his means, Nadeau had rented his small fishing station to a visitor while he worked to clear a second property that would bring additional revenue. Unfortunately his new wharves, flakes, and sheds were not ready in time, and without revenue poor Nadeau was faced with losing both his assets. A court hearing that permitted him to cancel the lease of his first property cruelly exposed his managerial shortcomings; the tavern talk of hired fishermen would have been no less cruel.

Stories of hired men circulated just as widely. There was Nicolas Equard of Petit-de-Grat, a hired fisherman of twelve years' experience, now fighting his employer over money and being portrayed as a master of the art of evading his work. If the employer could be believed, Equard had perfected techniques for neglecting his duty: he would abandon his lines to go hunting, steal wine from the station stores, lose boats and equipment by his recklessness, and carry on a regular private commerce on his employer's time. Or there was the sad career of Claude Amiot, who had drifted out to Ile Royale mostly from a desire to see other countries. His urge to travel was not matched by a commitment to work, and Amiot floated from one job to another, never establishing expertise in any of the specialized skills of the fishing industry. Slowly he became one of the marginal men doing odd jobs about the fishing stations, and after eight years he was no more than a brewery boy preparing the spruce beer at a large fishing station at Fourché. Finally he turned a worksite fight into an axe-wielding attempt at murder. For that Amiot went back to France with a life sentence in the galleys, leaving behind only a brief notoriety among the fishermen and a cursory notation in the court registers. [...]

III

Though Ile Royale generally kept its face turned to the sea, the thick spruce forests closing in behind the fishing stations made no impenetrable barrier to men like Renaut, who would occasionally venture through them to tap the inland resources of Ile Royale. During the winter, as the fishing activity slowed and snowshoes made the woods accessible, Charles Renaut probably had opportunities to put down his fishing lines and join the stream of colonists heading into the interior.

Woodcutting might have occupied a gang of Jean Phelipeaux's men if a seasonal dearth of fish or a spell of rough weather kept the shallops ashore. Each winter a supply of firewood had to be cut and sledged to the shore or riverbank, mostly for the fishing station's own needs, but perhaps also for sale to Louisbourg's townspeople. As a by-product of the cutting, spruce boughs could be gathered for the *sapinette.* Or Renaut might have occupied himself cutting timber for boatbuilding. Little shallops lasted only three or four seasons under the hard usage of the fishing industry; proprietors always needed to have a few under construction, and off-season fishermen regularly tried their hand at ship carpentry. Renaut's co-workers might have attempted larger craft, for islanders like Phelipeaux usually owned at least one schooner, often built over the winter in a makeshift shipyard in a sheltered cove or inlet.

Renaut might also have penetrated inland to hunt. The coast swarmed with seabirds, seals, and other prey, but in the interior foxes and small furbearers could be trapped for their pelts, and there were partridges and rabbits for the stewpot. The partridges were so much in demand that hunting seasons had to be imposed throughout the island. No such protection seemed necessary for the easily killed passenger pigeons—their numbers were so great as to blacken the sky as they passed overhead in vast flocks. In ice-covered ponds and shallows eels were speared and fish taken with hook and line. Both for the thrill of the chase and the sake of the stewpot, Renaut and others might have borrowed muskets and dogs from their masters and gone in search of deer or even bear.

Ranging into the interior, a transient like Renaut glimpsed more of the colony that employed him. Though none of Ile Royale's towns and settlements lay inland, the woods were rarely deserted. A network of roads provided interior communications for journeys by foot or by wagon. Cattle and horses grazed in open range much of the year, and many settled colonists went seasonally to the forests to cut wood, to hunt, and to fish. It was subsistence as well as sport—garrison soldiers sometimes received months of leave to hunt or cut firewood. A few colonists even farmed. Had Renaut's tramping taken him to the valley of the Miré, a fertile crescent curving into the island's interior, he would have found pastureland and farmers struggling to raise grain and livestock. But most of the people Renaut met if he went to the woods were like himself: men of the shoreline making brief forays inland. Anyone more committed to the land and its resources was alien and slightly suspect in a community that lived by the wealth of the surrounding ocean.

Among those who had chosen the woods over the shore were renegades from the industry that employed Charles Renaut. Profoundly committed to stern standards of authority, Ile Royale offered neither redress nor sympathy to employees at odds with their masters. Since disobedience was an offence against hierarchy—and so against society—employers held almost every advantage in disputes against individual fishermen. The skilled workers like Charles Renaut might escape from harsh masters merely by waiting a few months: one fisherman was soundly whipped for fighting with his employer, but another had the sense to await the end of his contract before striking his hated master, and he escaped lightly. Less fortunate were the unskilled, who were frequently obliged to commit themselves to three years of servitude in exchange for passage from France, room and board, and a token wage. Called *engagés,* or "thirty-six-months men," these workers had no opportunity to recover their freedom if they regretted their bargain, and they had little protection against a brutal employer or one who neglected his side of the contract. Desertion was a disgruntled *engagé*'s only escape.

Some bold deserters from the fishing stations would steal a shallop and flee toward the west coast of Newfoundland, where a colony of outsiders had established itself beyond the reach of French law. Other rebellious employees simply took to the woods.

Those to whom the woods offered refuge were known simply as the vagabonds. Most had been fishermen at some time in their careers, though not all had run afoul of the law before leaving that work. Voracious for labour, skilled or unskilled, the fishing industry recruited any man expressing a willingness to work, and many footloose young men were tempted to join the steadier professionals in the migration to the New World. If pressed, they would say they came with a desire to see the world, to earn a better living, to seek adventure, but the hard, routine labour of the fishing stations could not always oblige them.

In 1737 Jean Galon was one who had learned how little adventure the world offered men with neither talent nor protectors. The son of a Norman stonemason, Galon claimed no profession. He had been offered passage to Louisbourg in his teens, and in over two decades he had never gone home. After working off his three years of servitude, Galon hired out as a salter for one fisherman or another, but he grew to prefer the quiet seasons when hunting and odd jobs replaced the drudgery of tending the cod. Gradually he gave up on the fishing industry, subsisting with like-minded friends on whatever work came their way—hunting, haymaking, piecework labouring. Slowly they slipped out of organized society altogether. By 1736 Galon and his companions lived more or less permanently in a shack in the woods. Inevitably they fell into conflict with a hardworking community naturally suspicious of their apparently idle ways. When they ran short of food during the winter and began helping themselves to the sheep and cattle pastured in the natural prairies, hostilities became overt. Galon and his fellow vagabonds were soon arrested, convicted of cattle theft, and shipped out for punishment; but as they ceased to trouble society, some other disgruntled fishermen probably drifted away from the shores to take their place.

The other, more tolerated aliens of the interior woodlands were the nomadic Micmac bands. It is not very likely that Charles Renaut encountered these people during his ventures into the interior, but had he done, the meeting would not have put his scalp at risk, for the Indian nations of Atlantic Canada were old allies of the French. Christianized by French missionaries, the Micmacs had united with the French to resist the expansion of New England's settlements. In war they made common cause; in peace they lived separately, meeting for trade and diplomacy but rarely transgressing on each other's domains. Missionary influence on the tribes was strong, but the priests had to earn their authority. Father Gaulin so totally adopted the rough nomadic life of the Indians that his fellow Frenchmen distrusted him, and Abbé Mailliard would eventually change his fealty from France to Britain rather than leave the Micmac people.

On the whole, distance had helped to preserve the friendship of the Micmacs and the French over several centuries of contacts between them. Transient or settled, Ile Royale's colonists lived in European towns, eating imported food and wearing imported clothing, their careers and attitudes shaped by international exchanges and global military priorities. The Micmacs, for their part, still lived in their traditional houses, preferring their own dress and cuisine. They resisted French pressure to have them settle in permanent towns on Ile Royale. Instead, the nomads ranged from the island to the mainland and back, ignoring imperial boundaries to follow the cycles of the game, the fish, and the wild crops, feasting when the harvest was good, accepting deprivation when it was not. Within Catholic rituals they preserved traditional ceremonies, and they retained many cultural values alien to the newcomers. Like all the tribes of the eastern woodlands, the Micmacs had been shaped by the austere life of a hunting and gathering people—the accumulation of material possessions was not a Micmac priority. Though they were canny bargainers when they sought muskets, metals, and woollens from the French, the woodland nomads must have found the Europeans' striving for security behind the walls of Louisbourg barely comprehensible.

Hunting skill was greatly esteemed by the Micmac. Each year their hunting parties sought the moose, deer, and bear of Ile Royale's rugged northern peninsula, and a trade in skins was one of the few enticements that brought Micmac bands to the coastal towns of the French. Despite his occasional hunting forays, and the Micmacs' skills in small-boat sailing, Charles Renaut and the natives of Ile Royale were most likely to meet when both the fishermen and the Indians were visiting Louisbourg to trade.

For Renaut as for most of his contemporaries, the presence of Indians was largely an exotic tale he could take back to amaze his children in Normandy. The land was not really his element, and his usual perspective on Ile Royale was the view from the fishing boat that demanded most of his attention. Struggling with his fishing lines or making sail in his little vessel, he glanced up to see only a hazardous rocky shore, a stretch of wind-cleared moor, and the forested hills. By contrast, his sense of the ocean around and under him was three-dimensional: he knew the depths of water off every headland, the bottom samples that identified each fishing bank, and the warmer or colder currents that guided him to the cod. Tossing in the ocean rollers he was in his element—a ceaselessly hazardous one, but more real to him than the forest frontier around his outport mooring.

IV

The winter of 1730 may have marked the first time Charles Renaut and his brother stayed a full year in Ile Royale, but already the colony was familiar territory to them. In earlier seasons they had worked at several fishing outports up and down the coast. They would have sailed occasionally to Louisbourg and ranged inland to cut wood or to hunt. In the fishing industry they were veterans, and throughout the colony they had a network of friends, co-workers, and potential employers. Transient though they were, little in the colony was strange to them, and probably much was appealing. Was their decision to winter at Scatary a prelude to bringing out their families, making a permanent commitment to the New World?

The incentive for fishermen to settle was what had given outports like Scatary their small permanent populations, and Jean Phelipeaux offered the brothers a close-at-hand example of a man who had seized the opportunity. The Renauts' employer was a man of obscure background and limited means, who shared his crews' hard work, but where the Renauts were employees, labouring for a fixed and small share of their catch, Jean Phelipeaux was an independent entrepreneur with property, equipment, and employees at his service. Scatary offered few amenities to anyone, but Phelipeaux had at least a permanent house there, with his wife and family and a servant, and the pride of a householder and master of men. He knew that the small proprietors bore the greatest share of the risks of the fishing industry, but he could also look around and see men who had risen from fishing stations like his to wealth and prestige in Ile Royale.

Michel Daccarrette for instance. Daccarrette and his brothers had begun as fishermen, travelling annually to Terre-Neuve with the fleets of migrant Basques. They began to prosper soon after they settled in the New World, and their business expanded mightily once they made Ile Royale their home. Soon Daccarrette fishing stations at the outports of Baleine, Fourché, Saint-Esprit, and Niganiche were employing as many as 170 fishermen every summer. Few of their employees earned more than 300 *livres* a season, but the Daccarrettes' annual haul of cod was worth at least 100,000 *livres.* Small profit margins sufficed to make the brothers rich.

Michel, the youngest brother and apparently the best educated, led the firm from fishing into trade. Just forty in 1730, Daccarrette commanded a commercial empire: fishing properties, trading ships, and commercial warehouses raised the name of Daccarrette to eminence. Despite his humble origins and alien mother tongue, Daccarrette was becoming a power in the colony. His Louisbourg house was tended by servants and slaves; his daughters could look ahead to ennobling marriages, his sons to dignified mercantile careers far from the smell of drying fish.

Jean Phelipeaux may not have aspired to match the Daccarrette fortune, but he could read and write, which gave him an advantage over some proprietors, and in 1730 his catches were cause for optimism. The fundamental support for his aspirations was the property he owned. In France and Canada the law of *nulle terre sans seigneur,* no land without its lord, still reigned supreme, but the Crown preferred to grant freehold tenure in its fishing colonies, whether the property in question was a Louisbourg town lot, a Scatary fishing station, or an inland woodlot. Owners had only to clear and put to use their newly granted land to gain permanent title. With property in hand, a man like Phelipeaux acquired collateral for the supplies he borrowed each fishing season, and success beckoned so long as his crews produced more fish than he owed to his creditors—among whom merchant-fishermen like Michel Daccarrette would have been prominent. In 1730 bountiful catches were beginning to repay Jean Phelipeaux's gamble on settlement.

By comparison, the migratory life offered no springboard to a hired fisherman, who would take home only some small savings. And even a labourer should have been able to discern a slow decline in the migratory fishery that had supported Charles Renaut's people for generations. In his grandfather's day, scarcely anyone had wintered in Terre-Neuve, but the steady increase in colonial settlements from New England to Newfoundland proclaimed the advantages held by resident fishermen. Closer to their work, the permanent residents could fish longer and concentrate on fishing, leaving the annual crossings of the Atlantic to merchant ships specialized for trade. The rise of men like Daccarrette and Phelipeaux was the personal side of a trend that would one day reduce the westward flood of migrant fishermen to a trickle. Already resident proprietors like Phelipeaux, with their crews of migrant workers, took nearly three-quarters of the total catch around their island. Each time some hardship afflicted the industry, the transients suffered a little more than the colonists and the balance shifted further. The future seemed to lie in the colonies, where a fisherman of experience and standing could quickly acquire title to land, then outfit his own fishing station and pursue the opportunities of proprietorship.

But the rise of the resident fishery was a trend for the centuries; even the prospect of personal advancement need not have been a powerful lure for Charles Renaut. Jean Phelipeaux might have property, authority, and hopes of wealth to show for his decision to settle on the stormy shore of Scatary Island, but his title to land would mean little if the cod harvest failed for a few seasons, or if a raiding privateer landed to loot and burn. There were as many risks as opportunities in the New World.

Despite all incentives, the Renauts had ties to hold them back from settlement. Their ancestry, running through generations of migrant fishermen, had shaped men who served their clan and community at least as diligently as they pursued personal fortune. More than a livelihood, not just the economic support of the towns devoted to it, the migratory fishery went deep into the folkways of a traditional society, shaping men like Charles Renaut to accept long exiles and slim prospects of advancement. In exchange, Normandy assured them an established place in a reassuringly changeless home society, for home bonds remained strong in a community that had always sent its men to sea. Renaut travelled and worked with brothers and cousins and friends from his own community, and went home with them to Normandy to rejoin wives and families bound in a seamless web of neighbours and kin. When emigration meant the snapping of such ties and traditions, community seemed more important than some dubious chance at fortune. The raw newness of an outport fishing village in Ile Royale seemed little compensation for losing the settled stability of his Normandy home. Even when he agreed to winter in Ile Royale in 1730, Charles Renaut seems to have declined the chance to settle there, and in the spring of 1731 his wife was writing in expectation of seeing him back home soon.

Had he been able to see a decade or two ahead, Charles Renaut would have seen much to sustain his conservatism. Whatever the long trends, the 1730s and 1740s would be hard years for the owners of Ile Royale fishing stations. Already, when the fish catches were large, employers like Jean Phelipeaux were finding it hard to recruit enough labourers, and the workers used the shortage of men to extract a better share of the catch and better conditions. Phelipeaux could not push his prices up to meet the rising wage bill, for Europe would do without Ile Royale's cod if the price should creep too high. Though settled proprietors were beginning to bully the authorities to help them with wage restrictions, that would hardly ease the shortage of workers. The diminishing gap between costs and revenues was starting to pinch many small proprietors.

Power had already shifted toward the men who had come in early, men like Daccarrette who now dealt in supplies and transport as well as fish. Indebted to these men every season, Phelipeaux had to keep up his cod production or risk the loss of his property and his business; but soon even the cod would cease to oblige him. Abundant as it was, the cod resource was not limitless. Late in the 1730s the shallopmen's relentless attack on local fish populations would cross an invisible boundary between harvesting and overfishing. Catches would plunge. Soon afterwards war between Britain and France would bring privateers and naval vessels to harry the fishermen of the coast. By the 1740s the survival of his business and then even his physical survival were going to preoccupy Jean Phelipeaux. There would be no gentle rise to wealth and prominence. If he were prospering in 1730, still his future was not one to entice men to join him in the gamble of proprietorship.

Charles Renaut could not see into the future, of course, and he would not be there to experience it. But he had made his choices, and through the winter of 1730 he simply did his job. Day by day, out in the boat, around the fishing station, off in the woods, he tolerated the extended hardships and limited pleasures of a transient workman on an Ile Royale fishing station, sustained by the home ties so well expressed in the occasional letters arriving from his wife.

V

The badly spelled, awkwardly phrased, and none the less moving letter that Marie-Joanne Renaut sent her long-absent husband in the spring of 1731 represented a small triumph of literacy. Renaut and his wife made unlikely correspondents, for even in prosperous Normandy literacy remained largely the preserve of the church and the leisured aristocracy. Three-quarters of the people of France were illiterate, and many in authority were content to have it so. Why educate one's servants beyond their needs? Since Charles Renaut's training in seamanship had probably required no book-learning, there was nothing in his vocation to demand that he, let alone his wife, be able to read.

Yet their literacy is perhaps symptomatic of the way their community had shaped itself to an economy built upon the distant fishing grounds of Terre-Neuve. A village that sent most of its men away for half the year or more had either to become a matriarchal niche in a powerfully patriarchal society or else it had to find a way for its men to retain some contact with their homes and families. Undoubtedly the women had shouldered some traditionally male responsibilities, but the effort to unite far-flung families had given the fishing towns a special motive for valuing and encouraging literacy. Though most of his fellows seem to have been illiterate, Charles Renaut was not the only hired man to send and receive occasional letters.

That such letters actually reached Charles Renaut in his Scatary Island isolation makes his communication with his wife a double triumph, a victory over distance as well as ignorance. Floods of mail reached Louisbourg each year, but little of it was personal correspondence. The mail was dominated by official dispatches, and even more by commercial exchanges: stacks of bills and credit notes passing between businessmen, orders from merchants to their distant agents, price news, market reports, and political summaries to support a global commerce. An individual might write to order goods, to manage a legacy, or to seek royal preferment, but even the literate seem to have cut home ties and let family contacts slip once they settled in the New World. Renaut's correspondence went against the colonial grain. It was proof of the migrant's bond to home and to family. Among the meagre possessions stowed in his sea-chest, the key to Charles Renaut's loyalties was the portfolio stuffed with letters.

Like any family letter, Marie-Joanne Renaut's began with wishes of health. "I let pass no occasion to inquire about your health which I pray God with all my heart is perfect as mine is good, thank God, and also that of our little girl who is doing well and who sends you her best compliments. She has been walking since two months after you left." Then the reference to the months that had passed led to an expression of need and longing. "All I ask is that you come home this year, for such a long absence is truly wearisome to me. Nothing has gone along well since you have been out." The importance of the husband's administering hand to set the family affairs aright was still acknowledged, even if he did absent himself for much of the year.

The traveller's wife cast around for news of home. Finding little, she fell back on a report of the weather. Four months of drought and cold winds were threatening ruin that spring, she wrote, and prayerful processions were being held daily. Still, the family apple orchard was looking very well. Next Marie-Joanne Renaut turned to family news, running through the activities of long chains of cousins and in-laws from the neighbourhood. Her brother Jacques would soon be coming to Ile Royale. A family inheritance had recently been divided; the Renauts now shared ownership of a house and land. A cousin and two aunts held the rest of the estate. No mere financial windfall, such a legacy underpinned the network of family ties that bound Renaut to his home. Temporary custodians of the wealth of their lineage, the Renauts would one day in their turn bequeath these holdings to new generations of cousins, sons, and in-laws.

Marie-Joanne summarized other letters she had sent, ones that might have gone astray. By Monsieur de la Vigne's ship she was sending her husband some more clothes—boots, two leather aprons, and a pair of shoes. By Captain Voisin's ship she had sent a twelve-pound pot of butter, a cheese, and some herbs. Such rations were items the migrant men took along in their sea-chests in the spring voyage to the fishing grounds. Since Renaut's stay had been extended, his wife sent these foods to revive his rations after a winter of dried vegetables and fish. Another tribute to the reliability of the transatlantic post, the dispatch of these parcels also underlined the couple's interdependence across the ocean.

Having covered all the family correspondent's eternal topics—health, the weather, family news, and the contents of previous letters—Marie-Joanne Renaut found herself without more to add, and she closed her letter with a brief prayer for her distant husband's good health. "I wish you perfect health and I am always, dear husband, your affectionate spouse, Marie-Joanne."

Concern for her husband's health was an expression of well-grounded fear as well as affection. Charles Renaut practised a dangerous trade: his wife need only look around her town to count the fishing industry's widows and disabled men. A dismembering injury, a bout of arthritis, or some debilitating disease brought on by his arduous work might wreck Charles Renaut's ability to work and earn a living. Pneumonia or smallpox or any of a dozen ill-understood diseases might strike him down in his exile. Above all he might succumb at any time to the numberless perils of the sea.

By the end of an unlucky fishing season, Ile Royale could have lost fifty or sixty fishermen in great storms, in sudden accidents, in unexplained disappearances. Each day that Renaut took a shallop out of Scatary harbour, he risked sudden squalls that could come down to swamp his small and laden boat. On the fishing grounds he kept a wary eye open for fast-moving merchant ships. More than one of his fellows had been run down in the heavy traffic at the approaches to Louisbourg. Whenever a fog came down upon the boats, he redoubled his vigilance and checked his position against signal bells and shots, for in fog a piloting error could doom a crew to death by exposure before they found the land. When he crept back to harbour, no matter what the weather, he was duly cautious of the hazards ringing every small and surf-wracked anchorage. And despite his ingrained caution the risks remained, in every voyage, in every season, only increased by winter storm and ice. Renaut's wife had cause to worry for his safety. All too often an outport fishing proprietor found himself auctioning away the scant possessions of a drowned employee, totalling his debts and wages and sending off what remained to benefit the widow and heirs.

Such an end, oddly enough, was almost the only way for an obscure migrant fisherman to draw some kind of recognition to himself. For all his skill and his dedication, a transient like Renaut could come year after year to one outport or another, earning his wage and contributing his share of the precious catch, and never leave a record of his presence in the colony. Yet should he die in his bunk or drown with his shallopmates, a tiny but permanent dossier reporting the disposal of his paltry estate would be drawn up by the clerks of the admiralty service, who would often add some note about his career and his end.

Inevitably, it is from such a dossier that we chart the career and read the letters of Charles Renaut. The slim admiralty file does not inquire about Charles and Mathurin Renaut's motives for setting out from Scatary three days after Christmas of 1730. Perhaps they planned a duck-hunting expedition along the coast. Perhaps the brothers hoped to celebrate the Christmas feast-days with a sociable visit to compatriots down the shore. Or it could have been a routine fishing trip like a hundred others they had undertaken for Jean Phelipeaux. Whatever the plan, something went wrong. The veteran boatmen got into trouble, and suddenly the shallop was lost, the men quickly drowned in the frigid waters.

When Marie-Joanne wrote in April 1731, Charles Renaut was already four months dead. He would never eat the cheese and butter she was sending, never see his daughter walk. When some messenger faithfully delivered the letter to Scatary that summer, Jean Phelipeaux could only add it to the papers of the dead brothers and go on with the hard routines of his trade. Because he died without seeing it, Charles Renaut's useless letter still lies in the registers with a note on his belongings and how he died, as if the cold Ile Royale waters that closed over his head in December 1730 had conferred on this obscure transient visitor some small and unsought immortality.

Travels in North America, 1749 (excerpts)

PETER KALM

August the 15th

The New Governor Arrives. The new governor-general of all Canada, the Marquis de la Jonquière, arrived last night in the river before Quebec; but it being late he reserved his public entrance for to-day. He had left France on the second of June, but could not reach Quebec before this time on account of the difficulty which great ships find in passing the sandbars in the St. Lawrence River. The ships cannot venture to go up without a fair wind, being forced to sail in many windings and frequently in a very narrow channel. To-day was another great feast on account of the Ascension of the Virgin Mary which is very highly celebrated in Roman Catholic countries. This day was accordingly doubly remarkable both on account of the holiday and of the arrival of the new governor-general, who is always received with great pomp, as he is really a viceroy here.

About eight o'clock the chief people in town assembled at the house of Mr. de Vaudreuil, who had lately been nominated governor of Trois Rivières and lived in the lower town, and whose father had likewise been governor-general of Canada. Thither came likewise the Marquis de la Galissonnière, who had till now been governor-general, and was to sail for France at the first opportunity. He was accompanied by all the people belonging to the government. I was likewise invited to see this festivity. At half an hour after eight the new governor-general went from the ship into a barge covered with red cloth. A signal with cannons was given from the ramparts for all the bells in the town to be set ringing. All the people of distinction went down to the shore to salute the governor who, on alighting from the barge, was received by the Marquis de la Galissonnière. After they had saluted each other, the commandant of the town addressed the new governor in a very elegant speech which he answered very concisely. Then all the cannon on the ramparts gave a general salute. The whole street up to the cathedral was lined with men in arms, chiefly drawn from among the burgesses. The governor then walked towards the cathedral, dressed in a suit of red, with an abundance of gold lace. His servants went before him in green, carrying firearms on their shoulders. On his arrival at the cathedral he was received by the Bishop of Canada and the whole clergy assembled. The bishop was arrayed in his pontifical robes, and had a long gilt tiara on his head, and a great crozier of massy silver in his hand. After the bishop had addressed a short speech to the governor-general, a priest brought a silver crucifix on a long stick (two priests with lighted tapers in their hands, going on each side of it) to be kissed by the governor. The bishop and the priests then went through the long aisle up to the choir. The servants of the governor followed with their hats on, and arms on their shoulders. At last came the governor and his suite and after them a crowd of people. At the beginning of the

Peter Kalm, Excerpts from his *Travels in North America* (New York: Dover Publications, 1964), vol. 2: 415–447.

choir the governor and the General de la Galissonnière, stopped before a chair covered with red cloth and stood there during the whole time of the celebration of the mass, which was celebrated by the bishop himself. From the church he went to the palace where the gentlemen of note in the town afterwards went to pay their respects to him. The members of the different orders with their respective superiors likewise came to him to testify their joy on account of his happy arrival. Among the numbers that came to visit him none stayed to dine but those that were invited beforehand, among which I had the honor to be one. The entertainment lasted very long, and was as elegant as the occasion required.

The governor-general, Marquis de la Jonquière, was very tall, and at that time above sixty years old. He had fought a desperate naval battle with the English in the last war, but had been obliged to surrender, the English being, as it was told, vastly superior in the number of ships and men. On this occasion he was wounded by a ball which entered one side of his shoulder and came out at the other, so that he walked slightly bent over. He was very complaisant but knew how to preserve his dignity when he distributed favors. [...]

A Catholic Procession. The procession in memory of the Ascension of the Holy Virgin, which was held to-day in Quebec, was in its way quite magnificent. Believing that She ascended on this day, the Catholics marched from one church to the other through the whole city. The people flocked to see the procession, as though they had never seen it before. It was said that they were always anxious to behold such sights. First came two boys who were constantly ringing bells, followed by a man carrying a banner with a painting of Christ on the Cross on one side and one of Mary, Joseph and the Christ-Child between them on the other. Then came another man bearing a painted wooden image of the Savior on the Cross. Both the banner and the image were on long poles. Then followed the Recollets, or Mendicant Friars, dressed in the costume described above, walking far apart and two abreast; and since they affected poverty they carried aloft a plain wooden cross. Next, borne on a pole, part of which was of silver, came a silver image of the crucified Savior. Then followed several pairs of boys, about ten or twelve years old, clad in red tunics with white cottas over them and wearing red, cone-shaped caps. Then came some more boys with black tunics and caps, followed by the priests. Some of the latter wore white chasubles, others long silk mantles of various colors, with black, cone-shaped hoods on their heads and bluish bands. A priest swinging a censer followed. Then came two priests bearing a silver image of the Virgin enclosed in a silver-plated shrine, surrounded on all sides by men carrying lanterns with wax-candles, and after came the most distinguished clergymen in their long robes. The bishop in full dress with his official crosier ended the religious group of the procession. After him marched the governor-general's private guard with guns on their shoulders, followed by the governor himself, de la Jonquière, and General de la Galissonnière, walking abreast. Last came a number of distinguished residents and a large group of common people. As the procession passed the castle the soldiers presented arms in salute, the drums were beaten, and the cannon roared from the forts, as was customary on such occasions. Those who stood nearest where the procession passed kneeled as the image of the Holy Virgin was carried by; but at the figure of Christ they remained standing. Onlookers who watched at some distance did not kneel. Thus the procession went on, the priests singing as they marched. [...]

August the 17th

The Ursuline Convent. To-day I went to see the nunnery of the Ursulines, which is located on nearly the same plan as the two other nunneries. It lies in the town and has a very fine church. The nuns are renowned for their piety and they go abroad less than any others. Men are not allowed to go into this convent either, except by the special license of the bishop, which is given as a great favor. The royal physician and the surgeon are alone entitled to go in as often as they please to visit the sick. At the desire of the Marquis de la Galissonnière the bishop granted me leave to visit this nunnery together with the royal physician M. Gauthier. On our arrival we were received by the abbess, who was attended by a great number of nuns, for the most part old ones. We saw the church; and it being Sunday, we found some nuns on every side of it kneeling by themselves and saying prayers. As soon as we came into the church, the abbess and the nuns with her dropped on their knees and so did M. Gauthier and myself. We then went to an apartment or small chapel dedicated to the Virgin Mary, at the entrance of which they all fell on their knees again. In several places which we visited we found images and paintings and candles which burned in front of some of these. The nuns explained that these pictures and images were not kept here for worship, because God alone is to be worshipped, but only to arouse piety through them. We afterwards saw the kitchen, the dining hall and the apartment they work in, which is large and fine. They do all sorts of neat work there, gild pictures, make artificial flowers, etc. The dining hall is similar to those in the other two nunneries. Under the tables are small drawers for each nun to keep her napkin, knife and fork, and other things in. Their cells are small, and each nun has one to herself. The walls are not painted; a little bed, a table with a drawer, a crucifix and pictures of saints on it, and a chair, constitute the whole furniture of a cell. We were then led into a room full of young ladies about twelve years old and below that age, sent hither by their parents to be instructed in reading and in matters of religion. They are allowed to go to visit their relations once a day, but must not stay away long. When they have learned reading and have received instructions in religion they return to their parents again. Near the nunnery is a fine garden which is surrounded with a high wall. It belongs to this institution and is stocked with all sorts of kitchen herbs and fruit trees. When the nuns are at work, or during dinner, everything is silent in the rooms, unless some one of them reads to the others; but after dinner they have leave to take a walk for an hour or two in the garden, or to divert themselves within doors. After we had seen everything remarkable here we took our leave. [...]

August the 21st

Indians. To-day there were representatives of three Indian nations in this country with the governor-general, *viz.* Huron, Mickmacks and Anies,[1] the last of which are a nation of Iroquois and allies of the English. They were taken prisoners in the last war.

The Hurons are some of the same Indians as those who live at Lorette, and have received the Christian religion. They are a tall, robust people, well shaped, and of a copper color. They have short black hair which is shaved on the forehead from one ear to the other. None of them wear hats or caps. Some have earrings, others not. Many of them have the face painted all over with cinnabar; others have only strokes of it on the forehead and near the ears; and some paint their hair with the same material. Red is the color they chiefly use in painting themselves, but I have also seen some who had daubed their face with black. Many of them have figures on the face and on the whole body, which are stained into the skin, so as to be indelible. The manner of making them shall be described later. These figures are commonly black; some have a snake painted on each cheek, some have several crosses, some an arrow, others the sun, or anything else their imagination leads them to. They have such figures likewise on the breast, thighs and other parts of the body; but some have no figures at all. They wear a shirt which is either white or blue striped and a shaggy piece of cloth, which is either blue or white, with a blue or red stripe below. This they always carry over their shoulders, or let it hang down, in which case they wrap it round their middle. Round their neck they have a string of violet wampum, with some white wampum between them. These wampum are small, of the figure of oblong pearls, and made of the shells which the English call clams *(Venus mercenaria* L.) I shall make a more particular mention of them later. At the end of the wampum strings, many of the Indians wear a large French silver coin with the king's effigy on their breasts. Others have a large shell on the breast, of a fine white color, which they value very highly; others again have no ornament at all round the neck. They all have their breasts uncovered. In front hangs their tobacco pouch made of the skin of an animal with the hairy side turned outwards. Their shoes are made of skins, and bear a great resemblance to the heel-less shoes which the women in Finland use. Instead of stockings they wrap the legs in pieces of blue cloth, as I have seen the Russian peasants do.

The Mickmacks are dressed like the Hurons, but distinguish themselves by their long straight hair of jet-black. Almost all the Indians have black straight hair; however, I have met with a few, whose hair was quite curly. But it is to be observed that it is difficult to judge the true complexion of the Canada Indians, their blood being mixed with the European, either by the adopted prisoners of both sexes or by the Frenchmen who travel in the country and often contribute their share towards the increase of the Indian families, to which the women, it is said, have no serious objection. The Mickmacks are commonly not so tall as the Hurons. I have not seen any Indians whose hair is as long and straight as theirs. Their language is different from that of the Hurons; therefore there is an interpreter here for them on purpose.

The Anies are the third kind of Indians which came hither. Fifty of them went to war, being allies of the English, in order to plunder in the neighborhood of Montreal. But the French, being informed of their scheme, laid an ambush, and killed with the first discharge of their guns forty-four of them so that only the four who were here to-day saved their lives, and two others who were ill at this time. They are as tall as the Hurons, whose language they speak. The Hurons seem to have a longer and the Anies a rounder face. The Anies have something cruel in their looks; but their dress is the same as that of the other Indians. They wear an oblong piece of white tin in the hair which lies on the neck. One of those I saw had taken a flower of the rose mallow, out of a garden where it was in full blossom at this time, and put it in the hair at the top of his head. Each of the Indians has a tobacco pipe of gray limestone which is blackened afterwards and has a stem of wood. There were no Indian women present at this interview. As soon as the governor came in and was seated in order to speak with them the Mickmacks sat down on the ground, like Laplanders, but the other Indians took chairs.

There is no printing press in Canada, nor has there formerly been any: but all books are brought from France and all the orders made in the country are written, which [as I have shown] extends even to the paper currency. They pretend that the press is not yet introduced here because it might be the means of propagating libels against the government and religion. But the true reason seems to lie in the poverty of the country, as no printer could make a sufficient number of books for his subsistence; and another reason may be that France now has the profit arising from the exportation of books hither.

Food. The meals here are in many respects different from those in the English provinces. This depends upon the difference of custom, taste, and religion, between the two nations. French Canadians eat three meals a day, *viz.* breakfast, dinner and supper. They breakfast commonly between seven and eight, for the French here rise very early, and the governor-general can be seen at seven o'clock, the time when he has his levee. Some of the men dip a piece of bread in brandy and eat it; others take a dram of brandy and eat a piece of bread after it. Chocolate is likewise very common for breakfast, and many of the ladies drink coffee. Some eat no breakfast at all. I have never seen tea used here, perhaps because they can get coffee and chocolate from the French provinces in America, in the southern part, but must get tea from China. They consider it is not worth their while to send the money out of their country for it. I never saw them have bread and butter for breakfast. Dinner is exactly at noon. People of quality have a great many dishes and the rest follow their example, when they invite strangers. The loaves are oval and baked of wheat flour. For each person they put a plate, napkin, spoon and fork. (In the English colonies a napkin is seldom or never used). Sometimes they also provide knives, but they are generally omitted, all the ladies and gentlemen being provided with their own knives. The spoons and forks are of silver, and the plates of Delft ware. The meal begins with a soup with a good deal of bread in it. Then follow fresh meats of various kinds, boiled and roasted, poultry, or game, fricassees, ragouts, etc. of several sorts, together with different kinds of salads. They commonly drink red claret at dinner, either mixed with water or clear; and spruce beer is likewise much in use. The ladies drink water and sometimes wine. Each one has his own glass and can drink as much as he wishes, for the bottles are put on the table. Butter is seldom served, and if it is, it is chiefly for the guest present who likes it. But it is so fresh that one has to salt it at the table. The salt is white and finely powdered, though now and then a gray salt is used. After the main course is finished the table is always cleared. Finally the fruit and sweetmeats are served, which are of many different kinds, *viz.* walnuts from France or Canada, either ripe or pickled; almonds; raisins; hazel-nuts; several kinds of berries which are ripe in the summer season, such as currants, red and black, and cranberries which are preserved in treacle; many preserves in sugar, as strawberries, raspberries, blackberries, and mossberries. Cheese is likewise a part of the dessert, and so is milk, which they drink last of all, with sugar. Friday and Saturday, the "lean" days, they eat no meat according to the Roman Catholic rites; but they well know how to guard against hunger. On those days they boil all sorts of vegetables like peas, beans and cabbage, and fruit, fish, eggs, and milk are prepared in various ways. They cut cucumbers into slices and eat them with cream, which is a very good dish. Sometimes they put whole cucumbers on the table and everybody that likes them takes one, peels and slices it, and dips the slices into salt, eating them like radishes. Melons abound here and are always eaten without sugar. In brief, they live here just as well on Fridays and Saturdays, and I who am not a particular lover of meats would willingly have had all the days so-called lean days. There is always salt and pepper on the table. They never put any sugar into wine or brandy, and upon the whole they and the English do not use half so much sugar as we do in Sweden, though both nations have large sugar plantations in their West Indian possessions. They say no grace before or after their meals, but only cross themselves, a custom which is likewise omitted by some. Immediately after dinner they drink coffee without cream. Supper is commonly at seven o'clock, or between seven and eight at night, and the dishes the same as at dinner. Pudding is not seen here and neither is punch, the favorite drink of the Englishmen, though the Canadians know what it is.

August the 23rd

The "Poor Man's Horse". In many places hereabouts they use their dogs to fetch water out of the river. I saw two great dogs to-day attached to a little cart, one before the other. They had neat harnesses, like horses, and bits in their mouths. In the cart was a barrel. The dogs were directed by a boy, who ran behind the cart, and as soon as they came to the river they jumped in of their own accord. When the barrel was filled, the dogs drew their burden up the hill again to their house. I frequently saw dogs employed in this manner, during my stay at

Quebec. Sometimes they put but one dog before the watercart, which was made small on purpose. The dogs were not very large, hardly of the size of our common farmer's dogs. The boys that attended them had great whips with which they urged them on occasionally. I have seen them fetch not only water but also wood and other things. In winter it is customary in Canada, for travellers to put dogs before little sledges, made on purpose to hold their clothes, provisions, etc. Poor people commonly employ them on their winter journeys, and go on foot themselves. Almost all the wood, which the poorer people in this country fetch out of the woods in winter, is drawn by dogs, which have therefore got the name of "the poor man's horse". They commonly place a pair of dogs before each load of wood. I have likewise seen some neat little sledges for ladies to ride in, in winter. They are drawn by a span of dogs, and go faster on a good road than one would think. A middle-sized dog is sufficient to draw a single person when the roads are good. I have been told by old people that horses were very scarce here in their youth and almost all the transportation was then effected by dogs. Several Frenchmen who have been among the Esquimaux on Terra Labrador have assured me that they not only make use of dogs for drawing drays, with their provisions and other necessaries, but are likewise employed for pulling the men themselves in little sledges. [...]

August the 25th

Shipbuilding. They were now building several ships below Quebec, at the king's command. However, before my departure an order arrived from France prohibiting the further building of ships of war, except those which were already on the stocks; because they have found that the ships built of American oak did not last so long as those of the European variety. Near Quebec is found very little oak, and what grows there is not fit for use, being very small; therefore they are obliged to fetch their oak timber from those parts of Canada which border upon New England. But all the North American oaks have the quality of lasting longer and withstanding rot better the further north they grow, and *vice versa.* The timber from the confines of New England is brought in floats or rafts on the rivers near those parts and near St. Pierre which empty into the great St. Lawrence River. Some oak is likewise brought from the country between Montreal and Fort St. Frédéric, or Fort Champlain; but it is not held so good as the first, and the place it comes from is further distant. [...]

August the 29th

The Women of Canada. The ladies in Canada are generally of two kinds: those who come over from France, and those who are natives. The former possess the politeness peculiar to the French nation; the latter may be divided into those of Quebec and Montreal. The first of these are equal to the French ladies in good breeding, having the advantage of frequently conversing with the French gentlemen and ladies, who come every summer with the king's ships, and stay several weeks at Quebec, but seldom go to Montreal. The ladies of this last place are accused by the French of being contaminated by the pride and conceit of the Indians, and of being much wanting in French good breeding. What I have mentioned above[2] about their dressing their head too profusely is the case with all the ladies throughout Canada. Their hair is always curled, even when they are at home in a dirty jacket and a short coarse skirt that does not reach to the middle of their legs. On Sundays and visiting days they dress so gayly that one is almost induced to think their parents in origin and social position to be among the best in the realm. The Frenchmen, who consider things in their true light, complain very much that a great number of the ladies in Canada have gotten into the pernicious custom of taking too much care of their dress, and squandering all their fortune and more upon it, instead of sparing something for future times. They are no less attentive to having the newest fashion; the best and most expensive dresses are discarded and cut to pieces; and they smile inwardly when their sisters are not dressed according to their fancy. But what they get as new fashions are often old and discarded in France by the time they are adopted in Canada, for the ships come but once every year from abroad, and the people in Canada consider that as the new fashion for the whole year which the people on board brought with them or which they imposed upon them as new.

The ladies in Canada, and especially at Montreal, are very ready to laugh at any blunders strangers make in speaking; but they are very excusable. People laugh at what appears uncommon and ridiculous.[3] In Canada nobody ever hears the French language spoken by any one but Frenchmen, for strangers seldom come there, and the Indians are naturally too proud to learn French, and compel the French to learn their language. Therefore it naturally follows that the sensitive Canadian ladies cannot hear anything uncommon without laughing at it. One of the first questions they put to a stranger is whether he is married; the next, how he likes the ladies in the country, and whether he thinks them handsomer than those of his own country; and the third, whether he will take one home with him. There are some differences between the ladies of Quebec and those of Montreal; those of the latter place seemed to be generally handsomer than those of the former. The women seemed to me to be somewhat too free at Quebec, and of a more becoming modesty at Montreal. The ladies at Quebec, especially the unmarried ones, are not very industrious. A girl of eighteen is reckoned very poorly off if she cannot enumerate at least twenty lovers. These young ladies, especially those of a higher rank, get up at seven, and dress till nine, drinking their coffee at the same time. When they are dressed they place themselves near a window that opens into the street, take up some needlework and sew a stitch now and then; but turn their eyes into the street most of the time. When a young fellow comes in, whether they are acquainted with him or not, they immediately lay aside their work, sit down by him, and begin to chat, laugh, joke, and invent "double-entendres" and make their tongues go like a lark's wings; this is considered *avoir beaucoup d'esprit.* In this manner they frequently pass the whole day, leaving their mothers to do all the work in the house. In Montreal the girls are not quite so flighty, and more industrious. It is not uncommon to find them with the maid in the kitchen. They are always at their needle work or doing some necessary business in the house. They are likewise cheerful and content; and nobody can say that they lack either wit or charms. Their fault is that they think too well of themselves. However, the daughters of all ranks, without exception, go to market, buy watermelons, pumpkins, and other food and carry it home themselves. They rise as soon and go to bed as late as any of the people in the house. I have been assured that in general their fortunes are not great and are rendered still more scarce by the number of children and the small revenues in a house. The girls at Montreal are very much displeased that those at Quebec get husbands sooner than they. The reason for this is that many young gentlemen who come over from France with the ships are captured by the ladies at Quebec, and marry them; but as these gentlemen seldom go up to Montreal the girls there are not often so happy as those of the former place.

Notes

1 Probably Oneidas.—F.

2 See diary for July 25, 1749.

3 Apparently the Canadian ladies laughed at Kalm's French.

1755–1784: Exile Surmounted

BY NAOMI E.S. GRIFFITHS

The years of proscription, from 1755–64, were years of bitter trauma for the Acadian community. They were the years during which the authorities at Halifax attempted to enforce a policy of banishment and exile on all members of the Acadian community. They were the years when the Acadians were dispossessed of all rights to own land within Nova Scotia. The events of these years, whether labelled as "the deportation," "the time of exile," or "le grand dérangement," have become so central to the self-definition of later generations of Acadians that the reality of what actually happened has often been overlooked.[1] Yet the broad outlines of the cataclysm are clear enough. For more than a hundred years, the Acadians had been the dominant society of European descent within the territory covered by the present-day provinces of Nova Scotia, New Brunswick, and Prince Edward Island. In 1755 this pre-eminence was ended, never to be regained. It took more than seventy years for the Acadian population within the Maritimes to reach the level that it had been in the summer months before the boats left. When the numbers once more reached the pre-deportation level of some 20,000 people, the Acadian communities were to be found, geographically, politically and economically, in a very different situation than they had been in 1755. The policy carried out by Lawrence had both succeeded and failed. It had destroyed Acadian power but not Acadian identity.

Politically after 1755, the Acadian communities would be marginal, if not peripheral, to a majority made up of several collectivities of newcomers: above all to the Planters and the Scots in Nova Scotia, Cape Breton and Prince Edward Island, and to the Loyalists in New Brunswick. Economically, in the 1780s, the Acadian communities were primarily dependent on subsistence farming, fishing, and the lumber trade. Acadians never regained control of the rich lands of the Annapolis Valley, the Minas Basin, and the largest salt-marsh lands in the world, the Tantramar. Instead, significant Acadian communities were to be found much where they are now: on the northern sea shores of New Brunswick, in the upper Saint John River Valley, around the Petitcodiac and the Memramcook valleys, with a bare scattering of settlements around Cape Breton Island and St Mary's Bay in Nova Scotia, and on the northern shores of Prince Edward Island.[2] From 1755 onwards, the Acadians were a minority where they had once been a majority. They were a community often excluded from the norms of the political life of a broader polity of which they formed part,[3] and their legal rights to establish themselves in certain areas were often successfully challenged.[4] But from 1755 onwards, as in the years leading up to that date, the Acadians lived as a collectivity, as a people with a sense of their distinctiveness, as members of communities with specific and deeply held beliefs in their unique identity.

Naomi E.S. Griffiths, "1755–1784: Exile Surmounted," in *The Contexts of Acadian History, 1686–1784* (Montreal: McGill-Queen's University Press, 1992), 95–127.

Even when the sense of identity is despairing, a bitter cry of defeat and powerlessness in the face of an uncomprehending majority,[5] an Acadian sense of self endured.

But how did the Acadians survive as a distinct people? What are the connections, other than the purely genealogical, between the pre-deportation Acadian community and later manifestations of Acadian distinctiveness? What is the relationship between the Acadians who returned from exile after 1764 and the shattered remnants of the Acadian society that continued in the Maritimes after 1755, despite every effort of the authorities to complete the banishment of the Acadians. Many of the answers to these questions are to be found in the complexities of what exactly occurred between 1755 and 1763. First and foremost, the Acadian reaction to exile has to be understood. How was it that they did not disappear as a distinct people, that they did not end up by being assimilated into the societies of other British North American colonies or in France? How was it that a significant and important number of them, if by no means the majority, made their way back to Nova Scotia?

But the history of what actually occurred provides only part of the answer to questions of Acadian identity after 1755. A second part of the answer lies in the Acadians' interpretation of the deportation and its aftermath. By the end of the eighteenth century, a shared Acadian belief had evolved about why the deportation had occurred and what it had meant for the Acadian community. This belief was and is crucial for their continued existence as a separate people within New Brunswick, Nova Scotia, and Prince Edward Island. The Acadian history of the exile, as much as the history of the exile itself, needs to be examined. The Acadian interpretation of the deportation became the framework for the development of a rich and distinct identity in the nineteenth and twentieth century.

In the first instance, exile scattered the Acadians into the other British North American colonies from Massachusetts to Georgia. But this was only in the first instance. One of the most important factors which influenced the fate of the Acadians during their exile is that these were years of war. The places of exile were themselves embroiled, to a greater or lesser extent, in the Anglo-French battle for dominance of North America. What happened to the Acadians immediately on arrival in new lands was often only the beginning of their travails. The Acadians would nowhere find the conditions of their exile stable and unchanging. For many Acadians the deportation meant far-ranging voyages, quite beyond anything imagined by those who had supervised their embarkation in Nova Scotia.

For example, a number of those sent to Maryland, South Carolina, and Georgia went on to Santo Domingo and some of these journeyed to either Louisiana or British Honduras. Others first landed in Massachusetts but after 1763 went to the banks of the St Lawrence. Some voyaged to the Channel Islands and then to the islands of St Pierre and Miquelon. Most of those who were first landed in Virginia were sent on to England and then to France. Many of those who survived this trek sailed from Nantes in 1785 for Louisiana at the expense of Spain, whose territory Louisiana then was.

There is as yet no single-volume history of the Acadian experiences in exile during the years 1755–84, from the deportation to a time when an Acadian community can be considered to have achieved, once more, a legitimacy in the territory, if not on the actual lands, previously settled by their ancestors. There are a considerable number of works which either relate the whole story of some particular group of Acadians or some part of the experiences of most of the exiles. Works such as Emile Lauvrière's *La tragédie d'un peuple*[6] give an overview of what occurred. Others, such as O.W. Winzerling's *Acadian Odyssey*,[7] and the more recent work by William Faulkner Rushton,[8] both of which are concerned with the history of how the majority of Acadians that reached Louisiana did so, concentrate on events that only some of the Acadian exiles experienced.[9] Few works have attempted to discuss the available information in order to answer wide-ranging questions about how various jurisdictions dealt with the Acadians on their arrival or what impact exile had on the Acadian sense of identity. The widely scattered nature of the sources available, both for the North American narrative and for the more far-ranging paths of exile (resources which include the Vatican archives[10] and the graveyards of British Honduras[11]), has understandably tended to encourage the writing of the more restricted accounts of a particular local group. Even the magnificent work of collection which has been undertaken by the Centre d'études acadiennes, at the Université de Moncton, has not yet gathered all known archival deposits. In sum, the history of the Acadians during exile has been recorded either in broad but shallow overviews or narrow but detailed accounts.

The very strength of those incidents of the exile that have entered public knowledge has overshadowed the intricate reality of the exile as a whole, in much the same way as the episode of the deportation itself has thrown so very much of Acadian experience into shadow. Longfellow's poem *Evangeline,* for example, has led many to believe that the deportation of the Acadians entailed the wholesale and deliberate separation of close-knit families, as well as the removal of the whole community directly to Louisiana.[12] The incompatibility of these two ideas is not often noticed. Both remain powerful images of the deportation and both have enough connection with reality to make them enduring myths.

In fact, no one was deported *directly* from Nova Scotia to Louisiana, for, in 1755 Louisiana was Spanish territory and the Acadians were destined for the British North American colonies from Massachusetts to Georgia.[13] As noted already, the majority of those Acadians who did reach Louisiana were those who had initially landed in Virginia.[14] There were some Acadians who, having been landed in South Carolina, made their way by land to the mouth of Mississippi, although the most used "other route" was via Santo Domingo.[15] The essential plot of Longfellow's poem could have happened and perhaps did. Longfellow heard of the story from an Acadian who was a serving maid, and the legend of lovers parted by the deportation to meet only as death strikes one of them is found in varying forms among several groups of people whose ancestors were Acadian. As suggested already, the years of exile were years of wandering, not years of stability. However inaccurate the detail of incident in the work of this American poet, there is an essential element of truth: the deportation meant the end of a way of life and, for many, the need to construct the pattern of the days in a foreign land.

Similarly, the popular image of the separation of loved ones is both true and false. The break-up of communities was a calculated part of the deportation but, as will be seen in a moment, the separation of closely connected groups was not part of the original plan and was rarely deliberate. As has been noted, when the decision was made to deport, Colonel Lawrence and those associated with him were well aware of the danger of adding to the strength of France in North America. It was for this reason above all that it was decided to split up the various settlements and divide them among the British colonies in North America. To repeat the words of Lawrence again, it was agreed "to divide them [the Acadians] among the Colonies....and as they cannot easily collect themselves together again it will be out of their power to do any mischief."[16]

Very detailed plans were drawn up to organise the deportation, based largely on the work of surveyor Charles Morris, elaborated by the lieutenant-governor and other members of council.[17] Each major collection of Acadian villages was to be divided up among several colonies. It bears repeating that the Acadians deported from Nova Scotia in 1755, who constituted the vast majority of those sent into exile between 1755 and 1763, *without exception* had as their appointed destination one of the British colonies in North America. The instructions sent to Lieutenant-Colonel Winslow, who would be in charge of the removal of the Acadians from the Grand-Pré, instructed him to ship "To North Carolina... Five hundred persons or thereabouts...to Virginia... one thousand persons;... To Maryland... Five hundred persons."[18] Major Handfield, who was in charge of deporting those who were to be removed from the Annapolis Valley, was ordered that the community was to be divided approximately as follows: 300 persons to Philadelphia; 200 persons to New York; 300, to Connecticut; 200, to Boston.[19] The instructions to Colonel Moncton, who was in charge of the Chignecto Isthmus, were to divide those deported as follows: "528 [persons] to Georgia; 1020 to South Carolina and 392 to Philadelphia."[20]

This division of the Acadians can be seen as characteristic of the deportation: it was conceived as a military tactic and designed to mean the end of the Acadian community. It was an act of war. It was not, however, a policy aimed at the extermination of the individual; it was not a "Final Solution" bred out of the madness of racial hatred. It was an action comparable to the Highland Clearances. There was no deliberate intention in the plan itself to separate nuclear families, to divide husband and wife, parents and children. In fact, during most of the embarkation proceedings, special efforts were made by Winslow and some of the other officers to bring parents and children together.[21] At the same time, however, there was no attempt to keep the extended family together, as can be seen from cases such as that of René Leblanc, the notary who was landed with his wife and two of his youngest children in New York, with the rest of the family being sent on to Philadelphia.[22]

But it is important to remark that the plan sketched above was only a plan. It was carried out with all the mishaps and bungling which attend most large-scale human endeavours. Those carrying it out found that it was subject to modification in many details. Most of the changes increased the distress of the Acadians. Some changes were made because certain of the Acadians proved much more recalcitrant than had been expected. For example, some eighty-six men who had been held in Fort Lawrence awaiting the arrival of the ships, "got away...by making a Hole under ground from the Barrack through the South Curtain above thirty feet."[23] Further, as the months passed, Lawrence became impatient and ordered his officers to be more zealous in getting the ships away, and hence to take less account of embarking the men with their families.[24] Yet other changes came about because of the difficulty of organizing and provisioning the transports.[25] Perhaps the most devastating changes came because of the weather, which delayed embarkations and then blew many ships from their approved destinations.[26]

The deportation destroyed a way of life and broke a close-knit kin group into fragments, but it was no massacre. Yet limited horror and controlled disaster are horror and disaster nonetheless. Those who survived the voyage often found on disembarkation that their distress had only just begun. The initial separation from neighbours and the break-up of the extended family was often immediately compounded once disembarked. The authorities frequently then split the Acadians into their nuclear families of five to eleven persons in order to ensure that the newcomers would constitute no danger to public order, and to provide for the support of the Acadians according to the norms these polities had evolved for the sustenance of their own sick and poor.

These policies towards the Acadians were adopted in haste by the various colonies. In most cases, the first the new hosts of the Acadians knew about the deportation was on the delivery of a letter when a shipload of exiles arrived in the major colonial port, whether that was Boston, Massachusetts; Annapolis, Maryland; Columbia, South Carolina; Savannah, Georgia; or some other port. The captains of the ships on which the exiles left carried a copy of the circular from Lawrence to the "Governors on the continent," dated 11 August 1755. None of the colonies had received any previous official notification, let alone been consulted, about the deportation. Thus, the general pattern of the Acadians' reception was that of an administration having to make some immediate provisions to house and feed unexpected and unwelcome newcomers.

On arrival, therefore, the Acadians were the subject of extensive official discussions and much public scrutiny. They were immediately recognized everywhere as a distinct people: they were unexpected refugees, they spoke French, they were Catholic, and they were in desperate need of succour after the long sea voyage. None of the authorities, whose charge they now were, knew whether to greet them as fellow subjects of the British Crown, removed from a battle zone, prisoners-of-war, "neutrals," or—as Governor Dinwiddie of Virginia wrote to Governor Shirley of Massachusetts—"intestine Enemies."[27] In Pennsylvania the Acadians were considered, and accorded treatment, as "Subjects of Great Britain,"[28] while in South Carolina their treatment wavered between that accorded prisoners-of-war and that which would be given to "natural-born subjects of the Crown" who were yet in need of surveillance.[29] The Acadians were certainly seen as different from those among whom they had been sent to live. And this distinctiveness was further emphasized at the outset by the poor physical condition of the Acadians on arrival. The ill-health of the Acadians meant that the authorities had to intervene decisively and immediately on their behalf. Without exception, all colonies had to set about provisioning the exiles, coping with the impact on them of typhoid and small-pox, and deciding whether they permitted them to land, as did Massachusetts, or to keep them temporarily on board ship, as did Pennsylvania, Virginia, and Georgia.[30]

The debate about what should happen next to the exiles was considerably influenced by how sharply the colony felt the threat of the coming hostilities, for by the fall of 1755 there was no longer any question that a formal declaration of war would very soon regularize the fighting of England and France. If Nova Scotia saw danger in the presence of French-speaking Catholics, the other colonies were equally as aware of the possibility of the Acadians giving aid and comfort to the French cause. The Governors of the differing jurisdictions wrote to one another in great perturbation. Governor Belcher[31] of New Jersey expressed a common view in his letter to Governor Morris of Pennsylvania dated 25 November 1755. "I am, Sir," he wrote, "truly surprised how it would ever enter into the thoughts of those, who had the ordering of the French Neutrals, or rather Traitors and Rebels to the Crown of Great Britain, to direct any of them into these Provinces where we have already too great a number of foreigners for our own good and safety." He was of the opinion that the Acadians "should have been transported already to old France."[32] In Massachusetts, a petition to the governor in February of 1756 complained that about 1,000 Acadians had been landed in the Commonwealth, all in great want and distress, and that "the receiving among us so great a Number of Persons whose gross Bigotry to the Roman Catholick Religion is notorious and whose Loyalty to His Majesty Louis XV is a thing very disagreeable to us."[33] Even in colonies where there was an immediate expression of sympathy for the bereft, there was also wariness and fear. *The Maryland Gazette* of December 1755 remarked: "Sunday Last [Nov 30th] arrived here the last of the vessels from Nova Scotia with French neutrals for this place, which make four within this fortnight who have brought upwards of 900 of them. As the poor people have been deprived of their settlements in Nova Scotia, and sent here for some very political reason bare and destitute Christian charity, nay common humanity, calls upon everyone according to their ability to lend their help and assistance to these objects of compassion."[34] Considerable concern was also expressed, however, that the Acadians would prove to be spies. The first act which Maryland passed on their account was one in May 1756 to keep them from witnessing any training manoeuvres.[35]

There were some common characteristics in the reception of the Acadians by the governments of the varying colonies on arrival, although the provisions then made for the exiles varied. In general, the exiles were put in the charge of those responsible for the poor of the colony, and distributed, in small groups, throughout the colony in question. As might be expected, colonies north of, and including, Pennsylvania took greater pains to circumscribe the exiles than did the colonies to the south, Maryland, for example, or the Carolinas and Georgia. The actions of the Commonwealth of Massachusetts were followed, to a greater or lesser extent, by Connecticut, New York, and Pennsylvania. A first step taken by the commonwealth was not followed by any other jurisdiction, however. Lawrence was advised, in November 1755, that Massachusetts expected to be reimbursed for any money spent on the Acadians.[36] No other jurisdiction, to my knowledge, took this path. As a second step, the commonwealth passed an act on 16 December 1755 to cope "with divers of the Inhabitants and Families in Nova Scotia...sent by the Government...to prevent their suffering by sickness and Famine."[37] By its provisions, a committee was brought into being to organize the immediate supply of food and shelter to the Acadians. Once the immediate needs of the Acadians were met, the commonwealth endeavoured to disperse them among various towns and villages of the colony in order that no danger could arise from the exiles gathering together and threatening public safety. Thus, on 27 December 1755, another act was passed which provided for the dispersal of the Acadian families among "several towns" and the binding out of children as servants and apprentices.[38]

There was an immediate outcry against this practice from the Acadians. They organized petitions to Governor Hutchinson, one of which reads in part: "La prève que nous avons souffrir de nos habitations et a mene ici et Nos Separations les Uns les autres n'est Rien a compare a Cell que de prendre Nos Enfans devant nos yex: La Nature meme ne peut souffrir cela."[39] As a result of this and similar petitions,[40] a committee was appointed by the Council of Massachusetts to look into the matter. The report, which they made within two days, and which was concurred in by Council on the day it was presented, recommended that "Selectmen or Overseers should desist binding them out."[41]

The people of Massachusetts, in the words of Doughty, "Loved not Catholics and Frenchmen,"[42] but they were affected by the distress of the Acadians, even though they feared both the expense they would incur on their behalf and the danger that the Acadians might prove to the commonwealth. By June 1756 the roaming of Acadians about Massachusetts, in search of relatives and friends, led to an investigation.[43] On 11 August 1756 an act was proposed "for the better ordering of the late inhabitants of Nova Scotia," which made the penalty for such wanderings "imprisonment and return to their district."[44]

The more time passed the more complicated the problem became. By mid-summer 1756, Massachusetts had not only to cope with those Acadians who had been directly sent to her shores but also had news that "ninety of the French inhabitants of Nova Scotia having coasted along shore from Georgia and South Carolina...had put into harbour in the southern part of this province."[45] An attempt was made to put an end to such voyagings, as well as to the comings and goings of Acadians within the commonwealth. The records show remarkably little success. Repeated acts and resolutions of the colony's administration reveal a continuing problem, part of it caused by humanitarian reactions. Some voyagings were permitted as Acadian petitions to be allowed to join with relatives were granted.[46] In January, Dedham's answer to a request as to the whereabouts of the Acadians ends with the sentence: "There is another girl who is sometimes here and sometimes not."[47]

On 13 August 1757 the commonwealth made yet another effort to deal directly with the security problem posed by the Acadians who wandered their towns and villages. A circular was issued to all sheriffs, under-sheriffs or deputies, pointing out that "there may be great Danger in allowing the French people, late Inhabitants of Nova Scotia, too great a Liberty at this critical Juncture."[48] But nothing really changed. In 1759, General Wolfe was complaining that "some of the said Nova Scotians have deserted the Province and gone to Canada,"[49] and he demanded a closer surveillance of them. As a result, one more survey was undertaken which reported as follows:[50]

January 25th, 1760:	
Acadians able to Labour	304
Incapable by reasons of old age, 50 and up	61
Incapable by reasons of Sickness	107
Children under 7	240
Children capable of being put out from 7 to 14	187
Employed in attending and nursing sick	28
	947 [sic]

As was to be expected, considering the resolution that had been made when the Acadians first arrived, Massachusetts kept accounts of the cost of their support. For the year 1759 it was calculated as £1478 2s. 9d. Over the years more than one community complained, as did Salem, that "by reason of this addition of Neutrals, the poor of our Town are kept out of the almshouse."[51] The sort of support that the Acadians received is typified by the records of Medway, which spent £711s. 3d. to support nine people from 28 October 1756 to 7 March 1757. The full report reads as follows:[52]

	£	s	d
To House Rent for One Family from October 28th, 1756 to March 7th, 1757		2	8
To nine Bushels of rye meal	1	10	
To nine Bushels and one half of Indian mealand corn	1	2	9½
To 286 pounds of Beef	1	18	1½
To 64 pounds of Pork		8	6½
To 32 pounds of cheese		5	9
To 3 pounds of Butter		1	10
To 8 pounds of Mutton		1	1
To 10 gallons of milk		4	6
To 13 loads of wood		13	
To half a bushel and a peck of Salt		1	9
To Bread		4	
To five gallons of Cyder		1	2½
To 2 pounds of wool		4	8
To mending a pot		8	
To a wheel and an Axe		16	8
To Mr. John Thibault for Trouble as an Interpreter			8
	7	11 [sic]	3

The nine persons above mentioned the head of the family...aged 53, his wife 48, they are not well and healthy, not capable of constant labour; their eldest son aged 28, his wife, 23, well and healthy, the next son aged 20 and healthy, the next son aged 16 has been poor and weakly, the next aged 13, next aged 9, the

> youngest son aged 6, the four last mentioned are small and not capable of doing much for their support. The men are all fishermen. They can handle an axe But do not understand our common husbandry; By reason thereof we can't find 'em Constant Labour.

The final bill for the monies spent by Massachusetts for the support of the Acadians was computed in September of 1762 as £6,000 and by August of 1763 as £9,563 9s. 10d.[53] As far as I know, these accounts were never paid.

But while the archives of Massachusetts are full of evidence concerning the expenditures of the commonwealth on the Acadians, that is really the least part of the matter. The decision to deport the Acadians might have seemed a swift and simple solution to a longstanding and thorny problem to the Governor's Council in Halifax in 1755, but its outcome was an exacerbation difficulties for other British colonial administrations in North America and a calvary for the Acadians. In truth, the deportation was a matter of perplexity and confusion for the officials of the colonies to which they were sent, as much as for the Acadians themselves. Further, all involved would find that the repercussions of the policy did not end with Peace of Paris in 1763. In January 1764, Bernard, then Governor of Massachusetts, wrote to the House of Representatives, on the occasion of an epidemic of small-pox in the colony:[54] "The case of these people [the Acadians] is truly deplorable. They have none of them had the small-pox and they depend upon their daily labour for their bread. If they don't go about town they must starve; if they do go about they contract the distemper, and as they are crowded in small apartments and wanting the necessaries of life, they must have a common chance to escape perishing.... I am therefore obliged to apply to you to help to save these people." Some measures were taken to lessen the misery of the Acadians, but their circumstances continued to be pitiable.[55]

In the summer of 1764 there seemed to be a possibility for a new and better life for the exiles, albeit in very foreign circumstances. An invitation was made "to all the Acadians residing in New England" to go to Santo Domingo where they "shall have grants of land made to them and they shall be maintained by the King [Louis XVI] during the first months of their abode."[56] Bernard was much against this. In January of 1765, he sent a message to the House of Representatives that he had been informed that "the Acadians belonging to this province were going hence in large numbers to form a settlement in French Hispaniola." He continued: "Their case is truly pitiable; if they go to Hispaniola they run into certain destruction very few escaping with life, the Effects of the bad climate there and yet they have no Encouragement in this Country; Humanity more than Policy makes me desirous to prevent the remainder of them taking this fateful voyage; I want not so much to make them British subjects as to keep them from perishing."[57]

At least some Acadians reacted bitterly to this well-meant paternalism. They informed the governor that "for nine years we have lived in hopes of joining our Country men and it seems to us that you have caused a door which was open to be shut upon us. We have always understood that in times of Peace and in all countries the prison doors are open to Prisoners. It is therefore astonishing to us, Sir, to be detained here.... This is very hard upon us. It is hard to reflect upon our Present situation, to see ourselves by one sudden blow rendered incapable of affording ourselves relief."[58] The governor's desires, however, prevented them leaving.

One scheme might have been thwarted, but another avenue opened. In the spring of 1766 Governor Murray of Quebec wrote to Governor Bernard suggesting that under certain circumstances the Acadians might be settled in his province "for the Good of the British Empire."[59] By 2 June, some 890 Acadians had agreed to be transported to the banks of the St Lawrence. The *Quebec Gazette* of 1 September 1766 reported the arrival of a sloop from Boston with "forty Acadians who, for the Benefit of their Religion, are come here to settle." On Monday 8 September, 1766 "At the Council Chamber in the Castle of St. Louis in the City of Quebec"[60] an order was given to provide one month's supplies to some ninety Acadians, men, women and children.

After this date, information in Massachusetts archives about the Acadians dwindles. In 1766, eleven years after the first Acadian exiles arrive in Boston harbour, noticeable numbers begin to depart. How many made their way back to Nova Scotia is debatable and will be considered later in this chapter. For present purposes, suffice it to say that the Acadians who were sent to Massachusetts were treated as some peculiar form of prisoners-of-war, although such a status was never officially accorded them. Since the majority of the Acadians had been born since 1713, on British territory, there was grave doubt as to what their legal rights might be. The question of subjecthood and citizenship is complex enough in the eighteenth century, whether the state be France, England, or a British North American colony. The rights of non-juring, native-born subjects posed a sufficient conundrum to colonial officials to make them cautious in their treatment of the Acadians. The Acadians were convinced that, if they were prisoners-of-war, then they should be treated as such: confined as a group, provided for by their enemy. If they were other than prisoners-of-war, then the limits placed on their freedom were utterly without justification. In either case, in Acadian eyes, forced separation of parents and children was monstrous. Massachusetts avoided any final pronouncement on the matter of Acadian legal status, referring to Acadians whenever possible as "inhabitants of Nova Scotia" or "exiles from Nova Scotia." The binding out of children, however, was halted. In the final analysis, however, whatever rights the Acadians might have had, their situation in Massachusetts was one of poverty, sickness, and limited freedom of movement. Their final disposition was as arbitrary as much of their treatment had been: a gradual and relatively unrecorded dispersal to destinations out of province.

From Massachusetts to Pennsylvania the governors, councils, and assemblies received the Acadians with considerable displeasure but made some sort of provision for their subsistence and something of an effort to keep them under surveillance until 1763. All these more northerly colonies attempted a distribution of the exiles among different towns and villages in order both to minimise the impact of the exiles on the public purse of any particular settlement and to prevent any conspiracy of the Acadians against their hosts. New York received some five hundred of the exiles and by 9 July 1756, had passed an act empowering the justices "to bind out such of his Majesty's Subjects, commonly called Neutral French...to the End that they may not continue, as they now really are, useless to his Majesty, themselves and a burden on the Colony."[61] The justices were further urged to treat "the said people committed to their Care, with all the Justice in their Power, observing to make the most favourable contracts for them."[62]

Connecticut received perhaps 400.[63] They were divided into groups of no more than seventeen persons, and usually of only six or seven, and the groups were distributed among fifty different settlements throughout that colony.[64] In 1760 there is a report that about twenty-two vessels arrived in Boston from Connecticut and were refused permission to land the Acadians they had on board.[65] The next destination of these Acadians would almost certainly have been Santo Domingo.

The history of the Acadians who went to the Caribbean is difficult to piece together. What is known at present can be summarized as follows. The Caribbean was, in every case, the exiles' second destination. In some cases, it was their third or fourth halt.[66] According to present knowledge, some 418 left from New York for Santo Domingo in 1764 and of these, 231 left in 1765 for Louisiana. In 1765, another 600 are reported as arriving in the Caribbean from "Acadie." It was thought they had been encouraged to do so by the English.[67] Parish registers indicate that the "Acadians were decimated by disease during the first months following their arrival."[68] What happened to them after that is a matter of debate. A large number went on to Louisiana, with either French or Spanish government aid. But there is no doubt that others remained, and in 1770 Acadians are still recorded in the records of Martinique, Guadaloupe, and Santo Domingo. In the mid-1820s a French government enquiry was undertaken for purposes of indemnifying former planters of Santo Domingo who had suffered losses during the Revolutionary year.[69]

Only six Acadian names appear on this list.[70] In sum, the Acadians can be distinguished in the records of Santo Domingo from 1764 until 1790. After that date, information about them is sparse indeed.

To return to the experiences of the exiles in their places of first landing, the number sent directly to Pennsylvania does not seem to have been much more than that sent to New York and Connecticut. But the plight of the exiles seems to have produced much more concern among the legislators and leading men there than anywhere else except France. Approximately 400 Acadians were landed in Pennsylvania on December 1755.[71] The governor requested an immediate opinion of his council as to what should be done with them.[72] It was not until the spring of 1756 that Benjamin Franklin received the commission as the printer of the act for "dispersing the Inhabitants of Nova Scotia, imported into this Province, into the several Counties of Philadelphia."[73] The act made provisions much like those of Massachusetts, placing the Acadians in the hands of the overseers of the poor, but it added to the powers the command to settle the Acadians on farming families.[74] By January 1757, Pennsylvania had decided to follow the procedure of Massachusetts and bind out children, while continuing to make provision for the "aged, sick and maimed at the charge of the province."[75] The Acadians reacted as they had in Massachusetts: they wrote petitions saying that the law should be revoked. In one petition it was stated that "to separate innocent Children who have committed no Crime from their Parents appears contrary to the Precept of Jesus Christ."[76] This particular petition ended with the point that the Acadians should be permitted to depart as soon as they were able if they would give assurance that they would not join the French. "If we had inclined to War," they claimed, "we should have been still perhaps in our own Country."[77]

The records of the province show that binding out was halted and that the Acadians were supported "in great Measure by private Charities, whence they are become extremely burdensome to the well-disposed Inhabitants."[78] In 1760 an Acadian petition was sent to the Penn brothers in London, accompanied by a covering letter signed by several of Philadelphia's leading men. Pemberton, Hantin, Emton, and others wrote that the Acadians had been struck by all manner of diseases, but above all by smallpox. "Those who have survived," the letter continued, "have flattered themselves with a hope that at the End of the Warr, they should be restored to their former Possessions, which we conceive, arises in part from a Consciousness that they were dispossessed out of Political Considerations rather than by way of Punishment for any Offence."[79]

Pennsylvania records fall silent after this point until 1771 when an account was made of some twenty-two families still in Philadelphia, most of them burdened with sickness of one kind or another.[80] This account is very different from the contemporary accounts of the Acadians in Massachusetts during the 1760s, or from the comparable reports from France at the opening of the 1770s, when officials in both places counted up to ten children a family. The Philadelphia list is filled with details of the blind, of sick children, of children that were "Foolish." In general a picture is painted of the very depths of misery. Apart from the records of death, there is no clear indication in the archives of Pennsylvania whether the fate of those Acadians sent there led back to Nova Scotia or southward to the Caribbean and to Louisiana.

Maryland and colonies further south did not allow the Acadians complete freedom of movement, but the attempts of these colonies to circumscribe Acadian activities were less efficient and less long-lasting than the efforts of the more northerly colonies. As has been noted, the immediate response of Maryland to the Acadians was a mixture of fear and compassion, with fear predominating. The Act already cited, which banned them from witnessing any training manoeuvres, was followed five days later by an act to empower the justices of the county courts to make provision for the Acadians, who were to be dispersed through various settlements.[81] By 1757 various county supervisors were asking for help from the authorities at Annapolis. Talbot County commissioners reported that the Acadians "are become a grievance; inasmuch as we are not at present in a Situation and in a Circumstance capable of seconding their own Fruitless Endeavours to support their numerous families, as a People Plunder'd of their Effects: for tho' perhaps our Magistrates have taxed us, perhaps sufficient to feed such of them as cannot feed themselves, they cannot find Houses, Cloathing and other Comforts, in their Condition needful, without going from House to House Begging."[82]

By 1763 Maryland records show that about one-third of those landed in 1755 had died or emigrated.[83] In 1765 a petition by the Acadians was presented to the Justices of the Peace of Cecil County, asking for help to leave for the Mississippi.[84] Some ships did leave for this destination two years later. The *Maryland Gazette* reported that the schooner *Virgin* with some Acadians aboard cleared Annapolis in 1767.[85] But reports show that the passengers of this ship almost certainly ended up in Sante Fe.[86] The story of the Acadians sent to Maryland dwindles into the occasional genealogical detail and the fate of the majority becomes, once more, a matter for conjecture.

Once south of Maryland, the treatment meted out to the Acadians becomes even less uniform. As has been noted, Virginia exported the problem one more time. This colony introduced a bill into its House of Burgesses on 1 April 1756 to "enable certain persons to contract for the Transportation of the Neutral French to Great Britain."[87] The cost was about £5000.[88] North and South Carolina and Georgia kept less than total control of the exiles that came their way. North Carolina, in fact, had no Acadians actually destined for her shores. However, in Cape Few, on 22 April 1756, one Jacques Morris appeared: "on behalf of himself and one hundred French, being part of the French Neutrals sent to Georgia and come coastwise in small boats, having a pass for himself from Governor Reynolds [Georgia] and Governor Glen [South Carolina]."[89]

The exiles were allowed to continue north. There is considerable debate about whether any particular group that left a southern colony was the one which is reported as being held in custody in a more northerly jurisdiction. It is, however, probable that this group made it as far as New York.[90]

South Carolina received more than 1,000 Acadians.[91] The policy evolved in Charleston was a combination of the actions of Massachusetts, but with occasional forced labour, and the dispatch of a few families to England.[92] In general, however, exiles to this colony had their lives regulated by the legislation of 6 July 1756; this was entitled "An Act for disposing of the Acadians now in Charleston, by settling some fifth part of their number in the parishes of St. Philip and St. Michele and the four other parts of them in the other Parishes within this Province."[93] On 14 November 1755, Georgia received notice that Acadians had arrived. There was "great Confusion and Consternation"[94] and no coherent policy of any sort emerged from the discussions of governor and council. There were perhaps 600 to 700 Acadians in Savannah at any one time, and some of them were provided with boats and allowed to attempt the journey back. Lawrence was writing indignantly to the Board of Trade in August 1756 that "French Inhabitants sent to Ga...have been assisted at the Public Expense and are making for Nova Scotia."[95] Georgia did not manage to draft an act for "providing and disposing of the Acadians now in this province" until February 1757. At that point the provisions were similar to those of Massachusetts: the Acadians were divided among the townships and power was given to the Justices of the Peace to bind out the healthy into labour.[96]

The general impression one has of the deportation and years of exile is of the misery and distress of the Acadians. The entry for 8 October 1755 in Capt. Winslow's diary reads, "began to Embark the Inhabitants who went off Very Solentarily and unwillingly, the women in Great Distress Carrying off their children in their Arms, Others Carrying their Decript Parents in their Carts and all their Goods moving in Great Confusion and it appeared a scene of Woe and Distress."[97] His words are vivid and he is reporting a scene of human suffering accurately. But these words are utterly inadequate as a summary of Acadian reaction to what occurred. After all, the Acadians *survived* deportation and exile. Not only do some descendants of those loaded on the ships live as a coherent group in the Maritimes today, but others live as part of a coherent community which was established some 2,000 miles south. A 1930s survey of French-speaking peoples in the southern part of the state of Louisiana noted that "out of 120 families...[there were] 108 reporting lines of descent on both sides as French...11 families reporting the use of both French and English in the home but French was the language stated to be most commonly used...solidly Catholic in religion, not a single exception to be found... [further] 72 of the families have as their nearest neighbour...the family of a some relative...[and this report] takes no account of relationships more remote than first cousin."[98]

The Acadians were nowhere merely passive recipients of the policies imposed on them by others. Even during the process of embarkation, some Acadian communities were able successfully to resist the plans for their exile. Once disembarked in new lands, the exiles continued to behave as if they were much more than just a body of refugees, or victims of war, and began to act with considerable political acumen. As soon as the Acadians had made even a minimal adaption to their new situation, they gathered their wits and wrote, or employed the local legal talent to write, petitions which set forth the totally unjustified nature of the punishment they had suffered and requested a variety of alterations in their situation.[99] This motif, that the deportation was basically unjust, is present no matter where the petitioners were and irrespective of whether the petition in question was made by an individual asking for consideration of a specific wrong, or by a group aimed at righting a more general wrong. Whether the petitions were written to the authorities of the British colonies in North America, to the British authorities in London by those Acadians sent abroad by Virginia, to the French authorities by the Acadians who arrived there between 1758 and 1764, or to the Spanish authorities at the time of the removal of Acadians from France to Louisiana in 1785, the tenor of the petitions is similar: for various and particular reasons, the deportation was unjustified and the authorities were asked to do something about the unfortunate situation in which the Acadians now found themselves.[100]

It is fascinating to compare the way in which this belief—that the deportation was a matter of singular injustice—was expressed to the different jurisdictions. In North America, of course, such petitions often contained assertions of past loyalty to British interests. For example, Joseph Michelle, in a protest sent to Governor Shirley of Massachusetts about the way in which his son was treated, remarked that he and his family had "been employed in repairing the forts at Annapolis, as an overseer of all Carts in bringing up Timber which I was obliged to do in the Night Time for fear of the Indians where I and my family run the risk of our Lives."[101] Similarly, in a handbill circulated in Philadelphia in 1758, the Acadians asserted "Almost numberless are the Instances which might be given to the Abuses and Losses we have undergone from the French and the Indians, only on account of our adherence to our Oath of Fidelity."[102]

Those Acadians whose exile took them to England and to France also petitioned about the conditions under which they lived and the payment of the government support which both countries accorded them. In neither country were the Acadians over-awed by the status of those whose business it was to oversee their lives. The Acadians who arrived in England did so in early summer 1756. They are reported as numbering over 1,044.[103] They remained in England for nearly seven years and never hesitated to dispute measures that the British government took towards them. As peace approached in 1763, steps were taken to ask those Acadians then living in Liverpool, Southampton, Penryn, Falmouth, and Bristol what they hoped for. In no uncertain terms, the Acadians demanded that they be returned to Acadia. "We hope We shall be sent into Our Countries," their petition noted, "and that our Effects etc., which We have been dispossessed of (notwithstanding the faithful neutrality which We have always observed) will be restored to Us."[104] That these views were ignored does not alter the fact that those who expressed them had a clear idea of what their future should be. The immediate fate of these particular Acadians was to be shipped to France in the summer of 1763. They were fewer than the number that had arrived from Virginia, being in total no more than 866.[105]

These were by no means the first Acadians to arrive in France.[106] As early as 1749 an English vessel was reported as arriving at Nantes with "Acadians" from Louisbourg.[107] Almost ten years later, in 1758, separate arrivals were reported at Boulogne, Brest, Cherbourg, and St Malo; in 1759, further listings are given for ships arriving at Boulogne, Dunkerque, and St Malo; in 1760 there is a listing for Cherbourg; in 1761 for Rochefort; and in 1763 for Marlaix.[108] The numbers are difficult to establish. I would estimate that, including those sent on from England, there were some 3,000 Acadians in France at the end of 1763.

Their attitude towards French officialdom was as trenchant as it had been to English bureaucracy. The first reply of the exiles to French proposals for their settlement in Belle-Ile-en-Mer, a small island off the south coast of Brittany, was less than grateful. In the Acadians' view, the land was poor, and the island far too near English power for comfort.[109] This response set the tone for much of the future interaction between the Acadians and French authorities. The two major attempts at resettlement, at Belle Ile and at "La ligne acadienne" in Poitou, both failed.[110] The majority of the Acadians left France in 1785 for Louisiana.[111]

At first sight, this seems surprising. Acadians were, after all, French-speaking Catholics: there was at least a supposition of commonalty of interest with the French nation, and one of the proposed sites for their resettlement was in a part of France from which many of their ancestors had emigrated. Superficially, having been given considerable aid from the French government and having had the experience of exile in British communities, assimilation into eighteenth-century France would appear a distinct possibility. But this did not happen: the Acadians were French-speaking and Catholic, but they were also North American. The norms of the Acadians during the twenty years they spent in France were dominated by the Acadian identity that had been forged in "Acadia or Nova Scotia." They did not prove malleable to French influence. Some reasons for this are suggested in a letter by a lawyer of Dinan in 1759 to the naval commissioner at St Malo, asking help for the twenty-two Acadians he had established on his own farm.[112] He wrote in part as follows: "Premierement ses peuples sont elévés dans un pays d'abondance, de terres a discretion, par consequent moins difficile a cultiver...de plus les hommes...ressentent déjà les chaleurs quoy aye point encore sensibles pour nous, ils mannient un peu la hache pour logement et assez mal quelques chose a leurs usages, ce qu'on n'appeller que hacheur des bois, les femmes filent un peu des bas." According to this same source, the Acadians wanted a great deal of bread, demanded milk and butter, and would not be weaned to cider: the desire for North American foodstuffs had replaced an appetite for French staples.

But material customs, however, are only a part—if an important part—of the life of a distinct community. The Acadians confronted not merely a different agricultural environment but a fundamentally different social and political context. As was shown very early on in the Belle Ile experiment, the Acadians were not used to the structured organization of eighteenth-century French bureaucracy.[113] Acadians did not like tithes, bitterly resented the idea that they should stay in one place, and found little in common with their new neighbours, the original inhabitants of Belle Ile. Similarly, the efforts made in the 1770s to establish the Acadians on the estates of the Marquis de Perusse des Cars came to naught.[114] Although one can find traces that record the treatment of Acadians as a distinct group in France as late as 1828, after 1785 their history there is once again a matter of genealogical interest in individuals rather than a question of the survival of a community.

The reactions of a group in exile are influenced not only by conditions existing within the group but also by their new external environment. The binding nature of Acadian kinship ties was reinforced by their total lack of such ties, at least during the early years, with the people among whom they were exiled. The Acadians retained their identity in exile partly because of official policies that designated them a group. Thus, the ways in which governments organized the exiles, paid them pensions, or settled them in areas reserved exclusively for them all helped preserve the Acadian sense of their unique identity. But when all is said and done, the Acadians remained a coherent group in exile because they were a coherent people before they went into exile. It is the sense of community that was part and parcel of the Acadians as individuals that led to behaviour which caused a Georgia official to comment, "such is the Bigotry and Obstinacy of these People that they have chosen rather to live miserably than to separate and live comfortably."[115]

The most important resources that the Acadians took with them into exile were social and political strengths. Acadian society was really built on the extended family. Thus, while brutal family separations did take place during the exile, there always remained a web of family linkages which supported the individuals in the strange new lands. The network of inter-marriages, which brought together people from different settlements as well as from within the same village, is documented in the registers compiled by the French government for Belle Ile.[116] The psychological impact of the trauma, the impact of death and sickness, would be somewhat mitigated by the presence of people who were obviously kin. The political experience of the Acadians before 1755 gave the exiles not only a known pattern of leadership, but forged a people accustomed to arguing with an authority that, in its own eyes, was stronger and more righteous.

There was a third factor which not only sustained the Acadians who went into exile but was also a significant factor in the continuance of the Acadians in Nova Scotia. This was the belief, held by the community as a whole, that the Acadians were a people distinct from others. Their legitimate country was "Acadia or Nova Scotia." The eighteenth century Acadians were not a nation, but they were a distinct culture. The Acadian sense that the lands surrounding their villages were theirs to exploit, coupled with a clear sense of the family connections which ran from village to village and a distinctive lifestyle, was by 1755 the fundamental background for Acadian political action. The Acadians considered that they had developed a political culture which fitted the needs of the society that they had built between two empires. In the Acadian view, a view that is repeated over and over again in the petitions they presented in exile, they had done nothing, nothing at all, to deserve deportation. It is the sense of being a society, of possessing both a group identity and the right to live in a particular place, that allowed the Acadians to surmount the exile and later rebuild their community in the Maritimes, as well as establishing another in Louisiana.

The deportation was not an incident which took place in a single year, but a policy pursued until 1763. Despite the zeal with which the policy was prosecuted, however, the colony was never entirely without Acadians.[117] On 26 July 1764, the Lords of Trade informed the governor of Nova Scotia that he should allow the Acadians to settle in Nova Scotia, provided they took the oath of allegiance, in spite of their "having taken up Arms in support of France during the late war."[118] Nine years after the transports first left, the Acadians were admitted once more as subjects with legal status in the colony. There were at that time about 1,500 of them actually within Nova Scotia.[119]

From the moment they left the coast of Nova Scotia, the Acadians had made every effort to return. Even those who escaped to Quebec did not find that society to their liking. Bishop Pontbriand wrote in 1756 that "le sort des Acadiens m'afflige; a en juger par ceux qui sont ici, ils ne veulent par demeurer parmi nous."[120] They returned from all points of the globe, Massachusetts as well as France. On arrival in Nova Scotia they found their former lands occupied, their villages truly conquered territory. They found that those who had escaped deportation had relocated in new settlements, some within the peninsula, but most on the very boundaries of the territory once called "Acadia or Nova Scotia." They had some choice. They could attach themselves to the Acadian communities within Nova Scotia on the lands which had been specifically assigned to them: in particular, they could join those living along Baie St Marie, district of Clare.[121] They could elect to join the tiny communities on Cape Breton Island or to join those established in what after 1798 would be called Prince Edward Island. They could go to the Acadian communities that existed in what would become New Brunswick in 1784, either to those of the St John River Valley or to those on its coast between the Baie de Chaleurs and Baie Verte.

Wherever the Acadians were established after 1764, one thing became clear: their sense of themselves as a people was undiminished. As far as it lay in their power, they attempted to recreate the same self-contained and independent life they had had before 1755. The circumstances were very different. They were no longer a border people but were now merely one group within a large empire. By the end of the 1780s, the Acadians had recovered some of their former demographic strength, but they were still a minority in the three Maritime colonies and would remain so over the ensuing decades. Yet the reports sent by Quebec missionaries to the Archbishop of Quebec in the late 1780s still characterize the Acadians as stubborn, argumentative, and clearly determined to assert their right to argue the politics of their lives with all those who considered them subject to their authority.[122] The subsequent growth and development of the identity of this Acadian society is as complex as the history of its genesis. It was an identity that included not only the experience of the cataclysmic events of the Deportation but also beliefs about the pre-deportation Acadian society. It was an identity that would be built not only on a common language and religion, and on a common culture, but on a common interpretation of the history of the Deportation. The Acadians of the nineteenth century would find an extraordinary force for unity in their adherence to a particular interpretation of the events of 1755. One thing is clear, the policy initiated by Colonel Lawrence at mid-century failed to destroy the Acadian community. Further, in the very circumstances of its failure, it provided the Acadians with one of the foundations of their unique identity in the centuries to come.

Notes

1 Michel Roy, in his work *L'Acadie Perdue* (Quebec, 1978), 39, considers that the task is both the historian's challenge and the historian's inevitable defeat. Both he and Leon Theriault, the latter in a work entitled *La question du pouvoir en Acadie* (Ottawa, 1982), struggle with what the dominance of the idea of the deportation means to Acadian identity today.

2 In 1981, Statistics Canada reported that those with French as a mother tongue made up 5 percent of the population of Prince Edward Island, 4 percent of the population of Nova Scotia, and 34 percent of the population of New Brunswick. Recognition of the Acadians as a French-speaking people with a recognizable community identity encapsulated by the word "Acadian" has not yet been accorded them by the Canadian federal government.

3 N.E.S. Griffiths, "The Acadians," *DCB* 4: xxvii–xxxi.

4 The organization of Acadian settlements after 1764 was controlled by the authorities at Halifax and, later, by those in Fredericton and Charlottetown. There is no question that an Acadian's absolute title to land was often abrogated. On the question of Acadian holdings in the Saint John River Valley see E.C. Wright, *The Loyalists of New Brunswick* (Moncton, 1955).

5 The poems of Hermenegilde Chiasson are a riveting expression of such emotion, especially those collected in the volume *Mourir à Scoudouc* (Moncton, 1979). It is in his works that one reads: "Comment faire comprendre, faire sentir, faire vivre que l'Acadie ce n'est pas le lèpre que nous ne voulons plus qu'on vienne faire ses bonnes oeuvres parmi nous," 33.

6 Emile Louvrière, *La Tragédie d'un peuple,* subtitled: *Histoire du peuple acadien de ses origines à nos jours* (Paris, 1923).

7 O.W. Winzerling, *Acadian Odyssey* (Lafayette, 1955).

8 William Faulkner Rushton, *The Cajuns From Acadia to Louisiana* (New York, 1987).

9 The best bibliographic references for this subject are the relevant pages of *Bibliographie acadienne: Liste des Volumes, Brochures et Thèses concernant l'Acadie et les Acadiens des debuts à 1975* (Moncton, n.d.); and Helene Harbec and Paulette Leversque, eds., *Guide bibliographique de l'Acadie, 1976–1987* (Moncton, 1988).

10 Archivo Segreto Vaticano, Collegione Nunziatura de Fiandra, 22 November 1763, Leg. 135, which was used by O.W. Winzerling, *Acadian Odyssey: Exile Without End* (Louisiana, 1955).

11 Winzerling notes that he spent several years in the colony where there "were graves of scores of Acadians who had once sought refuge on the shores between Monkey River and Point Diable." Ibid., 70.

12 For a survey of the historical roots of this poem and of the circumstances in which it was written, see N.E.S. Griffiths: "Longfellow's Evangeline: The Birth and Acceptance of a Legend," *Acadiensis* 11 (1982): 28–41.

13 R. Cole Harris, ed., *Historical Atlas of Canada: From the Beginning to 1800* (Toronto, 1987), 1: Plate 24.

14 Winzerling, *Acadian Odyssey.*

15 The best collection of essays on the way in which the Acadians arrived and settled in Louisiana is that edited by Glenn R. Conrad, *The Cajuns: Essays on their history and culture,* The University of Southwestern Louisiana History series no. 11, (Lafayette, LA, 1978).

16 "Circular from Governor Lawrence to the Governors on the continent, Halifax, August 11th, 1755," in *Report Concerning Canadian Archives for the Year 1905,* 3 vols. (Ottawa: Public Archives of Canada, 1906), 2: App. 3, 15–16.

17 Brown Manuscripts, Add. Mss. 1907, 11–73, British Museum. Lawrence's letter of instructions are in *Northcliffe Collection Reports* (Ottawa: Public Archives of Canada, 1926), 80–3.

18 "Instructions for Lieut. Colonel Winslow, Halifax, August 11th, 1755," in T.B. Akins, *Selections from the Public Documents of the Province of Nova Scotia* (Halifax, 1869), 271–4.

19 Ibid., "Instructions to Major Handfield, Halifax, 11th August," 275.

20 "Instructions to Moncton, August 11th, 1755," in *Northcliffe Collection,* 65–7.

21 "Winslow's Journal," *Collections of the Nova Scotia Historical Society* 3 (1883): 97 ff.

22 "Petition to the King of Great Britain, c. 1760," in L. Smith, *Acadia: A Lost Chapter in American History* (Boston, 1884).

23 "Moncton to Winslow, October 7th, 1755," *Report for 1905,* 2: App. B, 30.

24 "Lawrence to Moncton, September 1755," Vernon-Wager Mss., Library of Congress (Washington, DC).

25 See "Winslow's Journal," vol. 3.

26 The first Acadians to be landed in Boston arrived there as a result of stormy weather. *Report for 1905,* 2: App. E, 81.

27 "Dinwiddie to Shirley, 28th April, 1756," in R. Brooks, ed., "Dinwiddie Papers," *Virginia Historical Society Collections* (Richmond, 1899), 2: 394.

28 "Minutes of the Provincial Council, September 1756," *Colonial Records: Minutes of the Provincial Council of Pennsylvania from the Organization of the Termination of the Proprietary Government,* 16 vols., (Harrisburg, Pa., 1852–3), 7: 239–41.

29 28 November 1755: *Extracts from the Journals of the Provincial Congress of South Carolina* (Charlestown, 1775–6), 513.

30 Massachusetts: 7 November 1755, Boston State House, Hutchinson Papers, vol. 23; Pennsylvania: "Minutes of the Provincial Council," 6: 712–3; Georgia: George C. Candler, ed., *The Colonial Records of the State of Georgia,* 26 vols. (1904–13), 7: 301 ff.; Virginia: Robert Dinwiddie, *The Official Records of Robert Dinwiddie, Lieutenant-Governor of the Colony of Virginia, 1751–1758,* ed. Robert A. Brock, 2 vols. (Richmond, VA, 1883–84), 2: 269 ff.

31 He was the father of Jonathon Belcher, at that time Chief Justice of Nova Scotia and much involved in the organization of the deportation.

32 Pennsylvania Archives, First Series, 1748–56, 2: 514.

33 Massachusetts State Archives, Council Records, Commonwealth of Massachusetts, 21: 80.

34 Cited in Placide Gaudet, "Acadian Genealogy and Notes," *Report for 1905,* 2: v.

35 Proceedings and Acts of the General Assembly of Maryland (Baltimore, 1930), 24: 461.

36 *Report for 1905,* 2: App. E, 81. Massachusetts nagged at this question throughout the years that Acadians remained a public charge; the final account of £9563 9 shillings and 10 pence was submitted in August 1763, ibid., App. F, 133.

37 *The Acts and Resolves, Public and Private of... Massachusetts Bay to which are Prefixed the Charters of the Province,* 21 vols. (Boston, 1869–1922), 3: 951.

38 Ibid., 887.

39 Boston State House, *Hutchinson Papers,* vol. 23. This petition is translated and printed in *Report for 1905,* 2: App. E, 88. It is important to consider the original, in which the spelling and grammar indicate that it was most probably written by the Acadians themselves.

40 *Report for 1905,* 2: App. E, 100 ff.

41 13 April 1756, Boston State House, *Hutchinson Papers,* vol. 23. See also Massachusetts State Archives, Council Records, Commonwealth of Massachusetts, 21: passim.

42 A.G. Doughty, *The Acadian Exiles: A Chronicle of the Land of Evangeline* (Toronto, 1916) 184.

43 10 June 1756, Boston State House, *Hutchinson Papers,* vol. 23.

44 Boston State House, *Hutchinson Papers,* vol. 23. Gaudet, "Acadian Genealogy," *Report for 1905,* 2: 89 has the Act as 28–30 August 1756. *Acts and Resolves...Massachusetts Bay,* 3: 986.

45 23 July 1756, Boston State House, Hutchinson Papers, vol. 23. Much of the documentation of this episode is printed in Akins, *Nova Scotia Documents,* 302 ff.

46 A good collection of these can be found in *Report for 1905,* 2: 104 ff.

47 Boston State House, Hutchinson Papers, vol. 23.

48 *Report for 1905,* 2: 114.

49 5 October 1759, *Acts and Resolves...Massachusetts Bay,* 4: 102.

50 Massachusetts State Archives, Council Records, Commonwealth of Massachusetts, 23: 210.

51 15 January 1757, Boston State House, Hutchinson Papers, vol. 23.

52 (no day given) March 1757, ibid.

53 6 September 1762, *Acts and Resolves...Massachusetts Bay,* 5: 104; and *Report for 1905,* 2: App. F, 133–4.

54 18 January 1764, *Report for 1905,* 2: App. E, 90.

55 A somewhat muddled, but exhaustive account of this can be found in Pierre Belliveau, *French Neutrals in Massachusetts* (Boston, 1972), 22 ff.

56 *Report for 1905,* 2: App. E, 90.

57 24 January 1765, *Acts and Resolves...Massachusetts Bay,* 6: 105.

58 "Jean Trahant, Castin Thibodet, Jean Hebaire, Charles Landry, Allexis Braux to the Governor and Commander in Chief of Massachusetts Bay, Boston 1st Jan. 1765," in *Report for 1905,* 2: App. E, 92–3.

59 Ibid., 96–9. See also *Acts and Resolves... Massachusetts Bay,* 4: 911.

60 Account published in Gaudet, "Acadian Genealogy," 100.

61 W. Livingstone and W. Smith, eds., *Laws of New York from the 11th November, 1752 to 22nd of May, 1762,* 2 vols. (New York, 1762), 2: 103–4.

62 Ibid.

63 Trumbell, James Hammond, and C.J. Hoadley, eds., *Public Records of the Colony of Connecticut, May, 1751–February, 1757,* 15 vols. (New Haven, 1850–90), vol. 10.

64 "An Act for distributing and well-ordering the French people sent into this colony from Nova Scotia, January 1756," *Report for 1905,* 2: App. K, 254.

65 L.W. Cross, *The Acadians and the New England Planters* (Cambridge, NS, 1962).

66 J.T. Vocelle, *The Triumph of the Acadians* (1930), is the best short account but see also Gabriel Debien, "The Acadians in Santo Domingo," in Conrad, *The Cajuns,* 21–96.

67 Archives Colonial de Commerce de Guyenne, c. 4328, 1765, in 1F2161, AD, Ile-et-Vilaine (Rennes).

68 Debien, "The Acadians in Santo Domingo," in Conrad, *The Cajun,* 87.

69 *The Detailed List of Indemnities, Drawn up by the Commission Charged with Indemnifying the Former Planters of Santo Domingo, According to the Law of April 10th, 1826,* 6 vols. (Paris, 1827–33), cited in Conrad, *The Cajuns,* 90.

70 A. Therior, Jacques Genton, Victoire Jourdain, Joseph Giroir, Michael Poirier, and Marie-Madeleine Poirier.

71 Samuel Hazard et al., eds., *Pennsylvania Archives: Selected and Arranged from the original documents in the Office of the Secretary of State of the Commonwealth...* 138 vols. (Harrisburg and Philadelphia 3 PA, 1852–1935). Eight Series, 1931, 6: 4159.

72 9th of December, 1755, Minutes of the Provincial Council, *Colonial Records, Pennsylvania,* 6: 751.

73 J.T. Mitchell and H. Flanders, eds., *Statutes at Large of Pennsylvania from 1682 to 1801,* 17 vols. (1896–1915), 5: 215–19.

74 Hazard et al., *Pennsylvania Archives,* 6: 4408.

75 Mitchell and Flanders, *Statutes at Large of Pennsylvania,* 278–80.

76 Public Archives of Pennsylvania, Votes of Assembly, 4509–12.

77 Ibid., 4512.

78 Hazard et al., *Pennsylvania Archives,* 6: 4901.

79 *"Pemberton Papers"* (Harrisburg, n.d.), 1: 99.

80 2 November 1771, Pennsylvania Historical Society Collections, printed in *American Catholic Historical Review* 18 (1901): 140–2.

81 27 May, 1756, *Proceedings and Acts of the General Assembly of Maryland* (Baltimore, 1930), 24: 542 ff.

82 Cited in B. Sollers, "The Acadians (French Neutrals) Transported to Maryland," *Maryland Historical Magazine* 3 (1907): 18.

83 Census of Acadians, July 1763, photostat in Hall of Records, Annapolis, Maryland. The original is in the Archives Nationales (Paris), Affaires Etrangères, Politique Angleterre, vol. 451, f. 438.

84 Printed in J. Johnston, *History of Cecil County, Maryland* (Elkton, 1881), 263.

85 9 April 1767 (Annapolis).

86 B. Sollers, "Report on Smyth, *A Tour of U.S.A.* (London, 1784)," *Maryland Historical Magazine* 4 (1909): 279.

87 McIlwaine, ed., *Journals of the Houses of Burgesses of Virginia* (Charlottesville, 1909), 353. The bill was given assent by the Governor on 15 April 1756.

88 "Governor Dinwiddie to Dobbs, June 11th, 1756," in Dinwiddie, *The Official Records,* 2: 442–3.

89 W. Saunders, *Colonial Records of North Carolina,* 1752–59, 5: 655.

90 Doughty, *The Acadian Exiles,* 147.

91 Figures derived from the reports of the arrival of various ships in *Carolina Gazette,* 13–20 November 20–27 November, and 4–11 December 1755. See also C.J. Milling, *Exile without End* (Columbia, SC, 1945).

92 The best short account of this episode is Milling, *Exile without End.*

93 T. Cooper and David James MacCord, eds., *The Statutes at Large of South Carolina, 1682–1838.* 10 vols. (S. Carolina, 1836–41), 3: 31.

94 "Letter of Council to the Board of Trade, 5th January 1756," in Allan D. Candler, ed., *Colonial Records of the State of Georgia,* 7: 207.

95 Akins, *Nova Scotia Documents,* 302–3.

96 *Statutes enacted by the Royal Legislature, Georgia* (1757), 18: 188.

97 "Winslow's Journals," *Collections of the Nova Scotia Historical Society,* 3: 166.

98 T.L. Smith, "An Analysis of Rural Social Organization Among the French Speaking People of Southern Louisiana," *Journal of Farm Economics* 16 (1937): 682–4.

99 N.E.S. Griffiths, "Petitions of Acadian Exiles, 1755–1785. A Neglected Source," *Histoire Sociale / Social History 11,* no. 21 (mai–May 1978): 215–23 presents a summary of many of these.

100 A selection of these petitions has been printed in *Report for 1905,* vol. 2; and L.H. Gipson, *The British Empire Before the American Revolution,* 6: chapter 6.

101 *Report for 1905,* 2: App. E, 100.

102 Hazard et al., *Pennsylvania Archives, First Series, 1752–1756,* 3: 566.

103 N.E.S. Griffiths, "Acadians in Exile," *Acadiensis* 4 (1974): 70.

104 "L.G. and J.B. to John Cleveland, 4th January, 1763, Admiralty Records 98/9," partially printed in ibid., 74.

105 *Report for 1905,* 2: 150.

106 For a general survey of Acadian experience in France see N.E.S. Griffiths, "The Acadians Who Returned to France," *Natural History* 90 (1981): 48–57.

107 There is not much information about these people, save that they are called Acadian in the port listings of arrival, 1F2160, Archives d'Ille-et-Vilaine (Rennes).

108 Ibid.

109 Petition dated Morlaix, 31sr 8bre 1763, c. 5058, AD, Ile-et-Vilaine (Rennes).

110 Winzerling, *Acadian Odyssey,* describes the arrival in France of those who had been sent to England. The works of Milton P. Rieder and Norma Gaudet Rieder, including *The Acadians in France,* 3 vols. (Lafayette, 1973), are most useful. Ernest Martin, *Les exiles Acadiens en France au xviii siècle et leur établissement en Poitou* (Brissard, 1979) gives a solid narrative of Acadian experience in one area of France from 1763 to 1785.

111 N.E.S. Griffiths, "Les Acadiens et leur établissement en Louisiane," *France-Amérique* 35 (1983): 1–4.

112 "Dinan, l'avocat de la Crochais to Guilot, St. Malo, 10 mai 1750," IF2159, Archives d'Ille-et-Vilaine, Rennes.

113 Griffiths, "The Acadians Who Returned to France," 53 ff.

114 On this see Martin, *Les exiles Acadiens.*

115 "Report of the Committee...12th July, 1760" in the Journals of the House of Assembly, State Archives, Columbia, South Carolina. These records are now part of a publication series, viz: Easterby, J.H., ed., *The Journal of the Commons House of assembly of South Carolina, South Carolina colonial Records.*

116 Rieder and Rieder, eds., *The Acadians in France,* vol. 2.

117 *Censuses of Canada, 1665–1871* (Ottawa, 1876), 4: xxviii.

118 "Lords of Trade to Wilmot, July 16th, 1764," NA, CO 218/6, B 1115.

119 PANS, "Early Descriptions of Nova Scotia," *Reports* (Halifax, 1943), App. B, part 2, 32.

120 "Pontbriand a Belair, 23rd juillet, 1756," Archives Archévêque de Québec (Quebec), 2: 620.

121 M.A. Tremblay, "Les Acadiens de la Baie Francaise: L'histoire d'une survivance," *Revue de l'histoire de l'Amerique francaise* 20 (1962).

122 "Etat de la Mission de l'Acadie," Archives Archévêque de Québec NE/1–12, 1786.

PART III

The Origins of British North America 1749–1821

National Archives of Canada/C17

Imperial rivalries did not end with the Seven Years War. In 1776, thirteen of Great Britain's colonies along the Atlantic seaboard declared independence. France took advantage of the war between Great Britain and the newly declared United States to hit back at its old enemy. When the American Revolution ended in 1783, only colonies that had once been claimed by France remained under British control. They became the foundation upon which the future nation of Canada would be built, but the building occurred in a difficult context. In 1789, the French Revolution erupted, drawing most of Europe and, for a brief time, the United States into a long struggle known as the French and Napoleonic Wars (1793–1815). Despite the embarrassing loss of the Thirteen Colonies, Great Britain emerged as the dominant power in the new world order that emerged in the nineteenth century.

In addition to seeking territorial gains, the combatants in these wars fought over political ideas. The American and French revolutions signalled the birth of a new era characterized by liberal democratic political systems, capitalist commercial relations, and new social values focused on individualism and secularism. In this period Great Britain fought a rearguard action against the more advanced tenets of liberalism, which called for separation of church and state, abolition of monarchies, and universal manhood suffrage. Such a position in part explains the policies adopted toward Quebec, the name given to its newly conquered colony in 1763. While designed to placate their new subjects in the context of impending wars, both the Quebec Act of 1774 and the Constitutional Act of 1791 were also crafted to preserve and even strengthen conservative elements in colonial governance.

The arrival of 35 000 Loyalists in the Maritime colonies and another 12 000 in Quebec following the American Revolution further strengthened the bias toward conservatism. While in no way a uniform group in their culture or political values, many Loyalists were initially reluctant, because of their experience in the United States, to champion the republican cause. Moreover, British authorities kept a watchful eye on their remaining North American colonies, especially the new ones designed to accommodate the Loyalists: New Brunswick and Upper Canada (now Ontario). The War of 1812, which found the British North American colonies caught in another war between Great Britain and the United States, served to harden political lines, especially in Upper Canada, where the bulk of the fighting occurred. Following the war, a conservative backlash helped to maintain a hierarchical, class-structured society in Upper Canada that many hoped would preserve British institutions in the face of American republicanism and territorial expansion.

The readings in this section focus on the social adjustments that accompanied the warfare and political turmoil of the late eighteenth and early nineteenth centuries. In the conclusion to his study of culture in New France, Peter Moogk explores the conservative values that, he argues, link modern French-speaking Canadians with their colonial past. Moogk contends that the religious and ideological conformity that prevailed in New France is reflected in the ethnic nationalism and strong role of the state in Quebec today. Some historians reject this interpretation of society in New France, claiming that it was the trauma of the Conquest and the defeat of the rebellions of 1837–1838, rather than the experiences of New France, that produced a conformist society for many generations in Quebec. As we saw in Part 2, for example, it is frequently argued that the harsh control of seigneurs over censitaires was a product of British rather than French rule.

As was noted in the articles on Jacques Cartier and Madeleine de Verchères, history has frequently been used to serve current political ends. Nowhere is this approach more widely practised than in the history of the Loyalists. Often believed to have been the founders of English Canada, they were imbued with a variety of attributes—loyalty, of course, but also elite origins, civic virtue, and conservatism—that do not always stand the test of historical analysis. Norman Knowles here deconstructs the mythology surrounding the Loyalists who came to the colony of Upper Canada.

While most Loyalists were drawn from the farming and artisan classes, and left few personal records to describe their experience of exile, the minority who became office holders and professionals left behind a wealth of documentary evidence. Ann Gorman Condon uses personal letters written by these Loyalists to explore how families coped with the migration to what would become the province of New Brunswick. The family letters, she notes, are "delicate, witty, warmly demonstrative," suggesting that close family relationships for Loyalist refugees, as for the Acadians, played an important role in accommodating the difficulties posed by being uprooted. Interestingly, the elegance, the exclusivity, and the intensity reflected in the Loyalist letters were transferred to their children but not to their grandchildren. By that time oral history transmitted by families was giving way to written accounts of the Loyalist experience that, as Knowles has shown, were prompted more by public motives than a desire to preserve family lore.

Much of the work of historians today is devoted to exposing the political baggage that encumbers many events of the past. The War of 1812 is one event in Canadian history that has gathered a lot of baggage. After the fact, Upper Canadians often boasted about their loyalty to the British Crown and their commitment to militia duty. Their historical memory, it appears, quickly became distorted. As George Sheppard argues, most Upper Canadians were "cool calculators," hoping, like so many ordinary people trapped in a war zone, that they would not lose everything by backing the wrong side. Indeed, he concludes, "avoidance of militia duty was the norm for Upper Canadian males throughout the struggle."

As Carolyn Podruchny shows, men working on the fur trade frontier between 1780 and 1820 reluctantly conformed to the ideals laid down for them in labour contracts. Instead, both masters and servants constantly renegotiated their relationships, with labour disputes and power struggles punctuating the process. While Podruchny is unable to determine whether accommodation or confrontation predominated as a means of settling disputes, she is certain that what she calls the "social contract" had more impact than the legal one in a world where employers sustained their authority by controlling European necessities, carefully dispensing perks, and keeping their employees in indebtedness.

The last article in this section also dispels historical myths, in this case around the violent clash between Metis and Selkirk settlers at Seven Oaks (in present-day Manitoba) in 1816. By carefully analyzing various accounts of the event, Lyle Dick shows how the version of this event commonly accepted by academics in the twentieth century had its origins in the late nineteenth century when Anglo-Canadian immigrants began to dominate Western Canada. This version trumped earlier versions, both written and oral, that offered a more balanced account of what became commonly called a "massacre." Dick's claim that academic historians ignored available evidence to perpetuate their ethnocentric account is a warning to all aspiring historians of the pitfalls awaiting them in the pursuit of objectivity.

"The Apples Do Not Fall Far from the Tree": The Legacy of New France in Modern Canada

PETER MOOGK

It may seem like a long stretch to link the modern French-speaking Canadians with a colony that was absorbed by the British Empire in the 1760s. There are, however, traces of *la Nouvelle France* that have endured into the twentieth century, and their survival attests to the social conservatism of the European emigrants who settled in French North America. Most white newcomers before 1760 were single men who did not intend to make a home in the New World. Their sojourn overseas as soldiers or contract workers was a temporary exile to escape unemployment and hunger at home; it was not meant to be the prelude to permanent settlement abroad. The men, even the soldiers, were mostly urban craftsmen who knew little about their destination, and they embarked, trembling at the hazards, real and imagined, that awaited them. New France had a terrible reputation. One intendant wrote in the 1680s that "Canada has always been regarded as a country at the end of the world, and as a [place of] exile that might almost pass for a sentence of civil death, and also as a refuge sought only by numerous wretches until now to escape from [the consequences of] their crimes."[1]

Most migrants, both men and women, came as dependents whose passage across the Atlantic Ocean was paid by others. Religious dissenters and political rebels were to be screened out. The educated wastrels who were transported to the colony at their families' request did not remain in it for long. In New France, the newcomers were quartered in colonists' homes for three or more years, which helped them adjust to their new setting. After the 1670s, the minority who stayed married women from established families, which completed their absorption into the new society. The fusion of people from France's western provinces, from the Paris region, and from foreign countries and colonies was rapid. By 1700, Acadians and Canadians were well-defined colonial types with distinctive traits. The very mixed origins of the original settlers were forgotten and nineteenth-century *Canadiens* would boast of the purity of their French ancestry in contrast to the mongrel races that surrounded them.[2] Later immigrants to Quebec were expected to assimilate into the established culture and to adopt the same religious faith, if they were not already Roman Catholics. That assumption,

Peter Moogk, "'The Apples Do Not Fall Far from the Tree': The Legacy of New France in Modern Canada," in *La Nouvelle France: The Making of French Canada—A Cultural History* (East Lansing: Michigan State University Press, 2000), 265–281.

minus the religious requirement, is implicit in the Province of Quebec's requirement that children of foreign immigrants must enroll in French-language schools.

Latecomers had a modest impact upon the Franco-Canadian identity, although, thanks to nineteenth-century Irish immigrants, there are strong Celtic elements in French-Canadian folklore. The jig and reel were generally accepted as the *gigue* and *rille,* which are now "traditional" French-Canadian country dances. By contrast, other areas of Canada depended on a never-ending and increasingly diverse flow of immigrants for growth. These newer settlements always included a high proportion of newcomers, who came with families and formed ethnic subcommunities that remained culturally distinct. Multiculturalism, even before it received the Canadian federal government's blessing in the 1970s, has long been a fact of life in the provinces west of Quebec.

Many Italian and Irish immigrants to Quebec after 1760 met the expectation that they would assimilate to the majority's culture. Amerindian converts to Christianity during the French Regime were supposed to do the same, and the Hurons of Lorette took this route. Descendants of the Iroquois converts who settled in the St. Lawrence Valley were resented because, despite being Roman Catholics, they became English-speakers. That choice was encouraged by their work as steel-frame construction workers in the adjacent state of New York. Franco-Quebeckers' frustration with their Iroquois neighbors exploded in 1990, after a native blockade of the Mercier Bridge to support another band's claim. White Quebeckers stoned cars carrying aboriginal families out of the Kahnawaké reserve at the bridge's south end.

The religious and ideological conformity of New France had various consequences. Unity of faith and the settlers' conservatism produced a coherent society in which fidelity to the dominant belief system was a social virtue. That cohesion was reinforced by later historical experiences. Defensiveness, aroused by restrictions on publicly funded French-language education outside Quebec in 1870–1920, demanded a unified response to meet the challenge. Deviants, such as the abstract artist Paul-Emile Borduas, who had rejected the conservative Catholic nationalism of the 1940s, went into exile.

Historians know that cultural continuity is maintained by transference or substitution and that what appears to be a break with the past is usually the displacement of one creed by a similar belief system. In Quebec ethnic nationalism has taken the place of religion. In "the Quiet Revolution" of the 1960s, Quebec's government assumed the Roman Catholic Church's role as guardian and promoter of French-speaking culture. For politicians of the only province with a French-speaking majority, this seemed to be a natural role. Because French Canada extended beyond the frontiers of Quebec, the provincial government could not claim to be the national government of all French Canadians. The Acadians of the Atlantic provinces would not accept such an assertion of power by Quebec's government. The pan-Canadian identity of French-speakers was an impediment to the assertion of Quebec's special status. In the late 1960s the Québécois nation was "discovered," which justified the Quebec government's claim to the rank of a "national"—not provincial—government within Canada.[3] Since then, Quebec has been redefined by its politicians as a nation-state, and the provincial legislature has become a "national assembly."

With the secularization of social values and the disappearance of visible distinctions that set French Canadians apart from other North Americans, language has become the key distinguishing characteristic and the focus of nationalist concern. Solidarity is still enjoined, not out of religious fidelity, but out of loyalty to a language group that feels it is besieged by an English-speaking world. It is a cliché of Quebec nationalists to describe their province as a French-speaking island in an Anglo-Saxon sea. They, however, enjoy swimming in that sea. The American entertainment industry and fashions from the United States have made inroads into Quebec, as they have elsewhere in the world. Quebeckers surpass other Canadians as consumers of "Big Mac" hamburgers—translated as "Gros Mac"—at McDonald's restaurants.

The customary French-Canadian emphasis on group solidarity and collective rights has been attributed to a defensive mentality awakened by assimilationist pressures; it is, however, a natural development from the religious, governmental, and legal heritage of New France, which placed family obligations above personal interests. Individualism in the colony meant family autonomy rather than personal individualism. The strong familial ethos is evident in the apartments built in Quebec's cities in 1890–1930; these buildings are really single-family dwellings stacked one on top of another—up to three floors, each with its own exterior staircase to the street below, its own entranceway, and a separate verandah. Despite the advantages for heat conservation and economy, a shared, internal stairwell and a common entrance for all of the resident families did not appeal to French-speakers. The interior distribution of space, as well, left little scope for the personal privacy that British-Canadians prized. As in the houses of New France, there might be a small entrance vestibule, but to get to the back of the residence, one passed through several rooms.[4] These buildings are a visible statement of French-Canadian social values in the early twentieth century.

Family solidarity has been an outstanding trait of French-Canadians: in 1954–55, when Philippe Garigue interviewed fifty-two Montrealers, he found that, on average, each informant knew of 215 relatives and could trace the family's lineage beyond three generations. "While awareness of descent and pride in the history of the family name is shown by the majority of informants, frequency of contact is highest between members of the same generation" with the same social status. One man saw 40 to 45 relatives every month, and kin were preferred by all when seeking professional services or personal advice, buying goods, hiring an employee, or finding a business partner.[5] The same preference for relatives and for functioning within a kinship network was evident in eighteenth-century New France.

French-speakers have long regarded insistence on individual freedom of action and independent self-expression as an Anglo-Saxon peculiarity. During the 1745 siege of Louisbourg, a town resident marveled at the lack of coordination between the two enemy commanders and commented, "only the English are capable of such oddities, which nevertheless form a part of that precious liberty of which they show themselves so jealous."[6] Among French colonists, family interests took precedence over individual rights and the *père de famille* defined those interests. The patriarchal family, which was blessed by the Roman Catholic Church and upheld by Quebec's civil law until the 1960s, meant that, even after the establishment of an elected, legislative assembly for Lower Canada (part of the Old Province of Quebec) in 1792, French-speaking voters were still drawn to authoritarian father figures who promised to protect and rule their people as a good father would do. Maurice Duplessis, a Quebec provincial premier who died in 1959, embodied the patriarchal tradition in Quebec politics. The Quebec Civil Code described the father and husband as the "chef de famille," and Duplessis was nicknamed "le chef."

The way in which elected, representative government came to French Canadians explains the historic deference to one man's leadership, despite democratic political structures. The division of the Old Province of Quebec in 1791 and the introduction of an elective assembly had come about because newly arrived American

Loyalist refugees and British merchants in the province had insisted on representative government as the birthright of every British subject; it was not done in deference to the French-speaking population. Most educated *Canadiens* at the time distrusted elected legislatures as instruments of taxation and opposed the creation of a house of assembly.[7] Representative government was imposed on the French Canadians, despite their opposition to it.

Authoritarianism was always tempered by compassion, even two centuries after the end of the French Regime. The humane aspect of paternalism was evident in the attitudes of French-Canadian entrepreneurs interviewed by Norman W. Taylor in the 1950s. They valued long-serving employees and were reluctant to fire an inefficient worker whose family depended upon his earnings. One manufacturer said, "my manager is inept, but he has been with us for a long time; he was hired by my father. So what can I do?" The *patron,* or boss, had an obligation to old employees that overrode an objective appreciation of their value to the business.

Taylor's French-Canadian entrepreneurs displayed the same preoccupation with family independence and security shown by craftsmen and by Roman Catholic merchants in New France. These twentieth-century businessmen refused equity capital from outsiders because it meant a loss of control over their enterprise, and they were unwilling to borrow money from banks for expansion. In most cases, they had no desire to expand their enterprise if it meant bringing non-family members into the company's management and losing a personal relationship with the workers or direct supervision over all operations. "I don't like to owe money, I wouldn't consider a partnership or anything like that, I want to run my business myself," said a furniture manufacturer. These attitudes in the 1950s limited the size of French-Canadian firms; if the business were providing family members with jobs and a good living, that was enough. Expansion of the family business or a new line of goods carried risks. Compared with English-speaking businessmen, French-speakers were more concerned with enjoying life than with getting rich. Extra profits were put into government bonds and into real estate—the safest investments possible.[8] Family autarky and material security were then as important as they had been for farmers and artisans in *la Nouvelle France.*

During "the Quiet Revolution" of the 1960s the Quebec provincial government took over education and social welfare from the Roman Catholic Church. The creation of a provincial department of education in 1964 was the first step in taking French-language instruction out of the clergy's hands. Hospitals and asylums—traditionally an ecclesiastical domain—became the responsibility of Quebec's government. A Ministry of Cultural Affairs was also established. While assuming many of the church's functions, the state acquired some of the attitudes of an ecclesiastical establishment. The church was an authoritarian institution whose leaders expected to provide intellectual and moral guidance for the population. Populism—belief that political representatives should be guided by their constituents and faith in the wisdom of the common man—is not a part of French Canada's political tradition. The educated elite knows what is necessary for the public good, without having to consult the people. The old aristocracy of seigneurs and military officers has long since been displaced by elected politicians, of humbler origins, trained in the law. Commercial and technical expertise is now valued in the government bureaucracy, yet there remains a paternal condescension toward the general population. In the late 1960s I saw provincial civil servants being given a bulletin called *Mieux Dire,* which, with text and diagrams, showed them how to *properly* enunciate French words. I could not imagine a provincial or state government elsewhere trying to regulate how its employees pronounced words.

The population, then and sometimes now, was not organized to effectively challenge paternalistic leadership and its respect for authority is strong.[9] The French colonial government's hostility to self-constituted groups among the lowest social ranks, and the colonists' pursuit of family independence and material self-sufficiency, hindered voluntary cooperation with strangers. Family networks provided the associates one needed. France's communal traditions were not transplanted to the St. Lawrence Valley. Only in Acadia was there a form of village self-government provided by elders, and that exception was due to the French government's indifference to what happened in Acadia. The collective building of dikes to reclaim tidal marshes for cultivation and the maintenance of the embankments also encouraged interfamily cooperation among the Acadians. In nineteenth-century Ontario, friends and neighbors came together in "bees" to erect the massive, timber framework of a neighbor's barn or for some other major task. The helpers were rewarded with food and drinks and the beneficiary of one "bee" was expected to render the same service to others. Baptists, Presbyterians, and other Protestants organized and administered their own congregations; they hired and dismissed their ministers. If a school were needed, the local people would create one. Such spontaneous, self-organized cooperation with other families was rare in French Canada, apart from community dances.[10] In small, French-speaking settlements throughout Canada, the priest provided social leadership and the parish provided the institutional framework for community life. It was not a framework that the people created for themselves and it was always subject to external authority. The genesis of this pattern could be seen in eighteenth-century New France.

The unique cohesion of the estate-owning gentry of *la Nouvelle France* gave this group an advantage in the postconquest era. About 1,600 people left New France as a result of the defeat. The civil administrators, many wholesale merchants, and serving military officers departed with the French troops in the 1760s. Their fortunes were tied to the French empire, and the British empire's administration offered no employment to Roman Catholics, just as Protestants and Jews had been excluded from all public offices during the French Regime. The remainder of the elite, which had stayed in Canada, banded together to win the patronage of King George III, their new sovereign. The state church, however, was now the Protestant Church of England, and British oaths of office required the candidate to disavow the Roman Catholic faith and to swear fidelity to the Protestant monarchs of the royal House of Hanover. The oaths' intent was to detect and exclude Roman Catholics who might support the Stuart pretenders to Great Britain's throne. Without government appointments and military commissions, Canada's gentry were reduced to the role of seigneurs, formerly an incidental role for the privileged leaders of society. For a group accustomed to enjoying the benefits of royal patronage, this was a distressing situation.

The British crown accepted collective petitions from all ranks of society. Just as they had made individual appeals to the French monarch on behalf of family members, the remaining Canadian gentlemen were quick to present addresses to the throne seeking readmission to government positions, financial rewards, and other concessions. In 1767 the Montreal region's seigneurs begged, "that all the subjects in this province [of Quebec], without any Distinction of Religion, may be admitted to any Office, the only basis of selection being that of capacity and personal merit. To be excluded by the State from participating in it, is not to be a member of the state."[11] This was not a plea for popular participation in government; it was a request for patronage appointments.

A 1770 petition to George III from "the Canadians of your Province of Quebec," both seigneurs and educated townsmen, repeated the appeal for admitting Roman Catholics to public offices and for a restoration of French laws and regulations, "the Basis and Foundation of their possessions, and...the rule of their families." They noted "how humiliating it had been to them to be excluded from the offices which they might fill in this Province, for the Service of Your Majesty, and the Comfort of Your Canadian People.... Could the religion we profess, Sire,...be a reason...for excluding a number of Your submissive and faithful Children from participation in the favors of the best of Kings, of the tenderest of fathers?"[12] The obsequiousness, the appeal to a paternal monarch, and the piteous wish for positions of profit and honor came naturally to a class nurtured on royal patronage under the Bourbons.

This address was entrusted to Sir Guy Carleton, the governor-general of Quebec, when he returned to England to make the case before a parliamentary committee for adapting the government and laws of the province to the traditions of the *Canadiens.* Like other British newcomers, Carleton mistook the seigneurs for a landed aristocracy—people of his own class—and called them "the Noblesse of Canada." British officers, such as Carleton, also admired the Canadians' martial valor and treated them as social equals. Naturally, the Canadian seigneurs were not going to correct the British officials' belief that the landlords were the aristocracy of the colony. Language was not an issue, and educated Europeans, like the British officers, conversed easily in French, then regarded as the language of high culture and intellectual discourse. There was no government plan to impose English on the conquered population before the 1790s. Language was not a political issue, strange as it might seem to the current generation of Canadians. One's religious faith, however, was another matter.

Religion was an impediment to public appointments because it had been the key to political loyalties in Europe since the sixteenth century. Just as the French army defending New France had contained English-speaking Roman Catholics, like James Johnstone, the British forces of occupation included Protestant French-speakers, both Huguenot and Swiss, such as Frederick Haldimand, a future governor-general of Quebec. Nonetheless, the British permitted Monsignor Jean-Olivier Briand to go to France in 1766 to be consecrated bishop of Quebec by French Roman Catholic archbishops. Briand provided a head for the Canadian church, which had been without a bishop for six years, and, with episcopal power to ordain priests, he ensured the continuation of the church. Thus did a major institution of the French regime, with educational and charitable functions, survive the change of rulers. By reassuring the Roman Catholic clergy and by conciliating the seigneurs, Sir Guy Carleton hoped to win the fidelity of the entire population of Canada. He assumed that the gentlemen-landowners commanded the obedience of their tenant-farmers and that the priests could also determine the Canadians' political allegiance.[13]

With the formal transfer of New France to Great Britain in 1763, the disappearance of French legal traditions seemed certain. British government policy assumed that a British territory ought to have English legal and political institutions, like those in the other British North American colonies. The Royal Proclamation of 7 October 1763 authorized the introduction of "the Laws of our Realm of England" by courts "hearing and determining all Causes, as well Criminal as civil."[14] Soon, that policy was compromised and then abandoned in favor of perpetuating the *Coutume de Paris,* which was familiar to the French-Canadian majority in Quebec. In 1767 Sir Guy Carleton complained to his superiors about the confusion and "chicanery" that had resulted from the mixture of French and English legal practices. His solution was to revoke the 1763 proclamation, "and for the present leave the Canadian laws almost entire," or to prepare an amended version of these laws "as a Canadian Code."[15] At Carleton's request, François-Joseph Cugnet compiled *An Abstract of Those Parts of the Custom of the Viscounty and provostship of Paris, which were received and practised...in the time of French Government,* which, after further revision, was published in London in 1772. The seigneurs' property rights and prerogatives were embodied in that legal code; without it, they could not exist as a privileged class.

The British government had been moving toward the compromise of retaining English criminal justice while sanctioning continuation of French civil law in those areas most dear to the Canadians: property ownership, inheritance, matrimonial rights, and paternal authority. In 1766 the Rockingham government accepted this compromise in principle, and Solicitor-General Alexander Wedderburn's 1773 report provided the outline for the 1774 Quebec Act. Recent research has found no evidence to support the American revolutionaries' claim that the Quebec Act was passed to refashion the northern province into a model for ruling the rest of British North America and to make Quebec into a base for punishing mutinous colonists in the other territories.[16]

The 1774 Quebec Act, as passed by the British parliament, provided a new oath of office, inoffensive to Roman Catholics, and recognized the validity of French civil law, seigneurial land tenure, and the tithe collected by the Roman Catholic Church. Given the strong religious prejudices of the day, these provisions and the reaffirmation of the Canadians' right to freedom of worship, were remarkably liberal. Catholic emancipation from legal disabilities occurred in Canada fifty-five years before it was granted in Great Britain. The 1774 act stated that "in all Matters of Controversy, relative to Property and Civil Rights, Resort shall be had to the Laws of Canada, as the Rule for the Decision of the same."[17] Sir Guy Carleton, who imagined that the customary laws of Paris had "established subordination, from the first to the lowest, which preserved the internal harmony they [the Canadians] enjoyed until our arrival," took this concession as a license to restore the entire body of French civil usages, including those affecting commerce—an area where English law was to have been admitted. In this way, the British government's humane pragmatism combined with one governor's naïve enthusiasm for the French Regime to bring about a continuation of French civil law in the Old Province of Quebec and in its successor, the modern Province of Quebec.

Half of the twenty men appointed in January 1775 to the Governor's Council—an advisory *and legislative* body in the absence of an assembly—were French-speakers. Eight came from the old military-administrative elite of landowners.[18] When rebellious American colonists invaded Quebec in 1775, Carleton distributed military officers' commissions to the seigneurs, on the mistaken assumption that leadership of their tenants in war was one of their customary functions. The Canadian seigneurs gladly accepted this role because being an officer was the traditional role of a French noble. Despite the bishop of Quebec's call to enroll in the militia to defend the colony, most rural folk resisted military service and rejected their landlords' military leadership. Some handed their seigneurs over to the invading Continental Army. Carleton and other British administrators were astounded by this conduct; they had expected loyal gratitude for the Quebec Act. The presumed social leaders of French Canada were shown to have little influence over the rest of the population, and, once a legislative assembly was established in the 1790s, elections allowed political leadership to pass to men of humbler origins. Although discredited as the natural leaders of French Canada, the seigneurial families continued to be favored in governmental and judicial appointments. They reciprocated with active loyalty to the British crown in war and during the *Patriote* rebellions of 1837–38 in Lower Canada.

The British government's willingness to compromise on the principle that a British colony should have English Common Law assisted the survival of French-Canadian culture, yet that very flexibility perpetuated the divergent intellectual traditions of the two language groups and increased the chances for later, mutual incomprehension. Educated *Canadiens* retained the bias for deductive reasoning that would distinguish them from the English-speaking newcomers. The 1791 severance of the Old Province of Quebec into Lower Canada, based on the St. Lawrence Valley, where most French-speakers resided, and Upper Canada, the principal destination for immigrants from outside the colony, created a political unit that was and would remain the home of a Roman Catholic, French-speaking majority. The division of the old province had been undertaken to appease the American Loyalists concentrated in the western region, who wanted freehold land tenure, Common Law, and representative government. Once that fast-growing area had been severed from the eastern portion, called Lower Canada, it was possible to maintain the legacy of the Quebec Act. The seigneurial system, embodied in the civil laws, survived in Lower Canada until 1854, far longer than the same landholding system in France. Despite reorganization and amplification in 1866, the civil law of the new Province of Quebec (created in 1867) retained principles and values from the French regime: contracts could not offend "good morals," articles 173–84 and 242–45 upheld the patriarchal family, and divorce was not recognized. In domestic matters, in its social conservatism and in its support for Roman Catholic morality, the Civil Code perpetuated the legacy of *la Nouvelle France.*

In the years after 1774, the civil code and church-run schools perpetuated a cultural preference for argument from abstract principles and, by corollary, a distrust of pragmatism. Louis-Joseph Papineau, as speaker of the Lower Canadian House of Assembly, became leader of the majority party in the early nineteenth century. He was a rigid man of principle who scorned all compromise. Historian Fernand Ouellet treated Papineau's inflexibility as a temperamental peculiarity.[19] This disposition, however, would have been reinforced by his training in a church-run college at Montreal and at the Quebec Seminary, as well as by his apprenticeship in French civil law. Law offices and Roman Catholic classical colleges have, for generations, been the training ground for French-Canadian politicians, from Papineau to Premier Lucien Bouchard of Quebec.

The course of the liberal-democratic rebellions against British imperial authority in Lower Canada during the 1830s revealed another legacy of New France. The inexperience of the *Canadiens* with voluntary self-organization resulted in confusion, indecisiveness, and a reliance on outsiders for military leadership.[20] French-speaking *Patriotes* preached democracy, republicanism, and cultural nationalism in fiery speeches. Having led their followers to the threshold of insurrection with verbal fireworks and a strategy of unyielding confrontation, the political leaders faltered. The principal *chef,* Louis-Joseph Papineau, who had served during the War of 1812, fled to the United States when the fighting began. Rank-and-file *Patriotes* fought under the leadership of a Swiss, an Irishman, and British and American immigrants. Only three commanders, Bonaventure Viger, Dr. Cyrille Côté, and Dr. Olivier Chenier, were French Canadians. The *Canadiens* produced few dynamic military leaders and were inclined to remain passively on the defensive rather than seize the initiative in combat—a fatal strategy. Their strongholds were reduced one by one by British troops and the loyal militia.

Their dependence on outsiders for leadership is surprising in what was, reputedly, a

French-Canadian nationalist uprising, unless we consider French Canada's past. Some of the timidity and disorder can be blamed on the rebels' unfamiliarity with warfare and their inferior weapons, yet to these factors one must add the loss of a tradition of self-organization, resulting from the decline of popularly constituted organizations and communal traditions in New France. Rural *Patriotes* tried to take control of existing, local institutions created by outside authority, such as the parish or the militia companies, rather than create alternative institutions.[21] In the later development of Quebec's secular trade unions, Irish immigrants and English-speakers were often the principal initiators of workers' organizations. The French-speaking clergy organized tame Catholic workers' associations to counteract the appeal of the international unions.

The defeat of the anticlerical *Patriotes* and the rarity of voluntary associations among French-speakers explains the ease with which the Roman Catholic clergy assumed the social leadership of French Canada after the rebellions. Priests were free to define French-Canadian identity, and politicians deferred to their cultural leadership. The clergy's conservative, Roman Catholic version of nationalism dominated in French-speaking Canada until the 1950s. In school texts New France was recast as a missionary colony whose saintly colonists were models for the current generation. The young were told that they belonged to a heroic and apostolic race, whose duty was to remain faithful to the traditions of their devout ancestors. The life of a farmer, after a religious vocation, was held to be the most moral of occupations and one suited to the spiritual nature of the French Canadians. When the surplus rural population started to migrate to cities and even to New England in search of industrial work, the church and province created colonization programs to resettle these people on the land within Quebec. Clerical belief in the agrarian vocation of the French Canadians meant that church-run schools provided very little preparation for careers in commerce and the sciences.

The puritanical Catholicism of the seventeenth century was also extolled. The successful revival of Counter-Reformation asceticism may be measured by the absence of the naked human body in paintings exhibited by French-Canadian artists before Joseph Franchère's *Sylphide* (c. 1916). A voluptuous nude, such as *A Venetian Bather*, painted by Paul Peel of London, Ontario, and acquired by the National Gallery of Canada in 1895, would have shocked French-Canadian viewers. There was not much of the legendary Gallic joie de vivre in French Canada from 1840 to 1945. Rather, the religious atmosphere was one of repression, guilt, and shame.

The providential view of human affairs held by the faithful did not offer much optimism. In a divinely regulated universe, human action counted for little. The fatalism of the lower classes was summed up in the French-Canadian proverb "celui qui est né pour un petit pain, n'en aura un gros (whoever is born for a small loaf of bread, will never have a big one)." The socially conservative ideology propagated by the clergy was not seriously challenged. In Canadian provinces outside Quebec, the dominance of parish institutions, including schools and credit unions, in French-speaking communities ensured their survival, at a price. The church, however, was more concerned with preserving Roman Catholics than with maintaining the French language, and when insistence on French instruction imperiled public funding of parochial schools then language might be sacrificed. With the secularization of social values, there was an urgent need to find lay leaders to take over the priests' role as community spokesmen and to establish cultural institutions and schools outside the parish framework. For a population inexperienced with self-constituted, secular associations, that was a challenge. The evidence that spontaneous self-organization still does not come easily to many French-speakers is that peculiarly Québécois institution: the *animateur sociale.* An appointed social initiator is required to coordinate and activate social groups. Among English-speakers, an "animator" is someone who makes live-action cartoons.

The patriarchy upheld by French Canada's legal and religious traditions has had a long history. Even the republican *Patriotes* could not conceive of an active political role for women. What helped to discredit the British monarchy in their eyes was the 1837 accession of Victoria as monarch of Great Britain. It was considered unnatural for a young woman to exercise political authority.[22] That bias was consistent with the law: the married man exercised paternal authority (*la puissance paternelle*) over his dependents. Article 174 of Quebec's 1866 Civil Code stated, "a husband owes protection to his wife; a wife obedience to her husband." The words may have been borrowed from France's *Code Napoléon* (1804), but the sentiment was identical in the *Coutume de Paris,* which made husbands the sole lords and governors of a couple's joint property and deprived wives of financial independence. Not until 1931 were married women in Quebec given legal control of their pay and of any purchases made with those earnings. Wives were not granted complete legal equality until 1964. Quebec's women had obtained the right to vote in provincial elections in 1940—being the last women in Canada to receive the provincial suffrage. The word "receive" is used advisedly. Female suffrage had been achieved nationally in 1918, largely at the instigation of English-speaking feminists. Most French-speaking women were indifferent to the cause of female suffrage, and the Roman Catholic clergy was hostile to the movement. The senior clergy in Quebec resisted the legal and political emancipation of daughters and married women because, according to Monsignor Louis-Adolphe Paquet, it would destroy masculine authority and repudiate the natural inequality of the sexes.[23] Since the 1960s the tendency of French-Canadian men to mistake virility for virtue has faded.

The masculine bias of the civil law and church doctrine was counterbalanced by a compassion for the weak. Roman Catholic teachings about the need for forgiveness and for charity gave a humane aspect to French-Canadian culture. New France was ahead of the British colonies in providing assistance and shelter to the unfortunate, and, starting with the foundation of Quebec's hospital in 1639, religious orders provided these services. In the nineteenth and twentieth centuries a separate, parallel system of schools and hospitals developed in Quebec for Protestants and Jews. After the 1950s social welfare provided by church-run institutions, organized on a diocesan basis, was replaced by a province-wide, government-run system of health care and social assistance. Just as the provincial government took over the church's role in running schools, it has inherited the ecclesiastical responsibility for the needy, the sick, and the aged. The result is a highly integrated and centralized system of welfare and medical services. The range of social services provided by the Quebec government exceeds that supplied by other provinces: it comprises day-care for children, income supplements, automobile insurance, consumer protection, and generous family allowances.[24]

A cynical explanation for the "unique nationalist and social-democratic political culture" in Quebec is that the self-interest of the French-speaking "technocratic elite" is served by an expanding, interventionist state because of the jobs it generates and the power it accords to this social group.[25] This argument of bureaucratic self-interest overlooks the heritage of government paternalism from New France and the Roman Catholic Church's doctrine of good works. Quebec's so-called "social democratic ethos" is a new label for a very long established outlook. Roman Catholic social teachings are probably more influential than socialist theory in ensuring general acceptance of the provincial government's welfare state.

Both aspects of church and state in New France, compassion and authoritarianism, are present in the policies of Quebec's provincial government. Quebec's parliamentarians, like lawmakers of the French Regime, believe that there is a legislative solution to every social problem, and they are attracted by categorical rules. As in *la Nouvelle France,* the legislative reach is extensive. The interest of the Franco-Québécois nation provides the ideological rationale for intervention formerly supplied by royal absolutism. Place names can be changed, whatever residents may wish, and there is a preference for French nomenclature. When a province redefines itself as the nation-state of one language group, it necessarily reduces all other language groups to subordinate status. Ethnic nationalists are uncomfortable with the visible evidence of cultural diversity. Thus, St. Andrew's East, founded by the Scots, was renamed Saint-André d'Argenteuil and the Payne River is now Rivière d'Arnaud. The personal names of the newborn must pass official scrutiny before registration in Quebec. Immigrants who have not been educated in English within Canada are obliged to send their children to French-language schools. Quebec's draconian regulations on the language of public signs are the best-known examples of intrusive authority in action.[26] The explanation is that the preeminence of the French language must always be visible and that the use of any other language, especially English, threatens the survival of French.

In the late twentieth century, the patriarchal and Roman Catholic values in Quebec's civil code have been replaced by egalitarian and secular standards shared by the rest of North America, such as the legal equality of women. Alteration of content has not meant an abandonment of deductive logic, which is characteristic of French legal reasoning and still affects intellectual debate in the Province of Quebec. The 1989 program of the *Parti Québécois* (PQ)—a separatist party established in 1968—is a modern example of the idealism and deductive reasoning inherent in the province's legal tradition. The principles that are the basis for political arguments come from nineteenth-century European cultural nationalism and are presented in a declaratory fashion as self-evident truths. Language is treated as the defining trait of nations: "Without the French language, the Québécois nation would no longer exist." Within Quebec people are classified by language as *francophones* (French-speakers), *anglophones* (English-speakers), or *allophones* (those whose mother tongue is neither French nor English). The political platform uses the terms *peuple* (people) and *nation* interchangeably. Nations are spoken of as organic beings with a single mind and "a national will (*une volonté nationale*)"; they are objective realities. The French-speaking residents of Quebec are assumed to be so distinctive as to be a nation apart from French-speaking Canadians residing elsewhere. That distinctiveness is asserted rather than defined.

Parti Québécois speakers, when addressing outsiders, often begin by insisting that the listeners must acknowledge that "Quebec is a nation; it is a people." What is the point of this demand? This insistence has as its objective the establishment of a basic premise from which logical deductions—in the rhetoric of European nationalism—may be drawn. Each nation, it is said, has its own national homeland, and, for the Franco-Québécois, that homeland is the province of Quebec. To be *"un peuple normal,"* in the PQ argument, a people must have its own sovereign nation-state. "Normal" does not mean according to a statistical norm, but rather how things ought to be in a perfect world. The everyday expressions "ça, c'est normal (that's normal)" or "c'est naturel" are an assertion of what is right and proper and not, as English-speakers might imagine, what is generally done by people. Every "nation" has the right of self-determination, and, in the best of all possible worlds, each nation should have its own politically independent state. This is the idealism in the PQ argument. Multinational states may outnumber nation-states, but the latter represent the right way. The coexistence of aboriginal nations within Quebec is acknowledged, but their territories necessarily have a subordinate status in the Québécois homeland.

Canada, it is said, cannot be the homeland of the Franco-Québécois because it is not a "true" federation of autonomous states and because Canada, according to the late PQ leader René Lévesque, contains "two nations in the same land." The other nation, the PQ postulates, is a monolithic and homogeneous "English Canada."[27] That bigger "nation" is said to control the federal government, which, reputedly, uses its power to impose English Canada's will upon the smaller Québécois nation. *Péquistes,* as PQ supporters are called, see Canadian history as the story of an eternal antagonism between two nations, which makes their continued coexistence impossible: "this incompatibility is unconquerable (*irréductible*), irreversible." "Quebec," states the tract, "must be master of its own house," and "is on the march to becoming a complete and normal society." If one accepts the initial and the following premises of this argument, then it proceeds with relentless logic: the Franco-Québécois are a nation; all nations have the right of self-determination; and self-determination means a politically independent state of Quebec.

To this sequential deduction from abstract principles are added some pragmatic arguments, such as a promise of financial savings by eliminating one level of government or the assertion that only an independent Quebec can guarantee the survival of the French language, "threatened, if not excluded, everywhere else on the North American continent." *Péquistes* believe that, historically, French-speakers in North America have been a victimized people. This can be sustained by a selective reading of the past. Dislike of compromise is evident in the statement that "it is no longer acceptable that the future of the Quebec people be constantly subjected to the complicated arbitration" of federalism. There is even an echo of past values in the assertion that "the family constitutes the [basic] unit, par excellence, of our societies and the source of their dynamism."[28] It is appropriate that the platform of Quebec's most nationalist, political party, by reasoning deductively from unquestioned axioms, is faithful to the intellectual tradition of New France.

Given the different patterns of reasoning favored by French- and English-speaking Canadians, it is not surprising that they often misunderstand each other or resent the other language group's resistance to arguments that seem utterly convincing to one's own group. Arguments of principle collide with appeals to pragmatism, to what is achievable. The pragmatic approach follows English Common Law practice of appealing to precedents: previous court decisions in similar cases. Case law invokes what has been done in the past as a guide for the future. This is the pattern of legal argument in every Canadian province but Quebec and in every American state except Louisiana. To someone reared in the intellectual traditions of French Canada, such an approach to problems seems like unprincipled expediency and, indeed, English-speaking Canadians have been indifferent to federal government initiatives that have encroached upon the provinces' jurisdiction over education and social welfare. The original constitutional division of powers between the federal and provincial governments, made in deference to Quebec's distinct institutional heritage, is forgotten in the pursuit of national standards for health care and post-secondary education. It is usually politicians from Quebec who, fortified by their belief in provincial autonomy, must point out that the constitutional division of authority, a principle of federalism, has been violated.

The *Parti Québécois* argument is most persuasive to someone whose intellectual tradition is rooted in French civil law and has been shaped by Roman Catholic doctrines, whose truths are defined by those in authority. Cultural nationalism appeals to the heart as well as to the mind, and so one cannot treat it as a cerebral exercise in persuasive logic. Yet, it seems that these two intellectual traditions, rooted in law and experience, which foster different approaches to problem solving, help to distinguish Canada's two major language groups, one from another. When the August 1992 Charlottetown Accord of Canadian provincial premiers and the country's prime minister stated that "Quebec constitutes within Canada a distinct society, which includes a French-speaking majority, a unique culture and a civil law tradition," it was acknowledging a historical truth. Moreover, those distinguishing traits of language, culture, and civil law are traceable to the French colony of *la Nouvelle France.*

Much has changed in Quebec, Acadia, and the other parts of French Canada in recent decades: religious practice has declined, family bonds have been loosened, technology and urban society have been embraced. In 1984 Quebeckers had the lowest birth rate in Canada: 1.45 children born to every woman of child-bearing age, as opposed to a national average of 1.7. This result of artificial birth control, a practice condemned by the Roman Catholic Church, reveals the collapse of clerical authority. In the 1990s, 40 percent of the children born in Quebec were born out of wedlock—an indication of the changed relationship between the sexes and the weakening of matrimonial conventions. As elsewhere in North America, there has been a sizable Asian, Caribbean, African, and Latin-American migration into the French-speaking regions of Canada. This makes the definition of Canada, even of French-speaking Canada, difficult. The pre-1945 stereotype of the French-Canadian "Habitant farmer," contained in the poems of William Henry Drummond and immortalized in the drawings of Edmond Massicotte, as deeply religious, conservative, blessed with numerous children, and living in a small, culturally homogeneous parish, has nothing to do with the lives of most French-speakers in Canada today.

There still remains a perceptible legacy from New France that sets French-speaking Canadians, especially those in Quebec, apart from their diverse compatriots. It is a legacy that goes beyond language. There are still elements of compassionate authoritarianism, of Christian humanity, of family solidarity, and of dogmatic idealism that are traceable to *la Nouvelle France.* How much of that legacy, now altered by the passage of time, will survive into the twenty-first century I cannot say. Historians usually face backward, and this makes them unreliable prophets of the future. Twentieth-century French Canadians were the heirs of New France and, in some respects, the apples had not fallen far from the tree.

Notes

1 Archives nationales de France, Archives des Colonies, série F3, vol. 2, f.198: De Meulles to the king, c.1684.

2 The theme of racial purity has now been superseded by an emphasis on the present generation's personal link with settlers from France. Thus Marcel Fournier, in Les *Européens au Canada, des origines à 1765* (Montreal: Editions du Fleuve, 1989), 32, writes, "all serious authors...are in agreement in saying that 97 percent of Quebec and Canada's French population comes from France." It is equally certain that most French-speakers have ancestors from countries other than France.

3 Apart from the circumstantial differences of being in a province with a French-speaking majority and being subject to a civil code rooted in French

jurisprudence, there are few outward differences to set French-speakers within Quebec apart from French-speaking Canadians in other provinces. The lack of tangible or visible differences is not critical to one's outlook. The wonderful thing about cultural nationalism is that if enough people believe that they belong to a group whose interests are incompatible with those of other peoples, then they will be a nationality, whatever the external evidence indicates. Nationalism is, after all, a state of mind.

4 Claude Bergeron, *Architecture du XXe siècle au Québec* (Montreal: Editions du Méridien, 1989), 58–61, provides floor plans of this urban, low-income housing, which is still plentiful in Quebec's cities.

5 Philippe Garigue, "French-Canadian Kinship and Urban life," in Marcel Rioux and Yves Martin, eds., *French-Canadian Society* (Toronto: McClelland and Stewart, 1964), 358–72.

6 G.M. Wrong, ed., "Louisbourg in 1745: The Anonymous lettre d'un Habitant de Louisbourg," *University of Toronto Studies—History,* 2d ser., 1 (1897): 2–74. The original reads, "Les Anglais sont les seuls peuples capables de ces bisarreries, qui font cependant partie de cette précieuse liberté dont ils se montrent si jaloux."

7 See the opposing petitions from the two language groups, for and against an elected assembly, reprinted in A. Shortt and A. G. Doughty, eds., *Documents relating to the Constitutional History of Canada, 1759–1791* (Ottawa: Dawson, 1907), 502–20, 524–27, 541–47.

8 N.W. Taylor, "French Canadians as Industrial Entrepreneurs," *Journal of Political Economy* 68 (February 1960): 37–52.

9 In 1999, when the proposition "respect for authority is important" was presented to Canadians, those who were most likely to agree were residents in areas with a preponderance of French-speakers, such as southern Manitoba, northern New Brunswick, and the Province of Quebec. See *Saturday Night* 114, no. 4 (1 May 1999), 22.

10 One can see the consequences of relying on one family's labor and of subsistence farming with few animals in the size of Quebec barns built in the early 1800s: they are much smaller than contemporary barns constructed in the adjoining Province of Ontario.

11 Shortt and Doughty, *Documents,* 189.

12 Ibid., 294.

13 Ibid., 197–98.

14 Ibid., 121.

15 Ibid., 203.

16 Philip Lawson, *The Imperial Challenge: Quebec and Britain in the Age of the American Revolution* (Montreal and Kingston: McGill-Queen's University Press, 1989), has put to rest the claim, contained in the 1776 Declaration of Independence and endorsed by historian Chester Martin, about the counterrevolutionary aims of the Quebec Act. The late Professor Lawson showed that abandonment of the 1763 Royal Proclamation was considered, as was a compromise with French legal and administrative traditions, well before the outbreak of violence in New England. Lawson also diminished the role of Sir Guy Carleton in effecting this reversal of British administrative policy for Canada.

17 Shortt and Doughty, *Documents,* 404.

18 Ibid., 420. Elizabeth Arthur, "French-Canadian Participation in the Government of Canada, 1775–85," *Canadian Historical Review* 32 (1951): 303–14, suggested that these appointees were compliant "yes-men" who could never be independent spokesmen for French Canada.

19 F. Ouellet, *Louis-Joseph Papineau: A Divided Soul* (Ottawa: Canadian Historical Association, 1961).

20 A coincidental rebellion in Upper Canada in 1837 also suffered from a lack of coordination because of poor communication, but its leadership was indigenous and the plan of William Lyon Mackenzie's followers to seize the provincial capital in a surprise attack showed enterprise and daring.

21 Allan Greer, *The Patriots and the People: Rebellion of 1837 in Rural Lower Canada* (Toronto: University of Toronto Press, 1993), 100–107, 229–33.

22 The masculine prejudices of the Patriotes are discussed in Greer, *The Patriots and the People,* 197–210.

23 L. A. Paquet, "Le féminisme, un mouvement pervers," from the December 1918 issue of *Le Canada français,* reprinted in G. R. Cook and W. Mitchinson, eds., *The Proper Sphere: Woman's Place in Canadian Society* (Toronto: Macmillan, 1976), 84–91.

24 The expansion and extent of these services are described in A. Beaudoin, ed., *Services sociaux à l'enfance, la famille, aux personnes âgées et dans le domaine de la santé: État de la situation au Québec* (Sillery: École de service social, Université Laval, 1988). The limitations and problems within this system are discussed by the Commission d'Enquête sur les Services de Santé et les Services sociaux, *Les services de santé et les services sociaux: Problématiques et* *enjeux* (Quebec: Gouvernement du Québec, 1987).

25 Marc Renaud, "Quebec's Middle Class in Search of Social Hegemony: Causes and Political Consequences," *International Review of Community Development,* n.s., 39/40 (1978): 1–36; reprinted in A. D. Gilbert, C. M. Wallace, and R. M. Bray, eds., *Reappraisals in Canadian History: Post-Confederation* (Scarborough: Prentice Hall, 1992), 451–87.

26 Under Bill 101, passed by Quebec's Parti Québécois government in 1977, English and bilingual signs were made illegal and all commercial enterprises with fifty or more employees were obliged to conduct their business in French. Even the international "stop" sign must read "arrêt," which reveals the nationalist antipathy to English. Quebec's linguistic minorities opposed the law on the grounds that it violated freedom of expression, guaranteed by the federal Charter of Rights and Freedoms. The Quebec Superior Court and the Supreme Court of Canada agreed, but the provincial government exercised the "notwithstanding clause" in the Canadian constitution to override these decisions. The absence of a populist tradition among French-speakers raises the question of other missing elements, in comparison with the rest of Canada. Political separation from France in 1760 and a period of cultural isolation during the Anglo-French wars from 1793 to 1815 meant that French Canada was scarcely touched by eighteenth-century Romanticism, which celebrated nature as a source of spiritual renewal. Later, French historical romanticism did inspire paintings of past military glories and poems that nostalgically recalled the French Regime. Landscape painting was a late development in French Canada, as was literature in praise of natural beauty. Joseph Légaré (1795–1855) was called by Barry Lord "the father of Quebec landscape painting." Légaré's views contain figures or some manmade structure, and this "father" had few children. In the 1800s unpopulated scenes of Quebec's countryside were painted by English-speakers such as Lucius O'Brien, Homer Watson, and John A. Fraser. The charming landscapes produced by Clarence Gagnon (1881–1942), a French Canadian, show picturesque country villages, purged of telephone poles and wires, automobiles, and power lines. His paintings were a visual expression of the idealization of rural life among French Canadians in a postindustrial era. Symmetrical and formal private gardens were part of the French tradition. Naturalistic public parks, such as Montreal's Mount Royal Park or Quebec City's Battlefield Park, were introduced to Quebec by English-speakers in the 1800s. The botanical garden was so closely associated with British Canadians that, during the nineteenth century, many French Canadians referred to Montreal's botanical garden (*jardin botanique*) as the "jardin britannique." The absence of romantic naturalism in French-Canada's past explains the slow acceptance of the ecology movement in that province.

27 I realize that anyone who knows the nature of Canada will find this claim that all the other peoples of the country form a single cultural nation bizarre. Canada has a political nationality; it is not a single cultural entity, even if one subtracts Quebec from the equation. Talking about "Canada" and "Quebec" as mutually exclusive entities, when one comprises the other, presents another intellectual challenge.

28 Parti Québécois, *Programme du Parti Québécois: Édition 1989* (n.p., 1989).

"Chiefly Landholders, Farmers, and Others": The Loyalist Reality

NORMAN KNOWLES

In his 1861 work *The History of the Settlement of Upper Canada*, the Belleville physician and amateur historian William Canniff described the United Empire Loyalist as "one who advocated, or wished to have maintained, the unity of the British Empire" and "who felt as much a Briton in the colony of America, as if he were in old England." Guided by "higher motives," Canniff proclaimed, many of "this noble class relinquished comfortable homes, rather than live under an alien flag" and "preferred, above all measure, to enter a wilderness and hew out a new home." "They would live anywhere, endure any toil, undergo any privation," he insisted, "so long as they were in the King's dominion, and the good old flag waved over their head, and their families." Finding themselves in a threatening landscape with few resources, these "honest, devoted, loyal, truthful, law abiding" refugees overcame repeated hardships and setbacks and transformed the Upper Canadian wilderness into a fruitful field through collective cooperation and hospitality. Ever vigilant in their guard against American aggression, Canniff concluded, the "U.E. Loyalists have been as a barrier of rock, against which the waves of Republicanism have dashed in vain."[1] Canniff's portrayal of the Loyalists as an elite group of anti-American Anglophiles and aristocratic imperialists is a classic statement of what historians have labelled the *Loyalist tradition*. Canniff's description of the Loyalists, however, bears little relationship to the historical reality.

Surprisingly little is known about the approximately 7,500 Loyalists who by 1785 had settled in what would become Upper Canada. The Loyalist settlers fell into three distinct categories. The largest group encompassed the 3,500 soldiers and dependants of the provincial regiments. These Regimental Loyalists were supplemented by a much smaller group of unincorporated civilian Loyalists who had migrated to the province overland and by two companies of Associated Loyalists who had sailed from New York City under the leadership of Captain Michael Grass and Major Peter Van Alstine.[2] These groups of Loyalists were joined in Upper Canada by over 2,000 of Britain's Native allies among the Six Nations and the tribes of the Ohio country. One group, under the leadership of John Deseronto, settled at Tyendinaga on the Bay of Quinte in 1784. The following year a second, larger group settled with Joseph Brant along the Grand River on lands purchased for them by the British government from the indigenous Mississauguas of the region.[3]

While some Loyalists were undoubtedly ideologically dedicated to the preservation of

Norman Knowles, "'Chiefly Landholders, Farmers, and Others': The Loyalist Reality," Chapter 1 of *Inventing the Loyalists: The Ontario Loyalist Tradition and the Creation of Usable Pasts* (Toronto: University of Toronto Press, 1997), 14–25. Reprinted with permission of the publisher.

the Empire, the motives of many were decidedly mixed.[4] Patronage and commercial ties dictated the position of many Loyalists; others were merely opportunists who pledged allegiance to whichever side appeared to be on the ascendancy locally; still others were reluctant Loyalists, who took sides only when forced out of a preferred state of neutrality by Patriot harassment or Loyalist intimidation.[5] The motives of the Loyalist refugees did not impress Major Robert Mathews, the secretary to the governor of Quebec, Frederick Haldimand. Most of the refugees, Mathews asserted, were "in fact only Mechanics... removed from one situation to practice their Trades in another."[6] Natives had their own reasons for allying themselves with Britain during the American Revolution. The tribes that sided with the British did so as allies, not as subjects of the Crown, and they fought largely to preserve the integrity of their tribal lands against the rising tide of white settlement.[7]

In a report to the Loyalist Claims Commission in January of 1786, the administrator of Quebec, Lieutenant-Governor Henry Hope, observed that the Loyalists were "chiefly landholders, farmers, and others from the inland part of the continent" and that there were few "persons of great property or consequence" among them.[8] Although no comprehensive analysis exists of the backgrounds and occupations of the Upper Canadian Loyalists, two studies shed considerable light on the nature of the Loyalist migration. Bruce Wilson drew a rough portrait of Upper Canadian Loyalists from the 488 compensation claims filed between 1783 and 1789 with the commission established by the British government to investigate the losses and services of the American Loyalists. Wilson discovered that 90 per cent of the claimants were pioneer farmers of modest means. Almost half of those seeking compensation indicated that they had cleared less than ten acres of land. The remaining 10 per cent of the claimants included five public office holders, a teacher, a physician, two surgeons, and a handful of merchants and tavern-keepers. Just over half of those applying for compensation were foreign born and only 8 per cent were English by birth.[9] A similar picture emerges in Larry Turner's study of the Associated Loyalists of Adolphustown. Of the 240 Associated Loyalists who settled at Adolphustown in 1784, Turner found that only five of the families had accumulated any significant degree of wealth before the revolutionary war. The majority were drawn from the middle and lower strata of society. Farmers were by far the largest occupational group, although there were a number of skilled craftsmen. The Associated Loyalists of Adolphustown were also an ethnically and religiously diverse lot. Turner estimated that about 37 per cent were of Dutch ethnicity, 28 per cent British, 20 per cent French, and 15 per cent German. The overwhelming majority appear to have been Methodists, although there were a significant number of Quakers and only a few Anglicans.[10]

The Loyalists who settled in Upper Canada were not members of a "noble class" representing gentle birth, wealth, and learning. While a small officer class did exist, the Loyalist rank and file consisted primarily of farmers and artisans of modest means. Most Upper Canadian Loyalists were in fact recent immigrants to the American colonies who had yet to establish themselves. Not yet fully assimilated into American society and feeling themselves threatened by more powerful elements within the colonies, many immigrants chose loyalty as an alternative to economic and political subjugation. Loyalists also tended to be members of ethnic and religious minorities who feared domination by their more numerous neighbours. A culturally diverse group, the typical Upper Canadian Loyalist would not, as Canniff asserted, have "felt as much a Briton in the colony of America as if he were in old England."

Discontent, disappointment, and division characterized the resettlement process. Rumours that all the best land had been granted to Native peoples or that the settlements would be of a military nature and the settlers obligated to serve at any time produced unrest and unease among the anxious refugees. Loyalists encamped in Quebec during the winter of 1783 constantly complained about their primitive accommodations and besieged government officials with petitions for supplies and assistance. One particularly "extravagant" petition demanded that each family be equipped with a complete set of tools, building supplies, arms and ammunition, one year's clothing, a supply of seed, two horses, two cows, and six sheep.[11] At one point, an exasperated Haldimand curtly advised the Loyalist refugees that he would find passage for them at the earliest date for Nova Scotia. Disenchanted with conditions, many left the camps, not for Nova Scotia, but to return to their former homes in the new republic to salvage what they could.

Matters did not improve once the Loyalists arrived at the site of their new homes. Incomplete surveys, inadequate supplies, and disputes over location tickets produced widespread bitterness and resentment. In July of 1784, for example, Robert Mathews informed Sir John Johnson that "the settlers at Cataraqui are in great disorder, not yet having got upon their Land, many of them unprovided with a Blanket to cover Them, scarce any Turnip seed and neither Axes or Hoes for Half of them."[12] Civilian settlers charged that Regimental Loyalists received favourable treatment and had been allotted the best land. Officers complained that the process had been too impartial and that special provision should have been made so that they were assured the prime parcels of land. Such were the divisions among the Loyalists that in the Royal Townships laid out along the St Lawrence settlers were divided, at their own request, according to their ethnicity and religion. The first township was consequently allotted to Catholic Highlanders, the second to Scottish Presbyterians, the third to German Calvinists, the fourth to German Lutherans, and the last to Anglicans.[13]

Once the Loyalists were settled, their economic and political behaviour was far removed from the cooperative and communitarian spirit idealized by Canniff. "Disputes amongst the Loyalists frequently arise," observed Major Ross in July of 1784.[14] Officers of the Loyalist regiments often complained that they were unable to exert any influence over those formerly under their command. Loyalist society was essentially atomistic. Settlers consistently acted as individuals, refusing to lay aside their self-interest for the common good or to merge their identity into some greater whole. In this respect, Loyalist society differed little from that in the United States.[15]

There is little truth in the image of the Loyalist as an Anglophile who venerated all things British and detested all things American. Governor Haldimand was shocked when Associated Loyalists insisted upon "a form of government as nearly similar as possible to that which they Enjoyed in the Province of New York."[16] Contemporary observers noted that "passions mutually subsided" shortly after the Revolution and that "the natural feelings of consanguinity, amnity, and personal friendship revived."[17] Articulate Loyalist leaders, such as Richard Cartwright, were consciously Anglo-American and vigorously resisted efforts to transform the Upper Canadian wilderness into a little Britain. During the first session of the Upper Canadian legislature in 1793, Cartwright complained that the province's lieutenant-governor, John Graves Simcoe, "thinks every existing regulation in England would be proper here" and "seems bent on copying all the subordinate establishments without considering the great disparity of the two countries in every respect." Cartwright advised Simcoe that "a government should be formed for a Country and not a country strained and distorted for the Accommodation of a preconceived and speculative scheme of Government."[18] A Loyalist background did not provide a sure guide to political affiliation. While Loyalists of the officer class tended to be firm supporters of the social and political status quo, rank and file Loyalists were much more likely to advocate reform and support the opposition.[19] Preoccupied with carving out an existence on the Upper Canadian frontier, most Loyalists had neither the time nor the inclination to devote much attention to politics or abstract questions about the nature of government.

By the outbreak of the War of 1812, the Loyalist element was scarcely noticeable among the diversity of people that had come to the province to take up land or engage in trade.[20] The Loyalist response to the call to arms during the war was, at best, equivocal. A government report at the war's end declared that the son or daughter of a Loyalist would not be entitled to land grants unless able to demonstrate "that the Parent retained his Loyalty during the late War, and was under no suspicion of aiding or assisting the Enemy—and if a Son, then of Age, that he was also Loyal during the late War, and did his duty in defence of the Province—and if a Daughter of an U.E. Loyalist married, that her Husband was loyal, and did his duty in defence of the Province."[21] The government obviously had serious doubts about the contributions of the Loyalist community to the war effort. Contrary to conventional belief, the War of 1812 did not enhance or create a Loyalist identity in Upper Canada. Divided by race, origins, and religion before the war, Upper Canadians emerged from the war even more divided. Disputes over compensation, militia pay, land grants, pensions, and medals for heroism were the source of considerable postwar acrimony.[22]

The militia legend—the belief that the war was fought and won by the Upper Canadian militia—originated as a piece of wartime propaganda designed to cover up the extent of disaffection and desertion in the province and to encourage wavering elements within the population to respond to the government's call to arms.[23] For men like John Strachan, who were not of Loyalist background, the militia legend provided a usable past that was more inclusive and integrating than the Loyalist experience. After the war, the militia legend was used by members of the governing "Compact" to justify their continued hold on the province's positions of privilege and authority. It was not until the 1850s, when the memory of wartime grievances began to fade and many of the remaining veterans had passed away, that the war began to be looked back upon as a great national achievement and to be interpreted as a Loyalist victory.[24]

The Loyalist reality differed significantly from Canniff's idealized treatment. The original Loyalist settlers of Ontario lacked a coherent and cohesive identity. Mixed motives, ethnic and religious diversity, preoccupation with the everyday work of surviving in the wilderness, frequent relocation, marriage into non-Loyalist families, and the influx of large numbers of American settlers all contributed to the failure of the Loyalists to develop a distinct self-awareness.[25] The question remains: when and why was the image of the Loyalist as an aristocratic, principled, Yankee-hating Anglophile invented?

If the original Loyalist settlers lacked a coherent and cohesive identity and ideology, they shared a fundamental common interest: land. It was land that attracted the Loyalists to Upper Canada in the first place or induced them to stay once they had arrived. Land was the main and for several years virtually the only source of wealth. For the Loyalists, land also had a symbolic value. Deprived of their landholdings during the Revolution, Loyalists viewed land grants from the Crown as recognition that their service and sacrifice had been worthy, their allegiance was legitimate, and their claims were valid. It was the successful battle to subdue the land, not the lost battles of the Revolution, that assumed the largest place in the reminiscences of the Loyalist pioneers. Not surprisingly, then, government land policy and the debates that it aroused played a critical role in the early evolution of the Upper Canadian Loyalist tradition.

It was land that initially set the Loyalists apart as a distinct group. In 1783 General Frederick Haldimand, governor of the Province of Quebec, received royal instructions directing him to allocate lands to all Loyalist refugees desiring to become actual settlers. Grants were to be free, unencumbered by survey and patent fees, and would vary according to rank and status. Heads of families were to receive 100 acres with an additional fifty acres for each member of the family. A single man was entitled to fifty acres. Grants to those who served in one of the Loyalist regiments ranged from 100 acres for privates to a 1,000 acres for field officers. An exception was the 84th Regiment, which had been recruited with the understanding that field officers would receive 5,000 acres, captains 3,000 acres, subalterns 2,000 acres, and non-commissioned officers 200 acres. In the face of considerable resentment over the 84th Regiment's favoured treatment, an order-in-council was passed in 1788 extending the 84th's generous terms to the other Loyalist regiments. In 1787 Lord Dorchester increased the grant by 200 acres to heads of families who had already improved their lands. "Lord Dorchester's bounty" was interpreted by the Land Boards established to oversee the settlement process to mean that all those who had borne arms would be entitled to 300 acres or more, according to their rank, and that other Loyalists would receive an initial grant of 200 acres.[26]

It soon became obvious, however, that not all of the settlers flocking into the province were genuine Loyalists. Dorchester resolved in 1789 "to put a mark of honour upon the families who had adhered to the Unity of Empire and Joined the Royal Standard in America before the Treaty of Separation in the year 1783." An order-in-council was passed directing the Land Boards to compile lists of Loyalists "to the end that their posterity may be discriminated from future settlers...as proper objects...for distinguished benefits and privileges." As a first step in this direction, it was resolved that the Loyalists and "all their children and their Descendants by either sex are to be distinguished by the following capitals affixed to their names: U.E., alluding to their great principle, the Unity of Empire." Although this "mark of honour" was to appear in all parish registers, militia rolls, and other public documents, it was not consistently or widely used in the province.[27] A more tangible gesture was the decision that sons of Loyalists on their coming of age and daughters at the time of their marriage were to receive a land grant of 200 acres free of all survey and patent fees. Although the Loyalists were to be set apart from all subsequent settlers as a group deserving of special recognition, Dorchester was not very precise in his definition of who was a Loyalist. Acceptable wartime service remained unprescribed and no cut-off date for residence in the province was established. Given such loose definitions, inclusion on the U.E. List can hardly be said to identify committed Loyalists.

The text of Dorchester's order-in-council became the subject of considerable controversy over the next three decades. The terms of the order-in-council stipulated that such grants were limited to the children of Loyalists already in the province and would be made only if there were "no default in the due Cultivation and Improvement of the Lands, already assigned to the Head of the Family, of which they were members." It was also clear that the children were expected to conform to all settlement regulations and were thus expected to occupy and improve the grants. Unlike the "mark of honour," the land grants to children, or "U.E. Rights" as they came to be known, were never intended to be "perpetual" or to constitute an imprescriptible right.[28] Loyalists and their descendants, however, imposed an entirely different construction upon the meaning of the order-in-council. It was repeatedly argued that Dorchester was simply implementing the royal will to recognize, reward, and compensate the Loyalists for their services and sacrifices on behalf of the Crown during the

Revolution. All Loyalists, irrespective of their time of arrival in the province, it was maintained, were entitled to land free from all conditions and expenses for themselves and their children.

The controversy that came to surround these "U.E. Rights," perhaps more than any other single factor, accounts for the earliest attempts to transform the Loyalists into heroic figures who endured untold sufferings and privations on behalf of their unwavering allegiance to the Empire and British constitutional principles. Whenever the government attempted to put an end to Loyalist claims, to purge the U.E. List of fraudulent names or to impose settlement duties on U.E. grants, it was confronted by a storm of protest from surviving Loyalists and their disaffected offspring and descendants. The careers of early reformers such as Robert Thorpe and William Weekes were based to a considerable extent on the discontent arising from the government's handling of U.E. Rights. With each confrontation the Loyalists' sacrifices, their services to the Crown and Empire, in short, their claims to special status and recognition, reached new heights.[29]

In 1832 an order-in-council was issued stipulating that patents would not be issued for land held on location tickets until it was proved that a resident settler had been established on part of the grant. The following year even more stringent regulations were introduced: U.E. Rights were not to be located unless the original grantee was prepared to settle in person on the lot, and patents were not to be issued until two years' residence had been completed.[30] The government's actions produced a wave of dissent among speculators in U.E. Rights. The protests culminated with "An Address to His Majesty on the subject of U.E. Rights" from the Assembly in 1834. The petitioners described the Loyalists as "the most faithful and loyal subjects of His Majesty King George the Third." "Uncompromising" in their "zeal and fidelity to His Majesty's cause, person, and government," the Loyalists "unhesitatingly sacrifice[d], not only their possessions and worldly effects, but also the peace and comfort of themselves and their families, by voluntarily joining the Royal Standard." Land grants from the Crown, the petitioners insisted, "were always considered and understood in the shape of a debt due by the government...as a reward for meritorious services performed, and for which they considered they held the pledge and faith of government."[31] Underlying the increasingly elevated rhetoric, however, was a very real economic interest. U.E. Rights had become the object of considerable speculation, and any restriction on their use or transfer threatened to reduce their value. Significantly, 1834 also marked the fiftieth anniversary of the Loyalists' settlement in the province. A year earlier, New Brunswick Loyalists had marked the occasion with a number of celebrations.[32] Despite the continuing debate over U.E. Rights, the anniversary passed without comment in Upper Canada.

Closely related to the land issue was the question of immigration. The desire to recognize the Loyalists immediately came into conflict with the imperatives of settling and developing the province. In the end, the forces of development prevailed. Upper Canada's first lieutenant-governor, John Graves Simcoe, lured settlers into the province from the United States with the promise of free grants of land. The Loyalist population soon found itself swamped and its power and influence reduced. By 1812 there were approximately 100,000 people in the province, 80 per cent of whom were recent arrivals from the United States.[33]

The Loyalist response to this influx was mixed. Many welcomed the Americans: without additional settlers, U.E. Rights had little speculative value. During the Alien controversy of the 1820s members of the House of Assembly of Loyalist stock and representatives from centres of Loyalist settlement were among the most vocal critics of the government's policy to prescribe the rights of Americans already in the province and to exclude additional American settlers from entering the province.[34] A Loyalist correspondent to the *Upper Canada Herald* insisted that American settlers were "faithful subjects" and contributed as much as the first Loyalists "to the clearing of the settlement, and improving of the country."[35] Only the relatively few Loyalists who had entrenched themselves within the provincial establishment vehemently opposed the influx of American settlers. Opponents of American immigration portrayed Upper Canada as the exclusive preserve of those persons whose loyalty had been tested and found true during the American Revolution and subsequently in the War of 1812. Recent arrivals from the United States were described as radicals who threatened to subvert the very foundations of Upper Canadian society. Characteristic of this viewpoint were the words of a correspondent to the Kingston *Chronicle* of 1 February 1822 opposing the election of Barnabas Bidwell to the Legislative Assembly:

> Well can I remember how I was driven from them [the scenes of my youth], and from the spot where my father fell, fighting for his King against rebels. By whom was I robbed of my patrimony—by whom was my parent deprived of life? Even by such as him who now claims equal privileges with the best of us. I was driven, like many of you, from my home, for I scorned to join the rebels, or to desert my King:—it makes my blood boil within me to think of it. Not only the leader of a violent democratic faction, one who had betrayed a public trust, who has committed crimes...who held a seat in their House of Congress, and was amongst the loudest and most inveterate enemies of Great Britain...comes now forward after a lapse of years, to enjoy one of your highest prerogatives, to amend and make your laws, to sit, cheek by jowl, with your honorable men, and like himself up in your Council Chamber as one whose hands are clean.... What are you about ye sons of U.E. Loyalists? What are you about? Will you suffer these things?[36]

Beneath such heated rhetoric lay questions of power, influence and income. On the one hand, American settlers threatened to undermine the power and privileges of the established leaders of the province. On the other, they promised to increase the speculative value of U.E. Rights.

As politics began to polarize around issues such as the Alien Question, the question of allegiance assumed a central position in the political discourse of the period. Loyalty, narrowly defined, became essential for entry into and advancement within the provincial power structure. The Tory establishment appropriated the example of the Loyalists as a weapon against the voices of opposition and reform. Every movement which questioned the position and privileges of the governing compact was dismissed as a manifestation of subversive republicanism and a deviation from Loyalist principles. An address delivered by Richard Cartwright to a Kingston town hall meeting in March of 1832 was typical of the manner in which the Loyalist experience was arrogated for partisan purposes during the divisive years prior to the 1837 rebellions. "As the son and the grandson of an U.E. Loyalist," Cartwright attacked "the machinations of the disloyal and disaffected who are now industriously endeavouring to persuade the ignorant and unstable that certain weighty grievances exist." Cartwright reminded his audience that the province "owes its origins" to the Loyalists—"a set of gallant men, many of whom were the greatest Landholders in the United States," who "contended for the constitution, and rights of the Crown" and "hazarded their lives and fortunes, in attempting to put down Rebellion and preserve the unity of the Empire."[37] As David Mills has noted, such rhetoric forced reformers to appropriate and reshape the language of Loyalism for themselves. In their defence, reformers claimed to be equally loyal to the British Crown and constitution, frequently claimed to be of Loyalist background, and often cited the Loyalists' dedication to principle to justify dissent against what they perceived to be the narrow and self-serving interests of the provincial administration.[38]

After the resolution of the land and Alien questions in the 1830s, the province's Loyalist origins became increasingly peripheral to political debate in Upper Canada. The experience and example of the Loyalists were rarely referred to following the 1837 rebellions and the subsequent debates over responsible government. By the 1840s the exclusive definition of loyalty that had been used by the governing elite to support its power and privileges was gradually displaced by an assimilative concept of loyalty that acknowledged the place of newcomers and of party in the political system. Loyalty ceased to be a birthright, but it could be earned through commitment to the community and the achievement of respectability.[39] No longer useful as a political or social weapon, the experience and example of the Loyalists became a distant memory throughout most of the 1840s and 1850s. Although the seventy-fifth anniversary of the arrival of the Loyalists was marked by substantial celebrations in New Brunswick in 1858, the milestone passed virtually unnoticed in Canada West.[40] Forces were building, however, that were to revive interest in the province's Loyalist past over the next few years.

Notes

1 William Canniff, *History of the Settlement of Upper Canada with Special Reference to the Bay of Quinté* (Toronto 1869), 616, 617, 625, 634.

2 The Loyalist migration to Upper Canada is discussed in Robert Allan, ed., *The Loyal Americans: The Military Role of the Loyalist Provincial Corps and Their Settlement in British North America* (Ottawa 1983); A.L. Burt, *The Old Province of Quebec,* vol. II (Toronto 1968), chap. 15; Gerald M. Craig, *Upper Canada: The Formative Years, 1784–1841* (Toronto 1963), chap. 1; Bruce Wilson, *As She Began: An Illustrated Introduction to Loyalist Ontario* (Toronto 1981).

3 On the settlement of the Six Nations see C.M. Johnston, *The Valley of the Six Nations* (Toronto 1964).

4 The best discussion of Loyalist ideology is Janice Potter, *The Liberty We Seek: Loyalist Ideology in Colonial New York and Massachusetts* (Cambridge 1983). Potter maintains that the Loyalists presented a "comprehensive, logical, and consistent alternative to Patriot proposals" based on the political thought of Blackstone, Bollingbroke, and Burke (viii). Potter's study is particularly relevant to Upper Canada, since the majority of Loyalists who settled there came from New York. Very few of the vocal elite studied by Potter, however, actually settled in the province. See also Ann Gorman Condon, "Marching to a Different Drummer: The Political Philosophy of the American Loyalists," in *Red, White and True Blue: The Loyalists in the Revolution,* ed. Esmund Wright (New York 1976) and John E. Ferling, *The Loyalist Mind and the American Revolution* (University Park and London 1977).

5 For a discussion of the Loyalists' mixed motives see Wallace Brown, *The King's Friends: The Composition and Motives of the American Loyalist Claimants* (Providence 1965); Robert McCluer Calhoon, *The Loyalists in Revolutionary America, 1760–1781* (New York 1973); William Nelson, *The American Tory* (Boston 1964).

6 Major Robert Mathews to Stephen DeLancey, 15 April 1784 in *The Settlement of the United Empire Loyalists on the Upper St Lawrence and Bay of Quinte in 1784: A Documentary Record,* ed. Ernest Cruikshank (Toronto 1934), 67.

7 On Native involvement in the American Revolution see Barbara Graymount, *The Iroquois in the American Revolution* (Syracuse 1972) and Francis Jennings, "Tribal Loyalty and Tribal Independence," in *Red, White and True Blue,* ed. Wright.

8 Quoted in Burt, *The Old Province of Quebec,* vol. II, 79.

9 Wilson, *As She Began,* 13–18, 120.

10 Larry Turner, *Voyage of a Different Kind: The Associated Loyalists of Kingston and Adolphustown* (Belleville 1984), 141–4.

11 "Major Mathews to Major Ross, 29 March 1784" and "Memorial of the Associated Loyalists, January 1784" in Cruikshank, ed., *Settlement of Loyalists,* 41–2

12 "Major Mathews to Sir John Johnson, 19 July 1784" in Cruikshank, ed., *Settlement of Loyalists,* 138.

13 On the settlement process see Craig, *Upper Canada,* chap. 1, and Wilson, *As She Began,* chaps 3 and 4.

14 "Major Ross to Major Mathews, 7 July 1784," in Cruikshank, ed., *Settlement of Loyalists,* 132.

15 Donald Akenson, *The Irish in Ontario: A Study in Rural History* (Montreal and Kingston 1984), chap. 2.

16 "Memorial of the Associated Loyalists, January 1784," in Cruikshank, ed., *Settlement of Loyalists,* 41–2.

17 Robert Gourlay, *Statistical Account of Upper Canada* (1822; Rpt. Toronto: S.R. Publishers, 1966), 115. For a discussion of the Loyalists' decidedly ambivalent attitudes towards Britain and the United States see Jane Errington, *The Lion, the Eagle and Upper Canada: A Developing Colonial Ideology* (Montreal and Kingston 1987).

18 Errington, *The Lion, the Eagle, and Upper Canada,* 30–2.

19 J.K. Johnson has calculated that 36 per cent of Conservative members of the House of Assembly between 1791 and 1841 were of Loyalist stock compared with 25 per cent of Reformers. During the same period, the main centres of Loyalist settlement in eastern Ontario returned forty-five Reformers and only forty-two Conservatives; *Becoming Prominent: Regional Leadership in Upper Canada, 1791–1941* (Montreal and Kingston 1989), 140–9.

20 For a discussion of the diffusion of Loyalist power and influence see ibid., chap. 5; H.V. Nelles, "Loyalism and Local Power: The District of Niagara, 1792–1837," *Ontario History,* 58 (1966), 99–114; Bruce G. Wilson, *The Enterprises of Robert Hamilton: A Study of Wealth and Influence in Early Upper Canada, 1776–1812* (Ottawa 1983), chap. 3.

21 Quoted in Craig, *Upper Canada,* 89. For a detailed discussion of the rather halfhearted and lacklustre Loyalist contribution to the war effort in Leeds and Landsdowne townships see Akenson, *The Irish in Ontario,* chap. 3.

22 On the controversies that followed the War of 1812 in Upper Canada see George Sheppard, *Plunder, Profit and Paroles: A Social History of the War of 1812 in Upper Canada* (Montreal and Kingston 1994).

23 R.A. Bowler, "Propaganda in Upper Canada," M.A. thesis, Queen's University, 1964, 37–40. For a discussion of the evolution of the militia legend see Keith Walden, "Isaac Brock: Man and Myth. A Study of the Militia Myth of the War of 1812 in Upper Canada, 1812–1912," M.A. thesis, Queen's University, 1971.

24 S.F. Wise, "The War of 1812 in Popular History," in *God's Peculiar Peoples: Essays on Political Culture in Nineteenth-Century Canada,* ed. A.B. McKillop and Paul Romney (Ottawa 1993), 149–68.

25 For an analysis of the frequent relocation of Loyalist settlers see Darrell A. Norris, "Household and Transiency in a Loyalist Township: The People of Adolphustown, 1784–1822," *Histoire Sociale—Social History,* 13 (1980), 399–415.

26 Lillian F. Gates, *Land Policies of Upper Canada* (Toronto 1968), 15–21.

27 *Fourth Report of the Ontario Bureau of Archives, 1906* (Toronto 1907), 184–5.

28 Gates, *Land Policies of Upper Canada,* 20–1.

29 For a detailed description of the controversy surrounding U.E. Rights between Dorchester's order-in-council of 1787 and their abolition in 1835 see Gates, *Land Policies of Upper Canada,* chaps. 5 and 9.

30 Ibid., 132–3.

31 "Address to His Majesty on the Subject of U.E. Loyalist Rights," *Journal of the Legislative Assembly of Upper Canada,* 4th session, 11th Parliament, 1834, Appendix, 51–2.

32 Murray Barkley, "The Loyalist Tradition in New Brunswick: The Growth and Evolution of an Historical Myth, 1825–1914," *Acadiensis,* 4 (1975), 10.

33 R.C. Harris and John Warkentin, *Canada before Confederation* (Toronto 1974), 116–7.

34 Gates, *Land Policies of Upper Canada,* 99–100.

35 Cited in Mills, *Idea of Loyalty,* 47.

36 Kingston *Chronicle,* 1 Feb. 1822.

37 Cited in Mills, *Idea of Loyalty,* 76.

38 Ibid., 99–104.

39 This transformation in the understanding of political allegiance is admirably described in ibid.

40 Barkley, "Loyalist Tradition in New Brunswick," 18–20.

The Family in Exile: Loyalist Social Values after the Revolution

ANN GORMAN CONDON

"All happy families are alike but an unhappy family is unhappy after its own fashion." Thus begins Leo Tolstoy's *Anna Karenina,* that extraordinary fictional journey into the private lives of the Russian aristocracy in the nineteenth century.[1] While modern anthropologists might gasp at Tolstoy's willingness to make such sweeping generalizations about the family, no one can deny his success in creating a vivid world of intimacy and intrigue, devotion and deceit, noble suffering and base humiliation, climaxing, of course, in the necessary self-destruction of its flawed heroine, followed by a ringing affirmation of traditional, and very Christian, family values.

Culturally, Tsarist Russia was a far different place than colonial Canada, but they did, for a short while, have one thing in common: an official ruling class. Until the mid-nineteenth century, the British North American provinces were ruled by a group of privileged officers who held their powers independently of the people they governed and reinforced their authority by elaborate social codes and extensive family connections. Indeed, so powerful and so notorious were these sets of provincial oligarchs that they are known pejoratively even to this day in the former colony of Upper Canada, now Ontario, as "The Family Compact."

Alas, thus far Canada's period of gentry rule has inspired no Tolstoyan masterpiece, no insider account of the intimate life, passions and pairings of this select group. In fact, it is both remarkable and regrettable that, for all the many treatises on the political operations of the Family Compact, we have so few accounts of its internal dynamics: its elaborate network of filiations and obligations, its shared aspirations and anxieties, and the mechanisms by which it ensured the transmission not only of property and power from generation to generation, but of a distinctive code of values.[2]

Using the new methodologies developed by family historians and the wealth of personal letters left by prominent Loyalist families (which extend in some cases through four generations), I have begun a research project aimed at discovering the personal bonds and ideals which united these people over such a long stretch of time. Eventually, I will include representative family writings from five of the British North American colonies, spread over three generations. I have started with the Maritime provinces because the Loyalist style of cultural leadership was established here so very quickly after their arrival in the 1780s and is so well chronicled in their letters to each other.

This essay represents the "first fruits" of my work, my first attempt to identify patterns and

---

Ann Gorman Condon, "The Family in Exile: Loyalist Social Values after the Revolution," in Margaret Conrad, ed. *Intimate Relations: Family and Community in Planter Nova Scotia* (Fredericton: Acadiensis Press, 1995), 42–53.

figures in this very complex material, based mainly on the Jarvis Papers and Robinson Papers in the New Brunswick Museum and the Bliss Papers in the Public Archives of Nova Scotia. Unfortunately editorial constraints will not permit me to explore the wealth of material in these letters fully, but let me at least hint at the tone and atmosphere of family life among the Loyalist grandees by quoting three sets of love letters from prominent Loyalists to their wives.

My first example is a letter from Edward Winslow, the unfailingly gallant, but perpetually impoverished, Massachusetts Loyalist, to his wife Mary. The two had married before the revolutionary war and she accompanied him on his circuitous flight pattern after 1775—from Boston, to Halifax, to New York City, to Annapolis, Nova Scotia, and finally, ten years later, to their permanent abode in Kingsclear, New Brunswick. Throughout this long hegira, Mary managed the family household which at times included the first eight of their 11 children, Edward's elderly parents and his two spinster sisters. The letter I quote was written in 1784, while Edward was in Halifax, looking, as always, for a profitable job, and apparently aware that his lonely, overburdened wife could use some cheering up. Winslow starts off with trumpets blaring:

> what do I care whether it's the fashion for men to write long letters to their wives or not.... In matters where my own feelings are concerned I will not be shackled by any of the rules which bind the generality of mankind.... I cannot enjoy a pleasure equal to that of writing to you, and that's sufficient for writing. If other men do not experience the same sensation they have not the same degree of affection.

He then launches into a hilarious description of the fashionable ladies of Halifax and, with mock pity, bemoans the fact that the

> immensity of False-Tops False Curls, monstrous Caps. Grease, Filth of various kinds, Jewels, painted paper and trinkets, hide and deform heads of Hair that in their natural state are really beautiful. Rouge & other dirt cover cheeks and faces that without would be tolerable, whilst the unfortunate neck and breasts remain open to the inclemency of the weather & the view of the World....

But his Mary, he notes, is the exact opposite: "From 16 years old to the present time you have literally set your Cap at no creature on earth but me. Regardless of Fashion you have only endeavoured by uniform cleanliness to make yourself desirable in my eyes." After declaring his continuing love for her, Winslow closes by saying he still hopes that she will be able once more to enter the world of fashion and elegance.[3]

My second example is a series of letters from Beverley Robinson, the dashing young military officer from New York. Beverley had married Nancy Barclay during the war, and he proved, in New Brunswick, to be a bit of a martinet. Even though Nancy had abandoned a comfortable home in New York City for a refugee farm on the Nashwaaksis River, and had borne 11 children during their marriage, Beverley cannot resist chastising her for "laziness" and negligence. In one 1799 letter, he gave her elaborate instructions on the proper way to cool down and curry horses, and then proceeded to remind her to wrap his doughnuts securely so they will remain moist. The last batch were so dry he could not eat them![4]

Yet the petty irritations of married life did not undermine Beverley's devotion to his wife. For example, when he heard that Nancy was worried about losing her attractiveness now that she was forced to wear spectacles, Robinson rushed to reassure her with this stunning declaration:

> ... my present feelings have nothing to do with the respectability of your appearance, no madam my imagination is not confined to the age of 45 but wanders back to those days of yore when you was all youth and beauty I all ardour and affection...you are and shall be my beloved and adored mistress and as such only I will cherish the recollection of you....[5]

A year later on their twenty-second wedding anniversary Beverley acknowledged, with exquisite sensitivity, that although many changes had taken place since "the day that gave my Nancy to me, I can truly say that she is dearer to me now than when I received her with the rapture of a Bridegroom...."[6]

My final example concerns Jonathan Bliss. A crusty, 47-year-old bachelor when he came to New Brunswick, Bliss had spent the revolutionary war in England, enjoying, to the full, the pleasures of London and Bristol. He came to New Brunswick for sake of a job, but candidly admitted that he was too old, too spoiled by England to appreciate such a new country, however promising.[7] Bliss performed his duties as Attorney General in a minimal sort of way and amused himself by writing political poetry. In 1789, after much deliberation, he decided to take a wife. He returned to his American home in Massachusetts and married the daughter of the richest man in Worcester County. She was Mary Worthington, a woman in her late 20s, and thus a full 20 years younger than Bliss. Her letters to her husband make it clear that she embodied the ideal of female grace and submissiveness so cherished by people in the eighteenth century.[8]

Unexpectedly, passionately, Jonathan Bliss fell in love with his young wife. She and the four sons she bore became the enchanted centre of his life. In his letters to Mary, this aging, cynical lawyer resorted to baby talk. He confessed to her that she had made him the "happiest man in New Brunswick"—but ruined him for living alone. Mary was more deferential and demure in her responses to this older man, but she did assure Bliss that his companionship supplied all the love and support she once drew from family and friends. When Mary died in 1799 delivering their fifth child, Bliss was crushed. He would never remarry, and for both Jonathan and their sons, her memory would profoundly shape their ideals of womanhood and of happiness.[9]

It seems to me that, on the surface at least, these are remarkable letters—delicate, witty, warmly demonstrative. They suggest deep mutual concern and enduring affection, the ideal of "companionate marriage" which Lawrence Stone has described so forcefully for the English gentry of the eighteenth century and which Bernard Bailyn finds so powerfully at work within the family of Thomas Hutchinson in colonial Massachusetts. It is an ideal, according to Richard Sennett, which calls for detachment and careful control in public roles, but a warm, expressive, supportive behaviour among one's intimates.[10]

Yet how are we, citizens of the late twentieth century, living as we do in the "Age of Deconstruction," to interpret these letters? Do we take them at face value? Or do we look for evasions, masks and ambiguities, which subvert and undermine the highly polished surface? These are some of the questions I am pursuing through the thousands of Loyalist family letters still available in our public archives. My goal is to uncover the inner workings of power and intimacy among the people known universally in Canadian history as The Family Compact. As for the all-important question of interpretation, my strategy is to pursue a dual track: to try to appreciate at full value the depth of feeling and mutual dependency radiating through these letters, and at the same time to recognize that these statements were also calculated performances, survival measures and personal defences against an undeserved fate and a relentlessly cruel world.[11]

Rather than digress into methodology, I would like to use the balance of this essay to describe the three major conclusions which I have reached at this stage in my research. I hope this will provide a concrete sense of the richness of the material contained in these Loyalists letters, as well as practical examples of my interpretive strategy.

First, it seems abundantly clear from the written sources that, for the Loyalist refugees, the family was the most important institution in their lives. Despite occasional attempts by historians (including myself) to embroider Loyalist life during their years in the Maritime provinces, the fact remains that these colonial gentry found their new physical environment forbidding and its public life totally lacking in beauty or grandeur. Even those Loyalists who came with money, servants and prestigious public posts found their new homes strange and alienating.[12]

Since there was little hope of returning to America, and neither their Christian beliefs nor their self-respect would permit them to give in to despair, these displaced people threw their energies into their immediate families—the one area of life they could control and also the one area capable of positive response. Within the day-to-day life of their families, within the houses so carefully constructed and tastefully furnished, they could reenact their days of glory. They could organize little entertainments for friends according to the remembered standards of colonial Boston and New York; they could dress in silks and velvets and dancing shoes; they could exchange gossip and wit and observe the courtesies of a world far removed from the frontier. In such ways, private life became far more important than the crude tedium of public affairs.

Second, the fact that the Loyalists were exiles, not simply immigrants, had important psychological repercussions. The mentality of exile has been described many times by novelists and essayists in our century. Indeed, exile has come to be the salient fact of modern existence. Put simply, exiles are rootless, mutilated people, who live two lives simultaneously: first, their ordinary life which they find dull, even repulsive; and second, their imagined life—their dreams, memories and feelings of nostalgia which are full of warmth, vitality and success. In a remarkable essay, "The Mind of Winter," the literary critic, Edward Said, notes how many outstanding chess players, novelists, poets and adventurers in the twentieth century are exiles—people to whom the imaginary life is much more important than the real world.[13]

The personal letters of the Loyalists provide multiple diverse glimpses into the imaginary world which they cherished during long exile in the Maritimes. And what were its contents? The answer is obvious: it was filled with remembered moments of glory and power in colonial America! It was the world painted so magnificently by John Singleton Copley and described most recently by Richard Bushman.[14] It was a world of refinement, taste and elegance—a world where men were so confident of their authority in both society and the family that they chose to display the feminine side of their nature in their portraits. Hence the silk stockings, ruffled shirts and velvet suits worn by Copley's subjects. Hence the private, domestic backdrops of sinuously carved furniture and bookcases full of the bound books which signified a man of taste. Their wives' appearance complemented the men's. Although their dresses and jewels were dazzling, their faces were those of the hostess—gentle, attentive, welcoming. Despite their elaborate garb, there was nothing worldly about these women. They were domestic creatures—decorative, dependent, nurturing of husbands and guests. Their pride came from domestic accomplishment—a piece of needlework, a fine table, an appealing bowl of fruit. Their personal world did not extend beyond the front door.[15]

These prescribed male and female roles were reenacted in their letters as they doubtless were in the actual homes of the Loyalists. In fact, the extraordinary charm and grace of the Loyalist letters were quite deliberate, expressing affirmations of their cultural ideals. Although fewer in number, the women's letters were as lively and extroverted as the men's. And they were cheerful, often deliberately so, for it was clearly against the common code for either men or women to complain about their fate. Unfortunately, we have no extant letters written by Edward Winslow's wife Mary. We do know that she was very upset when her husband decided to send their son Murray, aged 12, to military school in England. This could suggest that she had already experienced too many separations in her life. Otherwise, she seems to have borne her fate bravely and silently.[16]

Few letters from Beverley Robinson's wife Nancy have survived, but from her husband's comments it seems that she fell into a depression after moving with her 11 children to the howling wilderness. The fascinating response to her melancholy was that several members of her family—not only her husband, but her mother, her son and her brother—began writing letters urging Nancy to carry on and bear her burdens stoically.[17]

Jonathan Bliss's wife Mary wrote letters regularly to her family and her husband, many of which survive. They are marked by delicate sensitivity and a humorous vein of self-mockery. Clearly, Mary, too, went through a difficult emotional period during at least one New Brunswick winter. After admitting to her sister that she felt a certain loneliness while her husband was away on business, Mary blamed herself for her low spirits—not her four young children, nor her absent husband, nor the piercing cold. She ended this confessional letter by telling her sister not to worry, for she had just written out two pages of resolutions to improve herself and now felt much better![18]

It is notable that all letters from Loyalist women to men contained an apology for the "stupidity" of their letters, ascribed usually either to their allegedly poor handwriting or to the scattered nature of their thoughts. Although the letters themselves do not bear out this harsh judgment, it seems to have been an unwritten rule among these Loyalists that women must openly and repeatedly acknowledge their inferiority to men. Some historians call this trait "learned helplessness," but I find it more significant. Although they were encouraged to tease and flirt with the men of their circle, like other eighteenth-century women, Loyalist women did defer to male superiority—men's education and worldly knowledge. This seems to have been fundamental to the marriage bargain, an essential part of the reciprocal, complementary roles they performed as husband and wife. In accepting this deference, men implicitly agreed to protect and cherish such "stupid" but lovable creatures.

Third, the letters suggest that Loyalist children were deeply affected by their parents' history, and the most talented devoted a significant portion of their lives to redeeming their parents' fate by achieving great distinction in their professional lives. The impact of Loyalist values on their *redeemer children* is without doubt the most important finding of my research thus far. These children were raised with enormous affection and care, but also with firm discipline and fond expectations. Children were expected to carry the torch—maintain the codes of manner and dress and use their talents to bring honour to family.[19] Among the numerous examples available, consider the case of Henry Bliss. Perhaps the most talented of all the Loyalist sons, Bliss was educated at King's College, Nova Scotia, and the Inner Temple in London. He emerged laden with academic prizes, good looks and acclaimed charm. Bliss chose to settle in London where he painstakingly established a reputation as a distinguished lawyer, ran for Parliament, and, in his private moments wrote at least seven historical dramas in iambic pentameter, exalting Loyalist principles. Although he considered these verse plays to be the most important aspect of his productive life, they were anachronistic to English tastes and failed utterly to win Bliss any notice, much less any commercial success. Admittedly discouraged, Bliss nonetheless continued writing such plays to the end of his life, in order to affirm the parental code and his own unrealized sense of destiny.[20]

The lives of Edward and Maria Jarvis illustrate a similar pattern of frustrated idealism. He was the English-educated son of Loyalist merchant Munson Jarvis and she, the daughter of a prominent medical man in Saint John. Soon after their marriage they lived for four years in the British colony of Malta, where Edward held an appointment as a law officer, and they both enjoyed the elaborate social life of the colony's rulers. Eventually, Edward's appointment as Chief Justice of Prince Edward Island permitted the Jarvises and their growing family to return to North America. They were dismayed, however, by the dull, "bumpkin" life on the Island. In consequence, the two expended both their health and their limited fortune building a grand house—"Mount Edward"—near Charlottetown and giving heroic entertainments in order to expose the local population to the best British standards. Maria's exertions produced a heart condition, and she died soon after the house was finished. The disconsolate Edward remained heavily in debt for the rest of his life, and confessed to his brother that he was so short of funds he felt he could not comment on his children's choice of marriage partners, even though he disapproved! Such were the links between financial power and patriarchal authority.[21]

A variation on second-generation experience was that of William Bliss, son of Jonathan and brother to Henry. After English legal training, William returned to Halifax to marry the richest bride in that city, Sarah Ann Armstrong, the adopted daughter of his father's childhood friend, Loyalist Sampson Salter Blowers. Within a decade William's connections enabled him to get appointed to the Nova Scotia Supreme Court. But despite this great honour, his very comfortable life, and apparently happy family, William worried ceaselessly in his letters to his brothers that he had sold out, taken the easy road, instead of seeking fame by pursuing the law in London or risking his all on a literary career.[22]

The preoccupation of these Loyalist children with their parents' world—their lifelong efforts to redeem and vindicate the parental sacrifice—meant that they, too, lived a great deal of their existence in the "floating world" of the imagination. Unlike the sons of ordinary immigrants, they had difficulty sinking roots in the local Canadian soil, committing themselves to the realities of time and place. In 1825 Henry Bliss recognized the disadvantages of this outlook and told William that he was considering returning to New Brunswick and marrying a local beauty:

> To marry a local girl will give me come connexion in the country, some friends. I mean some common interests with others; and I shall find somebody to sympathize with me, or seem to do it. That is just what our family has always wanted. We have been alone and unconnected with all the society in which we lived; and had any of us stumbled how the world would have trod on us! But then our situation... had its advantages for when their daughters whored, or their sons got drunk, it touched not us.... I sometimes regret that Father did not take a different side, or that the side he did take was not more successful in the American Revolution. We should now have been great Yankees at Boston—full of money and self conceit.... But then I might never have seen Kean... nor the inside of the Louvre... nor the Pont du Gard, nor so much of this beautiful Earth. No I am well content with my destiny. How can people doubt that God is good.[23]

This introspective, ambivalent letter, written at the age of 27, perfectly captures the dilemma of second generation Loyalists—their cosmopolitan outlook, coupled with a severe, often crippling detachment from ordinary life. Only with the third generation do we find Loyalist heirs rooting themselves in the local soil, identifying with its landscape and people, including even the Protestant dissenting sects who once represented the antithesis of all the Loyalist gentry stood for.[24] Moreover, their obsession with Loyalist sacrifice lessened. It is true that genealogy became a hobby with the third generation, as did commemorating their ancestors in local churches and cemeteries, but such activities were not an unpaid debt, haunting their waking hours. As well, obsession with family life diminished. Relations between husbands and wives of the third generation were far more relaxed and informal, but also more separate. Husbands spent much of their leisure time in clubs or hunting camps or militia musters. This apparent preference for the exclusive company of males was a new development, an assertion of a type of "rugged" masculine identity which their grandfathers deliberately avoided.[25] Likewise, the third generation of Loyalist wives and mothers became more civic minded, more involved in such reform movements as temperance, public health and religious education. Their children were increasingly sent off early to boarding school where the girls were permitted to study an academic curriculum and even aspire to university by the end of the century, while the boys' training emphasized military drill from school days onward.[26]

As an inevitable part of this evolution, Loyalist elegance, Loyalist exclusivity and Loyalist intensity gradually dissolved. Although their grandchildren certainly respected their ancestors, they themselves had become Canadians and Victorians. In the words of the great conservative historian William L. Morton, grace had been transformed into respectability.[27]

Thus the special Loyalist culture—the special circumstances produced by the exile experience—seems to have lasted two generations at most. What we need to define is how it shaped, and perhaps even transformed English Canada in general and Planter society in particular. It is a striking fact that the rampant individualism that seized American culture in the nineteenth century—the exaltation of success, of the loner, the wilderness and even of violence—never took hold of nineteenth-century Canadian culture.[28] On the contrary, group loyalties to the community and the family, a cordial acceptance of the complementarity of the sexes, a strong emphasis on public duty as well as an equal insistence on the sheer joy of human companionship: all were values which the Loyalists brought with them from colonial America and kept vividly alive through most of the nineteenth century. Philosophically, these exiles were Aristotelians rather than Platonists, Arcadians rather than Utopians. Surely their dominance for 75 years left a residue which requires definition. Indeed, it seems singularly unfortunate that the ruling historical metaphor for the Loyalist contribution to Canadian culture is Northrop Frye's "the garrison mentality." Without denying the elements of arrogance and paranoia in the Loyalist personality, we must also recognize the social virtues of wit, learning, style and profound human solidarity. Sustained exploration of their private papers may bring both the positive and negative aspects of the Loyalist legacy into proper balance.

Notes

1 Leo Tolstoy, *Anna Karenina* (Rosemary Edmunds, tr., London, 1954), 13.

2 The *Jalna* series of Mazo de la Roche is, I believe, the closest fictional attempt to recreate the private life of Ontario's landed gentry but, unlike Tolstoy's novel, the *Jalna* novels are set in the period after the gentry's fall from political power and are essentially a romantic rejection of modern industrial Canada, not a depiction of the gentry in its years of power. More salient are several recent scholarly studies of Loyalist women. Especially noteworthy are Katherine McKenna, "Options for Elite Women in Early Upper

Canadian Society: The Case of the Powell Family," in J.K. Johnson and Bruce G. Wilson, eds., *Historical Essays on Upper Canada; New Perspectives* (Ottawa, 1989), 401–24 and her recently published book, *A Life of Propriety: Anne Murray Powell and Her Family* (Kingston and Montreal, 1994), as well as Janice Potter-MacKinnon, *While Women Only Wept: Loyalist Refugee Women in Eastern Ontario* (Montreal and Kingston, 1993). Also valuable are three doctoral studies: Robin Burns, "The First Elite of Toronto: An Examination of the Genesis, Consolidation, and Duration of Power in an Emerging Colonial Society," Ph.D. thesis, University of Western Ontario, 1975: Robert L. Fraser, "Like Eden in Her Summer Dress: Gentry, Economy and Society, Upper Canada, 1812–1840," Ph.D. thesis, University of Toronto, 1979; Beatrice Spence Ross, "Adaptation in Exile; Loyalist Women in Nova Scotia after the American Revolution," Ph.D. thesis, Cornell University, 1981. My study, *The Envy of the American States: The Loyalist Dream for New Brunswick* (Fredericton, 1984) deals briefly with family life.

3 Edward Winslow to his Wife, W.O. Raymond, ed., *The Winslow Papers* (Saint John, N.B., 1901), 225–27.

4 Beverley Robinson to Nancy Robinson, 21 November 1799, Robinson Family Papers, New Brunswick Museum.

5 *Ibid.*, 11 November 1799.

6 *Ibid.*, 20 January 1800.

7 Jonathan Bliss to S.S. Blowers, 19 September 1786, Bliss Family Papers, Public Archives of Nova Scotia, [PANS].

8 Phillip Buckner, "Jonathan Bliss," *Dictionary of Canadian Biography,* VI (Toronto, 1987), 74–6. Thomas Vincent, "The Image and Function of Women in the Poetry of Affection in Eighteenth Century Maritime Canada," in Margaret Conrad, ed., *Making Adjustments: Change and Continuity in Planter Nova Scotia, 1759–1800* (Fredericton, 1991), 234–46.

9 Jno. Bliss to Mary Bliss, 4 June 1792 and Mary Bliss to Jno. Bliss, 23 July 1792, Bliss Papers, PANS. The story of the devotion of the Bliss men to Mary Worthington Bliss has never been written, but can be traced through the family papers.

10 Lawrence Stone, *The Family, Sex and Marriage in England 1500–1800* (New York, 1977); Bernard Bailyn, *The Ordeal of Thomas Hutchinson* (Cambridge, Mass., 1974); Richard Sennett, *The Fall of Public Man* (New York, 1977), 98–107. For a fine survey of recent scholarship on the family in Europe and North America, see Tamara K. Hareven, "The History of the Family and the Complexity of Social Change," *American Historical Review,* 96 (1991), 95–124.

11 In developing my interpretive approach I have been especially influenced by the work of the French philosopher Paul Ricouer. For an explanation of this methodology see my "The Celestial World of Jonathan Odell: Symbolic Unities within a Disparate Artifact Collection," in Gerald L. Pocius, ed., *Living in a Material World: Canadian and American Approaches to Material Culture* (St. John's, 1992), 192–226. I find the recent effort by Edward Said to develop a "contrapuntal" approach to historical experience an equally rich, if less systematic attempt to capture both the pure and impure elements of literary texts within a single conceptual framework. See *Culture and Imperialism* (New York, 1993).

12 Neil MacKinnon captures this estrangement especially well in *This Unfriendly Soil: The Loyalist Experience in Nova Scotia, 1783–1791* (Kingston, 1986).

13 Edward Said, "The Mind of Winter: Reflections on Life in Exile," *Harper's,* 269 (1984), 49–55. For a subtle exploration of the imaginary worlds of exiled writers Joseph Conrad and Vladimir Nabokov, amongst others, see Michael Seidel, *Exile and the Narrative Imagination* (New Haven, 1987).

14 Richard L. Bushman, *The Refinement of America: Persons, Houses, Cities* (New York, 1992).

15 Margaret Doody, "Vibrations," *London Review of Books,* 5 August 1993, 13–14.

16 Edward Winslow to his wife Mary, 15 September 1784, *Winslow Papers.*

17 Beverley Robinson, Jr. to Anna Robinson, 29 October [1799?] and Thomas Barclay to Beverley Robinson, 1 November 1799, Robinson Papers.

18 Mary Bliss to Frances Ames, 13 February 1797, Bliss Papers, PANS.

19 The best book on parent-child relations for this period is Philip G. Greven, *The Protestant Temperament: Patterns of Child-Rearing, Religious Experience and the Self in Early America* (New York, 1977). Equally insightful is a three-generation study of Virginia families within almost the same time frame as this essay on Loyalist families: Jan Lewis, *The Pursuit of Happiness: Family and Values in Jefferson's Virginia* (New York, 1985).

20 Bertis Sutton, "The Expression of Second-Generation Loyalist Sentiment in the Verse Dramas of Henry Bliss," *Nova Scotia Historical Review,* 13, 1 (1993), 43–77.

21 Anna Maria Jarvis to Caroline Boyd, 6 March 1832; E.J. Jarvis to William Jarvis, 4 August 1835 and 30 January 1837; E.J. Jarvis to Mrs. William Jarvis, 21 September 1849, Jarvis Papers, New Brunswick Museum. J.M. Bumsted and H.T. Holman, "Edward James Jarvis," *Dictionary of Canadian Biography,* VIII (Toronto, 1985), 428–30.

22 William Bliss to Henry Bliss, 18 May 1828, Bliss Papers, PANS.

23 Henry Bliss to William Bliss, Marseilles, 7 January 1825, Bliss Papers, PANS.

24 See for example, Ann Gorman Condon, ed., " 'The Young Robin Hood Society': A Political Satire by Edward Winslow," *Acadiensis,* XV (1986), 120–43.

25 W.L. Morton, "Victorian Canada," in W.L. Morton, ed., *The Shield of Achilles: Aspects of Canada in the Victorian Age* (Toronto, 1968), 311–33. For the equivalent development in the United States, see E. Anthony Rotundo, *American Manhood: Transformations in Masculinity from the Revolution to the Modern Era* (New York, 1993).

26 These impressionistic findings are based on my reading of the letters of William Jarvis, Jr. and his two wives and children in the 1860s and 1870s, Jarvis Papers.

27 Morton, "Victorian Canada."

28 Alexis de Tocqueville was the first to recognize these traits in volume II of his *Democracy in America* (New York, 1957). For modern interpretations, see Richard Slotkin's trilogy: *Regeneration through Violence: The Mythology of the American Frontier, 1600–1860* (New York, 1973); *The Fatal Environment: The Myth of the Frontier in the Age of Industrialization, 1800–1890* (New York, 1985), and *Gunfighter Nation: The Mythology of the Frontier in Twentieth Century America* (New York, 1992). For the Canadian comparison, see Marcia B. Kline, *Beyond the Land Itself: Views of Nature in Canada and the United States* (Cambridge, Mass., 1970).

"Cool Calculators": Brock's Militia

George Sheppard

Despite the increased tempo of military preparations during 1812, most colonists still believed that war would somehow be avoided. Prideaux Selby, the receiver-general of the province, wrote to a friend in April 1812 that the British forces were acting "as if war was expected, but my own opinion is that all Jonathan's blustering will end in nothing of that sort."[1] It would seem that years of incessant rumours of impending conflict had made the inhabitants of Upper Canada somewhat complacent. A correspondent to the *St David's Spectator* would later recall that although "relations with our neighbours were very gloomy," most Upper Canadians were simply "not apprehensive of war" and the commencement of hostilities was a "totally unexpected...subject of wonder."[2] Thus, when the news reached York on 27 June that the long-dreaded event actually had occurred, the villagers appeared to be in a state of shock. Eli Playter, a farmer who lived north of the capital, rushed to the garrison and "found all York in alarm, everyone's countenance wore the mark of surprise."[3]

Isaac Brock was not startled by the news. Since April increasing numbers of "armed men in coloured clothes" had gathered on the opposite shore, and early in May he received a secret dispatch from Sir George Prevost advising that he "consider war as inevitable." The message went on to warn that hostilities would commence by July at the latest.[4] This information confirmed Brock's belief that the course of military preparations he had embarked upon the previous autumn had been the right one. At that time he had arranged to improve the fortifications at the various garrisons and had made plans to place his militia forces in a state of readiness. Brock considered those plans to be of prime importance since, in his opinion, the "active and efficient aid" of at least a portion of the population would be necessary if the colony was to be defended successfully.[5]

The Militia acts of Upper and Lower Canada dated from June 1793, when fears that the United States was intent on attacking the British colonies prompted the governments in those provinces to pass legislation allowing for the creation of official local defence forces.[6] In Upper Canada, John Graves Simcoe was the author of the colony's first Militia Act, and its governing principle was near-universal liability for service. All able-bodied men between the ages of sixteen and fifty were required to attend authorized militia parades or pay fines ranging from two to eight dollars an offence. The first muster in 1793, however, only produced an enrolment of 4213 men. Alarmed by the small turnout, the authorities amended the Militia Act the next year so that men up to the age of sixty were liable for service. From 1794 until 1812 the Militia Act of Upper Canada remained relatively unchanged.[7] The basic militia unit was the company, and each was to consist of between twenty

George Sheppard, "'Cool Calculators': Brock's Militia," in *Plunder, Profit, and Paroles: A Social History of the War of 1812 in Upper Canada* (Montreal: McGill-Queen's University Press, 1994), 40–67.

and fifty privates and three officers (a captain, a lieutenant, and an ensign). Regiments consisted of eight to ten companies, in other words 160 to 500 privates, commanded by one colonel, one lieutenant-colonel, one major, one adjutant, and one quartermaster. Officers and men were expected to bring to every muster their own firearms and at least six rounds of ammunition. Quakers, Mennonites, and Tunkers were excused from service but were required to pay twenty shillings a year in peacetime, and £5 a year in wartime, for that privilege.[8]

Brock was concerned that the annual musters had failed to prepare men for actual combat. The parades, usually held on 4 June every year, were looked upon by the men as an opportunity to socialize and by the authorities as a chance to engage in military census-taking. Brock's concern about the utility of the Militia Act was grounded in fact. By 1805, for instance, only 200 of the province's 8600 militiamen had received any genuine training.[9] To remedy this situation, Brock wanted to revamp the old law so that at least a portion of the militia had proper instruction in military matters. He also thought new regulations dealing with discipline and training were required. Though there were "many wise and salutory provisions" in the old act, Brock felt there were too few means of enforcing them.[10] When he addressed the provincial legislature in February 1812 he requested that the House of Assembly add an oath of abjuration to the Militia Act. He felt that the number of Americans in the province who openly professed that they would never fight against their former country made this amendment necessary. Under the proposed legislation, each militiaman would be required not only to pledge allegiance to the king but also to take an oath abjuring every foreign power. Yet many representatives, especially those born in the United States, refused to support the bill. Aware that an oath of abjuration would eliminate any pretext for claiming neutrality, they voted against the measure and managed to have it laid aside. According to Michael Smith, an American Baptist preacher in Upper Canada at that time, the assemblymen were only following the wishes of their constituents. Smith also believed that passage of the bill would have led to a rebellion by American settlers.[11]

Brock's request for legislation to suspend Habeas Corpus for a period of eighteen months met a similar fate. Had he been granted that power, Brock could have arrested and detained without trial anyone he felt was endangering the public peace. A majority of assemblymen, however, believed that the measure was unnecessary. They reasoned that hostilities would probably be avoided and that in any case the province had managed to survive over two decades without such radical legislation. In addition to this "dread of arming Government" with extraordinary powers, the American element in the Assembly was cognizant that Brock sought the change in order to "keep the numerous body of Americans in a proper state of subordination."[12]

Brock had better luck with the amendments to the Militia Act that dealt with organization, training, and discipline. The new legislation increased the size of militia companies from fifty to one hundred men. The old regulation, which stipulated that companies could not exceed fifty men, had offered a means for some settlers to escape attendance at musters. Apparently a number of Upper Canadians had approached the wording of the Militia Act as they would any contract, and their "sharp" business sense had uncovered a loophole. When their officers attempted to force them out, they replied that their company's fifty-man limit had already been met. Ralfe Clench complained that these absentees even managed to avoid paying any fines because local magistrates agreed with this strict interpretation of the law.[13]

The new regulations also called for the creation of two "flank companies" from every battalion. These forces were to be deployed on the sides, or "flanks," of a body of regular troops and each company was to consist of up to one hundred volunteers willing to undergo training as often as six times a month. Should the number of enlisted men fall short of one hundred, a ballot system would be employed to draft the remainder from those men under forty years of age who had failed to volunteer. To ensure that balloting was kept to a minimum, various inducements were offered to those men willing to enlist of their own free will. Flank volunteers were exempt from both statute labour and jury duty, and from personal arrest on any civil process. Widows and children of flank members killed on active duty were promised annual pensions of five pounds provincial currency, while disabled veterans would receive nine pounds a year.[14]

The amendments meant that a larger proportion of the nearly 13,000 militiamen in the province would be better prepared for war.[15] Under it, one-third of the eligible men under forty, totalling some 1800 recruits, would at least have a smattering of proper training. Over time that number would increase, since provisions had been made for new recruits to replace one-third of the flank members at regular intervals. The remaining men under forty, and those up to sixty years of age, would continue in "sedentary battalions" and were only to be called upon if absolutely necessary. With 1800 partially trained militiamen, and about 11,000 more or less untrained, Brock believed a successful defence of the province might be possible. Moreover, to ensure greater compliance with military decisions, all militiamen were now required to take an oath of allegiance if asked to do so. Members of both flank companies and the sedentary battalions were also subject to trial by court martial for misbehaviour. A new scale of fines and jail sentences was created so that a refusal to follow lawful orders would now prove costly.[16] Although pleased with these changes to the Militia Act, Brock was less than satisfied that the Assembly had limited the duration of these amendments to the end of the current parliamentary session. Having failed to acquire either the oath of abjuration or the suspension of Habeas Corpus, he was forced to accept this limitation rather than come away from the session empty-handed.

While Brock issued orders directing the various districts to establish flank companies, Joseph Willcocks did his best to discredit the new system. In the pages of his Niagara newspaper, Willcocks announced that all members of the provincial militia would be forced to train at least six days a month. The *Kingston Gazette,* in contrast, pointed out that only flank volunteers were liable to train so often and that it was highly unlikely this would be necessary. The editor expressed surprise that a member of the provincial legislature could be "so base, so wicked" as to spread lies that would only lead to increased disaffection.[17] To counter Willcocks's campaign, Brock released circulars to the various colonial newspapers which explained why flank companies were needed and which stressed the benefits of volunteering. These bands of "Loyal, Brave and Respectable Young Men" would serve only as a supplementary force to the British army.[18] Should an emergency arise, the authorities would have at their disposal a group of men able to assist regular troops, who were expected to do most of the fighting. Such explanations seemed to work. After a tour of the Niagara region in early May, Brock reported that an "almost unanimous disposition to serve is daily manifested." He felt that all the flank companies could be completed shortly if arms and accoutrements were sent from Montreal.[19]

What Brock failed to appreciate was that the eagerness to enlist in the flank companies was not proof that Upper Canadians were anxious to fight. Since most inhabitants thought war was unlikely, the volunteers looked upon enlistment quite differently from Brock. For most, enlistment meant only that they acquired exemptions from statute labour, jury duty, and personal arrest for small debts. There was, however, another incentive to peacetime service in the militia. In a new colony, where marks of distinction were rare, service in the elite flank units of the militia could enhance one's status. A few serious social climbers even went so far as to purchase their own swords to brandish over the heads of their subordinates.[20]

In addition to the militia forces, Brock also had a group of volunteers gathered primarily from the eastern portion of the province. A proposal to raise a corps of volunteers from among the Scots of the Glengarry region had first been made after the *Chesapeake* incident in 1807 when a confrontation between a British warship and an American frigate nearly led to a full-scale conflict. Although not considered feasible at that time, the same proposal was understandably greeted with greater interest by Brock in 1811. He petitioned the British government to offer land grants and cash bounties to those volunteers willing to join the Glengarry Light Infantry Fencible Corps, led by Captain "Red George" Macdonell.[21] By May 1812 some four hundred "fine, young men" said to be "chiefly Scotch" in origin, were training at a camp near Three Rivers. The regiment was not made up solely of Upper Canadians, however, and recruiting parties went as far afield as Prince Edward Island in search of volunteers. Sir George Prevost believed that the recruiting had proved successful because of the "zeal of the Officers," who also received bounties for each private enlisted, and because the promised land grants had proven to be "a powerful Auxiliary."[22]

After the declaration of war, the regulations dealing with those "auxiliaries" underwent a change. From then on, privates who joined only for the duration of the American conflict were given four guineas bounty but were not entitled to land grants. Individuals willing to guarantee their services for three years, or until a general peace was declared in Europe, received slightly more money and were promised a one-hundred-acre farm. The change, therefore, meant that in order to acquire a land grant, volunteers also had to be willing to serve overseas. But these more demanding terms did not seem to hamper recruitment, and over 700 men eventually enlisted in 1812. Unfortunately for "Red George," some signed up only to receive the cash bounty and then disappeared. Thomas Armstrong, for instance, enlisted early in May at Kingston but was still missing in June. Apparently he was one of thirty-six men who had deserted after being awarded a bounty, and another thirty left after they reached headquarters. It was later discovered that five of those deserters were already wanted for similar incidents with other regular units.[23] A soldier who served with the British army in Upper Canada later recalled that once enrolled in the ranks, the "military ardor of the young Glengarrians had evaporated like the morning dew." Donald McLeod also noted that the high rate of desertions forced future recruiting parties to be far less selective. Eventually the Fencible companies "were soon filled up with runaway sailors, English, Irish, Dutch, Americans, Canadians, and a sprinkling of Africans, with a considerable portion of broken-down raftsmen."[24]

There were also problems meeting the quotas established for the militia flank companies. Recruitment of volunteers had been limited by shortages of rations and weapons, and only in the Niagara and Home districts were the flank companies well established. At the end of April some 700 men had been embodied but, with the arrival of the confidential dispatch in May warning that war was imminent, Brock decided to call out the 1800 men which the new Militia Act permitted. On 15 May he ordered the flank companies to begin training as often as the law allowed.[25] Brock then approached the Executive Council to supplement the incentives offered to flank-company volunteers. Four days after calling out the companies, he suggested that the Council request from the prince regent that militiamen be granted "UE" status if killed or wounded on active service. Following Brock's advice that "immediate disclosure" of this request was necessary, the adjutant-general of the militia, Eneas Shaw, announced a few days later that the government was seeking a "portion of the Waste lands of the Crown" for such individuals.[26]

In addition to recruitment difficulties, the militia suffered from problems dealing with training and discipline. Militiamen were expected to bring their own arms to training sessions, but some were too poor to afford weapons and others claimed to have lost those supplied by the government. Between 1795 and 1812 several thousand muskets were given to the militiamen of the province, but when Brock attempted to account for those weapons he found most were "lost to the service."[27] Since such a valuable item was not likely to be accidentally misplaced, it was probable that many inhabitants had sold the weapons for a profit. To prevent the "disappearances of guns so common in the past," Brock directed that all government-supplied arms were to be stored in depots after each day's training.[28] Although this procedure might have reduced the number of incidents, it did not prevent all weapons from going astray. In June 1812 Abraham Nelles, a captain of one of the Fourth Lincoln flank companies, reported that seven of his men had still managed to misplace their muskets.[29]

The policy of storing guns nightly also had been prompted by the uncertain loyalties of the Upper Canadian populace. Earlier in the year Brock had noticed that some of the "most dubious characters" in the province had expressed a desire to acquire arms from the government.[30] It was probably for that reason that Brock had also decided to create the flank companies. Not only would flank members be better trained than their fellow militiamen, but it was expected that the majority would be volunteers who, unlike unwilling conscripts, could be relied on to act properly. Sir George Prevost was convinced that only about a third of the militia in Upper Canada was loyal enough to be entrusted with arms.[31] The new militia system, which limited access to the king's stores, was a reflection of the suspicions and doubts that plagued the fragmented society of Upper Canada.

Meanwhile, the mistrust that existed between British and American Upper Canadians caused problems for Robert Nichol. Brock had appointed Nichol to the command of one of the Norfolk flank regiments, but on taking up his post, the men refused to follow Nichol's orders. Apparently his junior officers, because of some personal animosity, had spread rumours about him; among others, it was alleged that he believed no American should ever be trusted. Try as he might, Nichol could not erase the impression created by such gossip. After printing and distributing handbills denying the charge, he still found that the men refused to recognize his authority. "My wish is to *command* a regiment," complained Nichol to a superior, "and *not to be* the *leader* of a mob."[32] Problems between the officers and men of the Norfolk militia undoubtedly played a part in Nichol's being offered the full-time post of quartermaster general of the militia. The Scottish merchant, concerned as always about the effect such public duty would have on his private interests, at first refused the offer. But Brock persisted and eventually the "clever little Scotsman" was persuaded. His decision to undergo such "a great personal sacrifice" was made easier when Brock reminded him that the "British government was never backward in rewarding faithful and meritorious service."[33]

On the eve of war, therefore, Brock's situation had improved only slightly. The new militia system was well suited to provincial conditions and would eventually provide a portion of the male population with the skills needed for military operations. All the same, shortages of both money and recruits had hampered the complete implementation of the plan, and the province was still far from secure against invasion. Moreover, no assurances could be given about the loyalties of the large American element in the population. Worse still, even members of the British and Loyalist communities appeared to need added inducements to ensure their support. Members of the Six Nations also appeared to be indifferent. As a result, one could not blame Brock for having "no great confidence in the majority" of the provincial population.[34] Despite that realistic assessment, even he was surprised by how passively the inhabitants responded to the invasion of their province.

News of the outbreak of hostilities between the United States and Great Britain first reached General Brock on 24 June, but he decided against immediately informing the population of this development.[35] He reasoned that the information would eventually spread throughout Upper Canada anyway, and he was determined to use the interim period to his best advantage. He quickly ordered both the British regulars and the militia flank companies in the Niagara region to assemble and march to Fort George. Members of the flank companies were told only that muskets were to be acquired at the garrison and they were then to be sent home. According to Michael Smith, the volunteers "obeyed with cheerfulness," having no idea that war had already been declared.[36] This little act of deception served its purpose. Before they realized what was happening, some nine hundred militiamen reported for duty and found themselves distributed among the four posts along the Niagara frontier. Not surprisingly, when the real situation was made apparent to the men there were many expressions of dissatisfaction. Brock attempted to mollify the militia by announcing on 2 July that they would be entitled to the same pay and provisions as regular troops, but few seemed impressed by this offer. The next day Brock admitted to Prevost that the original cheerful disposition of the Upper Canadians had been replaced by "a spirit of impatience."[37]

Though his trick had brought the militia out, Brock's actions also meant that the volunteers had not been given the opportunity to bring blankets and other necessary equipment. Since the men were expected to supply their own kits, they demanded pay to buy the required items. When this was not given, the men began to desert. On 4 July 1812 Brock warned that if this behaviour continued, the enemy would soon "destroy and lay waste to the province."[38] That stern message appeared to have little effect, however, since the number of desertions continued to mount. To reduce the number of absentees, Brock announced on 10 July that half the men could return to their homes, but only if they left their muskets behind.[39] Of those who remained on duty, Brock was sure most would leave anyway once the harvest began in spite of the £20 fine for desertion. That possibility worried Brock immensely. Although many of the militiamen appeared willing to defend their own property, Brock felt that the majority were "either indifferent to what is passing, or so completely American as to rejoice in a change of government." Had he had a greater number of regulars at his disposal, Brock believed the population would offer its support more readily. As things stood, however, most were content to wait out events. Trying to put the best light on the situation, Brock reminded Prevost that such "cool calculators" were numerous in every society.[40]

The British were no more successful in acquiring Indian support. The New York Six Nations had adopted a position of neutrality at a council held at Buffalo on 6 July. Emissaries were then sent to their Canadian counterparts urging them to follow the same course. Previously, Brock had called on the Grand River settlements to send all their warriors to Fort George. To Brock's disgust only one hundred men of "that fickle race" appeared, and these only for a few days. Brock thought he might yet win their support, but he was sure that the crown would have to "sacrifice some money to gain them over."[41] For that purpose Joseph Willcocks, who was known to the Six Nations, was approached to serve as intermediary and he eventually achieved a good deal of success on this mission. In the meantime, the Canadian Six Nations returned the answer to the deputation from their American brothers: "We know not your disputes... We do not want to fight...but if you come to take our land, we are determined to defend ourselves."[42] Those were sentiments with which Upper Canadians of every background appeared to agree.

Meanwhile, without the support of the Six Nations and with half his trained Niagara militia on leave, Brock received word that Brigadier-General William Hull had entered western Upper Canada on 11 July. After arriving in the province, the American commander issued his proclamation asking the inhabitants to exchange British tyranny for "Civil and Religious Liberty and their necessary result—individual and general prosperity." He went on to request that the men remain at home, and he warned that any white man found fighting at the side of an Indian would be put to death. That last provision was designed to discourage the use of native warriors by the British. Tales of horrible atrocities had left many Americans, including Hull, with a considerable fear of the Indian style of fighting. News of the proclamation soon spread throughout the province, but the effect of this warning, while impressive, was not exactly what Hull had intended. A number of American settlers in Upper Canada were offended by the tone of the offer and upset by its terms. According to Smith, few of the inhabitants of the province considered themselves subjects of a tyrannical government. If they had, they would have crossed back over the border. Nonetheless, they did not wish to fight for either side in the contest; Smith said that originally many had decided they would run to the American lines and surrender when battles occurred. The threat of giving no quarter to anyone found fighting beside an Indian, however, would have made that ploy suicidal. Smith explained that the Upper Canadians were angry because they "were well assured that Hull knew every man in Canada to be under the controul of government, and that they were obliged to bear arms...and that they could not prevent the Indians from marching with them." As to Hull's "friendly advice" about staying home and remaining neutral, most would have done so if circumstances had permitted. "This proposal they would willingly have acceded to," Smith believed, "for they dreaded the war with their whole souls."[43]

The decision to remain at home was made easier if no strong British garrison was nearby. In the western regions, where there were few regulars, the proclamation "operated very powerfully on our Militia," reported Colonel Matthew Elliot of the First Essex. Nor should it be forgotten that the American offer promised greater prosperity and guaranteed the protection of private property if citizens remained neutral. For a people dedicated to improving their economic circumstances, these were powerful incentives to obey Hull's directions. Some months later an American spy reported to Major-General Van Rensselaer that the proclamation worked primarily because there was "a security for private property contained in it."[44]

In an attempt to limit the effect of Hull's proclamation, Brock countered with one of his own only ten days later. To those who thought that the economic prospects of the colony would improve under American control, Brock explained that the "unequalled prosperity" already enjoyed by the province was a product of government expenditure and access to British markets. Brock also warned the American element in the province that the United States actually intended to give Canada back to France after the war was over. Instead of enjoying American liberty, Upper Canadians would find themselves "slaves to the Despot" Napoleon. Finally, Brock reminded all inhabitants, including those who had never taken the oath of allegiance, to resist any American appeal for assistance. As "Canadian Freeholders," every citizen owed allegiance to Britain. Those who failed to heed this advice did so at their own peril, Brock warned, since Britain would eventually win the war.[45]

A recent occurrence added an air of plausibility to that statement. In the early hours of 17 July, a small British force from St Joseph Island captured the American post at Michilimackinac. The victory was bloodless, as the American forces surrendered after being caught completely by surprise. Having never been informed by their own forces that war had been declared, the Americans at Michilimackinac were not prepared to fight when Captain Charles Roberts and his redcoats appeared at the gates. The capture of this small post proved to be of monumental significance to the British war effort. For the western Indians, such as the Miami, Shawnee, Ottawa, and Delaware, it was proof that their old ally Britain was determined to defeat the Americans. As a result, hundreds of western warriors were now committed to the British cause.[46]

Encouraged by the success at Michilimackinac, Brock began preparations to regain control of the territory occupied by Hull's forces. On 22 July he ordered all militia furloughs cancelled. Colonel Thomas Talbot was directed to assemble the two hundred members of the flank companies of the Oxford, Norfolk, and Middlesex regiments at Moraviantown. Brock assumed that the one thousand Western militiamen, many of whom were French Canadian and not recent American arrivals, could offer a spirited defence until Talbot's London militia joined them. In combination with a force of Indian volunteers expected to number at least 150, and with the regular troops from that region, Brock thought he could force Hull to retreat. In this expectation, however, he was to be sorely disappointed.[47]

Those militiamen directly in Hull's path had originally assembled at Sandwich "with as much promptitude as could be expected."[48] On hearing of Hull's generous offer of protection for the property of neutrals, however, the majority of Essex and Kent militiamen left their posts and returned to their homes. The remainder retreated to Fort Amherstburg with some three hundred regulars of the 41st Regiment on 10 July 1812.[49] Three days later Lieutenant-Colonel T.B. St George reported to Brock that the retreat to Amherstburg had been prompted by the militia, which was "in such a state as to be totally inefficient in the field." Even after leaving Sandwich the local men continued to desert, and St George noted they were "going off in such numbers" that half the men had left in only a few days. The desertion of more than five hundred Western militiamen meant that Brock's front-line defences were too weak to offer resistance to the invaders.[50]

At that point Brock turned to the men of the London District, but here he had even less luck. Colonel Talbot had managed to assemble the militia from the Long Point region and they set out for Moraviantown, but along the way the whole force, except for a handful of officers, mutinied and turned back.[51] The number of other volunteers from the London District was described as "very small," and Charles Askin said on 21 July 1812 that only fifty Grand River Indians appeared willing to fight the invaders.[52] Brock reported that the other four hundred warriors, after hearing from emissaries sent by General Hull, had determined to "sit quietly in the midst of war." He also noted that the refusal of the Six Nations to follow the British standard had produced a "domino effect" among their white neighbours. Some militiamen claimed they could not leave their families and property so long as the "fickle" natives remained behind.[53]

Not only had most western Upper Canadians refused to follow orders, but one group had even decided to aid the invaders. The most prominent members of that disloyal body, Ebenezer Allan, Andrew Westbrook, and Simon

Zelotes Watson, had crossed over to the American camp and offered to form a cavalry unit to help distribute copies of Hull's proclamation. Allan had served as a spy for the British during the revolutionary war, but in 1783 he had been imprisoned for ten months by his superiors who suspected that he was acting as a double agent. Nonetheless, after the war he moved to Upper Canada and in 1798 he received 2000 acres as a reduced officer. Allan proved to be a particularly "fractious misfit" and, after numerous disputes with neighbours, he was again arrested in 1806. This second jail term may have soured Allan's views towards the British government. One of his biographers has noted that his "allegiance to higher authority was never strong" anyway and that he was "primarily motivated by self-interest."[54]

Watson and Westbrook had both quarrelled with Thomas Talbot over business matters. Apparently Watson had sought to enter into a partnership with the colonel to settle immigrants, but the deal was never formalized and the two men had nearly come to blows over this misunderstanding. Brock remarked that Watson had paraded as far as Westminster Township in the London District distributing news of Hull's offer while at the same time vowing "bitter vengeance against the first characters of the province."[55] For his part, it seems Westbrook had quarrelled with Talbot about a number of issues in the past and he may have harboured a grievance over not being appointed an officer in the local militia.[56] His decision to support Hull in 1812, however, was probably related to more immediate concerns over property losses. A successful blacksmith, Westbrook was described as a "large, red-haired, rough featured man" who had managed to acquire land in four townships. According to Captain Daniel Springer, Westbrook had publicly declared he would not take up arms against Hull's force because "he had too much at stake."[57] Whatever Watson and Westbrook's motivations were for their actions, they could at least take some pride in knowing that they had succeeded in acquiring more followers than their old enemy. While Talbot's men deserted to their farms, Brock noted that Watson and Westbrook managed to gather about fifty individuals to assist in spreading word of the American offer.[58]

Reports of these events unnerved Brock. Though aware that most inhabitants desired to avoid war at all costs, the numerous desertions and evidence of widespread treasonous activity surprised him. "The population, although I had no great confidence in the majority," he informed Prevost on 28 July, "is worse than I expected to find it." Such an opinion is understandable. The Essex and Kent militia had done nothing to impede Hull's progress. The London area militia appeared equally unreliable, although Brock had previously placed great store in the loyalty of the settlers in that region. To prevent the "impending ruin of the country," he had determined two days earlier to go west himself and drive the enemy from the province.[59] Before embarking on such an expedition, however, Brock required a greater degree of control over the militia forces and population of the province. To acquire that power, he gathered together the members of the new sixth parliament for an emergency session on 28 July 1812.

During his speech at the Assembly's introductory session, Brock found himself offering contradictory messages about the state of the province. He claimed that the number of disaffected was few and that the militia had responded to the recent American invasion with conduct "worthy of the King whom they serve."[60] Yet his renewed request that Habeas Corpus be suspended and that more rigorous laws be enacted to deal with militia desertions revealed that the province was as threatened from within as it was from without. Aware that his speech would be published in colonial newspapers, Brock tried to put the best light on the situation, although that meant distorting the truth.

Only a few days later, for example, he would admit to the Executive Council in a private session that the militia was in a "perfect state of insubordination." His purpose in addressing the Assembly had been to acquire a partial suspension of the Habeas Corpus Act. Once that was accomplished, Brock intended to begin wholesale prosecutions and he hoped the arrests would "restrain the general population from treasonable adherence to the enemy."[61] By lying to the Assembly, however, Brock had undercut his case for wider powers. Although most members of the legislature had surely heard rumours about the situation in western Upper Canada, Brock's speech offered them a way out of a difficult situation.

It seems that almost all of the assemblymen were convinced that the province would soon become part of the United States. In what they perceived to be the waning moments of British power in the colony, none wished to offend prospective American masters by offering Brock everything he wanted. Therefore, instead of authorizing a declaration of martial law, the assemblymen agreed only to amend certain aspects of the Militia Act. They spent the next eight days discussing the repeal of the 1807 School Act. In Brock's opinion those men had abandoned the "honest fulfillment of their duty" to avoid "incurring the indignation of the Enemy." Knowing that little further would be gained from the session, he prorogued the Assembly on 5 August 1812 after it had voted £10,000 for the militia.[62] For their part, the assemblymen were angered by Brock's actions and on 5 August they issued an address to the people of Upper Canada explaining the legislation adopted during the last session. They noted that "owing to the loyalty of the great body of the people," there was no need for a declaration of martial law. They also observed that the changes to the Militia Act permitted the use of very strict discipline. New regulations made it a crime to sell or barter arms and equipment, to counsel others not to appear for duty, and even to use disrespectful language against the royal family. Moreover, court martials were now empowered to deliver death sentences for desertion to the enemy and for fomenting mutiny or desertion.[63]

Of course, Brock had sought more than changes to the Militia Act, and this experience with the Assembly marked the lowest point in his career as leader of Upper Canada. The day after the Assembly began proceedings, Brock informed a fellow officer, Edward Baynes, that his situation was "most critical, not from anything the enemy can do, but from the disposition of the people—the population, believe me, is essentially bad—a full belief possess them all that this Province must inevitably succumb—this prepossession is fatal to every exertion. Legislators, magistrates, militia officers, all have imbibed this idea.... Most of the people have lost all confidence. I however, speak loud and look big." But that bravado had turned to desperation as the session dragged on without any movement on the question of wider powers for the executive. Eventually, as he later admitted to Prevost, Brock considered declaring martial law on his own authority but was warned that, if he did so, the whole of the provincial militia would disperse.[64]

After deciding to prorogue the legislature, however, Brock appeared reinvigorated. W.D. Powell remarked that after taking that step, Brock immediately "proceeded to the Barracks and harrangued the militia." Apparently this tirade impressed a number of the York militiamen. Several hundred volunteered that same day for service in any part of the province, and Brock selected 100 men and ordered them to march to Long Point. A further 150 militiamen from the Home and Niagara districts eventually followed that first group of volunteers. In this manner over the next two weeks, Brock managed to assemble a motley force for the relief of Amherstburg. He detached just over 300 regulars from the Niagara frontier and eventually acquired 600 native allies, including a handful of Six Nations warriors. He also managed to assemble 400 militiamen, including 150 from the London and Western districts; altogether, the British relief force totalled just over 1300 men.[65]

On 13 August Brock's force reached Amherstburg, only to find that the Americans, after surviving food shortages and outbreaks of disease, had retreated to their own shore. Although outnumbered two to one by the Americans, Brock decided to cross the Detroit River in pursuit of Hull's army. To fool the enemy into believing that the British force was much stronger than it actually was, the militia were supplied with the red jackets usually worn by regular soldiers. Before launching this audacious attack, Brock warned the Americans that the Amerindian warriors attached to his force would "be beyond control the moment the contest commences."[66] This announcement must have been chilling to Detroit's defenders since even British soldiers who served with the native volunteers were frightened by their appearance. Thomas Verchères recalled that the warriors afforded an "extraordinary spectacle," with bodies covered in red or blue clay, or tattooed black and white from head to foot. He described the scene as "horrifying beyond expression" and said watching the assembly of warriors made him feel as if he were "standing at the entrance to hell."[67] Hull, who was also deathly afraid of the Amerindians, heeded the British warning and surrendered Fort Detroit without firing a shot. Brock's gamble had paid off and, when later accused of being reckless, he countered by arguing "that the State of the Province admitted of nothing but desperate remedies." Yet he also denied that the unconditional surrender of the numerically superior enemy had been a matter of luck, preferring instead to see it as a product of the "cool calculation of the *pours* and *contres*."[68]

The 400 volunteers who followed Brock to Detroit, however, constituted only about 7 per cent of the 5850 militiamen eligible for service in the Home, Niagara, London, and Western districts. If the 500 men who remained on duty on the Niagara frontier are added to that number, about 85 per cent of the militiamen from those areas are still not accounted for, although the authorities had called out both the flank companies and the sedentary battalions in those districts. Where had the rest of the "Spartan Band" gone? Almost all, it seems, had returned quietly to their farms or had never left them in the first place.[69]

Most of the militia in the London and Western districts had simply returned home after Hull issued his proclamation, and many of their officers had quickly followed suit. On his arrival at Amherstburg, Brock had issued a general order expressing his discontent over the numerous desertions that had taken place during the last few weeks. Instead of fining deserters, however, Brock only asked commanding officers to transmit the names of those few militiamen who had remained faithful so "that immediate measures may be taken to discharge their arrears of pay."[70] A court of enquiry, appointed by Brock after the capture of Detroit, recommended that ten officers of the Essex and Kent militias be removed from their positions. But the court also announced that there were many others "to whom no share of blame can justly attach."[71] With no realistic means of punishing the hundreds of deserters in that region, it seems the British authorities were forced to settle for the token chastisement of a few of the most prominent offenders.

In the Niagara District, those who had been granted leave to attend to their farms early in July had refused, almost to a man, to return to their posts when called for by Brock. That left only 500 members of the Lincoln flank companies on duty, and many of them served very reluctantly. Colonel Christopher Myers, in charge of the district after Brock's departure for Amherstburg on 5 August, reported that "desertion to their homes is rather prevalent among them."[72] It seems likely that had no regular forces been present in central and eastern Upper Canada, militiamen in those areas, like the citizen-soldiers in the Western District, would have dispersed completely. For instance, a muster roll for Lieutenant Eli Playter's militia company during the month of August reveals that the men of the Home District were quite anxious to avoid service. Although by law the company could contain up to one hundred men fit for duty, the corps never reached half that total in August. Apparently one of the men had only recently discovered that he was near-sighted and therefore ineligible for duty. Beside another man's name was the notation "delirious," while others were simply classified as "deserters." Interestingly, Playter seems to have differentiated between those men who had left the ranks and two men who were listed as "gone to the States."[73] This would seem to imply that, at least for Playter, deserters were those who had returned to their farms and might yet be forced back on duty. Whether that was true or not, the muster roll for Playter's company illustrates how a fighting unit could quickly become a "paper force."

In the Niagara and Home districts, however, refusal to attend a militia summons could lead to arrest and imprisonment at the hands of British regulars. For that reason many individuals evidently decided to follow the path chosen by Playter's two men. The *Buffalo Gazette* and other American newspapers carried regular articles detailing the "escapes" made by "native born citizens of the United States."[74] Donald McLeod, a British soldier who served in the colony during the war, remarked that hundreds of people "escaped to the United States to avoid being drafted in the militia" at this time. It seems that most of those who chose to cross over were young tradesmen with little stake in Upper Canada. Those Americans with large holdings were more inclined to remain and guard their property, although the fear of military service induced a number of them to leave as well. An official list of landowners in the province who abandoned their farms during the war to flee south contains 336 names.[75]

In view of the behaviour of most Upper Canadians, it is scarcely surprising that Brock considered the men actually willing to do their duty to be particularly deserving of praise. After his western expedition he wrote to the earl of Liverpool in August 1812 about the exploits of his "little Band" of regulars, Indians, and militia. Brock claimed that he had never "witnessed greater cheerfulness and constancy" among any other troops. That attitude apparently proved infectious. Later, Brock told his brothers that other inhabitants had been inspired with confidence by the recent successes, and he noted that the whole situation of the province was "of late much improved."[76] Because of that change he now felt sure he could repeat the experience in the eastern region of the province. Within days of his victory at Detroit, Brock was making plans to attack the American posts along the Niagara River.

But on his arrival at Fort George on 22 August he discovered that Sir George Prevost had negotiated a temporary armistice five days before.[77] Since the militia were anxious to deal with their crops, Brock announced on 26 August that four-fifths of the flank members would be granted indefinite furloughs. Before being sent home, the men were warned that they should be prepared to return at a moment's notice. He then directed that general inspections of the Home, Niagara, and London militias take place weekly. At these drills the officers were expected to call upon the men to take the oath of allegiance and to note the names of those who refused. Some officials apparently went beyond these instructions and jailed men who declined to repeat the pledge. "Many took the oath," observed Smith, "rather than suffer this."[78] Of course, not all officers acted this way, and those who ordered colonists disarmed and jailed without proper recourse to the law were described by McLeod as "insolent, cruel, and oppressive" men.[79]

Brock was in a position to grant furloughs, not only because of Prevost's armistice, but also because he had finally acquired the support of the Grand River Six Nations. The warriors had originally stood back because they feared that the contest might lead to a fratricidal struggle. The Iroquois were afraid they might end up fighting members of the New York Six Nations and most, therefore, simply chose to ignore Brock's first appeals. Apparently the recent British victories, and the offer of "good wages to engage in the war," had led the Indians to reconsider their position of neutrality.[80] By 7 September some three hundred warriors had arrived in the Niagara District. Aside from frightening the American soldiers, however, Brock feared he would get "no essential service from this degenerate race." At the same time, he noted that the warriors appeared "ashamed of themselves" and had promised "to whipe away the disgrace into which they have fallen by their late conduct."[81]

Unfortunately for Brock, those flank members who remained on active duty seemed to share none of the determination now evinced by the Six Nations warriors. Although only 20 per cent of the militia were required to remain on duty, their officers were hard pressed to keep even that small number. On 21 September deserters were informed that Brock was willing to overlook their offence if they returned voluntarily. As the problem increased, however, Brock realized that the indifference of the majority of the inhabitants made a successful defence of the province increasingly unlikely. "I am quite anxious for this state of warfare to end," he wrote his brothers on 18 September, "I scarcely can think the people will suffer it to continue."[82]

On 13 October the war between Britain and the United States came to an end for Major-General Isaac Brock. At Queenston, on the Upper Canadian side of the Niagara River, he lost his life attempting to halt the second invasion of the colony by American troops. The next day his successor, Sir Roger Hale Sheaffe, managed to drive back the invaders, but not without loss of life on both sides. British dead, aside from twelve regulars, included two York militiamen and five Six Nations warriors. A further thirty-one York and Lincoln militiamen were wounded. Compared with casualty rates for battles in Europe, however, the losses at Queenston Heights were modest. A little over one month before, for example, Napoleon's army of 130,000 soldiers engaged a Russian force at the Battle of Borodino where casualties on both sides totalled over 70,000.[83]

Historians have sometimes said that the Battle of Queenston Heights was a turning point for Upper Canadian morale. C.P. Stacey, for instance, saw it as a "victory which further raised the spirits of the people of Upper Canada."[84] Yet an examination of the subsequent actions of the provincial militia reveals that the mood and behaviour of the inhabitants remained fundamentally unchanged. Immediately after the battle, Sheaffe called out both the flank companies and the sedentary battalions in the London, Niagara, and Home districts. This action, designed to bring together a force of 5000 men, was considered necessary in the face of further American invasions.[85] A majority of the inhabitants, however, were unwilling to answer that call. A British soldier who served in the colony during the war said that at this time hundreds of colonists "absolutely declined doing any kind of duty, civil or military, under the colonial authorities."[86] If caught, of course, shirkers could be jailed, and some chose to avoid punishment by leaving their homes. In Whitchurch Township, north of York, some seventy men chose to hide out in the woods rather than serve in their units. By December 1812, when Smith passed through the region, more than three hundred rebels had banded together. At that time Smith spotted a fifty-man contingent walking brazenly "on the main road, with Fife and drum beating for volunteers, crying Huzza for Madison."[87]

The republican sympathies of the Whitchurch rebels, and their determination to endure life away from their farms, certainly set them apart from other Upper Canadians. Most men in the province who managed to avoid service never abandoned their cozy farms for caves in the countryside. The experiences of Eli Playter with his militia company were probably typical. His diary describes the situation after the Third York regiment was once again called into service: "17th [October] I waited for the Men's coming till late the P.M. not more than ½ the company appeared...18th went early to some of the peoples Houses but they kept out of the way—I was much vexed at their conduct." Eventually Playter managed to gather about twenty men together. They set out for York, where two-thirds were excused and seven were balloted for service at the Niagara front.[88]

In addition to running off to the bush, or just lying low until their commanding officers had given up in frustration, Upper Canadians also avoided militia service through other means. Owing to recent amendments to the Militia Act, those with enough money could employ substitutes. Previously, the militia regulations had required draftees to appear for service whenever a partial call of the militia occurred. As of 5 August 1812, however, a draftee was permitted to send an able-bodied man in his place.[89] For a number of reasons, the use of substitutions, although a time-honoured and acceptable practice in most armed forces, was not as common in Upper Canada as one might expect. Since substitution was never permitted during a general call of the militia, the original draftee was still liable for service in the unlikely event that the whole regiment was called out. Also, it seems that it was exceedingly difficult to entice anyone to take the job. Those lucky enough to find a willing candidate were forced to barter away valuable items—such as a yoke of steer or as much as £50 cash—in exchange for a year's service.[90] For some Upper Canadian confidence artists, these transactions proved to be both profitable and relatively risk free. Philip Philips, for instance, deserted from the Third York militia only days after he took the place of William Shaw.[91]

As a traditional and respectable means of avoiding service, substitution was obviously a preferred method of steering clear of the fighting, but other legal means were also available. Amendments to the Militia Act passed by the Assembly in August had created a host of newly exempt occupations. According to the revised regulations, the following people now joined religious groups such as Tunkers, Quakers, and Mennonites in being excused from duty: "The Judges of the court of Kings bench, the Clergy, the Members of the Legislative and Executive Councils and their respective Officers... His Majestys Attorney General, Solicitor General, the Secretary of the Province...as well as all Magistrates, Sheriffs, Coroners, Halfpay Officers, Physicians, Surgeons, the Masters of Schools, ferrymen and one miller to every Grist Mill." Of course, the assemblymen thought it wise to include exemptions for themselves, at least "for the time being."[92]

If by some misfortune a well-to-do colonist did not qualify for an exemption or was unable to find a substitute, he could choose to remove himself from danger by simply ignoring the call and paying any fine that was levied. It has been estimated that in peacetime a farmer with thirty to forty acres cleared could expect a gross annual income of at least £110. During the war, however, inflationary pressures meant farmers' gross incomes doubled, and this prospective prosperity was a tremendous incentive to avoid militia duty. Since calls for service often came at harvest time and the largest fine that could be levied against a militia deserter in 1812 was only £20, risking punishment was often worthwhile.[93] Job Lodor, from the London District, admitted after the war that he "always procured a substitute when his tour of duty came" except when a general call for the militia was made. When that occurred, he would merely "go home & secure his many goods & property" and then await a fine. Of course, those who wished to avoid paying fines could also leave the province. That was the course chosen by Samuel Sherwood, who departed for Lower Canada as soon as war was declared. Sherwood, the son of a prominent Loyalist and a former member of the Assembly for Grenville, was apparently anxious about remaining in a region where the militia was "liable to be called out en masse." He therefore decided to go east to a safer area until hostilities had ceased.[94]

Some militia officers shielded their friends and relatives from serving by sending ineligible replacements in their stead. One such case involved Philip Lang, a private in the First York militia, who was described as being "lame an[d] sick better than two years." Nonetheless, Lang was balloted and sent to the garrison at the capital as part of the quota of men from the First York militia. His commanding officer, Captain James Mustard, was told by a superior: "Do not for the future have any man or men drafted for Actual Service that you know is sick or anyway not fit." Lieutenant-Colonel Graham went on to explain that such deception was "great trouble to me and a disappointment to the Public Service."[95] It also seems that a good number of settlers avoided militia service by simply announcing that they were Americans and, therefore, could not be forced to fight against their fellow countrymen. Brock had sought an oath of abjuration in February precisely because he foresaw that some inhabitants would take this position, but the refusal of the Assembly to pass the measure meant that the issue remained unresolved throughout the summer and it was not until 9 November that steps were finally taken to eliminate the practice. On that date, Sheaffe issued a proclamation directing the "divers Persons" claiming exemptions because of American citizenship to appear before boards that had been established in every district. Those who could prove they were Americans were to be given passports and escorted to the border. Any American who failed to appear before such a board by 1 January 1813 was warned that he would be considered an "enemy Alien" and was therefore "liable to be treated as a Prisoner of War, or a Spy."[96]

Declaring oneself an American, and therefore a noncombatant, sometimes proved risky even before Sheaffe announced his program of deportation. Some of those who had refused to take the oath of allegiance in August had been arrested and jailed for that refusal. Donald McLeod recalled that after hostilities had broken out, those Americans suspected of being disloyal were disarmed "and strictly watched."[97] Others were harassed by militiamen or British regulars who "thought it hard and unreasonable that they must bear all the burden and danger of war." Some Indian warriors, if they came across a "Yankee" who refused to serve, would threaten to kill him. According to Smith, the Indians sometimes made good on their threats.[98] In the end, however, a number of Americans who continued to refuse to fight were permitted to remain in the country even after reporting to the alien boards. Despite all Sheaffe's tough talk, it quickly became apparent that some well-established gentlemen who had purchased land and had never taken the oath of allegiance would be ruined by this order. For that reason, Sheaffe allowed such men to remain in the province under a "modified allegiance, or security of good conduct."[99] Other Americans, who it was felt knew too much about the defences of Upper Canada to be sent back to the United States, were also granted permission to remain in the colony.[100]

Whether they remained at home through legal or illegal means, or left their farms for Lower Canada, the United States, or the backwoods, the majority of Upper Canadians managed to avoid service in the militia. After the

Battle of Queenston Heights on 13 October, Sheaffe had summoned 5000 colonists to duty on the front lines, but on 24 October the paymaster recorded the presence of only 846 militia officers and privates in the Niagara peninsula.[101] Instead of increasing as time passed, the number of men on duty actually declined and, as another Canadian winter set in, the British authorities knew they would be faced with the difficult task of trying to keep even that small contingent on duty.

In addition to worsening weather, the British forces were experiencing problems with logistics. Although Sheaffe had ordered out 5000 men, he had neither the rations nor the equipment to feed and house additional soldiers. On 3 November he informed Prevost that the militia on the frontier was "in a very destitute state with respect to clothing, and in all regards bedding and barrack comforts in general." Not surprisingly, Sheaffe also went on to report that such conditions were prompting desertions. Ten days later he announced that the "many absentees" would not be punished if they returned voluntarily. The next day he sweetened the offer by promising to supply trousers, shoes, and jackets to flank members free of charge. Even men absent without leave could receive these items providing they returned "voluntarily and without delay."[102]

Other steps were also taken to reduce the number of absentees and to entice men back to duty. To help in uncovering desertions, officers commanding militia units were ordered to institute three roll calls a day. They were also instructed to establish squads comprising "a trusty sergeant and a file of men" to search for and apprehend any deserters.[103] Finally, a local resident, Samuel Street, Sr, was appointed as paymaster to the militia forces. It seems that the official formerly employed by the regular forces had often ignored the calls of the militia for pay and this, in turn, caused much dissatisfaction.[104] Several weeks after implementing this program, Sheaffe was able to report that the combined policy of bribes, strict discipline, coercion, and prompt payment had worked. On 23 November he informed Prevost that the number of militia in the field had increased recently and he was pleased to report that the men "continue generally, to evince the best disposition."[105]

Sheaffe's appraisal of the morale of the militia was optimistic. It was clear that miserable camp conditions were taking an enormous toll. The combination of inadequate hygiene and the lack of basic camp equipment, such as tents, blankets, and kettles, made disease the principal killer of Upper Canadians in the first year of the war. James Mann, a surgeon who served on the American side of the lines, reported that soldiers in nearby New York were struck by waves of different diseases. From July to September most men suffered from dysentery, diarrhoea, and fevers but, once winter arrived, there were also outbreaks of measles and severe pneumonia. The same sort of conditions existed on the British side, with predictable results. Pension lists record the deaths of only three members of the provincial militia during battles at Queenston and Fort Erie in late 1812. Disease, however, accounted for at least forty-six casualties among men on duty. As winter progressed, so too did the number of deaths from disease. The two men who died in September were followed by five the next month, and by eleven in November. Finally, in December, a minimum of twenty-eight militiamen died from diseases contracted while on duty.[106]

The large concentration of untrained men and dangerous weapons also ensured that accidents were commonplace. On 27 September 1812 Brock was forced to issue a general order reminding Upper Canadians to guard against "careless negligence" in the handling of weapons. He informed the militiamen that no greater military offence could be committed than the reckless use of firearms or the "willful waste" of ammunition. Nonetheless, at his own headquarters four days later, Brock was forced

TABLE 1 | LINCOLN MILITIA SERVICE, 1812

	30 Nov.	4 Dec.	11 Dec.
Captain Crook's Lincoln Flank Company			
Active	32	23	15
Ill	18	14	15
AWOL	31	44	51
Total	**81**	**81**	**81**
Captain Macklem's Lincoln Flank Company			
Active	40	27	15
Ill	6	7	7
AWOL	8	20	32
Total	**54**	**54**	**54**

Source: AO, Abraham Nelles Papers, Field Reports, 1812–14. These designations are a simplified version of the various systems of notation used at that time. "Active" includes "Present and Fit" or "Present under Arms," those on leave or on duty elsewhere. "Ill" includes sick at home, in hospital, or in barracks. The "AWOL," or absent without leave, designation was at times noted explicitly, but sometimes had to be determined by eliminating other designations from the original total.

to specifically forbid the "practice of individuals firing in the swamp or any other place within the neighbourhood" of Fort George. Such activities had predictable results. Pension lists record four militia casualties from accidents between September and December 1812. It would appear that at this point in the war colonists were more likely to be wounded by their comrades than by the enemy.[107]

Hungry, cold, fearful of becoming sick or injured, and worried about their families, it is hardly surprising that Upper Canadians simply walked away from the war. After all, most considered it none of their affair in the first place. Surviving muster rolls of two flank companies from the fall campaign of 1812 reveal the course of action adopted by most militiamen (see table 1). In less than two weeks, Crook and Macklem found themselves with more men absent without leave than on duty. The situation seems to have prevailed throughout the district. Captain Applegarth's flank company of the Second York militia had only three men present and fit for duty on 11 December.[108]

In their anxiety to return home, a number of deserters may have unwittingly spread the diseases ravaging the men at the front. Militia officer William Hamilton Merritt wrote to his fiancée in the United States on 8 December 1812: "You cannot conceive the state our frontier is in. Not a woman to be seen and you, I hope, hardly know that war exists. I am sorry to say that we have had a very sickly season, many young men have died through fatigue, and fifty people from the 10 and 12 Mile Creek with a fever which is equal to a plague."[109] Apparently even some Upper Canadians who managed to remain at home found they could not escape the wider effects of the war.

The muster rolls represented in table 1 suggest that most men seemed unconcerned about the possibility of court martial, and it appears that the desire to get away from careless and diseased comrades was greater than the fear of potential punishment. The leniency with which both Brock and Sheaffe had dealt with previous instances of mass desertion no doubt helped foster that attitude. Thus, when permission to leave was not forthcoming, the men took matters into their own hands. For Sheaffe this action represented a threat to his authority as commander of the forces in Upper Canada. Faced with the complete collapse of the militia defence system, Sheaffe was forced into action. On 11 December he dismissed almost all the militia, and five days later he allowed most of the remaining flank members to return home.[110]

The expedient of letting the men return home when it appeared they were all going to go anyway had been resorted to already by Brock in July. When Sheaffe confronted the same problem he was wise enough to perceive that nothing could be done to halt the numerous desertions. These militiamen were not hardened regular soldiers but settlers with families to care for and farms to tend. Dragging the men back to the field would only have made the British army unpopular; besides, the effort was not likely to work for long. There was also another benefit to the granting of a general leave. By adding official sanction to what had occurred, Sheaffe saved face since he at least maintained the appearance of being in control of the situation.

Sheaffe could consider himself lucky in one respect. On the opposite shore, General Alexander Smith was experiencing even greater difficulty with the New York militiamen. Their refusal to cross the Niagara River had led to the American defeat at the Battle of Queenston Heights. After that loss, the men began to desert in great numbers. The New York *Evening Post* reported on 11 November 1812 that the militia companies along the Niagara River were "dwindling to mere skeletons."[111] By the end of November the remaining men had mutinied and then "disembodied themselves." According to one witness, later taken prisoner by the British, the militiamen responsible for this mutiny declared that the Upper Canadians "were brothers and sisters, with whom they had always been at peace." Determined to keep matters that way, the American mutineers posted a $200 reward for Smith's head and then left for their farms.[112]

On the British side of the border there was also little enthusiasm for the war. Robert Nichol believed that the situation of the province had changed for the worse since Brock's death. "Confidence seems to have vanished from the land," he informed Colonel Talbot, "and a gloomy despondency has taken its place." One individual who refused to submit to the general miasma of depression was John Strachan. Reports of the frightful conditions at the front already had alarmed some members of the colonial elite and, on 22 November 1812, they met at York for the purpose of raising funds to buy supplies for the militiamen still on duty. Strachan chaired the meeting and told those in attendance that it was their duty "to comfort those who are fighting our battles."[113] By the end of the evening the Loyal and Patriotic Society of Upper Canada had been formed. A proposal to restrict voting rights in the organization to those who had paid a £10 fee was rejected and that privilege was instead automatically granted to members of the Executive and Legislative councils and, not surprisingly, to clergymen of the Church of England. Apparently, a good deal of resentment still existed over the Assembly's refusal to assist Brock, and only the speaker of the House was granted voting rights.[114]

Rather than simply assist active militiamen, the new society agreed to fund a number of projects. Families in distress because of the war were to be offered relief, and disabled militiamen were also considered fit objects for the society's bounty. The group even decided to award medals to those men who had distinguished themselves while on service. Aware that desertion was rampant at the front, the directors announced they would withhold medals from any "militiaman or soldier who has been or shall be convicted of desertion or absenting himself from duty." Of course, few of the directors themselves were on active service, chiefly because they had been lucky enough to have acquired exemptions. Chief Justice Thomas Scott was too old for militia service, but most of the other directors were under sixty years of age. Thomas Ridout was fifty-eight, William Powell had just celebrated his fifty-seventh birthday, and Alexander Wood was only forty. John Strachan, who was thirty-four years of age when he founded the society, later remarked that everywhere in the province "inhabitants rejoiced" to see those "who were exempted from their age or situation" coming forward to "comfort those who were called out." Although ostensibly designed to assist war sufferers, the society also served another purpose. It allowed Strachan and the other members of the colonial establishment to claim later that they had taken an "active part in the war" even though most of them never left the comfort of their homes.[115]

Avoidance of militia duty was the norm for Upper Canadian males throughout the struggle. Despite the high number of desertions during the first part of the war, participation in the militia actually reached a peak before Brock's death in October 1812. One researcher who has examined the postwar "cult of Brock worship" thinks that Upper Canadians idolized the British officer because they thought he was "merely a striking specimen of the men he led."[116] Yet Isaac Brock died less than four months after hostilities had commenced, and the war would rage for more than two years after his death. The victory at Michilimackinac had been gained without his direct participation, and the capture of Detroit was as much a product of Hull's cowardice as it was a result of careful planning on Brock's part. Why, then, was he chosen as an object for praise and raised to near demigod status by Upper Canadians? To answer that question one need only examine the conduct of the colonists after 1812. While the level of militia participation was certainly low before Brock's death, it dwindled even further in the months that followed. In contrast to this pitiful record, the dismal display of the first four months of the war appeared positively remarkable. Years later, writers would focus on Brock and the first few weeks of the conflict because there was at least a grain of truth to the claim that large numbers of Upper Canadians had responded with "unwearied exertions" when called to arms by their "immortal" leader.[117]

Notes

1 Selby quoted in Ermatinger, *The Talbot Regime,* 47.

2 *St David's Spectator* quoted in *Kingston Gazette,* 11 May 1816, 2.

3 AO, Eli Playter Diary, 27 June 1812, 397.

4 NA, RG 8, C Series, British Military Documents (hereafter NA, RG 8, C Series), volume 675, Brock to Prevost, 22 April 1812, 3; CO42/146, Barclay to Prevost, 5 May 1812, 209.

5 NA, CO42/352, Brock to Prevost, 3 December 1811, 55.

6 Hitsman, *Safeguarding Canada,* 57. There were unofficial militia musters prior to the passage of the 1793 act.

7 HPL, Jones, "The Militia," 3–4.

8 *Documentary History,* "Militia Law of 1808," 3:3–18.

9 HPL, Jones, "The Militia," 5.

10 NA, CO42/352, Brock to Prevost, 3 December 1811, 58–9.

11 Ibid., Brock to Liverpool, 23 March 1812, 8; Smith, *A Geographical View,* 80–1.

12 *Documentary History,* Brock to Prevost, 25 February 1812, 3:43.

13 Ibid., "An Act to Amend the Militia Act," 6 March 1812, 4:5–11, NA, UCS, vol. 14, 1811, Clenche to Shaw, 8 June 1811, 5456.

14 *Documentary History,* "An Act to Amend the Militia Act," 6 March 1812, 4:5–11.

15 NA, UCS, vol. 13, 4 June 1811 Militia Return, 5437. Altogether the militia numbered 12,801 in 1811. That was an increase of 924 from 1810 and, therefore, it is safe to assume that by 1812 the total was at least 13,000.

16 *Documentary History,* "An Act to Amend the Militia Act," 6 March 1812, 4:5–11.

17 *Kingston Gazette,* 24 March 1812, 3.

18 Ibid., 19 May 1812, 2.

19 NA, CO42/146, Brock to Prevost, 16 May 1812, 215.

20 At least three militia officers submitted claims for the loss of swords and belts; NA, RG 19, E5 (a), Board of Claims, Thomas Humberstone, claim 443; Nathaniel Bell, claim 467; Eli Playter, claim 1328. One historian has noted that officers sometimes purchased other items including special uniforms; Johnson, *Becoming Prominent,* 71–9.

21 Stanley, *Canada's Soldiers,* 146; NA, UCS, Edward Baynes's Notice, 22 February 1812, 5990.

22 NA, CO42/146, Prevost to Liverpool, 26 May 1812, 205.

23 For Armstrong see *Kingston Gazette,* 26 May 1812, 205; information on recruits and desertions is in Cruikshank, "Records of... The Glengarry Light Infantry," 13.

24 McLeod, *A Brief Review of the Settlement of Upper Canada,* 41.

25 Brock to Prevost, 22 April 1812, quoted in HPL, Jones, "The Militia," 7–8. Prevost discussed the 15 May call in NA, CO42/146, Prevost to Liverpool, 9 June 1812, 237.

26 NA, CO42/352, Brock to Executive Council, 19 May 1812, 101; Eneas Shaw circular, 23 May 1812, 103.

27 *Documentary History,* Brock to Prevost, 11 December 1811, 3:25–6; NA, UCS, vol. 13, 4 June 1811 Militia Return, 5437. The return lists only 1926 weapons brought by the 12,801 men.

28 *Kingston Gazette,* 19 May 1812, 2.

29 AO, Abraham Nelles Papers, June memorandum.

30 NA, CO42/352, Brock to Liverpool, 23 March 1812, 9.

31 NA, CO42/146, Prevost to Liverpool, 18 May 1812, 197.

32 *Documentary History,* Nichol to Glegg, March 1812, 3:15.

33 The description of Nichol is from Scott, *John Graves Simcoe,* 206, while his philosophy on government work is from NA, CO42/352, Nichol to Halton, 25 April 1811, 31. Brock's assurance is in Cruikshank, "Sketch," 22.

34 *Documentary History,* Brock to Prevost, 28 July 1812, 4:148–9.

35 Richardson, *Richardson's War of 1812,* 11.

36 Smith, *A Geographical* View, 81.

37 The pay offer is in NA, RG 9 UCM, IB3, vol. 1, General Orders, 1812–16, 2 July 1812, 58. *Documentary History,* Brock to Prevost, 3 July 1812, 3:97, discusses the attitudes of the men.

38 *Documentary History,* Militia General Order, 1 July 1812 3:97–8.

39 NA, RG 9 UCM, General Orders, vol. 2, 1811–21, 4 July 1812, 8; 10 July 1812, 12.

40 *Documentary History,* Brock to Prevost, 12 July 1812, 3:65.

41 Stanley, "The Significance of Six Nations Participation," 218; *Documentary History,* Brock to Prevost, 3 July 1812, 97.

42 Stanley, "The Indians in the War of 1812," 155–6.

43 NA, CO42/352, "Hull's Proclamation," 12 July 1812, 122; Smith, *A Geographical View,* 82–3.

44 Stanley, "The Contribution of the Canadian Militia," in *After Tippecanoe,* 33; *Documentary History,* spy to Van Rensselaer, 16 September 1812, 3:268.

45 NA, CO42/352, "Brock's Proclamation," 22 July 1812, 124.

46 Stanley, *The War of 1812,* 6–7; Stanley, "The Indians in the War of 1812," 150–2.

47 NA, RC 9 UCM, IB3, vol. 2, General Orders, 1811–21, 22 July 1812, 17; *Documentary History,* Militia General Order, 22 July 1812, 3:138.

48 NA, C.676, Elliot to Claus, 15 July 1812, in Stanley, "The Contribution of the Canadian Militia," 33.

49 NA, CO42/147, Prevost to Liverpool, 30 July 1812, 31–2, St George to Brock, 15 July 1812; CO42/352, Brock to Liverpool, 29 August 1812, 105.

50 T.B. St George to Brock, 15 July 1812, in *Documents Relating to the Invasion of Canada,* 61.

51 *The John Askin Papers,* Charles Askin's Journal, 24 July to 12 September 1812, 713.

52 AO, Percy Band Collection, no. 238, G. Hamilton to A. Hamilton, August 1812; no. 237, Charles Askin to A. Hamilton, 21 July 1812.

53 NA, CO42/352, Brock to Liverpool, 29 August 1812, 105.

54 "Ebeneezer Allan," *Dictionary of Canadian Biography,* 5:13–15.

55 Ermatinger, *The Talbot Regime,* 44–6, discusses the failed partnership, *Documentary History,* Brock to Prevost, 26 July 1812, 3:145–6.

56 "Andrew Westbrook," *Dictionary of Canadian Biography,* 6:808–9, notes the business deals between Talbot and others. In his fictional work *Westbrook the Outlaw; Or the Avenging Wolf,* 1, John Richardson said that Westbrook harboured a grievance over being refused a militia commission.

57 Springer to Brock, 23 July 1812, in *Documents Relating to the Invasion of Canada,* 85–6.

58 *Documentary History,* Brock to Prevost, 26 July 181, 3:45–6.

59 Ibid., Brock to Prevost, 28 July 1812, 3:148–9; Brock to Prevost, 26 July 1812, 3:145–6.

60 NA, CO42/352, Assembly Reply, 27 July 1812, 115.

61 Ibid., Executive Council Minutes, 3 August 1812, 109.

62 Ibid., Assembly Reply, 27 July 1812, 115; Brock to Liverpool, 29 August 1812, 105.

63 The address is in York *Gazette,* 5 September 1812, 2; and the new regulations in *Kingston Gazette,* 19 December 1812, 4; 26 December 1812, 4.

64 *Documentary History,* Brock to Baynes, 29 July 1812, 3:152–3; Brock to Prevost, 28 July 1812, 3:148–9.

65 NA, MG 23, H14, vol. 3, W.D. Powell Papers, "First Days in Canada," 1058. The composition of the force is discussed in NA, CO42/352, Brock to Liverpool, 29 August 1812, 105; and Stanley, *The War of 1812,* 106–7.

66 Stacey, "The Defence of Upper Canada," in *The Defended Border,* 18; Verchères in *War on the Detroit,* 107.

67 Verchères, *War on the Detroit,* 107.

68 NA, CO42/353, Brock to Brothers, 3 September 1812, 226.

69 NA, UCS, vol. 13, 4 June 1811 Militia Return, 5437. The militia of those four districts amounted to 5850 men in 1811. These calculations are an overestimate of the proportion of active men, since the total number of militiamen would have increased over the previous twelve months.

70 NA, RG 9 UCM, IB3, vol. 2, General Orders, 14 August 1812, 22.

71 *Documentary History,* Militia General Order, 18 August 1812, 3:188–9; Militia General Order, 23 January 1813, 5:46–7.

72 Ibid., Myers to Prevost, 17 August 1812, 3:185–6.

73 AO, Eli Playter Diary, August Muster Roll, 401–2.

74 *Documentary History, Buffalo Gazette,* 11 August 1812, 3:170; New York *Gazette,* 24 July 1812, 3:127.

75 McLeod, *A Brief Review of the Settlement of Upper Canada,* 44; Cruikshank, "A Study of Disaffection in Upper Canada," in *The Defended Border,* 223.

76 NA, CO42/352, Brock to Liverpool, 29 August 1812, 105; CO42/353, Brock to Brothers, 3 September 1812, 226.

77 Cruikshank, "The Battle of Queenston Heights," in *The Defended Border,* 22.

78 *Documentary History,* Militia General Order; 26 August 1812, 3:212–13; Smith, *A Geographical View,* 92.

79 McLeod, *A Brief Review of the Settlement of Upper Canada,* 44.

80 Smith, *A Geographical View,* 82.

81 *Documentary History,* Brock to Prevost, 7 September 1812, 3:243.

82 Ibid., Militia General Order, 21 September 1812, 3:285. NA, CO42/353, Brock to Brothers, 18 September 1812, 227.

83 *Kingston Gazette,* 31 October 1812, 3; *Documentary History,* Return of Casualties, 13 October 1812, 4:73; Brett, *The Wars of Napoleon,* 115–16.

84 Stacey, "The Defence of Upper Canada," in *The Defended Border,* 19.

85 Smith, *A Geographical View,* 90.

86 McLeod, *A Brief Review of the Settlement of Upper Canada,* 42.

87 This group is discussed in Smith, *A Geographical View,* 90, and *Documentary History, Baltimore Whig,* 5 June 1813, 5:269.

88 AO, Playter Diary, October 1812, 405.

89 York *Gazette,* 10 October 1812, 2.

90 For examples of substitution and costs see AO, Abraham Nelles Papers, John Frennett's Deposition, 11 September 1812; NA, Upper Canada RG 5, A1, UCS, Traitors and Treason, vol. 6, 6646; CO42/355, Baynes to Prevost, 18 June 1814, 404.

91 The Philips case is in AO, Military Records, Miscellaneous no. 5, Cameron's Company, 3d York, 1812.

92 *Kingston Gazette,* 9 January 1813, 3.

93 Peacetime figures for gross income are from Russell, *Attitudes to Social Structure,* 21, 75. Assumptions about wartime incomes are based on prices of goods sold to the commissariat; see chapter 6.

94 NA, RG 19, E5 (a), Board of Claims for War Losses, vol. 3735, file 3, claim 116, Job Lodor testimony. *The Constitutional History of Canada, 1791–1818,* Drummond to Bathurst, 27 February 1816.

95 AO, Captain James Mustard Papers, 26 March 1813.

96 *Kingston Gazette,* 1 December 1812, 2.

97 Cruikshank, "A Study of Disaffection in Upper Canada," in *The Defended Border,* 210; McLeod, *A Brief Review of the Settlement of Upper Canada,* 50.

98 Smith, *A Geographical View,* 90.

99 *Kingston Gazette,* 1 December 1812, 2.

100 Cruikshank, "A Study of Disaffection in Upper Canada," in *The Defended Border,* 212.

101 HPL, Special Collections, "Estimate of Sums Wanted," 25 September to 24 October 1812.

102 *Documentary History,* Sheaffe to Prevost, 3 November 1812, 4:176; Militia General Order, 13 November 1812, 4:207–8; Militia General Order, 14 November 1812, 4:211–12.

103 Ibid., Militia General Order, 28 October 1812, 4:169.

104 Ibid., District General Order; 29 October 1812, 4:170.

105 NA, CO42/354, Sheaffe to Prevost, 23 November 1812, 5.

106 Mann, *Medical Sketches,* 1. Battle casualties were determined from pension lists published in the *Niagara Spectator,* 11 December 1817. Since pensions were granted to widows or orphans, the pension lists did not include the names of single men who died on duty. For example, at least two other militiamen died in battle in late 1812 according to lists in CO42/354, Sheaffe to Prevost. Return of Casualties, 30 November 1812, 16.

107 NA, RG 9 UCM, IB3, vol. 2, General Orders, 1811–21, District General Order, 27 September 1812, 30; *Documentary History,* District General Order, 1 October 1812, 4:27; *Niagara Spectator,* 11 December 1817.

108 AO, Abraham Nelles Papers, Field Reports 1812–14. The experiences of Crook, Macklem, and Applegarth were shared by other commanders. Captain Hatt's flank company had 35 men fit for duty on 30 November 1812 but only 26 by 11 December. Abraham Nelles's company had 53 present on 24 November but only 38 six days later.

109 *Documentary History,* Merritt to Pendergrast, 8 December 1812, 4:4.

110 Ibid., Shaw to Talbot, 11 December 1812, 296; Militia General Order, 16 December 1812, 324; NA, CO42/352, Sheaffe to Bathurst, 31 December 1812, 176.

111 *Documentary History,* New York *Evening Post,* 11 November 1812, 4:179–80.

112 Ibid., Bill Sherman's statement; David Harvey's statement, 3 December 1812, 4:247–9.

113 Ibid., Nichol to Talbot, 18 December 1812, 327; Robinson, *The Life of John Beverley Robinson,* 61.

114 AO, Strachan Papers, draft constitution, 15 December 1812.

115 Ibid., society history, 1813?; Spragge, *The John Strachan Letterbook,* Strachan to Stewart, winter 1814, 58.

116 Walden, "Isaac Brock: Man and Myth," iii. The deification of Brock began as early as 1813 when John Rolph informed a friend that the former administrator was a man "who ardently loved the country and whom every lisping child would follow into the field." NA, MG 24, J48, J.W. Whittaker Papers, 1813.

117 AO, Strachan Papers, society history, 1813?

Unfair Masters and Rascally Servants?

Labour Relations Among Bourgeois, Clerks and Voyageurs in the Montreal Fur Trade, 1780–1821

Carolyn Podruchny

The history of working peoples in the fur trade has recently become a subject of concentrated interest. The publication of Edith Burley's *Servants of the Honourable Country*, which explores the master and servant relationship between Orkney workers and Hudson's Bay Company (HBC) officers stands as an important development in focussing attention squarely on the workers themselves, and demonstrates the extent of their power through insubordination and resistance.[1] A general pattern of master and servant relations existed among most fur trade companies and their labour forces which was similar to other 18th-century labour contexts. Servants signed a contract for several years, agreeing to be obedient and loyal to their master in exchange for food, shelter, and wages.[2] However, labour relations were highly influenced by local conditions. The personality of individual masters, the availability of food resources, the difficulty of work, and the cultural conventions of the labour force all affected the nature of the master-servant relationship. As many fur trade scholars have contended, there was never just one fur trade: it varied tremendously in different contexts.[3] The same can be said of labour relations in the fur trade. Process and flexibility were dominant characteristics in the relationships between masters and servants.

French Canadian *voyageurs*[4] working in various Montréal-based fur trade companies developed a distinct culture which emerged in the early 18th century and lasted to the mid-19th century. During the most active period of the Montréal trade, the labour force grew from 500 men in the 1780s, to over 2000 by the time the North West Company (NWC) merged with the HBC in 1821. As voyageurs travelled from their homes in Lower Canada to the Native interior, they underwent continuous transformations in identity and their culture came to be shaped by liminality.[5] Voyageur culture was also structured by masculinity. The cluster of values that permeated voyageur culture and became markers of the ideal man included being tough, daring, risk-taking, hard-working, jovial, and carefree.[6] The voyageurs made direct links between their work and their gendered identity as men. This was a means in which to ground themselves in their passage out of French Canadian society as adolescents, and into the adult world of the exotic and dangerous *pays d'en haut* or "Indian country" where they had to become courageous and tough adventurers. Their masculine identity was influenced by their French Canadian peasant and Catholic upbringing, the Native peoples they met in the interior, and of course the hege-

Carol Podruchny, "Unfair Masters and Rascally Servants? Labour Relations Among Bourgeois, Clerks and Voyageurs in the Montreal Fur Trade, 1780–1821," *Labour/Le Travail* 43 (Spring 1999): 43–70.

monic rule of their masters. Although many voyageurs became freemen (independently trading and living off the land)[7] and joined Native families or emerging métis communities,[8] their occupational culture remained distinct from these groups. Voyageur culture was also different from that of other labour forces, such as the Kahnawake Iroquois, and Orcadians. The men from these groups did not often work together, and language barriers prevented close communication.

As the fur trade in North America varied tremendously during its long history and expansive presence, it is not surprising that its paternalistic structure also varied tremendously.[9] Patterns between regions and among different companies changed over time. Fur trade historian Jennifer Brown contends that the managers of Montréal companies had greater difficulty in controlling their servants than did the HBC officers. The more fortunate HBC officers could rely on the London committee to lay down the standard rules of conduct which served as a basis for governing their men's behaviour. The Montréal companies not only lacked this central disciplining influence, but they also had further obstacles with which to contend. Discipline was not easy to administer while voyageurs traded *en derouine* (out on their own among Native peoples), or on long journeys requiring their support and assistance. Brown goes on to assert that not only were Montréal masters outnumbered by French Canadian voyageurs, but:

> they also generally lacked the vertical social integration that helped to hold the Hudson's Bay men together. Differences of status, without the mitigating prospect of promotion, and of ethnic background meant that relations between the two groups were often characterized more by opposition, bargaining, and counter-bargaining, than by solidarity. In addition, the French Canadians could draw on a long tradition of independent behaviour, social and sexual, in the Indian country.[10]

The particular form of paternalism in the post-Conquest Montréal fur trade was shaped by the high degree of control exercised by voyageurs in the labour system. Flexibility in contracts, frequent labour shortages, and continual re-postings gave the voyageurs bargaining power. Voyageurs' power was also augmented by isolation which increased their masters' dependence on them.

Burley challenges Brown's characterization of the HBC workforce as more rigidly controlled and less independent than the French Canadian voyageurs. She contends the Orcadians opposed and bargained with their masters like the voyageurs.[11] Although the culture of voyageurs was distinct from other fur trade labourers, all engaged in similar types of resistance and agency. These correlations are worth serious note, but the fractured nature of the sources prevents scholars from arguing convincingly that voyageurs were either more or less independent and 'rascally' than other fur trade labourers. The partners and clerks in the NWC did not keep detailed or consistent reports of their activities at fur trade posts, and they commented less on the behaviour of their men. It is thus difficult to compare quantitatively the extent to which voyageurs and other fur trade labourers resisted the rule of their masters. This paper instead focuses on the nature and patterns of voyageur and master relations, providing comparisons with other fur trade labourers where possible.

After the 1763 conquest of New France, the fur trade operating out of Montréal reorganized under the direction of Scottish, English, American, and a few French Canadian managers who called themselves *bourgeois*.[12] These companies, which eventually merged into the NWC, hired French Canadian men mainly from parishes around Montréal and Trois Rivières to transport goods and furs from Montréal to the North American interior during the summer months. They were also hired to work year-round at the company posts and handled trading with Native peoples. There is no question that the job of voyageurs was difficult. They performed near miraculous feats of transporting goods and furs over immense distances and undertook challenging canoe routes. Work at the interior posts was easier than that on the summer canoe brigades, but voyageurs were responsible for a tremendous range of duties, which included construction, artisan crafts, hunting, fishing, and trading. Threats to voyageurs' well-being, including starvation and physically debilitating overwork, came mostly from the harsh environment, but hostile Native peoples and cruel masters could contribute to the misery. Despite the harsh working and living conditions, voyageurs developed a reputation as strong, capable, and cheerful, although sometimes unreliable, servants. The writings of the bourgeois and clerks working in the trade reveal a deep admiration for their skill and effectiveness as workers, and a tolerance for petty theft and minor insolence.[13] This article concerns itself with two questions: why did voyageurs put up with their tough lot without overt revolt, and what was the substance of the relationship between voyageurs and their masters? Because voyageurs were primarily non-literate and left little record of their experiences, we must rely on the writings of a diverse group of literate outsiders, including the powerful fur trade partners, lowly clerks, and assorted travellers to the north-west interior. A close and extensive examination reveals a complex network of accommodation and resistance in the master and servant relationship. This article maps out some patterns in the period from 1780 to 1821, which was the height of competition between trade companies and the expansion into the interior.

The Montréal fur trade labour system was organized around indentured servitude, paternalism, and cultural hegemony. The fur trade managers and clerks acted as paternal masters directing the labour of voyageurs. Voyageurs signed a legal contract, or *engagement,* which established the framework for the paternal relationship. The principal tenet of the contract dictated that servants obey their masters in exchange for board and wages. Voyageurs and their masters, however, interpreted the contract differently in particular contexts. Their diverging and situational "readings" of the legal contract led to the emergence of a "social contract" which constituted the actual working relationship between the two groups. The "social contract" was expressed in the customs which came to characterize the fur trade workplace and the dialogue between servants and masters over acceptable working conditions. Masters tried to enforce obedience, loyalty, and hard work among voyageurs, while the voyageurs struggled to ensure that their working conditions were fair and comfortable, and that masters fully met their paternal obligations. Voyageurs exercised relative cultural autonomy on the job, and often controlled the workpace and scope of their duties. Their masters, however, maintained ultimate authority by exercising their right to hire and fire voyageurs and by successfully profiting in the trade.

Although masters and servants can be understood as constituting two loose but distinct "classes" within the fur trade, it is important to be aware of the ranges within each class in terms of power, authority, and duty. Some masters were junior clerks, bound in a paternal relationship with senior clerks and partners. These clerks were paid a smaller annual salary than senior bourgeois, and did not hold shares in the partnerships which made up the Montréal fur trading companies. Partners were granted voting privileges in business meetings, in addition to their company shares and higher salaries.[14] *Engagés* also had varying status. At the bottom were seasonally employed summer men, referred to as *mangeurs du lard,* or Porkeaters, who paddled between Montréal and the Great Lakes. Wintering *engagés,* or *hommes du nord,* who paddled canoes to and worked at the interior posts, scorned these greenhorns. Within the canoe, paddlers called middlemen or *milieu*, were subject to the authority of the foreman and steersman, or *devant* and *gouvernail*, who usually acted as canoe and brigade leaders. Some estimates suggest that these *bouts* could earn from one third to five times as much as paddlers.[15] Interpreters and guides, paid usually twice or three times as much as other *engagés*, also assumed more authority by their greater wealth and knowledge.[16]

Although the ethnic divisions did not entirely follow occupational lines, the Montréal bourgeois became more and more British after the 1763 Conquest, while the voyageurs were primarily French Canadians. British discrimination against French Canadians, and fellow-feeling among voyageurs contributed to the social distance between masters and servants. Voyageurs lived within a different cultural ethos than that of the bourgeois, one which emphasized independence, strength, courage, and cultural adaptation rather than profit, obedience, and cultural supremacy. These different frames of reference distanced voyageurs from their masters, and frequently impeded harmonious workplace relations. Despite the range of roles within each group, the division between bourgeois and voyageur, or master and servant, served as a basic social organization of the fur trade.[17] Class, ethnic, and cultural differences operated in conjunction to create a paternalistic and hegemonic labour system.

Masters and servants accepted their positions as rulers and ruled. Voyageurs could challenge the substance and boundaries of their jobs and loyalty to their masters without contesting the fundamental power dynamics. Voyageurs' acceptance of their masters' domination was based on a deeply held belief in the legitimacy of paternalism. Voyageurs certainly became discontented, resisted their masters' authority, and sometimes revolted, but it was outside of their conception of the world to challenge the hegemonic culture.[18] Thus, the structure of cultural hegemony was not inconsistent with the presence of labour strife. Although voyageurs participated in the formulation of the master and servant relationship, they challenged the terms of their employment and contracts without fundamentally challenging their position in the power relationship. Voyageurs, clerks and bourgeois engaged in a dialogue of accommodation and confrontation as a means of constructing a workable relationship.[19] To assert the power and agency of the voyageurs does not deny the framework of subordination; rather it looks within it. Hegemony did not envelop the lives of the voyageurs and prevent them from defending their own modes of work, play, and rituals. Hegemony offered, in the words of E.P. Thompson, writing of the 18th-century English plebians, a "bare architecture of a structure of relations of domination and subordination, but within that architectural tracery many different scenes could be set and different dramas enacted."[20]

What "scenes of rule" were enacted in the north-west fur trade? The mutuality intrinsic to paternalism and hegemony governed social relations and made up the substance of the "social contract" between the bourgeois and voyageurs in the north west. Each party accepted their roles and responsibilities in the master and servant relationship, but they pressed the boundaries, and tried to shape the relationship to best suit their desires and needs. The difficulty masters encountered in enforcing authority, and the precariousness of survival meant they had to be particularly responsive to their servants. Part of hegemony involved appearances.[21] Masters often engaged in self-consciousness public theatre, while voyageurs offered their own form of counter-theatre. Through this means of communication masters and servants came to accept common ideas of the way things should work. The formula laid out in the labour contracts served as the crux from which both parties tried to digress. In the "social contract," or "ritual theatre," masters attempted to evade their provision of welfare, and the voyageurs tried to ease the strain of their work and to control aspects of the workplace. A dialogue of resistance and accommodation kept the paternalistic relationship fluid and flexible, which was crucial to its resilience. Paternalistic hegemony was constantly being negotiated and, in the fur trade, management authority never came close to being absolute or ubiquitous.

Because the NWC and XY Company (the second most significant of the Montréal companies, hereafter XYC) were co-proprietorships, contracts were made in the names of the various firms or individuals comprising the shareholders and joint partnerships. No engagements were issued specifically in the name of the NWC or XYC, as all of the outfitting was carried out by shareholder partners and firms.[22] The labour contracts of all partnerships, both within and outside of the NWC, however, were remarkably similar. Contracts reveal voyageurs' names, parishes of origin, destinations in the north west, job positions, lengths of term, and salaries. The language of most contracts underscored the paternal nature of the relationship, requiring voyageurs to obey their masters, to work responsibly and carefully, to be honest and well-behaved, to aid the bourgeois in making a profit, and to remain in the service. For example, a contract form for the firm McTavish, McGillivrays & Co., and Pierre de Rocheblave, Ecuïer clearly instructs the *engagé:*

> to take good and proper care, while on routes, and to return to the said places, the merchandise, provisions, furs, utensils, and all the things necessary for the voyage; to serve, obey and to faithfully carry out all [orders] of the said Bourgeois, or all others who represent the Bourgeois, which are required by the present contract, he lawfully and honestly commands, to make his profit, avoid misfortune, warn him if you know of danger; and generally do all that a good and loyal servant must and is obliged to do, without doing any particular trading; do not leave or quit the said service, under the pain carried by the laws of this Province, and the loss of your wages.[23]

Masters were bound to pay the voyageurs' wages and provide them with equipment. The substance of the equipment, and the provision of food and welfare for the *engagé,* were rarely specified in contracts, and thus provided one of the few places for obvious negotiation between the masters and servants.[24] Custom came to dictate that equipment consisted of one blanket, one shirt, and one pair of trousers.[25]

In order to enforce the terms of the legal contracts, bourgeois tried to regulate their servants through legal and state sanctions. In January 1778, an official of the NWC sent a memorandum to Governor Guy Carleton asking him "that it be published before the Traders and their Servants that the latter must strictly conform to their agreements, which should absolutely be in writing or printed, and before witnesses if possible, as many disputes arise from want of order in this particular." The memorandum goes on to ask that men be held to pay their debts with money or service and that traders hiring men already engaged to another company should purchase their contracts.[26] Lower Canadian law eventually recognized the legality of notarial fur trade contracts, and a 1796 ordinance forbade *engagés* to transgress the terms or desert the service.[27] In Lower Canada, the legislature empowered Justices of the Peace (JPS) to create and oversee the rules and regulations for master and servant relations.[28]

Bourgeois on occasion turned to the law to enforce the terms of the contract. Voyageurs were charged with breaking contracts, mainly for deserting, rather than for insolence or disobedience.[29] The files of the Court of Quarter Sessions in the District of Montréal reveal a range of cases: voyageurs accepted wages from one employer while already working for another, they obtained advance wages without appearing for the job, and they deserted the service.[30] Cases of voyageur desertion and theft can also be found in the records of the Montréal civil court.[31] In 1803, the British government passed the Canada Jurisdiction Act by which criminal offenses committed in the "Indian territories" could be tried in Lower Canada, and the five JPs named were all prominent fur trade bourgeois, although the court's power remained limited.[32] It is difficult to determine the effectiveness of court action to control workers, especially since prosecution rates have not survived in most of the records. Presumably the bourgeois would not continue to press charges if their efforts did not pay off. Yet pressing charges against voyageurs did not seem to deter them from continuing to desert, cheat contract terms, and steal from their employers.

Other efforts to control workers included cooperation between companies to limit contract-jumping and blacklisting deserters. In 1800 NWC officer William McGillivray wrote to Thomas Forsyth of Forsyth, Ogilvy and McKenzie:

> I agree with you that protecting Deserters would be a dangerous Practice and very pernicious to the Trade and fully sensible of this when any Man belonging to People opposed to The North West Company have happened to come to our Forts, we have told the Master of such to come for them and that they should not be in any way wise prevented from taking them back.

McGillivray assured Forsyth that he was not protecting one of their deserters and had told his master to come and claim him. He went on to discuss the case of the NWC *engagé,* Poudriés, who was allowed to return to Montréal because of ill health on the understanding that he was to pay his debt in Montréal or return to the north west to serve out his time. McGillivray explained that when the NWC discovered that Poudriés engaged himself to Forsyth, Ogilvy & McKenzie they attempted to arrest him. McGillivray accused Forsyth of protecting him, and requested that he be returned to NWC service or that his debt be paid, continuing:

> With regard to paying advances made to Men I wish to be explicit, we have alwise made it a practice and will continue so to do to pay every shilling that Men whom we hire may acknowledge to their former Master such Men being free on the Ground. We hire no Men who owe their Descent considering this a principle not to be deviated from in determining to adhere strictly to it we cannot allow others to treat us in a different manner - if a Man was Free at the Point au Chapeau we do not consider him at liberty to hire until he has gone to it.[33]

McGillivray decided to purchase voyageurs' engagements from their previous masters rather than paying their wages, and warned other fur trade companies against hiring any deserters.[34] The other fur trade companies soon followed suit.[35]

Voyageurs occasionally took their employing masters to court, most often to sue for wages.[36] Cases of this kind were widespread in all sorts of labour contracts in New France and Lower Canada, so it is not surprising that voyageurs followed suit. However, servants were not usually successful in claiming wages for jobs which they had deserted, or where they had disobeyed their masters.[37] The colonial government and legal system supported fur trade labour contracts, but the contracts were difficult to enforce because of the limits of the policing and justice systems in the north west. Masters thus relied more on the "social contract" which they were constantly negotiating with their servants.

Masters and voyageurs had different views of their "social contract," which frequently resulted in rocky negotiations. They agreed that servants were supposed to obey their masters' requirements to trade successfully in exchange for fair board and wages. Their divergent readings of "the deal" were based on different ideas of what was fair. Establishing a mutual understanding of obligations was easier if servants respected their masters. Servants respected those masters whom they regarded as tough but evenhanded.

How did masters command and maintain their authority? In many historic circumstances, masters turned to physical might or the law as a principal vehicle for hegemony. But at the height of fur trade competition, the arm of the law was short and the high value of labour discouraged masters from physically intimidating their workers. Masters relied on paternalistic authority as an accepted ideology to justify and bolster their might. The ideology was expressed in the "theatre of daily rule."[38] Bourgeois and clerks imposed their authority believing that they were superior and were obliged to control their inferior servants. Masters also contributed to a dominant public discourse of their superiority, or enacted the "theatre of rule" in material ways. They ensured their access to more and better food, fancier clothing, and better sleeping conditions than voyageurs.[39] Further in the interior, away from the larger fur trade administrative centres, bourgeois and clerks had to rely on inexpensive symbols and actions to enforce their authority. Carefully maintained social isolation, differential work roles, control over scarce resources, reputation, and ability all symbolized masters' authority.[40]

Differentiation in work roles was very apparent in travel. Bourgeois were usually passengers aboard canoes, and only helped their men paddle and portage in cases of extreme jeopardy. At times the rituals of travel situated bourgeois at the head of a great procession. In his reminiscences of a fur trading career, Alexander Ross described how the light canoe, used for transporting men and mail quickly through the interior, clearly positioned the bourgeois as a social superior:

> The bourgeois is carried on board his canoe upon the back of some sturdy fellow generally appointed for this purpose. He seats himself on a convenient mattress, somewhat low in the centre of his canoe; his gun by his side, his little cherubs fondling around him, and his faithful spaniel lying at his feet. No sooner is he at his ease, than his pipe is presented by his attendant, and he then begins smoking, while his silken banner undulates over the stern of his painted vessel.[41]

HBC surveyor Philip Turnor, both envied and criticized that the NWC

> give Men which never saw an Indian One Hundred Pounds pr Annum, his Feather Bed carried in the Canoe, his Tent which is exceedingly good, pitched for him, his Bed made and he and his girl carried in and out of the Canoe and when in the Canoe never touches a Paddle unless for his own pleasure all of these indulgences.[42]

At posts, bourgeois and clerks did not participate in the vigorous round of activities which kept the post functioning smoothly, such as constructing and maintaining houses, building furniture, sleighs and canoes, gathering firewood, hunting, and preparing food. Rather, these masters kept accounts, managed the wares and provisions, and initiated trade with Native peoples.

Bourgeois and clerks were encouraged to keep a distance from their labourers. Junior clerks in particular, whose authority in isolated wintering posts was threatened by experienced labourers, had to establish firm lines of control. When the NWC clerk George Gordon was still a novice, he received advice from a senior clerk, George Moffatt, to be independent, confident, very involved in the trade, and

> Mixt. very seldom with the Men, rather retire within yourself, than make them your

> companions—I do not wish to insinuate that you should be haughty—on the contrary—affability with them at times, may get You esteme, while the observance of a proper distance, will command respect, and procure from them ready obedience to you orders.[43]

In 1807, John McDonald of Garth was sent out as a novice to take over the NWC's Red River Department which was notorious for its corruption and difficult men. A French Canadian interpreter, who had long been in the district managing to secure great authority among voyageurs and Native peoples, had to be reminded by McDonald: "you are to act under me, you have no business to think, it is for me to do so and not for you, you are to obey."[44]

Probably the greatest challenges the bourgeois and clerks faced in asserting authority and controlling workers came from the circumstance of the fur trade itself—the great distances along fur trade routes and between posts, and the difficulties of transportation and communication. The arduous job of traversing an unfamiliar and inhospitable terrain led to frequent accidents. The incomplete nature of the sources obscures any measurement of mortality rates, but the writings of the bourgeois are filled with literally hundreds of cases of trading parties losing their way along routes, injuring themselves or perishing in canoeing accidents, being attacked by bears, and starving, to name a few of the mishaps.[45]

Masters and voyageurs dealt with the danger which infused the fur trade in a particular way. Both social groups idealized strength, toughness, and fortitude. Voyageurs competed with each other to perform awesome feats of dexterity and endurance.[46] They played rough and risk-taking games and tried to push themselves beyond their limits. In doing so, they tried to distract themselves from, and desensitize themselves to the risks inherent in fur trading and the deaths, accidents, and illnesses around them. Rather than being overwhelmed by the danger and tragedy, they made a virtue of necessity and flaunted their indifference. By incorporating manly violence and aggression into daily life, in their competitions and brawling, men could toughen themselves for the challenges of their jobs.[47] For example, in August of 1794, the Athabasca brigade raced the Fort George brigade from the south side to the north side of Lake Winnipeg. Duncan McGillivray, in charge of the Fort George crew, explained that

> The Athabasca Men piqued themselves on a Superiority they were supposed to have over the other bands of the North for expeditions marching [canoeing], and ridiculed our men *a la facon du Nord* for pretending to dispute a point that universally decided in *their* favor.

Despite the fact that the Fort George crew was more heavily loaded than the Athabasca crew, the two groups were evenly matched. They pressed on for 48 hours before agreeing to call a truce and set up camp on shore. Not surprisingly, McGillivray was delighted with their progress.[48] During a return trip to Montréal in 1815, John McDonald's crew of Canadians raced McGillivray's crew of Iroquois all day. The Canadians allowed the Iroquois to pull ahead at the start of the day, but they raced past them in the evening.[49]

Bourgeois encouraged the 'rugged' ethos of the voyageurs, which conveniently suited their agenda for quick, efficient, and profitable fur trade operations.[50] In some instances, bourgeois had to remind voyageurs of their manly pride in skill and endurance. During a particularly difficult journey, Alexander Mackenzie began to hear murmurs of discontent. The desire to turn back increased when one of the canoes was lost in a stretch of rapids. In order to encourage them to continue, Mackenzie

> brought to their recollection, that I did not deceive them, and that they were made

> acquainted with the difficulties and dangers they must expect to encounter, before they engaged to accompany me. I also urged the honour of conquering disasters, and the disgrace that would attend them on their return home, without having attained the object of the expedition. Nor did I fail to mention the courage and resolution which was the peculiar boast of the North men; and that I depended on them, at that moment, for the maintenance of their character....my harangue produced the desired effect, and a very general assent appeared to go wherever I should lead the way.[51]

Whether or not Mackenzie's "harangue produced the desired effect," it seems clear that both bourgeois and voyageurs valued the strength and courage required to paddle farther into the north west.

Accommodation among voyageurs, clerks and bourgeois made up part of the master and servant relationship. They worked closely for long periods of time, often shared living quarters, and faced many calamities and adventures together. As many disputes were caused by shortages of provisions, the surest way in which bourgeois and clerks could ensure loyalty was to provide plenty of good food for their men. Bourgeois and clerks fostered accommodation by meeting other paternal duties, such as attempting to protect their men from dangers in the workplace, providing medicines, and treating men with respect. Masters also solidified their hegemony through generosity and kindness, reminiscent of a kind of feudal largesse. Extra rations of alcohol and food, known as *regales,* were provided on significant occasions, such as settling accounts and signing new engagements.[52] Routine "rewards," such as the customary provision of drams at portages, were also incorporated into the more tedious aspects of fur trade work.[53] Sometimes masters' generosity was self-interested. When McKay gave his men moose skin to make themselves shoes, mittens, and blankets to last them through the winter, he warned them that "we have a strong opposition to contend with this year" and that they must be ready to go at a moment's notice.[54] His gifts no doubt consolidated his authority, but they also helped the voyageurs to perform their duties more effectively.

Despite these points of accommodation, harmony in the workplace was continually under stress as voyageur resistance to master authority characterized labour relations in the fur trade. Voyageurs' discontents focused on such unsuitable working and living conditions as poor rations, or unreasonable demands by masters. Voyageurs turned to strategies such as complaining to their bourgeois and attempting to bargain for better working conditions to highlight their concerns and initiate change. Like the Orcadians working for the HBC, individual action was a more common form of worker resistance than was organized collective protest.[55]

Complaining by the voyageurs became a form of "counter-theatre," which contested bourgeois hegemonic prerogatives. Just as the bourgeois often asserted their hegemony in a theatrical style, especially with canoe processions, the voyageurs also asserted their presence by "a theatre of threat and sedition."[56] In one illuminating example in the summer of 1804, while trying to travel through low water and marshes, Duncan Cameron's men ceaselessly complained about the miserable conditions and difficulty of the work. They cursed themselves as "Blockheads" for coming to "this Infernal Part of the Country," as they called it, damning the mud, damning the lack of clean water to quench their thirst, and damning the first person who chose that route. Cameron tried to be patient and cheerful with them, as he knew that complaining was their custom.[57] Voyageurs sometimes chose to limit the theatre of resistance to a small, and perhaps more effective scale by complaining to their bourgeois in private, so that they would not appear weak in front of the other men. During a difficult trip from Kaministiquia to Pembina, Alexander Henry the Younger commented that little or nothing was said during the day when the men had "a certain shame or bashfulness about complaining openly," but at night everyone came to complain about bad canoes, ineffective co-workers, and shortages of gum, wattap, and grease.[58] Often voyageurs restricted their complaining in front of their bourgeois to avoid losing favour. If they approached the bourgeois or clerk individually with strategic concerns, their demands were more likely to be met than if they openly abused their masters for unspecified grievances.[59]

When labour was scarce, men often bargained for better wages, both individually and in groups. In a large and organized show of resistance in the summer 1803, men at Kaministiquia refused to work unless they received a higher salary.[60] However, these types of group efforts to increase wages were more rare than the relatively common occurrence of men trying to individually bargain for better remuneration or conditions. Daniel Sutherland of the XYC instructed his recruiting agent in Montréal, St. Valur Mailloux, to refuse demands made by a couple of *engagés* for higher wages, and to appease the men with small presents. One *engagé* named Cartier caused turmoil by telling the XYC wintering partners that Mailloux was hiring men at significantly higher wages and by asking for his pay to be increased to that amount. Sutherland became angry with Mailloux, warning him "Always [offer more to] oarsman and steersman, but never exceed the price that I told you for going and coming [paid to the paddlers]."[61] Voyageurs could refuse to do tasks outside the normal range of their duties without extra pay as a means of increasing their wages.[62] They also frequently demanded better working conditions. Most often their concerns centred on safety, and they could refuse to take unreasonable risks.[63] Men with valued skills and knowledge, such as interpreters and guides, were in the best position to bargain for better working conditions and more pay.[64] Because fur trade labour was frequently scarce, and the mortality rate was high, skilled men were valued. Masters often overlooked servant transgressions and met servant demands in an effort to maintain their services.

Voyageurs also attempted to deceive their masters by pretending to be ill, or by lying about resources and Native peoples in the area to evade work. It is difficult to judge the extent to which voyageurs tried to trick their masters, especially when they were successful. However, hints of this practice, and suspicions of bourgeois and clerks emerge frequently in fur trade journals, suggesting that the practice was widespread. In December 1818, stationed near the Dauphin River, George Nelson became frustrated with one of his men, Welles, who frequently sneaked in "holiday" time by travelling slowly or claiming to be lost.[65] Less suspecting bourgeois probably did not catch the "dirty tricks" more careful voyageurs played on them regularly. Some masters, however, questioned their men's dubious actions and sent out "spies" to ensure that voyageurs were working honestly.[66] Other deceptions were of a more serious nature. Alexander Mackenzie was suspicious that his interpreters were not telling prospective Native trading partners what Mackenzie intended, which could have serious repercussions for the trade.[67]

When efforts to deceive their masters were frustrated, voyageurs could become sullen and indolent, working slowly and ineffectively, and even openly defying bourgeois orders. In one case in the fall 1800, while trying to set out from Fort Chipewyan, James Porter had to threaten to seize the wages of a man who refused to embark. When the voyageur reluctantly complied he swore that the devil should take him for submitting to the bourgeois.[68] More serious breaches of the master and servant contract included stealing provisions from cargo. Though Edward Umphreville kept up a constant watch over the merchandise in his canoes, a father and son managed to steal a nine gallon keg of mixed liquor.[69] George Nelson described the pilfering of provisions as routine.[70] Men also sometimes stole provisions to give extra food to their girlfriends or wives.[71] For the Orcadians working in the HBC service, Burley characterizes this type of counter-theatre—working ineffectively and deceiving masters—as both a neglect of duty and as an attempt to control the work process.[72] The same applies to the voyageurs.

One area of particular unease between voyageurs and masters was the issue of voyageurs freetrading with Native peoples. Unlike the HBC, the Montréal fur trading companies did not prohibit voyageurs from trading with Native peoples on the side to augment their income; some masters even expected them to do so as long as they did not abuse the privilege.[73] However, masters were often upset to find their men trading with Native peoples, because they wanted to concentrate the profit into their company's hands, and considered freetrading as "contrary to the established rules of the trade and the general practice among the natives."[74] In an 1803 trial over trading jurisdiction, John Charles Stuart, a NWC clerk, testified that when any men brought skins from the wintering grounds for the purpose of trading on their private account, "it was by a Special Favour" granted by their bourgeois, supported in the clause "Part de pactons" in their contracts. Although the practice was customary, the bourgeois retained the right to grant or refuse it.[75] After the 1804 merger of the XYC and NWC, the bourgeois decided to restrict private trade to increase profitability in the newly reformed company. Any man caught with more than two buffalo robes or two dressed skins, or one of each, would be fined 50 livres NW currency, and any employee caught trafficking with "petty traders or Montréal men" would forfeit his wages. The bourgeois were able to enforce this new restriction because the merger had created a surplus of men, so that employment became tenuous, and many voyageurs were concerned that their contracts would not be renewed.[76] In the minutes of the 1806 annual meeting, NWC partners agreed to ban men from bringing furs out of the interior in order to discourage petty trading.[77]

Voyageurs sometimes moved out of the "counter-theatre of daily resistance" to engage in "swift, direct action" against their masters' rule. Deserting the service was an outright breach of the master and servant contract.[78] Desertion should not be viewed as the single and straightforward phenomenon of voyageurs quitting their jobs. Rather, voyageurs deserted for a variety of purposes. Temporary desertions could provide a form of vacation, a ploy for renegotiating terms of employment, and a means of shopping for a better job. Men deserted when they were ill and needed time to recuperate.[79] Men also deserted when they thought their lives might be in danger, as was the case in March 1805, when servants of both the NWC and XYC ran off from the fishery at Lac La Pluie because they feared the Native people there wanted to kill them.[80] Voyageurs felt they could desert because they had a clear notion of their rights as workers which was instilled by the reciprocal obligations of paternalism. This may be one of the more significant differences between Orcadians working for the HBC and the voyageurs. Orcadians did not desert very often because of the lack of "desirable places to go." Orcadians would most often desert to NWC posts, while voyageurs more often became freemen, joined Native families, or returned to the St. Lawrence valley.[81]

As part of the continual negotiation of the master and servant "social contract," bourgeois and clerks responded to voyageurs' counter-theatre with intense performances of authority. They disciplined their men for transgressions of the master and servant contract, and sought to encourage voyageur obedience. Servant privileges, such as the provision of regales or sale of liquor might be curtailed or denied.[82] Bourgeois and clerks also frequently humiliated and intimidated their men. In one case during a journey to the Peace River in summer 1793, Alexander Mackenzie was confronted with a man who refused to embark in the canoe. He wrote:

> This being the first example of absolute disobedience which had yet appeared during the course of our expedition, I should not have passed it over without taking some very severe means to prevent a repetition of it; but as he had the general character of a simple fellow, among his companions, and had been frightened out of what little sense he possessed, by our late dangers, I rather preferred to consider him as an object of ridicule and contempt for his pusillanimous behaviour; though, in fact, he was a very useful, active, and laborious man.[83]

He also confronted the chief canoe maker during the same trip about his laziness and bad attitude. Mackenzie described the man as mortified at being singled out.[84] This kind of ritualized public shaming reinforced masculine ideals of effectiveness and skill. On an expedition to the Missouri in 1805, one of Larocque's men wished to remain with Charles McKenzie's party. Larocque became angry and told the man his courage failed him like an old woman, which threw the man into a violent fit of anger.[85] On occasion, a voyageur could be whipped for delinquency,[86] and bourgeois and clerks sometimes used the fear of starvation as a means of asserting authority over their men.[87]

In cases of severe dereliction, bourgeois could take the liberty of firing their employees.[88] In some cases, voyageurs were happy to be let go because they desired to become freemen. Nelson fired Joseph Constant, for example, for his "fits of ill humour without cause and Constant went on to become a prosperous independent trader."[89] However, it was a very serious matter when voyageurs decided to quit. Bourgeois and clerks made efforts to recoup deserters, and could punish them with confinement.[90]

The usual difficulties of the weather, accidents, and the constant challenge of the strenuous work could lead to high levels of stress and to anxieties among bourgeois, clerks, and voyageurs. Voyageurs' blunders, lost and broken equipment, and voyageur insolence often exacerbated tensions.[91] Alexander Henry the Younger grew frustrated with one of his men named Desmarrais for not protecting the buffalo he shot from wolves. He grumbled:

> My servant is such a careless, indolent fellow that I cannot trust the storehouse to his care. I made to-day a complete overhaul, and found everything in the greatest confusion; I had no idea matters were so bad as I found them.... Like most of his countrymen, he is much more interested for himself than for his employer.[92]

On rare occasions violence punctuated the generalized tension of master-servant relations in the fur trade. Mutual resentments could lead to brawls between the masters and servants.[93]

More typically tensions in the master and servant relationship were expressed in nastiness and unfairness, rather than violence. Motivated by the desire to save money and gain the maximum benefit from their workers, bourgeois pushed their men to work hard, which could result in ill will. Most serious cases of ill will and injustice concerned bourgeois selling goods to voyageurs at inflated prices and encouraging voyageurs to go into debt as soon as they entered fur trade service. It is difficult to find many instances of "bad faith" in bourgeois writings, as they would not likely dwell on their cruelty as masters, nor reveal their unfair tricks. However, travellers, critics of fur trade companies, and disgruntled employees provide clues. The French Duke de La Rouchefoucault Liancourt, travelling through North America in the late eighteenth century, commented that the NWC encouraged vice among their men by paying them in merchandise, especially luxuries and rum, so that none of them ever earned a decent wage.[94] Lord Selkirk, certainly no fan of the NWC, criticized the bourgeois further for exploiting their men, pointing out that *engagés* often left their French Canadian families in distress, and were unable to provide for them because the cost of goods in the interior was double or triple the price in Lower Canada, and men were usually paid in goods rather than cash. The NWC saved further costs on men's wages by encouraging addiction to alcohol, and then paying wages in rum at inflated prices. The Company placed no ceiling on its men's credit, so that many of them fell deeply into debt.[95]

Despite Selkirk's obvious bias against the NWC, he was not alone in his misgivings about Montréal fur trade company labour practices. As a new clerk in the XYC, George Nelson was instructed to provide any trade goods his men might ask for, and to encourage them to take up their wages in any of the trade goods on board the canoe. Nelson was initially uneasy with this mode of dealing,

> for thought I what is there more unnatural, than to try to the get the wages a poor man for a few quarts of rum, some flour & sugar, a few half fathoms of tobacco, & but verly little Goods who comes to pass a few of his best years in this rascally & unnatural Country to try to get a little money so as to settle himself happily among the rest of his friends & relations.

Eventually Nelson came to justify his participation in this system of exploitation because he felt that the men would ruin themselves anyway, and that most of them were disobedient "blackguards" for whom slavery was too good.[96] Nelson was also surprised that these men could live such a carefree existence while deeply in debt and with few material possessions.[97] His comment reveals one of the deep cultural fissures between masters and servants.

Voyageur responses to the cruelty of bourgeois and clerks could reach intense heights in the ongoing counter-theatre of resistance. Ill will between servants and masters could impede work. Sometimes the tensions were so strong that voyageurs refused to share the fruits of their hunting and fishing with their masters.[98] The more outrageous instances of masters abusing servants could lead to collective resistance among the voyageurs in the form of strikes or mass desertion. When a voyageur named Joseph Leveillé was condemned by the Montréal Quarter Sessions to the pillory for having accepted the wages of two rival fur-trading firms in 1794, a riot ensued. A group made up largely of voyageurs hurled the pillory into the St. Lawrence River and threatened to storm the prison. The prisoner was eventually released and no one was punished for the incident.[99] Voyageurs seemed to have developed a reputation for mob belligerence in Lower Canada. Attorney general Jonathan Sewell warned in a 1795 letter to Lieutenant Colonel Beckworth that officers in Lower Canada should be given greater discretionary power to counter the "riotous inclinations" of the people, especially of the "lawless band" of voyageurs.[100]

Instances of mass riots or collective resistance were not unknown in New France and Lower Canada. However, the small population, diffuse work settings, and not too unreasonable seigneurial dues usually restricted expressions of discontent to individual desertions or localized conflicts.[101] Yet, the instances of collective action could have created a precedent and memory for future mass protest.[102] On occasion voyageurs deserted en masse during cargo transports or exploration missions. In these cases men worked closely in large groups doing essentially the same difficult and dangerous tasks. Communication, the development of a common attitude to work, and camaraderie fostered a collective consciousness and encouraged collective action. In the summer of 1794 a Montréal brigade at Lac La

Pluie attempted to strike for higher wages. Duncan McGillivray explained:

> A few discontented persons in their Band, wishing to do as much mischief as possible assembled their companions together several times on the Voyage Outward & represented to them how much their Interest suffered by the passive obedience to the will of their masters, when their utility to the Company, might insure them not only of better treatment, but of any other conditions which they would prescribe with Spirit & Resolution.

When they arrived at Lac La Pluie the brigade demanded higher wages and threatened to return to Montréal without the cargo. The bourgeois initially prevailed upon a few of the men to abandon the strike. Soon after most of the men went back to work, and the ringleaders were sent to Montréal in disgrace.[103]

Efforts at collective action in the north west did not always end in failure. In his third expedition to the Missouri Country in fall 1805 and winter 1806, Charles McKenzie's crew of four men deserted. They had been lodged with Black Cat, a chief in a Mandan Village, who summoned McKenzie to his tent to inform McKenzie of their desertion. The men had traded away all of their property to Native people and intended to do the same with McKenzie's property, but Black Cat secured it. When McKenzie declared he would punish his men, Black Cat warned that the Native people would defend the voyageurs. When McKenzie tried to persuade the men to return to service, they would not yield.[104] Men who spent their winters in the *pays d'en haut* became a skilled and highly valued labour force and felt entitled to fair working conditions; they were not afraid to work together to pressure the bourgeois.[105]

Despite the occasions of mass actions, voyageurs more often acted individually than collectively. Their most powerful bargaining tool in labour relations was the option of desertion. The decision to desert could be caused by any number of poor working conditions, such as bad food, an unfair master, and difficult journeys. Voyageurs used desertion often as a means of improving their working conditions rather than quitting their jobs. Although bourgeois took voyageurs to court for deserting their contracts, the measure had little effect as voyageurs continued to desert anyway. The option to desert acted as a safety valve, relieving pressure from the master and servant relationship. If voyageurs were very unhappy with their master, they could leave to work for another company, return to Lower Canada, or become freemen. This safety valve worked against a collective voyageur consciousness. Collective action was also hindered because voyageurs valued independence.[106] They left farms where feudal relationships prevailed to enter into contracted servitude, but part of their pull to the north west may have been the promise of a more independent way of life than that on the Lower Canadian farm. Voyageurs idealized freemen and many chose this path, becoming independent hunters and petty traders, living primarily off the land with their Native Families.[107]

Some permanent deserters maintained a casual relationship with fur trading companies, serving the occasional limited contract, or selling furs and provisions. One man, Brunet, was forced to desert because his Native wife insisted on it. He rejoined the company under a freer contract. His wife began again to pressure him to desert the company and live with her Natives relatives.[108] Another man named Vivier decided to quit his contract in November 1798 because he could not stand living with Native people, as he was ordered to do by his bourgeois, John Thomson:

> he says that he cannot live any longer with them & that all the devils in Hell cannot make him return, & that he prefers marching all Winter from one Fort to another rather than Live any Longer with them.

Thomson refused to give him provisions or equipment because in the fall he had provided him with enough to pass the winter. Thomson was frustrated with his behaviour all season, as he had refused to return to the fort when ordered. Vivier had become so disenchanted with the trade that he offered his wife and child to another voyageur, so he could return to Lower Canada, but his wife protested. Thomson finally agreed to provide him with ammunition, tobacco and an axe on credit, and Vivier left the post. It is unclear whether he remained with his Native family. A month and a half later Vivier returned to the post, and appeared to take up work again.[109] Voyageurs may have returned to work for fur trade companies because they could not find enough to eat, or desired the protection that a post provided. Fear of starvation and the dangers of the north west may have discouraged voyageurs from deserting in the first place. In one case, Alexander Henry the Younger came across a pond where André Garreau, a NWC deserter, had been killed in 1801 with five Mandans by a Swiss party.[110]

Although it is difficult to quantify the occurrence of turbulence and accommodation in the relations between masters and servants, negotiations over acceptable labour conditions dominated the north-west fur trade. Masters controlled the workforce by ensuring that all men immediately became indebted to their company, and by being the sole providers of European goods in the interior. Masters also capitalized on the risk-taking and tough masculine ethos to encourage a profitable work pace. However, their best way to maintain order was to impress their men with their personal authority which was garnered by a strong manner, bravery, and effectiveness. Formal symbols, such as dress, ritual celebrations, access to better provisions, and a lighter work load reminded voyageurs of the superior status and power of their bourgeois. This "theatre of daily rule" helped to lay out the substance of the hegemonic structure of paternal authority. Masters also turned to the courts to prosecute their men for breaches of contract, and attempted to cooperate with other companies to regulate the workforce, but these methods were far from successful in controlling their voyageurs. The "social contract" overshadowed the legal contract between masters and servants, establishing an effective working relationship that was key to ensuring a well-functioning trade and high profits.

In turn, voyageurs asserted their cultural autonomy and resisted master authority. Their "counter-theatre" shaped the working environment. Voyageurs generally had very high performance standards for work, which were bolstered by masculine ideals of strength, endurance, and risk-taking. Nonetheless, voyageurs created a space to continually challenge the expectations of their masters, in part through their complaining. They also set their own pace, demanded adequate and even generous diets, refused to work in bad weather, and frequently worked to rule. When masters made unreasonable demands or failed to provide adequate provisions, voyageurs responded by working more slowly, becoming insolent, and occasionally freetrading and stealing provisions. More extreme expressions of discontent included turning to the Lower Canadian courts for justice, but, like the bourgeois and clerks, voyageurs found that their demands were better met by challenging the social, rather than the legal, contract. Their strongest bargaining tool proved to be deserting the service, which they sometimes did *en masse.* Overall, voyageurs acted more individually than collectively, as the option to desert the service acted more as a safety valve against the development of a collective voyageur consciousness.

The master and servant relationship was thus a fragile balance, constantly being negotiated. Ruling-class domination was an on-going process where the degree of legitimation was always uneven and the creation of counterhegemonies remained a live option. E.P. Thompson's emphasis on theatre and the symbolic expression of hegemony ring true for the voyageurs and bourgeois, whose power struggles were as often about respect and authority as about decent wages and provisions.[111] The difficult working conditions, regular fear of starvation, and absence of a police force positioned labour mediation in the forefront of the trade and strengthened the symbolic power of the "theatre of daily rule." The "social contract" between the masters and servants overshadowed their legal contract, and determined the day-to-day relations between the two groups. Frequently, accommodation allowed the fur trade to run smoothly, and voyageurs and bosses cooperated, especially in the face of external threats. Yet just as often, labour disputes and power struggles characterized the trade.

Notes

1 Edith I. Burley, *Servants of the Honourable Company: Work, Discipline, and Conflict in the Hudson's Bay Company, 1770–1879* (Toronto, New York and Oxford: Oxford University Press 1997); Philip Goldring first began to compile information on labourers in *Papers on the Labour System of the Hudson's Bay Company, 1821–1900,* Volume I, Manuscript Report Series, no. 362, Parks Canada, (Ottawa: Ministry of Supply and Services 1979). Also see Ron C. Bourgeault, "The Indian, the Métis and the Fur Trade: Class, Sexism and Racism in the Transition from 'Communism' to Capitalism," *Studies in Political Economy: A Socialist Review,* 12 (Fall 1983), 45–80 and Glen Makahonuk, "Wage-Labour in the Northwest Fur Trade Economy, 1760–1849," *Saskatchewan History,* 41 (Winter 1988), 1–17.

2 For a brief report of master and servant law in a colonial setting see Douglas Hay and Paul Craven, "Master and Servant in England and the Empire: A Comparative Study," *Labour/Le Travail,* 31 (Spring 1993), 175–84.

3 Daniel Francis and Toby Morantz, *Partners in Furs: A History of the Fur Trade in Eastern James Bay, 1600–1870* (Montréal and Kingston: McGill-Queen's University Press), 167.

4 Louise Dechêne uses the term *voyageur* to identify the small-scale independent fur traders, working alone or in small groups, with some financial backing from merchants, from the late 17th century to the mid-18th century. Louise Dechêne, *Habitants and Merchants in Seventeenth-Century Montreal,* trans. Liana Vardi, (Montréal: McGill-Queen's University Press 1992), 94. Later, the term came to be used more widely to refer to contracted labourers, or *engagés.* I use the term *voyageur* interchangeably with *engagé,* servant, and worker.

5 The term "liminal" is used by cultural anthropologists to mean interstitial, implying both margins and thresholds, and a transitional state. The concept was first suggested by Arnold van Gennep in his work *The rites of passage,* trans. by Monika B. Vizedom and Gabrielle L. Caffee, (London: Routledge and Kegan Paul 1909). The concept was further developed by Victor Turner, *The Ritual Process: Structure and Anti-Structure* (Chicago: Aldine, 1969), 94–5 and *Blazing the Trail: Way Marks in the Exploration of Symbols* (Tuscon: University of Arizona Press 1992), 48–51. For a theoretical discussion and cross cultural comparisons of *communitas* or the development of community in liminal spaces see Turner, *The Ritual Process,* 96–7, 125–30 and *Blazing the Trail,* 58–61.

6 My understanding of masculinity as a category for historical analysis is informed by Joan Scott, "Gender: A Useful Category of Historical Analysis," *American Historical Review,* 91, (December 1986), 1053–75 and R.W. Connell, *Masculinities* (Berkeley and Los Angeles: University of California Press 1995), 67–92.

7 John E. Foster, "Wintering, the Outsider Adult Male and the Ethnogenesis of the Western Plains Métis," *Prairie Forum,* 19, 1 (Spring 1994), 1–13.

8 See Jacqueline Peterson and Jennifer S.H. Brown, eds., *The New Peoples: Being and Becoming Métis in North America* (Winnipeg: University of Manitoba Press 1985) and Gerhard J. Ens, *Homeland to Hinterland: The Changing Worlds of the Red River Métis in the Nineteenth Century* (Toronto: University of Toronto Press 1997).

9 See Palmer, *Working-Class Experience,* 41–51.

10 Brown, *Strangers in Blood,* 88.

11 Burley, *Servants of the Honourable Company,* 15–16.

12 The term "bourgeois" was used in 18th and 19th-century Canada to refer to the Montreal fur trade merchants and managers, which included company partners and all but the most junior clerks.

13 For a representative example see W. Kaye Lamb, ed., *Sixteen Years in Indian Country: The Journal of Daniel Williams Harmon, 1800–1816* (Toronto: The MacMillan Company of Canada 1957), 197–98.

14 Toronto, Ontario Archives (hereafter OA), North West Company Collection (hereafter NWCC), MU 2199, Box 4, No. 1 (photostat of original), "An Account of the Athabasca Indians by a Partner of the North West Company, 1795," revised 4 May 1840 (Forms part of the manuscript entitled "Some Account of the North West Company," by Roderick McKenzie, director of the North West Company. Original at McGill Rare Books (hereafter MRB), Masson Collection (hereafter MC), C.18, Microfilm reel #22. Photostat can also be found at National Archives of Canada (hereafter NAC), MC, MG19 C1, Vol. 55, Microfilm reel #C-15640); 51.

15 George Heriot, *Travels Through the Canadas, Containing a Description of the Picturesque Scenery on Some of the Rivers and Lakes; with an Account of the Productions, Commerce, and Inhabitants of those Provinces* (Philadelphia: M. Carey 1813), 254; and MRB, MC, C.27, Microfilm reel #13, Roderick McKenzie, Letters Inward [all the letters are from W. Ferdinand Wentzel, Forks, McKenzie River], 1807–1824, pp. 3, 23.

16 "An Account of the Athabasca Indians by a Partner of the North West Company, 1795," p. 51; and Alexander Mackenzie, Esq., "A General History of the Fur Trade from Canada to the North-West," *Voyages from Montréal on the River St. Laurence through the Continent of North America to the Frozen and Pacific Oceans in the Years 1789 and 1793 with a Preliminary Account of the Rise, Progress, and Present State of the Fur Trade of that Country,* (London: R. Noble, Old Bailey 1801), 34.

17 Brown, *Strangers in Blood* 35, 45–8. Also see E.P. Thompson's discussion of "patricians" and "plebs" in *Customs in Common: Studies in Traditional Popular Culture* (New York: The New Press 1993), 16–17.

18 For a discussion on cultural hegemony and the consent of the masses to be ruled, see T. J. Jackson Lears, "The Concept of Cultural Hegemony: Problems and Possibilities," *American Historical Review,* 90 (June 1985), 567–593.

19 Edith Burley also found that the relationship between masters and servants in the HBC was constantly subject to negotiation. Burley, *Servants of the Honourable Company,* 110–11.

20 Thompson, *Customs in Common,* 85–6.

21 This is suggested by Thompson, *Customs in Common,* 45–6.

22 Lawrence M. Lande, *The Development of the Voyageur Contract (1686–1821)* (Montréal: McLennan Library, McGill University 1989), 41.

23 Winnipeg, Provincial Archives of Manitoba (hereafter PAM), Fort William Collection (hereafter FWC), MG1 C1; fo. 33, contract form for McTavish, McGillivrays & Co. My translation.

24 For examples see Joseph Defont's 1809 contract with the North West Company, PAM, FWC, MG1 C1, fo. 32–1 and the contract of Louis Santier of St. Eustache with Parker, Gerrard, Ogilvy, & Co. as a *milieu* to transport goods between Montréal and Michilimackinac, 21 Avril [sic] 1802, NAC, MG19 A51.

25 Mackenzie, "A General History," 34.

26 NAC, Haldimand Papers, "Memorandum for Sir Guy Carleton," 20 January 1778, cited by Harold Adams Innis, *The Fur Trade in Canada* (Toronto: University of Toronto Press 1956, first published in 1930), 221.

27 *Ordinances and Acts of Quebec and Lower Canada,* 36 George III, chpt. 10, 7 May 1796.

28 Grace Laing Hogg and Gwen Shulman, "Wage Disputes and the Courts in Montreal, 1816–1835," in Donald Fyson, Colin M. Coates and Kathryn Harvey, eds., *Class, Gender and the Law in Eighteenth- and Nineteenth-Century Quebec: Sources and Perspectives* (Montréal: Montréal History Group 1993), 129.

29 For one example see Montréal, McCord Museum of Canadian History, North West Company Papers, M17607, M17614, Deposition of Basil Dubois, 21 June 1798, and Complaint of Samuel Gerrard, of the firm of Parker, Gerrard and Ogilvie against Basil Dubois.

30 Montréal, Archives nationales de Québec, dépot de Montréal (hereafter ANQM), Court of Quarter Sessions of the District of Montréal, TL32 S1 SS1, Robert Aird vs. Joseph Boucher, 1 April 1785, JP Pierre Foretier; Atkinson Patterson vs. Jean-Baptiste Desloriers dit Laplante, 21 April 1798, JP Thomas Forsyth; and Angus Sharrest for McGillivray & Co. vs. Joseph Papin of St. Sulpice, 14 June 1810, JP J-M Mondelet. These cases were compiled by Don Fyson as part of a one in five sample of the whole series.

31 ANQM, Cours des plaidoyers communs du district de Montréal (hereafter CPCM), Cour du samedi (matières civiles superieurs), TL16 S4/00005, pp. 37, 27 mars 1784, JPs Hertelle De Rouville and Edward Southouse; and TL16 S4/00002, no page numbers, 2 Avril 1778, JPs Hertelle De Rouville and Edward Southouse.

32 The JPs were William McGillivray, Duncan McGillivray, Sir Alexander Mackenzie, Roderick McKenzie, and John Ogilvy. Marjorie Wilkins Campbell, The *North West Company* (Toronto: MacMillan Company of Canada 1957), 136–7.

33 NAC, North West Company Letterbook, 1798–1800 (hereafter NWCL), MG19 B1, vol. 1, p. 131, William McGillivray to Thomas Forsyth, Esq., Grand Portage, 30 June 1800.

34 NAC, NWCL, MG19 B1, vol. 1, pp. 152–3, William McGillivray to McTavish, Frobisher and Company, Grand Portage, 28 July 1800.

35 NAC, Letterbook of Sir Alexander McKenzie and Company, kept by Daniel Sutherland (hereafter LAMC), p. 40, D. Sutherland to Henry Harou, 15 May 1803.

36 ANQM, CPCM, Cour du vendredi (matières civiles inferieurs), TL16 S3/00001, p. 41, 314–25, 3 juillet 1770 and 3 juillet 1778, JPs Hertelle De Rouville and Edward Southouse; and TL16 S3/00008, no page numbers, 13 janvier 1786, JPs Hertelle De Rouville and Edward Southouse, 6 octobre 1786 (followed by several other entries later in the month), JPs John Fraser, Edward Southouse and Hertelle De Rouville, and 27 octobre 1786, JPs Edward Southouse and Hertelle De Rouville; and Eliot Coues, ed. *New Light on the Early History of the Greater Northwest: The Manuscript Journals of Alexander Henry* (Minneapolis: Ross and Haines 1897), vol. 2, 860–1, Sunday, 27 March 1814.

37 Hogg and Shulman, "Wage Disputes and the Courts in Montréal" 128, 132, 135–40, 141–3.

38 Thompson, *Customs in Common,* 43, 45–6.

39 Elizabeth Vibert, *Traders' Tales: Narratives of Cultural Encounters in the Columbia Plateau, 1807–1846* (Norman and London: University of Oklahoma Press 1997), 110–12.

40 James Scott Hamilton, "Fur Trade Social Inequality and the Role of Non-Verbal Communication," Ph.D. Thesis, Simon Fraser University, 1990, 138, 261–3.

41 Alexander Ross, *Fur Hunters of the Far West; A Narrative of Adventures in Oregon and the Rocky Mountains* (London: Smith, Elder and Co. 1855), 1: 301–2.

42 J. B. Tyrrell, ed. *Journals of Samuel Hearne and Philip Turnor* (Toronto: Champlain Society 1934), Journal III, "A Journal of the most remarkable Transactions and Occurrences from York Fort to Cumberland House, and from said House to York Fort from 9th Septr 1778 to 15th Septr 1779 by Mr Philip Turnor," 15 July 1779, 252.

43 OA, George Gordon Papers, MU 1146G, Moffatt, Fort William, to George Gordon, Monontagué, 25 July 1809. See also Hamilton, "Fur Trade Social Inequality," 135–6. Burley found a similar pattern in the HBC, Burley, *Servants of the Honourable Company,* 122–3.

44 NAC, Autobiographical Notes of John McDonald of Garth, 1791–1815, written in 1859, photostat, MG19 A17, pp. 119–21. The original can be found at MRB, MS 406, and a typescript can be found at the OA, MU 1763.

45 For a few examples of becoming lost see MRB, MC, C.8, microfilm reel #14, Alexander McKenzie, Journal of Great Bear Lake, 18–26 June 1806, p. 20; MRB, MC, Journal of John MacDonell, Assiniboines-Rivière qu'Appelle, 1793–95, Thursday, 13 March 1794 and Monday, 8 December 1794, pp. 11, 22; and OA, Company of Temiscamingue, Microfilm #MS65, Donald McKay, Journal from January 1805 to June 1806, Thursday, 12 September 1805, p. 32 (I added page numbers). For examples of canoeing accidents see NAC, MC, MG19 C1, vol. 1, microfilm reel #C-15638, Charles Chaboillez, "Journal for the Year 1797," Wednesday, 16, 19 and 31 August 1797, pp. 4, 6; NAC, MC, MG19 C1, Vol. 4, Microfilm reel #C-15638, William McGillivray, "Rat River Fort Near Rivière Malique...," 9 September 1789 to 13 June 1790 (written transcript precedes original on reel, both badly damaged), pp. 73–4; and NAC, MC, MG19 C1, Vol. 8, Microfilm reel #C-15638, W. Ferdinand Wentzel, "A Journal kept at the Grand River, Winter 1804 & 1805," 9 October 1804, p. 9. On bear attacks see Toronto, Metropolitan Reference Library, Baldwin Room (hereafter MRL BR), S13, George Nelson's Journal "No. 7," describing the Lake Winnipeg d/strict in 1812, written as a reminiscence, pp. 283–4; NAC, MG19 A17, Autobiographical Notes of John McDonald of Garth, 1791–1815, written in 1859 (photostat), pp. 54–5, 65–6; and "First Journal of Simon Fraser from April 12th to July 18th, 1806," Appendix B, *Public Archives Report for 1929,* pp. 109–45, (transcript from a copy at University of California at Berkeley, Bancroft Collection, Pacific Coast Mss., Series C, No. 16; copy also at NAC, MG19 A9,

Simon Fraser Collection, Vol. 4; originals at the Provincial Archives of British Columbia), Sunday 13 July 1806, pp. 143–4. On starvation see MRB, MC, C.24, Microfilm reel #2, Archibald Norman McLeod, Journal kept at Alexandria, 1800, Thursday, 19 February 1801, p. 22; NAC, MG19 A14, Microfilm reel #M-130, John Stuart, Journal kept at North West Company Rocky Mountain House, 1805–6 (original at Provincial Archives of British Columbia), Saturday, 1 February 1806, p. 20; and MRL BR, S13, George Nelson's Journal "No. 5," June 1807 – October 1809, written as a reminiscence, dated 7 February 1851, pp. 209–10.

46 Coues, ed., *New Light,* 1: 11 August 1800, pp. 30–1; MRL BR, S13, George Nelson's diary of events on a journey from Cumberland House to Fort William, part in code, 3 June – 11 July 1822 (notes taken from a transcription made by Sylvia Van Kirk); Tuesday, 9 July 1822; *ibid.,* Nelson's diary of events on a journey from Fort William to Cumberland House, 21 July – 22 August 1822 (notes taken from a transcription made by Sylvia Van Kirk); Monday, 19 August 1822; and Alexander Ross, *Fur Hunters of the Far West: A Narrative of Adventures in Oregon and the Rocky Mountains,* (London: Smith, Elder and Co. 1855), II: 236–7.

47 Elliot J. Gorn describes this pattern as well in "Gouge and Bite, Pull hair and Scratch: The Social Significance of Fighting in the Southern Backcountry," *American Historical Review,* 90 (Feb. 1985), 18–43.

48 Arthur S. Morton, ed., *The Journal of Duncan McGillivray of the North West Company at Fort George on the Saskatchewan, 1794–5* (Toronto: The MacMillan Company of Canada Limited 1929), 11.

49 NAC, Autobiographical Notes of John McDonald of Garth, 215.

50 In a different case, Gunther Peck found that middle class commentators condemned miners' penchant for risk-taking in late 19th century Nevada. Gunther Peck, "Manly Gambles: The Politics of Risk on the Comstock Lode, 1860–1880," *Journal of Social History,* 26 (Summer 1993), 701–23.

51 See entries Friday, 31 May 1793 and Thursday, 13 June 1793, Mackenzie, *Voyages from Montréal,* 285, 295–6, 322–6.

52 For examples see Coues, ed., *New Light,* vol. 1, 10, 243, 23 July 1800 and 6 May 1804; Lamb, ed., *Sixteen Years,* 105, Sunday, 19 July 1807; and Ross Cox, *Adventures on the Columbia River* (New York: J. & J. Harper 1832), 304–5, 19 September 1817.

53 For examples see NAC, MC, MG19 C1, vol. 1, microfilm reel #C-15638, p. 3, Friday, 11 August 1797, Charles Chaboillez, "Journal for the Year 1797"; NAC, MC, MG19 C1, Vol. 9, Microfilm reel #C-15638, p. 16, Unidentified North West Company Wintering Partner, "Journal for 1805 & 6, Cross Lake," Sunday, 10 November 1805; MRB, MC, C.1, microfilm reel #55, p. 66, Duncan Cameron, "The Nipigon Country," with extracts from his journal in the Nipigon, 1804–5, (also found in the OA, photostat, MU 2198 Box 3, Item 3; and in triplicate typescript, MU 2200, Box 5 (a–c)); and Mackenzie, *Voyages from Montréal,* 325, Thursday, 13 June 1793.

54 Approximately 20 June 1807, described in TMRL, BR, S13, p. 186, George Nelson's Journal "No. 5," June I807 – October 1809, written as a reminiscence, dated 7 February 1851.

55 Burley, *Servants of the Honourable Company,* 118–20.

56 E.P. Thompson, *Customs in Common,* 67.

57 Cameron, "The Nipigon Country," 38–39.

58 Coues, ed. *New Light,* 1: 247–8, 28 July 1804.

59 A blacksmith named Philip earned the wrath of his bourgeois, McKay, when he abused him both behind his back and to his face. Nelson, Journal "No. 5," 2 (labelled p. 186). George Nelson felt pressured by the continual complaints made by his men about their rations. He worried that his men were spreading discontent among each other and preferred them to approach him directly with their concerns. Nelson, "A Daily Memoranda," p. 8, Friday, 10 February 1815.

60 Mentioned in Coues, ed., *New Light,* 1: 247, 1 July 1804.

61 NAC, LAMC, 1802–9, vol. 1, MG19 A7, pp. 18–19, 25–26, D. Sutherland to Monsr. St. Valur Mailloux, Montréal, 10 November 1802, 29 November 1802, and 20 December 1802, (originals in the Seminaire de Quebec). My translation.

62 For one example of men demanding their pay be doubled for extra duties see Chaboillez, "Journal for the Year 1797," 49, Tuesday, 20 March 1798.

63 MRB, MC, C.27, Microfilm reel #13, p. 2, Athabasca Department, Great Slave Lake, W.F. Wentzel to Roderick McKenzie, Letters Inward, 1807–1824, 5 April 1819.

64 NAC, MC, MG19 C1, vol. 3, microfilm reel #C-15638, pp. 8–15, François-Antoine Larocque, "Missouri Journal, Winter 1804–5"; and Nelson, "A Daily Memoranda," pp. 30–2, Saturday, 8 April 1815.

65 See entries Monday, 2 November 1818, and from Tuesday, 1 December 1818 to Wednesday, 30 December 1818, OA, MU 842, pp. 10–11, 18–23, Diary of George Nelson, in the service of the North West Company at Tête au Brochet, 1818–19.

66 NAC, MC, MG19 C1, Vol. 15, Microfilm reel #C-15638, p. 7, Fragment of a journal, attributed to W. Ferdinand Wentzel, kept during an expedition from 13 June to 20 August 1800, Friday, 26 June 1800.

67 MRB, MC, C.8, microfilm reel #14, p. 125, Alexander Mackenzie, Journal of Great Bear Lake, March 1806.

68 On trip from Athabasca to the McKenzie River, NAC, MC, MG19 C1, Vol. 6, Microfilm reel #C-15638, p. 50, James Porter, Journal kept at Slave Lake, 18 February 1800 to 14 February 1801, 29 September 1800. Porter quotes the man as saying "Si Je avait Point des gages que le Diable ma aport si vous ma Soucier Embarker." See also John Thompson, who records that this man, named Bernier, gave further trouble to Porter on the trip. Thompson's interpretation of Bernier's swearing is "swearing the Devel myte take him if he had stirred a Step." See entries Monday, 29 September 1800 to Saturday, 4 September 1800, MRB, MC, C.26, Microfilm reel #15, pp. 1–2, John Thompson, "Journal, Mackenzies River alias Rocky Mountain, 1800–1."

69 OA, NWCC, MU 2199, p. 8, photostat of original, Edward Umfreville, "Journal of a Passage in a Canoe from Pais Plat in Lake Superior to Portage de L'Isle in Rivière Ouinipique," June to July 1784, Wednesday, 23 June 1784. Forms part of the manuscript entitled "Some Account of the North West Company," by Roderick McKenzie, director of the North West Company. Typescripts can be found also in the OA, NWCC, MU 2200, Box 5, Nos. 2 (a), (b), and (c). Photostats and typescripts can also be found in NAC, MC, Vol. 55, Microfilm reel #C-15640; the MRB, MC, C.17; and the MHS, P1571. For other examples of theft see MRB, MC, C.24, Microfilm reel #2, p. 5, Archibald Norman McLeod, Journal kept at Alexandria, 1800, Friday, 28 November 1800; OA, Angus Mackintosh Papers; MU 1956, Box 4, pp. 2–3, Journal from Michilimackinac to Montréal via the French River, summer 1813, 16 July 1813; and NAC, MC, MG19 C1, Vol. 2, microfilm reel # C-15638, p. 10, Michel Curot, "Journal, Folle Avoine, Riviere Jaune, Pour 1803 & 1804," Lundi, 11 octobre 1803.

70 TMRL, BR, S13, p. 9, George Nelson's Journal "No. 1," written as a reminiscence, describing a journey from Montréal to Grand Portage, and at Folle Avoine, 27 April 1802 – April 1803, (a typescript can also be found in the George Nelson Papers of the TMRL, BR).

71 Coues, ed., *New Light,* 1: 25, 6 August 1800.

72 Burley, *Servants of the Honourable Company,* 139–44.

73 Mackenzie, "A General History," 34. On the HBC prohibition of private trading see Burley, *Servants of the Honourable Company,* 24–25. However, Burley suggests that the lack of reporting on this offense may indicate that the officers tacitly allowed their men to do so (144–52).

74 Described by Ross, *Fur Hunters,* 1: 159.

75 MHS, GLNP, Folder 7, P791, p. 2, NWC Letters, 1798–1816, Dominique Rousseau and Joseph Bailley v. Duncan McGillivray, (originals from the Judicial Archives of Montréal).

76 Campbell, *The North West Company,* 155.

77 Wallace, W. Stewart, ed., *Documents Relating to the North West Company* (Toronto: Champlain Society 1934), Minutes of the Meetings of the NWC at Grand Portage and Fort William, 1801–7, with Supplementary Agreements (originals in Montréal, Sulpician Library, Baby Collection), 216, 15 July 1806.

78 For an example see MRB, MC, C. 7, microfilm reel #4, p. 4, Journal of John MacDonell, Assiniboines-Riviere qu'Appelle, 1793–95, (typescript copy in NAC, MC, MG 19 C 1, vol. 54, microfilm reel #C-15640), 5 December 1793 to 6 December 1793.

79 McLeod, Journal kept at Alexandria, p. 40, Saturday, 30 May 1801; and "The Diary of John Macdonell" in Charles M. Gates, ed., *Five Fur Traders* of the Northwest (St. Paul: Minnesota Historical Society 1965), 72, 1 June 1793.

80 "The Diary of Hugh Faries" in Gates, ed., *Five Fur Traders,* 233–34, Monday, 25 March 1805.

81 Burley, *Servants of the Honourable Company,* 153–4.

82 For example, see McLeod, Journal kept at Alexandria, 15, Friday, 2 January 1801.

83 Mackenzie, *Voyages from Montréal,* 329, Saturday, 15 June 1793.

84 *passim,* pp. 373–4, Saturday, 29 June 1793.

85 MRB, MC, C.12, Microfilm reel #6, p. 41, Charles McKenzie, "Some Account of the Missouri Indians in the years 1804, 5, 6 & 7," addressed to Roderick McKenzie, 1809. Photostat and typescript copies can be found in NAC, MC, MG19 C1, Vol. 59, Microfilm reel #C-15640 and OA, NWCC, MU2204, Vol. 3 and MU2200 Box 5 - 4 (a), and the account is published by W. Raymond Wood and

Thomas D. Thiessen, eds., *Early Fur Trade on the Northern Plains: Canadian Traders Among the Mandan and Hidatsa Indians, 1738–1818; The narratives of John Macdonell, David Thompson, François-Antoine Larocque, and Charles McKenzie* (Norman: University of Oklahoma Press 1985).

86 For one example see McLeod, Journal kept at Alexandria, Saturday, 22 November 1800.

87 Nelson, Journal No. 1, p. 43, Saturday, 17 November 1809.

88 Nelson, "A Daily Memoranda," 8, Friday, 10 February 1815; and "The Diary of Hugh Faries," p. 235, Tuesday, 2 April 1805.

89 TMRL, BR S13, pp. 14–15, George Nelson's Coded Journal, 17 April – 20 October 1821, entitled "A continuation of My Journal at Moose Lake," (notes made by Sylvia Van Kirk), Thursday, 10 May 1821. Constant had been threatening to desert the service for years, and he did make arrangements with another bourgeois, William Connolly, to leave the service. *ibid.,* Thursdays, 10 and 24 May 1821, pp. 14–15, 20.

90 "The Diary of Hugh Faries," p. 206, Sunday, 26 August 1804.

91 Coues, ed., *New Light,* 1: 114, 9 October 1800.

92 *passim,* pp. 99–100, 18–19 September 1800.

93 Cox, *Adventures,* 166–7.

94 *Voyages dans l'Amerique par la Rouchefoucould Liancourt,* Vol. II, 225, Paris, An. 7.; cited by Thomas Douglas, Earl of Selkirk, *A Sketch of the British Fur Trade in North America; with Observations Relative to the North-West Company of Montréal,* 2nd edition (London: James Ridgway 1816), 36–7.

95 Selkirk, *A Sketch of the British Fur Trade,* 32–47.

96 Nelson, Journal, 13 July 1803 – 25 June 1804, 1–2, 34, Friday, 15 July 1803.

97 TMRL, BR, S13, pp. 7–9, George Nelson, Tête au Brochet, to his parents, 8 December 1811.

98 Nelson, "A Daily Memoranda," pp. 17–18, 40–1, Thursday, 9 March 1815, Tuesday, 23 May 1815 and Wednesday, 24 May 1815.

99 NAC, 'Civil Secretary's Letter Books, 1788–1829,' RG7, G15C, vol. 2, CO42, vol. 100, Sheriff Edward Gray to Attorney General James Monk, 9 June 1794; J. Reid to same, 12 June 1794; T.A. Coffin to James McGill, 21 July 1794; cited by F. Murray Greenwood, *Legacies of Fear: Law and Politics in Quebec in the Era of the French Revolution* (Toronto: University of Toronto Press 1993), 80, 285.

100 NAC, Jonathan Sewell Papers, MG23 GII10, Volume 9, pp. 4613–14, Jonathan Sewell to Lieutenant Colonel Beckworth, 28 July 1795. Donald Fyson brought this reference to my attention.

101 Terence Crowley, "'Thunder Gusts': Popular Disturbances in Early French Canada," *Canadian Historical Association Historical Papers* (1979), 11–31; and Jean-Pierre Hardy et David-Thiery Ruddel, *Les Apprentis Artisans à Québec, 1660–1815* (Québec: Les Presses de L'Université du Québec 1977), 74–80.

102 Jean-Pierre Wallot, *Un Québec qui Bougeait: trame socio-politique du Québec au tournant du XIXe siècle* (Montréal: Boréal 1973), 266–7.

103 Morton, ed., *The Journal of Duncan McGillivray,* 6–7.

104 Charles McKenzie, "Some Account of the Missouri Indians," 72, 77–8.

105 MRB, MC, C.5, Microfilm reel #5, abridged version on Microfilm reel #6, pp. 75, 79, Alexander Henry the Younger, travels in the Red River Department, 1806, Saturday, 26 July 1806 and Thursday, 7 August 1806.

106 Alexander Ross, *Fur Hunters of the Far West; A Narrative of Adventures in the Oregon and Rocky Mountains,* 2 vols. (London: Smith, Elder and Co. 1855), II: 236–237.

107 Toronto; Metropolitan Reference Library; Baldwin Room; S13; George Nelson, Tête au Brochet, to his parents, 8 December 1811; pp. 9–11; and Ross, *Fur Hunters of the Far West,* 1: 291–93.

108 Nelson, Journal, 13 July 1803 – 25 June 1804, pp. 22–3, Monday, 31 January 1804, Monday, 14 February 1804, Tuesday, 15 February 1804, and Thursday 17 February 1804.

109 NAC, MC, MG19 C1, Vol. 7, Microfilm reel #C-15638, pp. 19–24, John Thomson, "A Journal kept at Grand Marais ou Rivière Rouge, 1798," Sunday, 18 November 1798, Monday, 19 November 1798, Tuesday, 20 November 1798, and Friday, 4 January 1799.

110 Henry, Travels in the Red River Department, p. 50, Wednesday, 23 July 1806.

111 Thompson, *Customs in Common,* 74–5.

The Seven Oaks Incident and the Construction of a Historical Tradition, 1816 to 1970*

LYLE DICK

Voulez-vous écouter chanter
Une chanson de vérité?[1]

PIERRE FALCON,
"CHANSON DE LA GRENOUILLÈRE," (1816)

Each [the historian and the poet] is a maker of myths, only the historian has neglected his job of making myths in this decadent, analytical age.[2]

W. L. MORTON (1943)

It is to be regretted that in a war of this kind, a very painful duty devolves on the narrator...for lawyers and commissioners will not be satisfied with "I was informed of this," or "I was told of that," but, "Who were the persons that informed you," is the point in question.[3]

COLIN ROBERTSON TO PETER IRVING,
DECEMBER 1818

In 1891, the Manitoba Historical Society dedicated the province's first historical monument, a stone cairn to commemorate the Seven Oaks incident, a violent clash in 1816 between a group of Hudson's Bay Company officers and Selkirk settlers and a party of Métis traders from Red River and the upper Assiniboine. The monument's brief inscription contrasted with a growing body of writings on this controversial event, a collection made larger by the society's simultaneous release of a pamphlet to mark the occasion.[4] The pamphlet included excerpts from previously published accounts of the battle or its contexts by two prominent Manitoba historians of the period—George Bryce, an academic, and Charles N. Bell, an amateur. The combination of these excerpts had a retrospective historiographical significance: it was the last time that two competing interpretations of Seven Oaks appeared under one cover, the last time that one version was not rewritten, overwritten, or erased by its rival.

The pamphlet's publication simultaneously marked the eclipse of one tradition of English-language writing on Seven Oaks and the inauguration of another. The outgoing tradition, represented by Bell's text, comprised a series of writings on the event by amateurs with ties to Old Red River or witnesses with direct knowledge of the event. The ascendant tradition, represented by

Lyle Dick, "The Seven Oaks Incident and the Construction of a Historical Tradition, 1816 to 1970," *Journal of the Canadian Historical Association* (1991): 91–113. Lyle Dick, West Coast Historian, Parks Canada, Vancouver.

*The critical comments and editorial advice of Ron Frohwerk, John Thompson, Philip Goldring, and Jennifer Brown are acknowledged with gratitude.

Bryce's version and his academic successors in the West, drew instead from treatments earlier advanced by Lord Selkirk, the Hudson's Bay Company, and their sympathizers, and now promoted to orthodoxy by the newly dominant Anglo-Canadian immigrant group in the West. Yet Bryce's and Bell's texts contrasted in more ways than the interpretative conclusions they drew from the event. They differed sharply in techniques of collection, evaluation, and presentation of evidence; in the handling of contradictory or contentious material; even in the definition of what constituted appropriate empirical evidence. Further, the selection of particular structures of historical representation revealed the diverging ideological positions of these authors. The differences between Bryce and Bell in methodology, interpretation, and form bear upon larger issues than the reconstruction of the Seven Oaks incident and go to the root of history-making in Western Canada. They chart a trajectory from the raw pluralistic origins of prairie historiography in the early-nineteenth-century controversies over Seven Oaks to the polished hierarchical structures of twentieth-century historical writing. An intensive investigation of treatments of this single event reveals much about the historiographical process in Western Canada, and about the role of history in the construction of cultural traditions.

Such a reconsideration also occasions a reexamination of the respective roles of amateurs and professionals in Canadian prairie historiography. In *The Writing of Canadian History,* Carl Berger argues that serious written history only began with the creation of an academic discipline. Nineteenth-century "clergymen, lawyers, and journalists" wrote history "to amuse themselves, to commemorate the eminent, to strengthen patriotism, or to draw morals from the past"; twentieth-century professionals practised the "critical study of the Canadian past." For Berger, these developments represent "a decisive change in the nature of historical study."[5] Similar arguments have been advanced by other Canadian intellectual historians. M. Brook Taylor argues that nineteenth-century historical writing was characterised by amateur partisanship,[6] while A. B. McKillop credits the late-nineteenth-century academics George Wrong at the University of Toronto and George Bryce at the University of Manitoba with initiating a "serious attempt to examine original sources" and "introducing principles of historical criticism into Canadian historiography."[7]

None of these writers devotes much attention to the actual *writing* of history: methods of research, forms of argument, or structures of historical representation. Instead, these works are largely thematic discussions of the topics selected or interpretive approaches followed by Canadian historians, combined with group biographies of its practitioners. There is no substantive discussion of how twentieth-century professionals improved the techniques of the nineteenth-century amateurs.

A historiographical reconsideration of the Seven Oaks incident presents a rare opportunity to test Berger's thesis. With the exception of Bryce's early writings, all of the texts on the battle written before the 1890s were prepared by amateurs, while the English-language texts of historiographical significance thereafter were by professionals. Moreover, the survival of oral tradition on Seven Oaks, specifically Pierre Falcon's "Chanson de la Grenouillère," affords the opportunity for alternative perspectives on the event from outside the realm of the written word. The presence of oral tradition and amateur texts outside the mainstream historiography facilitates a reconsideration of long-standing notions about the boundaries of legitimate historical discourse in Canada.

Rather than provide a historiographical survey, culminating in an improved, factual reconstruction, this paper proposes to deconstruct the various versions of Seven Oaks by drawing on basic methods from literary and linguistic criticism, and focusing on the relationships between "story" and "discourse,"[8] two narrative functions integral to any historical reconstruction. Contemporary theorists have argued that all forms of historical narrative constitute a content independent of the "facts" they subsume.[9] An analysis of writing on Seven Oaks suggests that literary strategies not only influenced the writers' selection and ordering of particular historical data, but actually required both the production of supporting "facts" and the negation or omission of alternative "facts." Moreover, the inherently allegorical character of historical discourse inevitably generates meanings on both literal and metaphorical levels.[10] This paper will also consider the extent to which the discourse on Seven Oaks could be explained by the concept of "master narrative," an overarching cultural allegory which explains an entire tradition of writing on the event.

That said, history itself is not a text, though it can be apprehended only through the spoken or written word. There is an obvious need to investigate the existing literature and the primary sources to establish the reported facts or basic "story" from which the discourse on Seven Oaks has been constructed.

Most writing on Seven Oaks occurred in the period of controversy immediately following the event, and later in the hundred years between 1870 and 1970. The enormous volume of literature of the early period largely falls under the rubric of partisan pamphleteering by the contending parties or their representatives.[11] The primary source materials also include the transcripts of subsequent trials of participants in the battle,[12] the surviving sworn depositions of various witnesses to Seven Oaks and related events,[13] and a voluminous correspondence between government officials and representatives of either Lord Selkirk or the principals of the North West Company.[14] Finally, the period record includes the report of William Bachelor Coltman, the principal commissioner appointed to investigate the Seven Oaks incident and other violent episodes associated with the fur companies' rivalry.[15] Coltman's report in particular warrants close attention. The most detailed and comprehensive analysis ever prepared on the Seven Oaks incident, it has been largely ignored in the dominant Anglo-Canadian historiography. Its neglect in its own period might be attributed to several factors, beginning with the multipurpose mandate accorded Coltman and his fellow commissioner, John Fletcher, and its frosty reception by the Selkirk side. In his instructions to the commissioners, Governor Sherbrooke charged them with a number of roles, to serve, alternately, as investigators, enforcers, and peacemakers.[16] It was Coltman's prosecution of these latter powers as a justice of the peace which occasioned an almost immediate and continuing series of attacks on his impartiality by the Selkirk party.

Coltman's peacemaking and law enforcement roles apparently also disqualified his report from the serious attention of Anglo-Canadian historians after 1870. Not until 1910, when George Bryce praised the report as "admirable" and "fairly impartial," was it mentioned in the literature.[17] In summarising its contents in 1939, A. S. Morton stated that "the detailed report describes the acts of violence with great particularity, on the whole accurately and with a great show of impartiality."[18] Even John Morgan Gray, who was critical of Coltman's role as commissioner, endorsed aspects of his report.[19] When it came to Seven Oaks, however, these historians utilised neither the report's data nor its conclusions. Bypassing as well the original testimony on which it was based, they chose instead to rely on mediations of these sources, that is, on representations of representations.

Coltman's research methodology derived from his legal experience as a justice of the peace,[20] and more generally from the inductive approach of Baconian science. To establish the facts of Seven Oaks and related incidents, he or his colleague, John Fletcher, examined under oath a large selection of witnesses. Each voluntary deposition[21] was transcribed, sworn, and signed. Of the thirty-three depositions or statements concerning Seven Oaks which were identified by name, sixteen were taken from Selkirk settlers or HBC employees, and seventeen from Métis or NWC witnesses. Coltman therefore appears even-handed in the compilation of evidence and in bringing all of it forward in his analysis.[22]

Beyond the adducing of evidence, Coltman's techniques of examination were derivative of contemporary British courtroom practice. He endeavoured to determine the credibility of the individual witnesses by examining their depositions for internal consistency, or by comparing their statements on specific points made on different occasions. In keeping with contemporary civil procedure, he also made an effort to establish the relative weight of evidence. He operated according to the convention, current in eighteenth-century civil jurisprudence, that stress must be placed on the character of the witness.[23] Regarding evidence submitted by the fur companies, he was more skeptical. His approach was to consider these writings as "moral evidence," useful in establishing admissions by these parties, but not to be taken as proof.[24] Various legal issues pertaining to the broader conflict of which Seven Oaks formed a part were also discussed at length in both this report and in a shorter, confidential memorandum he sent to Sherbrooke a week before formally submitting the *Statement*.[25]

Coltman's reconstitution of Seven Oaks comprises a massive discussion in its own right. Here it is useful to focus only on those contentious points which have been most prominent in the event's subsequent historiography. These include the issues of which party fired the first shot, the extent to which the battle was a premeditated "massacre," the allegations of "finishing-off" the wounded, the alleged mutilation and plunder of the bodies, and the claim that the Métis abandoned them on the field to be devoured by wild animals.

Coltman unambiguously concluded that the first shot was fired by the Selkirk party. He referred to testimony by two Métis witnesses that a member of Semple's party fired the first shot at François Boucher, a ball which passed so close that it caused him to fall off his horse. Joseph Pelletier also claimed that the Semple side fired a second shot at an Indian in the Métis camp, before the firing became general.[26] Three other witnesses gave similar testimony.[27] The Selkirk witness Michael Hayden disputed their testimony, but acknowledged that Lieutenant Holte of Semple's party had fired a shot beforehand by accident.[28] Coltman concluded that the weight of evidence obliged him to reject the allegation of a precipitous Métis attack.

On a strict examination of the evidence, the commissioner also concluded that the battle could not appropriately be considered a "massacre." Noting that the Semple side had begun the battle, he surmised that it continued until "the whole either fell or ran off." In his opinion the casualties on the Hudson's Bay side had been increased by their "standing together in a crowd, unaccustomed to the use of fire-arms, or any of the practices of irregular warfare," while their opponents were "all excellent marksmen, advantageously posted in superior numbers around their opponents, and accustomed as huntsmen, and from the habits of Indian warfare, to every device that could tend to their own preservation, or the destruction of their enemy."[29]

On the other hand, in considering whether the wounded had been "finished off," Coltman found it self-evident that scarcely one half of those killed would have been mortally wounded by the first volley. He therefore concluded that the wounded must have been "finished off" after the outbreak of hostilities. Coltman judged that the evidence pointed to the northern members of the fur brigade; specifically mentioned were François Deschamps, a French-Canadian living in the Northwest, and three of his sons as the individuals responsible.[30] He attributed their actions to a Native custom of taking no prisoners, and suggested that a mercenary approach was the only security available to individuals operating in this context.

Coltman examined the issue of whether the wounded members of the Selkirk party tried to surrender, and concluded that the only two men to have done so were Pritchard, who was spared, and Rodgers, who was not. He noted that a number of Métis witnesses acknowledged that Rodgers had been finished off while pleading for mercy, but they identified "Grossetête," a son of Deschamps, as the guilty party. Coltman noted that Hayden also gave contrary testimony, alleging a general massacre of wounded men trying to surrender, but he found Hayden to be an unreliable witness.

Regarding the mutilation and pillaging of the dead bodies, Coltman concluded that these alleged occurrences were established by a "mass of evidence"; he cited nine depositions as proof. Yet, here again, he found it important to distinguish between the actions of particular individuals and the conduct of the group, as only a few persons were said to have "partaken of these spoils." The Deschamps were identified as the men carrying off the largest share of the plunder, although witnesses also claimed to have seen others with articles of clothing or arms.[31]

Coltman also examined the allegations of Frederick Damien Huerter that the Métis left the dead bodies of their fallen adversaries on the field for an extended period to be preyed upon by birds and animals. He referred to evidence to the contrary from both the Selkirk and Métis sides, which tended to confirm that the bodies were duly buried.[32] He therefore considered Huerter's testimony to be coloured by "exaggeration," and also questioned this witness's reliability in that he had abandoned the service of one employer, the NWC, to become "an open and active partizan" of the HBC.[33]

These highlights of Coltman's treatment of Seven Oaks hardly do justice to his extremely comprehensive analysis. Whatever his personal biases or the constraints of his mandate, his assemblage of a myriad of reported facts on Seven Oaks established most of the evidentiary base available to subsequent histories of this event. These data comprise much of the "story" to be considered in evaluating the "discourse" of the event's historians. His methods of collection, adduction, and evaluation of evidence also set a standard of historical research against which his successors might fairly be judged.

The indigenous historiography of Seven Oaks in Western Canada begins with Pierre Falcon's "Chanson de la Grenouillère," said to have been composed by a Métis witness immediately following the battle. Throughout the Red River period, and long afterward, the predominantly oral culture of the Métis preserved its memory of Seven Oaks by singing this song as an expression of ethnic pride and national identity.[34] Despite its status as an eye-witness account, or at least a version based on eye-witness accounts, it was almost never cited as a source in reconstructions of the event.[35]

With regard to its content, the song presented information on both the historical background and the event itself. Falcon treated the English as having come to pillage their country; he acknowledged that, prior to the engagement, the Métis had taken three prisoners; and he related that they discerned Semple's party as coming out to attack them, and that they turned to meet their adversaries. He stated that Semple ordered his men to fire on them, and recounted a number of other details, including an admission that the Métis killed most of Semple's men, chasing them from mound to mound.

On the level of discourse, Falcon's song made few concessions to rhetoric to enlist its audience's concurrence with its claims. The 1816 version was quite unpolished, showing irregular metrical patterns, imperfect rhyming, and an absence of alliteration. The contents of this hastily composed account evidently were determined more by the desire to relate particular details than the discourse needs of a particular literary structure.

Jan Vansina has drawn attention to the pitfalls of relying exclusively on oral tradition as historical evidence. In being passed on from the original observer to others by word of mouth, a story is reinterpreted by each performer in the chain of transmission.[36] Yet Falcon's song is a rare example of oral tradition on a historical event for which there is also voluminous textual evidence. Note that, in a number of its details, it corresponds closely to sworn testimony at the trials in central Canada and depositions taken by Commissioners Coltman and Fletcher. Its significance as a historical source derives principally from its status as an authentic expression of Métis perceptions and attitudes toward the events of 19 June 1816.

Alexander Ross's 1856 book *The Red River Settlement* is the first published account by an author from the region. Moreover, it is apparently the first account to rely largely on written evidence: the only specific references he cites are to a published transcription of the trials. Ross also pioneered in making Seven Oaks an episode in a structured version of the region's history, and in self-consciously employing literary models to this end.

Ross's interpretive framework is uncomplicated: it is a straightforward expression of the theme of "civilisation versus savagery" which was to become so prominent in Western Canadian historiography. On the critical issue of who initiated hostilities, Ross asserted that "there has never been a shadow of doubt...that the North-West Company did unquestionably fire the first shot, and almost all the shots that were fired."[37] As evidence, he cited both the testimony of Michael Hayden at the Seven Oaks murder trials in Canada, and Chief Justice Powell's charge to the jury, in which Powell is said to have accepted Hayden's testimony that the Métis fired the first two shots. (Ross here seems to have misread the transcript. Powell clearly states that the evidence on this point is contradictory.[38]) There is no reference to Coltman's report or any suggestion that Ross read it.

What Ross's account lacked in empirical data it made up in imaginative conjecture. The final "proof" offered of the North West Company's guilt was the author's assertion that twenty-six of Semple's opponents at Seven Oaks subsequently met violent or sudden deaths. Ross took their supposed fate as confirmation of a kind of divine retribution on sinners.[39] His foray into occult models of historical explanation has been reproduced occasionally over the course of Seven Oaks historiography, in books by J. J. Hargrave, Mercer Adam, George Bryce, A. C. Garrioch and, most recently, Peter C. Newman.[40]

Ross's account of Seven Oaks cannot be separated from the overall narrative structure of his book. For him, Western Canadian history began with the granting of the Hudson's Bay Company charter in 1670, while he hailed the "real object" of Selkirk's scheme as "the pious and philanthropic desire of introducing civilization into the wilderness."[41] The remainder of his book elaborated this theme. It was a sustained effort by Ross to privilege his own European ethnicity in opposition to the posited savagery of all Native peoples within the Red River settlement, including persons of mixed race.

The narrative purpose of these assorted characterisations becomes apparent at the end of the book, when a discussion of the Pembina Métis functions to set off the hero of Ross's narrative, the entrepreneur Alexander McDermot. The Métis are presented as creatures of whim, contrasting with the purposeful entrepreneurship of McDermot.[42] These depictions function as a backdrop to Ross's advocacy of several causes, including an enforced dispersal and separation of Native groups from the colony and the transfer of oligarchic control from the HBC to a core of formally educated residents such as himself.

Ross's partisan conclusions could command credibility because the book was published in London for an audience with little knowledge of the region or people he was writing about. The subordination of Seven Oaks to ideological imperatives far removed from the original disputes within which it occurred was a tradition which prevailed after 1870. While Ross was not an academic, his interpretations were embraced by post-Confederation professional and popular historians alike, and provided the basis for many of the stereotypes of the Métis that would be reproduced over and over again, to infinite regress.

A contemporary of Ross, Donald Gunn took a different approach to the representation of Seven Oaks. While Gunn's account was not published until 1880, it reflected local knowledge of the event and belongs to Red River historiography rather than the Canadian period after 1870. Gunn's career in Red River paralleled Ross's in a number of respects, in that he settled there in the 1820s, served as a teacher and magistrate in the community, and was critical of the Hudson's Bay Company's role in the settlement.[43] Unlike Ross, however, he did not aspire to political dominance in the community, and his writing reflects his more populist sympathies.

Gunn's *History of Manitoba*[44] differs from Ross's treatment in more than its interpretive conclusions. It reflects a completely different approach to collecting and presenting evidence and to the ways in which the author inserted Seven Oaks into his larger text. Gunn presented the battle as the culmination of a series of aggressions committed by the HBC on the NWC. Noting an initial lack of animosity between the NWC and the Selkirk settlers, he attributed the deterioration in their relations to attempts by Selkirk to use Red River as a base from which to destroy the Nor'-Westers' trade. Among the listed HBC "outrages" was Miles Macdonell's "Pemmican Proclamation" which, in his view, inflamed the situation to the point of confrontation.

Regarding Seven Oaks, his approach was to present two versions of the event—one from the HBC sympathizer John Pritchard, and the other from the North West Company side. He referred to evidence assembled after the coalition of the two companies: "When party interest required no longer to be propped up by any fabrications that would serve that purpose, all parties agreed in acknowledging that the first shot was from Lieutenant Holt's piece, which went off accidentally."[45] Gunn limited himself to a discussion of actions, without resorting to ontological explanations of innate Native savagery, as in Ross's account. Nor is there an obvious "point" to his history, which simply ends in 1835 without interpretive conclusions.

Gunn's more pluralistic approach was echoed by one other Red River historian, J. J. Hargrave. The son of Chief Factor James Hargrave and himself an employee of the HBC,[46] Hargrave, unlike Ross or Gunn, was a HBC sympathizer. His account of Seven Oaks reflected the company's viewpoint, although his relegation of the discussion to an appendix suggests the minor significance attributed to the event in the Red River era.[47] Hargrave summarised the respective versions of both sides of the conflict and also reproduced Falcon's song, observing that it "gives, I have no doubt, a truthful description of the light in which the author, along with doubtless the majority of his comrades, regarded the appearance and intentions of Governor Semple and his followers."[48] Never again was Falcon's song accorded credibility as a legitimate account of the Seven Oaks incident. Nor, with the exception of Ross, were any of the other amateur versions from the pre-1870 era given legitimacy as historical accounts.

In 1870 the HBC ceded Rupert's Land to Britain, Britain transferred it to Canada, and the Red River colony ceased to be. Within only two decades, the large-scale influx of Anglo-Ontarian immigrants radically altered Manitoba's ethnic mix from a mixed-blood majority of Red River settlers with approximate parity in numbers between French and English, to the overwhelming dominance of the white, Anglo-Canadian newcomers. These new arrivals rapidly became the region's ruling group. While they claimed the region's best farmlands[49] and established their business dominance in the cities,[50] they nevertheless lacked the cultural traditions that could legitimise their political and economic power. Their writers, and particularly their historians, played a key role in constructing these traditions, and Seven Oaks figured prominently in their work.

In constructing a historical role for the Anglo-Canadian newcomers, no other writer matched the contributions of George Bryce. The first professional historian in Western Canada, the founder of Manitoba College, cofounder of the University of Manitoba, Moderator of the Presbyterian Church of Canada, the first president of the Manitoba Historical Society and, later, president of the Royal Society of Canada,[51] Bryce was well positioned to rewrite the region's history from the perspective of his own ethnocultural group and class. He wrote for a mass readership across the new Dominion of Canada. His work represented a formal departure, as it constituted the first fully realised integration of the event within the narrative structures of European literature.

The quantity of texts Bryce produced on Seven Oaks and the Selkirk settlement reveals the enormous significance he placed on this event and period. He left six published accounts of the incident, more than any other historian.[52] To Bryce, Seven Oaks was "the most notable event that ever occurred on the prairies of Rupert's Land or in the limits of the fur country,"[53] and "the most shocking episode that ever occurred in North-Western history."[54]

Seven Oaks assumed significance in Bryce's books to the extent that his narrativisation of Métis violence and lawlessness in 1816 functioned to explain the conflicts of 1869–70 and 1885. In a paper read only a few weeks after Louis Riel's execution, Bryce stated:

> Having tasted blood in the death of Governor Semple they were turbulent ever after. Living the life of buffalo hunters they preserved their warlike tastes.... It needs not that I should recite to you the doings in the rebellion of 1869–70, it was simply the outbreak of the "Seven Oaks" and "Sayer" affair again. A too generous Government overlooked the serious nature of those events. It was reserved for what we may trust may be the last manifestation of this unruly spirit existent for three quarters of a century to show itself on the banks of the Saskatchewan in 1885.[55]

Bryce's plot form is the romance, a construction of the region's past as a struggle between forces of light and darkness.[56] In his narratives, Selkirk and his settlers were the unproblematic heroes, and the North West Company and the Métis the villains, underscored by their putative role at Seven Oaks.[57] Bryce's approach to historical evidence was also quite straightforward: in researching Seven Oaks, he simply looked for testimony from the Selkirk side alleging Métis savagery, quoted it at length, and ignored contrary evidence. His reliance on three witnesses in particular suggests that he found all he needed in a collection of partisan testimonies compiled by John Halkett,[58] Selkirk' s brother-in-law and ghost writer.[59] By quoting testimony from only one side, Bryce was able to rewrite the history of Seven Oaks to incorporate all of the old Selkirk party's allegations which had been rejected by Coltman and called into question by the Red River historiography. For example, he revived the charge that the Métis fired the first shot,[60] and Huerter's assertions that the Métis deliberately left the bodies on the field for the scavenging animals.

The allegorical function of these details was revealed in the concluding chapters to Bryce's books, as he introduced the collective hero for whom the Selkirk settlers were earlier stand-ins: "What, then, is to be the future of this

Canadian West? The possibilities are illimitable. The Anglo-Saxon race, with its energy and pluck, has laid hold of the land so long shut in by the wall built around it by the fur traders. This race, with its dominating forcefulness, will absorb and harmonize elements coming from all parts of the world...."[61] This justification for conquest explains Bryce's narrativisations of Seven Oaks. Just as a heroic role needed to be accorded Anglo-Canadians and their imaginary ancestors, the Selkirk settlers, so the Métis needed to be presented as lawless, violent, unstable, and irresponsible—in short, as embodying the attributes considered antithetical to the new Anglo-Canadian business civilisation. Representing Seven Oaks as a "massacre" was therefore integral to the construction of a new master narrative of progress in the West.

Bryce set the tone for the subsequent English-language historiography of Seven Oaks. With the notable exception of the amateur Charles Napier Bell,[62] Bryce's Anglo-Canadian contemporaries adhered to his interpretation, and it became entrenched as the orthodox version in academic, popular, and novelistic treatments of the event.[63]

With the work of Chester Martin, the academic historiography of Seven Oaks moves from the overdetermined figurative language of Bryce and his contemporaries to the assumed neutrality of the plain prose discourse.[64] Born in Nova Scotia, Martin established the Department of History at the University of Manitoba and taught there until 1929. His obituary in the *Canadian Historical Review* in 1958 characterised him as "a disciple of the school of 'objective history.'"[65] Yet Martin was also identified with the revival of British imperial sentiment in the early-twentieth century.[66] His choice of the biographical form for his book *Lord Selkirk's Work in Canada*[67] and his presentation of Selkirk as an unproblematic hero were evidence of the continuation of the romance genre even within the school of "objective history."

Martin's work on Selkirk was extensively footnoted and written in a measured, apparently nonrhetorical style. Its hidden rhetoric can only be apprehended by a careful reading of its textual signifying practices. Martin structured the paragraph comprising his narrative of Seven Oaks into a sequence of sentences which individually and cumulatively signify aggression by the Métis and passivity on the HBC—Selkirk side. For example, he referred to Semple's seeing the "formidable numbers and attitude of his opponents," while "panic-stricken settlers" confirmed an impending Métis attack on the colony. The statement that "Semple soon found himself surrounded" reinforces his party's implied passivity, while the passive voice was also used to refer to the outbreak of gunfire: "There was a shot and then a general fusillade. The first to fall was Lieutenant Holte of the colony, but in a few minutes," says Pritchard, "'almost all our people were either killed or wounded.'"[68]

This construction avoided the issue of who fired the first shot. The implication of the second sentence is that the Métis not only fired the first shot, but immediately followed with a coordinated round of gunfire, a predetermined military manoeuvre which explains the heavy casualties. This implication contrasts with one of Martin's footnotes, which referred to "the usual conflict of evidence regarding the first shot" but acknowledged that it was fired by one of Semple's men, "perhaps accidentally."

Martin's book on Selkirk provided an academic justification for the standard Anglo-Canadian interpretation of the battle. While he avoided the use of the term "massacre," his grammatical and syntactical techniques of representation pointed to this conclusion. The apparent contradictions between his text and footnotes suggest the author's unconscious ambivalence toward his own reconstruction; yet readers were left with their preconceptions of the battle essentially undisturbed.

Outside the Anglo-Canadian discourse, an alternative historiography on Seven Oaks emerged in this period in French-language accounts by Franco-Manitoban and Métis amateur historians. These writers included Louis-Arthur Prud'homme, a francophone judge who wrote extensively on Métis and other aboriginal topics from the time of his arrival in St. Boniface in 1880,[69] and Auguste-Henri de Trémaudan, whose *Histoire de la Nation Métisse*[70] was commissioned by the Union Nationale Métisse Saint-Joseph de Manitoba. Both of these accounts relied heavily on the Coltman report. Prud'homme's article in particular was a closely reasoned analysis, with little overt use of rhetoric.[71] As in Bell's pamphlet, the paper ended with a discussion of his sources, directing attention back to its evidentiary base. Neither of these works appears to have figured in any of the subsequent accounts of Seven Oaks.

De Trémaudan's book received a mixed review in the *Canadian Historical Review* in the same issue in which a very positive review of George Stanley's *The Birth of Western Canada* appeared.[72] Unlike the two francophone accounts, this book was to have a major impact on the historiography of the Métis. In uncritically reproducing stereotypes from Alexander Ross,[73] Stanley helped perpetuate the conventional wisdom of Métis inferiority in Anglo-Canadian discourse. He referred to Seven Oaks as a "massacre" and, like Martin, avoided assigning responsibility by resorting to a passive construction: "A gun was fired." As with Bryce, he was principally concerned with impressing on readers a connection between Seven Oaks, Métis "turbulence," and 1885: "Seven Oaks was only the first of several demonstrations by the half-breeds against the settlement of their country by the whites, and was, in consequence, the forerunner of the Riel Rebellions of 1869–70 and 1885."[74]

In 1939 the Hudson's Bay Record Society published the HBC trader Colin Robertson's correspondence book from 1817 to 1822, edited by the distinguished British economic historian E. E. Rich. This was the first time since Seven Oaks that Hudson's Bay Company documents pertaining to the event were published for general research use. Their interest resides in Rich's conclusion that the evidence confirmed that the HBC party initiated the shooting. Among the documents he published was a letter by Robertson, dated December 1818, in which he referred to "the accidental shot from the musquet of the deceased Maroni."[75] In the footnote to this statement, Rich identified "Maroni" as Patrick Marooney, a member of the Semple party who was killed at Seven Oaks. He added that "this reference would seem to point to Patrick Marooney as firing the first shot." Rich also quoted from a contemporary report by the HBC Factor James Bird, who wrote of the altercation between Boucher and Semple: "the insolence of this man [Boucher] so irritated some of the party which accompanied Mr. Semple that they rashly fired on the Half-breeds who stood round and who had hitherto remained quiet spectators of the scuffle with Boucher."[76] These testimonies are conspicuous by their absence in the subsequent historiography of Seven Oaks.

In 1945, Marcel Giraud published his monumental doctoral thesis, *Le Métis canadien*.[77]It has been long held that this study presented a more sympathetic portrait of the Métis than had appeared in Anglo-Canadian writing. Reliance on Hudson's Bay Company primary sources and secondary works by Ross, Bryce, Agnes C. Laut, Martin, A. S. Morton, and Stanley helped ensure, however, that his interpretations were in the mainstream of the Anglo-Canadian discourse.

The consistency of Giraud's interpretation with Anglo-Canadian writing on the event is immediately suggested in his terminology. Where Martin had been careful to avoid the loaded term "massacre," Giraud underlined this interpretation by entitling a chapter section "Le Massacre De La Grenouillère," and repeatedly invoking the term throughout his discussion.[78] These lexical signifiers were reinforced by grammatical use. Specifically, on the question of the first shot, Giraud obfuscated. After describing the angry exchange between Boucher and Semple and the governor's seizing Boucher's bridle, he stated that at this moment "des coups de feu éclatèrent." As with Martin and Stanley, he resorted to a passive construction to sidestep the problem of attributing responsibility, and added that since the eye-witness testimony was contradictory, it was impossible to verify where the shots came from. He supported his equivocation by referring to four sources: John Bird's "Edmonton Report" and depositions by Michael Hayden, John Pritchard, and Joseph Pelletier. Of these witnesses, Pelletier attributed the first shot to the Semple party, Bird's report was a tacit admission from a HBC employee that his own side fired first, and Pritchard testified that he could not tell which side initiated the gunfire. This leaves only Hayden (who had been discredited as an unreliable witness by Coltman) asserting that the Métis fired the first shot. Giraud then focused on the supposed inability of the Métis to restrain innate savage impulses, reflected in alleged mutilation of the bodies: "l'action une fois engagée, ces natures simples, dépourvues de conviction réligieuse, parurent donner libre cours à l'instinct sauvage que les North-Westers avaient éveillé en eux. Leur barbarie s'exprima dans la mutilation des cadavres."[79]

Presenting Seven Oaks as a manifestation of instinctive Métis savagery was consistent with English-language versions from the time of Bryce. Giraud's contribution was to give renewed credibility to the old stereotype by providing both extensive footnoting and the scientific gloss of eugenics theory.[80] Despite the trappings of academic references and the use of pseudo-scientific language, Giraud's overarching thesis of the Métis as the inherently flawed product of an unsound racial mixture was derived entirely from the encrusted prejudices of half a century of Anglo-Canadian writing on this mixed-blood group.

The Anglo-Canadian historiography of Seven Oaks culminates in the work of W. L. Morton. Morton was the most prominent post-Second-World-War historian in and of Western Canada, and he was the only regional historian to whom Carl Berger devoted an entire chapter in his *The Writing of Canadian History.* Morton wrote two versions of the battle, a shorter account in his survey history of Manitoba and a more substantial narrative in a book on Cuthbert Grant.

Recent scholarship has credited Morton's account in *Cuthbert Grant of Grantown* with being the "most detailed reconstruction of Seven Oaks,"[81] but it is consistent with the version in his provincial history, albeit with more detail and footnotes. As with Martin, Stanley, and Giraud, he employed passive constructions and apologies to soften the impact of the Semple party's firing the first shot, while shifting the emphasis to an assumed coordinated response. Morton discussed the killing of Semple and correctly attributed it to either Deschamps or Machicabou, an Indian. Nevertheless, he proceeded to extend the responsibility for this "savagery" to the entire group of Métis: "This piece of savagery was matched elsewhere. The wounded were knifed and tomahawked, the dead stripped and ripped up after the Indian fashion. The wild blood of the *brûlés* was boiling, and it was some time before Grant could check their savagery." Grant's entire party was also presented as a wild group of plunderers.[82]

Beyond attributing savagery to the entire group, the author presented them as a continuing menace to the colonists. He referred to the settlers' "terror-stricken night"; the "horrors of the massacre"; and the "horror of the colonists."[83] Morton asked: "What pity for man or woman could be expected from these savages?" Grant was presented as mercifully in control of his men; otherwise, it was implied, they would have massacred the entire settlement. Morton also discussed the appearance of the bodies after they were brought in: "Some of them were naked, some mutilated, all rent by spear or knife. The spectacle completed the terror of the colonists."[84]

Morton's views on the Métis role at Seven Oaks are clear enough from his reconstruction in *Cuthbert Grant of Grantown* but, as a collaborative text, the book does not reveal his reasons for this interpretation. An answer is found in his *Manitoba: A History*, in which a similar version of Seven Oaks was narrativised as part of a much larger interpretive framework.

Here, the selected form of emplotment was the epic, essentially a monumental prose poem narrating the progress of a hero. While the epic form all but disappeared in Europe with the rise of professional history in the early-nineteenth century, in North America it was given new life by the nation-building preoccupations of the occupying Anglo-Saxon groups in the United States.[85] In a similar way, Morton's book represents the deployment of an antiquated literary form to advance the historical role of his ethnic group, class, and profession.

Morton plotted *Manitoba: A History* as a succession of dialectical struggles between what he considered to be the progressive and reactionary forces at each stage of the historical process. In each successive era, the mode of production and social organisation considered to advance society swept away the old order. For example, the Métis were accorded a role in the fur trade era but, by 1870, they were viewed as resisting progress and had to be turned out. This narrative structure required that the Métis be presented in a negative light before the reader reaches the critical years of 1869–70 in the text. Accordingly, they were thematised as wild men throughout the approximately eighty pages devoted to the Red River period. This was achieved through the simple device of applying a large number of adjectives signifying their alleged unruliness and irresponsibility.[86]

The function of Seven Oaks within the larger narrative is revealed when Morton referred to the "sudden and deadly burst of passion" at Seven Oaks, a foreshadowing of the subsequent reference to the execution of Thomas Scott as a "sudden return to violence by Riel." He asked: "Why the resistance, hitherto so restrained rose so suddenly to this pitch of brutal violence, is an obscure and complex question," and then answered by attributing the violence to "the divisions and instability of his [Riel's] own people."[87] He thereby echoed the interpretation he advanced in reviewing Giraud's book in 1950: "it was their tragedy that the instability and violence of Riel, reflecting the inherent instability and ready violence of his own uncertain people, ruined his achievement and destroyed his nation."[88]

Morton's narrativisation of Seven Oaks can therefore be seen as integral to the discrediting of the legitimacy of the Riel Resistance and, by extension, the Métis rights it represented. Here Giraud's assertions of an inherent Métis instability and tendency to violence provided Morton with all that was required to justify their suppression in 1870 and, by implication, 1885.

Morton's version of Seven Oaks reveals a deeper allegorical structure beyond these narrative functions, which it shares with the broader Anglo-Canadian discourse. One has only to compare the optimistic tone of the conclusions to Bryce's books with the pessimism evident in Morton's concluding jeremiad to perceive that a very different conception is at work. That his text went beyond the agendas of the Anglo-Canadian discourse is also evident from a comparison of stereotypes in the respective accounts. Where such writers as Ross, Bryce, and Stanley presented the Métis in terms of both positive and negative stereotypes as a combination of Wild Man and Noble Savage, Morton's characterisation was almost uniformly negative.

Why Morton resorted to such hyperbole might well have had less to do with the Métis than a preoccupation with a perceived decline in the position of his own ethnic group and profession in the twentieth century. Morton's uneasiness with the increasingly multicultural composition of the province after 1900 is reflected in the statement that "many of them were to be alien in origin and of faiths and traditions unknown to the West, and with their coming was to begin a testing of the Canadian nationality such as it had not yet undergone." Here "Canadian nationality" signifies *Anglo*-Canadian nationality. Later, he referred to the "the gulf between the immigrant and the Canadian-born generation breaching family ties, delinquency among the younger generation, the decline of politeness, the debasement of English speech," and so on. Similarly decried was the decline in status of the academy: "The decadence of intellectual standards, the maintenance of which was the greatest need of a society emerging from pioneering, was increased by the contempt in which a materialistic community held the teaching profession. The really fine achievement of the University of Manitoba in its first generation was similarly threatened." Just as he wistfully recalled the leading role of the university in Bryce's day, he nostalgically looked back to the privileged role of Ross and other retired fur traders, men of "prestige and means" and "the natural aristocracy of the primitive community of Red River" in their own era.[89]

These assorted statements point to the author's deeper narrative purpose. In his statement quoted at the beginning of this paper, Morton suggested that historians had neglected their responsibility to produce "myths" to counter the "decadence" of the age. His own narrativisation of Seven Oaks approached the mythical in *Manitoba: A History,* a romantic epic in which the role attributed to the Métis functioned to set off the text's implied hero, an Anglo-Canadian aristocracy for the West.

Morton's account of Seven Oaks in *Cuthbert Grant of Grantown* was apparently the last detailed treatment of the event by a Manitoba-born Anglo-Canadian. Its status as the last archivally based version has ensured a continuation of elements of the Anglo-Canadian tradition in historical writing to the present. Morton's interpretation of a "massacre" survived in Frits Pannekoek's recently published study on the origins of the Red River Resistance,[90] and a current francophone history of St. Boniface relied on Giraud and Morton as sources on Seven Oaks.[91] In varying degrees the Anglo-Canadian version is also in evidence in current survey textbooks in Canadian history.[92]

Some regional histories of the fur trade or Western Canada have been more discriminating but they, too, reveal the influence of this tradition. For example, in his book on the Western Canadian fur trade, Daniel Francis reproduced the passive equivocation ("A shot was fired"),[93] as did Gerald Friesen in his textbook on prairie history. In chiding other writers for their use of the term "massacre,"[94] Friesen has been more judicious than most. Friesen's and Francis's treatments do not consciously conform to the master narrative but, as syntheses of secondary materials, these versions are unavoidably dependent on the existing literature.

Today, exaggerated accounts of Métis "savagery" persist largely in popular works by authors such as George Woodcock or Peter C. Newman,[95] or in fictional accounts, as in a particularly lurid version in a recent romance novel.[96] Writing on Seven Oaks appears to have come full circle. Anglo-Canadian academics seized control of the incident's historiography from Red River amateurs in the period between 1870 and 1970 but, in the last twenty years amateurs have returned to the fore. Where the nineteenth-century writers exemplified *vernacular* or grass-roots approaches to historical writing, however, the more recent amateur historians fall into the category of *popular* writing, essentially comprising the popular reproduction of conventional wisdom.[97] In stretching the gulf between story and discourse to absurd lengths, the popular historians have only extended a process of textual reification, pioneered by the Anglo-Canadian academics and entrenched in a discursive tradition of a hundred years duration.

The voluminous literature on the Seven Oaks incident illuminates far more than the event of Seven Oaks, and broadly bears on the practice of historical writing as it evolved in Western Canada. In different but complementary ways, each of the nineteenth-century amateur texts on Seven Oaks, apart from Ross, contributed suggestive models as to how writing on history within the region might otherwise have developed. Coltman contributed the judicial techniques of comprehensive compilation and review of all the available evidence and subjection of the data to the rigorous standards of courtroom examination. Falcon's "Chanson de la Grenouillère" constituted both an eye-witness account and a folk memory of one of the groups participating in the event. Gunn and Hargrave acknowledged the existence of more than one viewpoint on the event, while C. N. Bell took the remarkably progressive step of letting eye-witness representatives from both sides of the conflict speak for themselves. In the twentieth century, they were joined by Louis-Arthur Prud'homme and Auguste-Henri de Trémaudan, who preserved the memory of alternative perspectives on Seven Oaks in the French language.

Yet the amateur historical writings were virtually without impact on the post-Confederation historiography of the battle. In the hundred years between 1870 and 1970, writing on Seven Oaks was dominated by professionals who proceeded to rewrite its history to reflect the ideological imperatives of their ethnic group, the newly dominant Anglo-Canadians on the prairies. With the passage of time, the new tradition of writing became entrenched as "truth," while the more pluralistic Red River amateur accounts passed into oblivion. The problem was that the academics' forms of writing often owed more to the structures of the fictional genre than to scientific analysis, while their contents were based less on empirical research than on discursive tradition.

The Anglo-Canadian discourse on Seven Oaks might be best understood by referring to the concept of master narrative, an overriding interpretive paradigm informing an entire body of writing. After 1870, the master narrative of progress was apparent in the Anglo-Canadian erasure of Métis traditions and the rewriting of the historiography of the battle, as attested to by the works of Bryce, Martin, and a host of other historians and novelists. In these works, the year 1870 simultaneously heralded the end of a long period of stagnation for Red River, its rescue through Canada's acquisition of the region, and the introduction of an integrated national market economy. As a society of newcomers, however, prairie Anglo-Canadians needed to establish cultural traditions to justify their assumption of dominance in the region. A key element in their programme consisted of the Canadians' adoption of the Selkirk settlers as imagined ancestors in the West. Whatever shortcomings they might have perceived in them, these Scots were the only full-blooded European, anglophone settlers from the early-nineteenth century available for the purpose. Selkirk's claims to the occupation of Western lands therefore needed to be valorized, and rivals discredited. The narrativisation of Seven Oaks as a flashpoint in the imagined struggle of civilisation versus savagery was essential to promoting the legitimacy of these adopted ancestors.

In the context of the new master narrative of progress, however, it was important that the Métis assume broader allegorical roles. This was so because the Anglo-Canadians were essentially in competition with the Métis for lands to which this Western Native group held a prior claim, a fact which the resistances of 1869–70 and 1885 had made all too clear. The Métis needed to be seen as violent, volatile, easily led astray, and lacking in judgement—in short, as the antithesis of qualities considered essential to the development of a stable free market economy in the West. Seven Oaks provided a convenient vehicle for the presentation of an alleged Métis weakness of character, implicitly justifying the dispossession of their lands. The preoccupation with this event probably also had as much to do with the construction of Euro-Canadian identities in the West as with the discrediting of the Métis. The representation of a savage Métis "Other" was integral to the inculcation of a kind of "morality tale" in which the chain of stereotyped characteristics of the Métis functioned to set off all the attributes valued by the new capitalist order in the West.

The discourse on Seven Oaks also raises some questions regarding the master narrative of the Canadian historical profession, that the professionalisation of the discipline around 1900 enabled critical methods to supersede the partisanship of nineteenth-century amateurs. With specific reference to Western Canada, the intellectual historian Doug Owram has correctly identified Bryce with a major historiographical shift, focusing on the rehabilitation of the role of the Selkirk settlers. Yet this shift was not rooted in "a sense of alienation from the East"[98] so much as it reflected the demonstrable need of an immigrant group aspiring to preeminence in the West to establish a blood line of succession. This study of Seven Oaks also challenges Owram's conclusion that the "major proponents of this increasingly romantic view of life in Red River were those older settlers who had actually experienced life in the settlement before 1870 and their descendants,"[99] as opposed to Bryce and his successors. The historiography of Seven Oaks suggests that it was actually the other way around. The romance form was essential to the Anglo-Canadians' construction of a history favourable to their claims to dominance, and survivors of Old Red River acquired a romantic sensibility from newcomers such as Bryce, rather than *vice versa.* A case in point was Roderick G. MacBeth, an amateur historian and descendant of Selkirk settlers, whose life spans the transition from the Red River colony to the Canadian period after 1870. An indication of the shift in his own writing is provided by the titles of two of his books, *The Selkirk Settlers in Real Life,* published in 1897, and *The Romance of Western Canada,* published some twenty years later. The titles are also indicative of their contents; on Seven Oaks, MacBeth moves from a neutral, more realistic treatment in the earlier book to a romantic representation of a massacre, based on Bryce, in the second.[100]

What we witness in most of the Anglo-Canadian versions, then, is less a reconstruction of the Seven Oaks incident than the construction, through historical discourse, of the self-image of prairie Anglo-Canadian society. Bryce and his successors brought about the transformation of Seven Oaks historiography from Red River pluralism to Anglo-Canadian romance, while Morton presided over its final elevation to the realm of myth. As current writing on the event suggests, when the weight of discourse compresses its sedimentary layers into an ideological bedrock, such myths have been stubbornly resistant to revision.

Notes

1 Canada. National Archives (NA), Selkirk Papers, MG 2, A 1, fols. 9207–08.

2 W.L. Morton, comment on R. G. Trotter, "Aims in the Study and Teaching of History in Canadian Universities Today," Canadian Historical Association, *Annual Report* (1943): 61.

3 E.E. Rich, ed., *Colin Robertson's Correspondence Book. September 1817 to September 1818* (London, 1939), 28.

4 "Seven Oaks," Historical and Scientific Society of Manitoba, *Transactions* 43 (1891–92).

5 Carl Berger, *The Writing of Canadian History* (Toronto, 1976). The following quotations are from page 1 of this text.

6 M. Brook Taylor, *Promoters, Patriots and Partisans: Historiography in Nineteenth-Century Canada* (Toronto, 1989).

7 A.B. McKillop, "Historiography in English," *Canadian Encyclopedia,* rev. ed., 993.

8 "Story" is defined as a sequence of events to which historians refer in constructing their narratives, while "discourse," or plot, is a particular version of the referred-to events. See Wallace Martin, *Recent Theories of Narrative* (Ithaca and London, 1986), 108–29.

9 The literary or narrative analysis of historical texts comprises a growing subdiscipline within the field of intellectual history. Among various works now published in this area, see Hayden White, *Metahistory* (Baltimore, 1973); Dominick LaCapra, *Historical Criticism* (Ithaca, 1985); Sande Cohen, *Historical Culture: On the Recoding of an Academic Discipline* (Berkeley, 1986); and Hans Kellner, *Language and Historical Representation* (Madison, 1989).

10 See Hayden White, *The Content of the Form* (Baltimore, 1987), 26–57.

11 The published sources are listed in W. S. Wallace, "The Literature Relating to the Selkirk Controversy," *Canadian Historical Review* 13:1 (March 1932): 45–50.

12 A. Amos, ed., *Report of the Trials in the Courts of Canada Relative to the Destruction of the Earl of Selkirk's Settlement of the Red River with Observations* (London, 1820), and *Report of the Proceedings Connected with the Disputes Between the Earl of Selkirk and the North-West [sic] Company at the Assizes Held at York, in Upper Canada, October, 1818, From Minutes Taken in Court* (London, 1819).

13 See NA, Records of the Provincial and Civil Secretaries' Offices, Québec, Lower Canada, and Canada East, 1760–1867, RG 4, B 46, "Lower Canada, Commission of Enquiry into the Red River Disturbances, 1815–21," Vols. 1–5 (hereafter "Commission of Enquiry"); Manitoba. Provincial Archives, Hudson's Bay Company Archives, E. 8/5, '"Papers Relating to Disturbances Forwarded to Lord Bathurst, 1815–1819," and E. 8/6, "Papers Relating to Disturbances, 1814–1819"; McGill University Libraries, Department of Rare Books and Special Collections, Selkirk Papers, MS 403/12 and 403/13.

14 In addition to the assorted correspondence reproduced in *Papers Relating to the Red River Settlement,* see the original letters in NA, RG 4, B 46, "Commission of Enquiry," and NA, Colonial Office Records, MG 11, CO 42, Vol. 181.

15 "A General Statement and Report Relative to the Disturbances in the Indian Territories of British North America by the Undersigned Special Commissioner for Inquiring into the Offences Committed in the Said Indian Territories and the Circumstances Attending the Same." Two manuscript copies of the report were examined, in NA, Colonial Office Records, MG 11, CO 42, Vol. 181, fols. 74–232 and in NA, Fur Trade and Indian Records 1763–1867, MG 19, E 2, "Red River Settlement," Vol. 1. Both copies contain essentially the same text as the published version in Great Britain. Parliament, House of Commons, *Papers Relating to the Red River Settlement,* Paper 18, No. 584 (London, 1819), 165–250. This version has been republished in *Collections of the State Historical Society of North Dakota* 4 (1915): 451–653.

16 Instructions to W. B. Coltman and John Fletcher by Sir J. C. Sherbrooke, 11 November 1816, reprinted in *Papers Relating to the Red River Settlement,* 64.

17 George Bryce, *The Remarkable History of the Hudson's Bay Company* (3rd ed., Toronto, 1910), 255.

18 A.S. Morton, *A History of the Canadian West to 1870–71* (Toronto, 1939), 599.

19 John Morgan Gray, *Lord Selkirk of Red River* (Toronto, 1963), 320–21.

20 Roy C. Dalton et al., "William Bachelor Coltman," *Dictionary of Canadian Biography (DCB)* 6: 166.

21 W.B. Coltman to the agents of the North West Company, 27 December 1817, reprinted in *Papers Relating to the Red River Settlement,* 127.

22 For Coltman's defence of his approach to evidence, see NA, Colonial Office Records, MG 11, CO 42, Vol. 181, fol. 254, W. B. Coltman to Earl Bathurst, 30 November 1819.

23 See Sir William Holdsworth, *A History of the English Law* (London, 1926), 9: 210–11.

24 W.B. Coltman to the agents of the North West Company, 27 December 1817, reprinted in *Papers Relating to the Red River Settlement,* 127.

25 NA, Colonial Office Records, MG 11, CO 42, Vol. 181, fols. 3–17, W. B. Coltman to Sir J. C. Sherbrooke, 14 May 1818.

26 *Papers Relating to the Red River Settlement,* 190.

27 Ibid., 188.

28 At the Seven Oaks trials at York, two Selkirk settlers, Winnifred McNolty and Hugh Bannerman, testified that Hayden had admitted to them that his own side fired the first shot. Amos, ed., *Report of the Trials,* 315–16, and *Report of the Proceedings Connected With the Dispute,* 192.

29 *Papers Relating to the Red River Settlement,* 192.

30 Ibid., 219–20.

31 Ibid., 187, 191, 192, and 193.

32 NA, Fur Trade and Indian Records 1763–1867, MG 19, E 2, fols. 285–89, W. B. Coltman, "A General Statement and Report Relative to the Disturbances...."

33 Ibid., fols. 290–91.

34 Margaret Complin, "Pierre Falcon's 'Chanson de la Grenouillère,'" *Transactions of the Royal Society of Canada,* Section 2 (1939): 49–58.

35 Numerous renditions of this song have followed its publication in the Québec folklorist François Larue's 1863 compilation, *Chansons populaires et historiques.* For historiographical purposes, an early handwritten copy and an 1871 published version transcribed from a performance by the author may be considered to be the most authentic. The handwritten version was among papers seized by Lord Selkirk at Fort William in 1816 and now found in NA, Selkirk Papers, MG 2, A 1, fols. 9207–08; the 1871 published counterpart is found in Joseph James Hargrave, *The Red River* (Montréal, 1871), 488–89.

36 Jan Vansina, *Oral Tradition as History* (London, 1985), 29.

37 Alexander Ross, *The Red River Settlement: Its Rise, Progress, and Present State, With Some Account of the Native Races and its General History, to the Present Day* (London, 1856), 36–37.

38 Amos, ed., *Report of the Trials,* 173–74.

39 Ibid., 37–40.

40 Hargrave, *The Red River,* 489–91; G. Mercer Adam, *The Canadian North-West: Its History and its Troubles: The Narrative of Three Insurrections* (Toronto, 1885), 123; George Bryce, *Mackenzie, Selkirk, Simpson* (Toronto, 1909), 184; A. C. Garrioch, *The Correction Line* (Winnipeg, 1933), 39–41; and Peter C. Newman, *Caesars of the Wilderness* (Toronto, 1987), 175.

41 Ross, *The Red River Settlement,* 18. Ross's constructions of the Métis role at Seven Oaks and on other occasions reveal the "cultural ambivalence" that Sylvia Van Kirk has described in an insightful article on his family; see "'What if Mama is an Indian?': The Cultural Ambivalence of the Alexander Ross Family," in *The Developing West: Essays in Honour of L. H. Thomas,* ed. John E. Foster (Edmonton, 1983), 125–36.

42 Ross, *The Red River Settlement,* 404 and 401.

43 L.G. Thomas, "Donald Gunn," *DCB* 10: 324.

44 Donald Gunn and Charles R. Tuttle, *History of Manitoba* (Ottawa, 1880).

45 Ibid., 107–08 and 149.

46 Glen Makahonuk, "Joseph James Hargrave," *DCB* 12: 408–09.

47 Hargrave, *The Red River,* 485–91.

48 Ibid., 487–88.

49 See Lyle Dick, *Farmers "Making Good"* (Ottawa, 1989), Chap. 1, and "Factors Affecting Prairie Settlement: A Case Study of Abernethy, Saskatchewan in the 1880s," *Historical Papers/Communications historiques* (1985): 11–28.

50 See Alan F. J. Artibise, *Winnipeg: A Social History of Urban Growth* (Montréal, 1975), 23–37.

51 Henry J. Morgan, ed., *Canadian Men and Women of the Time* (Toronto, 1912), 163–64; George Bryce, *A History of Manitoba, Its Resources and People* (Toronto/Montréal, 1906), 689–92.

52 Bryce's versions of Seven Oaks appear in the following: *Manitoba: Its Infancy, Growth, and Present Condition* (London, 1882), 213–35; *Mackenzie, Selkirk, Simpson,* 177–84; *A History of Manitoba, Its Resources and People,* 80–85; *The Remarkable History of the Hudson's Bay Company,* 3rd ed., 229–37; *The Romantic Settlement of Lord Selkirk's Colonists (The Pioneers of Manitoba)* (Toronto, 1909), 117–32; and *The Life of Lord Selkirk: Colonizer of Western Canada* (Toronto, 1912), 67–73.

53 *A History of Manitoba, Its Resources and People,* 80.

54 *The Romantic Settlement of Lord Selkirk's Colonists,* 133.

55 George Bryce, *The old settlers of Red River, a paper read before the Society on the evening of 26th November 1885* (Winnipeg, 1885), 6. In 1903, he reiterated this interpretation: "their attack on Fort Douglas, in 1816, gave them a reputation for turbulence, which again showed itself in the rebellions of 1849, 1869, 1885." See his "Intrusive Ethnological Types in Rupert's Land," *Transactions of the Royal Society of Canada,* Section 2 (1903): 412. Contemporaries who also attributed the conflicts of 1869–70 and 1885 to the unleashing of Métis turbulence at Seven Oaks include John Reade, "The Half-Breed," *Transactions of the Royal Society of Canada,* Section 2 (1885): 12 and G. Mercer Adam, *The Canadian North-West.*

56 For a discussion of the formal characteristics of the romance genre, see Northrop Frye, *The Secular Scripture: A Study of the Structure of Romance* (Cambridge, Mass., 1976).

57 Essentially, the Métis role is constructed from stereotypes originating with Ross. See *Manitoba: Its Infancy, Growth, and Present Condition,* 200 and 204.

58 *Narratives of John Pritchard, Pierre Chrysologue Pambrun and Frederick Damien Huerter, Respecting the Aggressions of the North-West [sic] Company Against the Earl of Selkirk's Settlement Upon Red River* (London, 1819).

59 W.S. Wallace, "Lord Selkirk's Ghost Writer," *The Beaver* 271, No. 2 (September 1940): 31.

60 See, for example, *Manitoba: Its Infancy, Growth, and Present Condition,* 223; *Mackenzie, Selkirk, Simpson,* 181; *A History of Manitoba, Its Resources and People,* 81–82.

61 Bryce, *A History of Manitoba, Its Resources and People,* 306.

62 Emigrating from Perth, Ontario to Manitoba in 1870, Bell was a cofounder and president of the Manitoba Historical Society and a fellow of various geographical societies in the United States and Europe. His account of Seven Oaks appears in his pamphlet, *The Selkirk Settlement and the Settlers: A Concise History of the Red River Country From its Discovery, Including Information Extracted from Original Documents Lately Discovered and Notes Obtained From Selkirk Settlement Colonists* (Winnipeg, 1887). Basing his conclusions on oral and documentary research, he acknowledged that "it is difficult to get at the exact truth of what followed this meeting of the rival traders" (17). He therefore quotes representative eye-witness accounts from both sides—the familiar testimony of John Pritchard favoured by pro-Selkirk historians, and a statement by François Firman Boucher of the North West Company. He added that "many of the settlers are of the opinion that the first shot fired was by Lieut. Holte, whose gun went off by accident, thus precipitating the conflict" (19).

63 See Alexander Begg, *History of the North-West* (Toronto, 1894), 183; F. H. Schofield, The *Story of Manitoba* (Chicago, 1913), 1: 138; Robert B. Hill, *Manitoba: History of Its Early Settlement, Development, and Resources* (Toronto, 1890), 50–56; Louis Aubrey Wood, *The Red River Colony: A Chronicle of the Beginnings of Manitoba* (Toronto, 1915), 91–107; and John Perry Pritchard, *The Red River Valley, 1811–1849: A Regional Study* (New York, 1942), 162–80. Among the many fictional accounts acknowledging their debt to Bryce, or reproducing the essentials of his accounts, were: Agnes C. Laut, *Lords of the North* (Toronto, 1900), v; J. H. McCulloch, *The Men of Kildonan: A Romance of the Selkirk Settlers* (New York, 1926), vii; Frederick Niven, *Mine Inheritance* (London, 1940), 285–88; John Jennings, The *Strange Brigade: A Story of the Red River and the Opening of the Canadian West* (Boston, 1952), 367; and J. W. Chalmers, *Red River Adventures: The Story of the Selkirk Settlers* (Toronto, 1952), 99–103.

64 See Robert Adolph, *The Rise of the Modern Prose Style* (Cambridge, Mass., 1968), and Hayden White, *Tropics of Discourse* (Baltimore, 1978), 94–95.

65 *Canadian Historical Review* 39:3 (September 1958): 264.

66 Carl Berger, *The Sense of Power* (Toronto, 1970), 215.

67 Chester Martin, *Lord Selkirk's Work in Canada* (Oxford, 1916).

68 Ibid., 111.

69 L'abbé Elie-J. Auclair, "L'honorable Juge Prud'homme," *Mémoires de la Société Royale du Canada,* Section 1, Série III, 35 (1941): 135–40; Morgan, *Canadian Men and Women of the Time,* 921.

70 Auguste-Henri de Trémaudan, *Histoire de la nation métisse dans l'ouest canadien* (Montréal, 1935), 105–12.

71 L.-A. Prud'homme, "L'engagement des Sept Chênes," *Mémoires de la Société Royale du Canada,* Section 1, Série III, 12 (décembre 1918/mars 1919): 165–88.

72 *Canadian Historical Review* 17:4 (December 1936): 452–54 and 454–57.

73 George F. G. Stanley, *The Birth of Western Canada* (Toronto, 1936), 6–9.

74 Ibid., 11 and 12.

75 E.E. Rich, ed., *Colin Robertson's Correspondence Book, September 1817 to September 1822* (London, 1939), 27.

76 Ibid., 27, n. 2.

77 Marcel Giraud, *Le Métis canadien: son rôle dans l'histoire de provinces de l'Ouest* (Paris, 1945).

78 Ibid., 1: 591, 594, and 596.

79 Ibid., 1: 594 and 596.

80 Eugenics, an ideology and programme of fostering racial betterment by genetic manipulation, generated an enormous literature in the early-twentieth century. See Samuel J. Holmes, *A Bibliography of Eugenics* (Berkeley, 1924).

81 J.M. Bumsted, "Introduction," *The Collected Works of Lord Selkirk, 1810–1820* (Winnipeg, 1987), 2: Ixxxix, n. 285. The narrative in *Cuthbert Grant of Grantown* has been attributed incorrectly to both Morton and his coauthor, the amateur historian Margaret Arnett MacLeod. In the preface to the second edition, Morton disassociated himself from what he considered MacLeod's overly romantic view of Grant as a "heroic" figure, and he assumed sole responsibility for authoring various chapters, including the one which treats Seven Oaks. See W. L. Morton, "Introduction to the Carleton Library Edition," in Morton and MacLeod, *Cuthbert Grant of Grantown* (Toronto, 1974), ix–xv.

82 Morton and MacLeod, *Cuthbert Grant of Grantown,* 49.

83 Ibid., 51 and 52.

84 Ibid., 51–52.

85 At least five leading American historians of the nineteenth century wrote epic histories to reflect the national experience of the United States. See Ernst Breisach, *Historiography: Ancient, Medieval, and Modern* (Chicago, 1983), 255–56.

86 W.L. Morton, *Manitoba: A History* (Toronto, 1957). The adjectives used to depict the Métis include six applications of the term "wild"—twice on page 51 and on pages 56, 62, 65, and 70; one instance of "half-wild" (56); one case of "Ishmaelite wildness" (67); four instances of "turbulent" (56, 70, 102, and 119); another of "turbulent and lawless" (82); and references to "barbarism" (56 and 62), "but half-won from barbarism" (39), and "slovenly barbarism" (90). Other modifiers used for the Métis include "slovenliness" (65), "volatile" (77), "fickle" (63), "careless and amiable" (63), "restless" (102), "reckless" (145), "insoucient" (66), and "lawless" (61 and 64). He also refers to their "divisions and instability" (138) and to their "primitive and slovenly agriculture" (88), and speaks of "a lazy fecklessness a Métis could not have exceeded" (67).

87 Ibid., 54, 136, 138, and 137.

88 W.L. Morton, "The Canadian Métis," *The Beaver* 281 (September 1950): 7.

89 Morton, *Manitoba: A History,* 274, 467, and 67.

90 Note Pannekoek's reproduction of Morton's terminology ("the horrors of the Seven Oaks Massacre") in *A Snug Little Flock: The Social Origins of the Riel Resistance of 1869–70* (Winnipeg, 1991), 76.

91 Luc Dauphinais, *Histoire de Saint-Boniface,* tome I, *À l'ombre des cathédrales* (Saint-Boniface, 1991), 45–46.

92 For example, the revised edition of J. M. S. Careless's *Canada: A Story of Challenge* (Toronto, 1974) characterises Seven Oaks as a "massacre" (143), while Desmond Morton's *A Short History of Canada* (Edmonton, 1983) perpetuates the image of the Métis as North West Company dupes who "shot down twenty-one men from the colony and mutilated some of the corpses" (66). Even J. L. Finlay and D. N. Sprague's *The Structure of Canadian History* (Scarborough, 1979), an account generally sympathetic to the Métis, states that the incident is remembered as an "atrocity" and a "massacre" (104).

93 Daniel Francis, *Battle for the West* (Edmonton, 1982), 121.

94 Gerald Friesen, *The Canadian Prairies: A History* (Toronto, 1984), 78–79.

95 George Woodcock, *The Hudson's Bay Company* (Toronto, 1970), 115–16; Newman, *Caesars of the Wilderness,* 173–75.

96 Alfred Silver, *Red River Story* (New York, 1988), 382–84.

97 For a discussion of the character of Canadian popular history writing, and of the approach of Peter C. Newman in particular, see Lyle Dick, "Renegade in Archives: Peter C. Newman and the Writing of Canadian Popular History," *Archivaria* 22 (Summer 1986): 168–81.

98 Douglas Owram, *Promise of Eden: The Canadian Expansionist Movement and the Idea of the West, 1856–1900* (Toronto, 1980), 203.

99 Ibid., 208.

100 R.G. MacBeth, *The Selkirk Settlers in Real Life* (Toronto, 1897), 26 and idem., *The Romance of Western Canada* (Toronto, 1918), 42–43.

PART IV

Maturing Colonial Societies

1815–1867

National Archives of Canada/C1242

The British North American colonies went their separate ways between 1815 and 1867, but they drew closer in culture and values. As population expanded in the Atlantic region and the Canadas, colonial politicians demanded a larger measure of self-government. In the Hudson's Bay Company territories, agricultural settlements first supplemented and eventually supplanted the fur trade as the *raison d'être* for the European presence in areas still overwhelmingly populated by First Nations.

At one point historians painted the movement toward self-government in this period as one of virtual inevitability, part of an inexorable move toward democracy in the Western world. Certainly, the colonists had reasons to congratulate themselves on their successes. In 1848, Nova Scotia became the first colony in the British Empire to achieve "responsible government"; that is, a government that enjoyed the confidence of the majority of the members of the elected Assembly. Later that year, the United Province of Canada, formed by the forced union of Upper and Lower Canada in 1841, also achieved responsible government, and the remaining three Atlantic colonies had won the same victory by 1855.

As the readings in Part 4 suggest, the achievement of responsible government involved popular struggles and, in the Canadas, outright rebellion. Although the political changes ushered in during the period covered in Part 4 gave more political control to the common people, the extent to which democracy was extended remained circumscribed. The vote was largely limited to European-origin male property-holders, leaving all women and Natives, as well as the colonial poor among white males, without a formal political voice. Government priorities reflected the concerns of those who held the franchise, often completely ignoring the interests of the disenfranchised.

Ian Robertson's article locates a progressive reform in Prince Edward Island—the provision of free public education to all Island children—within a broader reform agenda: The Reform politicians who espoused both responsible government and public education had as their ultimate aim a social transformation in which an island made up largely of tenants exploited by often absentee landowners would become a colony made up of self-governing small landholders. Education was perceived as a first step along the way. As long as many tenants remained illiterate or barely literate, they could not understand the contracts that bound them to the landowners, much less prevent the landowners from imposing conditions that the contracts forbade.

The wishes of the landholding class also prevailed in New Brunswick. As Gail Campbell indicates, the province passed a restrictive franchise law in 1791 that limited the vote to male property-holders whose freeholds were assessed at a minimum value of £25. Only minor changes to the law occurred by the early 1850s. But how restrictive did that law prove in practice? Campbell carefully mines the demographic and electoral data for Albert County, a fairly typical area in terms of average incomes. She demonstrates that in 1851, over 70 percent of the men in the county were eligible to vote while another 8 percent, though technically ineligible, were allowed to vote because they were regarded as solid citizens of the county.

Newfoundland was the last of the Atlantic colonies to receive representative government and eventually responsible government. Britain, having resisted for many generations the notion of allowing a settler-colony to become established in Newfoundland, was in no hurry to grant representative government even as the colony's population expanded rapidly in the early eighteenth century. Jerry Bannister demonstrates that public pressure, initiated by the merchant elite, but eventually joined by the colony's general population, forced Britain's hand in 1832. As in other colonies, settlers became upset with arbitrary laws imposed by Britain and insensitive administration by appointed colonial governors. Efforts by British officials to raise finances for public expenditures by imposing a tax on imports caused widespread opposition. They raised the same issue that had caused the American Revolution: taxation without representation.

The gains that white men in Newfoundland and other colonies made with regard to representation were of little benefit to Native peoples, particularly the Beothuk of Newfoundland, the only First Nation in today's Canada known to have been eradicated in the period that followed European contact. Ralph Pastore analyzes the complex issue of why the Beothuk disappeared. Earlier works had focused both on the ravages of European diseases and the loss of resources faced by the Beothuk as English settlement expanded along the coast, forcing the Beothuk to move inland. Pastore adds to this sorry tale the immigrations of Basques and Inuit along the Strait of Belle Isle, and Mi'kmaq to the southern third of the island. Hemmed into the areas of least resources in the Newfoundland interior, the Beothuk had little chance of survival.

While Native peoples experienced the rise of democracy that accompanied growing white settlements in terms of dispossession, it was hardly the case that all whites benefited equally from the landholders' democracy that was spreading across British North America at mid-century. Many men owned no land, and existed on the margins of these societies. As for women, almost none owned land. Patriarchy, the control of men over women, was embedded both in the customs of the colonists and the law of the land. Marjorie Griffin Cohen traces the Upper Canadian (Ontario) laws that made women simply extensions of their menfolk, lacking personhood in the ownership of property. While women fought to gain property and legal rights in this period, they won only token victories.

This situation was in direct contrast to the democratic temper of the times for men. Allan Greer points out the extent to which both the urban middle classes and the "rural plebeians " embraced democratic ideals in the days that led to the Rebellion of Lower Canada in 1837. As the British authorities remained resolute in their opposition to calls for responsible government in the Canadas, the Patriotes, who easily won Assembly elections with their calls for a democratic transformation of the colony, became more radical. They used rallies, boycotts, and conventions to demonstrate their unwillingness to accept British domination. Many farmers went much further, using charivaris to force out British-appointed officials, and electing their own judges and militia leaders.

The democratic spirit of the times in Upper Canada is evident as well in the constitution proclaimed by William Lyon Mackenzie and the radical reformers whom he led. The influence of ideas borrowed from the American Revolution is much in evidence.

The "frontier" is often seen as the inspiration for democratic ideas in this period. The former Europeans and their descendants, who were carving out new societies in the North American environment, were supposedly unprepared to allow European class-based norms to flourish in their midst. While the Hudson's Bay Company leadership was resolute in its efforts to ensure a hierarchical society in the fur-trading West, frontier realities often upset its plans. Despite the company's initial efforts to prevent sexual relations between traders and Native women, these became the norm early on in the trade. Sylvia Van Kirk traces the essential roles of Native women, and discusses why, despite their central importance to the fur trade, they faced discrimination in fur-trading society on the Prairies.

Adele Perry, focusing on the campaigns of immigration promoters in British Columbia, demonstrates similar prejudices in the coastal colony. As she observes, colonial promoters' discourse regarding desirable settlers revealed a great deal about the class, gender, and race prejudices that had been transplanted from Britain to the settlement frontier, where settlement was fast replacing the fur trade in the years preceding British Columbia's entry into Confederation. She also demonstrates that the immigration promoters largely failed in their goals during these years, and that early British Columbia society did not become the society of hardy backwoodsmen married to righteous middle-class women that the promoters craved.

Reform, Literacy, and the Lease

The Prince Edward Island Free Education Act of 1852*

IAN ROSS ROBERTSON

The first administration formed in Prince Edward Island under the constitutional system of responsible government passed legislation popularly known as 'the Free Education Act' in 1852.[1] George Coles, the leader of that government, stated with pride that the colony was "the first place in the British dominions, in which a complete system of free education was established."[2] The new law meant that the colonial treasury would pay teachers' salaries; thus teachers would be guaranteed their salaries regardless of the local tax base, and children would be admitted free of tuition charges. Teachers would not have to consider the resources of the district before accepting a position, and students would not be denied entry to school for lack of money. In the following year the government imported a Scottish school visitor, John Murdoch Stark, from David Stow's pioneering Normal Seminary in Glasgow, to oversee the system. While criticizing the quality of instruction he found in the district schools, the vigorous and candid Stark was full of praise for the policy initiative of the government. "This small colony," he wrote, "has solved for herself the question which has been agitating the public mind of Britain for so many years, and which is still at issue."[3] That task, as defined by Stark, was to establish a system for imparting the basic elements of education to the whole community.[4]

Prince Edward Island Reformers had taken a remarkably progressive step in educational policy in 1852, demonstrating convincingly that they placed exceptional value on access to primary education. They were the first of the Maritime provinces (the usual reference group for colonial Islanders) to establish 'free education,' and, if Coles was correct, they had not been deterred by the prospect of being the first in the British empire to do so. The importance they placed on popular access to education was underscored by the fact that they had passed their legislation a mere one year after achieving responsible government. Nova Scotia was the next in the Maritimes to adopt free education, and it did so in 1864, 12 years later, and a full 16 years after being the first British colony to achieve responsible government. New Brunswick, which attained responsible government in a series of stages culminating in 1854, did not take the step until 17 years later, in 1871.

Ian Ross Robertson, "Reform, Literacy, and the Lease: The Prince Edward Island Free Education Act of 1852," *Acadiensis* 20, 1 (Autumn 1990): 52–71.

*This article grew out of a paper delivered at the Atlantic Canada Studies Conference in Edinburgh in May of 1988. The author wishes to thank Paul Thompson, chair of the Division of Humanities, Scarborough College, University of Toronto, who made attendance possible, and Phillip Buckner, who encouraged development of the paper into an article; special thanks are also due to F.A. Cunningham and A.R. Gillis.

Why did an overwhelmingly agrarian colony, whose inhabitants were unusually cash-poor, place such value on education in an era before significant numbers could realistically harbour aspirations of climbing the ladder of social mobility, as conventionally understood? Why did the Island act so much earlier than its mainland neighbours, and why was it the first of all the colonies?

Explanations for increasing plebeian access to education in the 19th century which have apparent plausibility elsewhere have little application to Prince Edward Island in 1852. Some writers have conceptualized the spread of popular education as a means of preparing the population for the discipline of the Industrial Revolution—and the term "bourgeois state formation" has been used.[5] But it would require considerable distortion of perspective to visualize the Island as a whole as being poised on the brink of industrialization; and 1852 is rather early to imagine Island legislators as consciously preparing the mass of the population for migration to the mills and factories of New England.

Another possible motive for educating poorer elements would be to mould their attitudes in such a way as to make them unreceptive to potentially dangerous radicals who might threaten property.[6] But radicalism on the Island was at a low ebb in 1852. The radical movement known as Escheat had been discredited through the failure of its simplistic proposal for solution of the land question, and its leaders had either become marginal or entirely irrelevant politically.[7] William Cooper was out of politics, and indeed had been in California during the latter stages of the struggle for responsible government; John MacKintosh was defeated at the polls in both 1850 and 1853; and John W. LeLacheur left the Island (for Iowa) permanently sometime between 1850 and 1852, the uncertainty of the public record as to the date of his departure bearing eloquent testimony to his political insignificance by the early 1850s.[8] As historian Harry Baglole has written, the decisive defeat of the Escheat movement at the election of 1842—a full ten years before the passage of the Free Education Act—meant that "as a coherent, thrusting political force, the Escheators were through."[9] The 'ideology of Escheat'[10] constituted a threat to no one in 1852, and in any event, the conservative elements in the assembly, those with most to lose through any plebeian susceptibility to radicalism, steadfastly opposed the reform. The crucial vote on the principle of the legislation passed 15-3, with Tory leader Edward Palmer, a landlord, and James Yeo Sr., a wealthy shipbuilder, merchant, and land agent, among the three opposed. The main resolution passed 16-3, with the minority comprising Palmer, Yeo, and Lord Selkirk's agent, William Douse[11]—in Reform journalist Edward Whelan's words, the "extreme proprietary party."[12] The legislation was certainly a matter of partisan division, but those identified most strongly with the rights of property did not support it as a measure of social control, effectively giving the lie to any interpretation of the measure as one of enlightened conservatism. In fact, Douse stated explicitly that "The scheme [the Free Education Act] was calculated injuriously to affect their [the proprietors] interests,[13] and Palmer was candid enough in discussing the measure and explaining his opposition to be reported as follows: "He confessed that he had always been an advocate for the rights of proprietors."[14]

Thus ready-made (or made-on-the-mainland) hypotheses provide little assistance in explaining the Island's primacy in easing popular access to basic education. Nor can the Prince Edward Island of 1852 be portrayed as besieged by a growing horde of impoverished immigrants whose integration or assimilation to local norms was urgent. The census data do not support any notion that the Island was facing increasing immigration—and they are especially incompatible with the hypothesis that the number of immigrants from areas with traditions of agrarian insurgency might be increasing. Both in percentage terms and in absolute numbers the non-native born were declining. The census closest to 1852, that of 1855, revealed that 24.2 per cent of the population were non-native born, a decline of 5.2 per cent since the census of 1848. In absolute numbers the decrease in non-natives was from 18,437 to 17,276—1,161, or 6.3 per cent—and in the same interval the native-born increased by 9,110 or 20.8 per cent. Of course the pattern of decline within the non-native portion of the population was not uniform across the recorded groups. The two which declined most significantly in the intercensal period were the Irish-born (841, or 13.1 per cent) and the Scots-born (870, or 12.9 per cent), the groups likeliest to fit the mould of the angry and dispossessed immigrants inclined to listen to demagogues.[15] Indeed, the more closely all available data are scrutinized, the less comfortable the empirically-minded researcher is likely to be with any thesis that a propertied elite designed the Free Education Act of 1852 with the purpose of exerting control over the unpropertied elements and preventing them from becoming unruly.

An examination of the state of education on the Island prior to passage of the Free Education Act yields some insight into the motivation of the Reformers. The pre-1852 educational system was underdeveloped and chaotic, with little regulation and attention to common standards and practices. In addition, there were periodic lapses in instruction in individual districts. Stark's predecessor as school visitor, John MacNeill, estimated in 1853 that before implementation of the statute, only two-thirds of the school houses in Queens County, the most populous and prosperous of the three Island counties, had ever been in operation at any one time.[16] A major part of the problem was financial, for poor and possibly irregular pay made it difficult to retain the more capable teachers. Even when well-motivated persons could be attracted, the itinerant and insecure life of the teacher tended either to undermine the morale and hence the effectiveness of the teacher or to encourage a change in occupation.[17]

The Free Education Act of 1852 addressed the financial issue directly, for teachers were to be paid in full by the colonial treasury. This provision meant an end to reliance on two other potential sources of revenue: local assessment and tuition fees. Teachers paid under the act were specifically forbidden to demand the latter, and the former was only to be used for the erection and maintenance of school buildings, which were the responsibility of the local trustees (who were chosen by the resident householders of the district). The changes meant that after 1852 poor districts and poor children would be much less likely to be disadvantaged. In two years the number of students enrolled doubled.[18]

But pre-1852 educational conditions, although essential for understanding the background and significance of the Free Education Act, do not explain the Island's pre-eminence in educational reform, for similar conditions existed elsewhere. The explanation, like so much else in the history of the Island as a British colony, is rooted in the unique system of leasehold land tenure which had been established in the 18th century and the legislation of 1852 must be seen in relationship to the land question. Much of the existing literature on the history of education in Prince Edward Island in the 19th century has tended to focus on institutions and legislation as such, and to neglect historical context.[19] In fact, the drive for public education in the years 1852–1877 was part of a general 'age of reform' in Prince Edward Island, and the history of education cannot be understood adequately without noting its relationship to other aspects of Island history in this turbulent era.[20] In turn, the general reform movement revolved around the land question, and specific proposals were advocated or opposed in large measure because of their perceived bearing on the parties to the land question.

Virtually everything in colonial Prince Edward Island, including the particular perspective of George Coles himself, has to be interpreted in relation to the land question, which distinguished the Island from its neighbours. Coles was a relatively wealthy Islander committed to the widest possible access to education. At first glance, it would seem strange that Coles, a leading capitalist in his economic life, should be in his political life the leader of the Reform movement supported by impoverished tenant farmers. Yet as a manufacturer of goods of common consumption, namely beer and spirits, his class interests ran contrary to the status quo: it was to his benefit that common Islanders have in their hands the greatest possible purchasing power. Understood in this light, it is not surprising that Coles favoured liquidation of a system which scooped up whatever cash many settlers had, and placed it in the hands of a small elite dependent upon the existing relationships centring on leasehold tenure. In the particular circumstances of Prince Edward Island, whatever measures—such as wider literacy[21]—would undermine the pillars of the leasehold system (short of endangering public order and property itself) would be attractive to Coles.[22] Likewise, the opposition of proprietary spokesmen like Palmer, Yeo, and Douse to the Free Education Act is significant.

Evidence drawn from a variety of sources indicates that, without basic literacy and within their own environment, with leasehold land tenure as the predominant mode of production, many ordinary Islanders in the middle decades of the 19th century were incompetent to manage their own affairs. The reason is that the unique situation of Prince Edward Island placed an emphasis upon written contracts which was not parallelled anywhere else in British North America. It is this context of mid-19th century Prince Edward Island which is the focus of the present paper and which provides the explanation for the early acceptance by the colony of the principle of free education. In brief, popular access to basic, primary-level education was a means to redress in part the imbalance in power between the landowners who controlled most of the Island, and the working settlers.

The alienation of almost all the land to private owners in 1767 had created special difficulties for the government and inhabitants of the Island. In the first instance, it meant that the local government had virtually no public lands whose sale or lease could generate revenue. Second, the nature of the leasehold system placed enormous importance upon the relationship between the land occupier and the landowner or his agent. This relationship would usually be formalized in a written contract consisting of either *a lease* or *an agreement to lease.* Testimony over many years underlined the absolutely crucial nature of the act of *attorning,* or acknowledging the landlord's title by accepting a lease or an agreement to lease. Once an occupier of land had attorned, the conditions of his holding the land had been set for as long as 999 years.[23] These conditions might include such matters as the farmer's access to timber growing on his property, his access to mill sites, the currency in which the rent was to be paid, and the liability for arrears of rent owing on the land, but almost certainly would not include any provision for compensation for improvements he might make. After the settler had attorned, he could make no effective legal challenge to the title of the landowner (or 'land claimant,' as some Island radicals referred to the proprietors). The decision to attorn was irrevocable.[24]

Thus the typical Island settler would, in the normal course of events, be required to decide upon acceptance of a document with sweeping implications and usually of perpetual duration. To appreciate properly the significance of basic literacy and hence the importance of access to education, it is essential to understand the circumstances in which decisions on attornment were made. In the first place, one must note that the land system had not functioned as had been intended in 1767.[25] It was to have provided for the orderly settlement of the Island under the supervision—the policy-makers appear to have assumed—of a resident landowning class; and the regular payment of quitrents by this neo-feudal class of 'proprietors' was to provide for the government of the Island without cost to the British treasury. These objectives were not realized. Only a small fraction of the number of settlers which the owners were required to establish on the land arrived in the first decade; only a handful of landlords took up residence in a place so lacking in the amenities associated with the existence of a substantial population; the owners fell far in arrears in quitrents, requiring London to intervene with annual grants to save local officials from ignominious penury, or even from perishing; and the officials adopted a predatory attitude towards the landlords. The consequence was a vicious circle of recrimination and suspicion between the landocracy and the local political elite. The landlords suspected the political elite of coveting their property and they feared to invest in the settlement of a place where they found it almost impossible to control or even monitor events to a satisfactory degree; as one authority has noted, in cold terms, the prudent landlord was the speculator who put nothing in and waited for the efforts of others or changes in the marketplace to increase the value of his property, for the landlord willing to invest in development was likely to lose a lot of money.[26] The resident political elite resented deeply the overseas owners, most of whom had never seen and would never see the colony, and, to put it bluntly, considered them to be fair game. The resident lawyers, politicians, promoters, and even some judges sought employment retainers, and powers of attorney from the nonresidents, consistently remitting little while demanding more, and all too often abusing trust.

For the colony as a whole, the result was the opposite of orderly settlement. Immigrants arrived in significant numbers after the end of the Napoleonic wars, but they did so, as a rule, without any assistance from landowners. The settlers were unevenly distributed throughout the colony, and they faced highly variable situations. Some found that they could not obtain a lease either because the proprietor had authorized no one to grant leases or because the authorized person was unavailable or indisposed to provide a lease. Others took up residence on a plot of land without bothering with formalities of any sort. Twenty years of squatting gave a settler freehold title, and many squatters hoped that the years would pass without challenge. For such persons the appearance of a surveyor was anathema. A report by lieutenant governor Sir Charles FitzRoy in 1837 gives some notion of the chaotic conditions of settlement in the colony. Under "Tenure of Settlers," for many townships he wrote "Tenants at Will" or "Mostly Tenants at Will," which meant that the tenant held the land by a verbal agreement which was not legally binding. Some properties were owned by persons or heirs of persons who had once been active on the Island, but had long since ceased being so.[27] An entire township was effectively tied up "in chancery." One large resident proprietor was known for his short leases and high rents—and also his unwillingness to apply sanctions to enforce collection of rent, which meant that he collected little. FitzRoy's "Return," as he termed it, was impressionistic in its explanations, and doubtless imperfect in some details.[28] Yet the overall picture he painted was accurate. Practices varied greatly; policies were often nonexistent, were sometimes based on utter lack of first-hand knowledge of local circumstances, and occasionally were patently irrational. Indeed, rational and systematic estate management could scarcely be said to exist.

Given the conditions of settlement on the Island in the early decades of the 19th century, and the fact that many landlords did not either live on the Island or even retain agents there for years at a stretch, many settlers had to make the decision on attornment after they had already established themselves, cleared some land, and built a dwelling.[29] Thus the stakes were high, and the consequences of being forced to depart were daunting. The settler's security of tenure depended on a minimum of two variables: the validity of the proprietary title and the decision whether to attorn. He had also to worry about false claims by persons purporting to be agents of proprietors who had valid titles. In such a circumstance, a properly authorized agent might appear on the scene at a later date, and naturally would not accept payments made to an imposter as counting against his demands. If the land claimant or the purported agent of the claimant were making an illegitimate claim, then defiance would carry no penalties aside from a period of uncertainty. Acknowledgement of the claim of such a person and payment of claims for rent and arrears of rent would mean loss of whatever money had been paid, with little or no hope of recovery, for he would probably never be seen again; and attornment and payment would carry no benefit (except, possibly, temporary peace of mind) since the claimant's title was not valid.

Acknowledgement of the title of a landlord with a valid title entailed serious consequences (including demands for rent and probably for arrears, and limitations on freedom of action), but at least offered the benefit of relative security of tenure. Defiance of an agent or landlord making a legally valid claim would probably result in, at the least, a costly lawsuit. Beyond the actual lawsuit and its costs lay the possibilities of seizure of assets; imprisonment for non-payment of the debts incurred through the claim for rent and probably arrears of rent and the associated legal costs; and eviction, with the necessity of leaving the land and starting over again elsewhere. These dire consequences were more than a merely theoretical extrapolation based upon assumption of a series of contingent possibilities. A reading of the evidence gathered in 1860–1861 by the royal commission on relations between landlord and tenant indicates that migration of settlers within the Island, that is, moving from one homestead to another one, was a fairly common occurrence.[30] The usual reason for moving revolved around inability of the settler to meet the demands of either the landlord or his agent. A researcher hired by the commissioners reported being told by "several persons" that "at least one half of the new settlers lose their farms, or hold them only until the landlord can get a tenant who will pay a part of the back rent."[31]

It is clear that from time to time ill-founded claims were made on settlers, and that these could be ignored or defied with impunity. But defiance of a legitimate claimant or agent carried an awesome cost. One squatter, Angus Macdougald, petitioning the Assembly from Georgetown Jail in 1844, reported that over his 21 years on the same piece of land six different individuals had demanded rent from him. He had paid none, and it would seem that he suffered no ill consequences until the sixth had him jailed; thus being right five times out of six did not protect him on the sixth occasion, when the person making the demand had the inclination and legal authority to take effective action.[32] The demand for rent, arrears of rent, and acknowledgement constituted, in effect, a test of the settler's nerve and competence, a test with life-changing potential. In this situation, there can be little doubt that widespread plebeian illiteracy was a major factor in the power equation between the land occupier or prospective occupier and the proprietor or his agent.[33] Many farmers simply could not be certain of the nature and contents of the document they were signing, and their only source of information on that score might be the proprietor or his agent.[34] Without even that necessary knowledge, it was difficult, if not impossible, for them to make an informed decision, let alone distinguish between a bluff and a demand with a legal basis. This situation left the door open to caprice and deception, as well as ordinary misunderstanding.

Seeking legal advice does not seem to have been an option which many settlers favoured. Reasons included the cost, the apparent abuses of legal process of which many settlers had heard, and a general distrust of the legal profession. This disinclination to put their affairs in the hands of a profession which was at the very centre of the local elite extended to the Island premier who established the land commission of 1860, Edward Palmer. One of his former clients stated baldly at the public hearings of the commission that "I think I was misled."[35] Another witness declared that the tenantry trusted only one member of the Island bar, Joseph Hensley, a Liberal and one of the two counsel appointed to represent the interests of the tenants before the commission.[36] The haste of the commissioners (two of whom were lawyers) and the barristers present in their professional capacity, including both counsel for the tenantry, to close ranks and repudiate entirely such views may have reinforced rather than allayed popular scepticism about the bar.[37] In some cases, distance from Charlottetown, where virtually all lawyers conducted their practices, was undoubtedly a factor inhibiting tenants from consulting a lawyer.[38]

To use a term borrowed from Canadian labour history, there existed a 'competence gap' or 'differential levels of capacity' between the two sides.[39] From one perspective, this can be illustrated most clearly in cases involving a highly competent and systematic agent. By 1838, the year after FitzRoy's "Return," there was one such agent on the Island: James Horsfield Peters, who had come to the Island from New Brunswick in order to manage the lands recently acquired by his in-laws, the Cunards, who would soon own one-sixth of the land surface of the Island. A brilliant lawyer, a man with a keen eye for economic opportunities, an excellent decision-maker, and endowed with an exceptionally formidable manner, Peters was a unique figure on the Island. He was the ideal estate agent. He was even familiar with the wilderness and the intricacies of the timber trade as a result of his youth in the Miramichi region, and therefore was effective in protecting the timber on the Cunard estate—which infuriated such shipbuilders as the Conservative leader Joseph Pope, who had previously taken his timber wherever he found it.[40] But it was in Peters' dealing with tenants that he became a legendary figure. He travelled the full extent of his in-laws' sprawling estate, which included property from one end of the Island to the other. In the course of doing so he was often bringing order to tenurial relationships on properties which previous owners had neglected for many years. He insisted that all occupiers of Cunard property take leases, and also that all who were owing back rent pay a portion. He would, he said in defending his record publicly, forgive a portion of arrears, but in no instance the entire amount.[41] In cases where there was honest doubt as to the boundaries or the acreages of farms he appears to have been willing to order surveys to resolve the problems.[42] But those who simply refused to pay rent to him, or were dragging their feet, did so at their peril. It was he who had Angus Macdougald placed in Georgetown Jail and over the years, on other occasions as well, he proved willing to make examples of those who crossed him.[43] One witness before the land commission of 1860 recalled that he had "kept clear [of the agent], but paid dearly for so doing. Peters sent and seized my vessel which was on the stocks, and compelled me to take a lease."[44] Peters' operating methods allowed little or no room for negotiation or compromise; in effect, his policies were set in stone, and the settlers had to conform. His systematic and relentless approach, conveyed in a style which was peremptory, if not dictatorial, provoked many protests, and made him the prime symbol of proprietary exaction.[45] A Gaelic bard presented him as the embodiment of what was wrong with Prince Edward Island's version of life in the New World, in his conclusion to *Complaint about America:*

We left there
and came out here
thinking we would receive consideration,
and that the rent would not be so exacting.
But Peters is oppressing us,
and, if he doesn't die,
we must leave this place
and Cunnard [sic], himself a beast.
A pity Peters wouldn't change
and give some thought to death;
if the good one doesn't have mercy on him
his deeds will cost him dearly,
oppressing the poor
and sending the constables after them.
He will ultimately receive retribution...[46]

According to one source, Peters had told "a poor creature that he must find money if he raked the ashes of Hell for it."[47]

Yet there is another perspective on the relationship between the tenantry and the landocracy or its servants, purported or real, which casts Peters, with his orderly, no-nonsense ways, in a more favourable light. There is no known surviving record of anyone complaining that Peters refused to give a lease or took money and failed to produce a lease, promising to do so at some time in the future. The tenant dealing with Peters at least received a written lease which, providing its obligations were met, offered security of tenure. Settlers confronted with less competent, less systematic, or less scrupulous agents—that is, with most, if not all, other agents—faced a much less predictable, and therefore less manageable, situation.

The record of an inquiry by a special committee of the House of Assembly in 1843 presents a strong contrast between the practices of Peters and those of H.D. Morpeth, agent for David and Robert Stewart of London. One Colin McPhail, residing on Lot 32, was asked by what authority he had settled on his land. He replied that Morpeth and another agent had told him he might do so. The questioning continued:

> Have you any written document from them to settle? No. I signed a kind of note of hand last summer twelve months, to Mr. Morpeth, to pay rent. He promised, a fortnight afterwards, to give me a lease and to run [survey] the land. Have you applied to him since for a lease? Yes; but did not get it. What reason did he assign for withholding the lease? He would make different excuses every time we would ask him. This paper we signed for him is a kind of agreement to attorn.... Do you find the want of a lease of any disadvantage to you?—does it discourage you to go on clearing? To be sure it must.... What terms were specified in the document you signed? Mr. Morpeth read it to me; I did not read it, not being very good at reading writing.[48]

Another witness, who "was himself a party to the attornment,... [also] knew the terms only from his [Morpeth's] reading."[49] In cases where the settlers lacked basic literacy, the decision on attornment, fraught with enormous significance, was consequently made in dangerous ignorance. FitzRoy reported in 1837 that some settlers had been the victims of one or another sort of deception; and, linked to this, he said, "many of the settlers are extremely ignorant men."[50] Testimony before a committee of the Assembly in 1840 included a claim by one tenant that for years he had been paying rent on 150 acres rather than the 102 actually contained in his farm. He stated that he had been unable to get the owner to authorize a survey, and only realized the discrepancy when he arranged for performance of the work himself.[51] His attorneys indicated in subsequent testimony that the law had provided no redress, and one cited a case in which another tenant was liable to pay rent on 200 acres although he held only 130.[52] Aside from ignorance in the usual sense, many settlers did not have competence in the English language. Farmers of Highland Scottish origin were probably at a disability in this respect at least as great as Acadians. With reference to Gaelic-speaking Scots, in 1841 Samuel Cunard testified before a select committee of the British House of Commons that "I know whole settlements where they cannot speak English among them."[53]

Tenants who testified before the royal commission on the land question in 1860 sometimes expressed or even emphasized their own sense of relative disadvantage. The former client of Premier Palmer who stated that his lawyer had "misled" him also claimed that "they"—apparently meaning both Palmer and Peters, the lawyer for the other party (the Cunard estate)—"took advantage of my ignorance."[54] Another witness recalled how, in 1831, influenced by the presence of the purported proprietor, David Stewart, who was making a once-in-a-lifetime trip to the Island, the presence of lawyers, and the liberal dispensation of rum, he and others had attorned. In his words, "I thought Mr. Stewart had a title."[55] Yet a witness from the same area also observed that one squatter who had boycotted the meeting with Stewart did not attorn, "and he has been a freeholder ever since."[56] The New Brunswick lawyer Samuel R. Thomson, who had been retained on behalf of the Island tenantry, stated that many of his clients

> do not enjoy the advantage of a good education, and so, to a great extent, would be disqualified from obtaining necessary information. These may, it is true, possess an abstract right to enter into the public offices of this Colony for the purpose of procuring necessary papers, but, even supposing they had the right, they would scarcely have known into which offices to have gone to obtain necessary documents. But the case was the opposite with the clients of the Counsel on the opposite side [the proprietors]. My learned friend on that side...was assisted by men who were fully posted up in these matters, and knew where to put their hands on any document which would favour their own cause and be adverse to the cause of our clients.[57]

The need to redress this 'competence gap' between tenant and landlord gave a special urgency to the drive for educational reform in Prince Edward Island. In no other colony was the ordinary resident virtually certain to be confronted by a similar situation, in which he had to decide upon signing an irrevocable contract with such sweeping consequences. A farmer gaining access to public lands in Nova Scotia or New Brunswick, a lumberer committing himself to a season in the woods, a fisherman going out to exploit a common resource after incurring a debt for supplies—none of these encountered even an approximate parallel to the Island settler who was being told that he must attorn. Access to a basic education could not provide any absolute protection, but it could reduce the 'competence gap' which was so advantageous to the landlord. The impact of that reduction in the 'competence gap' would be felt as soon as the younger members of a settler's family (assuming there were children) were sufficiently literate to read accurately a lease or an agreement to lease.

In a colony whose major natural resource, namely, its topsoil, had been alienated by the crown in 1767, it was certain that private landholders would be called upon to make major contributions to the Island treasury for any significant new expenditures; there was no alternative. Thus the landlords opposed new programmes for improvement because of the probable costs to themselves. As a consequence such proposals as 'free education'—education paid for entirely by the colonial treasury—became central points of contention between Reformers and proprietors, with the latter petitioning London against confirmation.[58] At one level, there was an irony to the proprietors' opposition to the Free Education Act, for their extraction of much of the scarce cash in the countryside in the form of rent had played a major part in creating the need for such a measure. In fact, the proprietors tended to suspect every such proposal as part of a hidden agenda to undermine the profitability of their Island estates. It is not surprising that they would harbour such suspicions, for George Coles' Liberals let it be known that, given the unacceptability to the British of compulsory measures to dispossess the landlords, they would use taxation as a means to persuade landlords to sell.[59]

The Free Education Act of 1852 was part of a comprehensive reform programme of the Liberals. Indeed, of all the provincial sets of Reformers in the Atlantic colonies who came to power with responsible government between 1848 and 1855, the Coles government had the most far-reaching agenda. More than anywhere else, again primarily because of the land question, responsible government was a means to a broader end, rather than an end in itself. In 1853 the Island Liberals extended the franchise to make it almost universal for adult males, and enacted legislation enabling the local government to make large-scale purchases of land from consenting proprietors for resale to its occupiers. Other reforms concerning the land question were either negated or diluted by the British government. But the local government was able to proceed with educational reform without hindrance from Downing Street.

The establishment of free education became a mark of epochal change on Prince Edward Island. It represented 'progress' in the 19th century sense of opening opportunities to a broad segment of the population. It was also the beginning of a remarkable 25-year period in the development of public education. In the quarter-century framed by passage of the Free Education Act and the Public Schools Act of 1877, the local government established a system of tuition-free public education, made attendance in the public school system compulsory, and entrenched the non-sectarian principle. Beyond the common schools, the Island government established a normal school, converted a public academy into a college, and rejuvenated the system of administration and inspection. Those 25 years witnessed, albeit with setbacks along the way, the transformation from an underdeveloped educational system, with an unpredictable impact on individual districts of the colony, to an early modern system which virtually guaranteed a minimum level of opportunity and quality to each district.

In the specific environment of the colony, free education also contributed to a change in the balance of power between the landocracy and the common settlers. Both sides, proprietors and their opponents, judged all reform measures, including responsible government and a wider franchise, according to their impact on the land question. When Edward Palmer argued against extending the elective franchise in 1853, he did so explicitly in class terms:

> Hon. Mr. Palmer took his stand against the Bill on the ground that it will give a political ascendancy to men destitute of property over those who possessed it. He argued that there could be no sympathy, on many probable occasions, on the part of the former with the latter—of the unpropertied with the propertied classes.[60]

In the same speech, Palmer chose the raising of funds for the free education system as his example of how the unpropertied could use the franchise to victimize the propertied. That sort of perspective, with its mirror image in the Reform camp, gave exceptional urgency to the Island's movement for free education, and ensured that district school education would have high priority on the agenda of Island Reformers. After passage of the Free Education Act, the progressive initiative became a source of local pride, with permanent and committed advocates.[61] For the next generation, education would always be a major concern of some prestigious and influential persons in public life.

There were undoubtedly other important factors in explaining the attention education commanded in the colony. It was more than coincidence that most prominent individuals involved directly in education, like Alexander Anderson, long-time principal of Prince of Wales College and later superintendent of education for the province,[62] and Stark and William McPhail,[63] crusading school visitors, were Scots. When the local government sought to remedy the lack of professional training and common methods of education on the part of teachers by establishing a normal school in Charlottetown in 1856, it was staffed with a Scottish master recommended by Stark and also from Stow's Normal Seminary. There was unquestionably a Scottish cultural hegemony on the Island in matters of education, especially in terms of key personnel.[64] But if an explanation for the Island's pre-eminence in establishing free education at the district level is sought, the place to begin is the land question. It was the central role of the lease, the nexus between landlord and tenant, which made access to primary education a matter of pressing urgency for most Island households. Prince Edward Island was not the only colony with leasehold tenure, and undoubtedly it was not the only one in which there was popular distrust of lawyers; but the combination of leasehold as the predominant form of land tenure, the lack of faith in the legal profession, and the chaotic way in which settlement had proceeded combined to create a uniquely urgent need for literacy. It was a necessary means of self-help, and at the core of the Island's 'age of reform.'

Notes

1 *Statutes of Prince Edward Island,* 15 Vic., c. 13. Its official name was "An Act for the Encouragement of Education, and to raise Funds for that purpose, by imposing an additional Assessment on Land in this Island, and on Real Estate in Charlottetown and Common, and Georgetown and Common."

2 See summary report of House of Assembly debates for 10 February 1852 in *Royal Gazette* (Charlottetown), 23 February 1852.

3 Prince Edward Island, Assembly, *Journal,* 1855, appendix M, p. 62.

4 For contemporary attitudes and struggles in Scotland, with which Stark was intimately familiar, see T.C. Smout, *A Century of the Scottish People 1830–1950* (London, 1986), pp. 209–16.

5 See in particular Philip Corrigan and Bruce Curtis, "Education, Inspection and State Formation: A Preliminary Statement," *Historical Papers* (1985), p. 168; and Bruce Curtis, *Building the Educational State: Canada West, 1836–1871* (London, Ont., 1988), pp. 366–82.

6 The differing attitudes among conservatives to the spread of popular education (was it dangerous to property or was it a means of social control?) are evident in Judith Fingard, "Attitudes toward the Education of the Poor in Colonial Halifax," *Acadiensis,* II, 2 (Spring 1973), pp. 15–42, particularly pp. 19, 30, 33, 39, 42. The contrasting perspectives might be characterized as reactionary versus enlightened conservative.

7 For a summary of the rise and decline of the Escheat movement, see Ian Ross Robertson, "Highlanders, Irishmen, and the Land Question in Nineteenth-century Prince Edward Island," in L.M. Cullen and T.C. Smout, eds., *Comparative Aspects of Scottish and Irish Economic and Social History 1600–1900* (Edinburgh, [1977]), pp. 229–31.

8 Harry Baglole, "William Cooper of Sailor's Hope," *The Island Magazine,* no. 7 (Fall–Winter 1979), pp. 8–9; Nicolas de Jong, "John MacKintosh," *Dictionary of Canadian Biography,* vol. XI (Toronto, 1982), p. 567; information on LeLacheur from the files of the *Dictionary of Canadian Biography,* courtesy of Mr. Robert Wuetherick, editor, on 15 February 1990.

9 Baglole, "William Cooper of Sailor's Hope," p. 7.

10 This term was coined by Baglole in his part of the book he co-authored with David Weale, *The Island and Confederation: The End of an Era* (Summerside, P.E.I., 1973), p. 59; also see Baglole's authoritative "William Cooper," *Dictionary of Canadian Biography,* vol. IX (Toronto, 1976), pp. 155–8.

11 See P.E.I., Assembly, *Journal,* 1852, pp. 57, 118.

12 *Royal Gazette,* 23 February 1852.

13 Summary report of Assembly debates for 17 February 1852 in *Royal Gazette,* 23 February 1852.

14 Summary report of Assembly debates for 18 February 1852 in *Royal Gazette,* 29 March 1852.

15 In making these calculations, I have relied entirely upon the censuses of 1848 and 1855, as published in P.E.I., Assembly, *Journal,* 1849, app. Y, and 1856, app. D, and I have obtained the totals of non-natives by adding together the number of non-natives under each category of non-Prince Edward Island birthplace (England, Scotland, Ireland, 'British Colonies,' 'Other Countries'). This method is different from that employed by Andrew Hill Clark, *Three Centuries and the Island: A Historical Geography of Settlement and Agriculture in Prince Edward Island, Canada* (Toronto, 1959), p. 121, Table V in analyzing the census of 1848. He apparently determined the number of non-natives by subtracting the number of natives from the total number of inhabitants. This is problematic because, by inference, it assigns all those listed under 'Country not stated' to the non-native category, thus increasing artificially the number and the proportion of non-natives; counting as non-native only those for whom non-Island birthplaces had actually been reported is surely a safer procedure. But in addition Clark's lumping together of the non-native and the 'Country not stated' numbers obscures a difficulty facing the researcher who attempts to compare data for 1848 and 1855: in that seven-year interval the number listed under 'Country not stated' rose 2,305.8 per cent, from 52 to 1,251. The net result of the combination of Clark's method with this problem in reporting is to understate the decline in non-natives over the seven-year period. Using his method, the decline in absolute numbers would be 292 (from 18,819 to 18,527) instead of 1,161; the percentage decline would be 1.6 per cent instead of 6.3 per cent; and the decrease in proportion of the population as a whole would be 4.1 per cent (30 minus 25.9) instead of 5.2 per cent (29.4 minus 24.2). Clark did not include calculations for 1855 in his Table V, and thus my comments on the results of applying his method for 1848 to the 1855 census represent my extrapolation.

16 P.E.I., Assembly, *Journal,* 1853, app. Z, p. 178.

17 The school visitors' reports, especially those of MacNeill, visitor for the entire Island from 1837 to 1847, are the best source concerning the pre-1852 situation. They were usually published in the *Journal* of the House of Assembly.

18 P.E.I., Assembly, *Journal,* 1858, app. T, p. 1.

19 See S.N. Robertson, "The Public School System," in D.A. MacKinnon and A.B. Warburton, eds., *Past and Present of Prince Edward Island...* (Charlottetown, [1906]), pp. 362a–390a; John C. Macmillan, *The History of the Catholic Church in Prince Edward Island from 1835 till 1891* (Quebec, 1913); A.H. MacKay, "History of Education in Nova Scotia and Prince Edward Island", in Adam Shortt and A.G. Doughty, eds., *Canada and Its Provinces,* vol. XIV (Toronto, 1914), pp. 511–42; Heber R. Matthews, "Education in Prince Edward Island," M.A. thesis, Mount Allison University, 1938; Derrill Ignatius McGuigan, "The Historical Antecedents of the Free School Act and the Public Schools Act of Prince Edward Island," Ph.D. thesis, University of Ottawa, 1956; Willard Brehaut, "Some Landmarks in Prince Edward Island's Educational History," paper delivered before Canadian Association of Professors of Education, Charlottetown, 1964; Sister Mary Olga McKenna, "The Impact of Cultural Forces on Commitment to Education in the Province of Prince Edward Island," Ph.D. thesis, Boston College, 1964, and "The History of Higher Education in the Province of Prince Edward Island," Canadian Catholic Historical Association *Study Sessions* (1971), pp. 19–49; Georges Arsenault, *L'Education chez les Acadiens de l'Ile-du-Prince Edouard 1720–1980 ou La survivance Acadienne à l'Ile-du-Prince-Edouard* (Summerside, 1982); G. Edward MacDonald, "'And Christ Dwelt in the Heart of His House': A History of St. Dunstan's University 1855–1955," Ph.D. thesis, Queen's University, 1984, and *The History of St. Dunstan's University, 1855–1956* (Charlottetown, 1989). There has also been an emphasis on institutions identified with Roman Catholicism, such as St. Dunstan's College, rather than public institutions. Pillars of the public system, such as the Central Academy (1836–1860), the Normal School (1857–1879), and Prince of Wales College (1860–1969), which absorbed the Central Academy in 1860 and the Normal School in 1879, await scholarly examination.

20 1877 was the year the government led by Louis Henry Davies passed the Public Schools Act, which entrenched the non-sectarian principle in the public school system, made attendance compulsory, provided for appointment of a well-paid superintendent of education, improved the status and training of teachers, reconstituted and secularized the Board of Education, clarified and strengthened the powers of local trustees, and completely reorganized the schools in Charlottetown, where the public system had been breaking down.

21 The definition of literacy for the purposes of this article is the same as that in *The Concise Oxford Dictionary,* 7th edition (1982), p. 588: "ability to read and write." There are no statistics on literacy in colonial Prince Edward Island, but first-hand observers who commented on this matter indicated that a large proportion of the population was illiterate. In 1844 school visitor MacNeill reported that he had attempted to determine the number of illiterates in each settlement, but found it too tedious and too large an undertaking. (P.E.I., Assembly, *Journal,* 1844, app. H, p. 39.) The prevalence of illiteracy, without doubt, varied greatly from district to district.

22 This interpretation is developed in Ian Ross Robertson, "George Coles," *Dictionary of Canadian Biography,* vol. X (Toronto, 1972), pp. 183–4, 187. According to Coles' own account, the Free Education Act also owed something to a visit he had made in 1848 to Ohio, where he had seen first-hand the benefits of state-paid education; see Robert Blake Irving, Reporter, *Normal School Soirée: Report of the Speeches and Proceedings at the Inauguration of the Normal School* (Charlottetown, 1856), p. 28.

23 Most leases were for terms of 999 years, and in 1838 Robert Hodgson, the attorney general, testified before the Durham commission that "long leases...is a technical term in the Island, meaning leases of 999 years." *Minutes of Evidence Taken under the Direction of a General Commission of Enquiry, for Crown Lands and Emigration, Appointed on the 21st June 1838, by His Excellency the Right Honorable Earl of Durham, High Commissioner, and Governor General of Her Majesty's Colonies in North America* (Quebec, 1839), Prince Edward Island section, p. 7. By implication, anything other than these leases, sometimes referred to as "perpetual," might, in a Prince Edward Island context, be considered "short leases."

24 In many years of research on the land question, the present writer has never encountered evidence of legal annulment of a lease resulting from alleged misrepresentation of its contents; yet allegations of such conduct by landlords and agents were frequent.

25 See J.M. Bumsted, *Land, Settlement, and Politics on Eighteenth-Century Prince Edward Island* (Kingston and Montreal, 1987).

26 J.M. Bumsted, "Sir James Montgomery and Prince Edward Island, 1767–1803," *Acadiensis,* VII, 2 (Spring 1978), p. 102.

27 See, for example, H.T. Holman, "John Cambridge," *Dictionary of Canadian Biography,* vol. VI (Toronto, 1987), pp. 107–10, and J.M. Bumsted, "John Hill," *ibid.,* vol. VII (Toronto, 1988), pp. 406–8.

28 See FitzRoy, "Return of Township Lands in Prince Edward Island, shewing their Extent, population, (from the Census of 1833), Names of the Principal Proprietors, the general Tenure of the Settlers, and the Causes which have tended to retard their improvement," in Colonial Office (CO) 226/54, pp. 267–9.

29 The disorderly, essentially unregulated system of settlement, and the resultant sequence of settlement preceding the establishing of terms distinguished the situation on the Island from that of pioneering New France, where leasehold also prevailed. One of the advantages of the seigneurial system which historians occasionally cite is the orderly process of settlement. The arrangements having been made at the start, the tenant in New France did not face the dilemma which many Island settlers did—and therefore the same incentive for literacy did not exist. Had the process of settlement on the Island proceeded in the orderly way policy-makers had intended in 1767, the situation there would also have been different.

30 See J.D. Gordon and D. Laird, eds., *Abstract of the Proceedings before the Land Commissioners' Court, Held During the Summer of 1860, to Inquire into the Differences Relative to the Rights of Landowners and Tenants in Prince Edward Island* (Charlottetown, 1862) (hereafter abbreviated to *Abstract...*); and P.E.I., Assembly, *Journal,* 1863, app. A. All the public hearings of the commission were held in 1860, but George Wightman, a researcher the commissioners hired, continued to submit information until 20 June 1861. Since historical causation was an integral part of the mandate of the commission, testimony before it (and the evidence gathered by Wightman) stretched decades back into the history of the land question.

31 See P.E.I., Assembly, *Journal,* 1863, app. A. For a concrete example, see the testimony by William S. McNeill, who had acquired his rented farm by paying the back rent owed by the original settler, in P.S. Macgowan, ed., *Report of the Proceedings before the Commissioners Appointed under the Provisions of "The Land Purchase Act, 1875"* (Charlottetown, [1876]), pp. 376–7.

32 See P.E.I., Assembly, *Journal,* 1844, pp. 63–4.

33 For an example of the crippling effect of illiteracy on a settler's self-confidence and hence on his effectiveness in negotiating with a landlord, see the testimony of Michael Lacey in Ian Ross Robertson, ed., *The Prince Edward Island Land Commission of 1860* (Fredericton, 1988), p. 115. This volume is an abridgement of Gordon and Laird, eds., *Abstract....* Because of its greater accessibility, the abridged version will be cited when possible; page references to the original will indicate whether the page occurs in the Proceedings or the Report, since the two are not numbered consecutively.

34 For an example of such a case, see the testimony of Patrick Dogherty in Robertson, ed., *The Prince Edward Island Land Commission of 1860,* pp. 112–3.

35 See testimony of Archibald Campbell in *ibid.,* p. 134.

36 See testimony of Robert Gordon in *ibid.,* p. 86.

37 See the cross-examination of Edward Palmer's former client by his brother, Charles Palmer, and by Hensley, in *ibid.,* pp. 134–5; and comments by Samuel R. Thomson and Joseph Howe on p. 135. Under pressure from all these, it is hardly surprising that the witness backed away from the imputation of actual wrongdoing by Edward Palmer. Also see the comment by Hensley on p. 86.

38 A good example of the convergence of some of these factors is the testimony of Thomas Hockin in *ibid.,* p. 80. Hockin stated that it cost 30s. to retain a lawyer. He also lived on Lot 3, which meant that he was at least 80 miles from the capital.

39 Concerning the concept of a 'competence gap' or 'title to authority by capacity,' see H.C. Pentland, "The Canadian Industrial Relations System: Some Formative Factors," *Labour/Le Travailleur,* IV (1979), p. 22; and H.C. Pentland, "The Western Canadian Labour Movement, 1897–1919," *Canadian Journal of Political and Social Theory,* II, 3 (Spring–Summer 1979), pp. 62, 76. In his writings, Pentland argued that this gap was not stationary, and varied greatly in different times and places in Canadian history.

40 See the observations of Sir George Francis Seymour, an absentee proprietor making his first visit to the colony, in Seymour of Ragley Papers, CR114A / 565, Miscellaneous Lot 13 Papers, "Memo Prince Edwd Island 1840," and CR114A/380, Tour Journal, 29 August 1840, Warwick County Record Office, Warwick, England.

41 See testimony of Peters in P.E.I., Assembly, *Journal,* 1840, app. P, p. 127. Also see Peters in summary report of Legislative Council debates for 13 April 1843 in *Royal Gazette,* 2 May 1843; and Peters to Thomas Heath Haviland Sr., 17 July 1843, in CO 226/65, p. 217.

42 See testimony of John Macgowan and Lawrence W. Gall in P.E.I., Assembly, *Journal,* 1843, app. P, pp. 126–8.

43 In 1843 Peters stated that "if in some cases, an apparent severity was exercised, it arose not from a disposition to be severe, but because in these instances, it was deemed necessary for the sake of example." (Summary report of Legislative Council debates for 13 April 1843 in *Royal Gazette,* 2 May 1843.)

44 See testimony of "Mr. Clements" in Robertson, ed., *The Prince Edward Island Land Commission of 1860,* pp. 135–6.

45 See Ian Ross Robertson, "James Horsfield Peters," *Dictionary of Canadian Biography,* vol. XII (Toronto, 1990), pp. 838–42. His quarrel with one tenant, which apparently originated in a boundary dispute between the Cunard estate and a piece of freehold land which the tenant owned (in addition to leasing a farm on Cunard land), attained vendetta-like proportions; see the entry on John Gordon Sr. in the Glossary of Names in Robertson, ed., *The Prince Edward Island Land Commission of 1860,* pp. 210–1. He could also be ruthless with members of the local elite. Note, in particular, proprietor P.D. Stewart's account of his treatment by Peters, who evidently believed him to have been less than candid in disclosing his means to pay a debt to the Cunards, in CO 226/74, pp. 317–408. Also see Public Archives of Prince Edward Island, RG 6, Supreme Court, Case Papers, Cunard & others vs. P.D. Stewart, 28 August 1845.

46 As translated in Margaret MacDonell, *The Emigrant Experience: Songs of Highland Emigrants in North America* (Toronto, 1982), pp. 123, 125. Peters, who later served 43 years as a judge, evidently provoked thoughts of death, retribution, and good and evil in the ultimate sense. In Sir Andrew Macphail's *The Master's Wife* (Montreal, 1939), his judgemental authority is compared with the judgement of God (p. 72).

47 P.D. Stewart to Peters, 16 June 1847, in CO 226/74, p. 362; also see Stewart to Peters, 12 May 1846, in CO 226/74, p. 357. Peters may have had a liking for such imagery, as one of the inscriptions on the monument to him in St. Peters Cemetery, Charlottetown contains the following, apparently directed towards his wife, who had predeceased him: "the gates of hell touch thee not." If the encounter between the landowner's interest and the settler in this period is viewed as being, to a degree, inherently confrontational and as involving a certain attempt on the part of the former to overawe the latter, as a means of bringing him to terms, it may be worth noting that Peters had an additional advantage, beyond his abilities, experience, and training: he was also solicitor general of the Island, a fact which can only have assisted in the task of intimidation.

48 P.E.I., Assembly, *Journal,* 1843, app. P, p. 134. Morpeth's own testimony before the committee smacked of ambiguity, if not evasion; see p. 132.

49 See testimony of Hugh Maclean in P.E.I., Assembly, *Journal,* 1843, app. P, p. 134.

50 FitzRoy, "To the Proprietors of Prince Edward Island. Circular" (accompanying his "Return"), 3 October 1837, CO 226/54, p. 266.

51 See testimony of James Douglas in P.E.I., Assembly, *Journal,* 1840, app. P, p. 121.

52 See testimony of Charles Binns and Charles Young in P.E.I., Assembly, *Journal.* 1840, app. P, pp. 125–6.

53 See "Extract from the Second Report from the Select Committee of the House of Commons appointed to inquire into the condition of the Islands and Highlands of Scotland, and into the practicability of affording the people relief by means of Emigration—24th May, 1841," *Colonial Herald* (Charlottetown), 30 April 1842.

54 See Robertson, ed., *The Prince Edward Island Land Commission of 1860,* p. 134. Of course the fear of collusion among lawyers engaged by contending parties in litigation, whether well-founded or not, reflected the popular lack of faith in the legal profession as a defence against the claims of landlords. For another example of tenants complaining that when they obtained their leases, "advantage was taken" of their ignorance, see *ibid.,* p. 50.

55 Testimony of Donald Mclnnis in *ibid.,* p. 93; in addition, see p. 92. There is also an undertone of distrust of lawyers in Mclnnis' testimony.

56 See testimony of Cornelius Howatt in *ibid.,* p. 92.

57 See *ibid.*, pp. 177–8.

58 See CO 226/80, pp. 587–8, 634–5.

59 See, *e.g.,* Coles' statement, made in 1855, cited in Gordon and Laird, eds., *Abstract....* Proceedings, p. 290.

60 Summary report of Assembly debates for 25 February 1853 in *Royal Gazette,* 7 March 1853.

61 In 1863, when the Conservatives, with a strong representation of landlords and agents, were returned to a second consecutive term in office, they would alter the Education Act so as to make the local districts responsible for a significant proportion of teachers' salaries. But the principle of 'free education' was restored by the Liberals in 1867. The Tories' modification of the system had failed, as even they admitted. See Ian Ross Robertson, "Political Realignment in Pre-Confederation Prince Edward Island, 1863–1870," *Acadiensis,* XV, 1 (Autumn 1985), pp. 44–5.

62 Regarding Anderson, Sir Andrew Macphail declared that "Of the many teachers I have since known he was the best.... He treated the crude boys as if they were grave young gentlemen determined to become scholars and win by their scholarship any highest place in the world." (Macphail, *The Master's Wife,* pp. 177–8). In 1888 McGill University conferred an honorary doctorate on Anderson.

63 See Ian Ross Robertson, "William McPhail," *Dictionary of Canadian Biography,* vol. XIII (forthcoming). McPhail would be especially vocal in the 1870s in directing attention to the decaying state of public education in Charlottetown. He was the father of Andrew Macphail, and 'the master' (*i.e.,* schoolmaster) of Andrew's semi-autobiographical memoir, *The Master's Wife.* As an adult, Andrew adopted a different spelling of his family name, substituting *Macp* for *McP;* William retained the older version.

64 This Scottish cultural hegemony was also evident in the Roman Catholic College, St. Dunstan's; see Robertson, "Highlanders, Irishmen, and the Land Question in Nineteenth-century Prince Edward Island," p. 235 and n. 52 on p. 240.

The Most Restrictive Franchise in British North America?

A Case Study

GAIL CAMPBELL

The exercise of the franchise is fundamental to the concept of representative government, but ideas about who should be allowed to vote have changed significantly over time.[1] Mature political democracies are characterized by a franchise that is private and universally accessible. During the nineteenth century, virtually every Western democracy moved to extend the franchise; in most countries, the adoption of the secret ballot either accompanied or preceded franchise reform. Such suffrage innovations set the stage for the emergence of mass politics and the organization of mass-based political parties. The decision to extend the vote was sometimes a response to pressures from below, but just as often the decision came as a result of contests for influence among competing elites. The history of the franchise is complex and central to an understanding of the history of the movement towards formal democracy in the West.[2]

To understand the development and nature of representative government in Canada, it is therefore necessary to examine the process followed in selecting representatives in the individual colonies prior to Confederation. In British North America, the basic assumption, unchallenged until the mid-nineteenth century, was that a man derived his right to vote from the ownership of property. After 1850 the movement for franchise reform brought extension of the suffrage. The colonial politicians responsible for such reform nonetheless remained convinced that the privilege of voting should be reserved to those men whose independence and tangible investment in their society could be demonstrated by their assessment for taxes.[3] Thus, the principle underlying the old property qualification was maintained. During the pre-Confederation period Britain's North American colonies operated under a variety of franchise laws, some more restrictive than others; even after Confederation these provincial laws continued to hold sway, and it was not until 1885 that the dominion government saw fit to enact the first comprehensive federal franchise law.

In his seminal monograph, published in 1969, John Garner provided a meticulous overview of the development of the franchise in British North America during the pre-Confederation period. He concluded that, despite significant differences in individual franchise laws, "no numerous and important segment of the [adult male] population" was excluded from the exercise of the franchise in any of the six colonies he examined.[4] Although the laws might differ significantly from colony

Gail Campbell, "The Most Restrictive Franchise in British North America? A Case Study," *Canadian Historical Review* 71, 2 (June 1990): 159–88. Reprinted by permission of University of Toronto Press.

to colony, in practice those laws worked in similar ways. In some colonies, such as the Canadas and Prince Edward Island, virtually all occupiers of land were legally entitled to vote, while in New Brunswick, the colony with the most restrictive franchise legislation, laws were regularly ignored by local officials and, in practice, the franchise was extended to all occupiers of land. Garner's conclusions concerning the breadth of the franchise, while based largely on aggregate election results, paralleled the findings of American historians who also argued that, despite restrictive franchise laws, a relatively broad male suffrage existed throughout the colonial period. Some American analysts agreed with J.R. Pole's assessment that "the suffrage was often exercised in fact by persons to whom it did not belong as a right under the law."[5] Others provided quite a different explanation for the broad suffrage, claiming that the majority of adult males were legally eligible to vote.[6]

American researchers have, however, begun to revise such interpretations. A careful analysis of election statistics for individual communities in each of the thirteen colonies suggests that the suffrage in colonial America, while fairly extensive, was by no means universal.[7] Similarly, two recent unpublished studies of the franchise in the Canadas in the pre-Confederation period have called Garner's assumptions about British North America into question.[8] Both studies are based on analysis of individual-level voting results and focus mainly on voter turnout. Turnout can, of course, be affected by a variety of factors, ranging from the degree of interest in the issues raised during the campaign to concrete obstacles, such as weather or distance, that might prevent voters from getting to the polls. Unlike voter turnout in the United States, which reached heights in the early nineteenth century that have not since been matched, turnout in British North America during the nineteenth century was not much higher than it is today.[9] But while low turnout does not by itself indicate a narrow franchise, the findings of these two researchers, paralleling as they do the conclusions of American researchers, suggest the need for a re-evaluation of previous assumptions concerning the universality of the franchise in British North America.

Franchise qualifications established by colonial administrations had been imported from England. Initially such qualifications had resulted in a broad franchise in colonies where land was still cheap and abundant. Fernand Ouellet has estimated that in Lower Canada, for example, at least one out of every eight inhabitants was qualified to vote.[10] Even though an increasing shortage of farm land made the franchise more restrictive as time went on, 83.8 per cent of the heads of families in Orléans voted in the election of 1834.[11] Ouellet's research, based on analysis of available poll books as well as aggregate election results, confirms Garner's conclusions concerning the near universality of the franchise in Lower Canada. Neither Ouellet nor Garner, however, argues that the men who voted in Lower Canada were not legally eligible.

The Lower Canadian experience, moreover, may have been quite different from that of colonists in other provinces, where the franchise laws were more restrictive. In 1791 the New Brunswick legislature had passed the most restrictive franchise law in British North America. The act had come into force four years later, having finally received imperial confirmation. Yet, Garner argues, the New Brunswick Assembly made no move to enforce suffrage restrictions and thus a class of *de facto* voters became a "feature of the New Brunswick franchise." By the 1840s "the convention had become firmly established that occupants of the proper quantity of landed property were eligible to vote, the law notwithstanding." The late 1840s saw a new influx of immigrants, the famine Irish. According to Garner, most of these "pauper Irish," along with substantial numbers of leaseholders and squatters, as occupiers of land, "exercised the franchise on sufferance and by convention."[12]

Colonial New Brunswick, with its extraordinarily restrictive franchise, provides the ideal setting for a case study. If Garner was correct in his assessment of the New Brunswick case, it seems likely that the franchise would have been at least as broad in other colonies which had less stringent qualifications for voters. A microstudy of a specific group of voting-aged males, who can be traced over a series of elections, will allow for a more accurate analysis of the breadth of the mid-nineteenth-century New Brunswick franchise and the extent of *de facto* voting. Conclusions concerning the breadth of the franchise have generally been based on an analysis of the proportion of voting-aged males who actually exercised the franchise and the extent to which the proportion voting varies over time. This approach has serious limitations, however. By developing voting profiles of a specific cohort of voting-aged males followed over a series of elections, some of the limitations inherent in the old approach can be eliminated and a new dimension can be added to the analysis. When the breadth of the franchise is measured as the proportion of voting-aged males who manage to achieve the vote over the course of a series of elections, the problem of equating eligibility, or access, with turnout is eliminated. Moreover, on the basis of such analysis, conclusions can be drawn about whether or not a man with specific demographic characteristics might reasonably expect to achieve the franchise in the course of a decade.

The richness of the source material for Albert County has provided the opportunity for just such a detailed case study. The population base for the study included all those men, twenty-one years of age and older, who were recorded as residents of the county in the 1851 manuscript census (1370 men in all). The survival of poll books for five of the six elections held between 1845 and 1858 (1846, 1850, 1851, 1854, and 1856) made it possible to determine which men actually voted during the period. Individual voter profiles were developed using the information contained in the poll books, which include each voter's name, his parish of residence, his parish of freehold, the names of the candidates for whom he voted, any objection registered against his vote, and a record of whether he was required to take an oath attesting to his eligibility under the law. Because Albert was one of the five counties for which voters' registers had been prepared prior to the 1857 election, in compliance with the 1855 Election Act, the new franchise law became operative in the county in that election. Therefore, the vote itself was secret, but a record of who voted in 1857 is available in the form of the returning officers' "checklists" of voters.[13] Of course, knowing who voted is not necessarily synonymous with defining eligibility, for not all those eligible will vote, while some men who are not legally eligible may well vote. Fortunately, a relatively complete set of assessment records for Albert County, covering the years 1847, 1854, 1855, 1856, and 1857, and including valuations of real and personal property as well as income for individuals, has survived. The revised voters' lists (which were based on the assessment records) for both the 1856 and the 1857 elections are also extant. Using these records, the eligibility of electors under the law could be determined.

Albert County thus offers a unique opportunity for a case study of the mid-nineteenth-century New Brunswick franchise.[14] While it was not representative of New Brunswick as a whole, this consideration in no way diminishes its suitability as the setting in which to determine the breadth and accessibility of the mid-nineteenth-century franchise. Since the people of Albert were not wealthier than other New Brunswickers, the proportion of men who were legally eligible to vote would not have been higher in Albert than in other counties. Conclusions based on a close analysis of a largely rural, anglophone county cannot provide definitive answers about the New Brunswick experience, but, because the vast majority of mid-nineteenth-century New Brunswickers were, like the people of Albert County, anglophone and rural, conclusions drawn from this study can provide the framework for a standard interpretation against which the experiences of the minorities can more accurately be assessed.

Albert County is located in the southeast region of the province between Saint John and Moncton, on the Bay of Fundy. Established as a separate county in 1845, Albert initially included just four parishes: Coverdale, Harvey, Hillsborough, and Hopewell. Elgin was added in 1847 and Alma was carved out of Harvey Parish in 1855. Of the 6313 people living within the county's boundaries in 1851, 1370 (21.7 per cent) were voting-aged males. Nearly 90 per cent of the county's population had been born in New Brunswick, but people had not forgotten their roots. Thus, only 42 per cent (580) of the men in the study group were classified as New Brunswickers in the 1851 census. Just over 20 per cent (292) identified themselves as Irish, although not all of those so classified had been born in Ireland. A further 15 per cent (209) were listed as English, while 9 per cent (129) identified themselves as German. The group also included, among others, Scots (45), Americans (32), and Nova Scotians (76).

The major occupation in the county was farming, accounting for 56.6 per cent (776) of the men in the study group. But crop failures had plagued the farmers of Albert during the late 1840s[15] and by mid-century recovery was as yet incomplete: their crop yields in 1851 remained quite low. Artisans and mechanics accounted for a further 16 per cent (219) of the county's adult males, while 6.6 per cent (91) were classified as labourers. Some labourers were employed in the county's small but diversified mineral industry, producing grindstones and mining coal and gypsum. Some were also employed in the woods industry, but the sawmills were generally small, with ninety-seven mills providing employment for only 237 hands, many of whom combined mill work with farming. Merchants and professional men accounted for just 4 per cent (62) of the study group, while government officials comprised less than 2 per cent (18).[16] The majority of the county's population (84.6 per cent) lived in nuclear families, although one-quarter of these households included one or more single or widowed relatives, lodgers, apprentices, or servants. The remaining 15.4 per cent lived in multiple family households. Thus, while most voting-aged males (67.5 per cent or 925) headed their own households, 32.5 per cent (445) lived in households headed by others. The vast majority of the latter were young men under the age of thirty (330 or 24.1 per cent of the study group). Spiritually, Albert was relatively homogeneous, planted firmly within an Evangelical Protestant mould.[17]

The period encompassed by the Albert County poll books (1846 through 1857) was particularly significant and provided the opportunity to determine the impact of changes in franchise laws. Under the 1791 Election Act, which remained the basis for the New Brunswick franchise in 1846, only those men who were twenty-one years of age or over and in possession of a freehold valued at £25 or more were legally eligible to vote. For non-residents the qualification was somewhat higher: for them a freehold of £50 was necessary. In both cases property titles were to have been registered at least six months prior to the teste of writ, but the property could be mortgaged so long as the elector remained in possession of it and retained the right to its revenue.[18] To be eligible to run for provincial office, a candidate was required to possess £200 of real estate in the county he sought to represent, and, while the candidate need not be a resident of the county, his property there must have been registered at least six months before the teste of writ.[19]

By the 1840s some members of the Assembly had begun to call for franchise reform. Charles

Fisher, a future Liberal premier, sponsored bills in 1840 and again in 1842 which would have extended the suffrage to leaseholders. Other legislators argued that current abuses of the system should be corrected before granting more men the right to vote. James Boyd, a Conservative from Charlotte County, believing himself to have been the victim of such abuse, strongly opposed the liberalization of the franchise. He advocated the establishment of a voters' registry, arguing that if there had been a Registry Bill in operation he would never have had to endure a controverted election in order to gain his seat. "The fact was," he complained, "the rabble would pour in from all quarters, who had no right whatever to vote, and yet they would and did vote during the last election." At least some of his colleagues proved sympathetic and bills which would have served to tighten enforcement of the current franchise through the establishment of a voters' registry were introduced annually from 1844 through 1848. But these bills, like the bill sponsored by Fisher, failed to pass.

In 1848, however, the conservative element in the Assembly succeeded in gaining passage of an amendment to the Election Law which raised the qualification for candidates from £200 to £300.[20] In the same year the Executive Council decided that those who were purchasing crown lands by instalments should receive conditional title to their land upon making the initial payment of one-quarter the purchase price. By this apparently minor shift in policy, purchasers of crown lands gained the status of mortgagors and, thereby, legal access to the franchise.[21] Although this change occasioned little noticc, in 1853 a bill which would have extended the franchise to leaseholders, established a voters' registry, and introduced vote by secret ballot aroused so much controversy that it was allowed to die.

Nevertheless, by the 1850s the pressure for such franchise reform was coming from outside as well as from inside the legislature. It is true that the petitions demanding franchise reform came almost exclusively from one county—Carleton[22]—but the newly emerging Liberal opposition were encouraged by this external lobbying campaign which called for changes they had long advocated, and they continued to press for reforms to the Election Act. In 1855, having achieved power, the Liberals introduced legislation which would extend the franchise to include owners of personal property, or personal and real property, assessed at £100 or more and to all those assessed as recipients of an annual income of £100 or more. The assessment rolls would form the basis for the new voters' register, and vote by ballot would replace *vive voce* voting. The amended Election Act was passed with the proviso that it would not come into effect until 1 January 1857, in order to allow ample time for the preparation of the voters' registers.[23]

Franchise laws, passed by elected legislators, represented the views and values of political elites. The degree to which those views and values were shared by society as a whole can be determined by examining the various responses to those laws. When they strongly disapproved of laws passed by their governments, nineteenth-century New Brunswickers, like their counterparts throughout North America, routinely petitioned their legislatures to change those laws. But there were other, more subtle ways of demonstrating dissatisfaction with current laws. Men who were not legally qualified but who regularly voted by custom, challenged the franchise law when they stepped forward to vote. And their friends and neighbours challenged the franchise law when they failed to demand enforcement of suffrage restrictions. Because New Brunswick was very much part of a British tradition in which custom and practice were at least as important as the letter of the law in establishing societal standards and values, any analysis of the actual nature of the franchise must consider both the law and the reality and the extent to which the two converged and diverged in practice.

Of the 1370 men in Albert County who were twenty-one years of age or over in 1851, just 515 (37.6 per cent) voted in the general election held in that year. This would seem to provide convincing evidence that the New Brunswick franchise was indeed restrictive. Yet such a conclusion, drawn on the basis of a single election, is misleading. Over 70 per cent of the men in the study group (970 men in all) voted in at least one of the six elections held between 1845 and 1858.[24] A further 100 men were eligible to vote but failed to exercise their franchise. Sixteen of the latter attempted to vote but were prevented from doing so, usually because they refused to take the oath attesting to their legal eligibility when objections were raised against them. Thus, 78 per cent of the study group had access to the franchise during the period (see table 1 for a breakdown by parish). Although falling short of universal male suffrage, by any standards this was a broad franchise. Yet the full implications of these statistics are far from clear. By themselves, the numbers provide no information concerning the ways in which voters may have differed from non-voters. Nor do they indicate the proportion of voters who exercised the franchise on sufferance. And they do not allow for a consideration of the impact of either the change in crown-lands policy in 1848 or the 1855 Election Act, which may have enfranchised some men while barring other long-time voters from the polls. These and other underlying issues can best be analysed through a consideration of individual cases. Four men, resident in Albert for the entire period from 1846 through 1857, may serve as examples of voters or potential voters to whom these laws applied.

Franchise laws and changes in those laws affected individual men in quite different ways. When Silas Bishop, of Hillsborough Parish, stepped forward to vote in the general election of 1856, he almost certainly knew that this would be the last time he would be required to state his vote publicly, before an audience of his friends and neighbours. The new election law, requiring a registry of eligible voters and a secret ballot, was scheduled to come into effect on 1 January 1857. One of over 900 Albert County men who went to the polls in this historic election that witnessed the end of the era of *vive voce* voting in the county, Bishop may well have viewed the change with more equanimity than some of his contemporaries. A native New Brunswicker, he traced his roots to the German settlers who had migrated from Pennsylvania in the eighteenth century. Like the majority of their contemporaries, he and his wife, Sarah Ann, were Baptists. Their seven children had been born and raised in the parish and their eldest, now married, had recently purchased his own farm there. At fifty-five, Bishop was well established in his community and his ownership of a farm in Hillsborough, valued at £150, ensured that he would be among those listed in the voters' register which was even now being prepared. He had voted in 1846, 1850, 1851, and 1854, and he would vote again in 1857. But not all of those who went to the polls in 1856 shared Bishop's previous experience or future prospects.[25]

Hugh Alcorn of Harvey Parish also participated in the election of 1856. A native of Ireland, Hugh had immigrated to New Brunswick at the age of eighteen. In 1830, just four years after his arrival, he made his first payment on a 200 acre tract of crown land in an area that would become part of the new parish of Harvey. Like Silas Bishop, Alcorn, now forty-three, listed himself as a farmer in the 1851 census. But his farm was not, apparently, very prosperous. By 1856 he had still not succeeded in paying off the principal. And, in that year, the value of his farm was assessed at just £15, thereby falling £10 short of the necessary property qualification for voters. Yet he and his wife Biddy, also an Irish immigrant, had lived on their farm for over twenty years: their eight chil-

TABLE 1 | ACCESS TO THE FRANCHISE FOR VOTING-AGED MALES LISTED IN THE 1851 MANUSCRIPT CENSUS FOR ALBERT COUNTY

Parish	Males 21 and over	% who voted at least once	% eligible but did not vote	% eligible but rejected	% not eligible and did not vote	% not eligible and rejected
Coverdale	199	71.9	4.0	0.5	22.6	1.0
Elgin	158	61.4	18.4	1.3	18.3	0.6
Harvey	437	65.0	8.0	1.6	24.7	0.7
Hillsborough	321	79.1	1.9	0.9	17.4	0.6
Hopewell	255	75.3	2.3	1.2	21.2	–
Albert County	1370	70.8	6.1	1.2	21.3	0.6

dren had all been born there. This Irish-born Episcopalian was an established member of the community and that, apparently, was enough to qualify him in the eyes of his peers, if not in the eyes of the law. Although ineligible under the law, Alcorn had voted in all the elections from 1851 to 1856, but his name would not be recorded in the voters' registry, and he would not vote in 1857.[26]

Some men who sought to exercise the franchise in 1856 were not as fortunate as Hugh Alcorn. Wesley Peck, the second son of a prosperous farmer, was turned away from the polls when he attempted to vote in that election. His grandparents had been among the Loyalists who had migrated from Massachusetts at the close of the American Revolution. Like the majority of Albert County residents, the Pecks were Baptists. Still a bachelor at twenty-eight, Peck, a shipwright by trade, lived at home with his parents and three younger siblings. His older brother, as well as two younger sisters, had already left home to begin their own families. In June of 1856 his parents, both approaching sixty, sold each of their two eldest sons a portion of the family farm. For the modest price of £10, Thomas, the farmer, received an upland section of farmland, while Wesley received a section of marshland, bordering on the farm of a neighbour, Laurence O'Regan. Four months later, "for and in consideration of the sum of £50," Wesley purchased an adjoining "lot of undyked marshland" from Laurence and Mary O'Regan. By 1856, then, Wesley Peck was not only well established in his chosen trade, but was also the proprietor of a £60 freehold in Hopewell, the parish of his birth. Yet the returning officer refused to record his vote in the election of that year on the grounds that his freehold had not been registered six months prior to the election, as required by law. Wesley was still living in his parents' home in 1857, and his £60 freehold ensured him a place in the voters' registry, although, as it happened, he would not vote in the general election of 1857.[27]

Not all of those men who were legally eligible to vote went to the polls in every election. William Howard did not go to the polls in 1856, nor had he voted in any previous election. He and his wife Mary had, along with thousands of other Roman Catholics, fled famine-ravaged Ireland during the 1840s. They settled on a section of unoccupied crown land in the parish of Elgin, where, with the birth of their first child in 1846, they began to put down roots. In 1852, with the help of Reuben Stiles, the local member of the Legislative Assembly and deputy surveyor for the district, Howard petitioned the lieutenant-governor, requesting permission to purchase 100 acres of crown land under the terms of the "Labour Act."[28] Howard and his family had, by that time, been living on the land for several years and had managed to clear over twenty acres. The lieutenant-governor apparently saw fit to grant his petition, for, by 1856, Howard, then forty-one, still married, and the father of six, was paying taxes on land assessed at a value of over £100. He had not yet finished paying for the land and, in fact, would not be granted full and free title to his farm until 1859. But under the crown-lands policy, as amended in 1848, he had the status of a mortgagor and was, therefore, eligible to vote on the basis of his assessed property. In 1857 William Howard's name, like that of Silas Bishop and Wesley Peck, would be recorded in the newly established registry of voters.[29]

The experiences of these four men illustrate both the subtleties and the complexities of the mid-nineteenth-century New Brunswick franchise. An electorate confined to men like Silas Bishop, who were legally eligible under the province's restrictive franchise laws, would, on the surface at least, suggest a conservative society where men deferred to their "betters," accepting laws imposed upon them by political elites. Under such circumstances, even those who had the right to vote might be expected to exhibit deferential attitudes in their choice of candidates, electing local elites—men of power and influence.[30] Yet the experiences of the other three men suggest a more open society, with a relatively accessible franchise. If, on the one hand, suffrage restrictions were not rigorously enforced, Albert County, with its recent history of crop failures, might be expected to have had a larger class of *de facto* voters than other rural counties. The presence of a significant number of men like Hugh Alcorn on the voters' rolls would tend to confirm the views of those contemporary politicians and journalists who believed that abuse of the system was widespread.[31] On the other hand, if the experiences of Wesley Peck and William Howard were typical, the New Brunswick franchise laws may not have been as restrictive as they appeared. Perhaps many young men coming of age in Albert County could, like Wesley Peck, look forward to a time when they would be able to purchase their own freehold, thereby gaining legal access to the franchise. Others, too poor to purchase a freehold outright, were able, like William Howard, to purchase crown land on instalments, payable in labour or in cash. And, after 1848, they, too, gained legal access to the franchise. Of course, this assumes not only that the majority of men who purchased crown lands on instalment were informed of the implications of this minor change in crown-lands policy, but also that they would be able to improve their farms to the requisite value before they had finished paying for them. An analysis of the experiences of individual men can provide useful insights concerning both the development and nature of representative government in colonial New Brunswick.

To understand the nature of the franchise, and the extent to which it was representative of the adult male population, it is first necessary to determine precisely who voted and who did not vote. Previous studies of the franchise in British North America have focused exclusively on household heads.[32] Yet, as demonstrated by the case of Wesley Peck, a man could meet the property qualification without heading a household. It is true, nonetheless, that the majority of those who voted were, like Silas Bishop, Hugh Alcorn, and William Howard, household heads as early as 1851. Heads of households were significantly over-represented among voters and significantly under-represented among non-voters. While 67.5 per cent of all males over 20 were household heads in 1851, 74.3 per cent of those who voted at least once during the period (721) were listed in the census as household heads. In contrast, just 39.7 per cent of all non-voters (116) headed their own households in 1851. Moreover, many of the remaining 249 voters may well have been household heads by the time they began voting.

Although the manuscript census for 1851 identifies which men were household heads in that year, the status of voters within their households cannot be delineated with any degree of precision. But by focusing only on the elections of 1850 and 1851, the significance of a man's status within his household as a predictor in determining which men were most likely to exercise the franchise can be measured. Of the 507 men in the study group who went to the polls in 1850, 439, or 86.6 per cent, were household heads. In 1851, 429 of the 515 voters (83.3 per cent) headed their households. Sixty-eight Albert County electors in 1850 and eighty-six in 1851, or approximately 15 per cent of all electors, lived in households headed by others. And if this were true in the case of a very restrictive legal franchise, limiting the analysis to household heads may well mean ignoring substantial numbers of eligible electors.[33] Heading one's household was not a prerequisite for voting, but household heads did have a significant advantage.

While the act of establishing his own household did demonstrate a man's intention to settle in the county, it was not, by itself, enough to secure him access to the franchise. For the poorer men in the county especially, persistence in a community over a prolonged period proved at least as important as household status in predicting a man's chances of gaining access to the franchise. Hugh Alcorn had established his own household in 1831, when he was twenty-three years old, yet he voted for the first time in 1851, at the age of forty-three. In 1851 William Howard headed a household which included his wife and four small children, but his status then on the land he had already begun to clear was that of a mere squatter. He would not vote until 1857, when he was forty-two and secure in the possession of the land grant for which he had first petitioned in 1852. For these men, as for many others, persistence was rewarded. Of the 1370 men in the study group, 738 resided in Albert County throughout the entire period. The men in this stable group—even men like Hugh Alcorn, who were not legally eligible—proved much more likely to vote than their more mobile contemporaries. Almost 89 per cent (654) of them voted at least once during the period, as compared to just over 78 per cent of the entire study group.

The likelihood that such men would gain legal access to the vote increased in direct relationship to their persistence over time. Thus, 786 of the 1370 men were listed on the 1847 assessment rolls, but only 63 per cent of them were, like Silas Bishop, able to meet the property qualification. By 1854, 1073 of those men who had been living in the county when the enumerator called in 1851 were listed on the assessment rolls, and 74 per cent were qualified to vote in the election held in that year. One-fifth of those men had disappeared from the rolls by 1856, while a few of the younger men in the study group were assessed for the first time. Of the 880 assessed, 79 per cent met the property qualification for voters. The names of even more young men, Wesley Peck among them, were entered on the assessment rolls for the first time in 1857 (perhaps in anticipation of the voters' register which was then being compiled), but the proportion who were legally eligible to vote did not rise significantly.[34] Of the 930 men who had been living in the county in 1851, 81 per cent were eligible to vote in the election of 1857 (see table 2). Of course, prosperous members of a community were less likely to leave the community and it is not surprising that this geographically stable element were more often able to meet

TABLE 2 | MEN LISTED IN THE 1851 MANUSCRIPT CENSUS WHO MET THE PROPERTY QUALIFICATION FOR VOTERS

	Eligible		Not eligible		
Year	Number	%	Number	%	Total
1847	493	62.7	293	37.3	786
1854	796	74.2	277	25.8	1073
1856	696	79.1	184	20.9	880
1857	752	80.9	178	19.1	930

the property qualification than were their more mobile neighbours. Nonetheless, the incremental increase over time in the proportion of eligible voters among those who stayed does indicate that persistence was rewarded.

Access to the franchise was conditional on a variety of other factors as well. A consideration closely related to both household status and persistence was age. Like Wesley Peck, many young unmarried men lived at home with their parents. Most, even those from prosperous, long-established local families, did not themselves own any property at all. Wesley Peck, for example, was nearly thirty before he was able to gain access to the franchise. Certainly some young men did vote, but those in the twenty-one to twenty-nine age category were under-represented among voters (23.8 per cent of all voters in 1851 compared to 34.4 per cent in the population as a whole). Yet the mean age of those who voted in 1851 was not significantly higher than the mean age of all voting-aged males recorded in the 1851 census (forty-one compared to thirty-eight).[35] Rare indeed was the young man who automatically qualified for the vote on his twenty-first birthday, but the majority could realistically expect to gain access to the franchise before their thirtieth birthday.

In New Brunswick, voting was a privilege reserved for those men who were perceived to have that tangible stake in their society which property provides. Thus it is not surprising that young farmers proved more likely than their contemporaries who had chosen other occupations to gain access to the franchise. Farmers, by virtue of their very dependence on the land, were more often prepared to make sacrifices to secure a freehold. And even if that freehold was not assessed at the requisite £25, the possession of it could sometimes be enough to secure such a man the vote. In contrast, the artisans, merchants, and professional men who made their homes in Albert County had less need of a freehold and were likely to postpone land purchases until they were well established in their chosen fields. As a result, like Wesley Peck, the shipwright, they were often slightly older than their farming contemporaries when they made their first trip to the polls. Farmers comprised 56.6 per cent of the total workforce in Albert County, but 64.4 per cent of the total electorate. Of those who failed to qualify, just 26.7 per cent were farmers. Thus, men like Hugh Alcorn, ineligible under the law, could gain access to the franchise through long persistence in the community, the stature that comes with age, and their occupation. Had Alcorn been a landless labourer, it is unlikely that he would ever have been allowed to vote. While 6.6 per cent of all voting-aged males were listed in the census as

TABLE 3 | VOTING AND RELIGION IN ALBERT COUNTY, 1846-57

	Voters		Non-voters		Total	
Religion	Number	%	Number	%	Number	%
Baptist	365	61.0	45	39.1	410	57.5
Free Baptist	13	2.2	3	2.6	16	2.3
Calvinistic Baptist	42	7.0	11	9.6	53	7.4
Episcopalian	28	4.7	8	7.0	36	5.1
Presbyterian	13	2.2	7	6.1	20	2.8
Wesleyan	55	9.2	10	8.7	65	9.1
Methodist	45	7.5	12	10.4	57	8.0
Roman Catholic	29	4.8	16	13.9	45	6.3
Universalist	3	0.5	0	–	3	0.4
Free Thinker	1	0.2	0	–	1	0.1
Not Given	4	0.7	3	2.6	7	1.0
Totals	598	100.0	115	100.0	713	100.0

general labourers, 21.2 per cent of those who never gained access to the franchise in the period under review were unskilled. A minimal 2.3 per cent of voters were unskilled. Of course, the majority of the unskilled were immigrants and transients, men who were not perceived to have a tangible stake in the society.

Men whose roots in the community extended back to their parents' generation proved more likely to vote than did immigrants, even long-established immigrants like Hugh Alcorn. But Alcorn's sons, regardless of their Irish ancestry, could, by choosing to settle in the parish of their birth, gain an advantage their father had lacked. Yet although native New Brunswickers had a slight advantage over their immigrant neighbours, all major ethnic groups were proportionately represented among voters.[36] Similarly, all major religious denominations were proportionately represented among the electorate. Over half (52 per cent) of the 1370 men in the study group were still living in the county when the census was taken in 1861, and the parish enumerators recorded religious affiliation for all but seven of them. Of this group, which included 713 men in all, 598 voted at least once during the period while 115 never voted. New Brunswick-born Baptists—men like Silas Bishop and Wesley Peck—were the most stable and well established sector of the county's population, and they were, predictably, significantly under-represented among non-voters. In contrast, Roman Catholics were over-represented among non-voters (see table 3). The Catholics, especially the Catholic Irish, tended to be the most recent arrivals and were often among the poorest. Those who did vote, like William Howard, proved far more patient than their Protestant counterparts, generally waiting until they were legally eligible before venturing to the polls. The experience of the men of Albert County provides no evidence to support the assertion that most of the pauper Irish were allowed to exercise the franchise on sufferance.[37] Rather, the Irish immigrants who gained access to the franchise despite their inability to meet the property qualification tended to be men like Hugh Alcorn: they were rarely recent arrivals and they were usually Protestant.

Even men like Hugh Alcorn were the exception rather than the rule. The majority of those who could not meet the property qualification did not seek to "exercise the franchise on sufferance and by convention." They simply did not go to the polls. Yet few men who did present themselves at the polls were turned away. For example, in 1856, the year in which Wesley Peck was refused the right to vote because he had failed to register his freehold in time, just forty-nine of the 962 men who went to the polls (5.1 per cent) were turned away. Two, like Wesley Peck, had the necessary freehold but had failed to register their purchases the required six months before the teste of writ. Two others were refused on the grounds that they had no freehold in the parish. The returning officer for the parish of Hopewell turned one man away because both his residence and his freehold were in the parish of Hillsborough. And three impatient young men were denied the right to vote because they were under age.[38] Eight men were denied access to the franchise because they refused to take the required oath when called upon to do so. Candidates or their representatives lodged objections against fifteen electors and the votes of those men were not counted as a result. The votes of a further seventeen men were rejected although no reason was recorded by the returning officer. While the reasons given for rejection tended to be more precise in 1856 than in earlier elections, the proportion of electors who were frustrated in their attempt to vote was typical for the period. The votes of 5 per cent of the electors were rejected.[39]

The majority of men who were unable to meet the property qualification stayed at home on election day. Of the 381 men in the study group who never achieved eligibility, 292 (76.6 per cent) never once attempted to vote during the period under review. Hugh Alcorn, then, was a member of a very select group of voters. Only eighty-nine men who went to the polls during the period proved consistently unable to meet the property qualification (eighty-one actually voted). Over 90 per cent of those who voted (881 of 970) were able to meet the eligibility requirements before the end of the period. A few attempted to vote in advance of qualifying, but most, like William Howard and Wesley Peck, were patient, waiting until they had accumulated sufficient property before stepping forward to claim the franchise as their right.[40] And if the disfranchised men of Albert County protested publicly about their lack of power, no record of their protest has survived. Nor did the enfranchised demand an extension of the vote to their less prosperous neighbours; the men of Albert sent numerous petitions to their legislature during the decade between 1846 and 1857, requesting, among other things, roads and bridges, improved mail service, farm subsidies, and liquor legislation, but they did not present a single petition demanding franchise extension or reform.[41] Not all New Brunswickers shared the apparent satisfaction of the people of Albert, however, and the law relating to the franchise did change over time.

To understand the development of the New Brunswick franchise, it is necessary to assess the impact of franchise extensions and reforms. The first extension of the franchise, which occurred in 1848, came not as a direct attempt at franchise reform but as a by-product of a change in crown-lands policy. Indeed, this first extension of the suffrage required no revision of the current Election Law. The sale of crown lands, payable in four equal instalments, had long been a common practice throughout the province. By deciding to award land titles to purchasers upon payment of the initial instalment, the Executive Council, in effect, gave purchasers of crown land the status of mortgagor, thereby making them eligible to vote under the current franchise law. Of the 1370 voting-aged males who were living in Albert County in 1851, 101 were purchasing crown land on an instalment basis. But thirty-two of those were already eligible to vote, by virtue of owning other land in the county. Of the remaining sixty-nine men, twenty-six had not yet made enough improvements on their land to raise its assessed value to the required £25. Just forty-three men (3.1 per cent of the total) were enfranchised as a result of this change in crown-lands policy. The majority of those did not go to the polls in 1850. Only nineteen men (44.2 per cent) exercised their newly gained franchise in that election; and seven of those had voted in 1846 as well. In 1851 the proportion of voters to be found among this recently enfranchised group rose slightly as twenty-four men (55.8 per cent) participated in the election held in that year. By 1854 the number of men in the study group who qualified on the basis of their crown-land purchases had declined to thirty, but twenty of those (66.7 per cent) were among the voters who went to the polls that year.[42]

This very gradual increase in participation among those enfranchised as a result of the change in crown-lands policy suggests that men were slow to recognize the broader implications of the policy change. Moreover, because this broadening of the franchise required no change in the wording of the Election Act, the potential implications of the crown-lands policy change may well have been misinterpreted by those election officials who did take note of it. Hugh Alcorn, for example, may not have realized that he was voting illegally when he went to the polls in 1851. After all, from the time he paid the initial instalment on his crown-land grant in 1830 until the change in the crown-lands policy in 1848, he had made no attempt to vote. When he stepped forward and declared his vote in 1851, both he and the election official who recorded his choices may have believed that the very fact of his now holding the title to a tract of 200 acres of crown land automatically qualified him under the law. Alcorn may have believed himself to be eligible until he discovered that his name was not listed in the voters' registry, compiled for the 1857 election. At the same time, William Howard may have had no idea that he was legally qualified to vote, merely by virtue of paying taxes on a tract of land he did not yet own. Perhaps he was surprised to discover his name among those listed in the voters' registry. But however the law was interpreted, the 1848 change in crown-lands policy was not conceived as a franchise reform and was not publicized as such.

In contrast, no one could mistake either the intent or the significance of the changes in the Election Law that were approved by the New Brunswick Assembly in 1855. For months, the local newspapers throughout the province had carried reports of the discussion and they publicized the final outcome. In every county, parish officials had begun the process of preparing voters' registers. Nonetheless, by 1 January 1857, the day the new law was scheduled to come into effect, the parish officials in nine of the province's fourteen counties had failed to complete the task. Faced with an impending election, the Assembly, determined to enforce the new law to the extent they were able, decreed that it should come into effect in the five counties for which the voters' registers had been completed. Albert County was one of the five. Although the new law brought little change in the actual number of voters, it did inaugurate significant changes in the traditional conduct of elections. Men were no longer required to declare their vote publicly. The returning officer for each parish was provided with an official list of those who were legally eligible to vote. Included on that list were men who may have been ineligible under the old property requirement, but who were able to qualify under the new assessment franchise.

In adopting an assessment franchise, New Brunswick was participating in a suffrage reform movement that was international in scope. But the little colony was scarcely in the vanguard of that movement.[43] The assessment franchise established by the new act was, at best, a modest reform. Few legislators agreed with James Brown, of Charlotte County, that "every man who is bound to obey the laws ought to have a voice in making them." Even fewer shared the fears of John Ambrose Street, the representative from Northumberland, who argued that the proposed franchise would "degenerate into universal suffrage." In supporting the proposed changes, Brown admitted that "some of our farmers may not see the expediency of these reformatory measures," but, he asserted, "that does not argue against them." Abner McClelan, one of the two Albert County members agreed. He welcomed the reforms, although he recognized that a franchise based on personal property would benefit people in towns and cities rather than those in the country.[44] The people of McClelan's own county, like the majority of New Brunswickers, would be little affected by this extension of the franchise. In Albert, just eighteen men were enfranchised under the terms of the new act.[45] The new Election Act, then, represented but a tentative first step in franchise reform.

In contrast, New Brunswick was in the forefront of the movement towards the secret ballot and voters' registers.[46] The New Brunswick legislators who had pioneered in the introduction of these measures had perceived in them a method whereby corruption at elections might be curbed, if not altogether eliminated. If rigorously enforced, the use of a voters' registry, compiled from the assessment rolls, and revised annually, would eliminate the practice of allowing men who were legally ineligible to vote on sufferance and by convention. At the very least, returning officers, with a clear law before them, could be expected to be much more cautious in bending the rules for such men. Thus, in rural counties like Albert the Election Law of 1855 threatened to disfranchise as many men as it enfranchised.[47]

In 1857 men were enjoined to cast their ballots in their parish of residence, and the elimination of non-resident voters, who had previously comprised approximately 10 per cent of the electorate in each parish, undoubtedly made the task of the returning officers a good deal easier. This did not mean that the number of voters declined by a corresponding 10 per cent; rather, men made a greater effort to get to the polling station for which they were officially registered. The number of voters did decline, however, but in direct proportion to the decline in the number of legally ineligible voters. While the proportion of men voting on sufferance had remained consistent at 9 per cent throughout the period, it dropped to 6 per cent in 1857. Because the officials kept no record of rejected voters for that election,[48] there is no way to determine whether Hugh Alcorn and men like him, who did not vote in 1857 but who had, in the past, been permitted to exercise the franchise, were turned away from the polls. Yet the change was minimal and, at most, the decline suggests either that officials were more cautious than was the case in previous elections or that fewer men who had voted on sufferance in the past were willing to take what appeared to them a greater risk of being turned away.

Clearly, legislative changes had very little impact on the voting habits of rural New Brunswickers. Nevertheless, important shifts in electoral patterns did occur during the period. Patterns of voter turnout, for example, changed considerably between 1846 and 1857. But the change was gradual and the trend was unaffected by the new law. Silas Bishop, along with 160 other men in the county, voted in all six of the elections held during the period. Like Bishop, each of those 160 men met the property qualification as well as the age and residence requirements that would legally entitle them to vote. This cadre of consistent participants was in the minority, however; the majority of those who were legally eligible did not always choose to exercise their franchise. Because assessment records for 1850 and 1851 have not survived, a

TABLE 4 | ALBERT COUNTY VOTING PATTERNS, 1846-57*

Voted in	Frequency	%	Cumulative frequency	Cumulative %
0	12	2.6	12	2.6
1	28	6.0	40	8.5
2	33	7.0	73	15.6
3	38	8.1	111	23.7
4	73	15.6	184	39.3
5	124	26.4	308	65.7
6	161	34.3	469	100.0

*Includes only those men who were eligible to vote in all six elections.

complete list of eligible voters cannot be compiled for the elections held in those years. But by using assessment records for 1847 and for 1854–7, it is possible to identify a group of 469 men who were present and eligible throughout the entire period. Among this stable and established group, the core of non-voters was very small, comprising just twelve (3 per cent) of the 469 men (see table 4). Nonetheless, electoral participation during the first three elections was relatively low, with 68 per cent voting in 1846 and 1850, declining to 65 per cent in 1851, an election to replace William H. Steeves, who had been appointed to the Legislative Council. In the final three elections of the period, which witnessed the transition from candidate-based to party-based voting, turnout rose steadily: from 76 per cent in 1854 to 81 per cent in 1856 to 86 per cent in 1857, the final election of the period and the first to be conducted under the new Election Act (see table 5). The same upward trend emerges when the analysis is expanded to include the more geographically mobile element of the population, although, as might be expected, turnout was somewhat lower and the increase more gradual.[49] While aggregate turnout patterns tended to rise steadily, individual turnout patterns proved somewhat less predictable. It is true that 60 per cent of the stable group of 469 were regular participants, voting in at least five of the six elections, and that 97 per cent exercised their franchise at least once. Yet some men who had voted in every previous election and who were listed in the voters' register failed to go to the polls in 1857. In all, 63 per cent chose to vote in some elections and not in others. These shifting patterns of voter turnout among electors who were legally eligible throughout the entire period illustrate both the value of tracing individual voting patterns over a series of elections and the danger inherent in basing generalizations on fluctuations in turnout alone.

In New Brunswick, the upward trend in voter turnout, which began in 1854, was not the result of legislative change. In the past, men had gone to the polls to support local elites—men such as John Smith and William Henry Steeves who were much more than mere farmers. Steeves, in partnership with his two brothers, had established a highly successful mercantile and lumber export business, while Smith was engaged in the shipbuilding business as well as running a prosperous farm.[50] When they were elected as representatives for the newly established county of Albert in 1846, they were among an elite group of forty-one men in the

TABLE 5 | ELECTORAL TURNOUT PATTERNS, ALBERT COUNTY, 1846-57*

	Men who voted		Eligible but did not vote		
Election year	Number	%	Number	%	Total
1846	320	68.2	149	31.8	469
1850	318	67.8	151	32.2	469
1851	306	65.2	163	34.8	469
1854	357	76.1	112	23.9	469
1856	382	81.4	87	18.6	469
1857	405	86.4	64	13.6	469

*Includes only those men who were eligible to vote in all six elections.

county whose real property was assessed at over £1000. During the ensuing decade, no candidate would receive a higher proportion of the votes polled than these two men had won in the first election held during the period.[51] Smith retired from politics before the 1850 election, however, and Steeves, who once again topped the polls in 1850, resigned within the year upon being called to serve on the Legislative Council. Despite their unprecedented success at the polls, neither man had inspired high levels of voter turnout. And turnout threatened to dip even lower following their resignations. Those who participated continued in their traditional habits of deference, favouring neighbourhood elites over other candidates, but the proportion of eligible electors who took the trouble to go to the polls declined in each election.

This pattern of low voter turnout reversed itself in 1854 with the emergence of incipient political parties. The shift from candidate-based to party-based voting did not signal the end of a political system based on deference. Candidates for election in New Brunswick had always been drawn from a relatively small pool as fewer than 25 per cent of all voting-aged males were able to meet the required property qualification.[52] The rise of parties did nothing to change this. Now, however, distinctions among candidates could be more easily delineated. This clearer ideological choice resulted in a tendency towards polarization among voters while at the same time creating a renewed interest in politics. Yet it is unlikely that the emerging political parties would have elicited such enthusiasm had not the rise of the Reformers (or Smashers, as they were soon dubbed) coincided with the rise of temperance as a political issue. In Albert County, with its preponderance of Baptists, the Smashers, under the leadership of Samuel Leonard Tilley, Most Worthy Patriarch of the Sons of Temperance of North America, gained the ascendancy. In 1857, with turnout higher than in any other election held during the period, the Reform slate of John Lewis and Abner R. McClelan captured 47.6 per cent of the vote, while Conservatives Edward Stevens and Peter Duffy were supported by only 31.9 per cent of the electorate.[53] Only an issue that called their fundamental beliefs into question, coupled with what many viewed as a clear ideological choice between two opposing world views, could bring men to the polls in such numbers.

Nevertheless, old habits died hard and men continued to favour neighbourhood elites over their lesser known rivals: both Liberal and Conservative candidates continued to do best in their own parishes.[54]

Politics changed significantly during the period under review. But the most important changes that occurred were not the result of changes in the franchise laws. In Albert County, the number of men who were enfranchised as a result of the change in crown-lands policy in 1848 exceeded the number enfranchised by the electoral reforms of 1855. And together these comprised barely 5 per cent of the adult male population. Nonetheless, the findings emerging from the Albert County analysis suggest that Garner was correct in assuming that the nineteenth-century franchise was relatively broad. At the same time, he appears to have been incorrect in concluding that a broad franchise necessarily meant that the law and the reality diverged in any truly significant way. Silas Bishop, Hugh Alcorn, Wesley Peck, and William Howard were all typical men of the time. Taken together, their experiences have provided insight into the nature of the franchise in mid-nineteenth-century New Brunswick. They have shown that in rural areas, at least, the majority of men were able to meet the required property qualifications. Thus, while it is true that only two-thirds of all voting-aged men were eligible to vote in each of the elections which took place in 1846–57, over three-quarters of the county's adult males gained access to the franchise in the course of that decade. The New Brunswick franchise remained legally the most restrictive in British North America, yet, if the men of 1851 were typical, over 70 per cent of the men of Albert County were able to achieve legal access to the franchise under this apparently restrictive law. A further 8 per cent who were not legally entitled to vote were allowed, by custom, to exercise the franchise.[55] These were not the paupers and transients. Nor did they include a majority of the county's leaseholders and squatters. Instead, the suffrage, already broad, was cautiously extended by judicious local officials to include a small select group of solid and respectable family men, landowners who were just a little poorer than their legally enfranchised neighbours. The suffrage had not yet become a universal right, accorded to all voting-aged males, but it was, nonetheless, a right that the vast majority of young men could realistically expect to gain, and to gain legally. Indeed, it was probably because reasonable expectations were so readily fulfilled that there was no agitation for the extension of the suffrage in Albert County.

This case study of Albert County raises some interesting issues for historians seeking to understand the development and nature of representative government in the rest of Canada and in other countries as well. In considering why popular agitation for suffrage reform was endemic in some places and virtually non-existent in others, it may be useful to move beyond an analysis of the proportion of the male population eligible to vote in each election to a consideration of the equally important issue of men's expectations. Men who were not eligible to vote in one election might, as in Albert, prove reluctant to demand reform if they expected that they would be able to gain access to the franchise before the next election. Similarly, in examining the franchise and in analysing changes in the franchise over time, it may not be enough to focus only on the letter of the law. As Garner and others have pointed out, when the law is examined in the context of the society as a whole to determine precisely how it worked, interesting results may emerge. In the case of Albert County, an apparently restrictive franchise law was accompanied by a relatively broad franchise.

Notes

1 Even today the franchise remains a privilege, conferred by the government upon its citizens, and is not an inherent right. Thus the Canadian government retains the power to deny the franchise to certain categories of adults considered, for some reason, to be unworthy. Such groups have, in the twentieth century, included imprisoned criminals, Japanese Canadians, immigrants from Germany, and all women.

2 The foregoing discussion owes much to Stein Rokkan, "The Comparative Study of Political Participation: Notes Toward a Perspective on Current Research," in *Essays on the Behavioural Study of Politics,* ed. Austin Ranney (Urbana 1962), 67–76.

3 Nor was this conviction unique to colonial politicians. In his *Commentaries on the Laws of England,* William Blackstone stated: "If it were probable that every man would give his vote freely and without influence of any kind, then, upon the true theory and general principles of liberty, every member of the community, however poor, should have a vote in electing those delegates to whose charge is committed the disposal of his property, his liberty and his life. But since that can hardly be expected in persons of indigent fortunes, or such as are under the immediate dominion of others, all popular states have been obliged to establish certain qualifications; whereby some, who are suspected to have no will of their own, are excluded from voting." Cited in John Garner, *The Franchise and Politics in British North America, 1755–1867* (Toronto 1969), 8.

4 Garner, *Franchise,* 3–5.

5 J.R. Pole, *Political Representation in England and the Origins of the American Republic* (London 1966), 146.

6 See, for example, Robert E. Brown, *Middle Class Democracy and the Revolution in Massachusetts, 1691–1780* (Ithaca 1955), 21–37; or Richard P. McCormick, *The History of Voting in New Jersey: A Study of the Development of Election Machinery, 1664–1911* (New Brunswick, NJ 1953), 61–3.

7 For a discussion of the literature and a useful analysis of the statistics presented see Robert J. Dinkin, *Voting in Provincial America: A Study of Elections in the Thirteen Colonies, 1689–1776* (Westport, CT 1977), 41–6.

8 In his study of voter turnout in seven elections held in Haute-Ville de Québec, David DeBrou found a very low rate of voter turnout (ranging from a high of 47.6 per cent in 1814 to a low of 22.3 per cent in 1836) and concluded that such a "low response to the opportunity to vote underlines the inaccuracy in describing the franchise in Lower Canada as universal." DeBrou, "Voter Turnout in Haute-Ville de Québec, 1814–1836," presented to the Canadian Historical Association, Winnipeg, June 1986. Similarly, Elwood Jones, in a study of the franchise in Upper Canada, argues that "there seems considerable evidence...that the franchise was narrower than widely assumed." There, in 1854, new legislation introduced an assessment franchise and voters' registers, thereby extending the franchise to tenants. Voter turnout increased immediately, suggesting that occupiers of land had not been voting by convention prior to that time. Jones estimates that, by 1861, three-fifths of adult males had the right to vote and that two-fifths actually voted. Jones, "The Franchise in Upper Canada, 1792–1867," presented to the Canadian Historical Association, Winnipeg, June 1986.

9 See Gail G. Campbell, "Voters and Nonvoters: The Problem of Turnout in the Nineteenth Century: Southwestern Ontario as a Case Study," *Social Science History* 11 (1987): 187–210 (see especially table 1). My research on New Brunswick suggests that this was a British North American pattern rather than merely an Ontario pattern. It is of interest to note that one analyst has recently argued that voter turnout in the United States during this period was not as high as has previously been claimed. See Gerald Ginsburg, "Computing Antebellum Turnout: Methods and Models," and the rebuttal by Walter Dean Burnham, "Those High Nineteenth-Century American Voting Turnouts: Fact or Fiction?" *Journal of Interdisciplinary History* 16 (1986): 579–644.

10 Fernand Ouellet, *Lower Canada, 1791–1840: Social Change and Nationalism* (Toronto 1980), 25.

11 Ibid., 348, table 8.

12 Garner, *Franchise,* 55–65. Indeed historians have found that even after manhood suffrage had become a fact, governments often proved careless in enforcing franchise regulations. Thus, in Ontario "in the March 1891 federal election there were over 34,000 more names on the voters' lists than the 1891 census listed males age 21 or more." Even so, the number of men who actually voted did not exceed the number of men listed in the census as being of voting age in a single constituency. Ben Forster, Malcolm Davidson, and R. Craig Brown,

"The Franchise, Personators, and Dead Men: An Inquiry into the Voters' Lists and the Election of 1891," *Canadian Historical Review* 67 (1986): 18.

13 The New Brunswick election of 1857 was, curiously enough, based on two distinct franchises. In only five of the province's fourteen counties had voters' registers been completed by the time the writs were issued. Therefore, in those five counties—Albert, Carleton, Restigouche, Sunbury, and York—the new franchise went into effect, while the old franchise prevailed in the remaining nine counties. Garner, *Franchise,* 70–1.

14 This micro-study is based largely on a computer-based analysis which links poll books for six elections—1846, 1850, 1851, 1854, 1856, and 1857 (located in Record Group 18 [RG 18], Record Series 146 [RS 146], at the Public Archives of New Brunswick [PANB]); voters' lists for 1856 and 1857 (PANB, RG 18, RS 146); assessment rolls for 1847, 1854, 1855, 1856, and 1857 (PANB, RG 18, RS 146); manuscript censuses for Albert County for 1851 and 1861 (PANB); and land records including the *Consolidated Index of Deeds, Registry Office* (PANB, RG 9, RS 84) and Crown Land and Lands Branch Records (PANB, RG 10, RS 107, RS 108, RS 272, and RS 686).

15 This is attested to by the petitions from Albert County in the 1840s referring to near famine conditions in some parishes and requesting relief in the form of seed or seed potatoes. PANB, RG 4, RS 24, 1846/Petition 68; 1847/Petition 191; 1848/Petition 396; 1849/Petition 375.

16 The demographic profile of the county is based on information from the Manuscript Census of Albert County for 1851 (PANB). No occupation was listed for the remaining 14.9 per cent (204) of the study group. It is, perhaps, also worthy of note that the proportion of labourers in the workforce as a whole was 15 per cent, substantially higher than the 6.6 per cent in the study group. The majority of those who were listed as labourers in the 1851 census were under twenty-one years of age.

17 Religious affiliation was not recorded in the 1851 census, and, therefore, has had to be drawn from the 1861 Manuscript Census Returns. Almost 62 per cent of Albert's population identified themselves as Baptists when asked by the census enumerator to state their religious affiliation in 1861. A further 18 per cent claimed to be Methodists, while 9 per cent identified themselves as Roman Catholics, 6 per cent claimed to be Episcopalians, and 4 per cent listed themselves as Presbyterians. Of the 1370 men in the study group, only 713 were still living in the county in 1861. Their pattern of religious affiliation conformed quite closely to that of the population as a whole, although Baptists were slightly over-represented and Roman Catholics and Presbyterians were somewhat under-represented (67.2 per cent Baptists, 17.1 per cent Methodists, 6.3 per cent Roman Catholics, 5.1 per cent Episcopalians, and 2.8 per cent Presbyterians).

18 A minor revision in 1848 stipulated that "in cases where persons claim to vote upon a freehold derived by inheritance, devise, or as tenant by the courtesy, or any estate or interest contingent upon the life or lives of another," it was unnecessary for the voter to have possessed the land for six months so long as the person through whom he derived his title had possessed the land for six months prior to the election. *Acts of the General Assembly of Her Majesty's Province of New Brunswick,* 6 Vic., c 44; ibid., 11 Vic., c 65.

19 Garner, *Franchise,* 55–8.

20 Ibid., 63–4. See also *Acts of the General Assembly,* 11 Vic., c 65.

21 Garner, *Franchise,* 65.

22 With a single exception, all petitions to the legislature calling for the establishment of a voters' registry, vote by ballot, and franchise extension which were submitted prior to the passage of the new act in 1855 came from Carleton County. See PANB, RG 4, RS 24, 1851/Petition 463; 1853/Petition 22, Petition 63, Petition 85, Petition 104; 1854/Petition 104, Petition 114, Petition 115, Petition 183, Petition 217, Petition 420. The exception was an 1853 petition from York County which called for annual elections, the establishment of a registry of voters, and the introduction of vote by ballot. See PANB, RG 4, RS 24, 1851/Petition 461.

23 Garner, *Franchise,* 68–9. See also *Acts of the General Assembly,* 18 Vic., c 37.

24 Politically, the men of Albert proved somewhat more active than their counterparts in other counties. Poll books are extant for two other counties during the same period. In Charlotte County, 65 per cent of men who had reached voting age by 1851 voted in at least one election, while in Sunbury County, 62 per cent of voting-aged males went to the polls.

25 The profile of Silas Bishop is based on information drawn from the poll books for 1846, 1850, 1851, 1854, 1856, and 1857 (PANB, RG 18, RS 146), voters' lists for 1856 and 1857 (PANB, RG 18, RS 146), assessment rolls for 1847, 1854, 1855, 1856, and 1857 (PANB, RG 18, RS 146), and manuscript censuses for Albert County for 1851 and 1861 (PANB).

26 The profile of Hugh Alcorn is based on information drawn from the poll books for 1846, 1850, 1851, 1854, 1856, and 1857 (PANB, RG 28, RS 146), voters' lists for 1856 and 1857 (PANB, RG 18, RS 146), assessment rolls for 1847, 1854, 1855, 1856, and 1857 (PANB, RG 28, RS 146), manuscript censuses for Albert County for 1851 and 1861 (PANB), and Crown Lands and Lands Branch Records, Land Sold, Payable by Instalments (PANB, RG 10, RS 107, RNA/C/8/1, RNA/C/8/4, RNA/C/8/13).

27 The profile of Wesley Peck was developed using poll books for 1846, 1850, 1851, 1854, 1856, and 1857 (PANB, RG 18, RS 146), voters' lists for 1856 and 1857 (PANB, RG 18, RS 146), assessment rolls for 1847, 1854, 1855, 1856, and 1857 (PANB, RG 18, RS 146), and manuscript censuses for Albert County for 1851 and 1861 (PANB). Information concerning the details of Wesley Peck's land purchase was drawn from the *Registrar of Deeds,* vol. F (1856–8), 114–15, 256 (PANB, RG 9, RS 84).

28 Under this "Act to facilitate the sale and improvement of Crown Lands in certain cases," the lieutenant-governor, acting "with the advice and consent" of the Legislative Council and Assembly, could dispose of lots of crown land, not exceeding 100 acres, by private sale at three shillings per acre for money or labour in making roads. *Acts of the General Assembly,* 12 Vic., c 4.

29 The profile of William Howard was developed using poll books for 1846, 1850, 1851, 1854, 1856, and 1857 (PANB, RG 18, RS 146), voters' lists for 1856 and 1857 (PANB, RG 18, RS 146), assessment rolls for 1847, 1854, 1855, 1856, and 1857 (PANB, RG 18, RS 146), and manuscript censuses for Albert County for 1851 and 1861 (PANB). Documentation on William Howard's land petitions and grants is located in RG 10, RS 108, 1852; RS 272, 1845, vol. 28, no 136, and 1853, vol. 39, no 80; RS 686, 1850, grant no 5861, and 1859, vol. 56, grant no 9268.

30 Certainly historians have argued that this was the case in mid-nineteenth-century England. See, for example, TJ. Nossiter, *Influence, Opinion and Political Idioms in Reformed England: Case Studies from the North-East, 1832–74* (Hassocks 1975), 45–106, and David Cresap Moore, *The Politics of Deference: A Study of the Mid-Nineteenth Century English Political System* (Hassocks 1976), 281–324. The role of deference in the United States in a slightly earlier period, and the impact of the introduction of the secret ballot is discussed in Ronald P. Formisano, *The Transformation of Political Culture: Massachusetts Parties, 1790s–1840s* (New York 1983), 128–48.

31 See, for example, James Boyd and G.E. Fenety, cited in Garner, *Franchise,* 64. Of course, the assessments of contemporary observers, especially when those observers happened to be, like James Boyd, politicians dissatisfied with election results, are not always reliable. Writing at the end of the pre-Confederation era, G.E. Fenety, a long-time political journalist, painted a portrait of a House of Assembly immobilized as a result of the number of scrutinies that followed "every general election." Yet between 1784 and 1867, the New Brunswick House of Assembly was called upon to resolve only eighty-seven controverted elections. Ibid., 188.

32 Garner, for example, focuses on "occupiers of land," while Ouellet, DeBrou, and Jones all consider only heads of households. Garner, *Franchise;* Ouellet, *Lower Canada;* DeBrou, "Voter Turnout"; and Jones, "The Franchise."

33 This problem is less serious when researchers have been able to identify individual voters using poll books. However, for those researchers who have depended on aggregate statistics, the assumption that only household heads were eligible to vote could lead to potentially serious misinterpretations. Turnout among household heads may not have been as high as the statistics suggest, and the number of ineligible occupiers of land voting "by custom" may have been smaller than historians have generally assumed.

34 Since all the parishes in Albert County had a poll tax, all household heads were listed on the assessment rolls, whether they owned property or not. Yet the assessment rolls did not include all males twenty-one years of age and older, as might have been expected. Men who did not head households were not listed unless they were possessed of real or personal property. Thus Wesley Peck, although he resided in the county throughout the period, did not appear on the assessment rolls until 1857.

35 And in each case, the median age was very close to the mean age (thirty-nine among voters and thirty-six for the entire study group), indicating a normal curve.

36 Among non-voters, the New Brunswick-born were slightly under-represented (37.7 per cent as compared to 42.3 per cent in the study group as a whole) and the Irish were slightly over-represented (25 per cent as compared to 21.3 per cent in the study group), but these differences are not statistically significant at the.05 level and can be explained by other factors (the poverty of many of the more recent Irish immigrants as compared to native New Brunswickers, for example).

37 And while it is true that Albert County did not have a high proportion of pauper Irish, the experience of the famine Irish in Charlotte County demonstrates that Albert was not unique. The parish of St Andrews included a large number of poor Irish immigrants in 1851, many of them railroad labourers. Of the 960 voting-aged men living in St Andrews when the census was taken in 1851, only 43.9 per cent would vote in at least one of the elections held during the period under review. This was in marked contrast to the proportion of voters in Charlotte County as a whole. Of the 4542 voting-aged males listed in the census in 1851, 64.9 per cent (2948) would go to the polls at least once during the period.

38 All three young men could have been denied the right to vote on other grounds as well. Abner Kinne, of Harvey Parish, was just nineteen years old in 1856. His widowed mother was listed as a proprietor in the 1851 census, but neither she nor her sons possessed the necessary property qualification of £25. Levi Stevens was twenty in 1856 and was, like Abner Kinne, the son of a widow. But although Levi was too young to vote and was not yet on the assessment rolls himself, his three older brothers were eligible and all of them voted in that election, Thomas and William for the second time, John for the first. Levi Downie of Hopewell Parish was turned away from the polls for the same reason. He was nineteen in 1856. Like the other two young men who were denied the vote because they did not meet the age requirement, he was not on the assessment rolls in 1856. Both his father and older brother were eligible, however, and both voted in that election.

39 The proportion of rejected voters ranged from a low of 4.2 per cent in 1846 to a high of 6.6 per cent in 1854. PANB, RG 18, RS 146, J1–J6.

40 The proportion of voters who exercised the franchise on sufferance remained relatively consistent over time. By comparing poll books and available assessment records, voter eligibility could be determined for four of the six elections. For 1846, 9.3 per cent of voters could be identified as legally ineligible; for 1854, 8.8 per cent could be so identified; in 1856, the proportion rose again to 9.3 per cent; and in 1857, the first election held under the new rules, just 6.1 per cent of voters were not qualified under the law.

41 PANB, RG 4, RS 24, 1846/Petition, 1847/Petition, 1848/Petition, 1849/Petition, 1850/Petition, 1851/Petition, 1852/Petition, 1853/Petition, 1854/Petition, 1855/Petition, 1856/Petition, and 1857/Petition.

42 This discussion is based on an analysis of poll books (PANB, RG 18, RS 146), records of crown land sales payable by instalments (PANB, RG 10, RS 107, RNA/C/8/2, RNA/C/8/4, and RNA/C/8/9, PANB), and assessment records (PANB, RG 18, RS 146).

43 Pennsylvania had introduced a taxpayer suffrage as early as 1776. Other states soon followed suit. By the 1840s the United States had adopted universal white manhood suffrage. France adopted manhood suffrage in 1848, Prussia in 1849. In England, the Reform Bill of 1832 abolished local franchises and created a national system which enfranchised all leaseholders holding property of an appropriate value—most of them for the first time. At the same time, it should be noted that borough franchises had long been established by local practice. A few were very generous. Thus the Reform Bill of 1832 also disenfranchised voters in the more democratic boroughs, some of which had had an assessment franchise for centuries. Pole, *Political Representation,* 272–3, 494; Rokkan, "The Comparative Study of Political Participation," 75.

44 New Brunswick, House of Assembly, *Debates,* 1855, 52–72.

45 Professionals and the wealthier artisans in Woodstock (Carleton County) and Fredericton (York County) were the men most likely to benefit from the extension of the franchise. In Saint John, the impact of the new franchise would be much less significant. Traditionally, freeman of the city had always had the right to vote, and the vast majority of Saint John's professionals and artisans had freeman status.

46 Voters' registers became common throughout British North America only in the 1860s, and the Dominion of Canada followed the province's example in adopting the secret ballot only after the Liberal victory of 1874. Sweden adopted the secret ballot in 1866, Germany in 1867, Great Britain in 1872, France in 1875, and Belgium in 1878. Information on the European countries comes from Rokkan, "The Comparative Study of Political Participation," 75.

47 It should be noted, of course, that the establishment of voters' registers did not, in fact, eliminate corruption. For a discussion of the ways in which voters' registers could be manipulated see D.G.G. Kerr, "The 1867 Elections in Ontario: The Rules of the Game," *Canadian Historical Review* 51 (1970): 369–77; and Forster, Davidson, and Brown, "The Franchise, Personators, and Dead Men."

48 Yet even if such information were available, a decline of 3 per cent could scarcely be considered statistically significant and does not constitute a major change in electoral patterns.

49 Thus, if all the men of 1851 who either voted or were eligible to vote in each of the four elections for which the relevant assessment information is available are considered, turnout is somewhat lower and the increase more gradual, but the findings are consistent with the conclusions based on the analysis of the more stable group traced over all six elections.

	Men who voted		Eligible but did not vote		
Election Year	Number	%	Number	%	Total
1846	383	64.6	210	35.4	593
1854	674	71.2	273	28.8	947
1856	766	79.4	199	20.6	965
1857	720	82.4	154	17.6	874

50 Information on William Henry Steeves and John Smith was drawn from PANB, Graves Papers, vol. x, part II, 32, 127, and William Spray, "William Henry Steeves," *Dictionary of Canadian Biography,* x, 665.

51 Steeves, who was supported by 79.6 per cent of those who voted, topped the polls. In his home parish of Hillsborough, 98 per cent of the voters supported him. Smith topped the polls in his home parish of Harvey, winning the support of 74.5 per cent of the electorate. In the county as a whole, 67 per cent of those who went to the polls supported him. Steeves's support declined to 59.3 per cent in 1850, but nine candidates ran in that election. Moreover, Reuben Stiles, the man who replaced Smith in 1850, won the support of only 22 per cent of the voters. Of course, Stiles was a farmer and, although prosperous, was not nearly so wealthy as either Smith or Steeves. But in 1851, John Lewis, the man who won the seat vacated by Steeves, managed to garner just 48.3 per cent of the votes in a three-way contest. Lewis was a merchant, who, like his predecessors, owned property assessed at well over £1000.

52 At the same time, it should be noted that even in colonies without such rigorous restrictions, candidates for office were regularly drawn from among wealthy local elites.

53 Of the remaining 20.5 per cent of electors, some men split their votes, while others "plumped" for a single candidate. Thus McClelan topped the polls, supported by 57.3 per cent of the 886 voters. He was followed by his running mate, Lewis, who captured 55 per cent of the vote. Stevens placed third, with 41.2 per cent, and Duffy fourth with 38.5 per cent.

54 For a more detailed discussion of the rise of party within the New Brunswick electorate during this period see Gail G. Campbell, "'Smashers' and 'Rummies': Voters and the Rise of Parties in Charlotte County, New Brunswick, 1846–1857," Canadian Historical Association, *Historical Papers/Communications Historique,* 1986, 86–116.

55 Thus, 78.1 per cent of the men in the study group gained access to the franchise before the end of the period. Moreover, the 78.1 per cent may well underestimate the number of men in the study group who were able to gain access to the franchise during the period. Of the 300 men who did not vote and were not eligible to vote during the decade, 216 (72 per cent) had either died or left the county before the final election of the period. It seems likely that at least some of them gained access to the franchise elsewhere. Under this very restrictive franchise, then, the proportion of voting-aged males who had access to the franchise was actually higher than the proportion of Canadian men and women who choose to exercise their franchise today.

The Campaign for Representative Government in Newfoundland*

JERRY BANNISTER

The reform movement preceding the grant of representative government in 1832 has figured prominently in the writing of Newfoundland history. The traditional school of thought—which was established by D.W. Prowse and reached its apogee with A.H. McLintock—placed the reformers at the head of a colonial struggle to break the yoke of naval governors and absentee merchants responsible for the island's backward development.[1] In the first serious challenge to this orthodoxy, Keith Matthews asserted that the grant of representative government in 1832 marked simply the inevitable success of a colonial elite's ambition. As recent immigrants from Ireland and England, the reformers were merely following political currents in Britain, and they imposed a nationalist ideology which bore little relation to circumstances in the colony.[2] Matthews' thesis has been criticized by Patrick O'Flaherty, who maintains that the reform movement comprised a series of hard-fought battles against long-established injustices. According to O'Flaherty, reformers such as Patrick Morris and William Carson were responding to a legitimate sense of local grievance caused by systemic inequities suffered under naval rule.[3] In an analysis of how the reform movement shaped economic policy, Sean Cadigan has argued that while the reformers did respond to some local issues, they were a small mercantile and professional elite who based their ideas largely upon British-shaped gentry aspirations.[4] And in a recent study of sectarianism, John Greene claims that local disputes over religion formed the driving force of the reform movement. The campaign for representative government was the means by which Irish Catholics fought for their civil rights against a reactionary Protestant elite.[5]

This article offers an alternative interpretation of the rise of the reform movement and the fall of naval government. It argues that far from being inevitable, the demise of naval government, which had dominated Newfoundland since the mid-eighteenth century, came only after a protracted political campaign. Though the surrogate courts were abolished in 1824, the basic structure of naval rule remained intact until the grant of a local legislature in 1832. The first phase of the reform movement, which was dominated by Irish Catholics, repeatedly appealed for an end to naval government, but their efforts met with limited success in the face of opposition from both mer-

Jerry Bannister, "The Campaign for Representative Government in Newfoundland," *Journal of the Canadian Historical Association*, New Series, 5 (1999): 19–40.

*This article is a revised version of a paper which originally appeared in the *Journal of the Canadian Historical Association* in 1994. For their comments on earlier versions of this paper, I thank Melvin Baker, Sean Cadigan, Jane Errington, Allan Greer, and Jim Phillips. I also gratefully acknowledge the research funding provided by the Institute of Social and Economic Research at Memorial University and the Social Sciences and Humanities Research Council of Canada.

chants and government officials. The pivotal factor in the campaign for representative government was the formation of a broad-based coalition in 1828, when concerns over taxation brought together leading members of the Catholic and Protestant communities. In London the reformers overcame the imperial government's intransigence through a strategy designed to gain support in Parliament and to undermine the Colonial Office. Analysis of local meetings and petitions, as well as parliamentary debates, also indicates that the press played a crucial role in the reform movement's ability to embrace disparate socio-economic interests. The newspaper press worked to maintain the necessary image of unity and respectability, and it provided essential political momentum throughout the 1820s and early 1830s.

The movement in favour of reforming the island's legal system was part of a broader wave of political upheaval throughout the British Isles in the early nineteenth century. British and Irish reformers campaigned for an end to slavery, public whippings, and other practices deemed contrary to the natural rights of man. Irish politicians worked particularly hard to persuade the British government to repeal the penal laws affecting Roman Catholics.[6] Reformers in St. John's drew upon this larger cultural milieu to formulate their demands for an end to naval government, but the impact of events and trends in Britain and Ireland on the course of reform in Newfoundland can easily be exaggerated. The Colonial Office remained wary of bestowing legislative authority on British possessions, and prior to 1828 public opinion in Newfoundland was divided on the question of reform. Merchants remained generally opposed to the campaign for representative government until they became convinced that it was in their immediate economic interests. The struggle for an elected assembly had long-term ramifications for the development of both nationalism and democracy, as it created a political culture which persisted well into the twentieth century.

The Origins of the Reform Movement

Despite the evident strength of the naval government in the early nineteenth century, beneath the political surface surged forces that threatened the entire system of governance. The decade after the peace of 1815 witnessed the advent of bourgeois culture in St. John's. The roots of this social transformation grew out of the island's remarkable economic development during the French Revolutionary and Napoleonic Wars. As Newfoundland became a populous colony with a resident fishery, incipient political institutions emerged, such as the Society of Merchants and the Benevolent Irish Society.[7] Accompanying these organizations was a momentous development: the first local printing press. Operating under licence from the naval governor, in 1807 John Ryan began the *Royal Gazette,* a weekly paper published in St. John's devoted largely to government notices, official proclamations, and mercantile advertisements.[8] Although Ryan could initially publish only materials approved by the governor's office, the appearance of a local press marked a formative stage in the monitoring of state power. For the first time, the court calendar and the outcome of trials were published, providing a basis of accountability that far outstripped the traditional forms of communication. Under Sir Francis Forbes, Chief Justice of Newfoundland from 1817 to 1822, the judiciary also took a much more active role in upholding property rights and checking abuses by local officials.[9] The press facilitated this process by creating a *public* space in which the bourgeoisie could fix its place in the social environment, identify its local interests, and promote its own particular causes.[10] Early demands for reform had come primarily from St. John's merchants. The Society of Merchants petitioned repeatedly for advantages in trade, vowing to defend the colonists' rights secured by the British constitution. A significant challenge to the governor's authority emerged in 1811, when local merchants organized meetings to discuss grievances over a statute authorizing the lease of ships' rooms as private property.[11] In the island's first protest pamphlet, William Carson openly criticized the seizure of common property without the inhabitants' consent.[12] Carson's next tract warned the government not to insult the rights of Britons living in Newfoundland. The colonists deserved, he concluded, "what is unquestionably their right, a civil Government, consisting of a resident Governor, a Senate House, and House of Assembly."[13] From its beginnings, reform rhetoric identified social progress closely with the attainment of formal institutions comparable to other colonies and the constitutional rights granted to all British subjects. By 1820 the press contained newspapers that were clearly independent of the naval government. St. John's had two major papers—the pro-reform *Public Ledger* and the *Mercantile Journal*—and a third, the pro-Catholic *Newfoundlander,* appeared in 1827.[14] Newfoundland had lagged behind colonies such as Upper Canada in the early development of an independent press, but the public debates in St. John's were now as lively as those taking place in York.[15] Policies of the naval government were for the first time subjected to potentially critical public evaluation; the governor's office could no longer monopolize the process of political legitimization. Freedom of speech, which had emerged in England the previous century, eventually became a pivotal factor in the eventual downfall of the naval government. The press did not invent political opposition but rather revolutionized its means of expression.

Cause Célèbres and the Campaign against Naval Justice

In 1820 Newfoundland witnessed one of the most important *cause célèbres* in its history. The affair centred on the cases of two Conception Bay fishermen, James Lundrigan and Philip Butler, who were publicly whipped after receiving default judgements in surrogate court for outstanding debts. In 1818 Lundrigan had borrowed around £13 from a local supplier and, when the surrogate court met the following year, the merchant brought an action to recover the debt. The court ruled against the fisherman, whose property was attached, but Lundrigan and his wife, Sarah, successfully resisted efforts to take possession of their house. Summoned to appear before a surrogate court in July 1820, Lundrigan refused on the grounds that he had to go fishing to feed his hungry family. Arrested during the night, he was taken to a naval vessel, charged the next day with contempt of court and resisting arrest, and sentenced to receive thirty-six lashes on his bare back. Lundrigan, who was an epileptic, collapsed after fourteen lashes, and a surgeon stepped in to stop the whipping. The court ordered Lundrigan to relinquish his house and assets to his creditor, thereby evicting his wife and four children. Philip Butler's case, which took place the next day, followed a similar course. An indebted fisherman, Butler was sentenced to receive thirty-six lashes for contempt of court (he was given twelve), and he and his family were also evicted from their home. Supported by a group of reformers in St. John's, both Lundrigan and Butler took actions of trespass for assault and false imprisonment against the presiding surrogate judges in the Newfoundland Supreme Court.[16]

The reformers turned the cases of Lundrigan and Butler into a serious political issue. In 1820 they convened a meeting to protest against the cruel punishments inflicted for minor offenses.[17] Chaired by Patrick Morris, the meeting included many of the leaders of the Catholic community who formed the backbone of Newfoundland's reform movement.[18] The fact that Lundrigan and Butler were Irish only served to underscore the deep concerns among Catholics over the island's legal system.[19] Determined to win their place in the circles of power, middle-class Catholics also supported the campaign to repeal the religious penal laws. A committee was appointed to draft a petition to London: in addition to detailing the flaws in the surrogate system, the petition linked the need for a civil judiciary directly to the absence of local legislature. Stressing the reformers' patriotism and allegiance to the king, it appealed for all the rights and privileges granted to subjects in other British colonies.[20]

As had happened during the fishing admiral's controversy a century earlier, political protest involved manoeuvres on both sides of the Atlantic. After presenting memorials for legal reform to Governor Hamilton, the committee sent a representative, William Dawe, to convey its petition to the British parliament. Dawe also carried letters asking Lord Holland, who led a circle of liberal Whigs, and the prominent reform advocate Sir James Mackintosh, to represent the reform committee's interests.[21] When the House of Commons considered the petition in May 1821, Mackintosh asserted that he knew of "no other colony which more required the constant vigilance of a local assembly than Newfoundland." He took particular aim at the naval regime:

> The courts in question were called Surrogate Courts; the judges were principally composed of officers of the navy. Punishment for contempt was, he admitted, resorted to by courts of justice in England; but he believed the use of the lash in such cases was altogether unknown in this county; it was, however, the ordinary mode of punishment adopted in Newfoundland.[22]

As to the root of the problem, Mackintosh charged:

> The mode of proceeding in these floating courts was not regulated by the common law of England, so much as the discipline and practice of the navy. The system was a bad one, but was, he believed, the remains of a system which was still worse.[23]

The British government admitted that the island's judiciary required an overhaul, but warned of the problems associated with colonial assemblies. The Colonial Office had, in fact, already informed Governor Hamilton that it had no intention of granting Newfoundland a legislative assembly.[24]

Undaunted, the St. John's reformers organized a public meeting to place their case before a wider audience. Held in August 1821, the meeting established the principal arguments for representative government. Patrick Morris recounted how the island's long history of oppression under English merchants and naval officers had produced a legal system unequaled in the annals of despotic nations. Not only did the absence of a properly-constituted civil judiciary deny settlers recourse to British justice, but backward laws also prohibited exploitation of the island's agricultural resources and thus retarded economic development. The absence of electoral representation deprived Newfoundlanders of their constitutional birthrights as British subjects. Newfoundland was left to endure taxation without representation, while its revenues were ample to support a legislature. The committee concluded that all these problems were, at bottom, caused by the want of an elected assembly.[25]

History, Politics, and Law Reform

The public outcry against the surrogate courts marked only the first salvo in a larger struggle against the naval government. Reformers incessantly attacked naval government as arbitrary, outmoded, and incompetent. In doing so, they not only drew on previous writers, such as Chief Justice John Reeves, but they also crafted their own version of Newfoundland history. Like most other nationalist movements, the St. John's reformers constructed a cultural memory of oppression as a basis on which to mount attacks on the status quo.[26] For example, William Carson asserted with biting sarcasm that the island's legal problems stretched back to its earliest settlers:

> The inhabitants appear to have been considered, either as a race of savages untamable by civilization, and which could not be re-trained by any regular code of laws, or as Angels descended immediately from Heaven, pure and perfect, possessing minds which did not require instruction, and passion that needed not the control of terrestrious [sic] institutions.[27]

And, in a lengthy speech devoted largely to Newfoundland history, Patrick Morris offered a similarly harsh appraisal:

> Here, Gentlemen, a system of Government was established for this country unequaled in the annals of the most despotic nations, and a system better calculated to oppress and barbarize a country, was never framed by the perverted ingenuity of man. Under this authority the most wanton acts of violence were committed—the houses and property of the Inhabitants and Planters were burnt and destroyed, and every other means were resorted to, to drive them from the land of their birth, or their extirpate them altogether. It is scarcely creditable at the period we live in, that such a state of things could exist in a country calling itself civilized.[28]

In essence, Newfoundland under naval government had failed the test of civilized society.

The fervor in St. John's reached new heights with the publication of an anonymous pamphlet which detailed the history of legal abuses culminating in the whipping of Lundrigan and Butler. On the problem of finding the cause of this "mal-administration of justice," it contended:

> [I]t is easy to comprehend that portion that must be of widely spreading magnitude, when it is considered that every new squadron of ships of war, and every single ship that arrives on the station, in their commanding officers, furnishes a new set of itinerant judges, who, under every disqualification for the office, save the authority which they derive under the commission of the Governor, are dispersed along the coasts of the island to exercise the functions of judges, in criminal as well as civil causes, in the surrogate and sessions courts.

The indictment of the naval government did not end there:

> When to the numberless errors in judgment, inevitably incident to such judges, and the consequent injuries to the rights of parties, are superadded the intemperate and unlawful finings, imprisonments, and floggings which they have inflicted; it becomes to a reflecting mind, a matter of surprise, how the moral relations of society have been held together, amid the heart-burnings and resentments which such a system of judicature must inevitably generate.[29]

For three generations, official correspondence and printed accounts had portrayed the naval governor and the surrogate system as the very bastion of English justice in Newfoundland. Within the space of a few years, however, the reform press had savaged the navy's reputation.

By taking this approach, the reformers were following a well-established pattern—as Eric Hobsbawm has argued, the process of inventing a tailor-made history has been a key ingredient of most successful nationalist movements—and the only exceptional aspect of this rhetoric is the degree to which Newfoundland historians have accepted such polemics at face value.[30]

Constitutional Reform, 1824–26

In 1824 the reformers scored their first major victory. The British government introduced a bill that appeared to signal the dismantling of the naval government. The Judicature Act abolished the surrogate courts and provided for a charter of incorporation to make town bylaws.[31] With the end of the surrogate courts, the island had shed one of the principal features of naval government. Having sat as judges since the seventeenth century, naval officers in Newfoundland finally lost their prerogative to administer law. A second statute passed in 1824 finally repealed King William's Act.[32] In 1825 the British government issued a Royal Charter which authorized the creation of a revamped Supreme Court and a system of Circuit Courts.[33] Captain Thomas Cochrane, the island's new governor, was also instructed to appoint a council to aid and assist his administration. The governorship became a civil appointment, no longer under the Admiralty's control, and Newfoundland was nominally recognized as an official colony.[34] When Cochrane arrived in St. John's, he received a warm reception and was lauded in the local press. In January 1826 he presided over an elaborate public ceremony to mark the opening of the newly-constituted Supreme Court. With the streets jammed with onlookers, a long procession of officials and dignitaries marched from the governor's residence to the court house; an officer in the parade displayed the Royal Charter as salutes were fired by an honour guard and a warship in the harbour; and, to mark the occasion, the Governor pardoned and released most of the prisoners from jail.[35]

The Royal Charter altered the island's judiciary but did not transform its basic mode of governance. Although Newfoundland was now a colony with a civil governor, many aspects of naval rule persisted under Governor Cochrane's tenure. Like most of the earlier naval governors, Cochrane was a relatively young career officer with good political connections. He had attained the rank of captain at the age of seventeen, and then served in the West Indian and North American squadrons before receiving his Newfoundland appointment. Still a captain when he assumed the governorship at the age of thirty-six, Cochrane was a martinet who treasured pomp and circumstance.[36] In a report to the Colonial Office, he affirmed, "I am persuaded from what I have heard of the people that a governor ought to go among them with all the attributes of consequence and authority belonging to the situation to ensure him that respect they are not over anxious to observe to those placed over them."[37] Not only was Cochrane himself little different from his predecessors, but the powers he enjoyed under the Judicature Act were not much different from those wielded under the old regime. Added to the system of colonial government was a council—it comprised the chief justice, two assistant judges, and the commander of the army garrison—but this was merely an advisory body, appointed by the governor and effectively under his control.[38] Like generations of naval officers before him, Cochrane was left to govern Newfoundland as best he saw fit, without the encumbrance of an elected assembly.

In early 1826 Governor Cochrane moved to implement his instructions from the Colonial Office. He held meetings with merchants and prominent reformers in order to discuss the creation of a town council in St. John's. The proposals called for a mayor and fifteen-member council, with a franchise of £10 freehold property or £20 annual leasehold.[39] However, this initiative abruptly ground to a halt when a bloc of leading merchants opposed the plans for reform.[40] While Cochrane preferred the majority's view, he left the Colonial Office to determine the "species of government" best suited to the colony. Cochrane did recommend an *ad valorem* duty as a means to raise revenue in the colony.[41] In a September 1826 report James Stephen, legal advisor to the Colonial Office, proposed a legislative council for the colony as an alternative to "the many inconveniences" attended by an assembly, but the British government decided to wait until Cochrane clarified the situation in Newfoundland.[42] In November 1826 Cochrane informed Lord Bathurst that the populace remained heavily divided on the question of local government.[43] Moreover, Henry Winton, editor of the pro-reform Public Ledger, conceded that the colony seemed unprepared for a local assembly. "The truth is," Winton wrote, "that we want a few practical lessons...before we can venture from our political leading-strings."[44] Merchants in St. John's had never fully backed the early reform movement: with a conservative faction publicly objecting to the establishment of a town council, the split between conservative and reformist parties inhibited further political change. By mid-1827 representative government still appeared to be a rather distant goal.

To keep the campaign for a local legislature alive, the reformers clung to their crusade against the naval government. These polemics were no longer restricted to anonymous pamphlets and letters to the editor. In 1827 Patrick Morris launched a full broadside against the evils of the old regime:

> The government of Newfoundland by the Admirals of the British fleet exhibits examples of the danger of placing uncontrolled power in the hands of any man or set of men, and affords melancholy proofs that English gentlemen—the representatives of a constitutional king—of the highest rank in the truly honourable profession to which they belonged—did, in the exercise of power, act more like Persian satraps or Turkish bashaws than men who, it is to be supposed, were well read in the constitutional history of their country.[45]

The reformers kept invoking this argument as long as it boosted their cause. By doing so, naval government entered the realm of caricature and legend, alongside the fishing admirals, to form one of the core myths of Newfoundland nationalism. By the time Judge Prowse published his seminal history of the island, the eighteenth-century had become a dark age of anarchy.[46]

Taxation without Representation: Making a Political Coalition

The proposals for new taxes quickly provoked St. John's merchants into political action. In October 1827 the Chamber of Commerce petitioned against the import duty "with painful apprehension" of the effects on the depressed fish trade.[47] After Cochrane forwarded the petition to London, George Robinson, a partner with Thomas Brooking and the Tory M.P. for Worcester, voiced the merchants' concerns in an interview with the Colonial Secretary, William Huskisson. The free importation of fishery supplies had long been a mercantile tenet, but Huskisson reportedly justified the new duty on the grounds that the colony now had "to pay its own expenses."[48] Robinson then took action in Parliament and, on 30 May 1828, asked the government to postpone Newfoundland's grant for civil expenditure until it investigated Governor Cochrane's financial management. With the five-year term of the Judicature Act soon to expire, Robinson demanded a select committee to inquire into the state of Newfoundland.[49] In August 1828 the Chamber of Commerce, led by

Thomas Brooking, publicly denounced the import duty as a grave threat to the fishery.[50] In a form of political protest, merchant vessels sailing to St. John's refused to carry the mail in order to prevent Cochrane from receiving instructions on the new tax.[51] The Newfoundland case reflects T.W. Acheson's model of Saint John's merchants: though often fractured, merchant interests could unite rapidly when threatened with increased taxation.[52]

In the meantime the question of Newfoundland's governance surfaced in the English press. In an April 1828 pamphlet Patrick Morris entreated the government to grant the neglected colony a local legislature. He argued that those merchants who resisted the reform movement were "vainly putting forth their paralyzed arms to arrest the progress of justice and civilization—they have all the *will* to keep us in bondage and barbarism; but, thank God, they have not the *power*." "Newfoundland will no longer be a plantation of Poole," Morris declared, "and her people will no longer be their slaves."[53] Although the surrogate courts had already been abolished, the island's naval government remained a principal target: "The absurd, and ridiculous, and often unjust and arbitrary proceedings of the surrogates are well known.... I have seen so many acts of cruelty and oppression committed at Newfoundland under the authority and pretense of summary justice, that I lose all patience even at the very mention of its being established."[54] He also insisted that Newfoundland possessed the elements necessary for representative government: a population of sufficient education and property, an environment able to support agriculture, and the means to raise adequate revenues. The pamphlet drew a rejoinder from a writer in Poole who attacked Morris' flagrant distortions, rejected notions that the island could sustain a viable agriculture, and termed the possible benefits of a local assembly too slender to alter existing policy.[55] A review of Morris' pamphlet in the *Sphynx* nevertheless lauded the triumphant refutation of the view of Newfoundland as a country too undeveloped for a local legislature.[56] In Newfoundland these exchanges received extensive coverage and editorial comment in local newspapers.[57]

The Newfoundland papers went much further than simply reporting on debates in England. With the creation of a bourgeois public sphere in St. John's, the press exerted a formative influence on political discourse.[58] In a series of editorials, the newspapers published by John Shea and Henry Winton soon transformed concerns over the proposed import duty into a cogent argument for representative government. When John Shea reported the duty in 1827, he noted the economic implications but then continued: "such a tax on a colony like ours, without representation, would be a direct violation of the pledge given by the Government to the Colonies after the American Revolutionary War."[59] That pledge was the Declaratory of 1778, which stated that the King and Parliament of Great Britain would not directly impose any duty or tax on any British colony, except for the regulation of commerce, in which case the funds could be allocated only for the internal use of the colony.[60] In April 1828, Shea appealed for the duty not to be "exacted from us upon the principle of 'taxation without representation.'"[61] A letter by "Mercator," published in the *Public Ledger* in December 1827, argued: "taxation without representation is contrary to the express promise of Great Britain to her colonies, and to the spirit of the British Laws."[62] Henry Winton claimed that he did not object to the duty itself, but to the absence of the "*right* to collect and appropriate the sums so raised." He concluded: "a new and very powerful argument arises out of this subject to confirm the necessity of introducing a change in the government of this country."[63] Three days later Winton warned that under the present system the tax would be imposed "while the people remain relatively unconscious of the indirect burthens" imposed on them.[64]

The press repeatedly urged the public to unite and act upon these grievances. Upon hearing that the government intended to use the duty to pay for new public buildings, Winton warned of dire consequences if the colonists could not "agree to solicit that the appropriation of the money so exacted may be placed within their own control."[65] An editorial in the *Newfoundlander* also affirmed that the time had arrived "when the most active steps should be taken to endeavour to obtain for the people a voice in the appropriation" of the any duties.[66] In August 1828 the Public Ledger called for a public meeting of "qualified" individuals to recommend changes to the colony's government.[67] During the fall of 1828 Winton encouraged a gentlemanly discussion and asked that "former prejudices and prepossessions upon the subject be thoroughly forgotten."[68] A letter from "Atomus" called for public meetings to discuss the issues and "to sooth down all angry feelings and conflicting sentiments." The letter held that "on the present occasion, I consider the great object of *all* should be—UNANIMITY."[69] Finally, on 18 November 1828 Winton reported that objections to a local legislature had abated: "upon *that* important question," he declared, "no obstacles are likely now to be raised."[70]

In early December 1828 the local papers printed an announcement for a meeting to discuss both the proposed import duty and the question of a legislative assembly. Strongly endorsed by Shea and Winton, the meeting marked a watershed in the colony's reform movement.[71] The list of signatures on the notice and the subsequent petition for an assembly reveals that many of the leading merchants who had opposed a charter of incorporation in 1826, such as Benjamin Bowring, Robert Alsop, James McBride, Robert Brown, and John Brine, now publicly supported the campaign for representative government.[72] Most importantly, the campaign for representative government received backing from the leadership of both the Irish Catholic community and the Protestant mercantile interests. Representing firms which would be directly affected by the new import duty, the leaders of the Chamber of Commerce—Thomas Brooking, John Dunscombe, William Thomas, and Newman Hoyles—became heavily involved in the campaign for a local legislature.[73] The Roman Catholic Church maintained excellent relations with the Protestant elite, and the lay leadership of the Irish community remained committed to political reform.[74] Tensions loomed beneath the political surface, but the apparent harmony between the Protestant and Catholic communities persisted largely because Catholics saw a colonial legislature as a means to acquire religious rights.[75] Driven by different impulses, then, the colony's two main factions came together in a coalition to work for a local assembly.

The data contained in the petitions of the 1820s reveal that political participation was not wholly restricted to a small colonial elite. The February 1826 petition against a charter of incorporation listed an occupation for each signature and provides a rough indication of the social range of political involvement in St. John's: of the 172 residents on the list, just over a quarter belonged to the elite, about forty per cent were from the middling ranks, and almost a third were artisans. A comparison of the 1829 memorial with data on an earlier petition reveals significant political involvement among the middling and working classes of St. John's. While the vast majority of identities on the 1829 memorial remain unknown, the list did contain a number of planters, shopkeepers, and artisans. The non-elite names that could be positively identified included several coopers and sailmakers, as well as a baker, wheelwright, carpenter, smith and shoemaker.[76]

The public sphere in St. John's appears to have been largely a male preserve. Six women signed the 1826 petition: Elizabeth McLean and

TABLE 1 | POLITICAL PARTICIPATION IN ST. JOHN'S, 1826

Occupation	Number of Signatories	Percentage of Total Signatories
Merchant	40	28%
Land Proprietor	2	
Landowner	3	
Gentleman	3	
Notary Public	2	41%
Surgeon	2	
Apothecary	1	
Shopkeeper	13	
Planter	32	
Farmer	8	
Fish Culler	6	
Innkeeper	2	
Spirit Dealer	3	
Schoolmaster	1	
Watchmaker	3	31%
Cabinet Maker	1	
Cooper	6	
Wheelwright	1	
Mason	2	
Smith	4	
Tailor	2	
Sailmaker	3	
Carpenter	19	
Shoemaker	5	
Painter	1	
Baker	3	
Butcher	3	

Source: PANL, CO 194/72, p. 158, Cochrane to Bathurst, 27 May 1826, enclosure 7.

Jane Dameral, both described as landholders in Riverhead; Ann Curtice, who was listed as a farmer; Mary Ann McCalman and Ann Matthews, both Water Street Shopkeepers; and Emily Hill, who signed for her husband, Nathaniel, an innkeeper. Yet only one woman, Anastasia McCarthy, was among the 498 signatories to the 1829 petition. The level of women's participation in the reform movement seems to have been lower than in New Brunswick, where women were significantly involved in petitions for political reform.[77] As in Prince Edward Island, women in nineteenth-century Newfoundland were largely excluded from the public arena of formal politics, though this did not extend to the informal politics which suffused rural communities.[78] Patriarchy was, as Sean Cadigan argues, actively supported by the naval government, which took a dim view of women who overstepped their roles as obedient wives and virtuous mothers.[79] Reformers may have attacked the system of naval government as unjust, but they also viewed women through the lens of their domestic responsibilities. For example, when Patrick Morris argued that Newfoundlanders had a strong moral character, he quoted at length from Lewis Anspach's *History of Newfoundland:*

> *[T]he natives, of both sexes, are equally remarkable for their ingenuity and industry;* the women, besides the very valuable assistance which they afford during the season for curing and drying fish, generally understand the whole process of preparing the wool from the fleece, and of manufacturing it, by knitting it into stockings, caps, socks, and mittens. Their worsted stockings are strong, and well calculated for the climate. *The women are also characterized by a steady attention to their domestic duties, and correctness of conduct in every point of view.*[80]

Like their counterparts in other British colonies, the reformers employed gendered language to construct arguments for political rights.[81] In reacting to a perceived violation of political rights, William Carson argued that "as Men, as British Subjects they hoped for better treatment."[82]

The reform movement encompassed a variety of arguments and political traditions as it evolved in a dynamic colonial environment. The situation in Newfoundland was far from unique: virtually every colony throughout British North America experienced similar political debates in the 1820s and 1830s, particularly over the twin issues of revenue and representation.[83] As elsewhere in the Empire, the reformers used language similar to trends in Britain, but the Newfoundland reform movement did not develop solely through the importation of British reform ideology. Evidence of a vibrant public discussion in St. John's contradicts Keith Matthews' assertion that the relative harmony after 1828 was the result of an ascendancy of a pro-reform elite of recent immigrants who imposed their own agenda on Newfoundland politics.[84] By the 1820s the burgeoning public debate in St. John's inhibited the political hegemony of a single clique. Fueled by anxieties over import duties, the reform movement had transformed into a fairly broad-based coalition united against "taxation without representation." And with the renewed drive for a local assembly came a nativist voice. In a June 1828 editorial John Shea commented sarcastically that it was "very kind of John Bull, truly, to allow us potatoes and salt *duty free.*"[85] Moreover, Henry Winton argued in October 1828 that Newfoundland "must be under the legislation of a body of men who are resident in the colony."[86] A letter from "A Native" opposed a local legislature and the influence of those with "no stake in the country."[87] In response to such concerns, William Thomas later asserted during a public meeting:

> I am not a native of this island, Sir, but my father was, and my children are natives. I have resided here nearly 30 years, and I look to this

> island as the future residence of myself and my family. To Newfoundland I am indebted for the property I possess... I am, therefore, attached by strong ties to Newfoundland.[88]

By protesting the proposed tax in 1828, Thomas was protecting his Newfoundland property.

The meeting to discuss taxation and representation, held 18 December 1828 in St. John's, had some dissension but ended in unanimity. It began with a brief conference, dominated entirely by merchants, which resolved to petition against any import duty. William Carson then began the meeting on a local assembly by stressing the need to end the colony's oppression, but the issue of taxation dictated the ensuing discussion. Several merchants noted that if the government went ahead with the duty, then the colony needed a voice in its appropriation. Thomas Bennett reportedly declared: "if they did not tax us, there would be no necessity for the institution of a House of Assembly," and he called for an adjournment until the tax became official. William Thomas maintained the need for a legislature but also said he was "no enthusiast" about the island's agricultural potential. Chaired by William Carson, the committee appointed to prepare a petition included members from both the older reform movement, notably Patrick Doyle, and the merchant elite, represented by William Thomas.[89] The resulting petition stressed the colony's economic development and argued that compared to other colonies the island deserved, and could financially support, its own legislature.[90] It also argued that the new import duty was unconstitutional because it contravened the Declaratory Act of 1778, which the reformers again quoted at length.[91] In taking this course, they were following a well established tradition in contemporary reformist rhetoric.[92]

Yet in spite of its recent growth, the reform movement met with little success throughout 1829–30. Governor Cochrane had already advised the Colonial Office to oppose the agitation for reform and to extend the Judicature Act for another year.[93] In February 1829 a report from the Poole merchants urged the government to repeal the provisions for local government in the colony.[94] Despite repeated attempts, George Robinson failed to persuade the government to form a Parliamentary committee of inquiry on Newfoundland.[95] The Public Ledger lamented that the petitions had "failed to become the subject of serious deliberation by the government."[96] Cochrane reported in late 1829 that the planned duty on imports continued to generate considerable excitement: "Unfortunately, as the various memorials in the Colonial Office will show you, there is mixed up with the question of taxation, that of colonial representation." He explained that "while one party pray to avert taxation because they cannot bear it, another entreat a legislature on the ground that they are equal to provide for their own expenses." In order to placate the agitators Cochrane recommended a "work popular in its character," i.e. road construction, funded from the new tax.[97]

A series of letters in the local press nevertheless formed a renewed political exchange which kept the question of a local legislature in front of the St. John's public. In the first of a series of letters, "Peregrinus" pleaded that "without the fostering aide of a local legislature, it is vain to talk of the improvement of the colony." Yet other letters by "Peregrinus" adopted the language on taxation and proclaimed: "*Taxation* and *representation* are inseparately united: God hath joined them; no British Parliament can separate them; to endeavour to do so is to stab our vitals." In response to "Peregrinus," "Hospes" questioned the "bare assertion" that a legislature assisting agriculture would cure all the colony's ills. "Quis" countered with a call for unity—"He who is not for us is against us"—and cited the *probable* good brought by a legislature. Finally, "Hospes" warned of merchant domination, stressed that all of the people should have a vote, and added a very perceptive comment on "Peregrinus": "Your writings are like a Jack-of-all-trades shop."[98]

On 15 September 1830 the reformers held a public meeting to discuss solely the issue of a colonial assembly. As a sign of the reform movement's growth, the meeting took place on the military parade ground in St. John's. The day before the meeting Winton repeated rumours that a cabal of merchants had resolved to support a town council instead of an assembly.[99] Though the report proved unfounded, it illustrated the tensions within the reform movement. Open opposition later appeared when an editorial in the *Royal Gazette* argued that Newfoundland could not afford a local legislature.[100] The meeting nevertheless went smoothly; in an apparent effort to represent the two main factions of the reform coalition, the Public Ledger printed the addresses given by William Thomas and John Kent, a new leader of the Catholic community.[101] Thomas reiterated the threat of import duties and, referring to the current gossip, asked rhetorically, "would a Town Council put a stop to this tax?" Kent argued that Newfoundland needed a legislature to ensure its economic development, and concluded that "the lovers of freedom...will support our cause." He also stressed that the political discussions enjoyed "a nearer approach to unity than at any previous period."[102]

The meeting then appointed a committee, chaired by William Thomas, to prepare a petition for a local legislature and to arrange for a delegation to present it to the British government.[103] Led by Thomas Brooking, the delegation arrived in London in December 1830 to find a new Whig government; after conferring with George Robinson, Brooking arranged for an interview with the King. On Christmas Eve they presented the petition, signed by over two thousand residents, to the Colonial Secretary, Lord Goderich. While Goderich affirmed the importance of Newfoundland, he neither voiced an opinion on the question of local government nor committed the government to any action.[104] The delegation in London nonetheless believed that the meetings had boosted their cause. When news of the interviews reached Newfoundland the Public Ledger observed that "the present government are likely to coincide with the views of the inhabitants."[105] During a meeting of the Benevolent Irish Society in St. John's, the gathering toasted the triumphant efforts of the reformers. Amid the cheers William Carson proclaimed there was every reason to expect that the authorities would grant a local legislature and thereby supply the constitutional rights needed to "consummate our happiness."[106]

Colonial Politics in London

Despite such optimism, the drive for representative government soon bogged down again. In June 1831 Lord Howick, the Under-Secretary for the Colonies, reaffirmed the official policy that local conditions prevented the establishment of a legislative assembly: the island's society had not developed sufficiently to support electoral politics.[107] While Howick's pronouncement met with astonishment in Newfoundland, it accorded with the broader trends throughout this period. The Whig administration's commitment to political reform in Britain did not necessarily extend to the colonies. Both Cabinet and Parliament typically paid little attention to colonial affairs, particularly during the intense debates over the Reform bill in 1831–32. Lord Howick, who wielded the real power in colonial affairs, remained ambivalent towards demands for colonial self-government. Within the Colonial Office, R.W. Hay's tenure as Permanent Under-Secretary epitomized conservatism.[108] Perhaps most importantly, the reform movement had failed to neutralize Governor

Cochrane's influence. In April 1831 Cochrane advised the Colonial Office against making any major changes to the existing political system.[109] Instead of an assembly he recommended the creation of a legislative council to enact laws for the internal government of the island.[110] And in July 1831 the Colonial Office informed Cochrane that the arguments against granting a local legislature were "so strong as to render it unlikely that the government will adopt such a measure."[111]

Meanwhile George Robinson struggled to keep the colonial reform movement alive in London. In July 1831 he again opposed the annual grant to Newfoundland on the grounds that the absence of a local assembly rendered its expenditure unaccountable. Robinson then quickly advanced three arguments for granting the colony a local legislature: the colony's economic development necessitated a local assembly; the Newfoundland people only wanted the legitimate right to control their own affairs; and the grant of a local legislature would eliminate the colony's cost to the British government.[112] When Howick defended the government's policy, Robinson responded:

> The people of Newfoundland have instructed me to say, that if you will grant them a local legislature they will not again ask for money. Here, then, is an inducement to alter the present system, under which it is impossible for you to tell what you pay for it.[113]

Though Robinson was chided for his "coarse game," a number of M.P.'s took the bait and voiced their indignation over the colony's financial mismanagement. By tapping into a theme which would draw an immediate response, Robinson reignited the case for a local legislature.[114]

When news of the debate reached Newfoundland, it revitalized the local reform movement. On 29 September 1831 the reform committee convened an open meeting in St. John's to discuss its next course of action. The application to hold a public assembly reveals that the coalition of the mercantile elite and Catholic reformers was still holding: Brooking, Thomas, Row and Bennett signed alongside Morris, Kent, Doyle, Beck and, of course, Carson.[115] Held on the parade ground in St. John's, the open meeting attracted a cross-section of the population. Henry Winton reported that the assembly involved "disreputable personalities" and declined to print speeches that served "simply to amuse the public."[116] Unfortunately, when the working people become visible, contemporary sources silence their voices. We can only conclude that, first, the "lower orders" were present in sufficient numbers to attract attention (and disapproval) and, second, some reform speakers were targeting a popular audience. In order to project a respectable image of the reform movement, Winton later printed a speech given by William Row. Row's address noted that while "but one opinion prevailed" on the issue of local government, it remained "highly important that this unanimity should continue, as on it must greatly depend the final success of our efforts."[117]

The meeting's other leading speeches reinforced the reform movement's established themes. William Thomas focused on the question of taxation and the need for an assembly to control the colony's revenue. John Kent concluded his appeal for a local assembly by noting that "the press—the index of public feeling, the mirror of the people's mind—loudly proclaims its necessity."[118] Carson and Morris then commented on the great strides made by the reform movement in the long struggle to overcome the colony's oppression. The meeting observed "with a degree of satisfaction the admission made in the House of Commons...that the wealth and intelligence of the people of Newfoundland have entitled them to have a direct control in the management of their own affairs." However, in an apparent contradiction, the next resolution noted that "the depressed condition of our trade and fisheries, and the infant state of our agriculture, absolutely require the fostering care and encouragement of a local legislature."[119] Yet the reformers had no difficulty with this paradox, for an eclectic mix of arguments characterized the discourse surrounding the campaign for local government. The themes of poverty and prosperity became intertwined into a vision of a local assembly as the ultimate panacea for the colony.[120]

As the St. John's reformers observed the growth of the campaign for a legislature, they increasingly discussed the issue of participation from outport communities.[121] The outports had in fact petitioned for reform as early as 1821, and in Conception Bay Robert Pack was an early proponent of a colonial legislature.[122] In 1829 the *Conception Bay Mercury* strongly endorsed a local assembly as a vehicle for improvement.[123] A letter from "An Out-Harbour Man" asked Winton to specify the reformers' plans for the operation of a local legislature.[124] But an organized campaign for a local legislature only emerged in the outports in 1831. Attached to the recent St. John's memorial were petitions from Carbonear, Port de Grave, Old Perlican, and Brigus. The texts massed population and trade statistics to illustrate rural economic development to prove that St. John's was not the colony's only town of importance.[125] Nonetheless, meetings held in Burin and St. Mary's underscored the depressed state of the fishery and, as the St. Mary's meeting noted, the hope for "practical and beneficial results" from a local legislature.[126] In 1831–32 the island endured a particularly harsh winter which saw outbreaks of looting for food.[127]

Unknown to those in Newfoundland, however, George Robinson had already pulled off a pivotal manouevre in the House of Commons. After consulting with Joseph Hume, Robinson introduced a motion concerning Newfoundland in the House of Commons at a time shrewdly calculated to achieve maximum publicity. On 13 September 1831, the evening reserved for the third reading of the Reform Bill, Robinson interrupted the proceedings to state that the government's neglect of Newfoundland had compelled him to speak on a local subject. After reading the colony's petitions he launched into three arguments for the establishment of a local legislature. First, he cited the colony's extensive trade and large population relative to other colonies with representative government. Second, Robinson argued that the government's financial mismanagement caused the fishery's state of great embarrassment and distress. Finally, Robinson referred to the practical difficulties entailed with Parliament's "meddling with the details of colonial legislation." Robinson concluded with a motion for an address to the Crown asking for a local assembly similar to the other North American colonies and in accordance with the principles of the British Constitution.[128]

In response Lord Howick complained of the embarrassment caused by the timing of Robinson's motion. Howick nevertheless went quickly onto the offensive and noted that a meeting of Poole merchants had declared against the establishment of a local assembly. He reiterated the government's position that Newfoundland's uneven development made it "practically impossible to have an assembly really representing the...inhabitants of the island."[129] Following some discussion Joseph Hume declared that any further delay in the establishment of a local legislature would be "extremely prejudicial" to the interests of both the island's populace and the British government. He then advanced in rapid succession three distinct arguments in favour of a local legislature:

> What is it that 80,000 or 90,000 British subjects ask for? It is that [1] they may be relieved from the arbitrary sway of an individual, and that they may be allowed to manage their own affairs; and, when they ask for this, they undertake [2] to relieve this country from every portion of the

> expense which has hitherto been incurred in the government of Newfoundland.... But let expense be what it may, I contend that [3] it is impossible for any body of men in Downing-street properly and satisfactorily to govern a distant and populace colony like that of Newfoundland.

Next, Hume targeted the neglect of the colonists' civil rights: "The present government profess to be guided by liberal principles—let us see if they will act upon them." Hume placed the onus squarely on the government and, therefore, transformed the issue of Newfoundland's governance into a question of the credibility of the Grey administration's commitment to reform.[130]

Lord Althorp, the Chancellor of the Exchequer, responded by recommending a committee of inquiry as the proper forum to discuss the colony's government. But with Hume's support, Robinson's motion quickly excited interest in the crowded House. Henry Labouchere, a prominent Whig and an acquaintance of Lord Howick, declared that Althorp's suggestion was inadequate because Robinson's motion concerned an issue too important for a committee.[131] Labouchere argued that Newfoundland deserved a constitution "founded upon those broad principles of British liberty which have been extended to the other colonies."[132] Forced on the defensive, Lord Howick professed that he had merely noted the difficulties entailed with giving Newfoundland an assembly. Howick's defense met with a barrage of reform rhetoric in which Daniel O'Connell argued that the "great principles of liberty" should govern colonial issues. Robinson then declared that he would withdraw his motion if the government guaranteed to appoint a committee of inquiry on Newfoundland. In response Lord Althorp stated cryptically that the government would "give to that colony as much freedom and independence as shall be considered consistent with its own prosperity and security."[133]

In October 1831 Governor Cochrane travelled to London for consultations at the Colonial Office. According to later testimony Cochrane believed that the interviews had gone well.[134] Yet Lord Howick had already instructed James Stephen to report on the type of legislature suited for the colony. Released on 19 December 1831, Stephens' report recommended a blended assembly, which would include elected representatives and officials appointed by the Governor. Emphasizing the problems which bicameral legislatures had wrought in other colonies, Stephen claimed that a single legislative body, like the one established in Demerara, would engender greater harmony and help to balance the colony's political factions.[135] On 22 December 1831 Thomas Brooking arrived in London and had a meeting with Lord Holland early in the new year. Pleased with the interview, Brooking informed William Thomas of his progress and mentioned a rumour, which was probably accurate, that the government had already made a decision regarding Newfoundland.[136] Finally, on 25 January 1832 Goderich told Brooking during a private meeting that the government had resolved to grant the colony a local legislature. Lord Howick also wrote a letter of congratulation to Robinson which claimed that the government had resisted making any promises simply out of anxiety not to raise false hopes.[137] After more than a decade of struggle, the Newfoundland reform movement had at last achieved its ultimate goal. Parliament passed legislation confirming the powers of the new assembly, and the first elections were scheduled for the autumn of 1832.[138]

Conclusion

A number of factors shaped the development of local opposition to naval government. The reform movement developed through a symbiotic process in which an inherited political culture interacted with colonial conditions. When the reformers dealt with local issues, such as the structure of the justice system, they viewed representative institutions as the proper solution to local problems. The colony's mercantile elite initially opposed the reform movement, and then publicly divided over the question of local government, but the Chamber of Commerce nevertheless maintained effective leadership of the St. John's merchant community. During the 1820s a bourgeois public sphere emerged in St John's and acted as a forum for reformist ideas. Although some people from outside the St. John's elite appear to have been involved in the reform movement's activities, the local press worked diligently to maintain an image of respectability. Following established imperial policies, the Governor and the British government both opposed granting Newfoundland a legislative assembly.

Public opinion in St. John's evolved in a dynamic colonial environment into an eclectic yet cohesive collection of arguments. While William Carson employed a sharp common rhetoric based on notions of the rights of British subjects, Patrick Morris relied on the emotive imagery of persecution suffered under despotic fishing admirals and naval governors. Carson and Morris both advanced a model of economic development in which a local assembly appeared as the key to prosperity. Reform rhetoric was never uniform, as a variety of notions permeated the malleable body of the campaign against naval rule. During the Lundrigan affair, reformers marshalled arguments of the rule of law, for example, while the view of an assembly as a panacea appeared in later petitions from rural communities. The various rhetorical strands within the reform movement came together during the 1828 crisis over taxation. After 1828 merchant-driven concerns over fiscal responsibility, and a nativist voice for local control of government, joined the public discussion. In effect, the campaign for representative government had become all things to all people.

Although one cannot pinpoint a single direct cause for the grant of an assembly in 1832, three developments were pivotal. First, in 1828 a proposed duty on imports prompted the Chamber of Commerce to mount a political protest against government policies. The colony's leading merchants soon became actively involved in the reform movement, and this led to the formation in 1828 of a viable political coalition. Second, through a series of editorials and public letters the local press sponsored a vigorous campaign against "taxation without representation." Active participants in the reform movement, Henry Winton and John Shea pushed for public meetings and a united campaign for a legislative assembly. Third, George Robinson represented the reformers' case in Parliament and, arguing that a local legislature would eliminate the colony's cost to the British government, obtained the backing of Joseph Hume. In September 1831 Robinson managed in a shrewdly timed motion in the House of Commons to make Newfoundland's governance a public litmus-test of the Whigs' liberalism. Forced to pledge a committee of inquiry, the Grey administration commissioned a Colonial Office report and, in a move that avoided further embarrassment, granted Newfoundland representative government.

The final element behind the success of the campaign for a local legislature was its ability to avoid divisive issues. The reformers were able to use diverse and sometimes contradictory arguments because their movement focused on a single, simple goal: the achievement of an elected assembly. Contentious issues surrounding how actually to govern the colony remained largely outside the political discussion. With the advent of electoral politics, however, the struggle for power within Newfoundland had only just begun. The coalition of interests which had held together since 1828 came apart at the seams soon after the first local elections; for the next three decades bitter sectarian factionalism dominated Newfoundland politics.[139] The establishment of representative government had marked the end of an era in the island's history. Although colonial governments continued to rely periodically on warships to help maintain law and order, the last vestiges of naval government had been swept away, as the Royal Navy became merely an ancillary to civilian rule.[140]

Notes

1 D.W. Prowse, *A History of Newfoundland from the English, Colonial, and Foreign Records* (Belleville, Ontario: Mika Studio, 1972 reprint of 1895 ed.); A.H. McLintock, *The Establishment of Constitutional Government in Newfoundland, 1783–1832: A Study of Retarded Colonisation* (London: Longmans, Green, 1941). For reviews of liberal historiography, see George Story, *People of the Landwash: Essays on Newfoundland and Labrador.* Melvin Baker, Helen Peters, and Shannon Ryan, eds. (St. John's: Harry Cuff, 1997), pp. 77–101 & 116–28; Peter Neary, "The Writing of Newfoundland History," in J.K. Hiller and P. Neary, eds., *Newfoundland in the Nineteenth and Twentieth Centuries: Essays in Interpretations* (Toronto, 1980), pp. 3–13; Olaf U. Janzen, "Newfoundland and the International Fishery," in M. Brook Taylor, ed., *Canadian History: A Reader's Guide, Volume 1: Beginnings to Confederation* (Toronto: University of Toronto Press, 1994), pp. 280–324; James K. Hiller, "Is Atlantic Canadian History Possible?," *Acadiensis* 30, 1 (Autumn 2000), pp. 16–22.

2 Keith Matthews, "Historical Fence Building: A Critique of the Historiography of Newfoundland," *Newfoundland Quarterly* 74 (April 1978): pp. 21–9; Keith Matthews, "The Class of '32: St. John's Reformers on the Eve of Representative Government," 6, 2 (1977), pp. 80–94; Keith Matthews, *Lectures on the History of Newfoundland, 1500–1830* (St. John's: Breakwater Press, 1988), ch. 30.

3 Patrick O'Flaherty, "The Seeds of Reform: Newfoundland, 1800–18," *Journal of Canadian Studies* 23 (Fall 1988), pp. 39–56; Patrick O'Flaherty, "Government in Newfoundland Before 1832: The Context of Reform," *Newfoundland Quarterly* 23 (October 1988), pp. 26–30; Patrick O'Flaherty, *Old Newfoundland: A History to 1843* (St. John's: Long Beach Press, 1999). O'Flaherty also probed the writings of Carson and Morris in *The Rock Observed: Studies in the Literature of Newfoundland* (Toronto: University of Toronto Press, 1979), pp. 49–71.

4 Sean Cadigan, "Economic and Social Relations of Production on the Northeast-coast of Newfoundland, with Special Reference to Conception Bay, 1785–1855." (PhD thesis, Memorial University, 1991), pp. 108–11, 179, 190, 326–7, 318–21; Sean Cadigan, "The Staple Model Reconsidered: The Case of Agricultural Policy in Northeast Newfoundland, 1785–1855," *Acadiensis* 21 (Spring 1992), pp. 54–9; Sean Cadigan, *Hope and Deception in Conception Bay: Merchant-Settler Relations in Newfoundland, 1785–1855* (Toronto: University of Toronto Press, 1995).

5 John P. Greene, *Between Damnation and Starvation: Priests and Merchants in Newfoundland Politics, 1745–1855* (Montreal & Kingston: McGill-Queen's University Press, 1999), chs. 1–4.

6 For overviews of the political environment in contemporary Britain and Ireland, see Linda Colley, *Britons: Forging the Nation, 1707–1837* (New Haven: Yale University Press, 1992), ch. 8; R. F. Foster, "Ascendancy and Union," in R.F. Foster, ed., *The Oxford History of Ireland* (Oxford: Oxford University Press, 1992), pp. 134–73.

7 In 1815 the island's population was over 40,000, and Irish Catholics comprised a large majority in St. John's. On the socio-economic transformation during the Napoleonic Wars, see Shannon Ryan, "Fishery to Colony: A Newfoundland Watershed, 1793–1815," in P.A. Buckner and David Frank, eds., *The Acadiensis Reader, Volume One: Atlantic Canada Before Confederation* (Second edition, Fredericton, 1990), pp. 138–56.

8 Patrick O'Flaherty, "John Ryan," *Dictionary of Canadian Biography* (14 vols. to date, Toronto: University of Toronto Press, 1966-), vol. 7, pp. 151–6 [hereafter *DCB*].

9 Patrick O'Flaherty, "Sir Francis Forbes," *DCB*, vol. 7, pp. 301–04; Bruce Kercher, "Law Reports from a Non-Colony and a Penal Colony: The Australian Manuscript Decisions of Sir Francis Forbes as Chief Justice of Newfoundland," *Dalhousie Law Journal* 19, 2 (Fall 1996), pp. 417–24.

10 On the creation of a public sphere generally, see Jurgen Habermas, *The Structural Transformation of the Public Sphere: An Inquiry into a Category of Bourgeois Society*. Thomas Burger, trans. (Cambridge, Mass.: Massachusetts Institute of Technology Press, 1991), esp. pp. 19–26; Craig Calhoun, "Hambermas and the Public Sphere," in C. Calhoun, ed., *Habermas and the Public Sphere* (Cambridge, Mass.: Massachusetts Institute of Technology, 1992), pp. 2–41. On the cultural impact of the growth of a local press, see Robert Darnton, *The Kiss of Lamourette: Reflections in Cultural History* (New York: Norton, 1990), chs. 7–9.

11 The Act 51 Geo. III, c. 45 (1811) empowered the governor to tender building lots for thirty-year leases. See Prowse, *History of Newfoundland*, p. 386; Sean Cadigan, "The Role of the Fishing Ships' Rooms Controversy in the Rose of a Local Bourgeoisie: St. John's, Newfoundland, 1775–1812." (Unpublished paper, Centre for Newfoundland Studies, 1992.)

12 William Carson, *A Letter to the Members of Parliament of the United Kingdom* (Greenock: W. Scott, 1812), pp. 3–4. In 1808 Carson emigrated from Scotland to St. John's, where he worked as a medical doctor: over the next thirty years he remained at the heart of colonial politics and the edge of agitation for reform. See Patrick O'Flaherty, "William Carson," *DCB*, vol. 7, pp. 151–56.

13 William Carson, *Reasons for Colonizing the island of Newfoundland* (Greenock: W. Scott, 1813), pp. 3–4, 6–8, 12–13, 24–6.

14 Suzanne Ellison, *Historical Directory of Newfoundland and Labrador Newspapers, 1806–1996* (St. John's: Memorial University, 1997), pp. 108–16 & 132–33.

15 For an incisive analysis of the role of the press in fostering public opinion, see Jeffrey McNairn, *The Capacity to Judge: Public Opinion and Deliberative Democracy in Upper Canada, 1791–1854* (Toronto: University of Toronto Press, 2000), esp. chs. 3–4.

16 Patrick O'Flaherty, "James Lundrigan," *DCB*, vol. 6, pp. 409–11.

17 Anon., *A Report of Certain Proceedings of the Inhabitants of the Town of Saint John, in the island of Newfoundland, with the view to obtain a REFORM of the LAWS, more particularly in the mode of their administration, and an INDEPENDENT LEGISLATURE* (St. John's: Printed by Lewis Ryan, 1821), esp. pp. iv, 10–11.

18 Morris had emigrated from Ireland in 1804, entered the mercantile trade, and soon became a prominent public figure. See John Mannion, "Patrick Morris," *DCB*, vol. 7, pp. 623–34.

19 *Report of Certain Proceedings*, p. 11. Eight of the thirteen men appointed to the committee were Roman Catholics. See John Mannion, "Henry Shea," *DCB*, vol. 6, pp. 709–11; Derek Bussy, "Patrick Doyle," *DCB*, vol. 8, pp. 234–35; O'Flaherty, "Seeds of Reform," p. 43.

20 *Report of Certain Proceedings*, pp. 12–13, 19–20.

21 The Newfoundland reformers were thereby able to capitalize on political trends in contemporary England. See Richard R. Follett, *Evangelicalism, Penal Theory, and the Politics of Criminal Law Reform in England, 1808–30* (New York: Palgrave, 2001), ch. 8.

22 *Parliamentary Debates*, New Series, vol. 5 (28 May 1821), pp. 1015–16; *Journals of the House of Commons*, vol. 76 (1821), p. 388.

23 Ibid.

24 On 17 May 1821 Governor Hamilton forwarded this letter to the reform committee. See *Report of Certain Proceedings*, pp. 31–2.

25 *Report of Certain Proceedings*, pp. 40–62.

26 See E.J. Hobsbawm, *Nations and Nationalism since 1780: Programme, Myth, Reality* (2nd ed. Cambridge: Cambridge University Press, 1992), ch. 1; Benedict Anderson, *Imagined Communities: Reflections on the Origins and Spread of Nationalism* (2nd ed. New York: Verso, 1991), ch. 9.

27 Carson, *Reasons for Colonizing Newfoundland*, p. 13.

28 *Report of Certain Proceedings*, pp. 43–44.

29 Anon., *Observations on the Present State of Newfoundland, in reference to its Courts of Justice* (London: A. Hancock, 1823), p. 2. The pamphlet was addressed to Lord Bathurst, the Colonial Secretary, and signed by "Britannicus."

30 Eric Hobsbawm, *On History* (London: Abacus, 1997), ch. 21.

31 5 Geo. IV, c. 67 (1824). The Judicature Act was limited to a five-year term. Two other acts passed in 1824 also revised aspects of the island's legal system: the Fisheries Act (5 Geo. IV, c. 51), and the Marriage Act (5 Geo. IV, c. 68).

32 5 Geo. IV, c. 51, s. 1 (1824). I thank Patrick O'Flaherty for kindly providing the statutory reference to the repeal of King William's Act.

33 The 1825 Royal Charter, which was promulgated on 2 January 1826, was printed in Henry Winton, ed., *Select Cases from the Records of the Supreme Court of Newfoundland* (St. John's: Henry Winton, 1829), pp. 559–74.

34 O'Flaherty, *Old Newfoundland,* pp. 139–40. As O'Flaherty points out, the fact that the statutes of 1824 referred to Newfoundland as a *colony* may have awarded a type of official colonial status, but they bestowed only piecemeal reforms.

35 *Mercantile Journal,* 5 January & 2 March 1826.

36 Frederic F. Thompson, "Sir Thomas John Cochrane," *DCB*, vol. 10, pp. 178–80. On Cochrane's administration, see Gertrude Gunn, *Political History of Newfoundland,* ch. 1; O'Flaherty, *Old Newfoundland,* ch.7; Cadigan, *Merchant-Settler Relations,* ch. 5.

37 Cochrane to Wilmot Horton, 29 July 1825, as quoted in McLintock, *Establishment of Constitutional Government,* p. 164.

38 Christopher English, "From Fishing Schooner to Colony: The Legal Development of Newfoundland, 1791–1832," in L. Knafla and S. Binnie, eds., *Law, Society, and the State: Essays in Modern Legal History* (Toronto: University of Toronto Press, 1995), pp. 85–88; O'Flaherty, *Old Newfoundland,* p. 141.

39 *Mercantile Journal,* 9 February 1826. See also Melvin Baker, "The Government of St. John's, Newfoundland, 1800–1921." (Ph.D. thesis, University of Western Ontario, 1980), pp. 30–5.

40 Provincial Archives of Newfoundland and Labrador [PANL], Colonial Office Papers, series 194 [CO 194], vol. 72, p. 158, Cochrane to Bathurst 27 May 1826, enclosures 1–7.

41 PANL, CO 194/72, pp. 160–3, Cochrane to Bathurst, 27 May 1826. In March 1827 the government asked Parliament to consider new duties on imports into Newfoundland. See *Journals of the House of Commons* 82 (1826–7), p. 359.

42 PANL, CO 194/73, pp. 158–62, Stephen to Wilmot Horton, 16 September 1826. A prominent figure in formulating Colonial Office policy, Stephen disdained partisan politics and stressed expediency over public opinion. See Phillip Buckner, "The Colonial Office in British North America, 1801–50," *DCB*, vol. 8, pp. xxx–xxxiv; A.G.L. Shaw, "James Stephen and Colonial Policy," *Journal of Imperial and Commonwealth History* 20, 1 (January 1992), pp. 11–34.

43 PANL, CO 194/72, pp. 332–3, Cochrane to Bathurst, 17 November 1826.

44 See editorial in *Public Ledger* (St. John's), 18 May 1827. After emigrating from England, Henry Winton founded (with Alexander Haire) the *Public Ledger* in 1820. See Patrick O'Flaherty, "Henry Winton," *DCB*, vol. 7, pp. 947–50.

45 Patrick Morris, *Remarks on the State of Society, Religion, Morals, and Education at Newfoundland* (London: A. Hancock, 1827), p. 10.

46 See O'Flaherty, *Studies in the Literature of Newfoundland,* ch. 4.

47 PANL, CO 194/78, pp. 131–4, Memorial of the St. John's Chamber of Commerce to Lord Bathurst, 9 October 1827. Thomas Brooking registered his opposition to oppose the duty in a letter to the local press. See the *Public Ledger,* 27 November 1827.

48 The proposed 2.5% duty covered all imported items except salt and potatoes; the government also planned new taxes on wine and spirits. See the editorial in the *Public Ledger,* 22 April 1828.

49 A transcript of the debate appears in the *Public Ledger,* 18 July 1828. Robinson's attack singled out the Governor's mansion which, paid out of unauthorized bills, had swelled beyond original estimates. The Colonial Office had already censured Cochrane for financial mismanagement: see McLintock, *Establishment of Constitutional Government,* p. 165.

50 Thomas Brooking succeeded Newman Hoyles as president of the Chamber of Commerce for 1828, and John Dunscombe and William Thomas were elected vice-presidents. All four men had supported the proposal for a charter of incorporation. As leading Protestant merchants they each served as grand jury foremen and leaders of local philanthropic societies. See *Royal Gazette,* 19 August 1828; Keith Matthews, "Thomas Brooking," *DCB,* vol. 9, pp. 84–6; Keith Matthews, *Profiles of Water Street Merchants* (St. John's: Memorial University, 1980).

51 PANL, CO 194/76, p. 385, Cochrane to Murray, 14 December 1828.

52 T.W. Acheson, *Saint John: the Making of a Colonial Urban Community* (Toronto: University of Toronto Press, 1985), pp. 55–9, 66.

53 Patrick Morris, Arguments to Prove the Necessity of Granting Newfoundland a Constitutional Government (London: Hunt and Clarke, 1828), pp. 11–12.

54 Ibid., pp. 27–28.

55 J. Bristow, *Brief Remarks on a Pamphlet entitled "Arguments to Prove the Necessity of Granting to Newfoundland a Constitutional Government"* (Poole: Moore and Sydenham, 1828), pp. 8–15, 19, 28.

56 The column was reprinted in the *Newfoundlander,* 2 October 1828.

57 The Newfoundlander reprinted Morris' pamphlets in extracts over several weeks from 23 February to

19 March 1828. In the *Public Ledger,* 25 August 1828, Henry Winton termed Morris' pamphlet "decidedly the best yet," and, on 29 August, Winton offered a critique of Bristow's essay.

58 The son of the reformer Henry Shea, John Shea established the *Newfoundlander* in 1827. See Mannion, "Henry Shea," *DCB,* vol. 6, p. 711.

59 *Newfoundlander*, 21 November 1827.

60 18 Geo. III, c. 12 (1778). This statute is referred to as either the "Colonial Tax Repeal Act" or the "Declaratory Act." On the evolution of the constitutional argument against "taxation without representation," see Bernard Bailyn, *The Ideological Origins of the American Revolution* (2nd ed., Cambridge, Mass.: Harvard University Press, 1992), esp. pp. 209–21.

61 In June 1828 Shea also questioned whether the new tax would be used to build "a new gaol, infirmary, work-house, treadmill...to improve our morals." See *Newfoundlander,* 9 April 1828, 19 June 1828.

62 *Public Ledger,* 25 December 1827.

63 *Public Ledger,* 22 April 1828.

64 *Public Ledger,* 25 April 1828.

65 *Public Ledger,* 17 June 1828. See also the editorial for 18 July 1828. In an 18 April 1828 editorial Winton had complained that the "Demon of Discord has attended our meetings."

66 *Newfoundlander,* 19 June 1828.

67 *Public Ledger,* 19 August 1828.

68 *Public Ledger,* 7 October 1828. See also the editorials on 3 & 24 October.

69 *Public Ledger,* 7 October 1828. "Atomus" declared in favour of a legislature but called for a "fair" discussion of all the options.

70 *Public Ledger,* 18 November 1828. The press played a similar role in other reform movements: see, for example, Linda Colley, *Britons: Forging the Nation, 1707–1837* (New Haven: Yale University Press, 1992), pp. 342–43; Carol Wilton, "'A Firebrand amongst the People': The Durham Meetings and Popular Politics in Upper Canada," *Canadian Historical Review* 85 (September 1994), p. 356.

71 Dated 1 December 1828, the notice requested the High Sheriff to convene a public meeting "for the purpose of taking into consideration the necessity of petitioning Parliament against any further imposts or duties upon imports or new duties upon exports, and the expediency of praying that His Majesty's Government will grant a Constitutional Legislative Government to this island." While Winton noted the announcement with "peculiar satisfaction," John Shea called for "a firm and unanimous appeal to the British Legislature." Both men signed the 1829 petition. See *Public Ledger,* 2 December 1828; *Newfoundlander,* 4 December 1828.

72 See PANL, CO 194/79, pp. 299–303, "Petition for a Legislative Government, 1 January 1829"; PANL, CO 194/72, p. 158 Cochrane to Bathurst, 27 May 1826, enclosure 7, "Memorial Against a Charter of Incorporation, 23 February 1826." Among the 498 signatories were several prominent figures: William B. Row, a merchant and lawyer; Edward Kielly, a Catholic surgeon; and John Ryan, the publisher of the *Royal Gazette.*

73 Imported items reported for sale 2 December 1828 in the Public Ledger include: tea (William Thomas); wine (Robinson and Brooking); rum and molasses (John Dunscombe); flour and beef (Brown, Hoyles).

74 John Edward FitzGerald, "Conflict and Culture in Irish-Newfoundland Roman Catholicism, 1829–1850." (PhD thesis, University of Ottawa, 1997), ch. 2; John Edward FitzGerald, "Michael Anthony Fleming and Ultramontanism in Irish-Newfoundland Roman Catholicism, 1829–1850," *CCHA Historical Studies* 64 (1998), pp. 27–44.

75 See Raymond Lahey, "Thomas Scallan," *DCB,* vol. 6, pp. 690–694; Raymond Lahey, "Catholicism and Colonial Policy in Newfoundland, 1779–1845," in T. Murphy and G. Stortz, eds., *Creed and Culture: The Place of English-Speaking Catholics in Canadian Society, 1750–1930* (Montreal and Kingston: McGill-Queen's University Press), pp. 50–1, 65–8; O'Flaherty, "Government in Newfoundland Before 1832," p. 30. Except for Morris, who was living in Ireland, the leaders of the older reform movement—notably Doyle, Shea, Hogan and Beck—were active in 1828. Laurence O'Brien, a Catholic merchant and later a prominent politician, was a recent addition.

76 By matching the signatures from the 1829 petition with those from the 1826 memorial, I was able to identify nineteen non-elite signatories: one cooper, one fish culler, one baker, one painter, three sailmakers, one smith, two planters, one carpenter, two spirit dealers, one shopkeeper, three coopers, one innkeeper, and one wheelwright. See PANL, CO 194/79, pp. 299–303, Petition for a Legislative Government, 1 January 1829; CO 194/72, p. 158, Cochrane to Bathurst 27 May 1826, enclosure 7, Memorial Against a Charter of Incorporation, 23 February 1826.

77 Gail Campbell, "Disenfranchised But Not Quiescent: Women Petitioners in New Brunswick in the Mid-19th Century," in Janet Guildford and Suzanne Morton, eds., *Separate Spheres: Women's Worlds in the 19th-Century Maritimes* (Fredericton: Acadiensis Press, 1994), pp. 39–66.

78 Rusty Bittermann, "Women and the Escheat Movement," in Guildford and Morton, eds., *Separate Spheres*, pp. 23–38. On the informal regulation of gender in rural Newfoundland, see Willeen Keough, "The Riddle of Peggy Mountain: Regulation of Irish Women's Sexuality on the Southern Avalon, 1750–1860," *Acadiensis* 31, 2 (Spring 2002), pp. 38–70.

79 Sean Cadigan, "Whipping them into Shape: State Refinement of Patriarchy among Conception Bay Fishing Families, 1787–1825," in C. McGrath, B. Neis, and M. Porter, eds., *Their Lives and Times: Women in Newfoundland and Labrador: A Collage* (St. John's: Killick Press, 1995), pp. 48–58.

80 Patrick Morris, *Remarks on the State of Society, Religion, Morals and Education at Newfoundland* (London: A. Hancock, 1827), pp. 13–14. Original italics.

81 Cecelia Morgan, *Public Men and Virtuous Women: The Gendered Languages of Religion and Politics in Upper Canada, 1791–1850* (Toronto: University of Toronto Press, 1996); Allan Greer, *The Patriots and the People: The Rebellion of 1837 in Rural Lower Canada* (Toronto: University of Toronto Press, 1993), ch. 7.

82 Carson, *Letter to the Members of Parliament*, p. 4.

83 There is not space here to discuss the historiography but see, *inter alia*, J. Murray Beck, *Joseph Howe, volume I: Conservative Reformer, 1804–1848* (Kingston & Montreal: McGill-Queen's University Press, 1982), esp. chs. 17–19; Rosemary Ommer, "The 1830s: Adapting Their Institutions to Their Desires," in Phillip Buckner and John Reid, eds., *The Atlantic Region to Confederation: A History* (Toronto: University of Toronto Press, 1994), pp. 300–01; Rusty Bittermann, "Agrarian Protest and Cultural Transfer: Irish Emigrants and the Escheat Movement on Prince Edward Island," in Tom Power, ed., *The Irish in Atlantic Canada* (Fredericton: Acadiensis Press, 1991), pp. 96–106; Peter Burroughs, *The Canadian Crisis and British Colonial Policy, 1828–1841* (Toronto: Macmillan, 1979); Paul Romney, "From the Types Riot to the Rebellion: Elite Ideology, Anti-Legal Sentiment, Political Violence, and the Rule of Law in Upper Canada," *Ontario History* 79 (1987), pp. 113–44; Allan Greer, "Historical Roots of Canadian Democracy," *Journal of Canadian Studies* 34, 1 (Spring 1999), pp. 7–26.

84 See Matthews, "Class of '32," pp. 80–94.

85 *Newfoundlander*, 19 June 1828.

86 Winton later attacked John Kent for not being resident in the colony long enough to sit in the Assembly. See *Public Ledger*, 3 October 1828, 18 September 1832.

87 *Royal Gazette*, 5 October 1830.

88 *Public Ledger*, 17 September 1831.

89 *Public Ledger*, 19 December 1828; *Newfoundlander*, 25 December 1828.

90 *Public Ledger*, 23 January 1829.

91 *Public Ledger*, 20 January 1829.

92 See Frederick Madden, ed., *Select Documents on the Constitutional History of the British Empire and Commonwealth, Volume III: Imperial Reconstruction, 1763–1840* (Westport: Greenwood Press, 1987), section B; John Belcham, "Republicanism, Popular Constitutionalism and the Radical Platform in early Nineteenth-Century England," *Social History* 6 (January 1981), pp. 1–32.

93 PANL, CO 194/78, p. 39, Cochrane to Murray, 13 December 1828.

94 PANL, CO 194/79, pp. 128–31, Bristow to Murray, 26 February 1826, enclosure, "Report of the Committee of Merchants Engaged in the Newfoundland Fishery at the Port of Poole." The report called for the repeal of section 35 of 5 Geo. IV cap. 67 (1824).

95 *Parliamentary Debates* 5 (6/7/13 April 1829), pp. 463, 533–5, 714; *Parliamentary Debates* 14 (11 May 1830), pp. 580–1.

96 *Public Ledger*, 12 May 1829.

97 PANL, CO 194/78, pp. 241–60, Cochrane to Murray, 11 December 1829. Cochrane also advised the government to add bread, flour, peas, and grain to the list of items exempted from the import duty.

98 The letters appear in *Public Ledger*, 13/23/30 July 1830 and 4/13/17 August 1830.

99 *Public Ledger*, 14 September 1830.

100 *Royal Gazette*, 28 September 1830. It is doubtful whether Ryan had written the editorial; Patrick O'Flaherty has suggested that the author was perhaps John Collier Withers. See Patrick O'Flaherty, "John Ryan," *DCB*, vol. 7, p. 765.

101 A nephew of Patrick Morris, Kent came to Newfoundland in 1820 and began working as a commission agent and auctioneer. Often compared to William Lyon Mackenzie, Kent was a combative

populist who espoused democratic principles. See P.B. Waite, "John Kent," *DCB,* vol. 10, pp. 398–400.

102 *Public Ledger,* 17 September 1830. The emphasis on unity also characterized public reform meetings in Upper Canada. See Wilton, "The Durham Meetings and Popular Politics in Upper Canada," p. 356.

103 The committee consisted of Protestant merchants and lawyers (Thomas, Bennett, Row, Job and Bland), Catholic reformers (Doyle and Shea), a representative from Harbour Grace, and William Carson. See *Public Ledger,* 17 September 1830.

104 *Public Ledger,* 18 March 1831, letter from the delegation to William Thomas, 29 December 1830. The paper reprinted all of the reform committee's correspondence.

105 *Public Ledger,* 15 March 1831.

106 *Public Ledger,* 25 March 1831.

107 *Parliamentary Debates,* 3rd series, 4 (27 June 1831), pp. 359–60.

108 P.A. Buckner, *The Transition to Responsible Government: British Policy in British North America, 1815–1850* (Westport, Conn.: Greenwood Press, 1985), pp. 15–18, 151, 294; C.A. Bayly, *Imperial Meridian: The British Empire and the World, 1780–1830* (London: Longman, 1989), pp. 194–5, 209; Peter Burroughs, "Liberal, Paternalist or Cassandra?: Earl Grey as a Critic of Colonial Self-Government," *Journal of Imperial and Commonwealth History* 18 (1990), pp. 33–5.

109 PANL, CO 194/81, pp. 73–81, Cochrane to Goderich, 14 April 1831.

110 PANL, CO 194/81, pp. 111–23, Cochrane to Goderich, 4 May 1831.

111 Hay to Cochrane, 6 July 1831, as quoted in McLintock, *Establishment of Constitutional Government in Newfoundland,* p. 182.

112 *Parliamentary Debates* 5 (25 July 1831), p. 283. The debate was also reprinted in the *Public Ledger,* 6 September 1831.

113 *Public Ledger,* 6 September 1831.

114 See *Parliamentary Debates* 5 (25 July 1831), pp. 288–9. On the cost of the colonies as an important political issue, see Bayly, *Imperial Meridian,* pp. 194–5.

115 *Newfoundlander,* 6 October 1831.

116 *Public Ledger,* 30 September 1831.

117 *Public Ledger,* 7 October 1831.

118 *Newfoundlander,* 6 October 1831.

119 *Public Ledger,* 30 September 1831.

120 The *Public Ledger* reprinted the petition to the Crown and Parliament on 7 October 1831.

121 Henry Winton noted that it was "gratifying to perceive that the inhabitants of the outports are unanimous in their desire to obtain the same object." See *Public Ledger,* 11 October 1831.

122 In 1821 Parliament considered a petition from Ferryland on the Lundrigan affair. See *Journals of the House of Commons* 76 (1821), p. 388. On Robert Pack's reform activities, see Keith Matthews, "Robert Pack," *DCB,* vol. 8, p. 674.

123 An editorial argued that if the island acquired a local legislature than "we have no hesitation in saying, that in five years its labours would be productive of incalculable advantage." See the *Conception Bay Mercury* (Harbour Grace), 21 August 1829.

124 *Public Ledger,* 24 September 1830.

125 *Journals of the House of Commons* 87 (1831–32), pp. 171–2, 298. The Harbour Grace and Carbonear petitions originated from meetings held 4 October 1831. A public meeting on 28 October 1831 had approved the memorial from Brigus. See *Public Ledger,* 12/21/18 October 1831, 18 November 1831.

126 The meetings occurred in Burin on 9 November 1831 and in St. Mary's on 6 December 1831. See *Public Ledger,* 13, 27 January 1832.

127 Cadigan, "Staple Model Reconsidered," p. 59.

128 *Parliamentary Debates* 6 (13 September 1831), pp. 1377–378. The *Public Ledger* printed a transcript on 15 November 1831. Hume admitted during the ensuing debate that he had offered advice to Robinson, and the quality of Robinson's address suggests substantial preparation and outside assistance.

129 Ibid.

130 *Parliamentary Debates* 6 (13 September 1831), pp. 1381–84. Hume's endorsement was important because he acted as a liaison between the Grey administration and the radicals on the fringe of the Whig party. During the crisis over the Reform Bill in 1831, the Whigs needed all the support they could muster. For a synopsis of the political situation in England, see Richard Brown, *Revolution, Radicalism and Reform: England, 1780–1846* (Cambridge: Cambridge University Press, 2000), ch. 4.

131 Labouchere had visited the Canadas in 1824, served on the select committee of 1828, and led the circle of Whigs with whom Howick studied in 1830. See Buckner, *Transition to Responsible Government,* pp. 149, 255.

132 *Parliamentary Debates* 6 (13 September 1831), pp. 1381–84.

133 Ibid.

134 Gunn, *Political History of Newfoundland,* p. 11.

135 The report recommended that the Newfoundland Governor be given the same commission and instructions as the Governor of Nova Scotia, with the added instruction to ask the assembly to pass a bill incorporating a council. Stephens' report is reprinted in McLintock, *Establishment of Constitutional Government,* pp. 207–10. On the use of different legislative models in imperial policy, see J.M. Ward, *Colonial Self-Government: The British Experience* (London: MacMillan, 1976), esp. pp. 126–28.

136 *Public Ledger,* 2 March 1832, letter from Brooking to Thomas, 5 January 1832.

137 *Public Ledger,* 27 March 1832, letter from Brooking to Thomas, 25 January, and letter from Howick to Robinson, 25 January 1832.

138 2-3 William IV, c. 78 (1832).

139 After 1832 Winton became a harsh critic of the political influence of the Roman Catholic Church. In an episode which marked the violent sectarian conflict of the 1830s, Henry Winton was violently attacked in 1835 by a group of masked men, presumed to be Irish Catholics, and had his face and ears brutally mutilated. Two years later the *Public Ledger* urged the government to revoke representative government in Newfoundland, and in 1842 the elected assembly was amalgamated with an appointed council. See Patrick O'Flaherty, "Henry David Winton," *DCB,* vol. 8, pp. 467–70; Patrick O'Flaherty, "The Road to Saddle Hill," *Newfoundland Quarterly* 89, 3 (July 1995), pp. 21–26; Linda Little, "Collective Action in Outport Newfoundland: A Case Study from the 1830s," *Labour/Le Travail* 26 (Fall 1990), pp. 7–35.

140 On the use of warships in assistance of civil authority, see O'Flaherty, *Old Newfoundland,* pp. 164–78.

The Collapse of the Beothuk World*

RALPH PASTORE

Until recently, the Beothuks, Newfoundland's aboriginal people who became extinct in 1829, were a shadowy people whose origins, culture, and demise were little understood. In the past 15 years, however, archaeological, historical, and linguistic investigation has produced answers to a number of significant questions about them. It is now clear that the Beothuks were a hunting and gathering people of Algonkian stock,[1] whose ancestors in Newfoundland produced tools typologically similar to the late prehistoric Indian inhabitants of coastal Labrador and the Quebec North Shore.[2] It is also clear that, prior to the coming of Europeans, the Beothuks occupied, or at least used, all of the island of Newfoundland with the possible exception of the Avalon peninsula east of Trinity Bay. This island, despite its enormous size, has a simplified ecosystem characterized by a disproportionately small number of prey species relative to the large number of predators. Those predators included wolves, bears, lynx, marten, mink, weasels, otter, fox, and human beings. The major native interior prey species were caribou, beaver, and arctic hare (although the bones of the latter have never been identified from an archaeological site on the island). In essence, then, the island is a rather impoverished piece of the boreal forest in the mouth of the St. Lawrence. Of course, the surrounding waters are much richer in available food. Most important of the marine mammals to native hunters were harbour, harp, grey, and hooded seals, and walruses, all of which were once found in abundance off the coasts. Other marine resources available to the Beothuks included cod, salmon, flounder, smelt, capelin, mussels, soft-shelled clams, and lobsters. A number of avian species also contributed to the aboriginal diet including the now extinct great auk as well as murres and a wide variety of ducks and geese.[3]

The majority of prehistoric Beothuk sites are found along stretches of coastline that allowed them to exploit the resources of both the near shore and the interior of the island. This site distribution leaves the impression of a people who were not specialized in their hunting and fishing strategies,[4] an hypothesis strengthened by the few samples of prehistoric Beothuk food remains that have been recovered from archaeological sites.[5] A generalized subsistence pattern was probably necessary for the island's peoples because, despite the rich resources of the sea, prehistoric human populations in Newfoundland have always been vulnerable to changes in the availability of animal stocks. One of the most significant marine resources would have been the harp seal which is usually present, even today, in herds numbering more than a million. Yet there have been times in the historic period when, due to strong offshore winds, the unsuitability of the ice, or factors not yet understood, these seals unaccountably failed to arrive off the island's

---

Ralph Pastore, "The Collapse of the Beothuk World," *Acadiensis* 19, 1 (Autumn 1989): 52–71.

*An earlier version of this work was presented at the Seventh Atlantic Canada Studies Conference, Edinburgh, May 4–7, 1988. I am indebted to Laurel Doucette, Charles Martijn, Douglas Robbins and Jim Tuck for their comments.

coast.[6] There is no reason to believe that prehistoric harp seal stocks would have been any more reliable. The most important land resource, caribou, may have been equally unreliable. A successful caribou hunt involved intercepting the animals primarily upon their fall migration.[7] Caribou movements are notoriously unpredictable and may be affected by factors as diverse as insects and ice storms. Newfoundland's native peoples, like most hunting and gathering bands, had to time their own seasonal movements to coincide with the availability of their prey. If that prey was not there, hunters would have to fall back on less important substitutes. Unfortunately, the island of Newfoundland lacked many of the "fall-back" species—the moose, deer, and porcupine—found on the mainland. Even less important prey species such as beaver and freshwater fish are much less abundant than on the mainland. Newfoundland native groups, therefore, had little margin for survival if one of their major food resources, caribou or harp seal, failed. A few years of such failures might well cause the sort of extinctions that appear to be characteristic of Newfoundland's prehistory. Indeed, archaeological research has demonstrated that in least three instances before the arrival of Europeans, prehistoric native populations have become extinct—very likely because of changes in the availability of vital food resources.[8]

Although archaeology has provided at least the outlines of the prehistoric Beothuk subsistence pattern, it is not possible to determine the size of the Beothuk population at the time of European contact. Such a determination would require a systematic survey of the entire coast and much of the interior of the island as well as a programme of excavation designed to reveal site size and population and, given the expense involved, such an undertaking is unlikely. Even the fortuitous discovery of archaeological sites is less likely in Newfoundland. Elsewhere, many archaeological sites are discovered because of modern building and road construction, but the island's poverty, sparse population, and rugged terrain make extensive activity of this sort highly improbable. In the absence of such a programme of reconnaissance and excavation, estimates of Beothuk population can only be informed guesses. Perhaps the first recorded estimate was by Joseph Banks who noted in 1766 that Beothuks were "thought to be very few as I have been told not Exceeding 500 in number but why that should be imagind I cannot tell as we Know nothing at all of the Interior Parts of the Island nor Ever had the Least Connextion with them tho the french we are told had."[9] Although Banks believed that by the 1760s the Beothuks had retreated into the interior, there is evidence that they were still visiting the coast to hunt and fish, even if their permanent residence had shifted to the interior.[10] He was, however, correct in regarding that population estimate with some scepticism, for there really was no sound basis for estimating their numbers.[11]

Ignorance about the size of the Beothuk population at a time when the numbers of other native peoples of the northeast were quite well known to whites is not surprising. Some time after about the second decade of the 17th century, the Beothuks followed a pattern of withdrawal from contact with Europeans which culminated in their extinction early in the 19th century. The tragedy of that extinction, unique in Canadian history, has attracted a great deal of attention from both scholarly and popular writers. The Newfoundland geologist, James P. Howley, whose remarkable collection of documents pertaining to the Beothuks was published in 1915, concluded that the Beothuks had been hunted and harassed to extinction. Although Howley discounted many of the more lurid oral accounts of Beothuk persecution, his documentary collection was eagerly used by a number of popular writers, most notably Harold Horwood and Pierre Berton, to spin out a sensational tale of "the people who were murdered for fun."[12]

Given the fact that researchers limited to the documentary record were faced with a number of accounts, some trustworthy, others not, of Europeans killing Beothuks, it is perhaps not surprising that a monocausal explanation of the Beothuk demise was accepted. That would change after the results of James Tuck's archaeological investigations of a number of Newfoundland sites were published. He found that for thousands of years prior to the coming of Europeans, Newfoundland's inhabitants had depended upon the resources of the sea for most of their food. He also noted that when Europeans began to settle the island, of necessity they were drawn to the same resource-rich areas of the coastline that the Beothuks inhabited. As Tuck put it: "An unknown number of natives were actually killed outright by Europeans. But more important to the survival or extinction of the race, the remaining Beothuks were denied access to the coast and forced to try and survive on the resources of the interior."[13] In an important article published in 1977 Leslie Upton argued that "despite these tales of slaughter, common to all North American frontiers, the decrease in Beothuck population over a period of three hundred years was unspectacular." Positing a population of about 2,000 at the time of European contact, Upton found nothing unusual about a rate of decline due to epidemic disease and loss of hunting territory that was, in fact, less than what other researchers had found for New England. In a suggestive comparison between the Micmac and the Beothuk experience Upton speculated that "the Beothuks died because they did not have enough contacts with the whites." He noted that the course of Beothuk-white relations had been remarkably different from that of other Indian peoples in North America. Upton stated that "the Beothuk strategy of withdrawal has no parallel elsewhere in the region, and its cause cannot be known: epidemic disease may have been the catalyst that prompted the decision."[14] The problem with this explanation is that every other native people in North America also suffered the ravages of epidemic disease; none, however, withdrew so determinedly from European contact.

Throughout North America, the lure that drew native peoples to European contact was trade. The knives, axes, kettles, blankets and guns of the newcomers were immensely desired by Indians. Elsewhere in North America Indians endured disease, violence, alcoholism, and an assault on their most deeply held beliefs in order to trade furs for European goods. The fact that the Beothuks did not do so is remarkable, perhaps unique. Since Upton's work, archaeologists working on Beothuk sites have done much to suggest a possible reason for the Beothuk failure to participate in a fur trade.[15] In brief, it is argued that because of the unusual nature of the early Newfoundland economy, the Beothuks did not *need* to enter into a fur trade to obtain European goods—especially metal objects. Once European fishermen began to dry fish on shore, they left behind, each winter, flakes, wharves, stages and a variety of debris associated with an onshore fishery. For the Beothuks, these seasonally-abandoned fishing premises were treasure troves of metal objects, particularly nails. Archaeological work at two Beothuk sites in Notre Dame Bay, in fact, has resulted in the recovery of hundreds of nails (many of them modified into projectile points), as well as scraps of iron and brass kettles, fish hooks, awls, and numerous other metal pieces. Although a marginal trade between European fishermen and Beothuks may have existed in the 16th and early 17th centuries,[16] by the latter date the Beothuks had been drawn into a pattern of pilfering European goods from seasonally-abandoned fishing premises. As a result, the first European settlers on the island had to trap their own furs. The Newfoundland "furrier," as he was called, dates to at least 1612–1613.[17] Although more research is needed, the practise of whites trapping furs in the 17th century appears to have little parallel in the rest of North America.[18] When whites were forced to trap their own furs, there was, of course, even less possibility that a systematic fur trade would emerge on the island between settlers and Beothuks.

The absence of fur traders in Newfoundland was paralleled by an absence of missionaries. Elsewhere in North America, one of the more important ways in which native peoples were drawn into interaction with Europeans was through the activities of missionaries. Newfoundland's seasonal fishery and tiny year-round British population (estimated at about 1200 in the last quarter of the 17th century),[19] however, could not support a missionary effort to the Beothuks. Nor is there any evidence that the colony of Placentia, occupied by the French during the period, 1662–1713, sent missionaries to the Beothuks.[20] The other usual medium for peaceful contact between Indians and whites in the European colonies was the official assigned by the metropolitan powers to deal with native groups. Such officials generally had two functions: to secure the assistance or the neutrality of Indians, and to negotiate the sale of Indian land. But the British Crown did not make the commanders of the Newfoundland convoy governors nor did it provide for the creation of magistrates who would spend the winter on the island until 1724.[21] By then there was certainly no need for Indian agents since the Beothuk pattern of withdrawal was well established. Nor was there any need to secure the assistance of the Beothuks in the wars between Britain and France. As a people who lacked firearms, they would have counted for very little and, in any case, the contest for supremacy in Newfoundland would be won by the power which had naval, not land, supremacy.

Without these Indian agents, fur traders, and missionaries, there was no one to stand between the Beothuks and the white settlers, their competitors for the resources of the coast.[22] Because the vast majority of those European occupiers left no written records, the historian of the Beothuk experience is forced to rely much more than usual upon archaeological data even for information as basic as the plotting of the Beothuk retreat from encroaching white settlement. In an attempt to delineate the shrinking world of the Beothuks, evidence from published and unpublished archaeological reports, site record forms on file in the Newfoundland Museum in St. John's, and a few scattered documentary references, have been used to note the location of both prehistoric and historic Beothuk sites in Newfoundland and related sites in Labrador and Quebec.[23]

The question of what constitutes prehistoric Beothuk needs some explanation. It now is clear that the immediate prehistoric predecessors of the Beothuks on the island of Newfoundland were the possessors of the Little Passage complex. At two important sites in Notre Dame Bay, for example, there was no evidence of another occupation intervening between that of the Little Passage people and the Beothuks.[24] In addition, the strong resemblance between the stone tools used by both groups suggested a continuity over time. That hypothesis has been strengthened by a detailed attribute analysis of Beothuk and Little Passage stone projectile points which identified a number of trends in attributes extending from the prehistoric period to perhaps the beginning of the 18th century.[25]

On the other side of the Strait of Belle Isle, William Fitzhugh first identified a late prehistoric/early historic Indian presence extending along the coast of Labrador from Saglek Bay to the Quebec Lower North Shore, which he named the Point Revenge complex. "The geographic extent of Point Revenge occupation and its persistence into the historic period," he argued, "make it the most likely progenitor of the modern Indians of Labrador." He also noted that "sites related to Point Revenge in Newfoundland are thought to be ancestral to Beothuck culture, and on the Quebec north shore, prehistoric continuity into historic Montagnais is also suggested."[26] The posited relationship between Little Passage and Point Revenge is based both on a similarity of projectile point styles and an apparent preference in both cases for locating sites in similar areas. Little Passage and Point Revenge sites are often found in an inner coastal zone which suggests a subsistence pattern described by Fitzhugh as "Modified-Interior." *i.e.,* a "generalized" rather than "specialized" dependency on coastal and interior resources.[27]

Although more research on both Little Passage and Point Revenge is needed, current evidence does suggest a relationship and has revealed 16 Point Revenge sites on the central Labrador coast, two Little Passage sites in the Strait of Belle Isle, and three Little Passage or Point Revenge sites on Quebec Lower North Shore.[28] At present, James Tuck, the excavator of the Red Bay site, believes that the diagnostic artifacts of the two sites in the Strait of Belle Isle would fit generally within the assemblages recovered from prehistoric Beothuk (Little Passage) sites on the island. This should not be surprising. The much earlier Maritime Archaic and Palaeo-Eskimo traditions have been reported from both Quebec-Labrador and the island,[29] and it would be unusual if the Beothuks and neighboring Quebec-Labrador groups were an exception to the general rule that related subarctic hunter-gatherer cultures tend to be scattered over quite wide distances. Still, there are locations within these huge areas which were quite crucial for hunter-gatherers, and the Strait of Belle Isle would have been exactly such a place. It has quite rightly been referred to as a "resource funnel" for a variety of marine resources including many species of whales and seals.[30]

On the island itself, six prehistoric sites have been discovered in Bonavista Bay, five in Notre Dame Bay, five on the south coast, two each in the interior and Trinity Bay, and one each in Placentia Bay and on the west. One explanation for the preponderance of sites in the island's northeast is suggested by the migration of harp seals to this area and the high concentration of seal breeding areas off the northeast coast.[31] Clearly, Notre Dame Bay would have been very appealing to prehistoric Beothuk seal hunters. The attraction of the south coast is more difficult to explain, but since this coast tends to be ice-free all year long,[32] its coves and bays once had harbour and grey seals in abundance.[33] In addition, prehistoric hunters may well have been drawn to the south coast to hunt caribou in the winter since the largest winter concentrations of caribou on the island are to be found along the south coast and its interior.[34]

In the far southeast, the Ferryland site is also the location of Lord Baltimore's colony, founded in 1621, and evidence of an Indian presence here lies beneath a stone wall attributed to Baltimore and is found with European artifacts which date to the late 16th century. In the far northwest, material from Blanc Sablon in the Strait of Belle Isle is still undergoing analysis, but according to its most recent excavator, aboriginally produced stone tools have been found at the same level with European artifacts.[35] Preliminary work from the nearby site of Red Bay, a Basque whaling station occupied from ca. 1540 to ca. 1610, indicates an association of 16th century Basque features with an Indian occupation. The stone projectile points produced by those Indians, both at Blanc Sablon and Red Bay, may in fact be a variant of those produced by historic Beothuks on the island. The island itself is clearly visible from the Labrador side of the narrow (20 km) Strait of Belle Isle, and it is inconceivable that native groups on either side would have been prevented from traversing it throughout the year. Indeed, for much of the year travel by canoe across the Strait would be far easier than an inland journey of 20 km by foot. The Strait of Belle Isle, in fact, should be viewed as a highway, not a barrier.[36]

Whatever the nature of the relationship between the historic Indians of Quebec-Labrador and those of the island, it is clear that both groups had access to European goods in a similar manner. That access is clearly indicated by the presence of native hearths found at both Red Bay and Ferryland which are located in and among European structures. This has led the director of excavations at those sites to suggest that the Indians in question had been visiting the two locations to scavenge European iron from seasonally-abandoned shore stations. The one site from the southwest corner of the island, in St. George's Bay, was reported in 1594 by the master of the *Grace* of Bristol who found a Beothuk camp in that bay, along with the wrecks of two Basque ships. The other sites along the South Coast and Placentia Bay are either burials or archaeological sites, none of which can be dated with any confidence. The three sites from Trinity Bay are drawn from the account of John Guy who met a Beothuk group camped there in 1612, and from a work by an early Newfoundland entrepreneur who reported an encounter between Beothuks and European mariners around the turn of the 17th century. Only two sites are listed for Bonavista Bay, perhaps because of a lack of archaeological surveys in the area. Of these two, one is a burial, the other a living site. Unfortunately, neither has been dated with any precision.

The 28 sites in Notre Dame Bay and all but one of the 116 sites from the interior represent the Beothuk response to increased European utilization of Newfoundland. Most of these living sites date to the late 18th-early 19th centuries when the Beothuk presence in the bay was restricted to furtive fishing and hunting forays carried out under the guns of white settlers. Two of these sites, Boyd's Cove and Inspector Island, however, have been dated to ca. 1650–1730, and merit special attention.[37] They are situated in eastern Notre Dame Bay and were occupied at a time when English permanent settlement ended in Bonavista Bay, and a French migratory fishery was carried on in the western portion of the bay. These two living sites were positioned in an area safely between the two zones of European exploitation from which it was possible to visit the seasonally abandoned French fishery to the west for European iron, and occasionally to steal from the English settlements and fisheries to the southeast.[38] These sites may well have been occupied at a time when Beothuk culture entered a period of florescence—when it was still possible to hunt and fish in safety, and still possible to acquire the iron from which to fashion the tremendously useful metal cutting and piercing tools that made their lives so much easier. Faunal analysis of the animal remains from the Boyd's Cove site bears this out. The wide range of species taken prompted the analyst, Stephen Cumbaa, to note: "At Boyd's Cove we have a glimpse of a people at ease in their environment and obviously exercising a fair degree of control over use of its resources. The contrasting picture we have a century later of a beleaguered and dwindling population eking out a living on the run from a dominant culture is all the sadder for the comparison."[39] The other sites in Notre Dame Bay represent archaeological sites, both living and burial, and bone ornament caches. None has been dated with any more accuracy other than to the historic period.

The sites clustered along the Red Indian Lake-Exploits River system represent the last refuges of the Beothuk. Many of these sites have been excavated, and they have produced a large quantity of knives, scissors, trap parts, and other European objects.[40] The abundance of European objects, coupled with the relative lack of stone tools, as well as the dates assigned to a number of artifacts from the Wigwam Brook site, support the evidence from the documentary record that this region was intensively occupied during the late 18th and early 19th centuries.[41] This was a period when the Beothuks were hindered by white settlement from access to the resources of the coast and were forced to try to subsist on the meagre resources of Newfoundland's interior. The nature of those last days is graphically revealed in the archaeological evidence. Animal bones from one late 18th/early 19th century site on the Exploits River, for example, revealed that not only were the Beothuks subsisting almost entirely upon caribou, but they were attempting to do so all year round.[42] One leading authority on caribou hunting has noted that in an area such as Newfoundland, where caribou migrate over short distances, it would have been possible for aboriginal groups to prey on caribou year-round, but "humans usually found easier resources to harvest for part of the year, mostly anadromaous fish, beaver, or moose."[43] Moose, of course, were not introduced to the island until the late 19th century, and the island's fish and beaver populations are both much smaller than those on the mainland.[44] Conventional anthropological thinking has it that caribou "can theoretically supply all of the requirements of a human population, but the chances of this occurring are in fact extremely small."[45] In fact, Newfoundland's stark interior supported only 14 indigenous mammalian species, and there is no evidence in the archaeological record that any aboriginal culture lived there for 12 months of the year. When the Beothuks were forced to do so, the results were tragic. Detailed analysis of a child's garments from a contemporaneous burial provides a graphic picture of Beothuk life during those last days. The shroud of one child (now in the Newfoundland Museum) was found to be a woman's legging, made from five pieces of skin, most of which had been patched and repaired. The child's moccasins exhibited similar careful patching and repairing; most surprising was the use of spruce root rather than the usual caribou sinew to repair the moccasins. All of this suggests a people on the ragged edge of desperation who did not even have enough animal skins to clothe a child properly.[46]

This pattern of gradual Beothuk withdrawal from a territory which once encompassed almost all of Newfoundland and perhaps the Strait of Belle Isle to the banks of the Exploits River has been constructed largely on the basis of archaeological evidence. However, the same pattern is evident in the documentary record. For example, as late as 1612 John Guy noted the presence of Beothuks on the Avalon peninsula. Ten years later, the experienced sea captain Richard Whitbourne stated that although Beothuks from Bonavista Bay stole into Trinity Bay to pilfer "Hatchets, Hookes, Kniues, and such like" he implied that they no longer lived in Trinity Bay.[47]

The Beothuks who had once lived in Trinity Bay appear to have travelled back and forth across the narrow isthmus of the Avalon peninsula to gain access to the considerable resources of Placentia Bay, especially the harbour seals.[48] The Beothuks may have also occupied that narrow neck of land in order to intercept caribou herds passing from the main part of the island to the isthmus.[49] The importance of that isthmus to the Beothuks is underscored by the presence of two large prehistoric Beothuk sites there. Thus, the year-round occupation of Trinity Bay by the English by 1675 and the French occupation of Placentia Bay by at least 1662 had the effect of denying these two important food sources to the Beothuk.[50] By 1694, de Brouillan, the commandant of the French garrison of Placentia, could write about "la découverte des sauvages qui habitent au sud de l'isle," clearly indicating that the French at Placentia had not been in contact with the Beothuks, if indeed they ever had, for some time.[51] De Brouillan's information was given to him by a band of Micmacs who had come to Newfoundland from Cape Breton. Their arrival in Newfoundland meant yet another competitor for the island's resources. While it is possible that there were Micmacs in Newfoundland in the 16th century,[52] given the report by de Brouillan, it does not appear as if their presence on the south coast was intensive enough to disrupt Beothuk use of that portion of the island. However, it is clear that by the middle of the 18th century, Micmac use of the southern portion of the island from St. George's Bay to Placentia Bay had denied yet another area of the island—and its caribou and seals—to its aboriginal inhabitants.[53]

By the middle of the 18th century, then, the Beothuk range had shrunk considerably. The contraction of the Beothuk world would have meant more than just reduced access to food resources. Given the presence in a number of prehistoric Beothuk sites on the island of Ramah chert, a translucent silicate found only in Ramah Bay in northern Labrador, it can be assumed that a trade across the Strait of Belle Isle existed in prehistoric times. Since trade between band level societies also implies the exchange of marriage partners, it is possible that at the point in Beothuk history when contact with Indian peoples in Labrador was either lost or reduced, the subsequent reduced gene pool would have further imperiled the survival of the island's natives.

It is difficult to determine when contact with Labrador may have been interrupted. There is some evidence that the Basques who carried on a whale hunt in the Strait of Belle Isle, during the period ca. 1540 to ca. 1610, employed native people at the shore stations.[54] Although there is some controversy—and no direct evidence—relating to the incidence of European epidemic disease among the native peoples of the Northeast in the 16th century,[55] there are two factors about this Basque-native contact which might have made the transmission of epidemic disease more likely. First, the distance from Europe to the Strait of Belle Isle was shorter than that to New England or the Maritimes, thus increasing the likelihood that a disease carried by a crew member would not yet have run its course prior to landing. Second, if the Basques employed Indians in shore-based activities throughout the season, the prolonged close contact implied would have been more conducive to the spread of pathogens than would be the case in a fur trade where contacts between the two groups would have been of much shorter duration.

Assuming that the Indians of the Strait of Belle Isle survived the Basque whale fishery of the 16th century, they would have had to face an invasion of the Strait by Inuit in the 17th century. There is evidence that by the last half of the 17th century there was an Inuit population living in the region throughout the year,[56] and it is quite likely that Indian use of the Strait was either severely curtailed or ended. In 1705 Augustin LeGardeur de Courtemanche established a trading post at Brador, near Blanc Sablon, and it is significant that he had to bring a group of Montagnais families with him to hunt fur bearers and to prosecute a (salmon ?) fishery.[57] The well-documented hostility between the Inuit and French traders and fishermen in the Strait of Belle Isle casts further doubt on the likelihood that normal communication between the Indian populations of the Island and Labrador could have persisted in the last half of the 17th and first half of the 18th century.[58] Those French posts were established to trade with the Montagnais whose persistence today underscores the hypothesis that it was the Beothuk decision to withdraw from the fur trade which was the most important factor in their demise. The effects of that decision, however, were reinforced by the growing exploitation of Newfoundland's resources by other ethnic groups. Although the spread of permanent English settlement on the island may have been the most important factor denying the Beothuks access to vitally needed coastal resources, to that equation must now be added the Basque and Inuit presence in the Strait of Belle Isle, the Micmac use of the southern third of the island, and the French base at Placentia. A complete understanding of all of the effects of these arrivals upon the Beothuks may not yet be attainable, but the pattern revealed by the distribution of Beothuk sites over time is clear enough. As contact with Labrador was lost, and as the various regions of the island were denied to the Beothuks, they were forced to withdraw to the island's impoverished interior where there could be but one outcome for them.

Notes

1 John Hewson, *Beothuk Vocabularies: A Comparative Study* (St. John's, 1978), pp. 135–46. Hewson also noted that the Beothuk language "appears to show" a "feature... normally considered diagnostic" of Central rather than Eastern Algonkian (p. 146). The present-day Naskapi-Montagnais of Labrador are also classified as part of the Central Algonkian subgroup.

2 Ralph T. Pastore, "Excavations at Boyd's Cove—1984: a Preliminary Report," in J.S. Thomson and C. Thomson, eds., *Archaeology in Newfoundland and Labrador, 1984* (St. John's, 1985), pp. 322–37 and R.T. Pastore, "Investigations at Boyd's Cove: The 1985 Field Season, a Preliminary Report," in J.S. and C. Thomson, eds. *Archaeology in Newfoundland and Labrador, 1985* (St. John's, 1986), pp. 218–32.

3 A.T. Bergerud, "Prey Switching in a Simple Ecosystem," *Scientific American,* 249 (December 1983), pp. 130–41; J.A. Tuck and R.T. Pastore, "A Nice Place to Visit, but...Prehistoric Human Extinctions on the Island of Newfoundland," *Canadian Journal of Archaeology,* 9 (1985), pp. 69–80.

4 R.T. Pastore, "The Spatial Distribution of Late Palaeo-Eskimo Sites on the Island of Newfoundland", in *Palaeo-Eskimo Cultures in Newfoundland, Labrador and Ungava* (St. John's, 1986), pp. 125–34.

5 David Simpson, "Prehistoric Archaeology of the Port au Port Peninsula," M.A. thesis, Memorial University of Newfoundland, 1986. Fieldwork under my direction in the summer of 1987 at a Beothuk site on an island in Notre Dame Bay revealed a prehistoric Beothuk midden made up of bones from a broad range of food species.

6 L. Chafe, *Chafe's Sealing Book: A History of the Newfoundland Sealfishery from the Earliest Available Records Down to and Including the Voyage of 1923* (3rd ed., St. John's, 1924), p. 19.

7 Arthur E. Speiss, *Reindeer and Caribou Hunters: An Archaeological Study* (New York, 1979), p. 124.

8 Tuck and Pastore, "Extinctions."

9 A.M. Lysaght, ed., *Joseph Banks in Newfoundland and Labrador, 1766: His Diary, Manuscripts and Collections* (Berkeley, 1971), p. 132.

10 For example, see "The narrative of Lt. John Cartwright's journey up the Exploits River, 1768," in J.P. Howley, *The Beothucks or Red Indians* (Cambridge, 1915), p. 33.

11 For a discussion of the debate on Beothuk population size see Ingeborg Marshall, "An Unpublished Map Made By John Cartwright Between 1768 and 1773 Showing Beothuck Indian Settlements and Artifacts And Allowing a New Population Estimate," *Ethnohistory,* 24 (Summer 1977), pp. 223–49.

12 Harold Horwood, "The People Who Were Murdered for Fun," *Maclean's Magazine,* 10 October 1959; Pierre Berton, *My Country: The Remarkable Past* (Toronto, 1976).

13 James A. Tuck, *Newfoundland and Labrador Prehistory* (Ottawa, 1976), p. 75.

14 Leslie Upton, "The Extermination of the Beothucks of Newfoundland," *The Canadian Historical Review,* 58 (June 1977), pp. 133–53.

15 The following argument is a brief summary of the material presented in R.T. Pastore, "Fishermen, Furriers, and Beothuks: The Economy of Extinction," *Man in the Northeast,* 33 (Spring 1987), pp. 47–62.

16 For example, in 1612 when the would-be colonizer, John Guy, encountered Beothuks in Trinity Bay, the Beothuks attempted to trade with the English by leaving behind poles with furs on them, but the English were not equipped with trade goods. As Cell noted, the Beothuks, unlike this particular group of Englishmen, appear to have engaged in a fur trade before. John Guy's Journal of a Voyage to Trinity Bay, 7 October 1612 to 25 November 1612, in Gillian Cell, ed., *Newfoundland Discovered: English Attempts at Colonization, 1610–1630* (London, 1982), p. 76.

17 "Occurrents in Newfoundland," 1 September 1612–1 April 1613, in David B. Quinn, ed., *New American World* (New York, 1979), IV, pp. 166, 169, 170, 172–5.

18 Although the Hudson's Bay Company did allow its men to trap privately at least by the 18th century (see for example Instructions of Joseph Isbister, Chief Trader at Albany Fort to John Yarrow, Master at Eastmain House, 15 September 1753, HBCA B.59/a/22, fo 4, extract provided by Toby Morantz), Morantz believes that such trapping by whites "was on a very small scale."

19 Grant Head, *Eighteenth Century Newfoundland* (Toronto, 1976), p. 82.

20 See Ministère de la France d'Outre-Mer, Archives des Colonies, Serie C11C, Amérique du Nord, vols. 1–7, Terre-Neuve (Plaisance), Microfilm in the PAC.

21 Keith Matthews, *Lectures on the History of Newfoundland, 1500–1830* (St. John's, 1973), pp. 141–50.

22 Upton, "The Extermination of the Beothuks," p. 153.

23 Earlier results of this research were published in Graeme Wynn, Ralph Pastore, and Bernard Hoffman, "The Atlantic Realm" in R. Cole Harris, ed., *Historical Atlas of Canada,* I (Toronto, 1987). Results of archaeological research undertaken since the preparation of that volume have been incorporated in this work.

24 Ralph Pastore, "Excavations at Boyd's Cove, Notre Dame Bay—1983," in J.S. Thomson and C. Thomson, eds., *Archaeology in Newfoundland and Labrador, 1983* (St. John's, 1984), pp. 98–125; Ralph Pastore, "Excavations at Inspector Island, 1987: A Preliminary Report," in *Archaeology in Newfoundland and Labrador, 1987* (in press).

25 Fred Schwarz, "The Little Passage Complex in Newfoundland: A Comparative Study of Assemblages," Honours thesis, Memorial University of Newfoundland, 1984.

26 William W. Fitzhugh, "Indian and Eskimo/Inuit Settlement History in Labrador: An Archaeological View," in Carol Brice-Bennett, ed., *Our Footprints are Everywhere: Inuit Land Use and Occupancy in Labrador* (Nain, Newfoundland, 1977), p. 14.

27 Schwarz, "The Little Passage Complex," pp. 43–7.

28 At present there is some confusion in the usage of the terms "Point Revenge" and "Little Passage." While Fitzhugh designates Indian occupations on the coast of central Labrador from about A.D. 1000 to A.D. 1650, as Point Revenge, the excavators of the Quebec sites perceive Point Revenge as antecedent to Little Passage. Until the results of recent research on both sides of the Quebec-Labrador border appear, I have chosen not to attempt to reconcile the terminology, but simply to present the data as reported. William W. Fitzhugh, "Winter Cove 4 and the Point Revenge Occupation of the Central Labrador Coast," *Arctic Anthropology,* XV, 2 (1978), pp. 146–74; Hélène Taillon and Georges Barré, eds., *Datations au 14C des sites archéologiques du Québec* (Quebec City, 1987), pp. 480–1.

29 James A. Tuck, "Prehistoric Archaeology in Atlantic Canada since 1975," *Canadian Journal of Archaeology,* 6 (1982), p. 203.

30 F.A. Aldrich, "The Resource funnel of the Strait of Belle Isle," paper delivered to the International Symposium on Early European Settlement and Exploitation in Atlantic Canada, St John's, October 1979.

31 Based on A.W. Mansfield, *Seals of Arctic and Eastern Canada* (Ottawa, 1964), p.12, and D.E. Segeant, "Migrations of harp Seals *Pagophilus groenlandicus* (Erxleben) in the Northwest Atlantic," *Journal of the Fisheries Research Board of Canada,* 22 (1965), pp. 433–64.

32 Chesley Sanger, "The Evolution of Sealing and the Spread of Permanent Settlement in Northeastern Newfoundland," in J.J. Mannion, ed., *The Peopling of Newfoundland* (St. John's, 1977), p. 139.

33 Even now there are major concentrations of harbour seals found from Placentia Bay to the southwest corner of the island. J. Boulva and I.A. McLaren, "Biology of the Harbor Seal, *Phoca vitulina,* in Eastern Canada," Department of Fisheries and Oceans Bulletin, No. 200 (Ottawa, 1979), p. 2.

34 During the period 1957 to 1967, the largest concentration of caribou was found along the south coast and its interior. A.T. Bergerud, "The Population Dynamics of the Newfoundland Caribou," Wildlife Society, Wildlife Monograph No. 25 (Washington, D.C., 1971). Whether this was true in the prehistoric period is not known.

35 Jean-Yves Pintal, personal communication.

36 I am indebted to Marguerite MacKenzie, Memorial University Department of Linguistics, for this observation.

37 Pastore, "Fishermen, Furriers, and Beothuks" and "Excavations at Inspector Island, 1987." The Beothuk component at Inspector Island appears to date to ca. 1720–1730, although future analysis may result in modification of this conclusion.

38 Pastore, "Fishermen, Furriers, and Beothuks."

39 Stephen Cumbaa, "'Diverse Furres and Deeres Flesh'—Animal Use by a 17th Century Beothuk Population at Boyd's Cove, Notre Dame Bay, Newfoundland" (unpublished report, Zooarchaeological Identification Centre, National Museum of Natural Sciences, National Museums, Canada, 1984).

40 Don Locke, *Beothuck Artifacts* (Grand Falls, Newfoundland, n.d.); Helen Devereaux, "The Pope's Point Site," unpublished report, Newfoundland Museum, 1965; Helen Devereaux, "A Preliminary Report on the Indian Point Site, A Stratified Beothuk Site," unpublished report, Newfoundland Museum, 1970; Raymond LeBlanc, "The Wigwam Brook Site and the Historic Beothuk Indians," M.A. thesis, Memorial University of Newfoundland, 1973.

41 Ingeborg Marshall, "An Unpublished Map," pp. 223–49; Maps of the Red Indian Lake-Exploits River region drawn by Shanawdithit in 1829, in Howley, *The Beothucks,* pp. 238–45.

42 Frances L. Stewart, "Faunal Analysis of the Wigwam Brook Site, Newfoundland," Appendix 1, in LeBlanc, "The Wigwam Brook Site."

43 Speiss, *Reindeer and Caribou Hunters,* p. 138.

44 W.B. Scott, and E.J. Crossman, *Fishes Occurring in the Fresh Waters of Insular Newfoundland* (Ottawa, 1964); Thomas Northcott, "An Investigation of the Factors Affecting Carrying Capacity of Selected Areas in Newfoundland for the Beaver (*Castor canadensis caector* Bangs 1913)," M.Sc. thesis, Memorial University of Newfoundland, 1964, p. 117.

45 Ernest S. Burch, "The Caribou-Wild Reindeer as a human resource," *American Antiquity,* 37 (1972), p. 363, quoted in Speiss, *Reindeer and Caribou Hunters,* p. 139.

46 Ruth Holmes Whitehead, "I Have Lived Here Since the World Began: Atlantic Coast Traditions" in Julia D. Harrison, ed., *The Spirit Sings: Artistic Traditions of Canada's First Peoples* (Toronto, 1987), p. 40.

47 Richard Whitbourne, *A Discourse and Discovery in New Found-land* (London, 1622), in Gillian Cell, ed., *Newfoundland Discovered* (London, 1982), p. 118.

48 Guy, "Journal," p. 72. Boulva and McLaren "Biology of the Harbour Seal," p. 2, found the largest concentration of harbour seals on the island in Placentia Bay.

49 The narrow necks of peninsulas are ideal for intercepting caribou migrations. M.A.P. Renouf, "Prehistoric Coastal Economy in Varangerfjord, North Norway," Ph.D. thesis, Cambridge University, 1981.

50 Gordon Hancock, "English Migration to Newfoundland," in Mannion, ed., *The Peopling of Newfoundland,* pp. 16–7; Jean Pierre Proulx, *The Military History of Placentia* (Ottawa, 1979), pp. 9–12.

51 Jacques-François de Mombeton de Brouillan to the Minister of Marine, 25 October 1694, Archives des Colonies, C11C, II, 20.

52 The evidence for this is summarized in Charles A. Martijn, "Voyages des Micmacs dans la vallée du Saint-Laurent, sur la Cote-Nord et à Terre-Neuve," in Charles Martijn, ed., *Les Micmacs et la Mer* (Quebec, 1986), pp. 215–21.

53 Ralph T. Pastore, *The Newfoundland Micmacs,* Newfoundland Historical Society Pamphlet No. 5 (St. John's, 1978), pp. 9–19. While the present article was undergoing editorial review, Ingeborg Marshall's "Beothuk and Micmac: Re-examining Relationships," *Acadiensis,* XVII, 1 (Autumn 1988), pp. 52–82, appeared. While I would agree with Ms Marshall that the Micmacs played a greater role in the extinction of the Beothuks than has been previously recognized, I have argued that this was because of Micmac displacement of the Beothuks from an area necessary to their subsistence. Until some direct evidence is produced, I remain unconvinced that the French paid a bounty to the Micmacs for Beothuk heads. I find even more dubious Marshall's uncritical use of an oral account of an alleged "critical turning point" when a group of Beothuks discovered a number of Micmacs with the heads of Beothuks for which they expected a reward from the French. The Beothuks supposedly then invited the offending Micmacs to a feast and slaughtered the erstwhile murderers. This is in fact a variant of a European folk motif, Motif K811.1 "Enemies invited to a feast and killed," in Stith Thompson, ed., *Motif Index of Folk Literature* (rev. ed., Bloomington, 1955), IV, p. 340. I also find puzzling the use of a term such as "nations" to describe the Micmac and the Beothuk, and a sentence such as: "The Beothuks were evidently not in a position to enforce their claim on this territory and may have relinquished the land voluntarily in order to remain on good terms with their Micmac neighbors." Such terminology is inappropriate when dealing with hunting bands.

54 Selma Barkham, "A note on the Strait of Belle Isle during the period of Basque contact with Indians and Inuit," *Etudes/Inuit/Studies,* 4, 1–2 (1980), pp. 51–8.

55 Dean Snow and Kim Lanphear, "European Contact and Indian Depopulation in the Northeast: The Timing of the first Epidemics," *Ethnohistory*, 35 (Winter 1988), pp. 15–33; Bruce Trigger, *Natives and Newcomers* (Montreal, 1985), pp. 237–9.

56 Charles Martijn, "La présence inuit sur la Cote-Nord du Golfe St-Laurent à l'époque historique," *Etudes/Inuit/Studies,* 4, 1–2 (1980), pp. 105–25.

57 "Anonymous Memoir, 1715, Concerning Labrador," No. 1419, in Privy Council, *In the Matter of the Boundary Dispute Between the Dominion of Canada and the Colony of Newfoundland in the Labrador Peninsual* (Ottawa, 1927), VII, p. 3694.

58 François Trudel, "Les relations entre les Français et les Inuit au Labrador méridional, 1660–1760," *Etudes/Inuit/Studies,* 4, 1–2 (1980), pp. 135–46.

Division of Labour in a Staple-Exporting Economy

Marjorie Griffin Cohen

Without exception, the important economic histories of pre-industrial Canada focus on the labour of men while women's labour remains virtually invisible. This preoccupation with male labour is symptomatic of the way historians have tended to ignore women in history.[1] It is also a result of a widespread undervaluation of female labour that derives from the preoccupation with market activity that dominates economic study.[2]

Canadian economic historians have been most interested in how the exploitation of resources for export to European markets has affected the character of the economy. Canada's attraction for Europe did not arise out of a need for land or the desire to settle and develop an agricultural society, but rather because of what it could provide to England and France in the way of fish and fur. This stress on the significance of export staples to Canadian development is known as the staple thesis. While there is considerable controversy about the period of time for which this thesis has validity, its usefulness in explaining the unique features of Canada's early years has been widely accepted.[3]

In recent years the staple approach has been criticized for its exclusive focus on external factors as explanations for growth and change. To some critics this "dehumanized" approach to Canadian development tends to undervalue the significance of labour and class issues as formative aspects of that development.[4] For the most part the studies which have attempted to redress this imbalance in Canadian economic history have focused on labour in the staple-exporting sector or on waged labour in the early stages of industrial capitalism. That is, they are directed toward the labour relations immediately associated with market activity. These studies of waged labour are significant advances in understanding the complexity of the problems of development and in opening up for investigation the myriad facets of social relationships integrally linked to the process of change. Nevertheless, exclusive focus on labour directly associated with market activity neglects the major portion of the total labour involved in the production of commodities and the reproduction of labour. To fully understand the nature of the economy, productive relations, and economic change in the early periods of Canada's development, it is essential that the nature and significance of the work of individuals in non-wage sectors and the relationship between non-market and market activity be understood as well.

The staple thesis has also received criticism from economic historians for its single-minded focus on exports as the engine for growth. For some, such as Louise Dechêne and Jean Hamelin, the fact that only a small proportion of labour was directly involved in the staple-

Marjorie Griffin Cohen, "Division of Labour in a Staple-Exporting Economy," in *Women's Work, Markets, and Economic Development in Nineteenth-Century Ontario* (Toronto: University of Toronto Press, 1988), 29–58: 178–88. Reprinted with permission of the publisher.

exporting sector is a significant indication that other forms of economic activity have been dominant even from the earliest periods.[5] Kenneth Buckley also questions the validity of a staple-led growth on a national scale after 1820 by pointing to the enormous growth of the labour force in Quebec in the nineteenth century even though the staple trade in this province had been seriously eroded.[6] Likewise, Douglas McCalla points to continuous growth in Ontario during periods when wheat exports were in serious trouble.[7] The point of all these criticisms is that the economy was considerably more diverse than most formulations of the staple thesis have indicated.

Attempts to broaden the perspective on the formative issues in Canadian growth have focused either on hitherto neglected forms of market activity or on the ability of non-staple-exporting regions to appropriate the linkages from the staple products of other regions.[8] Research efforts in both directions are not incompatible and even those who look to the significance of the development of internal markets, such as McCalla, do not deny the importance of the export sector in shaping the direction of the economy.[9] John McCallum's "modified staple approach" does a great deal to explain how non-staple-exporting sectors of the economy are influenced by staple production, and the increased interest in the development of local markets deepens our understanding of the nature of growth.[10] Yet both these analyses explain economic development solely in terms of market-oriented activity. I attempt to add another dimension to the explanation of development in a staple-exporting economy by examining the nature of labour in the non-market areas of production and by trying to understand the relationship between market and non-market production. […]

Dual Nature of the Economy: Market and Non-market Production

The basic point of the staple theory is to explain how the technology and geographical circumstances associated with specific staple commodities affected patterns of development and how the character of the staple affected productive relations and social organization. The specific nature of productive relations varied considerably according to the nature of the staple produced and conditions of time and space. Some forms of staple production, such as timber production in the Ottawa Valley from the mid-nineteenth century, were organized as capitalist ventures. Others, such as wheat production in Ontario, were carried out by independent commodity producers.[11]

In the pre-industrial period, export-oriented staple production was primarily responsible for the pace, character, and direction of market development. However, market growth was not a constant or even a characteristic feature of economic life for substantial periods of Canada's history, and much of the economic activity of the country was not directly related to the staple trade. The tendency of economic historians to focus on market relations has obscured the significance of non-market production and the labour organization characteristic of this type of economic activity.[12]

Allan Greer has made the very important point that, in fact, the bulk of productive activity in the pre-industrial period operated outside a market system. Greer argues that the nature of this activity has been ignored because "these people and their productive efforts made little or no contribution to the accumulation of capital."[13] While I concur with Greer's understanding of the predominance of non-market activity, I think he underestimates its significance to economic development in general, possibly because his major study of subsistence rural production focused on areas where the economy remained relatively static during the periods he studied.[14] Greer's perspective considers capital accumulation only in the narrow sense of that accumulated directly through capitalist activity. I argue, rather, that the contribution of non-market production was integrally related to staple production and other forms of market-oriented activity. The labour involved in non-market activity was critical to the accumulation of capital both in those activities characterized by capitalist productive relations and in those characterized by independent commodity production.

CAPITALIST PRODUCTION

The process of capital accumulation in countries on the periphery of capitalist development is highly dependent on the existence of subsistence production in agriculture. The existence of subsistence production serves a variety of functions, but its primary importance for the capitalist sector is in supplying and maintaining a labour force at prices which permit capital accumulation in this sector.[15] This was particularly important in a staple-exporting economy where labour shortages tended to drive up wage rates. In Canada the capitalist staple-extracting sector relied on the subsistence sector for its labour supply, but even more important, the subsistence sector, by its very existence, was able to supply this labour relatively cheaply. The key to the availability of labour at prices which encouraged capital accumulation was a division of labour by gender such that women's primary economic activities were associated with non-wage, non-market work in subsistence production.

But first, the interconnections between subsistence production and capitalist organized production need to be explained. These will be examined from two perspectives: that related to the requirements of capital accumulation, given the nature of the economy; and that related to the strategy necessary for family units to cope with the economic constraints and conditions they faced.

The focuses of labour and capital in the development and settlement process were distinctly different. Mercantile capital was attracted to the economy because of high returns expected from staple exports. In the pre-industrial period the capital movement related to the domestic economy was primarily that which was brought by settlers. Foreign capitalists were relatively uninterested in domestic production in the colonies.[16] By contrast, the attraction of labour to Canada, particularly to central Canada, had less to do with the availability of employment in the staple trades than the interest in land. While initial transfers of labour, mostly male, were associated with staple trades, either directly for work in staple production or indirectly for military employment, agrarian settlement was usually the objective of families. As a result, a potential conflict emerged between the capitalist sector's demand for labour and the possibility of alternative employment for labour on the land. Nevertheless, the logic of staple development forestalled the economic integration necessary for the growth of independent agrarian units, at least for substantial periods of time. In spite of these competing demands for labour, a symbiotic relationship developed between the capitalist demand for labour and labour requirements in independent production.

The relationship between subsistence production and capitalist production varied depending on the dominant staple, but a broad pattern is distinguishable. Since staple production and the capital development related to it were often seasonal or temporary, there was not a high demand for a permanent labour force in this sector. Generally, there was a core of labour hired on a permanent basis, but for the most part labour was employed intermittently.[17] From the perspective of employers in the capitalized sector, the ideal labour force was readily available, but when necessary was capable of finding alternative support during slack seasons or years. In this way the responsibility for maintaining the labour force would not have to be borne totally by the employer. To this end the sexual division of labour, the underdeveloped domestic economy, and the need for domestic units to have money to pay for imported goods were factors that contributed to meeting the labour needs of capital.

The division of labour between males and females in pre-industrial Canada was rigid and distinct. Undoubtedly it was predicated on the notion that the basic responsibility of women was to feed, clothe, and care for family members and to supplement male labour in the male spheres of production when necessary. This perspective on the proper work for women was basically unchanged from that of European societies.[18] While labour shortages in Canada might have led to some different forms of the division of labour between the sexes,[19] the reinforcement of traditional customs as a result of successive waves of immigration, and the logic of peasant production which favoured high birth rates, kept women tied to the subsistence non-market activities associated with the household.

In recent years the significance of female labour in the subsistence sector has been recognized as being crucial to capital accumulation. This recognition follows from a more general analysis which has tried to explain the importance of domestic labour to capitalist industrial development.[20] In Ontario the significance of female non-waged labour in the pre-industrial period can be examined in relation to capital accumulation in both the capitalized areas of the economy and the commodity production of the family economy.

Carmen Deere and James Sacouman have argued that in economies where labourers' families have access to subsistence production, employers need not concern themselves with providing a wage that would maintain the worker and this family.[21] The fact that wages paid to labourers can be reduced by having a portion of the family's needs provided by non-wage labour means that a greater part of the labour time of the worker can be appropriated by the employer.[22] In an economy where the nature of market-oriented activity meant that temporary employment was more characteristic than permanent waged labour, such as in pre-industrial Ontario, the subsistence agricultural labour of families was particularly important.[23] Women's labour, then, in subsistence production served the process of capital accumulation in the capitalist sector in critical ways. By providing unpaid labour on the land, women "freed" men for varying periods of time for waged labour. Yet because a certain level of subsistence was provided by female agricultural labour, the capitalist sector could avoid paying wages equal to the cost of maintaining the worker and his family. This permitted accumulation in the capitalist sector to proceed at a rate higher than would have occurred had the price of labour power been greater.

The rationale for the division of labour within the family between market and non-market activities reflected the structure of the economy and was a strategy to cope with the imperatives of the dominant market activity. While this division of labour in agriculture was not simply a response to the desire to maintain low wages on the part of the capitalist sector, it nevertheless reflects the strategy necessitated by the specific conditions of staple production.

The most notable condition was the unstable nature of the economy, a factor which shaped the parameters of economic activity for the family. Because of the uncertainty of income obtainable from market activity (as either wage labourers or direct producers), families were forced to pursue strategies which would both permit them access to the market and protect them to some degree from the uncertainty of market behaviour. Subsistence agricultural production gave a measure of security by providing a substantial portion of the family's needs. That this has historically been significant in Canadian economic development was pointed out in the Rowell-Sirois Commission report: "However prices might fall and cash income from other sources might melt away, the farm household always produced enough to prevent abject poverty...the sharp and frequent trade fluctuations of the [pre-Confederation] period did not cause profound dislocations."[24] As Greer points out, the safety-first imperative of the rural economy required that dependence on the market be avoided.[25]

However, agricultural pursuits alone frequently were inadequate to meet a family's income needs, particularly in the early pioneering periods of any region in pre-industrial Ontario when markets were seriously underdeveloped. While agricultural units tended to operate on a subsistence basis, they were not entirely self-sufficient. Vernon Fowke has argued that the perception of pre-industrial agriculturalists as self-sufficient, a view which has become an integral part of Canadian folklore, is essentially wrong. He shows how the pioneer economy of the nineteenth century forced farmers "initially and continuously into reliance on an exchange and monetary economy."[26] Even from the beginnings of settlement, when fur was the dominant export staple, substantial amounts of goods were consumed which could not be produced on individual farm units or within the colony. Food, clothing, and implements were provided in varying degrees by foreign markets.[27] Although trading within the community, often by means of barter, direct labour exchanges, or various forms of payment in kind, provided many items which could not be produced by the household itself, the limited nature of colonial manufacturing meant that substantial amounts of goods for consumption and production could not be obtained except through foreign markets. For these transactions, cash was needed, and to the extent that agricultural markets could not provide the necessary income, some members of the family might be forced to engage in work for wages. Pointing out that the pre-industrial family economy was not entirely self-sufficient does not negate the essentially subsistence character of the economy. Although trade and waged work existed to some extent, production for the market did not dominate economic activity.[28]

INDEPENDENT COMMODITY PRODUCTION

The significance of subsistence activity with regard to capitalist production in a staple-exporting economy is clear: its function is to provide a cheap labour force for the dominant sector. However, the significance of subsistence production becomes somewhat more complex when it is understood that the semi-proletarianization of labour was not the only dimension of labour in staple production. In some forms of staple production, waged labour was insignificant, with the work being carried on by individual producers who owned the means of production. This method of production is frequently referred to as independent or petty commodity production. While there are some difficulties with using these terms, primarily because of the inappropriateness of the term "commodity production" when capitalist relations of production are not present, they are generally accepted as terms for market-oriented production carried on by individual household units where waged labour is not the primary source of labour power.[29] In the sense that the term "commodity production" implies expropriation of the fruits of labour for purposes of accumulation by the owner of the means of production, it will be an appropriate term here.

Generally, labour involved in independent commodity production is seen as undifferentiated labour; the members of a family unit are treated as a "collectivity" of labour whose economic objectives are compatible and whose contributions and rewards are symmetrical. A.V. Chayanov's study of peasant economy was path-breaking because it showed that the objectives of this type of family economy were not identical with those of an economy where wage labour was common.[30] However, in his study, because wages were not paid in the family economy, he treated family labour as essentially undifferentiated. This treatment is not untypical and is used even in studies concerned specifically with women. Generally the family is seen as a unit rewarded collectively for its work. For example, Ann Oakley, in a discussion of pre-industrial family industry, says its two basic characteristics were "the unity of capital and labour: the family both owned the stock and tools and contributed the labour (receiving the monetary return for labour as a 'family' wage)."[31]

The stress is usually on the interdependence between the labour of men and women, with the implication that the interdependence is reciprocal. In this sense a certain equality of labour is taken for granted. I take issue with this view of the family economy in the next section, where the nature of productive relations in the family will be discussed. But here it is necessary to point out that in the sense that ownership of the means of production was distinctly in the hands of the male head of the family, women's subsistence production served essentially the same function for the accumulation of capital in the family unit that engaged in commodity production as it did in the capitalist sector. That is, to the extent that women's productive efforts were able to feed and clothe the family, male labour was free to engage in production for exchange on the market; to the extent that the total income from market production need not be expended on consumption, accumulation of capital in the family productive unit could occur.

This is not to imply that female labour was confined solely to subsistence production. In some forms of commodity production women's labour at specific periods was crucial to the market-oriented production process. This was particularly evident in the work of Indian women in the fur trade and women's labour in shore work in the fishing industry. However, my point is that the non-market-oriented activity was critical to the accumulation of capital and that this work was more central to women's economic activity than was their market-oriented activity.

Patriarchal Relations of Production

PATERNALISM

Labour relations in an economy dominated by staple production, when they are discussed at all, are usually accepted as developing from those characterized as "personal" or "paternalistic" to those commonly recognized as the "classical (abundant) labour market of industrial capitalism."[32] Paternalistic labour relations refer specifically to relations between employers and employees, controlled less by market exchange than by personal relationships and bonds of mutual obligation. Because of the shortage of labour on the one hand and the unavailability of alternative forms of paid employment on the other, both the worker and the employer were obliged to respond to incentives other than those that would dominate a true labour market. The central obligation on the part of the paternalistic employer was to provide the "fixed costs" of subsistence and reproduction in exchange for a reliable supply of labour.[33]

The issue is not whether paternalistic relations of production existed, but the extent to which these were the most prevalent forms of labour organization in the economy. For the permanent labour force of the fur trade and very early industrial enterprises, which Pentland focuses on, the description is probably fairly accurate.[34] But for the labour force employed on an intermittent basis (which Pentland acknowledges was typical of pre-industrial societies) in the fur trade and other forms of staple production there was considerably less obligation on the part of the employer to supply the worker with his annual overhead, particularly if that cost included the worker's family as well.

In the period of the great staple exports, the concept of paternalistic labour relations pertains to only a small fraction of the total relations of production. The greatest proportion of production involving the largest number of working people was centred on the family: the productive relations of this unit, although certainly related to paternalism, were distinct. Paternalism clearly involved unequal power arising from the relationship to the means of production and the conditions affecting the supply of labour. The paternalistic employer acted toward dependants "as a father does to his wife, his children and his servants."[35] It was a case of transferring traditional forms of control and organization to market relations. But the more fundamental relations of production, the patriarchal relations of production within the household, were distinct because of the added dimensions of family ties and sexual subordination.

Patriarchal productive relations can be defined as the organization of labour in which males, as husbands, fathers, and even sons and brothers, have power over the productive activities of their children, wives, and sometimes their sisters and mothers. This power was not confined simply to non-waged labour in the home but, since family labour was the most prevalent form of labour in the pre-industrial period, it will be the focus of my discussion of patriarchal productive relations.

PATRIARCHY

In the agricultural sector, the non-waged labour of family members was the most important source of labour power. The significance of family labour to agricultural production is well known, but the social relations of this type of production are rarely considered.[36] The concept of a family economy implies an indivisibility of income and a community of effort that does not easily lend itself to the type of class analysis possible when the object of study is waged labour. Yet the issue of ownership and control of labour is as significant in the family economy as it is in more identifiably capitalist relationships.

In most analyses of productive relations the issue of ownership is understood to be critical to establishing power and control. The very principles of organization of labour within a society are based on who does and who does not own the means of production: ownership implies not simply possession but all the social institutions developed to recognize property rights. How property relations are recognized by society is most directly evident in the laws which protect property relations. But the issue of ownership extends beyond the strictly legal aspects of control, for all of the social standards, customs, and the entire complex of human relations are influenced by this fundamental relationship. The significance of who owns property at any stage in the development process has been summed up by Oscar Lange: "It is the ownership of the means of production which decides the ways in which they are used and which thereby determines the forms taken by co-operation and the division of labour. Moreover the ownership of the means of production determines the issue of who owns the products, and hence decides how they are distributed."[37]

The usual analysis of class relations deals with those clearly identified through market activity. That is, class interests are evident when owners are employers and workers receive wages. When there is no waged labour present, such as in simple or independent commodity production, the ownership is usually treated as being vested in the group which performs the labour—the family. When ownership by the family is understood to be communal, the issue of systematic domination and exploitation in the production process cannot be admitted as a possibility. Whatever accumulation of capital occurs is not seen as an expropriation of anyone's surplus labour if it is assumed that the group shares in ownership.

However, the family in nineteenth-century Ontario was not an egalitarian unit and neither custom nor law considered that the family *per se* owned the means of production. Only under exceptional circumstances did women own the means of production. For the most part property was owned by the male head of the family. Wives and children were the proletariat of the family farm, the workers whose labour was rewarded according to the good fortune or goodwill of the owner. The significance of male control over female labour has been obscured because of the conjugal relationship, their mutual dependence, and their shared standard of living, yet female labour was not in a position of equality with male labour in the family economy where the ownership and control of property were in the hands of the male alone.

The important point to be made here is that the question of power through property relations in general is not unique to capitalist relations, but is crucial to understanding productive relations within the family economy as well.[38] Male control over labour was established through the power of ownership. In the family economy the issue of power was complicated by the personal relationships of the family and the fact that the male head of the family was clearly part of the labouring unit. But his position was distinct from the others; all surplus produced by the non-waged workers who did not share in ownership was, in effect, expropriated by the owner.[39] Whatever accumulation of capital occurred was legally his. Non-waged family workers had certain rights with respect to their membership in the family: children and wives could claim support from their fathers or husbands, but the general understanding was that this support was their right, less by virtue of their contribution than by virtue of their economic helplessness. They had no legal rights to what they produced through their labour even though the contribution of family members was critical to the success or failure of the economy of the family unit.

The implications of patriarchal productive relations were distinct for different forms of labour within the family unit. While male and female children and wives were all labourers subject to the authority of the male owner of the means of production, there were significant differences in the duration and extent of patriarchal dominance. Until the father died or gave his property away he exerted considerable control over his children's labour. But male and female children were treated differently, particularly with regard to their ultimate relationship to property. For women, both as children and as wives, patriarchal control took a different form than it did for men in that it did not cease with the passing of time, but was likely to continue throughout their lifetimes.

THE LAW

Male domination in property issues was stipulated in law in nineteenth-century Ontario. The rights of women to own property and even to claim ownership of the product of their own labour were severely restricted. Single women over twenty-one years of age and widows were, by law, given the same rights as males over property. But inheritance practices and social and legal restrictions with regard to occupation and appropriate behaviour meant that most property was controlled by males. For single women the period of time during which they were likely to be legally free from the control of either a husband or a father was non-existent or comparatively short. For most women the property protection for single women was irrelevant.

The labour a single woman provided on the property of a male relative generally was understood to have been freely provided and did not provide the woman with either a claim on the property or a claim to a wage. Paul Craven's study of court cases in nineteenth-century Ontario indicates that the law upheld the assumption that any work a woman performed for a member of her family was part of her natural duty. In one striking case, where a woman unsuccessfully sued her brother for wages for the work she had performed for several years on his farm, the judge was explicit in this regard:

> Nothing was more natural than an unmarried young woman should live with and keep house for her brother, especially while he was also unmarried, and that without the idea of hiring or wages entering into the mind of either. It would be we fear a mischievous doctrine to lay down that in every case in which a niece, or cousin, or sister in law is proved to be living in a farmer's house, treated in every way as one of the family, and assisting in the work of doing all or most of the house-work, she could, in the absence of any evidence whatsoever as to hiring or wages, be held entitled to the direction of a judge that the law in such a case implied a promise to pay.[40]

Until 1859 married women in English Canada had no right to property in their own name. This legal disability was based on English common law where, in the words of the English jurist Sir William Blackstone, "the husband and wife are one and that one is the husband."[41] Upon marriage women were considered the responsibility of their husbands and in this respect the law recognized it as the wife's legal right to be supported by the husband.[42] But the price of protection was the loss of independence of action, and of ownership and legal control over the products of a woman's labour. Even the primary products of her labour, her children, were legally under her husband's control. Until about the mid-nineteenth century, she could not claim them as her own under any circumstances and even when her husband died she would not automatically be recognized as the legal parent. Her husband could, if he wanted, appoint someone other than their mother as their legal guardian. In fact, anything a woman might produce, sell, or earn through her labour was legally the property of her husband and she could not use or dispose of it without his approval.

By mid-century, legislation was enacted to expand women's rights with regard to both their children and their property. In 1855 an act was passed giving women in Ontario the possibility of obtaining custody of their children under twelve years of age in cases where the judge "saw fit."[43] It followed similar custody legislation passed in England in 1839. In some cases, the courts rendered progressive interpretations of the law and women were not only awarded custody of their children, but also provision for their maintenance. However, in the majority of cases, courts upheld the idea that the common law rights of fathers over their children was not abrogated by enactment of the new legislation. According to legal historian Constance Backhouse, improved custody rights for women had less to do with women's rights, *per se,* than with the growing recognition of the need to protect children and to award custody in their interests.[44]

In response to considerable pressure from women, the Ontario government in 1859 passed An Act to Secure to Married Women Certain Separate Property Rights.[45] This act gave women rights to property they had owned before marriage which had not been covered by a marriage contract or settlement. However, a wife's earnings still belonged to her husband and while the law legally entitled her to make a will, her heirs could only be her husband or her children.[46] Once again, while the intent of the law seemed fairly clear, the tendency of the courts was to continue to uphold a husband's control over his wife's property, including her ability to make contracts and to convey her land.[47] The Married Women's Act of 1872 extended women's property rights somewhat. With this act, married women were permitted to own and administer separate property and to enter into contracts as though they were unmarried.[48] However, they were not given increased control over family property; rather, women's power existed only with regard to property that was distinctly in their name alone. With the Married Women's Property Act, a woman's earnings were considered her separate property. However, this provision was limited to earnings specifically arising out of the woman's employment in a trade or occupation where her husband had no proprietary interest. So while a married woman would be permitted to retain the earnings she might receive from production on her own land, from waged work, or from any special literary or artistic talent she might possess, she would not be legally entitled to the income from her labour on the family enterprise because the family property was still legally the husband's. The change in the law regarding women's property did not change the control a man could exercise over his wife's labour. His consent was still needed if she wanted to work for wages or engage in some sort of business on her own.[49] Nevertheless, throughout the second half of the nineteenth century the law was gradually improved so that its intent in providing greater property protection was clear. By the end of the century, women's separate property rights were considerably more secure than they had been at mid-century.

INHERITANCE

While family practices may have mitigated the practical effects of the law for some women in their daily lives, the significance of male legal superiority became especially clear when the husband or father died. An examination of the wills in one county—Stormont, Dundas, and Glengarry, Ontario—for two periods, from 1800 to 1811 and from 1850 to 1858, gives a clear indication of the tenuous claim women had on all forms of property.[50] The wills indicate not only the infrequency with which property was transferred to women, but also the understanding of the will-maker that the family property was entirely his. This particular county was chosen because records of wills are available from the early period of settlement and a comparison can therefore be made between inheritance practices when land was relatively plentiful and when it became more scarce. For the purposes of this study it would have been preferable to use data from a county more oriented toward wheat production, but since such counties were settled later, the changes in inheritance practices over a fairly long period of time (i.e., from mid-century when data are available to the end of the century) also reflected changes in legislation regarding women's property rights. While the changes in inheritance are significant in indicating the relative strength of patriarchal control as the economy became more industrialized and laws changed, at this point I want to focus on patriarchal control of all forms of property before legislative changes occurred.

Although Stormont, Dundas, and Glengarry County did not generate the wealth typical of wheat-exporting counties farther west, the economy in the early period relied heavily on timber exports and later was strongly influenced by the staple-exporting trade of other sections of the province.[51] To establish the validity of using information from this county as an indication of the general nature of female inheritance in the first half of the nineteenth century, I have also examined the wills of a wheat staple-exporting county, Wellington, for comparison. Since the inheritance pattern in Wellington County indicates that men there were no more generous in their distribution of property to the women in their families, it is fairly reasonable to assume that the infrequency with which property was transferred to women in Stormont, Dundas, and Glengarry was not atypical.

WIVES' INHERITANCE

In 1801 the Surrogate Court for the Eastern District of Ontario received a petition from Mary Links for permission to administer the estate of her husband, Matthew, who had died intestate. The inventory of his property indicates that not only were all the farm stock and implements considered to be his possessions, but all of the household items as well. Since these items are usually the tools of women's labour, their express ownership by the husband is noteworthy. Included in the inventory were the following: "1 collender, half a dusen of knives and forkes, 1 dusen of spunes, 1 candle stick and snuffer, 2 chairs, 3 tin canasters, 1 cuking glass, 1 frying pan, 1 dresser, 3 tin tumblers."[52] This inventory was not an isolated instance. In most cases men did not leave wills, so the court, usually after petition from a relative, would assign someone to be an administrator of the estate and would order an inventory of property to be taken. The inventories overwhelmingly indicate that household utensils, furniture, and linens were the property of the husband.

Widows were legally able to own property, but inheritance practices were such that males exerted considerable control over their wives after their deaths. Only in rare circumstances in the first half of the nineteenth century was a woman given total control over her husband's property when he died. In the wills of males in Stormont, Dundas, and Glengarry County, Ontario, for the two periods studied, women inherited their husband's property outright in only 6 to 8 per cent of the cases (Table 1). Women appear to have been given complete control of the property to dispose of without restriction only when there were no children of the husband living. But generally even if there were no children, directions were explicit about what should be done with the property after the wife's death.

Frequently the wife was given the use of the property for her lifetime, with instructions for further inheritance clearly laid out. In the early nineteenth century this was a much more common practice than later. In Stormont, Dundas, and Glengarry about one-third of the wills from 1800 to 1811 stipulated that the wife should have the estate for her lifetime. By mid-century the proportion had dropped to one-sixth.

TABLE 1 | BEQUESTS TO WIVES IN WILLS BY MALES,* STORMONT, DUNDAS, AND GLENGARRY, ONTARIO, 1800-11 AND 1850-58 (%)

	1800–11	1850–58
Wife inherits outright	8	6
Wife granted usufruct	30	16
Children inherit major portion	46	55
(a) son to support mother	14	19
(b) wife inherits portion	32	35
No mention of wife	16	23
Wife disinherits upon remarriage	30	35

* There was one woman who died with a will in the 1800–11 period and three with wills in the 1850–58 period.
Sample size: 1800–11 = 37; 1850–58 = 31.

Source: Public Archives of Ontario, Wills Collection GS1-1251; GS1-1253.

Even when wives were left the right to the estate for life, there were many restrictions laid out. Some men were quite specific about what the wife could do with the land, including instructions about whether or not she could cut timber. But the most restrictive practice was the tendency for husbands to tie their wife's use of the property to what they felt was the appropriate way for her to live the rest of her life. It was fairly common practice for men to deprive their wives of the right to inheritance if they should remarry. For example, one farmer left his wife the management of the income from the farm for as long as she remained his widow:

> In case my wife should remarry then in that case my executors herein after named and whom I also appropriate as Trustees for my children shall then take the sole management of the said farms and stock and rent or let the same or shares as they see fit and apply the said income to the benefit of my children whom they shall take the management of and see them educated and placed in such situation as said income will admit of and to give my widow a cow and four sheep with a bed and bedding and for her to have no more to say of my affairs. But if she remain my widow and so continues after the children are all educated and of age she shall still have during her natural life the one half of the income of the said farm on which we at present reside.[53]

Roughly a third of the wills made by men in Stormont, Dundas, and Glengarry during the first half of the nineteenth century specifically limited wives' inheritance to the period they remained widows. This practice appears to have been widespread throughout Ontario, although in counties farther west the proportion of wills which explicitly forbid remarriage by mid-century was somewhat smaller.[54]

While the threat of disinheritance undoubtedly gave women few options for the future, they did have some choice over whether they would adhere to their husbands' wishes that they not remarry. But some husbands even went so far as to stipulate that their wives would lose all property rights if they cohabited.[55] Over the issue of the guardianship of children, the husband's will was paramount. Women had no legal right to the guardianship of their children, either while the husband lived or when he died, and when he died he was entitled to designate anyone he chose as guardian.[56] Usually the mother was named as guardian, but it was not at all uncommon for the oldest son or some other male relative to be put in control of the younger children, should the wife remarry. George Crites's instructions in his will of 1804 is typical of caveats found in many wills. "If my widow should marry I hereby obligate my said son George to bring up and maintain the rest of my children that are not able to do for themselves and use the best endeavour to see them instructed in reading and writing."[57] Considering that his wife, upon remarriage, was to be disallowed the produce of the land and stock, the furniture, and the third part of the land which her husband had left her for life, her ability to care for these children would have been severely limited. The point remains that even if she had wished to, or if a new husband were prepared to assume responsibility for their maintenance, she would not have been permitted legally to assume this responsibility.

The issue of dower rights is particularly interesting with regard to a widow's claim to her husband's property. In theory a woman was to receive one-third of her husband's real and personal property upon his death, unless he designated in his will that her portion be larger. In practice this was less strict than the law would indicate. Dower clearly did not mean that a woman would inherit one-third of the estate outright. As mentioned earlier, it was usual for a man to stipulate who would receive his property after his wife died, even if she was to have control of it during her lifetime. The exceptions to this practice are so rare that they are remarkable in themselves. For example, although Donald Fraser left his land to his grandson, his wife was given use of the household furniture, stock, and farming implements for her life. Her husband, in addition, permitted her to dispose of this property after her death "as she may think proper amongst her children with the consent of the majority of the executors."[58] Alexander McGruner did not leave his estate to his wife for her life but trusted her judgment to a degree which was extraordinary for his time and circumstances. McGruner willed that his land be divided among his male children and that "the dividing of the same to my said children be according to the judgment and discretion of my wife as she may think and see most suitable when said children come of age." He also permitted his wife to take what she would need when the lands were divided "and arrangements should take place so that as my widow she may not be dependent in her advanced age."[59]

It was rare for a husband to be concerned about his wife's dependency as she aged. Generally the husband ensured that his wife would be dependent upon her children through the conditions of his will. In a substantial number of the wills a son was specifically ordered to support his mother. One man, in a will which was not at all uncommon, left instructions for the care of his wife. The two sons were to share all of his property "except the lower front room in the home which I have for the use of my wife Catherine as long as she is my widow and likewise she is to have a decent maintenance of the place suitable to her condition. But if she will marry she shall have what property she brought to my home and no more, neither will she have any title to hire, rent, or let the room to any other person or persons but for her own use only, then to be the property of my sons aforesaid."[60] Generally the wills did not describe in detail how the wife would be maintained. Rather, sons were simply instructed to maintain their mother for life or as long as she remained a widow. In some cases it was specified that the support be "in a kind, comfortable and respectable manner" or suitable to her sex and station in life.[61]

Clearly the conditions of dower could be satisfied without specifically settling how much a widow would receive. And whatever protection dower gave a woman, it did not extend beyond her widowhood. The vague stipulation that the wife should be provided for by the heirs of the estate increased from 14 per cent of the wills in the beginning of the century to almost one-fifth by mid-century. This practice could be a reflection of the general tendency for estates to be settled on one son as land became more scarce and farm sizes decreased.[62]

The effect of making women so dependent on their sons could create real hardship and loss of position. Frances Stewart described her widowhood as a period of extreme dependency where she was never "allowed...to think or act but as...guided or directed."[63] While widows may have appeared to have exchanged dependency on their husbands for dependency on their sons, the loss of position in the family could drastically change their real circumstances. Susanna Moodie claimed that in some families, especially those newly in the middle class, a widow was little more than a drudge: "the mother, if left in poor circumstances, almost invariably holds a subordinate position in her wealthy son's or daughter's family. She superintends the servants, and nurses the younger children; and her time is occupied by a number of minute domestic labours, that allow her very little rest in her old age. I have seen the grandmother in a wealthy family ironing the fine linen or broiling over the cook-stove, while her daughter held her place in the drawing room."[64] In these circumstances the women rarely had any alternative but to submit to the conditions in their children's households.[65]

The most common inheritance practice and one reflected in about a third of the wills studied was for the wife to inherit for her lifetime a portion of the estate, with the bulk to go to the children. If the farmer was relatively wealthy her inheritance would include land, but if the farm was small the usual practice was for one son to inherit the land, with the mother receiving the produce from a specific portion of it. John Munro was a wealthy farmer who willed that his wife be supported from the income from the property and be given the use of the house until her son married. When the son married he was to repair another house on the property for his mother's use, but if she decided to live with any of her children she was to continue to receive the same allowance from the estate "in order to compensate them for her support." While John Munro envisaged this income from the estate as ultimately belonging to whoever cared for his wife, he urged his children to give their mother enough so that "she may have what will be sufficient to keep her comfortable during her lifetime." John Munro obviously felt somewhat guilty about his treatment of his wife and explained why she was not given control over his will: "I should have appointed her executrix, but being sensible of her disposition I conceived it dangerous to the interest of the family."[66]

Occasionally the will stipulated that the wife's share was to be in lieu of dower. In a few cases there appears to have been a conscious effort to see that the wife's one-third interest was actually what she received. But for the most part the wife's rightful and legal claim seems not to have been an issue. The fact that very few women made wills and none, during the periods examined, contested the wills of their husbands indicates the lack of control women had over property.[67] Women's main security in property rights was their husbands' sense of duty to provide for them after they died.

DAUGHTERS' INHERITANCE

Patriarchal control placed sons and daughters on significantly different footings as labourers in the family economy. The labour of sons was more likely to result in a substantial share of the father's assets than the labour of daughters. In an economy where labour was scarce and land relatively plentiful, the ability of the father to retain the labour of his children often was crucial to the success or failure of the family enterprise.[68] The father was frequently able to assure his labour supply through the promise of land transference to his sons. When there were sons and daughters in the family, the daughters seldom shared equally in the distribution of the family property when the father died (Table 2). This could be a reflection of the greater value placed on the labour of male children and the desire to retain these services as long as possible, or it could reflect the social and legal restrictions which would have meant that any part of the estate left to a daughter would ultimately have been controlled by her husband. Most likely both these factors influenced a father's decision to exclude his daughters from a substantial share of his estate. The sexual division of labour whereby females tended to work most often at tasks associated with family subsistence and household maintenance would undoubtedly have made the daughter's labour appear less valuable to the farmer than the labour of sons, who would be more associated with labour directed toward the market.

The division of property among sons took a variety of forms. Sometimes it was given to the oldest son outright, but more frequently it was divided among the sons in a way so that each would have some property.[69] While the more or less equal division of land among sons was fairly common in the early part of the nineteenth century, the effect of this sort of property transfer over time, coupled with land scarcity in certain areas, meant that smaller and smaller parcels of land were being transferred. In order to pass on enough land to ensure an adequate "man/land" ratio, repeated subdivisions of land had to be avoided.[70]

TABLE 2 | BEQUESTS TO DAUGHTERS IN WILLS BY MALES,* STORMONT, DUNDAS, AND GLENGARRY, ONTARIO, 1800-11 AND 1850-58 (%)

	1800–11	1850–58
Daughters not mentioned	38	25
Daughters left all	3	35
Daughters inherit equally	8	14
Daughters given lesser portion of land	22	3.5
Daughters paid small sum; given chattels, personal property, furniture; or to be maintained by brother	30	54

* There was one woman who died with a will in the 1800–11 period and three with wills in the 1850–58 period.
Sample size: 1800–11 = 37; 1850–58 = 31

Source: Public Archives of Ontario, Wills Collection, GS1-1251; GS1-1253

To this end a type of land transfer known as the "English-Canadian" system of inheritance developed.[71] In this system the bulk of the estate would be passed on to a single son, usually the oldest, and he in turn was obliged to settle certain amounts on other children in the family. Sometimes though, the younger sons were given lesser amounts of land and the principal inheritor was obliged only to provide the daughters with some amount specified in the will. Generally the daughters did not fare well regardless of the system of inheritance. In 1803, Adam Johnston of Cornwall, Ontario, left his sons equal shares of his 400-acre estate. His daughters Nancy, Margaret, Janet, Jane, and Mary-Ann were to be given "one shilling if demanded."[72] While this appears to have been a particularly spiteful way to single out daughters in a will, this may not have been the intention. In a large proportion of the wills daughters were not mentioned at all.[73] But sometimes their omission is explained by the father as a consequence of their having already received what he thought appropriate.[74] The usual practice was for a father to settle some form of property or money on a daughter as her dowry when she married. Sons who inherited the bulk of the estate were frequently instructed to maintain their sisters until they were married, at which time they were to be given a cow or some sheep, sometimes with a little money as well.

The majority of wills either did not mention daughters or specified a legacy which was a small sum of money, some personal property, a portion of the family furniture when the mother died, or a cow, pig, or sheep.[75] In the early part of the century almost a third of the wills left some portion of the land to daughters. Generally this consisted of a small part of the total estate, with the major part going to the male heirs. But by mid-century, no doubt because of the scarcity of land in the district, the practice of leaving any land at all to daughters was drastically reduced. While over one-fifth of the wills in the early period left daughters a small parcel of land from the estate, by mid-century this was reduced to less than 5 per cent.

The striking feature of the wills is the extent to which it is assumed that daughters would be totally dependent on a male, either a brother or a husband, for support. The few exceptions to this practice are interesting for what they indicate about women's work. Duncan McDonald, for example, wanted to ensure that his wife and daughters would have some source of income for themselves. In his will, although he left everything to his son with the usual caveat that he provide the women with "sufficient fuel, provisions and other necessaries usual with their sex and station," the son was further instructed to see that each daughter receive one cow and one fatted hog each year to dispose of as she wished. He also specified that "the females [are] to have all poultry and the produce as their sole property."[76]

A female had little recourse in law if she felt that her inheritance was an unfair reflection of her contribution to the family economy. Craven's study gives the example of one woman who had lived and cared for her father for years under the assumption that she would inherit from him when he died. Her suit for recompense for her labour was not found in her favour because, as the judge commented, "this young woman could not be living any where else more properly than with her aged and infirm parent; and if she did acts of service, instead of living idly, it is no more than she ought to have done in return for her clothes and board, to say nothing of the claims of natural affection which usually lead children to render such services."[77]

OWNERSHIP

The concentration of ownership of the means of production in the household by males meant that women's labour throughout their lives would be subject, either directly or indirectly, to male power and authority. No part of their productive activity could escape the potential power of male domination. In this respect the issue of ownership of property in the family economy is considerably more all-encompassing than the power over labour exercised by capitalist ownership. The capitalist employer exercised control over the labour purchased, but the subsistence production of the wage worker in the family economy was distinct, separate, and beyond the employer's control. In the family economy the means of production and the means of subsistence were inseparable: women had no productive sphere beyond the power of male authority. Although the effects of patriarchal productive relations were often obscured by the close personal relationships and the interdependence of family members in the family economy, and while the degree of oppressive male dominance undoubtedly varied from household to household, the general effect of male ownership was to exercise control over female labour. [...] Daughters, wives, mothers, and widows were dependent on the will of fathers, husbands, sons, and brothers

In the transference of property the tenuous claim women had on the means of production was most obvious. Susanna Moodie's comment that "death is looked upon by many Canadians more as a matter of business, and change of property into other hands, than as a real domestic calamity"[78] is something of a mystery to historians who feel that, considering what happened when property changed hands, there was a domestic calamity.[79] Many women certainly experienced real grief when a father or a husband died, but their relationship to property was likely to change little. Perhaps Susanna Moodie was thinking less of the sentiments of widows than of children when she spoke of their calm anticipation of a relative's death. For sons with a prospect of inheritance it could not have been calamitous. For daughters, whatever change in property occurred was likely to affect them to a small degree. If any property was settled on them, it would be more likely to occur when they married than when their father died.

A widow's position was considerably more precarious. While there was a possibility of increased control of property through the provisions of the husband's will, there was also the more likely possibility that her situation would deteriorate if the terms of the will made her dependent on her children. In another respect Susanna Moodie's analysis is apt for the wife as well as for the children. For the most part the intention of men's wills appears to have been that wives would maintain essentially the same position relative to property that they held while the husband was alive.

Notes

1 The preoccupation of historians with the history of males and the distortions that has caused in historical methodology has been a subject of considerable interest to feminist historians in recent years. Of particular note are the following: Nancy Schrom Dye, "Clio's American Daughters: Male History, Female Reality," and Jane Tibbets Schulenburg, "Clio's European Daughters: Myopic Modes of Perception," in *The Prism of Sex: Essays in the Sociology of Knowledge,* ed. Julia A. Sherman and Evelyn Torton Beck (Madison, WI: University of Wisconsin Press 1979); Natalie Zemon Davis, "'Women's History' in Transition: The European Case," *Feminist Studies* 3 (Spring/Summer 1976), 809–23; Gerda Lerner, "Placing Women in History: Definitions and Challenges," *Feminist Studies* 3 (Fall 1975), 5–13; Ruth Pierson and Alison Prentice, "Feminism and the Writing and Teaching of History," *Atlantis* 7 (Spring 1982), 37–46.

2 For a discussion of the inadequacy of using concepts designed to explain market behaviour to explain non-market behaviour, see Marjorie Cohen, "The Problem of Studying 'Economic Man,'" in *Feminism in Canada,* ed. Angela Miles and Geraldine Finn (Montreal: Black Rose Book 1982), 89–101; Marjorie Cohen, "The Razor's Edge Invisible: Feminism's Effect on Economics," *International Journal of Women's Studies* 8, 2 (May/June 1985), 286–98; Bonnie Fox, "Women's Domestic Labour and Their Involvement in Wage Work: Twentieth Century Changes in the Reproduction of Daily Life," PhD Dissertation, University of Alberta 1980), 160.

3 Some economists, most notably Mel Watkins, Daniel Drache, and Richard Caves and Richard Holton find the significance of export staples to the economy important in explaining Canada's economic dependence and its chronic economic problems even in the twentieth century. See H.M. Watkins, "A Staple Theory of Economic Growth," *Canadian Journal of Economics and Political Science* XXIX (May 1963), 141–8; Richard E. Caves and Richard H. Holton, *The Canadian Economy* (Cambridge, MA: Harvard University Press 1961); Daniel Drache, "Staple-ization: A Theory of Capitalist Development," in *Imperialism, Nationalism and Canada,* ed. Craig Heron (Toronto: New Hogtown Press 1977), 15–33.

4 Carl Berger, *The Writing of Canadian History* (2nd ed., Toronto: University of Toronto Press 1986), 98; H. Clare Pentland, *Labour and Capital in Canada 1650–1860* (Toronto: James Lorimer 1981); Gregory S. Kealey, *Toronto Workers Respond to Industrial Capitalism 1867–1914* (Toronto: University of Toronto Press 1980); Bryan D. Palmer, *Working-Class Experience: The Rise and Reconstitution of Canadian Labour 1800–1980* (Toronto: Butterworths 1983); David McNally, "Staple Theory as Commodity Fetishism: Marx, Innis and Canadian Political Economy," *Studies in Political Economy* (Autumn 1980), 35–63.

5 Louise Dechêne, *Habitants et marchands de Montréal au XVIIe siècle* (Montreal: Plon 1974); Jean Hamelin, *Economie et société en Nouvelle-France* (Quebec: Université Laval 1961).

6 Kenneth Buckley, "The Role of Staple Industries in Canada's Economic Development," *Journal of Economic History* (Dec. 1958), 439–50.

7 Douglas McCalla, "The Wheat Staple and Upper Canadian Development," *Historical Papers* (1978), 34–46.

8 See especially Douglas McCalla, "The Internal Economy of Upper Canada: Some Evidence on Patterns of Agricultural Marketing (to 1850)," paper presented to the Thirteenth Conference on Quantitative Methods in Canadian Economic History, March 1984; John McCallum, *Unequal Beginnings: Agriculture and Economic Development in Quebec and Ontario until 1870* (Toronto: University of Toronto Press 1980).

9 McCalla, for example, wants to correct the picture of Ontario as solely reliant on wheat exports and shows that it was, "in some sense *a mixed*-farming

economy," but still, wheat was critical for, as he says, the more complex economy was "founded in most areas on wheat as the central crop for market purposes" (McCalla, "The Internal Economy of Upper Canada," 19).

10 McCallum, *Unequal Beginnings,* especially Ch. 8.

11 For a discussion of the various labour requirements and methods of labour organization characteristic of each type of staple production, see Daniel Drache, "The Formation and Fragmentation of the Canadian Working Class: 1820–1920," *Studies in Political Economy* (Fall 1984), 43–89.

12 Canadian feminist historians, however, have begun to examine the significance of female labour to the staple trades. See especially Sylvia Van Kirk, *"Many Tender Ties": Women in Fur-Trade Society 1670–1870* (Winnipeg: Watson & Dwyer 1980); Jan Noel, "Les Femmes favorisées," in *The Neglected Majority,* II, ed. Alison Prentice and Susan Mann Trofimenkoff (Toronto: McClelland & Stewart 1985), 18–40; Marilyn Porter, " 'Women and Old Boats': The Sexual Division of Labour in a Newfoundland Outport," in *The Public and the Private* ed. Eva Gamarnikow et al.; Marilyn Porter, "She Was Skipper of the Shore-Crew: Notes on the History of the Sexual Division of Labour in Newfoundland," *Labour/Le Travail* 15 (Spring 1985), 105–23.

13 Allan Greer, "Wage Labour and the Transition to Capitalism: A Critique of Pentland," *Labour/Le Travail* 15 (Spring 1985), 21.

14 Allan Greer, *Peasant, Lord, and Merchant: Rural Society in Three Quebec Parishes 1740–1840* (Toronto: University of Toronto Press 1985).

15 Arthur Lewis, "Economic Development with Unlimited Supplies of Labour," *Manchester School of Economic and Social Studies* II (May 1957), 149.

16 Marr and Paterson, *Canada,* Ch. 4.

17 This was true in all forms of staple development where wage labour occurred. See, for example, Fernand Ouellet, "Dualité économique et changement technologique au Québec (1760–1790)," *Histoire sociale/Social History,* 257; Lower and Innis, *Settlement and the Forest,* 32; Sacouman, "Semi-Proletarianization and Rural Underdevelopment in the Maritimes," *Canadian Review of Sociology and Anthropology* 17 (1980); Pentland, *Labour and Capital,* 29; Allan Greer, "Fur-Trade Labour and Lower Canadian Agrarian Structures," Canadian Historical Association, *Historical Papers* (1981), 197–214.

18 In *Women, Work, & Family,* for example, Louise Tilly and Joan Scott explain the basic division of labour between men and women in the family economy. While there was considerable diversity of roles and frequent overlapping of tasks, women's work centred on the household. Tilly and Scott, *Women, Work, & Family,* especially Ch. 3.

19 Naomi Griffiths points out that while certain industries in Canada encouraged a division of labour strictly according to age and gender, such as lumbering and fishing, in small settlements "the personality of the individual and the immediate challenge of the day were more important than social conventions about gender-roles." Naomi Griffiths, *Penelope's Web* (Toronto: Oxford University Press 1976), 124–5.

20 There is an extensive literature on this subject which is now known as "the domestic labour debate." An excellent overview of the literature is provided by Eve Kaluzynska, "Wiping the Floor with Theory: A Survey of Writings on Housework," *Feminist Review* 6 (1980).

21 Carmen D. Deere, "Rural Women's Subsistence Production in the Capitalist Periphery," in *Peasants and Proletarians,* ed. Robin Cohen, Peter C.W. Gutkind, and Phylis Brazier (New York: Monthly Review Press 1979), 133–48. R. James Sacouman, in his work on the Maritimes, discusses how subsistence farming has been an integral part of capitalist accumulation in the staple trades of that region: "Subsistence farming has provided and still provides the principal base for the "super-exploitation"...of the petty inshore fishermen and woodlot cutter. The money value of fish and of logs can be lowered below the value of labour power replacement since subsistence production does, even in its most truncated form, provide material sustenance directly, without the intermediary of cash." R. James Sacouman, "Semi-Proletarianization and Rural Underdevelopment in the Maritimes," 235–7.

22 This analysis follows a Marxian explanation of capital accumulation where surplus value is extracted from labour when labour is not paid a wage equal to the total value it produces, but is paid a wage which reflects the socially necessary labour time expended in production. Deere argues that since the value of labour reflects socially necessary labour, it is possible to reduce the value of labour when some of the goods and services required to maintain and reproduce labour are produced by non-waged labour. Deere, "Rural Women," 137–8.

23 Generally the prevalence of female subsistence agricultural labour is most directly associated with underdeveloped Third World countries. See, for example, Esther Boserup, *Economic Development* (London: George Allen and Unwin Ltd 1970), 77–8. While there are important similarities in the function of female pre-industrial labour in Canada and that of women in Third World countries today, there are also significant differences. The critical distinction between conditions in Third World economies with large resource-exporting sectors and Canada's early staple development is that Third World countries typically have an abundant labour supply whereas Canada experienced labour shortages. Also, in Third World countries there often existed well-developed agricultural and market traditions which continued to have an impact after colonial domination. In Canada agricultural and market development did not precede resource development.

24 *Royal Commission on Dominion-Provincial Relations,* Book I, 27, cited in Vernon Fowke, "The Myth of the Self-Sufficient Pioneer," *Transactions of the Royal Society of Canada* 56 (1962), 26.

25 Greer, *Peasant, Lord and Merchant,* 205.

26 Fowke, "The Myth of the Self-Sufficient Pioneer," 27. For a recent evaluation of Fowke's thesis see Leo A. Johnson, "New Thoughts on an Old Problem: Self-Sufficient Agriculture in Ontario," paper presented to Canadian Historical Association, June 1984.

27 Marr and Paterson, *Canada,* 80; Vernon C. Fowke, *Canadian Agricultural Policy: The Historical Pattern* (Toronto: University of Toronto Press 1978 [1946]), 45, 48; Robert Leslie Jones, *History of Agriculture in Ontario 1613–1880* (Toronto: University of Toronto Press 1946), 307.

28 For an excellent discussion of the misconceived dichotomy between subsistence and market activity, see Greer, *Peasant, Lord and Merchant,* 202–5.

29 It is used frequently in this sense in Canada. Particularly important are the following: Max Hedley, "Domestic Commodity Production: Small Farms in Alberta," in *Challenging Anthropology,* ed. David H. Turner and Gavin A. Smith (Toronto: McGraw-Hill Ryerson 1979), 280–98; Max Hedley, "Independent Commodity Production," *Canadian Review of Sociology and Anthropology* 13 (1976), 413–21; Leo Johnson, "Independent Commodity Production: Mode of Production or Capitalist Class Formation?" *Studies in Political Economy* 6 (1981), 93–112; Sacouman, "Semi-Proletarianization and Rural Underdevelopment in the Maritimes." For a discussion of the necessity of a capitalist labour market for the term "commodity production" to be appropriate, see Michael Merrill, "Cash Is Good to Eat: Self-Sufficiency and Exchange in the Rural Economy of the United States," *Radical History Review* (Winter 1977), 42–71.

30 A.V. Chayanov, *The Theory of the Peasant Economy* (Urbana: University of Illinois Press 1966).

31 Oakley, *Woman's Work,* 16.

32 Pentland, *Labour and Capital,* 24.

33 Paul Phillips, "Introduction," in Pentland, *Labour and Capital,* xxvi.

34 Pentland, *Labour and Capital,* Ch. 2.

35 D. Roberts, *Paternalism in Early Victorian England* (London: Croom Helm 1979), cited in Judy Lowen, "Not So Much a Factory, More a Form of Patriarchy: Gender and Class during Industrialization," in *Gender, Class & Work,* ed. Gamarnikow et al.

36 In the major study on labour in Canadian agriculture there is a brief reference to the labour of unpaid family workers, but for the most part the author chooses to see farm units which did not hire labour as being "owner-operated," and refers only to the labour performed by the male owner. George Haythorne, *Labour in Canadian Agriculture* (Cambridge, MA: Harvard University Press 1960).

37 Oscar Lange, *Political Economy,* I, trans. A.H. Walker (Oxford: Pergamon Press 1963), 16–17.

38 James A. Henretta, "Families and Farms: Mentalité in Pre-Industrial America," *William and Mary Quarterly* 35 (Jan. 1978), 21.

39 Max Hedley, in his studies of family farms in twentieth-century western Canada, points to the inequalities in productive relations which are concealed by the term "family farm." He says: "we need to recognize that while there is private ownership of the means of production by an individual who applies his own labour to the productive process, there is also a considerable amount of labour by non-owners of the means of production. The commodities produced by this labour do not belong to the actual producer but to the owners of the means of production; therefore, any surplus labour embodied in them is in effect expropriated." Max Hedley, "Relations of Production of the 'Family Farm': Canadian Prairies," *Journal of Peasant Studies* 9 (1981), 74.

40 *Redmond v Redmond* (1868), 1 *Upper Canada Queen's Bench Reports* 220, cited by Paul Craven,

"The Law of Master and Servant in Mid-Nineteenth-Century Ontario," in *Essays in the History of Canadian Law,* ed. David H. Flaherty, I (Toronto: Osgoode Society 1981), 177.

41 Margaret E. MacLellan, "History of Women's Rights in Canada," in *Cultural Tradition and Political History of Women in Canada,* Royal Commission on the Status of Women in Canada, No. 8, p 1.

42 Linda Silver Dranoff, *Women In Canadian Life: Law* (Toronto: Fitzhenry & Whiteside 1977), 26.

43 Constance B. Backhouse, "Shifting Patterns in Nineteenth-Century Canadian Custody Law," in *Essays in the History of Canadian Law,* ed. David H. Flaherty, 212–48

44 *Ibid.,* 213.

45 Constance B. Backhouse, "Married Women's Property Law in Nineteenth-Century Canada," unpublished paper, April 1987.

46 Sheila Kieran, *The Family Matters: Two Centuries of Family Law and Life in Ontario* (Toronto: Key Porter 1986), 51.

47 For a full discussion of the specifics of the law and how it was subsequently interpreted by the courts, see Backhouse, "Married Women's Property Law in Nineteenth-Century Canada."

48 Similar acts permitting married women to own and control property were passed by other provinces in the following years: British Columbia 1873; Manitoba 1875; Newfoundland 1876; Nova Scotia 1884; Northwest Territories 1886; New Brunswick 1896; Prince Edward Island 1896; Saskatchewan 1907; Alberta 1922. MacLellan, "Women's Rights," 4.

49 National Council of Women of Canada, *Women of Canada: Their Life and Work,* ed. Isabel Aberdeen (Ottawa: Queen's Printer 1900), 39.

50 Bruce S. Elliott correctly points out the dangers in looking only at wills for inheritance patterns. They tend to be more representative of the wealthy than the poor, the old rather than the young, and the sick rather than the healthy. "Sources of Bias in Nineteenth-Century Ontario Wills," *Histoire sociale/Social History* 17, 35 (May 1985).

51 For information on the significance of this area as a supplier of waged labour in the timber camps on the Ottawa see Arthur R.M. Lower, *Great Britain's Woodyard: British America and the Timber Trade, 1763–1867* (Montreal: McGill-Queen's University Press 1973), 188; also, for the effect of increased immigration to more westerly points of province on income generating activities in Dundas, see James Croil, *Dundas, or A Sketch of Canadian History* (Montreal: B. Dawson & Son 1861), 152.

52 Public Archives of Ontario [hereafter PAO], Wills Collection, [hereafter WC], GS1-1251, Mary Links 1801.

53 PAO, WC, GS1-1253, William Cassidy 1853.

54 See David Gagan, *Hopeful Travellers: Families, Land, and Social Change in Mid-Victorian Peel County, Canada West* (Toronto: University of Toronto Press 1981), 55.

55 PAO, WC, GS1-1253, Hugh Shaw 1853.

56 The right of married women to guardianship of their children was introduced in provincial statutes from 1910 to 1923. McClellan, "Women's Rights," 5.

57 PAO, WC, GS1-1251, George Crites 1804.

58 PAO, WC, GS1-1253, Donald Fraser 1853.

59 PAO, WC, GS1-1253, Alexander McGruner 1857.

60 PAO, WC, GS1-1251, John Saver 1811.

61 PAO, WC, GS1-1253, Adam Cockburn 1854; PAO WC, GS1-1264, Robert Valance 1890.

62 Gagan, *Hopeful Travellers,* Ch. 3.

63 E.P. Dunlop, ed., *Our Forest Home: Being Extracts from the Correspondence of the Late Frances Stewart* (Toronto 1889), 80–1.

64 Susanna Moodie, *Life in the Clearings vs the Bush* (New York: DeWitt & Davenport 1855), 291–2.

65 Moodie seemed to see this as a matter of will more than of necessity, saying "they submit with great apparent cheerfulness, and seem to think it necessary to work for the shelter of a child's roof, and the bread they eat." *Ibid.,* 292.

66 PAO, WC, GS1-1251, John Munro 1800.

67 Women were given the right to dispose of property by testament in Ontario in 1801. Susan Altschul and Christine Caron, "Chronology of Legal Landmarks in the History of Canadian Women," *McGill Law Journal* 21 (Winter 1975), 476.

68 Gagan, *Hopeful Travellers,* 44; Folbre, "Patriarchy," 6; see also Lawrence Stone, "The Rise of the Nuclear Family in Early Modern England: The Patriarchal State," in *The Family in History,* ed. Charles E. Rosenberg (Philadelphia: University of Pennsylvania Press 1975), 13–57, for a discussion of inheritance as a means of strengthening patriarchy.

69 Herbert J. Mays, in a study of the settlement of Gore near Toronto, has shown that acquiring land through inheritance, rather than direct sales, became increasingly significant for males by mid-century as land became more scarce and the population aged. "'A Place to Stand': Families, Land and Permanence in Toronto Gore Township, 1820–1890," *Historical Papers* (1980), 185–211.

70 Gagan, *Hopeful Travellers,* 50.

71 A.R.M. Lower, *Canadians in the Making: A Social History of Canada* (Toronto: Longmans, Green & Company 1958), 336.

72 PAO, WC, GS1-1251, Adam Johnston 1803.

73 From 1800 to 1811 in Stormont, Dundas, and Glengarry County, 38 per cent of the wills filed did not leave a bequest to daughters. In some of these families there may have been no daughters, but still the percentage is high. By 1850–58 the proportion had dropped to 25 per cent.

74 PAO, WC, GS1-1264, John McKercher 1890.

75 In the early part of the century this accounted for more than two-thirds of all wills. By mid-century almost four-fifths of the wills either neglected daughters altogether or gave them only very small bequests.

76 PAO, WC, GS1-1253, Duncan McDonald 1850.

77 *Sprague and Wife* v *Nickerson* (1844), 1 *Upper Canada Queen's Bench Reports* 284, cited by Craven, "The Law of Master and Servant," 177.

78 Moodie, *Life in the Clearings,* 138.

79 Rosemary R. Ball, "'A Perfect Farmer's Wife': Women in 19th Century Rural Ontario," *Canada: An Historical Magazine* 3 (December 1975), 16; Gagan, *Hopeful Travellers,* 50–1.

Parish Republics

Allan Greer

What do we mean by the Revolution? The war? That was no part of the Revolution; it was only an effect and consequence of it. John Adams[1]

Meanwhile, as male republicans continued to insult the queen and revile the monarchy, the colonial government of her majesty suffered attacks of a more practically damaging sort in the parishes of western Lower Canada. The autumn months saw changes, momentous in their implications, in the way sovereign power was actually constituted and exercised at the local level. The "people" were beginning to rule themselves, and this phenomenon, more than the declarations published earlier in the Patriot press or the blood later spilled on the field of battle, is what made 1837 truly a revolutionary year.

Parish Government Democratized

Clashes over the allegiance of militia officers and justices of the peace were, by September, developing into something more serious in the rural District of Montreal than mere gestures of protest. As the anti-coercion meetings succeeded one another over the course of the summer, the governor's secretary had added more and more names to the list of revoked commissions; all the while sympathetic magistrates and officers who had escaped the purge continued to resign. Now patriot supporters were beginning to wonder about the allegiance of anyone who kept a government commission; indeed the decision to resign or to stay on as militia captain or justice of the peace emerged as the crucial political test for local notables. Only a few months earlier the issues and actors involved in the Lower Canadian crisis were rather remote from the experience of country people, but now the contest within the British empire had come right down to the level of the parish and its little elite. Now there were targets for popular ire closer to home than Governor Gosford in his palace on Cape Diamond. In the county of Richelieu it was reported that "the people are insisting that all remaining officers of Militia (Magistrates there are none, now) should throw up their Commissions, as they consider it a disgrace to serve under the present Government."[2] Initially, recalcitrant officeholders seemed, from the patriot point of view, selfish men who placed personal honours before civic duty, but as the crisis deepened in the fall of 1837, they came to be seen in a more sinister light, as voluntary agents of a hostile power whose pretensions to rule Lower Canada were quite illegitimate. Accordingly, the pressures to resign intensified enormously.

Victims of the government purge were lionized as heroes who had refused to bow down to despotism, and all across the rural District of Montreal honours were heaped upon them. By early September patriots in several parishes were holding public meetings for the purpose of symbolically reinstating dismissed officers, and maypoles played an appropriately prominent role in these grass-roots initiatives. "The people have elected the dismissed officers of the militia

Allan Greer, "Parish Republics," in *The Patriots and the People* (Toronto: University of Toronto Press, 1993), 219–257. Reprinted by permission of the publisher.

to command them," wrote the commander of her majesty's forces. "At St. Ours a pole has been erected in favor of a dismissed Captain, with this inscription on it—'Elu par le peuple.'"[3] This may have seemed at first nothing more than a symbolic gesture of defiance, but in fact something significant was afoot.

Not surprisingly, the troubled county of Two Mountains was at the forefront. A month after the alarms of July most of the justices of the peace and militia officers from the French-Canadian areas of the county had been dismissed; there were no magistrates left in the parishes of St Benoit and St Hermas, and elsewhere the judiciary of this highly polarized region was entirely in the hands of Constitutionalists. These events were of course reminiscent of the tempests under Governor Dalhousie ten years earlier, when the revoking of royal commissions to punish political opponents had been particularly flagrant in Two Mountains. The situation was more serious in 1837, however, and it deteriorated further when the government began naming "loyal" subjects to replace officers and magistrates who had resigned or been dismissed. Most shocking to patriots was the appointment of a violent Constitutionalist who, as justice of the peace for St Eustache, had led the anti-patriot forces during the election riots of 1834. It was in reaction to these developments that northern radical leaders went beyond simply honouring purged officers and began organizing their own judicial apparatus.

At a meeting of the "Permanent Committee of the County of Two-Mountains" held at St Benoit on 1 October 1837 a series of resolutions was passed arranging for the establishment of "Justices of the Peace and Pacificators" (an awkward translation from the French: "juges de paix amiables compositeurs").[4] Invoking "the authority invested in it by the people," the committee recommended that the inhabitants of every parish in the county meet to elect at least three "pacificators" to adjudicate disputes. Local "Reformers" (i.e., everyone but government supporters) were to bring their legal cases to one of these judges, who would listen to both parties, call in witnesses as required and render his decision "in conformity with the dictates of his conscience without being obliged to observe the forms and proceedings of courts." Two or more pacificators could preside jointly, and in serious cases they were to empanel a jury. To ensure the authority of the new judiciary, the permanent committee ordered that anyone who defied its rulings or undermined its jurisdiction by taking cases to the regular courts should be excluded from public office and rigorously ostracized by all good patriots. There was also provision in the resolutions of 1 October for a revolutionized county militia with elected officers, but the main emphasis was on the new judicial apparatus.

This plan for a system of adjudicating disputes in Two Mountains is an interesting document, and it is worth pausing a moment to examine its features and their origins and antecedents. Obviously the tribunals were modelled to some degree on the British judicial system that had taken root in Lower Canada, with its juries and its justices of the peace, the latter acting unilaterally or sitting with colleagues in quarter sessions. The patriots did not replicate existing institutions exactly. Their program embodied several departures from current practice. For one thing, it had no room for a rigid separation of civil and criminal jurisdiction; the pacificators in fact combined the functions of a justice of the peace and a "commissioner for the trial of small causes." More than was the case under the prevailing judicial arrangements, the patriot system of Two Mountains provided convenient local facilities rather than institutional specialization. It was also intended to be informal, a characteristic generally prized by popular revolutionary movements intent on making justice comprehensible and accessible to all. To that end also, no fees were to be charged. Finally, the judge-pacificators were to be locally elected rather than appointed by external authority.

Simplicity, accessibility, community control: these were the characteristics that the northern patriots tried to build into their upstart judiciary.

While the plan in its general features bears testimony to the political philosophy that the bourgeois Patriots shared with radicals throughout the western world, clearly many of its details grew out of the institutions and customs of rural French Canada. The procedure for electing local pacificators, for example, is an exact copy of the way in which churchwardens were selected in country parishes. Moreover, as in the case of a vestry board, one year's service was mandatory for anyone elected by his neighbours. Just as striking is the continuity between the new office of "juge de paix amiable compositeur" and that familiar Lower Canadian figure, the arbitrator. Extra-judicial conciliation, as we saw earlier, was a well-entrenched practice in French Canada long before the conquest. A trusted local resident, or perhaps a committee of three, would try to settle small suits "à l'amiable" when called upon by parties anxious to avoid the expense of a formal application to the courts. The "Justice of the Peace and Pacificator" clearly represented an effort to establish this function on a more regular basis while combining it with some of the powers and responsibilities of a JP.

No habitant could have drawn up the St Benoit resolutions instituting a revolutionary judiciary for the county of Two Mountains. Obviously, the initiative was not popular in that sense. Quite likely Jean-Joseph Girouard, together with other local doctors, merchants, and notaries, was the driving force behind this and other actions of the "Permanent and Central Committee." Nevertheless, it was scarcely a case of middle-class leaders ramming a doctrinaire program down the throats of passive followers. The institution of the elective judge-pacificator arose, in very large measure, out of the traditions and experience of the people—plebeian as well as professional—of rural Lower Canada. That is what made it "popular." Arising in dialectical response to repressive measures by the government, the new judiciary was shaped by the history of French-Canadian community life generally, as well as by the specific conflicts that had troubled Two Mountains over the course of a decade.

Just how the insurgent tribunals operated is impossible to say. If records were kept, the patriots involved must have had the sense to destroy them when Two Mountains was invaded by troops and loyalists. We do know that justices/pacificators were indeed appointed in accordance with the guidelines set down by the Central Committee. At a public meeting held in the middle of October in the parish of St Benoit, featuring speeches by regional Patriot leaders, twenty-two men were elected judges for St Eustache, Ste Scholastique, St Hermas, and St Benoit.[5] Most of those selected were merchants, doctors, and notaries, though there were also rank-and-file patriots like the habitants Pierre Danis and Joseph Robillard. The deference to middle-class candidates is unsurprising—these were the sort of literate and widely respected individuals who, along with priests, would normally be chosen as arbitrators—but it does reflect the continuing bourgeois hegemony within the movement. Since several of the professional men were former justices of the peace lately dismissed by the government, there was also in their election an element of righting wrongs and rewarding virtue.

Middle-class leadership was much less pronounced a month later as Lower Canada girded for war and parishes across the District of Montreal proceeded to elect officers for a revolutionized militia. One meeting in late November—also at St Benoit—was held to name officers "in opposition to those of the government."[6] About this time 150 to 200 men met for the same purpose in the rectory of St Eustache, traditional locale for vestry meetings and churchwarden elections. Six officers were elected, only one of whom was a merchant; the rest were all cultivateurs. A government spy who attended the meeting reported that Dr Jean-Olivier Chénier gave a speech urging the people "to attack and destroy Her Majesty's Troops," but according to François Mallet, one of the habitants elected lieutenant, Chénier was the only "notable" present.[7] Elections of this sort were by no means limited to the county of Two Mountains. There were several specific reports from other parts of the province of revolutionized militia commands, in addition to the early cases in the Richelieu mentioned above. Even the apparently quiet parishes of the Berthier area were not immune to the contagion of revolt, according to the loyalist seigneur James Cuthbert. "The parishes of St Cuthbert and St Bartholomew were almost universally impregnated, and large numbers in Berthier; most of the militia officers that were dismissed, and some of those who gave in their resignations, allowed themselves to be reappointed by their former militia men."[8]

Hesitant and uneven though they were, the steps taken in the fall of 1837 to establish a patriot local administration with elected judges and militia officers were of enormous significance. Rather than complaining about the current government, people were attempting to organize a new one with completely different foundations. This could mean only one thing, concluded the editor of the anti-patriot *Populaire* after reporting the meeting at St Benoit: "La révolution commence!"[9]

The Grand Meeting at St Charles

With a booming cannon shot, the "Great Meeting of the Five Counties" was called to order at noon on 23 October. Over the course of the previous day and night, some 1,000 to 5,000 people (depending on whether one consults Patriot or Constitutionalist sources) had descended on the village of St Charles, coming from the southern counties of St Hyacinthe, Rouville, Chambly, Verchères, and Richelieu. At the last minute they were joined by a delegation from L'Acadie to form the "Confederation of the Six Counties." The delegates and casual spectators assembled in a meadow at the edge of the village where they listened to speeches from all the most renowned Patriot orators; they passed a set of resolutions by acclamation and cheered loudly for their country and its leaders. There were tricolour flags and banners proclaiming "Fly Gosford, Persecutor of the Canadians," "Long live Papineau and the Elective System," and "Liberty! We'll Conquer or Die for Her." In many respects the proceedings resembled those of the county protest meetings that had succeeded one another in the summer of 1837. It was a more elaborate affair, however, extending over two days and involving various rituals not normally associated with a political meeting. Moreover, the St Charles assembly had been convoked, not simply to protest political injuries, but to establish a regional "federation" and to celebrate the unity and determination of the people. Surely the organizers had in mind the French Revolution and "those defensive pacts which in the winter of 1790 linked city to city, militia to militia, and which were accompanied by ceremonies which we might call 'festivals of federation.' "[10] Politics—indeed, collective life in general—seemed to be finding new channels outside the institutional structures of the colonial state, and it was this promise of a new departure that gave St Charles a genuinely revolutionary flavour. No wonder that the enemies of the Patriot movement observed preparations for the meeting with the greatest alarm.[11]

It is not clear who conceived the idea of a mass multi-county meeting, but it seems likely that the impulse came from the patriot leaders of the Richelieu like Doctor Wolfred Nelson of St Denis. The idea of a spectacular demonstration at St Charles would have been particularly appealing in the context of regional politics; for the "Village Debartzch," as it was known, was the home of "that prince of renegades," Pierre Debartzch, a powerful seigneur and sometime radical, recently named to the Executive Council.[12] Certainly Papineau and the other Montreal leaders approved the project and played a prominent part at the St Charles meeting. They helped to draft the formal resolutions to be put to the meeting and, along with middle-class leaders from the region, they dominated the platform when it came time for speeches. Papineau himself rambled on for two and a half hours.

The content of the speeches and the resolutions, like the men who populated the stage, suggested continuities with the parliamentary wrangles of the past. Four resolutions dealt with the composition of the Legislative and Executive councils, calling for the reform of long-standing "abuses." The thrust of most of the motions was much more revolutionary. Beginning with an excerpt from the preamble to the American Declaration of Independence, the resolutions of the Six Counties emphatically denied the legitimacy of the current régime and insisted on the right of the people to govern itself. An "Address of the Confederation of the Six Counties to the People of Canada" issued an ominous warning. Under conditions of oppression, it declared, "it becomes the imperative duty of the people to betake themselves to the serious consideration of their unfortunate position—of the dangers by which they are surrounded—and by well-concerted organization, to make such arrangements as may be necessary to protect, unimpaired, their rights as citizens, and their dignity as freemen."[13]

But how exactly were the people of Canada to "protect their rights"? The boycott of British goods had clearly failed to secure concessions, and accordingly there was little talk at St Charles of the non-importation campaign. Indeed, far from retreating in the face of patriot gestures of protest and defiance, the government was bringing in more troops to Lower Canada. The call for "well-concerted organization" made some sense under the circumstances, but those in charge of the St Charles meeting had precious little to offer in the way of specifics. The resolutions spoke of a "Convention" of delegates from across the province that would presumably form the basis of an insurgent régime, but the meeting went no further than to call on citizens "seriously to consider if the time is not at hand when it ought to meet." Even the Confederation of the Six Counties itself proved to have no lasting existence. No one seems to have thought of giving it institutional form, and so, once the resolutions had been passed and the manifestos published, the participants packed up and departed and the confederation effectively dissolved.

The St Charles meeting was not completely ineffectual. It did urge concrete and immediate action in the area of local administration. Expressing indignation over "the arbitrary dismissals from office, ordered by the Governor-in-Chief...against a number of justices of the peace, officers of militia, and commissioners for the summary trial of small causes throughout the parishes," the resolutions urged the region's patriots to follow the example of the county of Two Mountains.

> That it is of urgent necessity, under such lamentable circumstances, to replace the individuals whom an administration inimical to the country will name to those offices, by men worthy of confidence; that all the parishes of the Six Counties are hereby invited simultaneously to elect, between the first day of December and the first day of January next, pacificator justices of the peace and officers of militia; and that the regulations of the county of Two Mountains be provisionally adopted for their direction and jurisdiction.[14]

It was this call for a revolutionized local administration that was the most powerful and controversial of the proceedings at St Charles. Timothée Franchère, the St Mathias merchant who seconded the motion quoted above, had a good deal of explaining to do when he was interrogated four months later in the Montreal prison. According to the prisoner, he had objected to any call for the election of militia officers, since such a move was "too strong and tended to encroach on the rights of government."[15] Nevertheless, Papineau persuaded him to set his objections aside. One does not have to accept every detail of Franchère's story to acknowledge that both he and the examining magistrate were aware of the implications of this particular resolution. In the aftermath of the 1837 insurrections several other prisoners and witnesses dwelt on this aspect of the St Charles meeting, either because they found it particularly striking or because their interrogators were preoccupied with the issue of local elections. Joseph-Léon Beauchamps, for example, recalled Papineau's speech in these terms: "he also recommended to the people to hold elections for officers of militia and *amiables compositeurs* who would judge their affairs."[16] Such advice must have seemed particularly serious sedition to the magistrates of Montreal, because it did more than call into question the legitimacy of the government, it proposed—admittedly in a hesitant manner—measures to replace it.

But where did the idea of an elective militia and magistracy originate? Certainly not at St Charles and not in the mind of Louis-Joseph Papineau. It is essential to recognize that the campaign to revolutionize local government was well under way before 23 October. It had developed primarily in the county of Two Mountains, although it was not entirely limited to the northern region, and it depended heavily on the traditions, the initiative, and the active support of the habitants and artisans of the countryside. In contrast to the revolutionary mimetism of the boycott of British imports, this campaign developed organically out of the Lower Canadian confrontation of 1837. Responding directly to government actions that were generally considered unjust, northern patriots defended traditional rights while laying the foundations of a democratic administration. Certainly there was middle-class leadership from the start, but the campaign drew its potency from the fact that the plebeians of Lower Canada had fought for generations to make institutions like the parish, the militia, and the magistrature into expressions of their communities. The St Charles meeting had the effect of spreading and accelerating the revolution in local government; it did not create it.

Just as important as the manifest content of the speeches and resolutions—probably more significant in its effects—were the festive and symbolic aspects of the assembly of the Six Counties. This was no mere political meeting: it was a celebration of national unity and public determination. Accordingly, it was staged with all the pomp and circumstance that the Richelieu valley could muster. Martial themes were prominent, anticipating the coming military confrontation perhaps, but also reflecting the importance of the militia in rural community life.

> During the Meeting, a company of between 60 and 100 Militia Men attended, with arms on the ground, under the command of Capts. Lacaisse and Jalbert. They went through their manoeuvres in very good style; a volley was fired at the passing of every Resolution... A very handsome column, surmounted with "a cap of Liberty," was erected, on the occasion, in honor of PAPINEAU, on the ground. It bears an inscription:—"To PAPINEAU, by his grateful brother patriots, 1836 [sic]." After the meeting was over, Mr. PAPINEAU was led to the front of the column, and addressed by one of the gentlemen, to which the Hon. gentleman replied in a suitable manner. The young men who attended the meeting afterwards marched in procession to this pillar, before which they sung a popular hymn, and laying their hands

> on the column, swore that they would be faithful to their country, and conquer or die for her. This solemn vow was registered in the hearts of all present, amid vollies of musketry and the thunders of artillery. It was a solemn and impressive sight.[17]

Evidently the cult of Papineau was at its height. The irony of course is that the honourable speaker no longer possessed the initiative in Lower Canada; in fact, increasingly after 24 October he would find himself overwhelmed by events. For the time being, however, he played a tremendously important role at St Charles, not only rousing the multitude with his oratory but, above all, serving as the human embodiment of the Patriot cause and the Lower Canadian nation. Still, he was not the object of blind personal devotion. Note that the "young men" swore allegiance to "their country" rather than to their leader. Moreover, whereas Papineau's close associate, E.B. O'Callaghan, author of the lines quoted above, emphasized the dedication of the "Papineau column" to the great man, less eminent spectators viewed the event from a slightly different angle. An habitant from Varennes later remembered "a column topped with a red bonnet that was called 'the liberty pole.'"[18] There is no denying the politically primitive nature of hero-worship; yet we do have to recognize symbolic discourse when we see it. The festivities at St Charles tended to identify Papineau, the pillar, liberty, and the nation, but this does not mean that those present took the identification in a literal sense.

The "message" of these rituals is important, but the "medium" in which they were expressed is just as significant. The contribution of popular traditions is unmistakable: the "liberty pole" clearly was a transformed maypole, and its dedication to Papineau recalled, in almost every respect, the popular investiture of a parish militia captain. Native traditions like the musket salute blended neatly, with a touch—the red bonnet—linking St Charles with the festivals of the French Revolution. About this time there were similar, though more modest, ceremonies featuring the politicized liberty/maypole in different parts of the District of Montreal. A government report in the wake of the patriot defeats at the end of 1837 referred to a disloyal lieutenant named Jean Villicot dit Latour of Ste Anne des Plaines: "At the death of Séraphim Bouc his Captain, believing the command had devolved upon himself, his men collected and planted a liberty pole at his door and he entertained them." Captain Séraphin Robert of St-Jean-Baptiste was denounced for similar reasons. After returning from the St Charles meeting,

> The said Séraphin Robert invited the deponent and the militiamen of his company to go to his home and shoot at his maypole or mast [this is, of course, the custom of blackening the pole with gunpowder]; the deponent and part of the company went and passed almost a whole day there. The said Séraphin Robert supplied the powder and had a flag on his maypole for liberty on one side and on the other side in favour of Papineau, and having an inscription at the base to the same effect. The said Robert gave them speeches in favour of liberty.

One deposition refers to "un mai de liberté," demonstrating the degree to which the maypole and the liberty pole had come to be identified at a time when the militia officer corps was at the storm centre and when the traditions of community life were helping to sustain the national struggle.[19]

As local contingents made their way home from St Charles in little processions, they took with them flags and paraphernalia that would soon decorate their own villages. At Ste Marie-de-Monnoir, the notary had a picture of the St Charles "liberty tree" painted on the side of his house.[20] In its festive and symbolic aspects the Six Counties meeting clearly drew upon the long-standing cultural traditions of French Canada, traditions that were already in the process of being forged into a revolutionary weapon. At the same time, the assembly had the effect of stimulating and accelerating the political transformation of popular culture in the southern countryside. Exciting for some, the profusion of eagles, tricolours, and liberty poles was profoundly distressing for other Lower Canadians.

The Bishop Intervenes

Among those alarmed by the drift towards revolt was the Catholic clergy of Lower Canada, particularly the bishop of Montreal, Jean-Jacques Lartigue. Friction between priests and patriots was of course nothing new; they had clashed in the past over matters like education and local government. But now, as the existing government was coming under serious attack, Lartigue felt the time had come to condemn revolution in no uncertain terms. Accordingly, he issued a pastoral letter ("mandement") on the day that the St Charles meeting concluded and ordered that curés read it the following Sunday from the pulpit of every church in the diocese. The burden of the bishop's message is quite simple: no Catholic might join in a "revolt against the established government." It consisted largely of passages quoted from Gregory XVI's papal encyclical of 1832 against the Polish revolution, together with quotations from scripture and warnings of the bloodshed and misery that were sure to accompany civil war.[21]

There was nothing remarkable about a nineteenth-century pastor instructing his flock to respect authority and shun violence. Nevertheless, the mandement did represent a significant intervention by a prestigious figure—and at a crucial moment—in the Lower Canadian debate over the proper foundation of legitimate state power. Patriots had to take it seriously, because it was transmitted to the bulk of the population—literate and illiterate alike—and they were, with few exceptions, a population of believing and practising Christians. Middle-class radicals knew that there were flaws in Monseigneur Lartigue's theological reasoning; they also knew that a much more liberal line was conceivable even within the Catholic Church: witness the tolerant position of Belgium's bishops during the recent revolution in that country. But what about the uneducated mass of habitants and craft workers? Would they simply obey the instructions of their spiritual superior? No one familiar with the stormy relations between clergy and laity in the rural parishes of French Canada would have expected blind obedience to episcopal dictate. For over a century and a half settlers had resisted curés and bishops whenever the latter attempted to interfere in community matters that the people considered their own business. At issue in so many parochial struggles had been the question of the proper limits of clerical authority, and of course that was precisely the bone of contention in late October 1837. The peasantry of the diocese of Montreal hardly needed the help of bourgeois Patriots to conclude that in lecturing them on politics Bishop Lartigue had overstepped the narrow bounds of his legitimate authority.

Consequently, the episcopal mandement met with a hostile reception in many rural churches. When the curé of Chambly read the document from the pulpit, a group of parishioners stormed out of the church in protest, while about twenty others who stayed drowned out the reading in shouts of "Vive Papineau! A bas l'évêque!" Most of the congregation at St Charles also took their leave rather than listen to the bishop's words; here the protesters adjourned to the habitant's room of the rectory and held a critical discussion of the pastoral letter's doctrine. Feeling ran so high against Lartigue's manifesto that many parish priests tried to dissociate themselves from its contents by adopting an ironic tone of voice. The curé of

Ste Scholastique was afraid to read the mandement at all; "Ubi non est auditus, non effundas sermonem," was his motto. Some parish priests, particularly those of conservative political leanings, read the bishop's message to a hostile audience and added their own personal rebuke to local patriots. "Imbeciles!" shouted the curé of St Césaire at the parishioners who tried to interrupt him. This was not the end of the matter, of course, since the radicals were in no mood to tolerate insults; soon the priest had, "recd. notice that if he preaches next Sunday, he will be torn from the pulpit."[22]

Another overzealous priest, Monsieur Amiot of Napierville, wrote to Bishop Lartigue about the furore that had erupted in his parish:

> Since the publication of Your Grace's pastoral letter people have become more and more excited against the clergy, as evidenced by the impious and infamous resolutions passed after services the morning of the very day the *mandement* was read. Since that time, they have declared open war on the clergy. Everywhere, they spread the word that it is time to demolish the tithes as well as the seigneurial dues; everywhere one hears nothing but impious and irreligious speeches against both religion and its ministers. It has been said that they even plan to come and treat me to a charivari to force me to embrace their cause, or at least to make me evacuate the rectory, taking with me my belongings; as far as the latter are concerned, they have promised them to the poor... At the confessional, those who are asked about their loyalty to the king reply dryly: "Monsieur le curé, I did not come here to talk politics. If you do not want to take my confession, I shall leave." In vain does one attempt to prove to them that it is not at all a matter of politics but solely a duty of conscience: they do not listen to you and they leave promising never to return.[23]

Echoes can be heard here of the struggle, far less serious and purely local in scope, that had pitted Jean-Baptiste Boucher against the parishioners of La Prairie thirty years earlier. Like Boucher, the curé of Napierville was soon the object of an anti-clerical charivari: "Your Grace has no doubt learned that on the ninth [of November], at 11 o'clock in the evening, they came and sang my *libera* under the window of my bedroom; then at midnight they came back, knocking at my door and making me get up. They ordered me not to preach politics and let me know that they were determined to get along without a curé rather than to allow themselves to be led into error."[24]

Not every priest suffered this sort of indignity, but then few were as virulently anti-patriot as curé Amiot. Some were indeed quite sympathetic to the popular movement, and one, Abbé Etienne Chartier of St Benoit, was a prominent radical leader. Most were rather more ambivalent, opposed to strife and bloodshed, yet convinced that Britain was not dealing justly with the Canadians. It was one thing for Bishop Lartigue to condemn revolution from his episcopal throne in Montreal, but parish priests had more complicated loyalties. Besides being faithful members of the ecclesiastical corporation, most rural curés were also integrated to some degree into the communities where they served. Many had lived among their parishioners for decades, knew them well, and felt a bond with them, in spite of occasional disputes over vestry finances and other matters. They were also well placed to observe that the pastoral letter of 24 October was powerless to stem the revolutionary movement and succeeded only in turning people against the Church. Accordingly, a group of Richelieu valley priests met at St Hyacinthe on 4 November and drew up a petition to the bishop, asking him to moderate his anti-patriot stand. "It is clear," they warned, "that for some time now the clergy has been losing the attachment and the confidence of the Catholics of this diocese."[25] By then it was too late. In the political crisis that was moving rapidly towards a military confrontation, the Church had become a marginal force. When the troops moved into the Richelieu in late November, several curés compromised themselves with the authorities by blessing the patriot militiamen as they went off to fight the British,[26] while others scurried to bury the parish silver before fleeing to safer regions.

And what about the layfolk of rural Lower Canada? What did the Rebellion mean for them as far as their relationship with the Church and the clergy is concerned? Well, certainly there was no sudden abandoning of Catholicism. Many patriots seem to have been very glad to avail themselves of the confession and mass offered by sympathetic priests on the eve of engagements with the enemy. This is hardly surprising: they knew they were about to face death, and even the stray sheep is likely to be susceptible to the appeal of religion in such circumstances. More striking is the case of Bonaventure Viger, the hero of the skirmish at Longueuil that opened the fighting in November 1837. A few days before that action Viger was busy collecting money "to help pay for a high mass so that the rebels would win out in their cause against the British government."[27] While some patriots were persecuting priests, others were purchasing masses: this does sound like evidence of a confused and contradictory attitude! Yet both actions accord perfectly with the traditions of the French-Canadian peasantry. Habitants had always taken their religion seriously and accorded their curés respect, but they were never blindly obedient, and they would not brook clerical interference in the secular affairs of the community.

Plebeian patriots were well aware that there were "good" priests and "bad" priests and that the clergy did not form an undifferentiated bloc as far as politics was concerned. Nevertheless, it was clear in the wake of the failed insurrection of 1837 that the Church's stance had been, on the whole, a conservative one best epitomized by Lartigue's pastoral letter. This perception surely helped to alienate rural Catholics of the diocese of Montreal from the Church, just as the curés assembled at St Hyacinthe had feared it would. Operating in the same direction was the general tendency, characteristic of a revolutionary situation, for established institutions and relationships of subordination to come into question. Accordingly, there were more open calls for the abolition of the tithe as the crisis deepened. When the habitants rose again in November 1838, many displayed fierce hostility towards the "black pigs" and seemed intent on taking parish priests prisoner. One country priest was able to find a silver lining in the dark clouds of anti-clericalism: "These days the burden of work is not crushing here, especially in the last year since these political crises have broken out we have more time to ourselves." Previously overextended, this curé could now enjoy some leisure because his parishioners were learning to get along with less help from the mother Church. The habitants' disengagement from religion, I would like to emphasize once again, was not simply the product of "external influences," whether from reading Voltaire or listening to Papineau (although that was certainly part of it). It should be seen rather as a logical extension, accelerated by revolutionary upheaval, of the age-old spirit of lay autonomy. In 1839 a stipendiary magistrate stationed at La Prairie made the following observation: "The clergy I believe to be generally loyal, but they possess less influence with the people than the clergy do in any other Catholic country." By that time, however, the process of secularization was just about to be rolled back. Soon the clergy would take advantage of the disarray of its liberal opponents, capitalize on the credit its loyalty had earned with the government, and, with swelled numbers and a revitalized spirit, go forth to Catholicize French Canada root and branch. It would be an exceedingly long time before anyone could once again speak of Quebec priests lacking "influence with the people."[28]

Terrorism and Midnight Marauding

One evening in early November, about a week after the St Charles meeting and the bishop's pastoral letter, Captain Louis Bessette, his wife, their son, and their daughter-in-law were sitting down to supper when they heard the sound of a cart pulling up in front of their house in the parish of St Athanase, in the upper Richelieu. They paused, waiting for the visitors to enter, but no one came to the door. Voices could be heard outside, followed by the ringing of an axe as it bit into dry wood.

Bessette must have realized he was in for trouble; the Federation of the Six Counties had called for the resignation of all justices of the peace and militia officers and he still retained the queen's commission. Why he chose to defy the patriot majority is not entirely clear. He does seem to have been an unusually rich habitant, a "coq de village" who owned, not only a prosperous farm, but even some shares in a steamboat business.[29] Bessette was not a staunch and vocal supporter of the government as Eustache Cheval of St Eustache was. In fact, he had earlier attended a patriot meeting in his parish and voted for a resolution insisting that all local magistrates and officers return their commissions.[30] Yet somehow he could not bring himself to resign. Was he afraid of offending the government, worried about the bishop's condemnation of rebellion, or simply reluctant to give up the coveted office of captain? Or was this old and wealthy farmer coming to a belated realization of just how much he had to lose in any revolutionary upheaval? Whatever his motives, Bessette found himself in a delicate situation: the region he inhabited was quite thoroughly aroused against the government. He would reply evasively when neighbours asked about his intentions respecting the captain's position, but unfortunately for him, the patriots of St Athanase were losing patience. On the day before the strange visitation to the Bessette home, a local habitant named Jacques Hébert had warned him that the time for a decision had come. Turn in your commission today, the captain was told, because "we will wait no longer."[31]

Louis Bessette therefore cannot have been surprised when he went to the door and discovered a small group of men gathered by the roadside. Two of the band were busy chopping at the base of his captain's maypole, and this desecration sent Louis into a rage. "You'll pay for my mast, you cretin, you toad," he shouted, but he was answered with similar insults, followed by a volley of stones; he quickly retreated into the house. The chopping resumed; soon the mast was crashing to the ground, while the onlookers cheered loudly.

Bessette's was neither the first nor the last maypole to fall victim to patriot axes in the crisis of 1837–8. A colonel of the Rouville county militia reported about this time that "Capt. Alex. Nadeau and Lieut. A. Julien Piedaleu have tendered me their commissions as officers in the provincial militia in consequence of their Poles having been cut down and graves dug at the foot of them by bands of armed men during the night, and threats held out that unless they resigned in two days their houses and barns would be burned and their lives and that of their families destroyed." Another captain, named Doucet, had his mast felled, and he himself was forced to run around the prostrate pole crying "Vive Papineau!" Lieutenant-Colonel Théophile LeMay of Ste-Marie-de-Monnoir, the leading Constitutionalist in the region, was also a victim. His was "a magnificent maypole, 94 feet tall and decorated with a flag and all its accessories," but early in November, after the terror-stricken LeMay had fled to Montreal, it too was toppled. Across the upper Richelieu valley the patriot bands took a substantial harvest of militia officers' maypoles in the early part of November 1837; by the sixth of that month a Montreal newspaper reported that over forty masts had already been cut down.[32]

The victims of this form of assault did not take their losses lightly. Some, like Louis Bessette, were indignant; others were terrified. Perhaps the undertones of castration conditioned these responses to some degree, even if the people involved had no consciousness of this aspect of the gesture. At another level, both the choppers and the victims must have been well aware of the symbolic message conveyed by this particular form of vandalism. If the presentation of a maypole signified popular ratification of the appointment of a militia officers, then the destruction of the mast also had a clear meaning. Bessette must have seen that the men of St Athanase were telling him: you are no longer our captain.

The felling of the captain's mast did not bring an end to the disturbance at Louis Bessette's farm; it was only the prelude. Men continued to arrive, until there was a crowd of at least two dozen. They began shouting; stones and lumps of frozen earth were hurled at the house. Half an hour and several smashed window-panes later, there was a great pounding at the door and, rather than wait for the door to be broken in, Mrs Bessette let the men in. As they came into the light, she could see that they were disguised. "Here is a band of devils," she announced. "You may have masks and blackened faces, but I recognize you." (In fact, Louis Bessette and his son were able to name only six of the attackers, though the whole group seems to have been composed of St Athanase men; the disguises must have been effective.) The house filled to overflowing with the noisy intruders, some carrying clubs, others guns, and all of them contributing to the horrendous din. "We want the commission!" chanted the invaders at the top of their lungs. Captain Bessette tried to explain that his commission was not in the house, but he could hardly make himself heard. The men banged their sticks for emphasis and soon had smashed a table, broken several more windows, and knocked down the stove-pipe. Finally Bessette prevailed on them to stop by promising to deliver his commission the next day. The captain was as good as his word; he went into the village the following afternoon and gave his commission to the local notary public and Patriot leader, Eusèbe Bardy. "You will not be troubled in the future," the notary assured him, adding that he himself would stop the group if it tried to resume the charivari.

There were dozens of political charivaris in October and November 1837, mainly in the Richelieu valley and in the county of L'Acadie. We happen to know more about this one and about the individuals involved in it because three of the participants signed full confessions three weeks after the event.[33] What induced them to take this step remains a mystery, but they certainly named names, twenty-eight in all; moreover, the lists coincide almost completely and they include all of the six individuals Louis Bessette was able to identify. Of these twenty-eight, sixteen could be found in the 1831 census rolls for St Athanase parish. This in itself is a significant finding, one that shows that the majority of participants were not only well-established local residents but also local patriarchs, since the census provides the names only of household heads. Those not found in the census may have lived in another parish, they may have moved to St Athanase between 1831 and 1837, or they may not have had the status of household head at the time of the census. Though this source does not give ages, the figures on family size set out in table 1 indicate that even six years before the Rebellion most of these men already had substantial households. The charivari was scarcely the work of youths. Nor did the rootless and landless predominate: every one of those traced to the census was a proprietor and most were

TABLE 1 | PARTICIPANTS IN THE CHARIVARI AGAINST LOUIS BESSETTE, 2 NOVEMBER 1837

	Occupation	No. in family	Land (arpents)	Horses
François Macé*	labourer	4	0	0
Jean-Bte Arcand*	butcher	4	6	1
Jacques Hébert*	farmer	8	56	2
Paul Rougier	farmer	8	60	2
Louis Haché	farmer	7	38	1
François Ouimet	farmer	6	36	1
Joseph Ouimet	farmer	11	56	3
Pierre Duclos	blacksmith	5	1	1
Charles Bissonant	farmer	11	56	0
Louis Tremblay	farmer	10	56	1
Joseph Goyette	farmer	7	54	1
Louis Lavalleé	farmer	5	92	2
François Plante	farmer	5	54	4
Charles Tremblay	labourer	3	56	4
Dominique Lavalée*	farmer	8	56	2
Isaac Tremblay	farmer	5	112	2
Antoine Robert dit Lafontaine				
François-Xavier Bissonet				
Pierre Bombardier dit Labombarde				
Charles Sabourin père				
Amable Lamare				
Louis Chenville				
A.-Eusèbe Bardy				
Michel Hétier				
Etienne Robert				
Jean-Bte Choinière dit Sabourin				
Vincent Huot dit Duval				
Louis Gélinoux				

*Leader/spokesman

Source: Economic information comes from 1831 census MS, St Athanase parish.

habitant-farmers with modest holdings. Of the two "day labourers" one seems to have been incorrectly labelled, since he had one of the larger agricultural establishments; and we know that the other, François Macé, had set himself up as an innkeeper by 1837, since he was notorious as a patriot leader then. All in all, the profile of the St Athanase charivari crowd resembles that of the larger patriot rank and file, in so far as the latter can be identified from arrest records,[34] and, like that wider group, it seems to have constituted a rough cross-section of the rural population.

A certain amount of coordination and even a measure of discipline were required to get all these men together to mount an assault on the home of the victim. Our three repentant charivaristes give some idea of the preparations that preceded the descent on Louis Bessette's farm. Bessette had been issued an ultimatum the day before, but it was only on 2 November, the day of the charivari itself, that definite plans were made for action. Some men had gathered at Sancerre's tavern. Among them was an habitant named Joseph Ouimet, who recalled the conversation this way: "A number of people said, we must go to Louis Bessette's place and make him turn over his commission. They also said that they would take Captain Arcand's company to carry out the action, as well as a part of Vincent Huot's company, and that they would make them march."[35] Ouimet is rather coy about the identity of the speaker or speakers, but his host, the innkeeper and prominent local patriot François Macé dit Sancerre, likely took a leading part in the discussions. What seems most remarkable about this passage is the fact that the instigators immediately had recourse to the militia as an instrument of organization. The militia had always been onc of those ambiguous entities, partly community institution, partly government imposition, but now the two aspects had been sundered, and the people's militia was being turned against the governor's militia.

A party of men set out along the concession roads of St Athanase that afternoon, stopping at each house to summon the male residents to their duty. Their procedure prefigured almost exactly the patriot militia call-ups that were to occur in many parishes a few weeks later when the armed clash with the British broke out. Unlike the later musters, frequently brutal because of the emergency conditions, this one was fairly casual. The band arrived at Louis Gélinoux's house at about 4 p.m. and asked him to join. Gélinoux was busy at the time but promised to meet the men later, and the recruiting party went on to the next farm without him.[36] He caught up with the others two hours later at the assigned rendezvous, Gagnon's tavern; some of his comrades had by then already drunk a good deal of rum. It should be noted that participation in this expedition was not entirely optional. On the way from the tavern to Bessette's place, the party stopped at the home of a man who had failed to report and tried to induce him to come along; Captain Jean-Baptiste Arcand used the flat side of his sabre in a most persuasive way and in fact broke the weapon over the man's shoulder! Arcand was a fifty-five-year-old butcher from the village centre of St Athanase. He had resigned his commission in October 1837, but he continued to act as militia captain and was indeed the main leader and spokesman during the confrontation at Louis Bessette's house.[37] The captain of the parish's third company was Vincent Huot. He must have resigned his commission, but he showed no willingness to participate in the charivari. His company was therefore led by Dominique Lavallée, who seems to have been an habitant, though I have been unable to identify him with any certainty.

Were these habitants and artisans working entirely on their own? Remember that Louis Bessette turned over his commission, not to Captain Arcand, but to the notary Eusèbe Bardy. Was Bardy then the sinister guiding spirit behind Bessette's troubles? Or was his role more akin to that of a traditional charivari go-between, the respected local figure who handled the negotiations between persecutors and victims and then collected the fine and distributed the proceeds according to the agreement? The government and its supporters, naturally unwilling to believe that popular support for the Patriots could be deep and widespread, tended towards the former explanation. In these circles it was believed that the charivari and all other similar disturbances were carried out on orders from Bardy, as well as from a local shopkeeper, Charles Mongeon, and a physician, Joseph-François Davignon. The rank and file were seduced by rhetoric, so it was said, and bribed with gifts of "grog, whiskey, bread and cheese."[38] Across the Richelieu in L'Acadie county, Dr Cyrille Côté had a similar reputation, though his activities ranged over a wider area, and accordingly he was held responsible for many more charivaris than was Eusèbe Bardy.

If Bardy and his bourgeois cohorts pulled all the strings, it does seem strange that none of the members of the charivari party ever said so, even when they fell into the hands of the authorities and had every reason to deflect blame in the direction of their social superiors. In the days of fear and demoralization that followed the defeats of 1837, many plebeian prisoners did tend to plead that they had been coerced or manipulated by middle-class Patriots. Indeed, Jean-Baptiste Arcand, lying in the Montreal jail under charges of high treason, went so far as to testify that he had resigned his militia commission because Bardy and the innkeeper Sancerre had "threatened" him. Yet he never claimed that they had ordered him to take action against Bessette; he merely suggested that Sancerre had been "at the head" of the charivari, whereas all the other testimony indicates that Arcand himself had been leader on the spot.[39] It is true that Bardy and Côté actually accepted the commissions extorted by means of charivaris and transmitted them to Quebec City. But who in a Lower Canadian rural parish, besides the little elite of the professions, had the education, much less the experience with bureaucracy, to deal with formalities of this sort? Notaries and members of the Assembly would have been expected to handle such business whether they had initiated the affair or not.

On the other hand, when one looks beyond this specific example at the larger pattern of charivaris, it is true that a large number occurred over a fairly extensive area during the fortnight following the St Charles meeting. This fact does suggest some supra-local coordination of a sort that the bourgeois Patriots of the region would have been best equipped to provide. There is indeed no reason to doubt that Côté, Bardy, and the rest played a vital role in communicating news of wider political developments and in giving advice to their habitant neighbours on the timing and direction of demonstrations. Thus, while the conspiracy theory that would have events entirely manipulated by a scheming middle-class clique is to be rejected, there is no use in standing the interpretation on its head and insisting that the charivari campaign was the spontaneous work of the unaided masses. Though they did not control the rank and file, the local Patriot elites certainly did channel and direct its ire. It is important to note, however, that the actions against non-resigning officers and magistrates drew on the traditions of popular culture: the maypole and other customs connected with the militia, as well as the charivari.

What about this novel political use of the old charivari custom? One more example might help to illustrate the general phenomenon. This charivari occurred up the river from St Athanase, in the parish of St Valentin, four days before the attack on Louis Bessette. Dudley Flowers, the victim, recounted his ordeal two weeks later in a judicial deposition that is so rich in detail it bears quoting in extenso.

> I am a Lieutenant in the Militia. On the twenty seventh day of October last in the afternoon the following persons viz. C.H.O. Côté, Olivier Hébert, L.M. Decoigne, Julien Gagnon, Amable Lamoureux and Jacob Bouchard, came to my house and demanded my commission as such Lieutenant to which I made answer that I would give it up to none but the governor of the Province. Doctor Côté said that if I did not give up my commission I would be sorry for

it—to which Gagnon added, "Si vous ne voulez pas vivre en haine avec nous autres rendez votre commission." Upon this they went away. About eleven o'clock in the night of the same day the same persons returned—at least I have every reason to believe that they were the same persons... They began yelling in the most frightful manner. They threw stones at my house and broke the greatest part of my windows. A large stone passed very near one of my children and would have killed him if it had struck him. Julien Gagnon who had seen my barn full of oats when he came in the day time told me that I should not have to thresh them unless I gave up my commission and also said that my grain, my house and outhouses would be burnt. I saw one of the mob go with a firebrand to my barn with the intention as I verily believe of setting fire to it. But it was in a damp state from the recent rain and the fire would not take. On the night of the following day (18th October last) it might be about ten o'clock a masked mob, composed of about thirty or forty persons attacked my house in a similar manner, yelling and throwing stones as at first and repeatedly threatening to take my life and burn my property if I did not give up my commission... On the following day (Sunday) about seven in the evening, some sixty or seventy individuals attacked my house a third time in the same manner and with the same threats as on the former occasions but if possible with much more violence, beating kettles and pans, blowing horns, calling me a rebel, saying it would be the last time they would come as they would finish me in half an hour. They had in a short time with stones and other missiles broken in part of the roof of my house and boasted that it would soon be demolished. Fearing that such must inevitably be the case, I opened the door and told them that if four or five of their party would come in and give their names I would give them up my commission. Four or five of them did come in, disguised in the most hideous manner but refused to give their names. Finding that my life was actually in danger if I refused to comply with their requests, I handed them my commission. There were about fifteen of the last mentioned mob masked... The same persons have declared in my presence that they were determined to compel in the same manner all persons holding commissions from her Majesty to surrender them. One of these individuals told me boastingly that they had obtained no less than sixty two commissions in one day. I firmly believe that if Doctor Côté and some of the ringleaders were taken up and punished it would have the effect of alarming the others and keeping them quiet.[40]

To begin at the level of forms, notice that many of the features of the "traditional" charivari were present in this episode: the nocturnal setting, the "hideous" disguises, the raucous serenade of blaring horns, banging pots, and shouted insults. Even the lieutenant's initial encounter with the patriot delegation recalled the negotiating process by which charivari fines were normally set: the talks were businesslike and superficially polite, but with an undertone of menace, and they were held in daylight in an atmosphere that contrasted sharply with that of the charivari itself. Flowers resisted for some time the summons to resign, but following the example of an ordinary charivari crowd faced with a stubborn old widower, his attackers simply intensified their efforts, bringing more supporters and threatening ever more ferocious punishment on each successive evening. There were differences of course, notably the stone-throwing and the overt threats of serious violence.

That the patriots should have had recourse to the charivari custom at this juncture is not surprising. A coercive practice in which the aggressors' identities were concealed had obvious attractions at a time when arrest was still a real danger. "The method concerted to raise a mob," reported a L'Acadie county magistrate, "is to pass along ringing a bell, when all are to turn out with their faces blackened, to prevent detection; under these circumstances, no one is supposed to recognize another."[41] This anonymity probably also served an equally important psychological purpose for the participants, that of overcoming inhibitions against aggressive behaviour. Indeed, the entire ritualistic package of charivari surely had this function. After all, Dudley Flowers was apparently a long-time resident of the community and he knew his attackers personally; even though he was a political enemy, the lieutenant was also a neighbour and therefore someone with whom it was important to maintain peaceful, though not necessarily cordial, relations. To turn on him with overt hostility would be to go against ingrained habits; masks and a familiar ritual may have made easier the transformation of neighbourly Jekylls into frightening Hydes.

Alcohol, another renowned solvent of inhibitions, seems to have been used for much the same reason. Many charivari parties, including the one that attacked Louis Bessette, met in taverns, where the members fortified themselves with doses of rum before setting off on their business (usually a feature of traditional charivaris as well). Taverns were commonly used as meeting places for all sorts of purposes, and since the St Athanase innkeeper François Macé dit Sancerre was a leading instigator of the charivaris, it was only natural that men should gather at his public house. Nevertheless, it is clear that strong drink played its part on the evening of 2 November. Indeed, a repentant participant later tried to convince the examining magistrate that "If he had not been under the influence of intoxicating drink, he would not have done such a thing."[42] This was a clever ploy, playing upon the authorities' comforting illusion that the turmoil of 1837 resulted from the machinations of middle-class leaders who manipulated a benighted—indeed an intoxicated—peasantry. Yet these men had not gone to the tavern without a purpose, and they did not gulp down tumblers full of liquor merely to slake a thirst. The inebriation, like the masks, was, paradoxically enough, a sign of serious purpose: individuals who feared arrest and who no doubt entertained ambivalent feelings about the propriety of their enterprise prepared themselves for actions that seemed to be required for the common good.

The charivari custom offered more than simply a cover for fears and uncertainties. The turning over of a sum of money was the central event of a traditional charivari and much of the pageantry was designed to extort this gift from an unwilling giver. What a perfect vehicle for forcing loyalists to resign or, more precisely, to "turn over their commissions" as the patriot mobs usually put it. Participants in the political charivaris of this stage of the drama of 1837 were rather blunt in declaring their intention to overcome opposition to their demands, and low-level violence, consisting mainly of stone-throwing, was common. There was little or no damage in most cases, though men who, like Dudley Flowers, resisted the initial attack, were likely to have their windows broken. The charivari mounted against Louis Bessette was the most destructive of any on record. This toll of broken glass and damaged roofs, though severe by the standards of ordinary pre-Rebellion charivaris, seems quite light when seen in the context of serious political crisis. Even more striking is the complete absence of personal injuries. When one places this record against the cracked heads and burned houses that resulted from, for example, the anti-Irish riots of contemporary New England and New Brunswick—not to mention the destruction wrought by crowd action in revolutionary episodes comparable to 1837—the restraining influence of the charivari form becomes even more apparent.[43] [...]

It began with the government's attempt to suppress "seditious assemblies," followed by the campaign to remove disloyal officers and magistrates. These initiatives provoked resistance that four or five months later had effectively dismantled the established system of rural law enforcement; by October there was scarcely any government presence in the western countryside of Lower Canada. At the same time, new institutions of local government were beginning to emerge in defiance of the rule of the British empire. The elective magistracy and militia never had time to establish themselves firmly, but they were marked at conception by the notions of popular sovereignty and (masculine) democracy that were characteristic of the patriot movement as a whole. Moreover, the insurgent régimes derived their specific shape from the community traditions of rural French Canada.

The crisis was then moving in unanticipated directions, impelled by the clash of various agents and forces in rapidly changing circumstances. Governor Gosford played a part in the drama; so did Louis-Joseph Papineau and the other professional men of the Patriot party; the English-speaking businessmen of Montreal helped to shape events, as did the habitants of the French-Canadian countryside. It has to be said that the habitants, along with the artisans and cottagers of the Montreal District, were playing a more significant part as time passed. At the outset of agitation in May the initiative belonged to the middle-class politicians with their rallies, boycotts, conventions, and other strategies inspired by the history of the Thirteen Colonies. The role assigned to the grass-roots rural patriots had then been a rather passive supporting function. By the autumn of 1837 these activities were fading, as the focus shifted to charivaris, militia elections, and the transformation of parochial government, all of which brought events closer to home for the habitants in more ways than one. The fall campaign required them to take a much more active role and to draw upon cultural traditions and political experience reaching many generations into the past.

Even at this stage, however, the habitants were hardly an independent and a self-sufficient force. Village notaries and doctors remained indispensable local leaders, and Papineau and the radical press of Montreal continued to inspire peasants to see the struggle in larger than local terms. As in the past, the patriot movement brought together diverse elements—town and country, peasant and professional—and united them in a common anti-imperial cause. To be a patriot was, ideally, to overcome personal, class, and local interests and to join with others of goodwill to win independence and democracy for Lower Canada. Yet in spite of deliberate efforts to foster unity, there were bound to be divergent tendencies within the patriot alliance; for the outlook, background, and material interests of rural plebeians and urban bourgeois were quite dissimilar. Had the revolution not been snuffed out at such an early stage, these differences might well have led to serious conflict within the patriot camp. As it was, they remained largely submerged, revealing themselves clearly only where the troublesome issue of seigneurial tenure was concerned.

Notes

1 Quoted in Bernard Bailyn, *The Ideological Origins of the American Revolution* (Cambridge, Mass.: Harvard UP 1967), 1.

2 *Vindicator*, 1 September 1837.

3 Colborne to Gosford, 6 October 1837, quoted in Robert Christie, *A History of the Late Province of Lower Canada, Parliamentary and Political, from the Commencement to the Close of its Existence as a Separate Province,* 2nd ed., 6 vols (Montreal: Richard Worthington 1866), 5: 32–3. See also *La Minerve*, 11 September 1837, 19 October 1837; *Vindicator,* 15 September 1837.

4 *Vindicator,* 6 October 1837.

5 *La Minerve,* 16 October 1837; ANQ, 1837, no. 808, déposition d'Antoine Danis, 8 January 1838; ibid., no. 824, examen volontaire de Jean-Baptiste Dumouchelle, 3 February 1838; NA, LC Rebellion Records, 1: 359–64, affidavit de Joseph Robillard, 26 December 1837.

6 ANQ, 1837, no. 803, déposition de François Groux, 11 February 1838 (author's translation).

7 Ibid., no. 583, déposition de Joseph St-Aubin, 9 February 1838; no. 682, déposition de Jean-Baptiste Jubenville, 30 December 1837; no. 685, examen volontaire de François Guérin, 29 January 1839; no. 700, examen volontaire de François Mallet, 30 January 1838; no. 721, examen volontaire de Jacques Dubeau, 31 January 1838; no. 769, déposition de Pierre Lamoureux, 18 November 1837.

8 NA, LC Civil Secretary, 529: 18, Cuthbert to Walcott, 2 January 1838. See also ANQ, 1837, no. 125, déposition d'Amable Dupuis, 10 January 1838; no. 129, affidavit de Pierre Besse, 25 November 1837; no. 130, affidavit de Luc Bétourné, 2 December 1837; no. 131, déposition de Louis Fréchette, fils, 22 December 1837; *Le Populaire,* 20 November 1837.

9 Quoted in Félix Leclerc, "1837–1838, dates et événements," in *Les rébellions de 1837–1838: Les patriotes du Bas-Canada dans la mémoire collective et chez les historiens,* ed. Jean-Paul Bernard (Montreal: Boréal 1983), 102.

10 Mona Ozouf, *La fête révolutionnaire 1789–1799* (Paris: Gallimard 1976), 51 (author's translation).

11 *BPP,* 9: 72, Gosford to Glenelg, 12 October 1837.

12 *Vindicator,* 27 October 1837.

13 *BPP,* 9: 105.

14 Ibid., 9: 96.

15 ANQ, 1837, no. 49, examen volontaire de Timothée Franchère, 19 February 1838.

16 Ibid., no. 42, affidavit de Joseph-Léon Beauchamps, 11 December 1837. Cf. ibid., no. 40, affidavit de Jean-Louis Beauchamp, 6 December 1837; no. 44, affidavit de Joseph Petit, 7 December 1837.

17 *Vindicator,* 24 October 1837.

18 ANQ, 1837, no. 40, affidavit de Jean-Louis Beauchamp, 6 December 1837 (author's translation).

19 NA, LC Civil Secretary, 532: 175, report signed John Fraser on disloyal militia officers, Terrebonne county, 30 March 1838; NA, LC Adjutant General, vol. 52, déposition de Gabriel Sansoucy, 27 September 1839 (author's translation); ANQ, 1837, no. 1114, déposition de Joseph Beauchamp, 15 November 1837. Something similar occurred during the American Revolution: see Peter Shaw, *American Patriots and the Rituals of Revolution* (Cambridge, Mass.: Harvard UP 1982), 182.

20 ANQ, 1837, no. 1372, déposition de Louis Ostiguy, 28 February 1838; ibid., no. 110, examen volontaire de François Ranger, 17 February 1838.

21 *BPP,* 9: 98–100. An English translation can be found in Christie, *A History of the Late Province,* 4: 417–21. See also Fernand Ouellet, "Le Mandement de Mgr Lartigue de 1837 et la réaction libérale," in *Constitutionalism and Nationalism in Lower Canada,* ed. Ramsay Cook (Toronto: UTP 1969), 67–74; Gilles Chaussé, *Jean-Jacques Lartigue, premier évêque de Montréal* (Montreal: Fides 1980), 199–205. For European comparative background, see William L. Langer, *Political and Social Upheaval, 1832–1852* (New York: Harper & Row 1969), 519.

22 Chaussé, *Lartigue,* 205; NA, "Quelques notes historiques sur les événements politiques de 1837 en Canada," 7–8; *La Minerve,* 13 November 1837, 16 November 1837; Archives du diocèse de St-Jérôme, Bonin to Lartigue, 20 December 1837 (author's translation); ANQ, 1837, no. 3557, Chaffers to Gosford, 9 November 1837.

23 Amiot to Lartigue, 7 November 1837, reprinted in Richard Chabot, *Le curé de campagne et la contestation locale au Québec (de 1791 aux troubles de 1837–38)* (Montreal: Hurtubise 1975), 213 (author's translation).

24 ACEJQ, Amiot to Lartigue, 16 November 1837 (author's translation).

25 Quoted in Chaussé, *Lartigue,* 213 (author's translation). Bishop Lartigue himself seems to have had little confidence in the efficacy of his pastoral letter, because about this time he was making arrangements to flee to the relative safety of Quebec City. Mason Wade, *The French Canadians 1760–1945,* 2 vols (Toronto: Macmillan 1955), 169.

26 Ouellet, *Lower Canada,* 300–1.

27 ANQ, 1837, no. 62, affidavit de Jean-Marie Morin, 2 December 1837 (author's translation).

28 Ibid., no. 1665, déposition d'Agathe Vient, 30 December 1838; Chabot, *Le curd de campagne,* 121; ACESH, XVII, C25, Demers to Lartigue, 5 November 1838 (author's translation); ANQ, 1837, no. 3731, Weatherall to Civil Secretary, 14 November 1839.

29 ANQM, gr., P.-P. Démaray, transport par Louis Bessette h Richard Bowen, 25 March 1837.

30 ANQM, Affaires Criminelles, déposition de Jean-Baptiste Arcand, 7 December 1837

31 ANQ, 1837, no. 257, déposition de Louis Bessette, 5 November 1837. Cf. ibid., no. 258, déposition de Louis Bessette, fils, 11 November 1837; no. 259, déposition de Joseph Ouimet, 20 November 1837; no. 260, déposition de Louis Gélinoux, 20 November 1837; no. 261, deposition of Charles Stuart Pierce, 4 November 1837; no. 262, deposition of John Hill Roe, 27 November 1837.

32 NA, LC Adjutant General, vol. 48, McCallum to Duchesnay, 6 November 1837; *Le Populaire,* 6 November 1837, 26 July 1837, 10 November 1837; NA, LC Civil Secretary, 524: 3, Lemay to Walcott, 26 November 1837; *Le Populaire,* 6 November 1837. For other examples, see ANQ, 1837, no. 158, déposition d'Ambroise Bédard, 20 November 1837; ibid., no. 803, déposition de François Groux, 11 February 1838.

33 ANQ, 1837, no. 259, déposition de Joseph Ouimet, 20 November 1837; ibid., no. 260, déposition de Louis Gélinoux, 20 November 1837; ANQM, Affaires Criminelles, déposition de François Ouimet, 20 November 1837.

34 Cf. Lucie Blanchette-Lessard and Nicole Daigneault-Saint-Denis, "La participation des groupes sociaux aux rébellions dans les comtés de Laprairie et de Deux-Montagnes," in *Les rébellions de 1837–1838,* ed. Bernard, 327–37.

35 ANQ, 1837, no. 259, déposition de Joseph Ouimet, 20 November 1837.

36 Ibid., no. 260, déposition de Louis Gélinoux, 20 November 1837.

37 ANQM, Affaires Criminelles, déposition de François Ouimet, 20 November 1837; ibid., déposition de Jean-Baptiste Arcand, 7 December 1837; ibid., examen volontaire de Jean-Baptiste Arcand, 28 March 1838.

38 Ibid., deposition of John Hill Roe, 1 January 1838.

39 Ibid., examen volontaire de Jean-Baptiste Arcand, 28 March 1838.

40 ANQ, 1837, no. 146, deposition of Dudley Flowers, 3 November 1837. For accounts of similar charivaris, see the following depositions: ibid., no. 75 (Isaac Coote, 10 February 1838), no. 109 (Louis-Marc Decoigne, 17 February 1838), no. 122 (Pierre Gamelin, 9 November 1837), no. 90 (David Vitty, Rickinson Outtret, Robert Boys, and Thomas Henry, 5 November 1837), no. 103 (Nelson Mott, 6 December 1837), no. 128 (C.H. Lindsay, 8 November 1837), no. 87 (Antoine Bruneau, 17 December 1837), no. 314 (Jean-Baptiste Casavant, 12 November 1837), no. 115 (François St-Denis, 7 November 1837), no. 318 (Benjamin Goulet, 20 November 1837), no. 516 (Orange Tyler, 16 November 1837), no. 3557 (W.U. Chaffers, 9 November 1837), no. 158 (Ambroise Bédard, 10 November 1837); NA, LC Civil Secretary, 524: 11 (Loop Odell, 17 November 1837). Additional information appears in *Le Populaire,* 5 November 1837; *L'Ami du Peuple,* 8 November 1837; NA, LC Adjutant General, vol. 48, James McGillvary to David McCallum, 26 November 1837; ACESJQ, H.L. Amiot to Mgr Bourget, St Cyprien, 26 November 1837.

41 *BPP,* 9: 107, "Letter from a Magistrate...dated St. Valentine, 30 October 1837."

42 ANQM, Affaires Criminelles, déposition de François Ouimet, 20 November 1837 (author's translation).

43 Ray Billington, *The Protestant Crusade 1800–1860: A Study of the Origins of American Nativism* (New York: Macmillan 1938); Scott W. See, "The Orange Order and Social Violence in Mid-Nineteenth Century Saint John," *Acadiensis* 13 (Autumn 1983): 68–92. See also Sean Wilentz, *Chants Democratic: New York City and the Rise of the American Working Class, 1788–1850* (New York: Oxford UP 1984), 264–5.

William Lyon Mackenzie's Draft Constitution, 15 November 1837

To the Convention of Farmers, Mechanics, Labourers, and other Inhabitants of Toronto, met at the Royal Oak Hotel, to consider of and take measures for effectually maintaining in this colony, a free constitution and democratic form of government.

The Committee appointed to report a popular Constitution, with guards suitable for this Province, in case the British system of government shall be positively denied us, respectfully submit the following draft:

WHEREAS the solemn covenant made with the people of Upper and Lower Canada, and recorded in the Statute Book of the United Kingdom of Great Britain and Ireland as the 31st Chapter of the Acts passed in the 31st year of the reign of King George III, hath been continually violated by the British Government, and our rights usurped; *And Whereas* our humble petitions, addresses, and protests and remonstrances against this injurious interference have been made in vain—WE, the people of the State of Upper Canada, acknowledging with gratitude the grace and beneficence of GOD, in permitting us to make choice of our form of Government, and in order to establish justice, ensure domestic tranquility, provide for the common defence, promote the general welfare, and secure the blessings of civil and religious liberty to ourselves and our posterity, do establish this Constitution:

1. The legislature shall make no law respecting the establishment of religion, or for the encouragement or the prohibition of any religious denomination.
2. It is ordained and declared that the free exercise and enjoyment of religious profession and worship, without discrimination or preference, shall forever hereafter be allowed within this State to all mankind.
3. The whole of the public lands within the limits of this State, including the lands attempted, by a pretended sale, to be vested in certain adventurers called the Canada Company (except so much of them as may have been disposed of to actual settlers now resident the State), and all the lands called Crown reserves, clergy reserves and rectories, and also the school lands, and the lands pretended to be appropriated to the uses of the University of King's College, are declared to be the property of the State, and at the disposal of the Legislature, for the public service thereof. The proceeds of one million of acres of the most valuable public lands shall be specially appropriated to the support of Common or Township Schools.
4. No Minister of the Gospel, clergyman, ecclesiastic, bishop or priest of any religious denomination whatsoever, shall, at any time hereafter, under any pretence or description whatever, be eligible to, or

---

William Lyon Mackenzie's Draft Constitution, 15 November 1837 (See Cornelius J. Jaenen and Cecilia Morgan, *Material Memory: Documents in Pre-Confederation History*, Vol. 1 (Toronto: Addison Wesley Longman, 1998) 238–241.

capable of holding a seat in the senate or house of assembly, or any civil or military office within this state.

5. In all laws made, or to be made, every person shall be bound alike—neither shall any tenure, estate, charter, degree, birth, or place, confer any exemption from the ordinary course of legal proceedings and responsibilities where unto others are subjected.

6. No hereditary emoluments, privileges, or honours, shall ever be granted by the people of this State.

7. There shall neither be slavery nor involuntary servitude in this State, otherwise than for the punishment of crimes whereof the party shall have been duly convicted. People of Colour, who have come into this State, with the design of becoming permanent inhabitants thereof, *and are now residents therein,* shall be entitled to all the rights of native Canadians, upon taking an oath or affirmation to support the constitution.

8. The people have a right to bear arms for the defence of themselves and the State.

9. No man shall be impressed or forcibly constrained to serve in time of war, because money, the sinews of war, being always at the disposal of the Legislature, they can never want numbers of men apt enough to engage in any just cause.

10. The military shall be kept under strict subordination to the civil power. No soldier shall, in time of peace, be quartered in any house without the consent of the owner, nor in time of war, but in a manner to be prescribed by law.

11. The Governor, with the advice and consent of the Senate, shall choose all militia officers above the rank of Captain. The people shall elect their own officers of the rank of Captain, and under it.

12. The people have a right to assemble together in a peaceable manner, to consult for their common good, to instruct their representatives in the legislature, and to apply to the legislature for redress of grievances.

13. The printing presses shall be open and free to those who may wish to examine the proceedings of any branch of the government, or the conduct of any public officer; and no law shall ever restrain the right thereof.

14. The trial by Jury shall remain for ever inviolate.

15. Treason against the State shall consist only in levying war against it, or adhering to its enemies, giving them aid and comfort. No person shall be convicted of Treason unless on the testimony of two witnesses to the same overt act, or on confession in open court...

16. The real estate of persons dying without making a will shall not descend to the eldest son to the exclusion of his brethren, but be equally divided among the children, male and female.

16a. The laws of Entail shall be forever abrogated.

17. There shall be no lotteries in this State. Lottery tickets shall not be sold therein, whether foreign or domestic.

18. No power of suspending the operation of the laws shall be exercised except by the authority of the Legislature.

19. The people shall be secure in their persons, papers and possessions, from all unwarrantable searches and seizures; general warrants, whereby an officer may be commanded to search suspected places, without probable evidence of the fact committed, or to seize any person or persons not named, whose offences are not particularly described, and without oath or affirmation, are dangerous to liberty, and shall not be granted.

20. Private property ought, and will ever be held inviolate, but always subservient to the public welfare, provided a compensation in money be first made to the owner. Such compensation shall never be less in amount than the actual value of the property.

21. *And Whereas* frauds have been often practised towards the Indians within the limits of this State, it is hereby ordained, that no purchases or contracts for the sale of lands made since the _____ day of _____ in the year _____, or which may hereafter be made with the Indians within the limits of this State, shall be binding on the Indians and valid, unless made under the authority of the legislature.

22. The legislative authority of this State shall be vested in a General Assembly, which shall consist of a Senate and House of Assembly, both to be elected by the People...

29. In order to promote the freedom, peace, and quiet of elections, and to secure, in the most ample manner possible, the independence of the poorer classes of the electors, it is declared that all elections by the People, which shall take place after the first session of the legislature of this State, shall be by ballot, except for such town officers as may by law be directed to be otherwise chosen...

43. No member of the legislature, who has taken his seat as such shall receive any civil appointment from the governor and senate, or from the legislature, during the term for which he shall have been elected.

44. The assent of the Governor, and of three fourths of the members elected to each branch of the legislature, shall be requisite to authorize the passage of every bill appropriating the public monies or property for local or private purposes, or for creating, continuing, altering, or renewing any body politic or corporate; and the yeas and nays shall be entered on the Journals at the time of taking the vote on the final passage of any bill.

45. The members of the legislature shall receive for their services a compensation to be ascertained by law and paid out of the public treasury.

46. Members of the General Assembly shall, in all cases, except treason, felony, and breach of the peace, be privileged from arrest during their continuance as such members; and for any speech of debate in either House, they shall not be questioned in any other place.

47. No judge of any Court of law or equity, Secretary of State, Attorney General, Register of Deeds, Clerk of any Court of Record, Collector of Customs or Excise Revenue, Postmaster of Sheriff, shall be eligible as a candidate for, or have a seat in the General Assembly...

58. The Executive power shall be vested in a Governor. He shall hold his office for three years. No person shall be eligible to that office who shall not have attained the age of thirty years.

59. The Governor shall be elected by the People at the times and places of choosing members of the legislature...

61. The Governor shall have power to grant reprieves and pardon, after conviction, for all offences, except in cases of impeachment.

62. The Governor shall nominate by message, in writing, and, with the consent of the Senate, shall appoint the Secretary of State, Comptroller, Receiver General, Auditor General, Attorney General, Surveyor General, Postmaster General, and also all judicial officers, except Justices of the Peace and Commissioners of the Courts of Request, or Local Courts.

63. The Judicial Power of the State, both as to matters of law and equity, shall be vested in a Supreme Court, the members of which shall hold office during good behaviour, in District or County Courts, in Justices of the Peace, in Courts of Request, and in such other Courts as the legislature may from time to time establish...

66. A competent number of Justices of the Peace and Commissioners of the Courts of Request shall be elected by the people, for a period of three years, within their respective cities and townships...

69. The Governor and all other Civil Officers under this State, shall be liable to impeachment for any misdemeanor in office...

80. No religious test shall ever be required as a qualification to any office or public trust under this State.

[Constitution, *15 November 1837*]

The Role of Native Women in the Creation of Fur Trade Society in Western Canada, 1670–1830

Sylvia Van Kirk

In essence the history of the early Canadian West is the history of the fur trade. For nearly two hundred years, from the founding of the Hudson's Bay Company in 1670 until the transfer of Rupert's Land to the newly created dominion of Canada in 1870, the fur trade was the dominant force in shaping the history of what are today Canada's four western provinces.

This long and unified experience gave rise in western Canada to a frontier society that seems to have been unique in the realm of interracial contact. Canada's western history has been characterized by relatively little violent conflict between Indian and white. I would like to suggest two major reasons why this was so. First, by its very nature, the Canadian fur trade was predicated on a mutual exchange and dependency between Indian and white. The Indian not only trapped the fur pelts but also provided the market for European goods. Until very recently, the fur trade has been viewed as an all-male affair, but new research has revealed that Indian women played an active role in promoting this trade. Although the men were the hunters of beaver and large game animals, the women were responsible for trapping smaller fur-bearing animals, especially the marten whose pelt was highly prized.[1] The notable emergence of Indian women as diplomats and peacemakers also indicates that they were anxious to maintain the flow of European goods such as kettles, cloth, knives, needles, and axes which helped to alleviate their onerous work.[2]

The second factor in promoting harmonious relations was the remarkably wide extent of intermarriage between incoming traders and Indian women, especially among the Cree, the Ojibwa, and the Chipewyan. Indian wives proved indispensable helpmates to the officers and men of both the British-based Hudson's Bay Company and its Canadian rival, the North West Company. Such interracial unions were, in fact, the basis for a fur trade society and were sanctioned by an indigenous rite known as marriage *à la façon du pays*—according to the custom of the country.

The development of marriage *à la façon du pays* underscores the complex and changing interaction between the traders and the host Indian societies. In the initial phase of contact, many Indian bands actively encouraged the formation of marital alliances between their women and the traders. The Indians viewed marriage in an integrated social and economic

Sylvia Van Kirk, "The Role of Native Women in the Creation of Fur Trade Society in Western Canada, 1670–1839," in S. Armitage and E. Jameson, eds., *The Women's West* (Norman: University of Oklahoma Press, 1988) 53–62.

context; marital alliances created reciprocal social ties, which served to consolidate their economic relationships with the incoming strangers. Thus, through marriage, many a trader was drawn into the Indian kinship circle. In return for giving the traders sexual and domestic rights to their women, the Indians expected reciprocal privileges such as free access to the posts and provisions.[3]

As a result of this Indian attitude, it was soon impressed upon the traders that marriage alliances were an important means of ensuring good will and cementing trade relations with new bands or tribes. The North West Company, a conglomerate of partnerships which began extensive trading in the West in the 1770s, had learned from its French predecessors of the benefits to be gained from intermarriage and officially sanctioned such unions for all ranks (from bourgeois down to *engagé*).[4] The Hudson's Bay Company, on the other hand, was much slower to appreciate the realities of life in Rupert's Land. Official policy formulated in faraway London forbade any intimacy with the Indians, but officers in the field early began to break the rules. They took the lead in forming unions with the women of prominent Indian leaders, although there was great variation in the extent to which the servants were allowed to form connections with native women.[5]

Apart from the public social benefits, the traders' desire to form unions with Indian women was increased by the absence of white women. Although they did not come as settlers, many of the fur traders spent the better part of their lives in Rupert's Land, and it is a singular fact in the social development of the Canadian West that for well over a century there were no white women.[6] The stability of many of the interracial unions formed in the Indian country stemmed partly from the fact that an Indian woman provided the only opportunity for a trader to replicate a domestic life with wife and children. Furthermore, although Indian mores differed from those of the whites, the traders learned that they trifled with Indian women at their peril. As one old voyageur explained, one could not just dally with any native woman who struck one's fancy. There was a great danger of getting one's head broken if a man attempted to take an Indian girl without her parents' consent.[7]

It is significant that, just as in the trade ceremony, the rituals of marriage *à la façon du pays* conformed more to Indian custom than to European. There were two basic steps to forming such a union. The first step was to secure the consent of the woman's relatives; it also appears that the wishes of the woman herself were respected, as there is ample evidence that Indian women actively sought for trade husbands. Once consent was secured, a bride price had then to be decided; this varied considerably among the tribes but could amount to several hundred dollars worth of trade goods. After these transactions, the couple were usually conducted ceremoniously to the post where they were now recognized as man and wife.[8] In the Canadian West, marriage *à la façon du pays* became the norm for Indian-white unions, being reinforced by mutual interest, tradition, and peer group pressure.[9] Although ultimately "the custom of the country" was to be strongly denounced by the missionaries, it is significant that in 1867, when the legitimacy of the union between Chief Factor William Connolly and his Cree wife was tried before a Canadian court, it was found to have constituted a lawful marriage. The judge declared a valid marriage existed because the wife had been married according to the customs and usages of her own people and because the consent of both parties, the essential element of civilized marriage, had been proved by twenty-eight years of repute, public acknowledgement, and cohabitation as man and wife.[10]

If intermarriage brought the trader commercial and personal benefit, it also provided him with a unique economic partner. The Indian wife possessed a range of skills and wilderness know-how that would have been quite foreign to a white wife. Although the burdensome work role of the nomadic Indian woman was somewhat alleviated by the move to the fur-trade post, the extent to which the traders relied upon native technology kept the women busy.

Perhaps the most important domestic task performed by the women at the fur-trade posts was to provide the men with a steady supply of "Indian shoes" or moccasins. The men of both companies generally did not dress in Indian style (the buckskinned mountain man was not part of the Canadian scene), but they universally adopted the moccasin as the most practical footwear for the wilderness. One wonders, for example, how the famed 1789 expedition of Alexander Mackenzie would have fared without the work of the wives of his two French-Canadian voyageurs. The women scarcely ever left the canoes, being "continually employ'd making shoes of moose skin as a pair does not last us above one Day."[11] Closely related to the manufacture of moccasins was the Indian woman's role in making snowshoes, without which winter travel was impossible. Although the men usually made the frames, the women prepared the sinews and netted the intricate webbing which provided support.[12]

Indian women also made a vital contribution in the preservation of food, especially in the manufacture of the all-important pemmican, the nutritious staple of the North West Company's canoe brigades. At the posts on the Plains, buffalo hunting and pemmican making formed an essential part of the yearly routine, each post being required to furnish an annual quota. In accordance with Indian custom, once the hunt was over the women's work began. The women skinned the animals and cut the meat into thin strips to be dried in the sun or over a slow fire. When the meat was dry, the women pounded it into a thick flaky mass, which was then mixed with melted buffalo fat. This pemmican would keep very well when packed into ninety-pound buffalo-hide sacks, which had been made by the women during the winter.[13]

But pemmican was too precious a commodity to form the basic food at the posts themselves. At the more northerly posts, the people subsisted mainly on fish, vast quantities of which were split and dried by the women to provide food for the winter. Maintaining adequate food supplies for a post for the winter was a precarious business, and numerous instances can be cited of Indian wives keeping the fur traders alive by their ability to snare small game such as rabbits and partridges. In 1815, for example, the young Nor'Wester George Nelson would probably have starved to death when provisions ran out at his small outpost north of Lake Superior had it not been for the resourcefulness of his Ojibwa wife who, during the month of February, brought in fifty-eight rabbits and thirty-four partridges.[14] Indian women also added to the diet by collecting berries and wild rice and making maple sugar. The spring trip to the sugar bush provided a welcome release from the monotony of the winter routine, and the men, with their families and Indian relatives, all enjoyed this annual event.[15]

As in other pre-industrial societies, the Indian women's role extended well beyond domestic maintenance as they assisted in specific fur-trade operations. With the adoption of the birch-bark canoe, especially by the North West Company, Indian women continued in their traditional role of helping in its manufacture. It was the women's job to collect annual quotas of spruce roots, which were split fine to sew the seams of the canoes, and also to collect the spruce gum, which was used for caulking the seams.[16] The inexperienced and undermanned Hudson's Bay Company also found itself calling upon the labor power of Indian women, who were adept at paddling and steering canoes. Indeed, although the inland explorations of various Hudson's Bay Company men such as Anthony Henday and Samuel Hearne have been glorified as individual exploits, they were, in fact, entirely dependent upon the Indians with whom they traveled, especially the women. "Women," marveled one inlander, "were as useful as men upon Journeys."[17] Henday's journey to the Plains in 1754, for example, owed much of its success to his Cree female companion who provided him with much timely advice about the plans of the Indians, in addition to a warm winter suit of furs.[18] The Hudson's Bay Company men emphasized to their London superiors the value of the Indian women's skill at working with fur pelts. In short, they argued that the economic services performed by Indian women at the fur-trade posts were of such importance that they should be considered as "Your Honours Servants."[19] Indian women were indeed an integral part of the fur-trade labor force, although, like most women, because their labor was largely unpaid, their contribution has been ignored.

The reliance on native women's skills remained an important aspect of fur-trade life, even though by the early nineteenth century there was a notable shift in the social dynamic of fur-trade society. By this time, partly because of the destructive competition between rival companies which had flooded the Indian country with alcohol, relations between many Indian bands and the traders deteriorated. In some well-established areas, traders sometimes resorted to coercive measures, and in some cases their abuse of Indian women became a source of conflict.[20] In this context, except in new areas such as the Pacific Slope, marriage alliances ceased to play the important function they once had. The decline of Indian-white marriages was also hastened by the fact that fur-trade society itself was producing a new pool of marriageable young women—the mixed-blood "daughters of the country." With her dual heritage, the mixed-blood woman possessed the ideal qualifications for a fur trader's wife; acclimatized to life in the West and familiar with Indian ways, she could also adapt successfully to white culture.

From their Indian mothers, mixed-blood girls learned the native skills so necessary to the functioning of the trade. As Sir George Simpson, governor of the Hudson's Bay Company emphasized in the 1820s: "It is the duty of the Women at the different Posts to do all that is necessary in regard to Needle Work,"[21] and the mixed-blood women's beautiful beadwork was highly prized. In addition to performing traditional Indian tasks, the women's range of domestic work increased in more European ways. They were responsible for the fort's washing and cleaning; "the Dames" at York Factory, for example, were kept "in Suds, Scrubbing and Scouring," according to one account.[22] As subsistence agriculture was developed around many of the posts, the native women took an active role in planting and harvesting. Chief Factor John Rowand of Fort Edmonton succinctly summarized the economic role of native women in the fur trade when he wrote in the mid-nineteenth century: "The women here work very hard, if it was not so, I do not know how we would get on with the Company work."[23] With her ties to the Indians and familiarity with native customs and language, the mixed-blood wife was also in a position to take over the role of intermediary or liaison previously played by the Indian wife. The daughters of the French-Canadian voyageurs were often excellent interpreters: some could speak several Indian languages. The timely intervention of more than one mixed-blood wife saved the life of a husband who had aroused Indian hostility.[24] Indeed, in his account of fur-trade life during the Hudson's Bay Company's monopoly after 1821, Isaac Cowie declared that many of the company's officers owed much of their success in overcoming difficulties and in maintaining the company's influence over the natives to "the wisdom and good counsel of their wives."[25]

In spite of the importance of native connections, many fur-trade fathers wanted to introduce their mixed-blood daughters to the rudiments of European culture. Since the place of work and home coincided, especially in the long winter months, the traders were able to take an active role in their children's upbringing and they were encouraged by company officials to do so.[26] When the beginnings of formal schooling were introduced at the posts on the Bay in the early 1800s, it was partly because it was felt to be essential that girls, who were very seldom sent overseas, should be given a basic education which would inculcate them with Christian virtue.[27] Increasingly, fathers promoted the marriage of their daughters to incoming traders, as the means to securing their place in fur-trade society. In a significant change of policy in 1806, the North West Company acknowledged some responsibility for the fate of its "daughters" when it sanctioned marriage *à la façon du pays* with daughters of white men, but now prohibited it with full-blooded Indian women.[28]

As mixed-blood wives became "the vogue" (to quote a contemporary), it is notable that "the custom of the country" began to evolve more toward European concepts of marriage. Most importantly, such unions were coming to be regarded as unions for life. When Hudson's Bay Company officer J. E. Harriott espoused Elizabeth Pruden, for example, he promised her father, a senior officer, that he would "live with her and treat her as my wife as long as we both lived."[29] It became customary for a couple to exchange brief vows before the officer in charge of the post, and the match was further celebrated by a dram of liquor to all hands and a wedding dance. The bride price was replaced by the opposite payment of a dowry, and many fur-trade officers were able to dower their daughters quite handsomely.[30] Marriage *à la façon du pays* was further regulated by the Hudson's Bay Company after 1821 with the introduction of marriage contracts, which emphasized the husband's financial obligations and the status of the woman as a legitimate wife.

The social role of the mixed-blood wife, unlike that of the Indian wife, served to cement ties within fur-trade society itself. Significantly, in the North West Company, many marriages cut across class lines, as numerous Scottish bourgeois chose their wives from among the daughters of the French-Canadian *engagés* who had married extensively among the native people. Among the Hudson's Bay Company men, it was appreciated that a useful way to enhance one's career prospects was to marry the daughter of a senior officer.[31] Whatever a man's initial motivation, the substantial private fur-trade correspondence which has survived from the nineteenth century reveals that many fur traders became devoted family men. Family could be a source of interest and consolation in a life that was often hard and monotonous. As Chief Factor James Douglas pointedly summed it up: "There is indeed no living with comfort in this country until a person has forgot the great world and has his tastes and character formed on the current standard of the stage...habit makes it familiar to us, softened as it is by the *many tender ties* which find a way to the heart."[32]

However, the founding in 1811 of the Selkirk Colony, the first agrarian settlement in western Canada, was to introduce new elements of white civilization that would hasten the decline of the indigenous fur-trade society. The chief agents of these changes were the missionaries and white women.

The missionaries, especially the Anglicans who arrived under the auspices of the Hudson's Bay Company in 1820, roundly denounced marriage *à la façon du pays* as being immoral and debased.[33] But while they exerted considerable pressure on long cohabiting couples to accept a church marriage, they were in no way champions of miscegenation. In fact, this attack upon fur-trade custom had a detrimental effect upon the position of native women. Incoming traders, now feeling free to ignore the marital obligations implicit in the "the custom of the country," increasingly looked upon native women as objects for temporary sexual gratification. The women, on the other hand, found themselves being judged according to strict British standards of female propriety. It was they, not the white men, who were to be held responsible for the perpetuation of immorality because of their supposedly promiscuous Indian heritage. The double standard, tinged with racism, had arrived with a vengeance!

Racial prejudice and class distinctions were augmented by the arrival of British women in Rupert's Land. The old fabric of fur-trade society was severely rent in 1830 when Simpson and another prominent Hudson's Bay Company officer returned from furlough, having wed genteel British ladies.[34] The appearance of such "flowers of civilization" provoked unflattering comparisons with native women; as one officer observed, "this influx of white faces has cast a still deeper shade over the faces of our Brunettes in the eyes of many."[35] In Red River especially, a white wife became a status symbol; witness the speed with which several retired Hudson's Bay Company factors married the English schoolmistresses after the demise of their native wives. To their credit, many company officers remained loyal to their native families, but they became painfully anxious to turn their daughters into young Victorian ladies, hoping that with accomplishments and connections, the stigma of their mixed blood would not prevent them from remaining among the social elite. Thus in the 1830s, a boarding school was established in Red River for the children of company officers; the girls' education was supervised by the missionary's wife, and more than one graduate was praised for being "quite English in her Manner."[36] In numerous cases, these highly acculturated young women were able to secure advantageous matches with incoming white men, but to some extent this was only because white ladies did not in fact make a successful adaptation to fur-trade life. It had been predicted that "the lovely, tender exotics" (as white women were dubbed) would languish in the harsh fur-trade environment,[37] and indeed they did, partly because they had no useful social or economic role to play. As a result, mixed marriages continued to be a feature of western Canadian society until well into the mid-nineteenth century, but it was not an enduring legacy. Indian and mixed-blood women, like their male counterparts, were quickly shunted aside with the development of the agrarian frontier after 1870. The vital role native women had played in the opening of the Canadian West was either demeaned or forgotten.

Notes

1 Sylvia Van Kirk, *Many Tender Ties: Women in Fur Trade Society, 1670–1870* (Norman: University of Oklahoma Press, 1980; Winnipeg, Manitoba: Watson and Dwyer, 1980), pp. 72–73.

2 The most outstanding examples of Indian women who, although not married to whites, were active peacemakers and diplomats, are Thanadelthur, a Chipewyan, and Lady Calpo, a Chinook. See ibid., pp. 66–71, 76–77.

3 The few cases of violent conflict, such as the Henley House Massacre of 1752, were caused by the traders' failure to respect this bargain. See ibid., pp. 41–44.

4 Ibid., p. 28.

5 Ibid., pp. 28–29, 41–42.

6 After an ill-fated venture in 1686, British wives were officially prohibited from traveling to Hudson Bay. It was not until 1812 with the Selkirk settlers that women were again officially transported to Hudson Bay. A French-Canadian woman in 1806 was the first and one of the few white women to come west in the North West Company canoes. See Van Kirk, *Many Tender Ties,* pp. 173–80.

7 *Johnstone et. al.* v. *Connolly,* Appeal Court, 7 Sept. 1869, *La Revue Legale,* 1:280 (hereafter cited as Connolly Appeal Case, 1869).

8 Van Kirk, *Many Tender Ties,* pp. 36–37. For a discussion of the motivation of the Indian women, see chap. 4.

9 This does not mean that sexual exploitation of Indian women was unknown in the Canadian West. Prostitution certainly existed, and the marriage relationship could be abused as in white society.

10 *Connolly vs. Woolrich,* Superior Court, Montreal, 9 July 1867, *Lower Canada Jurist* 11:230, 248.

11 W. Kaye Lamb, ed., *The Journals and Letters of Sir Alexander Mackenzie* (Cambridge, England: Cambridge University Press, 1970), p. 220.

12 Van Kirk, *Many Tender Ties,* pp. 54–55.

13 Ibid., p. 56.

14 Toronto Public Library, George Nelson Papers, Journal, 29 Jan.–23 June 1815. See also Van Kirk, *Many Tender Ties,* pp. 58–59.

15 Van Kirk, *Many Tender Ties,* p. 57.

16 Ibid., p. 61.

17 J. B. Tyrrell, ed., *Journals of Samuel Hearne and Philip Turnor, 1774–1792,* Champlain Society, vol. 21 (Toronto, 1934), pp. 252–53.

18 Van Kirk, *Many Tender Ties,* p. 64.

19 Hudson's Bay Company Archives, B.239/b/79, fols. 40d–41 (hereafter HBCA).

20 Van Kirk, *Many Tender Ties,* pp. 90–91.

21 R.H. Fleming, ed., *Minutes of Council of the Northern Department of Rupert's Land, 1821–31,* Hudson's Bay Record Society, vol. 3 (London, 1940), p. 378.

22 Public Archives of Canada, James Hargrave Correspondence, vol. 21, Hargrave to Christie, 13 June 1832.

23 HBCA, D.5/18, fols. 535d–536.

24 One of the most famous cases was that of James Douglas, a clerk in northern British Columbia, whose high-handed treatment so outraged the Carrier Indians that he might have been killed but for intervention of his mixed-blood wife Amelia and the wife of the interpreter. See Van Kirk, *Many Tender Ties,* pp. 111–13.

25 Isaac Cowie, *The Company of Adventurers* (Toronto: W. Briggs, 1913), p. 204.

26 Van Kirk, *Many Tender Ties,* pp. 97, 99, 106, 131.

27 Ibid., pp. 103–104.

28 W.S. Wallace, ed., *Documents Relating to the North West Company,* Champlain Society, vol. 22 (Toronto, 1934), p. 211.

29 Connolly Appeal Case, 1869, p. 286.

30 Van Kirk, *Many Tender Ties,* pp. 108, 115.

31 Ibid., pp. 108–109.

32 G.P. de T. Glazebrook, ed., *The Hargrave Correspondence, 1821–1843,* Champlain Society, vol. 24 (Toronto, 1928), p. 381.

33 Van Kirk, *Many Tender Ties,* pp. 153–56.

34 They also violated "the custom of the country" by callously casting aside their former mixed-blood partners after the fact. For a full discussion of this episode see Sylvia Van Kirk, "The Impact of White Women on Fur Trade Society," in *The Neglected Majority: Essays in Canadian Women's History* (Toronto: McClelland and Stewart, 1977), pp. 27–48.

35 PAC, Hargrave Correspondence, vol. 21, Hargrave to Charles Ross, 1 Dec. 1830.

36 Glazebrook, ed., *Hargrave Correspondence,* p. 229.

37 Ibid., pp. 310–11.

Hardy Backwoodsmen, Wholesome Women, and Steady Families

Immigration and the Construction of a White Society in Colonial British Columbia, 1849–1871

Adele Perry*

Who was in and who was out? One of the primary ways in which mid-nineteenth-century British Columbians negotiated inclusions and exclusions was through the practice and discourse of immigration. Immigration derived its social and political significance from its double ability to dispossess local peoples and establish a settler-society in their stead. The settler society this process sought to build was explicitly racialized and deeply gendered. In seeking "hardy backwoodsmen," colonial promoters encouraged men committed to hard work, steadiness, and rural life; in demanding "wholesome women," they sought women who would simultaneously serve as beacons of imperial society and constrain the excesses of white men; in courting "steady families," they pursued stable units that would exemplify the virtues of the same-race, nuclear family. Together, "hardy backwoodsmen, wholesome women and steady families" were constructed as the immigrants able to transform British Columbia into the stable settler society of imperialists' dreams.

Studies of the flow of people between Europe and the Americas in the "Great Migration Era" have tended to leave a blind spot, namely their disinterest in interrogating the politicized character of nineteenth-century "new world" migration.[1] When people left Europe for the Americas or Australia, they did not simply move into large, empty spaces. Instead, they participated in a process of colonization in which Aboriginal dispossession and settler migration were irreparably linked. As Daiva Staisulis and Nira Yuval-Davis argue, migration is one of the chief ways in which settler societies constitute themselves.[2] For individuals and families, migration was probably motivated primarily by straightforward social and economic needs, but the overarching structure of imperialism transformed these needs into imperial acts.[3] Immigration sometimes troubled and sometimes nourished the politics of empire. In either case, it cannot be separated from them.

Adele Perry, "Hardy Backwoodsmen, Wholesome Women, and Steady Families: Immigration and the Construction of a White Society in Colonial British Columbia," in *Histoire sociale/Social History*, Vol. 33, no.66 (November 2000): 343–360.

*Adele Perry is assistant professor in the Department of History at St. Paul's College, University of Manitoba. This article is drawn from *On the Edge of Empire: Gender, Race, and the Making of British Columbia, 1849–1871* (Toronto: University of Toronto Press, 2001). She would like to thank the organizers of the conference "Recasting European and Canadian History" for their contributions to this paper.

A better acknowledgement of the connections between migration and imperialism necessitates a return to an older phase in the writing of Canadian history, albeit with newly critical eyes. The past two decades have witnessed an increasing emphasis on the social experience of immigrant peoples to Canada. Historians have rejected earlier studies in which "immigration was acknowledged as a key ingredient in transcontinental nation-building but the immigrants were largely ignored or relegated to cameo appearances."[4] They have embraced the vantage point of the immigrant instead of the policy-maker and analysed how these people, like women and the working class, were active agents who shaped their own history. This historiographic shift is premised on a needed critique of histories that artificially isolate the powerful from both the cause and effect of their authority. An unintended and less useful consequence of changing historiographic imperatives has been to detach the process of migration from its larger political context. Instead of treating the political and social history of immigration as distinct processes, historians need to reckon with the profound ties that connect the politician with the peasant and the policy-maker with the people.

Acknowledging these ties is crucial to understanding white settler colonies like British Columbia. The significance of immigration in colonial contexts derives from its central position in the very business of imperialism. Settler societies aim simultaneously to dispossess Aboriginal peoples and to replace them with relatively homogeneous settler populations, and immigration is one of the tools that has allowed them to do so. Colonies of settlement are distinguished from other kinds of colonies chiefly by their reproductive and gendered character. That colonizers *settle* implies more than residence. It denotes a reproductive regime dependent on the presence of settler women who literally reproduce the colony. Immigration must therefore provide more than non-Aboriginal bodies. Ideally, it must provide the right kind of bodies, those suited to building a white settler colony.

These connections between immigration, empire, and gender came together in mid-nineteenth-century British Columbia in an especially revealing way. Its society was the product of three sometimes conflicting imperial intentions: the fur trade, the gold rush, and the British tradition of settler colonies. North America's northern Pacific coast and the Columbia Plateau were densely populated by linguistically, culturally, and politically diverse First Nations people reliant on foraging, hunting, and fishing. The Hudson's Bay Company (HBC) began trading with local peoples in the late eighteenth century, and formal colonial authority was established in 1849 when Vancouver Island was made a British colony.

The discovery of gold on the mainland's Fraser River in 1858 precipitated the creation of a mainland colony called British Columbia. It was, according to imperial opinion, destined to be a major colony of settlement. "[N]ever did a colony in its infancy present a more satisfactory appearance," remarked one Anglican cleric. By 1866 and 1867, however, "those who once entertained most extravagant expectations began to despond."[5] Imperial downsizing followed despondency. In 1866 the two colonies were merged, retaining the name of British Columbia, and in July 1871 British Columbia joined Canada as a province, bringing the colonial period to a close.

These shifts in political form reflected widespread disappointment in British Columbia's performance as a settler colony. "The high tide of immigration expected never reached the Colony," explained Governor Frederick Seymour, "and the ebb proved much stronger than anticipated."[6] To be sure, the population expanded: there were fewer than 1,000 settlers in 1855 and over 10,000 in 1871. But the settler population never rivalled the Aboriginal one, which, despite massive depopulation wrought by smallpox, likely hovered around the 45,000 mark in the early 1870s.[7]

Settler British Columbia did not grow as quickly as imperial observers hoped it would, nor did it grow in the way they had hoped. The periphery, like the metropole, defied pretences of ethnic and racial homogeneity.[8] For a supposed white settler colony, British Columbia was not very white: Chinese, African-American, Latino, and Kanaka (Hawaiian) settlers were a significant presence. Jews and continental Europeans pressed operative definitions of whiteness, and Americans unsettled the colony's claims to Britishness. In 1861 the local official for Douglas, a small gold-rush town on the mainland, enumerated 97 Chinese, 40 Americans, 20 Mexicans, 17 Europeans, and 6 "coloured" people. They dwelled amongst "About 700 Natives."[9] "It would have been difficult to find in one place a greater mixture of different nationalities," wrote German mathematician Carl Friesach after visiting Yale, another small mining town. "Americans were undoubtably [*sic*] in the majority—California, especially had sent a larger contingent. Then followed Germans, French, and Chinese. Next came Italians, Spaniards, Poles, etc," he noted.[10]

The special plurality that characterized resource towns helped shape the entire colony. American missionary Matthew Macfie found Victoria, the capital city, a small and alarmingly cosmopolitan place in the early 1860s:

> Though containing at present an average of only 5,000 or 6,000 inhabitants, one cannot pass along the principal thoroughfares without meeting representatives of almost every tribe and nationality under heaven. Within a limited space may be seen—of Europeans, Russians, Austrians, Poles, Hungarians, Italians, Danes, Swedes, French, Germans, Spaniards, Swiss, Scotch, English and Irish; of Africans, Negroes from the United States and the West Indies; of Asiatics, Lascars and Chinamen; of Americans, Indians, Mexicans, Chilanoes, and citizens of the North American Republic; and of Polynesians, Malays from the Sandwich Islands [Hawaii].[11]

Macfie's fevered attempt to classify this population perhaps speaks more to his own discomfort with the mutability of racial boundaries, but it is not surprising that this discomfort was triggered in British Columbia. The diversity fostered by the gold rushes of the early colonial days diminished but never disappeared. When British Columbia entered Canadian confederation in 1871, its settler society was constituted, according to one probably conservative count, by 8,576 whites, 1,548 Chinese, and 462 Africans.[12]

That British Columbia's settlers were overwhelmingly male further suggested its failure to fit the norms of a white settler colony. While the female proportion ebbed and flowed over the colonial period, it never exceeded a high of 35 per cent of the white society and reached lows of 5 per cent.[13] Imperial discourse that accorded white women a special role as harbingers of empire rendered this demographic problem a political one. A popular emigration guide by "A Returned Digger," like so many others, despaired of what to do with a society so lacking in women. "The great curse of the colony," he explained, "is the absence of women. I doubt if there was one woman to a hundred men twelve months ago. I am quite sure that now, when I am writing, there must be at least two hundred men to every woman."[14] In colonial discourse, the continuing demographic dominance of First Nations people, the plurality of settler society, and its prevailing masculinity became irreparably intertwined, a three-part symbol of British Columbia's departure from dominant social norms and expectations.

Colonial promoters—a term I apply to a loose collection of journalists, politicians, officials, missionaries, and self-appointed do-gooders—looked to immigration to address the smallness, diversity, and masculinity of settler British Columbia and to render it a prosperous and respectable settler colony. They attributed the colony's lamentable imperial performance to the sparseness of its settler society. The *British*

Columbian newspaper argued that the colony's poor showing stemmed from its underpopulation, "because we have only a mere handful of population, a few thousand people living upon one another."[15] The colony lacked white population of nearly every description. The Victoria press noted,

> If we enter our churches, they want worshippers; our school houses want scholars; our streets and highways want pedestrians and vehicles; our merchants want trade; our traders want customers; our steamboats want passengers and freight; our workshops want workmen; our fertile valleys want farmers; our gold and silver mines want miners; in short, the two Colonies want population.[16]

While the colony had resources, wrote the *Cariboo Sentinel,* "without a population a country may remain forever a barren wilderness, dotted here and there with a few fisherman's huts and a few miners' and lumberman's cabins, and known only to the world as an inhospitable and poverty-stricken place."[17]

If colonial promoters suggested that British Columbia's ills stemmed from the sparseness of the white population, they had a related and almost boundless faith in the political potential of white bodies to make it a successful colonial enterprise. Even the most shameless boosters, however, recognized that British Columbia's distance from centres of white population meant that active state intervention was required for mass immigration to occur. If they wanted a white population, they would have to work for it, bidding it to come hither, assisting its passage, and supporting it on arrival. "To have our country filled up we must not only assist people to reach our shores, but we must show them the way to earn a living after they get here," wrote the *Colonist* in 1866.[18] The intervention of both the local and colonial state was required. "What right has the most remote of the British Colonies to expect immigration without even *asking for it,*" agreed the New Westminster press, "to say nothing of *assisting* it?"[19]

Colonial promoters' demands for immigration were part and parcel of a programme of asserting white supremacy in British Columbia. Himani Bannerji has recently dubbed immigration a "euphemistic expression for racist labour and citizenship policies."[20] In colonial British Columbia the process worked to exclude First Nations migrants and to minimize non-white settlers. It was difficult, although hardly impossible, to argue for the removal of First Nations with local and obvious territorial claims. Those from distant territories were easy targets for settlers committed to visions of racial segregation. The city of Victoria worked hard to control and limit the presence of the so-called Northern Tribes—people from the coastal societies of the Nisga'a, Hieltsuk, Nexalk, Kwakwaka'wakw, Tlingit, and especially the wealthy and politically powerful Haida and Tsimshian—who made annual spring visits to Victoria for trade, wage work, and festivity. In 1859 a police constable found 2,235 Northern peoples, the bulk of them probably Haida and Tsimshian, living on the outskirts of Victoria.[21] As annually as they arrived, local burghers demanded their eviction. The language they used to stigmatize Northern peoples invoked the overlapping discourses of morality, criminality, and gender that have often been used to identify and marginalize immigrant groups. "Vagrancy, filth, disease, drunkenness, larceny, maiming, murder, prostitution, in a multiplied form, are the invariable results of an annual visit from the Northern Tribes," raged the *Colonist.* "We unhesitantly declare for stopping the immigration."[22]

Those who defended the rights of Northern peoples to visit Victoria—and, by implication, their status as legitimate immigrants and thus colonial citizens—relied on another staple of immigration discourse, namely the argument that the Northern peoples' presence, however unpalatable, was sweetened by their cheap labour. When settlers demanded that Northern peoples be forcibly evicted, missionary William Duncan argued that "the driving-away policy is contrary to the interests of our Colony, which needs at least the labor of the Indians." He referred those who doubted the local need for Aboriginal labour to "the kitchens and nurseries, the fields and gardens around Victoria."[23] Governor James Douglas proposed schemes of moral and social regulation as an alternative to eviction, arguing that Northern peoples' willingness to serve as a colonial labour force made them valuable to whites. "[I]t is hardly creditable to the civilization of the nineteenth century, that so especial an element of health, as labour of the cheapest description should be, in a manner, banished from the Colony," he explained.[24]

The sweat and toil of the Northern peoples ultimately failed to buy them a legitimate role in settler Victoria. Those who wanted racial segregation of colonial space were bolstered and legitimated by the apocalyptic smallpox epidemic of 1862, when Northern peoples were repeatedly and forcibly evicted from Victoria, a process later condoned and organized by public health legislation.[25] A brand of settler imperialism premised on the removal and containment of local peoples ultimately won out over the version that positioned them as subservient labourers for the ruling minority. Historians need to broaden our understanding of migration to account for the plurality and movement of the so-called old world and to make room for the migrations of Aboriginal North America. Doing so complicates our analysis of migration and lays bare the extent to which immigration functioned as a mechanism of inclusion and exclusion.

That this process worked to include whites and exclude others is confirmed by the experience of settlers of Asian and African extraction. Douglas—himself an archetypal hybrid figure, hailing from a "creole" mother and a Scottish father and having married the half-Cree Amelia Connolly—encouraged the migration of mainly middle-class African Americans associated with the Pioneer Society of San Francisco in 1858. Other settlers did not share his enthusiasm. Despite the African Americans' apparent fit with the colony's putative values of hard work, Protestantism, and respectability, their sizable presence in Victoria was regarded by many white people as a problem. Whether Victoria would replicate or challenge American-style segregation in her churches, theatres, and saloons was a significant item of debate until the black population began to disperse in the mid-1860s.[26]

It was Chinese immigration that created the most ambivalence among British Columbia's white commentators. Representations of Chinese men celebrated industriousness and sometimes located them on the colonists' side of the local imperial divide. The Grand Jury of Cayoosh (later Lillooet) told the Governor in 1860 that Chinese settlers were a benefit to white traders and the government alike. The jury further requested that the state acknowledge the Chinese as settlers, asking that they "afford them every due protection to prevent their being driven away, wither by attacks from Indians or otherwise."[27]

More often Chinese men were positioned as undesirable immigrants who would imperil rather than bolster colonialism. The *Cariboo Sentinel* argued that Chinese men should not be colonists for a variety of reasons, all indicating their fundamental difference and many invoking explicitly gendered images. The Chinese, the newspaper argued, were "aliens not merely in nationality, but in habits, religion"; they never became "good citizens" or served on juries or fire companies; they never married or settled outside China and were "more apt to create immorality than otherwise"; they dealt "entirely with their own countrymen"; they hoarded their money and evaded taxes; and, lastly, they were, ironically for immigrants, "inimical to immigration."[28] No restrictions were imposed on

Chinese immigration, although colonists debated ways—prominent among them being a miner's licence fee levied on Chinese men alone—designed to regulate their place within settler society.[29] Such discussions anticipated the highly organized, pervasive, and vociferous attacks on Chinese people that began later in the nineteenth century and continue to shape contemporary life and politics.[30]

The role of immigration to colonial British Columbia was thus an explicitly racial one. The "'bone, muscle, and intellect,' that is required here," explained the Victoria press plainly, "differs materially from the Indian or the African. It is Caucasian—Anglo-Saxon bone, muscle, and intellect we want."[31] Class, and the politics of respectability that so often went with it, also helped determine who would be included and who excluded. Not all white people were created equal. British Columbia's colonial promoters did not want convicts, although one, tellingly, was willing to tolerate juvenile offenders as long as they were placed on First Nations settlements.[32] When the Colonial Office inquired about the emigration of distressed Lancashire mill operatives, local officials were similarly unreceptive. Douglas replied that "this Colony offers but a poor field for destitute immigrants," warning that "instead of improving their condition, it is to be feared, that by emigrating in great numbers to this Colony, they would only be involved in a more hopeless state of distress and poverty."[33] British Columbia's officials were ultimately as fearful of organized immigration's class implications—of the shovelling out of paupers—as were others in British North America.

Immigration to this settler colony was an issue of race and class, and also very much one of gender. British Columbia's colonial failure was linked, in critics' minds, not only to the smallness and diversity of the settler society but also to the failure of increasingly hegemonic gender norms to take root there. British Columbia was home to a small, highly mobile handful of settler men living amongst a large Aboriginal society. This particular demography fostered a rough, vibrant homosocial culture created by and for young men and the widespread practice of white-Aboriginal domestic and conjugal relationships. Immigration was sought as a corrective for both. When promoters called for immigration, they called for a process that would address the society's perceived gendered deficiencies as well as its racial peculiarities.

Three gendered images dominated discussions of immigration. First, the hardy backwoodsman—a steady, hard-working man willing to meet the difficulties of colonial life and permanently settle in British Columbia—shaped discussions of men and migration. The hypothetical hardy backwoodsman was constructed in contrast to the rough gold miners who so pervaded the colony. British Columbia had two major gold rushes—the Fraser River Gold Rush of 1858 and the Cariboo Gold Rush of 1862–1863—and a host of smaller ones. Waves of young, footloose men disillusioned with the false promises of capitalist, industrial society were attracted by each strike of gold. Prevailing discourse understood these men as wandering, immoral, and anti-social. George Grant, secretary of a surveying party, argued that the gold rushes brought "not an emigration of sober, steady householders, whose aim was to establish homes, and live by their own industry, but of fever-hearted adventurers from all parts of the world,—men without a country and without a home."[34]

Miners' inadequacies as colonists became axiomatic in popular colonial discourse. "It must be admitted that a very considerable section of our population is composed of adventurers, who, having been attracted to our shores by our gold, feel little or no interest in the permanent success of the Colony," wrote the *British Columbian*.[35] For British Columbia to fulfil its imperial potential, hardy backwoodsmen would have to replace the wandering miners. In 1859

Douglas told the Colonial Office, "The mining population are proverbially migratory and unsettled in their habits, seldom engaging in any other than their own absorbing pursuits, and therefore, it is he who tills the soil, the industrious farmer, who must clear the forest, bring the land into cultivation, and build up the permanent interests and prosperity of the Colony."[36]

The hardy backwoodsman stood in contrast not only to the wandering miner, but to another masculine drain on the colonial enterprise, the "croaker." This term, along with grumbler, was applied to men deemed unable to weather the difficulties of colonial life. Whether an erstwhile son of wealth or an urban loafer, the croaker was flummoxed by the realities of pioneering and proceeded to complain instead of work. Gilbert Malcolm Sproat, a sawmill owner, magistrate, amateur anthropologist, and promoter of immigration, described the croakers:

> [C]ertain persons came into the country who had a strong desire to make a living without taking off their coats—a desire which could not be gratified. The friends of these persons at home sent them money, which they put into silly investments. They rode to the diggings, and road [*sic*] back again. They hung, like mendicants, round the doors of the Government offices. They croaked in the streets, spent their time idly in bar-rooms, and finally disappeared.[37]

Here, the language of class is put to work in the service of gender and race: the croaker is idle and delicate, bearing the mark of both femininity and bourgeois laxity. The local press argued a similar position. Some settlers, one paper argued, "only remain to croak and whine for a season, and eventually, like sickly lambs or untimely fruit, unequal to the task of combatting [*sic*] and overcoming the hardships and privations incident to all new countries, drop off to their native land."[38] The test of manliness these "sickly lambs" fail is thus generated by the specificities of the colonial context.

This was a test that the hardy backwoodsman passed. Just as they repelled the weak, colonies were thought to attract the most manly of British men who stood in contrast not only to their less rugged fellows, but to the indigenous men they alternately feminized or feared.[39] "As a rule," commented the local press, "it is the most energetic, hardy, manly, self reliant of her sons who first people her Colonies."[40] Ideal male immigrants were hard-working, disciplined, and predisposed to rural life. The new colony, argued a supporter in 1860, "does not want the idle, the profligate, and sickly."[41] The hardy backwoodsman embraced diligent labour, especially agricultural labour, just as the gold miner rejected it. His single state meant that he was able to devote himself fully to labour, to define himself as an entirely economic being. One much-reprinted emigration guide advised, "A family is a burden till a man is established."[42]

The discourse of the hardy backwoodsman both reflected and masked single men's economic significance to a colony materially tied to resource extraction. Despite the significance of Aboriginal people to British Columbia's wage-labour force, employers persisted in seeking non-Native miners and farmers and believed, in keeping with the Anglo-American world, that only men could fulfil these roles. That a work force of single men was literally reproduced elsewhere spared the colony the costs of maintaining and creating labour in the next generation.[43] Labour-force politics reinforced the prevailing gendered patterns of immigration and ensured that single men formed the overwhelming majority of independent immigrants. They also comprised a surprising percentage of assisted ones. Between 1849 and 1852 the HBC imported over 400 people, 250 of whom were adult men mainly destined to labour on Island farms.[44] The search for hardy backwoodsmen persisted throughout the colonial period. A proposed 1864 Vancouver Island scheme put "farm labourers" alongside "unmarried female domestic servants" and "married couples" as people whose passages should be subsidized.[45]

Yet single men, hardy or otherwise, constituted an ambivalent force for colonial promoters. Sproat thought that their tendency to wander made them a waste of public funds.[46] More fundamentally, imperial regimes were consistently troubled by the large numbers of working-class men assigned responsibility for practically enforcing them.[47] White soldiers, miners, and farmers frequently failed to meet standards of racial distance and superiority set by imperial masters. Racial concerns about young, footloose men in colonial contexts were also gendered concerns. Colonial promoters were disturbed by how regularly white men formed relationships and families with local women. Settler men who opted to remain single were also a worry. Increasingly in the mid-nineteenth century the domestic family was constructed as a necessary component of adult life. To be rendered a responsible colonial citizen who was appropriately distanced from local peoples, the hardy backwoodsman needed a wholesome woman.

The scarcity of white women in British Columbia became, along with the smallness of the settler population, axiomatic for the colony's condition. As I have argued elsewhere, white women were constructed as "fair ones of a purer caste"[48] with three related roles in the local colonial project. White women would first compel white men to reject the rough homosocial culture of the backwoods in favour of normative standards of masculinity, respectability, and permanence. "Women! women! women! are the great want," wrote aristocrat Harry Verney from London. "The normal state is man with a help meet for him, and if something is not soon done, either by the Imperial or Colonial Government, or by some philanthropists at home, I know not what will become of us. Poor man goes sadly down hill if he remains long without the supporting influence of women."[49] White women were considered to be men's collective better half, as the only force capable of ensuring their proper behaviour. Such a discourse accorded them a role, albeit a limited one, as agents in both imperialism and immigration.

White women would secondly address shortages in the local labour market and relieve overpopulation in Britain. That the supposed need for domestic servants and wives in British Columbia neatly matched fears of "surplus women" in Britain gave calls for female immigration a special efficacy. A female immigration to British Columbia, wrote one observer, "would be as great a boon to the colony as I am sure it would be to many of the underpaid, under-fed, and over-worked women who drag out a weary existence in the dismal back streets and alleys of the metropolis."[50] Immigration was thus invoked as a mechanism for simultaneously resolving the different crises of gender that troubled the metropole and the periphery.

White women's third service to the colonial project was the explicitly racial one of discouraging mixed-race sexual, domestic, and conjugal relationships. As white men's "natural" objects of desire, they would draw men away from the temptations of Aboriginal women and, in doing so, shore up the colonial project as a whole. "That many of the native women are cleanly, industrious, and faithful, we do not pretend to deny," wrote New Westminster's *Mainland Guardian,* "but, we regret to to [*sic*] say, they are the exceptions. With the increase of our white female population, we look for new life in our agricultural pursuits and we hope that every inducement will be offered to healthy industrious women, who are desirous of finding good husbands and comfortable homes, in this province, to come out to us."[51] This discourse was premised on the construction of white women as uplifting and on the representation of First Nations women as base and threatening that circulated throughout colonial British Columbia.

In these ways, the discourse of wholesome women emphasized the political utility of ordinary, working-class women above those who held an official role in the colonial project like missionaries' or officials' wives. Their contribution lay not in independent action, but rather in their ability to transform plebeian men. Such a discourse imbued women migrants with an agency less often acknowledged in historiography. At any rate, the sheer ideological weight of the conviction that a society lacking white women could not be a moral or even adequate one provided the motivation necessary to orchestrate immigration schemes in 1862, 1863, and 1870. Organized as joint efforts of the local elite, missionaries, and British feminists, these immigration campaigns are remembered in popular lore as the "brideships," as colony- (and, later, nation-) building enterprises. Together, the *Tynemouth, Robert Lowe,* and *Alpha* carried roughly a hundred women, largely teenagers from working-class and sometimes indigent backgrounds. They were putatively destined to be domestic servants, but popular discourse ensured that their real destiny lay in the marriage market. As wives of miners and farmers, colonial promoters hoped, these wholesome women would render British Columbia's fragile colonial project a stable one.[52]

The young working-class women produced by these female immigration schemes ultimately unsettled the colonial project rather than securing it. Instead of behaving as beacons of imperial rectitude, the immigrants acted like the young, working-class women that they were. Colonial promoters were deeply disappointed. By the close of the colonial period, their faith in the political usefulness of white female migration was profoundly shaken. In 1872 Sproat looked back on his experience with three separate female immigration efforts, commenting, "How to send single women to Victoria safely across the continent, and through San Francisco, is a problem which I cheerfully hand over for solution to those who are more experienced in the management of that sex than I am."[53] The fundamental problem with white female migration, he argued, was that *single* women were necessarily a moral problem. "The very delicate and difficult question of introducing single unmarried women into British Columbia might be partly solved by sending out a few, in charge of the heads of families—the women being from the same district as the families, and thus having an addition[al] guard for their self-respect," he argued.[54]

Wholesome women, much like hardy backwoodsmen, challenged the colonial project at the same time as they bolstered it. The enthusiasm for white female migration was always tempered and eventually overwhelmed by the conviction that single women, like men, were a dangerous population that could only be properly contained by families. After the disasters of the assisted female migration efforts of 1862 and 1863, the "steady family" gained a special cachet in pro-immigration discourse that would only increase after the 20 servant-women transported on the *Alpha* in 1870 proved, like their predecessors, a disappointment to those who so sought their importation. The Female Immigration Board that oversaw this scheme recommended that the colonial government abandon the project of female immigration and shift its monies and attentions to the "assisted passages of Families, and relatives of Farmers, Mechanics, and others settled in this Colony."[55] In pledging their support for the importation of families, and not single women, members of the board endorsed the stable family as the best kind of immigration for the colony.

They were not alone in suggesting that same-race domestic families would be the best base for a settler society and thus the best immigrants. Families simultaneously constrained young women and encouraged men to be permanent and diligent settlers. The *Victoria Press* argued, "The very class which we want above all others is the married agriculturist—the man whose social circumstances will bring him to the soil, and make him a permanent as well as productive inhabitant."[56] Sproat agreed, writing that "the married farmer with modest means, and accustomed to work in the fields, is the best kind of immigrant for British Columbia."[57] The HBC supported family migration when it imported 36 married colliers to work Nanaimo's coalfields.[58] That the Colonial Office shared this familial ideal is suggested by its willingness to pay for the passage of the wives and families of the Royal Engineers, the soldier-settlers sent to enforce British claims to the mainland.[59] On rare occasions the colonial government subsidized the migration of individual families,[60] but more often used land law to buttress domestic family formation. In Vancouver Island, nuclear family formation was encouraged by laws that gave white men an additional 50 acres of free land if they were married and 10 more acres for each child under the age of 10.[61]

The overlap between immigration discourse and immigration practice was usually indirect. These demands for hardy backwoodsmen, wholesome women, and steady families were rarely parlayed into concrete action. Immigration was what colonial pundits always wanted and never got. In referring to immigrants as "mythical beings," politician John Sebastian Helmcken astutely recognized the somewhat hypnotic role immigration played in colonial discourse.[62] The mythic rather than actual character of immigration to colonial British Columbia was not for lack of heated rhetoric or wild scheming. Colonial promoters held mass meetings, struck committees, wrote passionate letters, and developed plans for using immigration to secure their imperial fortunes.[63] With the exception of the 20 servant women carried on the *Alpha* in 1870, however, the colonial government's immigration efforts were largely confined to the cheap and discursive: they subsidized mail, explored territory, printed essays, and hired lecturers to regale the masses of various urban centres. In 1861, for instance, British Columbia created an exhibit for the World's Fair designed to prove to "struggling, hard worked Englishmen how easily a livelihood may be earned here."[64]

The modesty of these efforts deeply disappointed those who considered immigration key to imperial success. They complained bitterly about the local government's apparent inability to organize immigration. In 1864 the mainland press commented that, excepting "fifty pounds paid to a parson at Lillooet for an Essay," the colony had "not yet expended a single dollar" on immigration.[65] Five years later, the same newspaper despaired that there was not one person responsible for immigration "[a]mongst the army of officials who absorb the revenue of the Colony."[66]

If British Columbia's local government was unable, its imperial masters were unwilling. The Colonial Office argued that, given its location, British Columbia could only reasonably expect emigrants from the Australasian colonies, not from Britain, and repeatedly announced that it had no intention of ever assisting emigration to the colony.[67] When pestered to subsidize steam communication, Colonial Office staff made it clear that they lacked the requisite political will. "When this Country was supposed to be overpeopled, there was the appearance of a domestic object in schemes for using the proceeds of English taxes to encourage emigration. But that state of things has long ceased to exist," one noted.[68] Domestic issues like overpopulation fuelled the various assisted emigration schemes of the 1830s and 1840s and would again motivate major emigration schemes in the *fin de siècle*. These efforts ground to a near halt when popular economic fortunes bettered and events like New Zealand's Maori Wars and the Indian Rebellion of 1857 challenged British faith in the imperial project.

Whether in London, Victoria, or New Westminster, many doubted British Columbia's ability to attract settlers, but only a few challenged its need for a large white population. In 1861 the *Victoria Press* argued that mass immigration was an impractical goal cooked up by those unaccustomed to colonial labour, race politics, and labour relations. "It may suit a number of lackadaisical beings who are entirely unfitted for Colonial, or in fact any practical useful life, to be enabled to obtain, by a superabundant supply of immigrants, civilized *servants* at the same price they now pay for Indians," the press wrote.[69] Yet those who questioned the merits or feasibility of mass white immigration never captured the mainstream of public discourse. Ultimately, British Columbia's apparent inability to attract white and especially British immigrants served not as a reason for challenging the viability of colonialism, but rather as a rationale for the colony's entry into Canadian confederation.[70] If British Columbia could not use immigration to become a stable settler colony in its own right, it would try to do so as a Canadian province. That British Columbia finally registered a white majority in the first census taken after confederation suggests that this strategy was effective. With continuing depopulation of First Nations and the arrival of the transcontinental railroad in 1886—that tangible technology of both capital and nation and conveyor of migrants *par excellence*—British Columbia would begin to look increasingly like a textbook white settler colony, but it would continue to be haunted by a spectre of hybridity that was, in the final analysis, more nurtured by immigration than vanquished by it.

British Columbia's colonial pundits spilled much ink on the topic of immigration. They did so because immigration was central to their effort to transform British Columbia into a white settler colony. For them, immigration was a mechanism of inclusion and exclusion, one that would marginalize First Nations people, minimize non-white settlers, and nurture white migration. It would do so in explicitly gendered ways that reflected the importance of gender to the construction of a settler society. In newspapers, government reports, and colonial circles, they called for the immigration of white, preferably British immigrants who would fit into three gendered models: the hardy backwoodsman, the wholesome woman, and the steady family. This discourse reflected a minority's aspirations rather than a society's social experience. However constant and blustery the pro-immigration discourse, British Columbia's settler society would continue to be small, dominated by men, and relatively diverse until the Canadian Pacific Railway integrated the province into more continental patterns of demography and settlement. Immigration was indeed a tool for negotiating exclusions and inclusions, but not always in predictable ways.

Notes

1 See, for instance, Bernard Bailyn, *The Peopling of British North America: An Introduction* (New York: Knopf, 1986). For a revealing example, see the explicit definition of Ontario's Leeds and Landsdowne townships as "empty" in Donald Harman Akenson, *The Irish in Ontario: A Study in Rural History* (Montreal and Kingston: McGill-Queen's University Press, 1984), p. 55.

2 Daiva Staisulis and Nira Yuval-Davis, "Introduction: Beyond Dichotomies—Gender, Race, Ethnicity and Class in Settler Societies," in Staisulis and Yuval-Davis, eds., *Unsettling Settler Societies: Articulations of Gender, Race, Ethnicity and Class* (London: Sage, 1995).

3 On this point in a later period, see Stephen Constantine, "Introduction: Empire Migration and Imperial Harmony," in Constantine, ed., *Emigrants and Empire: British Settlement in the Dominions Between the Wars* (Manchester: Manchester University Press, 1990). See also Rita S. Krandis, ed., *Imperial Objects: Essays on Victorian Women's Emigration and the Unauthorized Imperial Experience* (New York: Twayne, 1998).

4 On this shift, see Franca Iacovetta, "Manly Militants, Cohesive Communities, and Defiant Domestics: Writing about Immigrants in Canadian Historical Scholarship," *Labour/Le Travail*, vol. 36 (Fall 1995), p. 221. Also see Iacovetta with Paula Draper and Robert Vantresca, "Preface," in Iacovetta, Draper, and Vantresca, eds., *A Nation of Immigrants: Women, Workers, and Communities in Canadian History, 1840s–1960s* (Toronto: University of Toronto Press, 1998).

5 Henry Wright, *Nineteenth Annual Report of the Missions of the Church of England in British Columbia for the Year 1877* (London: Rivingtons, 1878), pp. 16–17.

6 British Columbia Archives (hereafter BCA), GR 1486, mflm B-1442, Great Britain, Colonial Office, British Columbia Original Correspondence (hereafter CO 60), CO 60/32, Frederick Seymour to Duke of Buckingham and Chandos, March 17, 1868.

7 All population figures from colonial British Columbia are at best guesses. These are from British Columbia, *Report of the Hon. H. L. Langevin, C.B., Minister of Public Works* (Ottawa: I. B. Taylor, 1872), p. 22; and Edward Mallandaine, *First Victoria Directory, Third [Fourth] Issues, and British Columbia Guide* (Victoria: Mallandaine, 1871), pp. 94–95. Also see R. Cole Harris and John Warkentin, *Canada Before Confederation: A Study in Historical Geography* (Ottawa: Carleton University Press, 1991), chap. 7.

8 Antoinette Burton, *At the Heart of the Empire: Indians and the Colonial Encounter in Late-Victorian Britain* (Berkeley: University of California Press, 1998).

9 BCA, "Colonial Correspondence," GR 1372, mflm B-1330, file 620/16, John Bowles Gaggin to W. A. G. Young, April 3, 1861.

10 Carl Friesach, "Extracts from *Ein Ausflug nach Britisch-Columbien in Jahre 1858*," in E. E. Delavault and Isabel McInnes, trans., "Two Narratives of the Fraser River Gold Rush," *British Columbia Historical Quarterly*, vol. 1 (July 1941), p. 227.

11 Matthew Macfie, *Vancouver Island and British Columbia: Their History, Resources and Prospects* (London: Longman, Green, Longman, Roberts & Green, 1865), pp. 378–379.

12 British Columbia, *Report of the Hon. H. L. Langevin*, p. 22.

13 On this, see Adele Perry, *On the Edge of Empire: Gender, Race, and the Making of British Columbia, 1849–1871* (Toronto: University of Toronto Press, 2000), chap. 1.

14 A Returned Digger, *The Newly Discovered Gold Fields of British Columbia* (London: Darton and Hodge, 1862, 8th ed.), p. 7.

15 "Our Great Want," *British Columbian,* January 9, 1869.

16 "Our Wants," *British Colonist,* June 5, 1861.

17 "Emigration," *Cariboo Sentinel,* June 18, 1868.

18 "Assisted Immigration," *British Colonist,* December 11, 1866.

19 "Population, Population," *British Columbian*, May 29, 1869.

20 Himani Bannerji, *On the Dark Side of the Nation: Essays on Multiculturalism, Nationalism and Gender* (Toronto: Canadian Scholars' Press, 2000), p. 4.

21 "Our Indian Population," *Weekly Victoria Gazette,* April 28, 1859.

22 "Invasion of the Northern Indians," *British Colonist,* April 18, 1861.

23 Wm. Duncan, "The Indian Question," *British Colonist,* July 4, 1861. On Aboriginal wage labour, see John Lutz, "After the Fur Trade: Aboriginal Wage Labour in Nineteenth-Century British Columbia," *Journal of the Canadian Historical Association* (1992), pp. 69–94.

24 National Archives of Canada (hereafter NAC), Great Britain, Colonial Office Correspondence, Vancouver Island (hereafter CO 305). CO 305/10, mflm B-238, James Douglas to Sir Edward Bulwer Lytton, May 25, 1859.

25 See Perry, *On the Edge,* chap. 5.

26 For an argument for black migration to Vancouver Island, see Mary A. Shadd, *A Plea for Emigration; or, Notes of Canada West, in its Moral, Social, and Political Aspect With Suggestions Respecting Mexico, West Indies, and Vancouver Island, for the Information of Colored Emigrants* (Detroit: George W. Pattison, 1842), pp. 43–44. On black people in Victoria society, see Irene Genevieve Marie Zaffaroni, "The Great Chain of Being: Racism and Imperialism in Colonial Victoria, 1858–1871" (MA thesis, University of Victoria, 1987), chap. 4; Crawford Killian, *Go Do Some Great Thing: The Black Pioneers of British Columbia* (Vancouver: Douglas and McIntyre, 1978).

27 NAC, CO 60/8, MG 11, mflm B-83, "Address of the Grand Jury at Cayoosh to Governor Douglas," in James Douglas to Duke of Newcastle, October 9, 1860.

28 "Our Chinese Population," *Cariboo Sentinel,* May 16, 1867.

29 See, for an explanation of why they were impracticable, NAC, CO 63/3, mflm B-1489, "Speech of His Honor the Officer Administering the Government at the Opening of the Legislative Council," *British Columbia Government Gazette.*

30 On this, see Kay Anderson, *Vancouver's Chinatown: Racial Discourse in Canada, 1875–1980* (Montreal and Kingston: McGill-Queen's University Press, 1991); Patricia E. Roy, *A White Man's Province: British Columbia Politicians and Chinese and Japanese Immigrants, 1858–1914* (Vancouver: University of British Columbia Press, 1989).

31 "Indian vs. White Labor," *British Colonist,* February 19, 1861.

32 "Convict labour," *British Columbian,* January 11, 1865; "Juvenile Offenders—Colonization," *British Columbian,* May 30, 1869.

33 NAC, CO 305/20, MG 11, mflm B-244, and CO 60/16, MG 11, mflm B-89, James Douglas to the Duke of Newcastle, July 14, 1863.

34 George M. Grant, *Ocean to Ocean: Sandford Fleming's Expedition Through Canada in 1872* (Toronto: James Campbell & Son, 1873), p. 308. Also see Adele Perry, "Bachelors in the Backwoods: White Men and Homosocial Culture in Up-Country British Columbia, 1858–1871," in R W. Sandwell, ed., *Beyond City Limits: Rural History in British Columbia* (Vancouver: University of British Columbia Press, 1998).

35 "Arterial Highways," *British Columbian,* January 2, 1862.

36 NAC, CO 60/4, MG 11, mflm B-80, James Douglas to Edward Bulwer Lytton, July 11, 1859.

37 Gilbert Malcolm Sproat, *British Columbia: Information for Emigrants* (London: Agent General for the Province, 1873), p. 4.

38 "The Soil of British Columbia," *British Columbian,* February 3, 1863.

39 On masculinity and colonization, see Mrinalini Sinha, *Colonial Masculinity: The "Manly Englishman" and the "Effeminate Bengali" in the Late Nineteenth Century* (Manchester: Manchester University Press, 1995); Elizabeth Vibert, *Traders' Tales: Narratives of Cultural Encounters on the Plateau, 1807–1846* (Norman: University of Oklahoma Press, 1997).

40 "The Colonial Policy of Great Britain," *British Colonist,* May 2, 1863.

41 "Testimonial to D. G. F. MacDonald, Esq., C.E.," *Weekly Victoria Gazette,* January 30, 1860.

42 A Returned Digger, *The Newly Discovered Gold Fields*, p. 8.

43 This is dealt with, to some extent, in Alicja Muszynski, *Cheap Wage Labour: Race and Gender in the Fisheries of British Columbia* (Montreal and Kingston: McGill-Queen's University Press, 1996). Muszynski, however, discusses the economics of the single male immigrant as unique to Chinese men, when in fact most non-Natives lacked co-resident families.

44 University of British Columbia Library (hereafter UBCL), CO 305/3, mflm R288, A. Colville to John Packington, November 24, 1852, p. 1.

45 British Library, BS 72/1, "England, Emigration Commissioners," *Colonization Circular,* no. 25, 1866 (London, Groombridge and Sons), p. 8.

46 BCA, Add Mss 257, file 3, Gilbert Malcolm Sproat to Lieutenant Governor, "Memo re European Immigration into B.C.," November 3, 1871.

47 See, for instance, Kenneth Ballhatchet, *Race, Sex and Class under the Raj: Imperial Attitudes and Policies and their Critics, 1783–1905* (London: Werdenfeld and Nicholson, 1980), chap. 5.

48 One of the Disappointed, untitled piece in the *British Columbian,* June 7, 1862; Adele Perry, "'Fair Ones of a Pure Caste': White Women and Colonialism in Nineteenth-Century British Columbia," *Feminist Studies,* vol. 23, no. 3 (Fall 1997), pp. 501–524.

49 "Sir Harry Verney Upon British Columbia," *British Columbian,* August 20, 1862.

50 A. D. G., "British Columbia: To the Editor of the Times," *London Times,* January 1, 1862.

51 "Immigration," *Mainland Guardian,* February 9, 1871.

52 See Perry, *On the Edge,* chaps. 6–7, for an analysis of female immigration to British Columbia.

53 BCA, GR 419, box 10, file 1872/1, British Columbia, Attorney General, "Documents," G. M. S., "Memorandum on Immigration, Oct 1972," pp. 95–96.

54 BCA, GR 419, box 10, file 1872/1, "Attorney General Documents," G. M. Sproat, "Memorandum of a few Suggestions for opening the business of emigration to British Columbia, referred to as Memo C. in a letter of G. M. Sproat to the Honourable the Provincial Secretary, dated 29th August 1972," pp. 4–5.

55 BCA, GR 1372, mflm B-1314, file 955/23, "Colonial Correspondence," Wm. Pearse, John

Robson, W. J. MacDonald to Colonial Secretary, July 12, 1870; E. G. A., "The Immigration Board," *British Colonist,* June 24, 1870.

56 "The Overland Route," *Victoria Press,* March 16, 1862.

57 BCA, GR 419, box 10, file 1872/1, British Columbia, "Papers Related to Immigration, 1972," G. M. S., "Memorandum on Immigration, Oct 1872."

58 BCA, Add mss E/B/M91A, Andrew Muir, "Private Diary," November 9, 1848—August 5, 1850 [transcript]; Add Mss A/C/20.1/N15, James Douglas—Joseph William McKay, "Nanaimo Correspondence, August 1852–September 1853" [transcript].

59 NAC, MG 11, CO 60/9, mflm B-83, G. C. Lewis to James Douglas, August 11, 1860, draft reply, in James Douglas to the Duke of Newcastle, May 12, 1860.

60 See, for instance, James E. Hendrickson, ed., *Journals of the Colonial Legislatures of the Colonies of Vancouver Island and British Columbia, 1851–1871,* vol. 1: *Journals of the Council, Executive Council, and Legislative Council of Vancouver Island, 1851–1866* (Victoria: Provincial Archives of British Columbia, 1980), pp. 133–134.

61 "The New Land Proclamation for Vancouver Island," *British Colonist,* March 8, 1861; "Salt Spring Island," *Victoria Press,* November 10, 1861; Macfie, *Vancouver Island and British Columbia,*. p. 205.

62 "Legislative Council," *British Colonist,* February 4, 1869.

63 See examples in Hendrickson, ed., *Journals of the Colonial Legislatures,* vol. 2: *Journals of the House of Assembly, Vancouver Island, 1856–1863,* vol. 3: *Journals of the House of Assembly, Vancouver Island, 1863–1866,* and vol. 4: *Journals of the Executive Council, 1864–1871, and of the Legislative Council, 1864–1866, of British Columbia.*

64 "Industrial Exhibition Circular," *British Columbian,* May 30, 1861.

65 "Emigration," *British Columbian,* June 15, 1864.

66 "What Shall We Do With Them?," *British Columbian,* June 4, 1869.

67 NAC, MG 11, CO 60/5, mflm B-81, T. W. C. Murdoch and Frederic Rogers to Herman Merivale, April 28, 1859; mflm 69.303, Great Britain, House of Commons, Parliamentary Papers, vol. 38 (1863); no. 430, "Emigration: Number of Emigrants who left the United Kingdom for the *United States, British North America,* the several colonies of *Australasia, South Africa,* and other Places respectively; distinguishing, as far as practicable, the Native Country of the Emigrants, 1860–1863," mflm 69.303, p. 7.

68 NAC, MG 11, CO 60/14, mflm B-87, H. M. [Herman Merivale], April 8, note *en verso,* in T. W. C. Murdoch to Frederic Rogers, March 31, 1862.

69 "The Immigration Bubble," *Victoria Press,* July 27, 1861.

70 BCA, GR 1486, CO 60/29, mflm B-1440, Frederick Seymour to Duke of Buckingham and Chandos, September 24, 1867.

PART V

Industrializing Canada 1840–1867

Notman Photographic Archives, McCord Museum of Canadian History, Montreal, N-0000.94.56

Between 1840 and 1867, the British North American colonies experienced dramatic changes at all levels: economic, political, social, and cultural. These changes were symbolized by Great Britain's adoption of free trade in 1846, the introduction of responsible government in Nova Scotia and the United Canadas in 1848, the controversy over public schooling, and the growing support for separation of church and state.

In this period the Industrial Revolution, characterized by steam power, railways, and factories, was the catalyst for many of the changes taking place. Industrial capitalism not only transformed the nature of work and the relationship between labour and capital, it also quickened the pace of communications, encouraged new political arrangements, and inspired nationalist movements in Europe and the Americas.

By the mid-nineteenth century, business leaders, professionals, and politicians in the British North American colonies began to dream of a nation from sea to sea, bound together by political institutions adapted from their British heritage. Despite widespread opposition to the idea, the promoters of Confederation were successful. A new nation called Canada, made up of New Brunswick, Nova Scotia, Ontario, and Quebec, came into being on 1 July 1867. By 1880 boundaries had expanded to include Prince Edward Island, Rupert's Land, British Columbia, and the Arctic, making Canada the second largest nation in the world.

The dizzying pace of change affected everyone. In small villages, community leaders lobbied for a railway line, parsons and priests warned against the dangers of the new secular order, and schooling became an experience in the lives of virtually every child. Families debated the merits of public schooling and in many colonies found themselves taxed to pay for such a system whether they supported it or not. Whatever one's position on how schools should be sustained, few could deny that literacy had become the key to survival in the new industrial order. As Claudette Knight shows in the first article in this section, black residents in Canada West were eager for their children to be educated but encountered deep-seated prejudices when they tried to send their children to public schools. Despite the misgivings of the Superintendent of Education, Egerton Ryerson, the Separate Schools Act of 1859 made provision for segregated schools in what became the province of Ontario. It was, Knight argues, a "reasonable response" for racist whites who opposed integrated schooling and for black residents who demanded access to the advantages that education could bring.

As with public schools, the foundations of Canada's university system were laid in the mid-nineteenth century. Although only a tiny fraction of men received a college education, it was increasingly required of those aspiring to a professional career in medicine, law, theology, and science. Brian McKillop's account of the manoeuvring that accompanied the founding of the non-denominational University of Toronto demonstrates the complex relationship between political values and public institutions in the mid-nineteenth century. In Canada West and elsewhere in British North America, church-supported colleges survived but politicians influenced by liberal values, such as Robert Baldwin, were increasingly inclined to argue that state-supported educational institutions would better serve a progressive society.

By focusing on railways, the first large-scale industry in the United Canadas, Paul Craven and Tom Traves explore the structural changes and managerial policies that the factory system imposed on workers. Written contracts for indentured servants in pre-industrial society included obligations and duties on the part of both employer and employee, but such documents rarely exceeded more than a page or two of writing and disputes between masters and labourers were more often settled by face-to-face negotiation than by judicial processes. In contrast, workers in the shops of the Grand Trunk and Great Western Railway companies were expected to carry elaborate rule books and fit into a complex job hierarchy. Although the structure of industry had changed,

Craven and Traves argue that earlier artisan traditions and notions of paternalism still prevailed in railway shops, which in the 1850s were "on the boundary" of old and new patterns of labour–capital relations.

Formal education was not the only form of self-improvement that attracted the attention of British North Americans in the age of industry. Mechanics institutes, reading clubs, and voluntary organizations of many kinds emerged to keep the general public up-to-date on the latest literary, mechanical, and scientific achievements. In the 1820s the idea of temperance in the use of alcohol took root in British North America and by 1850 had become a mass movement. Temperance societies sprouted like mushrooms across the colonial landscape and, even for a time, made inroads among francophone Roman Catholics. In her account of the circuitous career of Father Charles Chiniquy, Jan Noel explores how French Canadians came to an accommodation with a movement that promised to solve issues such as family violence, disease, and poverty, and bring people closer to heaven on earth.

The spectacular advances associated with the Industrial Revolution offered the promise of a better life for everyone. In British North America one of the vehicles favoured for achieving the good life for all—railways, new agricultural frontiers, an end to sectarian and political bickering, material comfort—was political union of the eastern colonies and territorial expansion to the Pacific. The Civil War in the United States (1861–1865), anti-imperialist sentiment in the British Colonial Office, and political deadlock in the United Canadas furthered this aim by creating a crisis atmosphere in which the idea of colonial union became increasingly attractive. The Fathers of Confederation and their imperial and corporate backers prevailed in 1867, with the result that the views advanced by the opponents of Confederation are often treated dismissively or ignored entirely. Ged Martin takes a careful look at what the anti-Confederates had to say, concluding that while they lost the battle, they at least won some of the arguments.

The arguments did not end with *confederation.* Over the years since its passage, the British North America Act, passed in the British Parliament in the spring of 1867, has been the subject of much debate. Was it just an act or was it really a pact between provinces? Was the breakdown between federal and provincial powers judiciously apportioned in Sections 91 and 92? Why was the issue of language not mentioned in Section 93 relating to education? We conclude this section with excerpts from the controversial act so that readers can make their own judgments on the wisdom of the Fathers of Confederation.

Black Parents Speak:

Education in Mid-Nineteenth-Century Canada West*

CLAUDETTE KNIGHT

During the mid-nineteenth century, many black residents of Canada West were ardent advocates of public education for their children. Government policy officially supported black access to public education, although local white prejudice often limited its scope. Some black children attended common schools regularly, but others were denied public education or were forced to enroll in separate schools. Despite the increasing regulation and centralization of education during this period, local white opposition to integrated schooling ultimately shaped the policy that governed black students and, in some circumstances, was ultimately more powerful than the law.

Black parents seeking education opportunities amid anti-integrationist white communities resorted to a variety of strategies to combat local prejudice. Appeals to local officials, letters of protest to government education officers, and civil suits were initiated by black parents committed to educating their children. These initiatives not only document the history of black access to education in mid-nineteenth-century Canada West, but also serve as an important social barometer.

> I'm on my way to Canada
> That cold and distant land
> The dire effects of slavery
> I can no longer stand —
> Farewell, old master,
> Don't come after me.
> I'm on my way to Canada
> Where coloured men are free.[1]

This excerpt from George Clark's song, "The Free Slave," depicts Canada as a desirable refuge from the indignities and injustice suffered by American blacks under slavery. During the mid-nineteenth century, especially between 1850 and 1860, Canada West received a substantial influx of American blacks. The enslaved and the free sought to enjoy the freedom, equality, and justice that they were denied in the United States. According to Robin Winks, blacks migrating from the United States prior to the 1830s were generally well received in Canada West. During this period the number of blacks in Canada West was relatively small, and cheap labour was needed in many frontier communities to fell trees, lay roads, cut ties, and introduce tobacco farming.

After 1840 several significant changes altered these conditions. First, during the 1840s blacks faced increased competition from Irish immigrants, who were equally willing to embrace physically demanding, low-wage work, and whose skin colour was less likely to create social opposition. Secondly, as the availability of cheap land declined, blacks tended to drift towards towns where racial and real or imagined

Claudette Knight, "Black Parents Speak: Education in Mid-Nineteenth-Century Canada West," *Ontario History* 89, 4 (December 1997): 269–284.

*I am indebted to Professor Ian Radforth and *Ontario History* for their faith and invaluable criticism. Many thanks to Guy and my family for providing constructive criticism and encouragement throughout the evolution of this manuscript.

social differences would be more easily observed. Finally, and perhaps most significantly, the number of black fugitives fleeing to Canada West increased substantially after the passage of the Fugitive Slave Act in 1850. This act required all Americans to assist in the recapture and return of fugitive slaves, regardless of whether these blacks had obtained freedom in the northern states. Prior to September 1850, ten thousand blacks lived in Canada West; ten years later, this figure had increased to between thirty and thirty-five thousand.[2]

Initially, black fugitives tended to settle near the border in order to farm in regions most geographically familiar. Lack of funds and easy return access to the United States also determined that small groups settled in Welland, St. Catharines, Colchester, Windsor, Amherstburg, London, Chatham, and Dresden. Settlement occurred more slowly in Toronto, Oro, and the Queen's Bush. It is not surprising that later arrivals tended to settle in these regions where the small, established black communities could provide assistance to incoming fugitives.

Employment opportunities for the fugitives varied in Canada West, but most were farmers. Nevertheless, during the 1830s and 1840s many waiters in hotels near Niagara Falls were black, while others were employed on road construction or hired themselves out as field hands in Oro, and a small number operated their own small businesses in various towns. Some worked as brakemen on the Great Western Railway, made rope, were fishermen, or laboured in brickyards and slaughterhouses. Black women worked on farms and as servants. Despite the opportunities and prosperity enjoyed by some of these fugitives, the majority struggled financially, were often poorly prepared for the winter months, and many suffered from consumption.[3]

Proscriptions placed on black education in both northern and southern states meant that most black fugitives were illiterate. Blacks residing in the free states were often barred from public schools or forced to attend separate schools. Educating blacks was illegal in all slave states except Kentucky. A Virginia state representative summarized southern white sentiment: "We have as far as possible closed every avenue by which light may enter their minds... if we could extinguish the capacity to see the light our work would be completed."[4]

Despite their restricted access to education in the United States, once in Canada West black fugitives eagerly sought access to public schools. Many believed that the popular myth of black inferiority would be quickly destroyed when blacks gained educational opportunities. Educated blacks would undermine racist ideology, obtain superior employment, and gain voting privileges. On 22 October 1851, three black abolitionists (Henry Bibb, John Fisher, and James Tinsely) summarized the importance of education in their *Address to the Coloured Inhabitants of North America:*

> As we value education as being one of the most important items connected with our destiny, and it is more dreaded by the slaveholders than bowie-knives or pistols, we therefore recommend that there should be no time or opportunity lost in educating people of colour. Let there be put into the hands of the refugee as soon as he crosses Mason's and Dixon's Line, the Spelling Book. Teach him to read and write intelligibly, and the slaveholder won't have him on the plantation among his slaves. It is emphatically the most effectual protection to personal or political liberty with which the human family can be armed.[5]

Recognizing the value of education, blacks sought to enroll their children in Canada West's common schools. Susan Houston and Alison Prentice state that black children, like their white peers, attended schools "when and where they could."[6] Local prejudice of varying intensity resulted in the segregation of black youth. The exclusion of many black children from public schools was not inconsistent with the aims of the elites who promoted centralized education in Canada West. Furthermore, the success of white opposition to integrated schooling reflected the inability of government officials to wholly usurp educational authority from local communities.

The School Act of 1816 provided for the establishment of schools by property owners. These local citizens were permitted to construct a school, hire a teacher, and select trustees; during this period the schools provided basic literacy for their communities. The nature of public education in Canada West was altered throughout the latter half of the nineteenth century by elite Upper Canadians who sought to wrest educational authority from local communities. These elites were not concerned with economic or social mobility for the lower classes; instead, they sought to inculcate the attitudes and values that would respect their power and authority to rule. Bruce Curtis contends that these elite school promoters "consistently stressed both the necessity and beauty of class differences and of the social subordination of women."[7] It is not unreasonable to suggest that education reformers seeking to maintain class divisions in the white community would also have preferred Canada West's black community to maintain its inferior status.

The creation of the office of the superintendent of schools, legislated in the School Act of 1841, launched the beginning of centralized education in Canada West. School acts introduced between 1843 and 1871 resulted in a significant increase in the number of public schools and a serious erosion of local control over schooling. The educational bureaucracy expanded its power through increased regulation and the appointment of regional and central education officials. Whereas the pace of bureaucracy was rapid in Canada West, the actual authority of education officials to implement school policy emerged more slowly. For example, the School Act of 1841 provided for the superintendent of education to inspect common schools, manage the provincial school funds and distribute funds to district councils, and create and publicize plans to improve the education system. It did not, however, legislate power to enforce new school policies. Furthermore, the superintendent of education technically had no power to resolve local educational disputes.

In 1844 Egerton Ryerson, a well-known Methodist minister and former principal of Victoria College, accepted the position of superintendent of education of common schools in Canada West. To support policy development and funding responsibilities, this office expanded to include collecting educational data, resolving educational disputes, and discouraging "inappropriate behaviour." Despite the wide range of administrative responsibilities, the superintendent's power to enforce school policy was limited to withholding school funds from uncooperative communities. Egerton Ryerson was passionately committed to the development and expansion of schooling in Canada West. He sought the successful training of youth whose Christian values and developed mind and body would ensure political and moral order. It is likely that Ryerson's commitment to the expansion of Canada West's education system created a reluctance to withhold funding from disobedient school districts; his vision of a vast and regulated school system was dependent on the increase, not decline, of functioning public schools.

Before 1850, whites often used "creative" strategies to deny blacks their legal right to attend common schools; for example, they would gerrymander school districts or declare that local common schools were private. As a last resort, white parents would simply remove their children from the common school, which invariably closed due to the reduction in attendance. In a response to the exclusion of black youth from common schools, several black women established separate schools. In 1851 Mary Bibb opened a school for black children in her home, eventually expanding to a larger building. Similarly, in 1856 Amelia Freeman operated a grammar school for Chatham blacks. Between 1851 and 1853 Mary Ann Shadd, partially under the auspices of the American Missionary Association, operated a school in Windsor and eventually joined Amelia Freeman in the teaching and management of the Chatham Separate School. By providing independent education for black children, these black teachers made a valuable contribution to their communities, but their schools were plagued by financial difficulties. Since black communities were often small and relatively poor, funding was meagre. Enrolments varied and school grants, which were based on attendance, suffered as a result.[8]

Although much of black education in Canada West took place in separate schools, integrated schooling was accepted in some regions. In the late 1830s white children attended the renowned "black" school in Brantford. Similarly, the excellent reputation of the Buxton school, in the black settlement of Kent County, as well as the Church of England's Mission School, founded in London in 1854, attracted both black and white students. Even though the residents in larger, more socially heterogeneous communities such as Toronto and Hamilton were not wholly committed to racial integration, these urban centres did have some integrated schools. Prentice and Houston suggest that the central administration of these common schools, combined with teachers, trustees, and politicians who were committed to racial integration, were important components that permitted and supported integrated schooling.[9]

The voices of individuals who did not gain access to public schools are difficult for the historian to detect. Fortunately, letters written to education officials between 1840 and 1860 provide some indication of the history of black access to education. These letters articulate parents' tenacity and commitment to public education and illuminate the opposition mounted by their prejudiced white neighbours. Despite laws that granted equal citizenship, racism was a component that circumscribed black life in Canada West.

One of the earliest available records of the black struggle for access to education was a petition to Governor General Charles Metcalfe from Hamilton's community. In a letter dated 15 October 1843, these parents protested that although they paid taxes, their children were denied access to local common schools. They had emigrated to Canada to escape racism in the United States believing that "there was not a man to be known by his colour under the British flag." Yet they encountered verbal and physical abuse from their white neighbours. The local police board, whose members were also the public school trustees, refused to protect their access to education. The letter concludes apologetically: "[We are] sorry to annoy you by allowing this thing, but we are grieved much, we are imposed on much, and if it please your excellency to attend to this grievance."[10]

Charles Metcalfe's office responded immediately to this petition. On 19 October 1843, it sought additional information from George Tiffany, president of the Hamilton Board of Police, about the number of black children in Hamilton, the attitudes of whites toward blacks attending the public schools, and requested a summary of police action concerning black education. Tiffany's response confirmed that racism was prevalent in the Hamilton community. He concluded that the Board of Trustees should not yield to prejudice, but "should enforce the law without distinction of colour...a firm stand will eventually destroy prejudice."[11] It appears that these board officials chose to ignore the plight of their black neighbours until queries from Metcalfe's office prompted them to reverse their discriminatory enrolment practices. As a result of their parents' petition, black children gained access to Hamilton's common schools.

Similar circumstances existed in Amherstburg in 1846, but the outcome here was not so favourable. The Reverend Isaac Rice, a white Presbyterian missionary, wrote a letter on behalf of the black citizens of Amherstburg on 23 January 1846. Addressed to the Reverend Alexander McNab, the former acting superintendent of education, the letter complained that black children were barred from the common school by prejudiced whites. These white residents stated that, rather than send their children "to school with niggers, they will cut their children's heads off and throw them in the road side ditch." The letter asserted that Amherstburg's black students, children of tax-paying parents, deserved access to the public school. Nonetheless, the school trustees and white residents falsely claimed that the school was private and barred black students. The white teacher's response to black children was to "turn them out doors."[12]

Egerton Ryerson responded promptly to the concerns of the Amherstburg residents. Before replying, he sought additional information from Robert Peden, Amherstburg's former education superintendent. In a letter of 23 February 1846, Robert Peden concurred with the black residents' assessment of their exclusion from educational opportunities. Peden had attempted unsuccessfully to assuage these black parents by creating a separate school, but they had adamantly rejected segregated education.[13]

Ryerson's response to Amherstburg's black community was sympathetic: "the exclusion of your children from the school was at variance with the letter and spirit of the law, and the ground of exclusion is at variance with the principles and spirit of British institutions, which deprive no human beings of any benefit which they can confer on account of the colour of their skin." Unfortunately the affirmation of black citizens' rights as British citizens was the extent of Ryerson's assistance. He acknowledged the recent election of Amherstburg school trustees and concluded that he "trusts that a sufficient remedy will be provided against the recurrence of the inquiries of which you complain."[14]

Although Egerton Ryerson's written response to the residents of Hamilton and Amherstburg was of little tangible use, he was not wholly insincere in the sympathy that he expressed. Ryerson was committed to educational opportunities for all children, but he was unwilling to jeopardize his burgeoning universal common school program by directly confronting racist opponents to integrated schooling. Instead he opted for an indirect resolution. Recognizing the possible destabilizing effects of attempting to compel local whites to accept integrated schooling, Egerton Ryerson chose to push for legislation aimed at ensuring that all black children had educational opportunities. The School Act of 1850 included a provision for the creation of separate schools for blacks which would permit any group of five black families to ask local trustees to establish a school for their children. Theoretically, this legislation was to provide an option for black parents seeking education for their children, and it was in fact used by some black communities. But racist whites also used it to establish separate schools for blacks who did not want segregated education. In the 1859 School Act, Egerton Ryerson encouraged more active separation by legislating that any "12 or more heads of families, Protestant or Negro, could open their own institutions and receive apportionments from the common school fund."[15] Again, this provision was problematic because white school supporters interpreted it as a legitimate way of barring black youth from local common schools and forcing them to establish their own schools. As a result, many black children were excluded from local common schools, and those who did not have access to separate schools received no education at all.

The School Act of 1850 received mixed reviews from Canada West's black residents. Despite the misuse of the separate school provision by some white school supporters, this legislation was welcomed in several black communities. Separate schools were established in Amherstburg, Chatham, Colchester, and Windsor and these parents embraced the opportunity for their children to learn on their own terms protected from prejudice.[16] Other blacks were passionately opposed to this legislation because it often prevented access to a superior common school, and they believed that such segregation encouraged racism. In the March 1857 edition of the *Provincial Freeman,* black editor H.F. Douglas condemned religious and educational segregation: "Separate schools and churches are nuisances that should be abated as soon as possible, they are dark and hateful relics of Yankee Negrophobia." It is difficult for the historian to determine whether the overall effect of the 1850 School Act was favourable or detrimental to black children. Clearly, the existence of separate schooling remained a contentious issue in Canada West's black community. Nonetheless, it is probable that black advocates, on both sides of the debate, were governed by a belief in the value of education and a commitment to uplifting the black race.

On 12 December 1851, black residents of Simcoe questioned the intent of the 1850 School Act. The community petitioned Egerton Ryerson because their children were denied access to the local common schools. Their letter stated that school trustees and teachers excluded black students even though their parents paid municipal taxes. These parents had "no desire for separate schools" and requested Ryerson's assistance since they had attempted by "every possible means" to gain access to the public schools. They were particularly distressed because their poverty eliminated the prospect of private tutoring: "We are poor and can't provide education for our kids." Aware of the provision for separate schools, the Simcoe residents requested a specific interpretation of the law: did they have the right to attend the public schools with their white neighbours?[17]

Again, Ryerson's response expressed his dismay and sympathy for the Simcoe residents: "I deeply grieve the painful circumstances which you state." He cited the 1850 act to prove that black children enjoyed the same rights and privileges as their white peers unless their parents chose separate schooling. If black parents did not establish separate schools they "have the same right of access for their children as the parent of any other children residing in the section." He advised the Simcoe parents to pursue legal action. He suggested they should sue the school trustees for denying their children the right to education. Egerton Ryerson's final remarks compassionately reaffirmed Simcoe blacks' rights and privileges as British citizens, declaring that it was a "deplorable calamity to be denied access to education...more especially for those who are seeking it...who have been greatly wronged and oppressed in a neighbouring country and who are assured of all the rights and privileges of British subjects in this country, which ought not be infected with the spirit any more than it is cursed with the curse of slavery."[18]

The battle to gain access to public schools in Canada West continued in Camden Township, Kent County. In November 1852 Dennis Hill, a black resident, wrote to Ryerson asking: "Is it presumptuous to expect my eleven year old be educated with whites?" White residents had denied Hill's son access to the public school for "no crime other than skin a few shades darker." Hill sought Ryerson's advice because he "refused to allow his children to grow up in ignorance." He was particularly angry because he had significant landholdings and paid more taxes than most of his white neighbours. Hill was further incensed by white school trustees who barred local black children yet invited white students from other districts to attend the Camden Common School.

Ryerson's response was again supportive in emphasizing his disgust at yet another case of injustice. "It is mean beyond expression as well as unjust for the Trustees and other supporters of the school to levy and receive taxes from you," he wrote, "for the education of their children and then refuse admission to yours." He again cited the 1850 School Act, highlighting black students' fundamental right to public education unless a separate school had been established for their benefit. Ryerson advised Hill to prosecute for damages.[19]

Letters concerning black access to education were not exclusively written by black parents. The provincial education office received several letters from white school supporters who were frustrated by their black neighbours' determined efforts to gain access to Canada West's common schools. In 1856 James Douglas, the school superintendent of West Flamborough, Wentworth County, sought Ryerson's advice on segregated schooling. In his letter he outlined the ongoing racial conflict that threatened the survival of the local common school. West Flamborough school trustees demanded that their public school teacher physically separate black and white students in the classroom. This action provoked the wrath of a black parent who disrupted classroom proceedings in his attempt to eliminate this segregation. Superintendent Douglas summarized the anti-black sentiment that dominated his township: "old Canadian families are unwilling to allow their children to sit promiscuously with Negroes and Mulattos."[20] James Douglas feared that his school would soon close because white parents would withdraw their children unless black students were relegated to a separate area of the classroom.

Discrimination against black students was also the topic of Samuel Atkinson's letter of 29 December 1856 to Ryerson. This school trustee from Malden, Essex County, explained that a separate school established for black students had fallen into disuse, and black parents were seeking admission to the local common school. Atkinson was firmly opposed to integrated schooling. He stated that "a mixed school with them [blacks] at present cannot be had!" Again, school closure would result if black parents persisted in their efforts to gain access to the public school because white parents would refuse to send their children to the school. Certain that the black residents would continue to "push themselves on us," Atkinson advocated the legitimacy of rejecting blacks from public schools. Ryerson responded immediately and succinctly. "The Trustees," he wrote, "are not required by law to admit into the public school the children of persons, whether Roman Catholic or coloured people for whom a separate school has been established. Should the persons for whom a Separate School has been established not keep open the Separate School they do not thereby acquire a right to send their children to the public school."[21] It is probable that Malden's black children received no education following Ryerson's decision that supported their exclusion from the local common school.

The persistence of black citizens in seeking public education was also a source of aggravation for white residents of the township of Harwich, Kent County. In March 1862, Duncan Campbell, a white school trustee, wrote to Ryerson asserting that blacks did not request separate schools because they rarely possessed the funds to maintain these institutions. As a result of the attendance of eight black students in the local common school, fifty white children had been withdrawn because "the white people are determined that they shall not send their children to any school while the coloured people have the privilege of sending their children." Anger at his inability to relegate blacks to a separate school had led him to resign as a school trustee, a position that he had held for ten years. Harwich school trustees corroborated his testimony, stating that their black neighbours had "never contributed to the support of our school as there is not one of them who owns a single foot of land." Legally unable to exclude blacks from the classroom, the

Harwich trustees proposed the construction of a connecting classroom in order to segregate black and white students.[22]

The struggle to gain access to common schools was also seen in Dresden, Kent County. In January 1852 William Newman informed Ryerson, on the behalf of his black neighbours, that he needed clarification of the 1850 Common Schools Act. These black citizens frankly inquired if "the spirit of the law was to aid Blacks or the prejudice against colour?"[23] As Dresden's black children were denied access to the common school, they were forced to attend a separate school seven miles away. Exasperated by the inequity of contributing taxes towards the Dresden Common School, these citizens asked whether "the law was intended to give blacks the same rights as whites?"

An incident in Windsor showed that although Egerton Ryerson was committed to the education of black children, he was resigned to the racism that relegated blacks to separate schools. In February 1859, Clayborn Harris wrote to a barrister, William Horton, on behalf of the blacks in Windsor who sought legal assistance to enable their children to attend the local common school. Confident in their rights and privileges as British subjects, their letter asked: "Shall the Trustees use government money to support a prejudice of one class of Her Majesty's subjects against another?"[24]

All levels of Windsor's educational hierarchy had united to exclude black students from the public school. The local school administration refused to teach or admit these students. The regional superintendent of education stated that he was subordinate to the trustees and "consequently he, too, must reject Black students." These white officials provided blacks with a separate school, described as a "16 by 24 feet coop," in order to satisfy their black neighbours' desire for education. Windsor blacks were adamantly opposed to separate education. They believed that segregated schooling provided inferior education and thus defied British principles of equity and justice. The "idea of us asking for a separate school when it will debar us from all the higher branches of literature," Clayborn Harris wrote, "would be like cutting off our noses to spite our faces... We as a people feel to love British Law and will ever defend it, but we shall equally stand up for all the rights that the law provides for us, otherwise we would be unworthy of the rights that we are guaranteed." Harris concluded his letter to Horton by suggesting that Superintendent Ryerson might provide some valuable assistance. The postscript remarked that black residents of Sandwich encountered similar injustices. Their children were barred from the local common school and forced to attend a separate school four miles from their homes.

In addition to retaining William Horton, the black residents of Windsor wrote to Egerton Ryerson themselves. These parents were willing to abide by the laws of their new homeland, but were angered by the "use of the general Government as a means of fostering for a moment that hydra-headed monster [prejudice] at the cost of any class either on account of complexion or religion." Their letter addressed the fundamental legislative obstacle encountered by blacks pursuing public education after 1850: "Have they [school trustees] power to decide without our request according to Section 19 that the coloured children shall go in a separate school?" William Horton also wrote to Ryerson on the behalf of his clients. He stated that he had advised Windsor's black parents to seek separate education, but that they were either unwilling or unable to accept his suggestion. Unable to advance an alternative, Horton requested Ryerson's advice.[25]

Ryerson came to the point quickly in replying that if no separate school had been established, black children had the right to attend the local common school. It seems that an increased awareness of the strength of local racism led Ryerson to qualify his view: "If however public feeling is very strongly expressed against such a course it may be expedient with the consent of the parties concerned to establish a Separate School under the section quoted by you [section 19], but it is very undesirable that such a prejudice be sustained."[26] In 1862 a separate schoolhouse was constructed for Windsor's black community. Defeated in their attempt to gain access to the local common school, these black parents probably resigned themselves to segregated education.

Petitioning Superintendent Ryerson was clearly not an effective strategy for black parents seeking integrated education. Although Ryerson supported principles of equity and justice for blacks, he reluctantly concluded that "the prejudice and feelings of people are stronger than the law."[27] Perhaps it was the recognition of the education system's inability to overcome white racism that prompted several black parents to pursue legal action. Between 1855 and 1864 four cases concerning black access to public education were resolved in Canada West's civil courts. The justices presiding over these legal disputes acknowledged the prejudice that restricted black children's education. Nonetheless, they were firmly committed to the education of black youth, either through integrated or segregated schooling.

The first case occurred in 1855 when a black man named Washington prosecuted the school trustees of Charlotteville. The plaintiff's son, Solomon Washington, was barred from the local common school, yet there was no separate school in the district. Previously, this child had attended the common school and his father had been assessed and billed for school tax. Mr. Washington continued to pay school taxes despite his son's exclusion from the school. The Charlotteville school trustees defended their actions by stating that Solomon Washington had exhibited poor behaviour when he attended the school. In 1850 two of the school trustees had altered the boundaries of the school district so as to exclude Washington's fifty acres of land, and had instructed the local school teacher to bar Solomon Washington because his attendance promoted conflict and the potential dissolution of the school. These trustees used the new school boundaries to legitimize their expulsion of the black student from school.

John Beverley Robinson, the chief justice of Upper Canada from 1830 to 1862, presided over this case. Robinson's ruling favoured Washington. He declared the case to be a clear example of gerrymandering. He was particularly concerned that, due to the lack of a local separate school, Solomon Washington had been denied access to public education. Robinson's concluding comments acknowledged that the formation of the School Act of 1850 was predicated on an acceptance of racism, but he believed that prejudice should not wholly deny black children their right to education. "The legislation," he found, "does seem to have meant, though reluctantly, to give way so far to any prejudice that may exist in the minds of white inhabitants as to allow the establishment of separate schools for the coloured people, if thought expedient, but not to shut them out from the only public schools that do exist, by leaving it discretionary in the school trustees to deny them arbitrarily, when they have no other school to go to."[28]

Washington's legal triumph over the Charlotteville school trustees was financially debilitating. The defendants possessed no property that could be sold and Washington was forced to sell his farm to pay for legal expenses. *Washington* v. *Trustees of Charlotteville* established a precedent rendering gerrymandering of school districts illegal and unacceptable, especially if there was no proximate separate school.[29] The issue of segregated education surfaced again in *Dennis Hill* v. *The School Trustees of Camden and Zone.* Failing in his attempt to elicit a solution from Ryerson in 1852, Dennis Hill resorted to legal action in 1855. On several occasions he had requested permission to send his two sons to the local common school. The school trustees, both individually and collectively, had refused to admit Hill's sons because they were black. Dennis Hill was particularly distressed because there was no proximate separate school and his children received no public education.

Contrary to Dennis Hill's testimony, the school trustees of Camden alleged that a separate school, located at the British American Institute, had been established for the exclusive benefit of black residents under a bylaw passed in 1850. One of the defendants explicitly stated that the establishment of the separate school was a direct response to the prejudice displayed by white residents.

Chief Justice Robinson's decision favoured the Camden school trustees. He concluded that the "legislature did not intend at that time that separate schools should be resorted to or not according to the choice of the persons in whose behalf they have been established, by which I understand not only the applicants of the school, but those individuals belonging to the class of persons in whose behalf they have been established." In addition to ruling that black children must attend separate schools in their district, Robinson identified the prejudice that supported segregated schooling:

> We are of the opinion that separate schools for coloured people were authorized, as the defendants have suggested, out of deference to the prejudice of the white population, prejudices which the Legislature evidently, from the language they used, disapproved of and regretted and which arise, perhaps not so much from the mere difference of colour, as from the apprehension that the coloured people, many of whom have lately escaped from a state of slavery, may be, in respect to morals and habits, unfortunately worse trained than the white children are in general, and that their children might suffer from the effect of the example.[30]

Robinson's ruling suggests that white racism fuelled the legislation for separate schools. His theory that white prejudice arises not from race but from substandard morals and behaviour exhibited by blacks may have some validity. Certainly, life in Canada West must have been considerably different from slavery in the American South. Many of the blacks in Canada West, however, had not recently escaped plantation slavery. Several writers, including Mary Ann Shadd, Benjamin Drew, Henry Bibb, and Samuel Gridley Howe, stressed the high moral standards and temperance exhibited by blacks. It is most likely that white prejudice stemmed from a variety of sources, including "mere difference of colour."

In 1861 gerrymandering was again at issue in the case of Simmons and the Corporation of the Township of Chatham. Simmons, a black parent, prosecuted the local school trustees who had established a school section according to the presence of black inhabitants. Chatham's School District No. 1 was vaguely defined and fluctuating because it included "every lot or parcel of land occupied, or which shall be occupied by any coloured person in front of the said township." By establishing a separate school in this manner, Chatham school trustees compelled all black residents to attend this school regardless of their proximity to the school. Their exclusionary objectives were addressed in Chief Justice Robinson's ruling. Identifying the trustees' attempt to deny all blacks access to local common schools, Robinson quashed the bylaw responsible for School District No. 1. He concluded that Chatham's school districts were "not intelligibly confined,... uncertain in nature and do not give the school section any limits that can be said to [be] ascertained or known at any point in time."[31]

In 1864, George Stewart, of Sandwich, Essex County, successfully prosecuted local school trustees for refusing to admit his daughter Lively to the local common school. This black parent requested permission to send his child to the common school on several occasions, but his requests were rejected by school trustees because "he and his daughter were coloured people." Despite Lively's exclusion from the school, George Stewart regularly paid school taxes. The Sandwich East school trustees attempted to justify Lively Stewart's exclusion from school by stating that a separate school had been established at the request of local blacks. The trustees also alleged that George Stewart had not been taxed to support the common school. Although a separate school had been established by the Refugee Home Society, financial difficulties had forced its closure in 1861.

Chief Justice William Draper's ruling favouring Stewart was predicated on his belief in the immutability of black children's right to receive public education. He concluded that "coloured people are not to be excluded from the ordinary common schools if there be no separate school established and in operation for their use. The creation of a separate school suspends but does not annul those privileges [conferred by the common school act], and when the separate school ceases to exist the rights revive." Draper awarded Lively Stewart the right to attend the Sandwich East common school, but his judgment recognized the prejudice that motivated the school trustees. "We do not question the sincerity of those who state their apprehension of the consequences of allowing coloured children to enter the common schools," his judgment read, "but this is an argument against the law itself, if it can have any weight. The law does give such a right, subject to certain defined exceptions. The existence of these exceptions is not proved in this case."[32]

Canada West's black community continued to seek access to public schools until the outbreak of the American Civil War. The war launched a massive exodus of blacks back to their homeland. By 1865 approximately three quarters of Canada West's black community had returned to the United States.[33] A desire to renew family ties and friendships, as well as to participate in the civil war and reconstruction, are plausible explanations for their departure. However, white racism in Canada was also a catalyst as William Henry Bradley, a black Dresden resident, accurately and succinctly summarized:

> There is a great deal of prejudice here. Statements have been made that coloured people wished for separate schools; some did ask for them and they have been established, although many coloured people have prayed against them as an infringement of their rights. Still we have more freedom here than in the United States, as far as the government guarantees... There are many respectable coloured people moving in, but I have not much hope of a better state of things. Public sentiment will move a mountain of laws.[34]

The history of black education in mid-nineteenth century Canada West establishes the presence of racism in the formation of Ontario's public education system. Although unpalatable to modern sensibilities, the introduction of segregated education in Canada West seems to have been a reasonable response to blacks who sought educational opportunities for their children and racist whites who opposed integrated schooling. Separate schools gradually fell into disuse during the 1890s, but the 1859 Separate Schools Act remained until 1964. Nonetheless, even today black parents struggle against the more subtle racism in academic curricula and the assessment of student ability. It is likely that the tradition of active concern for educational rights, initiated by black parents in the mid-nineteenth century and currently exhibited by blacks, will continue to influence the development of Ontario's education system.

Notes

1 Quoted in Daniel Hill, *The Freedom Seekers: Blacks in Early Canada* (Agincourt: The Book Society of Canada Limited, 1981), 25.

2 Robin Winks, *The Blacks in Canada* (Montreal: McGill-Queen's University Press, 1980), 142–44. James Walker, *The History of Blacks in Canada* (Quebec: Government Publications, 1980), 55. Alison Prentice and Susan Houston, *Schooling and Scholars in Nineteenth-Century Ontario* (Toronto: University of Toronto Press, 1988), 298.

3 Winks, *Blacks in Canada,* 144, 246.

4 Jason Silverman and Donna Gillie, "Pursuit of Knowledge under Difficulties: Education and the Fugitive Slave in Canada," *Ontario History* 74 (1982), 95. See also Donald G. Simpson, "Negroes in Ontario from Early Times to 1870" (Ph.D. diss, University of Western Ontario, 1971), 26–29.

5 "Address to the Coloured Inhabitants of North America," in Peter C. Ripley, ed., *The Black Abolitionist Papers, Volume II, 1830–1865* (Chapel Hill and London: The University of North Carolina Press, 1986), 173.

6 Prentice and Houston, *Schooling and Scholars,* 299.

7 Bruce Curtis, *Building the Educational State: Canada West, 1836–1871* (London: The Falmer Press, 1988), 13–15. See also 54–56, 102, 115.

8 Prentice and Houston, *Schooling and Scholars,* 299. See Afua Cooper, "Black Women and Work in Nineteenth Century Canada West: Black Woman Teacher Mary Bibb," in Peggy Bristow, ed., *We're Rooted Here and They Can't Pull Us Up* (Toronto: University of Toronto Press, 1994), 144, 155, and Walker, *Blacks in Canada,* 65.

9 Prentice and Houston, *Schooling and Scholars,* 301.

10 Public Archives of Ontario, Incoming General Correspondence 1842–1871 [hereafter RG2 C6C], petition, People of Hamilton to Charles Metcalf, 15 October 1843.

11 Public Archives of Ontario, Outgoing General Correspondence 1842–1860 [hereafter RG2 C1], Robert Murray to George Tiffany, 19 October 1843. RG2 C6C, George Tiffany to Robert Murray, 9 November 1843. Silverman and Gillie, "Pursuit of Knowledge," 99.

12 RG2 C6C, Isaac Rice to Reverend Alexander McNab, 23 January 1846.

13 RG2 C6C, Robert Peden to Egerton Ryerson, 23 February 1846.

14 RG2 C1, Egerton Ryerson to Isaac Rice, 5 March 1846.

15 Winks, *Blacks in Canada,* 368, 370. Simpson, "Negroes in Ontario," 498–500. Cooper, "Black Woman Teacher," 148.

16 Walker, *Blacks in Canada,* 61.

17 RG2 C6C, Coloured Inhabitants of Simcoe County to Egerton Ryerson, 12 December 1851.

18 RG2 C1, Egerton Ryerson to R. Henderson, 17 December 1851.

19 RG2 C6C, Dennis Hill to Egerton Ryerson, 22 November 1852. RG2 C1, Egerton Ryerson to Dennis Hill, 30 November 1852.

20 RG2 C6C, James Douglas to Egerton Ryerson, 3 February 1856.

21 Ibid., Samuel Atkinson to Egerton Ryerson, 29 December 1856. RG2 C1, Egerton Ryerson to Samuel Atkinson, 29 January 1857.

22 RG2 C6C, Duncan Campbell to Egerton Ryerson, 14 March 1862; Harwich School Trustees to Egerton Ryerson, 17 March 1862.

23 Ibid., William Newman to Egerton Ryerson, 13 January 1852.

24 Ibid., Clayborn Harris to William Horton, 15 February 1859.

25 Ibid., Committee for the Coloured People of Windsor to Egerton Ryerson, 2 March 1859; William Horton to Egerton Ryerson, 16 February 1859.

26 RG2 C1, Egerton Ryerson to William Horton, 21 February 1859. Silverman and Gillie, "Pursuit of Knowledge," 103.

27 Quoted in Winks, *Blacks in Canada,* 112.

28 Report of the Cases Decided in the Court of Queen's Bench, Vol. II (Toronto: Harry Rowswell, 1854), *Washington* v. *Charlotteville,* 569–70.

29 Robin Winks, "Negro Education in Ontario and Nova Scotia," *Canadian Historical Review* 50, 175.

30 Court of Queen's Bench, Vol. 11, *Dennis Hill* v. *The School Trustees of Camden and Zone,* 574, 575–78.

31 Ibid., Vol. 21, *In The Matter of Simmons* v. *The Corporation of the Township of Chatham,* 75–79.

32 Ibid., Vol. 22, *Re Stewart* v. *Sandwich East School Trustees,* 636–38.

33 Winks, *Blacks in Canada,* 61.

34 William Henry Bradley, in Benjamin Drew, *A North-Side View of Slavery* (New York: John P. Jeweth, 1856), 312.

Education and Authority

BRIAN MCKILLOP

The occasion was probably Bishop John Strachan's finest hour. The main chamber, the gallery, even the adjacent corridors of the Upper Canadian Legislature in Toronto, abandoned since the union of the Canadas three years earlier, were again crowded with distinguished visitors. For almost all of them it was a singular occasion. Despite their social eminence in Upper Canada, few had ever attended a university function. They were about to do so now, for their presence had been requested at the first convocation of the University of King's College, Toronto.

A contributor to the *Patriot,* a newspaper that supported the Lord Bishop of Toronto, was part of the throng that packed the gallery on that Friday, five days before Christmas, 1844. The scene on the chamber floor below impressed him. "The first object, which met the eye of the spectator," he recorded, "...was the Dais, on which were seated the authorities of the University, attired in full academic costume. In the centre, on an elevated platform, was the Lord Bishop of Toronto, President of the University..."[1] Strachan's place was on the spot where the chancellor of King's College would normally be; but the chancellor of the college was the governor-general of the United Canadas, Sir Charles Metcalfe, and he had another ceremony to attend. The second Parliament of a newly united Canada had opened in Montreal three weeks earlier, on 28 November.

Bishop Strachan had therefore assumed the chancellor's duties as well as his seat. Seated to the left was the vice-president, the Reverend Dr John McCaul. Slightly in front of both were the proctors, the Reverend Dr James Beaven and Professor Henry Croft. So the academic hierarchy continued, with professors in stalls located in front of the dais, graduates on benches immediately behind them, tiers for the students on either side. Altogether, it was most impressive, thought the *Patriot's* reporter. The "coup d'oeil," he concluded, "was most attractive and imposing—on the Dais, the sombre yet ornamental furniture, the blaze of the scarlet and pink and blue worn by some authorities, according to their degrees, beautifully contrasted with the grave black which was the predominant colour."

The convocation itself was not unlike hundreds that had preceded it in the ancient universities of Europe and were to follow it within the boundaries of this British North American province. Degrees were bestowed, academic prizes given, and speeches by university authorities delivered. Still, it was the first such ceremony in the province; many if not all of the guests probably left the old legislative building that December afternoon impressed with the proceedings and secure in the belief that the intellectual and cultural life of Canada West had reached a new plateau. The ceremonies that day may have stirred up pride, but they represented aspiration rather than accomplishment, for King's was a college more by force of will than by actual circumstance. The cornerstone of its one building had been laid only two years earlier, and it had begun to admit students only in 1843. The young men who had presented themselves

Brian McKillop, "Education and Authority," in *Matters of the Mind: The University in Ontario, 1791–1951* (Toronto: University of Toronto Press, for the Ontario Historical Studies Series for the Government of Ontario, 1994) 3–25.

at convocation were a mere nine in number, and they were matriculants, not graduating university students. Six degrees, it is true, had been awarded, but five of them were granted *ad eundem,* because the candidates had previously attended the universities of Aberdeen, Edinburgh, and Dublin. The sixth was a bachelor's degree in arts, awarded to F.W. Barron, principal of Upper Canada College.[2] The recipient of the first of thousands of such degrees in the province that became Ontario graduated without having attended a class at his Alma Mater.

In spite of the pomp of this first granting of academic degrees in Canada West, it was not at all certain that the University of King's College would survive. The fact was that King's was struggling for existence at a time when a new economic and political order was coming into existence. The 1840s would prove to be one of the most important decades of the nineteenth century for British North America, although it could only have been dimly seen as such at the time. Much more than an institution of higher learning was at stake in the struggle over King's College; also in question was the legitimacy of the complex, interconnected web of power and authority that had gradually come into existence after the passage of the Constitutional (or Canada) Act of 1791 and that had reached its apogee with the overwhelming victory of Lieutenant-Governor Francis Bond Head and his Tory supporters in the Upper Canadian election of 1836. Rebellion was one result, triggered in part by sheer frustration at the rigid and self-righteous exclusiveness of those in power as they attempted to maintain authority in the face of changing social and economic circumstances. It came within a year. The arrival of the Earl of Durham to assess the nature and cause of the breakdown of existing constitutional structures was another. He submitted his famous report in 1838. The political union of the Canadas in 1841 was yet a third.

Durham's *Report* heralded a new epoch in the political and economic history of British North America, one that was to witness a remarkable shift in the basis of political, economic, and social authority, and it would do so within the short span of a single decade. On 20 December 1844 the most influential members of the old colonial elite, members of the "Family Compact" all, had attended an academic convocation designed to assure them that education conferred legitimate authority, that the interests of King's College were also their interests and would help perpetuate that authority. Like the mastodons that had once roamed North America at will, they must have believed themselves to be impervious to the changing environment, to be blessed by providence. Yet the next day in Montreal a young Kingston lawyer, John Alexander Macdonald, made one of his first speeches in the Legislature of the United Canadas. Its purpose was to support a "radical" grocer's petition to have two sitting members of the Legislature removed.[3] The man who would later become Canada's first prime minister had assumed his place in politics, and with him a new species of politician not far removed from the status of upstart grocers had come into political prominence. These men of commerce, the heirs of Smith, Durham, and Cobden, dreamt of a political process in harmony with the imperatives of the market-place. One result would be the evaporation of Bishop Strachan's dreams for King's College.

Simcoe and Strachan

Upper Canada's first lieutenant-governor, John Graves Simcoe, had been fond of reminding its inhabitants that while they lived in a new land they were not a new people. They lived in a colony but they were part of an Empire. In numerous ways during his term in the 1790s Simcoe attempted to extend into his newly established province the principles and practices—as he understood them—of the eighteenth-century England he had left. Filtered through his experience defending British interests during the American Revolution more than a decade earlier, and through his repulsion at the spectre of a French Revolution not then ended, that understanding came to sharp focus in his resolve to establish the western province as a pivotal British citadel in an alien American continent. It was his utmost duty, he believed, to "inculcate British Customs, Manners & Principles in the most trivial, as well as serious matters" in order "to assimilate the colony with the parent state."[4]

Simcoe knew first hand that armies and fortifications were not in themselves sufficient to guard against the potential intrusion of the republican institutions and democratic excesses he so abhorred. The source of all authority—whether political, religious, or social—was to reside, in Simcoe's schema, in the island centre of the Empire. Only in this way would Upper Canada become what he hoped it would: the very "image and transcript" of the England in his mind. Education was central to this purpose, and Simcoe voiced these thoughts from the moment he reached Canadian soil, whether to the English naturalist Sir Joseph Banks or to colonial leaders such as Bishop Mountain of Quebec and others.[5] "Liberal education," he wrote to Mountain, "seems to me...to be indispensably necessary; and the completion of it in the establishment of a University...in my apprehension would be most useful to inculcate just principles, habits and manners, into the rising generation; to coalesce the different customs of the various descriptions of settlers, emigrants from the old Provinces of Europe into one form."[6]

To Simcoe higher education and social authority were inextricably linked. They were also central in the mind of John Strachan from the time he arrived in Upper Canada in 1799, three years after Simcoe's departure for England. These were men who shared many assumptions. Strachan was every bit as Scottish as Simcoe was English, yet each nevertheless held dearly to the preservation at all costs of the "balanced" eighteenth-century English constitution—in which, they assumed, the monarchical, aristocratic, and democratic elements in society upheld and stabilized the social order by keeping each other in check. They were therefore vehement in their denunciations of the republican and democratic experiment that was the United States. They were firm in their commitment to the belief that the Constitutional Act made the Church of England the established church of Upper Canada. They were also unwilling to concede, as others had done, that this rigid extension of British institutions into a colonial environment could cause a disjunction of mental expectation and social experience. The secretary of state, Henry Dundas, expressed this when, reacting to the lieutenant-governor's educational plans, he pointed out what to him and others was obvious: "the Country must make the University, and not the University the Country."[7]

Such misgivings stopped neither Simcoe nor Strachan. The former left British North America in 1796 still committed to the notion of a university for the perpetuation and enhancement of the "superior classes," but he had been checked by the scepticism of both colonists and colonial authorities. "In particular," he wrote to Mountain in the year of his departure, "I have no Idea that a University will be established though I am daily confirmed in its necessity."[8] John Strachan directed much of his energy towards the control by the "established"—Anglican—church of the clergy reserves, and the use of Crown lands for educational purposes. In this area, as in most others, his activities marked a direct continuation of Simcoe's aspirations. He was indefatigable in the attempt, for the transition from Simcoe to Strachan was one from enthusiasm to ambition. Strachan, in fact, was one of the few leaders of Upper Canadian society who took an active interest in educational matters, for on only four occasions from 1800 to 1827 were they raised in speeches from the throne, and only two of these (in 1816 and 1827) concerned university affairs. The arrival of Sir Peregrine Maitland as lieutenant-governor in 1818 encouraged Strachan, for Maitland was warm to the idea of a university in Upper Canada. Prompted by Strachan, now arch-deacon of York and president of the board for the general superintendence of education, Maitland in 1825 solicited and received clarification from the Colonial Office that the Upper Canadian Legislature could indeed substitute some of the more valuable Crown reserve lands for existing university tracts, allocated by the Crown in 1797.[9] So impressed was Maitland with Strachan's energy and ideas that he named the arch-deacon as special envoy to confer with Colonial Office authorities in England.

Strachan returned to Upper Canada in 1827 with a Royal Charter for the University of King's College in his hands. He had not always agreed with Colonial Office officials such as Lord Bathurst, and ironically enough it was Strachan who was the man of "advanced views" during the discussions, arguing for a less strong Anglican presence than they had.[10] But by Upper Canadian standards, Strachan's charter for King's College was still strongly Anglican—too strongly for some. No religious tests were to be required of any student, but the president and the professorial members of the governing council were required to be members of the Church of England and to subscribe to the Thirty-Nine Articles. (Non-Anglican professors could therefore teach at King's, but could not participate in college administration.) What was to be administered at this point before King's had either buildings or students? To begin with, there were the 225,944 acres of Crown land set aside for its use. Even before King's existed in any meaningful sense it was therefore already an economic enterprise of no mean importance, and with that importance came political strife. Strachan's difficulties with King's College had scarcely begun. Twenty years later they would still be with him.

Between 1832 and 1851 no fewer than fourteen university bills failed to pass in the legislatures of either Upper Canada or United Canada, and not because their sponsors lacked political acuity.[11] They were drawn up and supported in debate by some of the most successful politicians of the day, including Robert Baldwin, W.H. Draper, and John A. Macdonald. They failed for other reasons, rooted in the tensions and discontentment caused by two diverging conceptions of which social and economic groups should govern. With them also came competing notions about the role of government. Should it primarily be dedicated to ensuring social stability or fostering economic change?

By the 1830s Bishop Strachan had come to epitomize the old order then still in political power in Upper Canada. He had long been insistent, for example, on the necessity of social inequality. For him, it was rooted in the natural order. Different classes of men have different capacities, he proclaimed in numerous sermons of the 1820s and 1830s.[12] As one of Upper Canada's first educators—certainly its foremost—Strachan was able to give his assumptions concrete expression. The early graduates of his Grammar School in Cornwall gradually took their places, as they were intended to do, in positions of power.[13] By the end of the 1830s, although by no means a completely united political group and under considerable pressure by moderate reformers and radicals alike, they nevertheless maintained their hegemony in the upper reaches of power, especially in the Upper Canadian Legislative Council. There the support for projects such as King's College remained unsullied by compromise on the matter of its Anglican nature. Yet people resented Strachan's charter for King's College from the outset, and their objections increased with the passing years.

Citizens from various districts presented more than forty petitions (containing almost five thousand signatures) to the Upper Canadian Assembly within a few months of Strachan's return from England with the King's College Charter in hand. When demands for revision to it were made, however, the initiative came from the Legislative Council, not from Reformers in the Assembly. Following the major victory of the Tories in 1836, led by the recently arrived Francis Bond Head, the Tory faction held a sizeable majority in the Assembly. It was now possible to introduce a limited bill of amendment. When it was passed early in 1837 it had significantly reduced the formal Anglican presence in the administration of the college. For Reform members of the Assembly, such changes were entirely too meagre. King's College still had full control over the Crown lands intended to support the cause of education in the province. Their suspicions that the changes would not affect the actual practice of religious exclusivism were not allayed when the announcement was made of the new officials of King's College. All were members of the Church of England.[14]

The abortive rebellion of 1837–8, as might be expected, strained affairs still further. On the one hand, the rebellion itself confirmed in Strachan's mind the need for proper institutional mechanisms by which to stabilize a shaky social order; on the other, Lord Durham's subsequent *Report* on the causes and implications of the insurrection severely criticized the oligarchical nature of the Family Compact, thereby strengthening the conviction of Reformers that the apparent stranglehold of the Compact needed to be broken. In addition, one further development added to Strachan's unease. In 1836 the Methodists had succeeded in founding the Upper Canada Academy, intended "for the general education of youth, in the various branches of literature and science on Christian principles."[15] By 1838 Strachan well knew that it was only a matter of time before the Methodist leader, Egerton Ryerson, a man every bit as energetic and ambitious as himself, made his case for a university that would meet the needs of his own denomination.

Politics, Sectarianism, and the New Economic Order

Durham's *Report* of 1838 has become well known for its indictment of the hegemony of the old colonial oligarchies, its promotion of the idea of "responsible government," and its argument for the legislative union of Upper and Lower Canada. Yet it was also an eloquent, sustained, and powerful apologia for an economic and social order that by the time of the Canadian rebellions was already beginning to assume definite shape. Published at the very outset of Victoria's reign, it embodied two notions central to the Victorian mind: an optimistic materialism and a firm belief in the progressive beneficence of the unfettered expansion of the market economy. It was, in the words of one historian, a socio-economic vision that "was firmly rooted in the secular world..."[16]

The report began and ended with attention called to the great potential for material prosperity in British North America made possible by its unexploited natural resources.[17] Durham's task, as he elsewhere stated it, was to remove the obstacles preventing Canadians from sharing "in the progressive prosperity of a flourishing State." Accordingly, the best way of securing continued loyalty was to "rectify existing evils, and to produce in their place a well-being which no other dominion could give." Greater population and more capital, Durham said, were the means of bringing this about. Immigration schemes would encourage the former; relaxation of mercantilist restrictions on commerce would help accumulate the latter.

But the crisis of the Canadas was also a crisis of leadership and of authority—a matter, put simply, of who should rule. Durham's criticism of the Upper Canadian governing class was based only in part on his dislike of oligarchy; of more importance was his belief that the Family Compact impeded the degree of economic growth that was possible. "The statute book of the Upper Province abounds," he admitted, "with useful and well-constructed measures of reform, and presents an honourable contrast to that of the Lower Province." Durham had, then, no fundamental quarrel with the legislative record of the pre-rebellion rulers of Upper Canada. His objection was instead with the fact that their monopoly on power and authority had closed the doors of opportunity to a new class of potential leaders who represented the enthusiastic and aggressive spirits of commerce, industry, and general economic self-interest. "As long as personal ambition is inherent in human nature, and as long as the morality of every free and civilized community encourages its aspirations," Durham wrote near the end of his *Report,* "it is one great business of a wise Government to provide for its legitimate development." To this end he quoted one of his philosophical mentors, the great eighteenth century moral philosopher and economic theorist, Adam Smith: "we must provide some scope for what he [Smith] calls 'the importance' of the leading men of the Colony, beyond what he forcibly terms the present 'petty prizes of the paltry rattle of colonial faction.'" It was Durham's fervent hope that by means of legislative union and responsible government new leaders would assume their rightful and necessary place in the corridors of colonial power. The hegemony of the unrestricted self-regulating market economy, not of democracy, was the central element in his solution to the Canadian crisis.

Durham's materialistic and secular vision was a portent of events to come. Within a decade King's College was to be closed, its place taken by a state-sponsored, secular provincial institution, the University of Toronto. Durham had seen the clergy reserves question, and by implication the King's College controversy, as one of the major issues precipitating the Upper Canadian rebellion, but he foresaw no solution to the problem short of leaving the disposal of all such lands completely in the hands of the colonial legislature. The combination of a representative government and a less dominant position of Anglican adherents in Upper Canada (because of non-Anglican British emigration), he thought, would soon make the Church of England recognize the incongruity of "the supremacy thus given to it." The 1842 census of Upper Canada showed a total of 107,791 Anglicans, compared with a combined total of 261,632 Methodists, Presbyterians, Roman Catholics, and Baptists, in Canada West.[18] Yet the conduct of Church of England politicians after the Act of Union came into effect in 1841 was scarcely one of acquiescence or philosophical resignation. Unless they decided to withdraw from politics altogether, they were now confronted with a serious problem in addition to that of the continued opposition of the Reform element: they were deeply divided among themselves.

A first source of division was the very issue of the Union. Many of the old guard—John Beverley Robinson, John Strachan, Henry Sherwood, and others (those strong in defence of King's College)—had bitterly opposed it. Theirs was a politics whose emphasis was on class differentiation, on deference, rather than on the imperatives of the market-place.[19] In their view the levelling implications of a united group of Upper and Lower Canadian reformers in a single legislative assembly outweighed the potential economic advantages of a restored Laurentian trade axis. But other heirs of the "Constitutional Party" of 1836 held different priorities. During the 1840s the advocates of commercial expansion became increasingly vocal within both its leadership and its rank and file. Francis Hincks and John A. Macdonald, both of whom later became premiers of pre-Confederation Canada and whose politics largely were railroads, were two such men who entered the Legislature during the decade.

The man who dominated the new coalition of Conservatives, as they were coming to call themselves, was, however, William Henry Draper. In a very real sense he was a man caught between the shifting allegiances within his political group. Draper was by inclination a supporter of the old Constitution of 1791, a believer in both the established church and the emergent secular state. But as a director of the Bank of Upper Canada he was equally committed to the ongoing expansion of Canadian commerce.[20] As a result he became the spokesman of other men of business who supported the Act of Union. Draper's great political ambition was to foster the development of a political system that preserved conservative social values yet provided incentives to economic advancement. It was not easy, however, to wed social pedigree and economic ambition. Draper found this out when he sought to find a middle ground on the King's College question, now an unresolved issue in Canadian politics for more than a decade.

To the modern student of Canadian history, the political activity of the Union period appears Byzantine in its complexity. Political parties, in the strict sense, did not exist, the principle of ministerial responsibility was a novel theory that had not, in the early 1840s, been conceded, and the issues that dominated the political process were often ones that perplex the secular, twentieth-century mind. To discover that religious concerns shaped Canadian politics in major ways in the 1840s and 1850s is puzzling enough to such students that many avoid the subject altogether. Yet the fact remains that no politician in Canada in the middle years of the nineteenth century could survive in office without addressing religious issues, and without allying, formally or informally, with the major political lobbies of the day: the organized churches. William Draper was not the only Canadian politician who had to negotiate the dangerous shoals of the university question in the Union period. Nor was he the first. Making his difficulties worse, by the early 1840s more than one university existed in Canada West.

The Methodists had not been inactive in promoting their own plans for a college during the years of the King's College controversy. In 1841 they had secured an extension of the charter of Upper Canada Academy, founded at Cobourg in 1836, and the new Victoria College was receiving students within a year of Egerton Ryerson's appointment as its principal.[21] The story of the origins of the new Methodist college provides a capsule case study of the rather complex interaction of personalities, religion, and politics that faced William Draper—and for that matter all other politicians—in the united Canadas. One religious figure dominated the scene: Egerton Ryerson, the voluntarist counterpart to John Strachan.

Along with missions and temperance, education dominated the pages of the *Christian Guardian* in its years after 1829, when Ryerson, the young Anglican-turned-Methodist, became its twenty-six-year-old founding editor. This decision to put the need for non-sectarian general education in the province before his brethren helped generate sufficient debate on the subject that it became a matter of serious concern at the Methodist Conference of 1830. As if to prod delegates further, Ryerson had printed in June a letter from "A Methodist Youth" that demanded to know why nothing was being done to provide education for Methodists in Upper Canada, and, as if to shame his elders, the young man had pledged ten pounds sterling towards such a project. This ploy, as well as other items on education by the *Guardian*'s editor, worked. That autumn, a five-man committee of the conference was appointed to consider establishing an institution of higher education. It was decided that the institution would be governed by a board of nine trustees and five visitors, to be chosen by the conference. Most important of all, the institution was to be based on broad, liberal principles. The committee's declaration stated that "no system of Divinity shall be taught therein; but all students shall be free to embrace and pursue any religious creed, and attend any place of religious worship which their parents or guardians may direct."[22] Altogether, this was a truly extraordinary declaration, given the fierce sectarian loyalties of the day. Later, after the appointment of a committee of nine, the choice of site was made by secret ballot. The lucky location was the Lake Ontario town of Cobourg, chosen from six possibilities including Brockville and York.

By the autumn of 1831, 3,954 pounds sterling had been subscribed, providing sufficient encouragement for the conference to instruct the building committee to proceed with the construction of a brick edifice not to exceed 5,000 pounds in cost. The cornerstone of the academy was duly laid by Dr John Gilchrist, chairman of the building committee, on 7 June 1832, amidst jubilant celebrations. Construction continued through 1832 and early 1833 at a pace that exceeded that of financing the venture.

A bill of incorporation failed to pass in the province's Legislature in 1835, and the next year, with the academy about to open and already deeply in debt, the president of the conference commissioned Ryerson to visit England to petition its government for a royal charter and to seek donations. C.B. Sissons's biography of Ryerson documents at length the initial rebuff he received from Lord Glenelg, the colonial secretary, and his persistent courtship of the under-secretary, Sir George Grey.[23] The visitations and negotiations at Westminster and the canvassing of London and prominent towns took nineteen long months, but when at last Ryerson returned he held the first royal charter ever granted to a non-Anglican institution. He also brought with him a colonial office promise of 4,100 pounds sterling and individual subscriptions amounting to more than 1,200 pounds. Ten of these were promised by the Duchess of Kent, whose daughter Victoria would soon assume the throne of England and provide the successor of UCA with its name.

Ryerson's role in the foundation and early history of UCA was as a general publicist of the cause of education and as a troubleshooter: whatever his other interests and duties, he was always available when needed. Once the academy was opened, under the principalship of Matthew Richey, he played no direct role in its affairs. But he was not to be apart from it for long. Richey was an Irish-born Wesleyan in Canadian Methodist territory, and he soon ran afoul of John and William Ryerson, among others, who feared that the new academy would become unduly Wesleyan in tone. As a result, he received little moral support, was accused of financial mismanagement, and had difficulty retaining staff. By 1838 the coeducational academy was near a state of "hopeless insolvency," and within a year Richey had all but resigned, leaving Jesse Hurlburt, a graduate of Wesleyan University in Connecticut, as acting principal.

For the brief span of a year or two, all was relatively tranquil. Instructors gave classes in chemistry, physics, and astronomy, classics and mathematics, Greek, Hebrew, and rhetoric. Then Acting Principal Hurlburt discovered and began to pursue the future Mrs Hurlburt, in the form of Miss Maria Boulter, the preceptress. The unaccountable but regular absences of both principal and preceptress from daily functions of the college led to laxity of discipline. One student boasted fifty years later that Miss Boulter's own preoccupations had made possible "certain infringements of discipline" on the part of himself and one of the girl students. By 1841 the principal had demonstrated to his staff that he was capable of giving only varying versions of the same public speech, students were open in their disrespect for him, and the call came from members of the academy for Egerton Ryerson to take charge.[24]

Ryerson was officially offered the principalship by the Board of Conference in early September, 1841, although only after the bitter opposition of British Wesleyan delegates such as

Matthew Richey. It was a fortunate, if divisive, decision, for the Church of Scotland in Canada had just obtained legislative approval for the construction of what would become Queen's University at Kingston, and was at the time pressing for a royal charter. Thus stimulated, and perhaps threatened, the conference applied for and secured by unanimous consent of the Legislature an act incorporating "Victoria College" at Cobourg, with the power to grant degrees in several faculties. On 27 August 1841 the statute received royal assent. With it, but not part of it, came a much-needed bonus in the form of an annual grant of five hundred pounds.

Ryerson proved to be a valuable but peripatetic principal of Victoria College. He remained stationed in Toronto, and travelled to Cobourg only when necessary, as when he presided over the opening exercises of the new college in October 1841. He directed his commencement address to the "Gentlemen and young friends" of the college, an indication of the decision (fully supported by Ryerson) that the coeducational experiment had failed and would not continue. Not until the 1870s would women return to Victoria. Instead, Ryerson put forward a conception of the college that was consistent with that of other Victorian liberal arts colleges, dedicated to producing useful Christians, citizens of sound character. "Education," he warned, "is not a license for idleness, but a means of active, honorable and useful enterprise." The object of all education, he asserted, is self-discipline. Time was precious, and should not therefore be squandered: "He that rises at five instead of seven-thirty every morning gains fourteen of the best hours every week for study and devotion."[25]

For the first year Ryerson remained principal *in absentia,* conducting college affairs primarily by correspondence. He was formally inducted to the position in June 1842, at an unpretentious ceremony marked by his "Inaugural Address on the Nature and Advantages of an English and Liberal Education," a speech that took an hour and a half to deliver and that outlined and justified the future curriculum of the college. It was, altogether, a broad and balanced liberal arts program that at once recognized the growing importance of the sciences yet nowhere disparaged the classics. Victoria was to be a college founded on Christian principles, one in which "intellectual and moral powers" would be employed according to the principles of reason and truth. It would educate prospective candidates for the Methodist ministry but would make no formal attempt to ensure the doctrinal orthodoxy of its staff.

Ryerson's lengthy address, a careful pre-Darwinian virtuoso performance balancing the dictates of traditional evangelical piety and the emergence of the Victorian critical intellect, can in retrospect be seen as one of the cardinal documents not only in the history of nineteenth-century higher education in Canada but also of English-Canadian intellectual history. For this reason alone, despite the brevity of his tenure at Victoria College as principal, Ryerson must rank as one of its true "founders." He contrived the structure of Victoria and then gradually withdrew, like the providential watchmaker of William Paley's eighteenth-century natural theology. He gave the new college shape and purpose, but let others establish its place in nature.

Another university opened its doors in 1842, one also provoked into existence by the intransigence of spokesmen for King's College. Championed by the Brockville merchant William Morris, and supported by the recently formed United Presbyterian Synod (of Upper Canada), Queen's College at Kingston received its first charter in 1840 from the Upper Canadian legislature. But when its trustees decided to petition for a royal charter, English legal officers declared that the original legislation was objectionable since the granting of a charter was the direct prerogative of the crown.[26] Accordingly, the original charter was revoked by proclamation and a royal one granted on 16 October 1841.

From the outset, however, Queen's was beset with difficulties. In the first place, it was unsuccessful in obtaining sufficient revenues. It received no legislative endowment of land or money in spite of its supporters' claims that because of its denominational affiliation with the Established Church of Scotland it should split the Crown lands claimed by King's College for its own use. It received meagre support from Scotland, and its first endowment campaign was a very modest success, if that. This was not its only problem. In 1843 the Scottish church was rent by schism based on the question of lay patronage. The controversy soon carried over into the three-year-old Canadian Synod. In Canada the issue became linked by 1844 to the propriety of receiving patronage from any body, including the provincial government. Led by the Reverend Robert Burns in Toronto, the Free Church movement soon divided Queen's College as well as almost all Presbyterian congregations. Six of Queen's seven theology students announced that they intended to join the dissenting body and urged that a Free Church theological college be established. Five of them subsequently left for Toronto and attended classes with nine others in a room in the Reverend Henry Esson's house. That same year the new synod of the Free Church named the institution Knox College. It was to have an even more precarious early existence than did Queen's. Moving from house to house, constantly impoverished, it did not receive a charter until 1858. Instruction in it was to be confined to theology.[27]

Very soon after the Act of Union was declared, advocates of different stances on university reform began to make their positions known to religious adherents and to politicians. By 1842, for example, Principal Liddell of Queen's, supported by William Morris, had tested the possibility of amalgamating Queen's with King's College in order to solve the fledgling Presbyterian university's financial problems. Such an arrangement, Liddell thought, would allow both "established" churches—Anglican and Presbyterian—a roughly equal footing, teaching divinity, within a single "provincial" university. To this end, Liddell quietly sounded out the King's College council, and his proposals for amalgamation reached the governor general and his executive council. Fearing that government support would not be forthcoming unless there was participation by the growing body of Methodists, Liddell also communicated with Egerton Ryerson about the possibility of the Wesleyan Methodists entering the scheme.[28]

The religious community and its newspapers divided on the issue of university reform, as it did on almost every other matter. The King's College council (its voice being the *Patriot*) rejected the notion of union, as did most Anglicans. Ryerson rejected Liddell's suggestion that direct representation be made to the Wesleyan Methodist Conference in order to cement a reform alliance, preferring that the two churches act independently. The Free Church newspaper, the *Banner*, supported reform, if only to "rescue the University from the grasping hand of Prelate STRACHAN." Throughout the middle months of 1843, university reform sentiment increased, as did pressures on legislators.

Francis Hincks considered Robert Baldwin's University Bill, introduced in the Assembly on 12 October 1843, as the most important piece of legislation in the first Parliament of the united Canadas. Under its provisions, King's College would have become a non-sectarian arts college in a "University of Toronto." Queen's, Victoria, and Regiopolis—the last a Roman Catholic institution in Kingston founded by Bishop Alexander Macdonell in 1837—would have retained status as essentially divinity schools, without degree-granting powers and would be relocated in Toronto. They would be granted five hundred pounds per year for four years. The new university would be administered by a board representing various "provincial" interests. No religious tests would be required for staff or students in arts. In the public and legislative debate that followed, the university question vied with the principle of responsible government as the major issue of the day. Indeed, in 1843 the two political phenomena intersected in an important way, for William Draper defended the sanctity of the King's College charter against Baldwin's intrusions by arguing before the Assembly that the erection of universities by the Legislature effectively usurped the Crown's prerogative, as did its interference with the powers of a corporation granted by the Crown. Three days after Draper's lengthy defence of King's and the Crown, Governor General Charles Metcalfe accepted the resignation of Robert Baldwin and all but one member of his executive council.

Baldwin's first attempt at solving the university question had failed. Throughout the 1840s the Tory old guard, especially from Toronto, continued to be adamant in its opposition to any modification to the King's College charter. Others, such as Ogle Gowan of Brockville, William Morris of Perth, and John A. Macdonald of Kingston, were eager to reach some sort of *modus vivendi* on the issue, if only to allow the Assembly to turn to more pressing matters. Macdonald detested the continuing influence of the Compact in political affairs. The "Toronto Clique," as he sometimes called them, was an impediment to his own aching ambition and to that of others like him. As he wrote to Gowan: "I attribute the doubt and hesitation on the part of the Government altogether to the influence of the Family Compact, who cannot abide the promotion or employment of any one beyond their pale..."[29]

Draper tried to wend his way between these fierce antipathies by proposing, on several occasions in 1845, a moderate compromise relating to King's College. His first proposal, submitted to the legislature in March, sought to locate Queen's and Victoria in Toronto, in some vague relationship with a proposed "University of Upper Canada," in which King's College would be the teaching and examining body in arts and science. Proposed payment to the theological colleges was greater than that provided in Baldwin's bill, and unlike it, administration of the new university would be vested in members of the academic community. All students would have been required to belong to the college of their faith. In sum, as historian John S. Moir, has concluded, "the Bill attempted a happy compromise between national and sectarian interests by combining at one time and in one place the advantages of the residential college and centralized university, teaching secular education in a religious setting with state endowments for religious purposes."[30] It fully satisfied no one, although the Presbyterian Church and the Wesleyan Methodists gave their support. Opposition came, on the other hand, from Free Church Presbyterians, Baptists, Congregationalists, the Episcopal Methodists, the Primitive Methodists, and, of course, the Anglican community. By the end of the year, Draper's educational policy was in ruins, and his attempt in 1846 to reintroduce university legislation found little support.[31] The prospect of war with the United States generated by the Oregon Boundary dispute, and the fear of economic collapse as a result of English Prime Minister Robert Peel's repeal of the Corn Laws, understandably deflected public and political attention.

Both Baldwin and Draper, reform and conservative politicians, had failed to find an answer to the university question. Yet others were willing to try. John A. Macdonald was not especially devoted to the cause of university reform, but he did recognize just how emotional and powerful the issue was and feared that the electors, irate over the inability of a Conservative ministry to solve the problem, would register their objections at the polls. "Many questions of more real importance may arise," Macdonald wrote, "but none which operates so strongly on the principles or rather prejudices of the public, and if the Conservatives hope to retain power they must settle it before the General Elections."[32]

Macdonald's proposals took the form of two bills that he introduced in July 1847. The first revoked the amendments made to the King's College Charter in 1837, and gave full control of the college to the Church of England. The second provided for the creation of a board composed of one government appointee and one representative from each of the denominational colleges, whose major responsibility would be to invest and administer funds derived from the university endowment. Queen's, Victoria, and Regiopolis were to receive fifteen hundred pounds yearly, and King's three thousand on the basis of its vested rights. "These proposals," concludes John Moir, "recognized the inherent relation of religion and education, and established the principle of collegiate establishments under the kind of denominational control for which the High Churchmen and Roman Catholics had consistently contended. At the same time it provided an assured income to colleges for whom finances were the prime consideration. Macdonald envisaged nothing more, nor less, than a galaxy of independent denominational colleges scattered across the province, each receiving a modest income from the state."[33]

The non-Anglican denominations who were to be part of the scheme announced publicly their general approval of the scheme. Strachan, the president of King's College, accepted the proposed division of the endowment. Even so, it failed, in part because of the pluralism of the religious community in Canada West. Excluded denominations—the Free Church, the Episcopal Methodists, and the New Connexion Methodists, for example—protested loudly in religious newspapers. The *Globe* of Free-churcher George Brown called for a "flood" of petitions to the legislature, and got it. "Insist that all denominations shall have an equal claim to manage and enjoy the benefits of this great institution," wrote Brown, "and that not one copper of the funds shall be alienated from its original purpose." Speaking for the secularists in the Assembly, Robert Baldwin provided a different denunciation, claiming that the matter had been "settled" only "by sweeping the University from off the face of the earth, and giving the Country, in its stead, a few paltry Institutions, in none of which could there be any possible pretension to those attributes which it was the highest behest to a University to possess."[34] Faced with growing public and legislative opposition, his university bill rejected by all Roman Catholic members of his own party, Macdonald decided not to proceed to second reading with it. He, too, had failed to solve the most divisive and explosive issue of the day. In 1847, at the dawn of the era of responsible government, the university question, not ministerial authority, was the major issue on the hustings.

The accepted premises and practices of Canadian political life had changed a great deal since the beginning of the decade. In 1840 the presence of the Family Compact was a critical factor. Then, the idea of responsible government was simply a theory proposed by William Warren Baldwin and his son Robert, although it had been made a practical possibility by Durham's *Report.* Eight years later it was the sine qua non of political success. The arrival of Lord Elgin in January of 1848 and the election of a new Reform majority led by Robert Baldwin combined to give it constitutional legitimacy.

The triumph of responsible government marked the rise to dominance of the new agents of commercial enterprise, their vision of the future almost wholly a materialistic one. In the turbulent politics of their day, these men of moderate and pragmatic persuasion were drawn into factional alliance and for the most part they remained loyal to their political groups, for their era placed a high premium on loyalty. In truth, none was an unalloyed embodiment, in human form, of any eighteenth-century political "type."

Most were like the young Oliver Mowat, who described himself in 1843 as being "neither Radical nor Tory nor Whig."[35] They were nineteenth-century heirs of both Edmund Burke and Adam Smith, although most had probably read the writings of neither. Philosophically, they were conservative in their general belief in a natural order of social hierarchies and liberal in their acceptance of the market-place as the equally natural fulcrum for social development in the economic realm. They were Canadian lawyers and businessmen in politics.

As such, they were character actors in a political morality play the dynamics of which were rooted in the legitimation of the moral basis of the emerging economic order. Under the practice of responsible government the dispensation of patronage, special privilege, and power was no longer to be under the control of individuals as such: they were, instead, to be distributed by an agency, the secular bourgeois state, acting as the mediator of a system of commercial exchange. The authority of persons had in an important sense been banished. In its place was substituted the authority embodied in the institutional mechanisms of Adam Smith's "unseen hand."[36]

Robert Baldwin's successful University bill of 1849 marked the extension of the secular state into the realm of higher education. The measure brooked no compromise on the matter of secularization. It completely removed any form of denominational presence, except a provision for the possible affiliation of church colleges with the state. The chancellor of the new provincial university was not to be a cleric; there was not to be any faculty or professorship of divinity; no Crown appointees to the senate could hold religious office or be ordained. No degrees in divinity could be conferred, and no form of religious test was to be required of any student or faculty member. As the preamble to the lengthy Bill declared: "it is...necessary that such Institution... should be entirely free, in its government and discipline, from all Denominational bias, so that the just rights and privileges of all may be fully maintained, without offence to the Religious Opinions of any..."[37] As far as the source of its social authority was concerned, the new University of Toronto was very much the "Godless Institution" its King's College opponents said it was.

That authority was now vested in the secular state. The Crown, acting through colonial politicians, was to hold substantial powers of control over the affairs of the university, including control over the old King's College land endowment. The "Governor, or Person administering the Government of this Province," was to be a visitor with powers of commission. The government would appoint a number of "Crown seats" to the senate equal in number "in all time to come" to the number of "college seats." It could disallow any senate statute within two years of its passing. It would have the right to appoint a member of the university's five-man endowment board; the other four would be appointed by the senate. Finally, after consultation with the senate, it would have final authority in the appointment of all professors.[38] Baldwin's University Bill was read in the House of Assembly for the second time on 17 April 1849, and it was passed with a substantial majority. It received royal assent on 30 May. Canada West now had a centralized, state-controlled, completely secular provincial university with three faculties: law, medicine, and arts.

The Demise of King's College

"In destroying King's College by enactment, you have placed yourself in open defiance of God and his revealed word and turned an Institution in which the Saviour was worshipped into a nursery of infidelity and delivered, so far as you are able, the lands of Christ's flock into the hands of his enemy, the Prince of this world." That was Bishop Strachan's reply to Baldwin after the University legislation was passed.[39] The Crown reserves—"the lands of Christ's flock"—were, under Baldwin's successful measure, to be used for the purely secular, satanic purposes of the state and its agents, the "Prince[s] of this world." In educational affairs the division of church and state was gaining substantial ground. The Church of England was now considered a denomination not to be elevated above any other. Accordingly, Strachan fell back on a second line of defence. He would preserve "true religion" in higher education by creating a new denominational college. Within two years his efforts had met with success. The charter of Trinity College, once again secured by a special trip to England, was accepted by the Legislature in August 1851. It was King's College by another name.

Four years earlier, the Methodist newspaper, the *Christian Guardian,* had declared its support for the university bills proposed by John A. Macdonald. Since the bills would have preserved King's College while sharing its endowment with other denominations, the *Guardian* had praised them for their "comparative equality and liberality." "We believe," said its editor, "no reader of the Guardian would wish to have the secular education of his son severed from instruction in the principles and morals of the Christian Religion." The separation of religion and university education, he concluded, was "a monstrous conception" held in the province only by "certain wise-acres..."[40] In 1849 the "wise-acres" had triumphed, and the *Guardian* declared that their plan was "the most objectionable one ever submitted to the country," since it was characterized by "Infidelity." Moreover, said one Methodist leader, its object was simply "to swell up the power and patronage of the Colonial government" by obtaining the old King's College endowment.[41] However precarious their formative years, four church colleges with charters and power to grant degrees nevertheless existed when Baldwin's University bill was passed: King's, Queen's, Victoria, and Regiopolis. Together, they represented a sizeable proportion of the population of Canada West, from different regions in the province, a population clearly convinced that instruction at university should not be divorced from the guiding principles of the Christian religion. It can scarcely be said that the colleges acted as one voice in their objections to Baldwin's university bill, for each had its peculiar needs and strategies for survival. At the same time, their reaction to it reflected some fundamental shared concerns that were to become a leitmotif of much future discussion of university affairs in Ontario.

The basic objection of the colleges was, naturally, to the assumption—now embodied in provincial statute—that the training of minds could and should be divorced from the nurture of spirit. For once, all leaders of the major denominations in the province were in agreement with the words of John Strachan when in a petition he warned: "An institution which drives away all those who from their living faith, warmth of disposition and sincerity of purpose are best qualified to train the young to all that is pure, lovely and sublime in religion, and noble in science, must become the abhorrence of all Christian parents, who can look upon it in no other light than as an infidel college, dead to all sense of religious truth and unworthy of the blessing of Heaven."[42] Such an unequivocal dismissal of religion as the basis of social cohesion and character formation was, for Strachan and his clerical colleagues, a painful affront to their beliefs; but more politically dangerous for them was the centralist nature and implications of the Baldwin measure.

The title of the new university bill contained the words, "to provide for the more satisfactory Government, of the said University." The substitution of state control for that of the church was one means of establishing such "satisfactory" government, for it made efficiency and economy in university affairs easier to monitor. Centralization of provincial university education in Toronto was another. As they viewed the matter, the church colleges now had only two choices: either to continue their separate existences or to seek affiliation with the new University of Toronto. It was not a happy choice. The former promised continuing penury (for they now could expect no support from the government); the latter offered dependence and absorption. Affiliation required the surrender of the power to confer any degree except in divinity. The dubious quid pro quo was that the college would receive only a single vote in a senate of over twenty members who would control the endowment and the expenditure of income from it. In a certain sense the Tories of Toronto had achieved a measure of victory even though King's College ceased to exist, for all its former professors now held seats in the senate of the new University of Toronto. With the Scylla of self-righteous Anglicans on one side of the senate and the Charybdis of government-appointed secularists on the other, how likely was it, thought the denominational college authorities, that their own institutional interests and needs would be met, or even survive? Only Knox College, still without charter and quite content to instruct only in divinity, took immediate advantage of affiliating with the new "Provincial University."

Robert Baldwin left office in 1851, but on the university question he left his successor, businessman and entrepreneur Francis Hincks, his own monsters and whirlpools to contend with. Representing the former was the liberal journalist and politician, George Brown, editor of the Toronto *Globe* and a vociferous voluntarist in religious affairs. Brown and his supporters lobbied strongly for the complete secularization of the clergy reserves; he therefore opposed any form of state aid to church colleges and supported the secular University of Toronto. Representing the latter were the leaders and supporters of the denominational colleges, equally vocal in their swirling denunciations of the 1849 legislation. Faced with such opposition, Baldwin had retreated somewhat from his wholly secular stance. In 1850, confronted with accusations of infidelity from all religious camps, he had successfully proposed an amendment to his 1849 Act requiring the University of Toronto to make adequate provision for the religious instruction of students. In addition, the amendment allowed affiliated colleges to make their students meet college academic requirements before advancing to a degree. But this compromise scarcely met the colleges' objections to Baldwin's act. It merely antagonized Brown.

During the 1852–3 legislative session Francis Hincks put forward his own compromise measure, one that at once gave the university examining and degree-granting powers and stripped it of its teaching functions. The latter were to be given to a newly created non-denominational University College that would share surplus revenues with any denominational colleges choosing to affiliate under the new scheme. It was a proposal not without merit but its single inducement to the church colleges was illusory for, as the historian of Victoria University wrote of the financial clause, "no surplus for distribution was ever permitted to exist."[43] The complex of buildings that eventually arose to house University College cost the extraordinary sum of 95,000 pounds sterling. University College was visible evidence, forever engraved in stone, that independent church colleges would never see any of the old King's College endowment. In the end, Hincks's compromise satisfied few other than the new residents of University College. After seeing a draft of the bill, Brown asserted that "it would be a national calamity to split up and destroy Toronto University for a set of little paltry colleges."[44] Egerton Ryerson concluded, however, that the reorganized University of

Toronto was an institution "defended by nobody, cared for by nobody but its salaried officers and paid students."[45]

Baldwin's University Act of 1849 was now repealed, but in important ways its spirit remained intact. The University of Toronto was more than ever a centralized and secular institution with the full measure of state support, but also vulnerable to the whims of that state, whether leading to neglect or to control. The government-appointed members of the senate had a veto over statutes passed by both senate and the University College council and made all professional and administrative appointments.[46] In addition, the 1853 University Act removed the teaching of law and medicine from university hands and left them to what a later age would call the "private sector." If the intention of the political leaders of the province was to establish the authority of the state in the area of higher education, that aspiration had largely been met by 1853. Control over the provincial university was now firmly established, the sensitive issue of church and state seemingly resolved. Politicians could therefore turn without risk to more pressing and profitable schemes. The provincial university could fend for itself.

Symptomatic of the uncertain future relations between the University of Toronto and its new secular patron were the unsatisfactory circumstances of its location in the days before University College was completed. With priorities separate from those related to higher education, the Hincks government first took possession of the old King's College building in anticipation of the possible location of new parliament buildings on the site. The university, whose secular future had recently been so brightly painted in political rhetoric, was then summarily shunted to an abandoned medical building, recently gutted by the local board of works. The old college building was fitted up as a mental hospital, and was officially named "The University Lunatic Asylum."[47]

Notes

1 Quotations and descriptions on the subject of this convocation are from the *Patriot* (27 Dec. 1844); see also *Patriot* (24 Dec. 1844).

2 *Fasti Academici: Annals of King's College, Toronto* (Toronto 1850), 1–14; *Patriot* (27 Dec. 1844). See also *Patriot* (24 Dec. 1844).

3 *Patriot* (27 Dec. 1844).

4 Quoted in Gerald M. Craig, *Upper Canada: The Formative Years, 1784–1841* (Toronto 1963), 21. See also Ged Martin, "The Simcoes and Their Friends," *OH* 69 (June 1977), 110–12.

5 Simcoe to Banks (8 Jan. 1792), quoted in Marni de Pencier, "The Evolution of the Idea of the University in English-Speaking Canada," PHD thesis, U of T (1974), 134.

6 Simcoe to Mountain (30 Apr. 1795), quoted in E.E. Stewart, "The Role of the Provincial Government in the Development of the Universities of Ontario," EDD thesis, U of T (1970), 20.

7 Quoted in Craig, *Upper Canada,* 39.

8 Simcoe to Mountain (27 Feb. 1796), quoted in E.A. Cruikshank, ed., *The Correspondence of Lieut. Governor John Graves Simcoe, with Allied Documents Relating to His Administration of the Government of Upper Canada* 5 (Toronto 1923–31), Supplement, 264.

9 By 1832 George Markland, secretary to the General Board of Education, could report that 225,944 acres had been "reinvested in the Crown in lieu of scattered Reserves granted as an endowment to the University of King's College..." (Markland to the secretary of Lieutenant-Governor Sir John Colborne [14 Dec. 1832], in J. George Hodgins, ed., *Historical and Other Papers and Documents, Illustrative of Education in Ontario* 1 [Toronto 1911], 32). It should also be noted that during the first two decades of the 19th century Strachan had largely been preoccupied with matters of public education, both as schoolmaster and as educator/politician. See J.D. Purdy, "John Strachan's Educational Policies," *OH* 64 (Mar. 1972), 45–54.

10 Bathurst, against Strachan's strenuous objections, insisted that the presidency of King's College be united with the Archdeaconry of York. See Purdy,

"Strachan's Policies," 55–7; Stewart, "Provincial Government," 31–2.

11 See Hodgins, *Documents* I, 223–24, for a list of these bills.

12 See S.F. Wise, "Sermon Literature and Canadian Intellectual History" and "Upper Canada and the Conservative Tradition," in S.F. Wise, *God's Peculiar Peoples: Essays on Political Culture in Nineteenth-Century Canada,* ed. A.B, McKillop and Paul Romney (Ottawa 1993), 3–18, 169–84.

13 See Terry Cook, "John Beverley Robinson and the Conservative Blueprint for the Upper Canadian Community," *OH* 64 (June 1972), 79–94; S.F. Wise, "The Rise of Christopher Hagerman" and "John Macaulay: Tory for All Seasons," in Wise, *God's Peculiar Peoples,* 61–90.

14 Stewart, "Provincial Government," 57–8.

15 Upper Canada Academy charter quoted in de Pencier, "Idea of the University," 171.

16 William Westfall, *Two Worlds: The Protestant Culture of Nineteenth-Century Ontario* (Montreal/Kingston 1989), passim. On the nature and influence of "optimistic materialism," see Phillip Graham Reynolds, "Race, Nationality and Empire: Aspects of Mid-Victorian Thought, 1852–1872," PHD thesis, Queen's (1978), 17–74.

17 Lord Durham, *The Report of the Earl of Durham, Her Majesty's High Commissioner and Governor-General of British North America.* 3rd ed. (London 1922), 5. The quotations in the next few paragraphs are drawn from this *Report* at 136, 193–4, 202, 109–10, 231.

18 Regarding the availability and nature of pre-Confederation statistics relating to denominational affiliation in Upper Canada, information was recorded only in the years 1842, 1849, 1851–2, and 1861–2. These data are found in *Censuses of Canada, 1665 to 1871. Statistics of Canada* (Ottawa 1976), 135. The standard modern source of Canadian historical statistics, M.C. Urquhart and K.A.H. Buckley, eds., *Historical Statistics of Canada* (Toronto 1965), partly because of the paucity of the statistical record, is inadequate in this respect. It includes only two brief tables relating to any aspect of religion in Canada (and for any period), and neither makes any attempt to discriminate by region. The category "Sheep and Lambs" is bleatingly fulsome by comparison and regional breakdowns of the woolly population are happily provided.

19 The conclusion should not be drawn, however, that members of the Compact were not engaged in business ventures. They were, but they tended to speculate in land (as befits aspiring aristocrats). See David Gagan, "Property and 'Interest': Some Preliminary Evidence of Land Speculation by the 'Family Compact' in Upper Canada," *OH* 70 (Mar. 1978), 63–70: H. Pearson Gundy, "The Family Compact at Work: The Second Heir and Devisee Commission of Upper Canada, 1805–1841," *OH* 66 (Sept. 1974), 129–46; Leo A. Johnson, "Land Policy, Population Growth and Social Structure in the Home District, 1793–1851," *OH* 63 (Mar. 1971), 41–60; J.K. Johnson. "The U.C. Club and the Upper Canadian Elite, 1837–1840," *OH* 69 (Sept. 1977), 151–68. Johnson's article shows the existence by the late 1830s of "overlapping elites" making their fortunes both from land and from trade. It argues that by then members of the Compact were coming to share a "developmental" economic vision. This suggests that the old Upper Canadian oligarchy was not vanquished by Mackenzie's attacks but was instead absorbed and transmogrified by Cobden's commercial vision.

20 See George Metcalf, "William Henry Draper," in J.M.S. Careless, ed., *The Pre-Confederation Premiers: Ontario Government Leaders, 1841–1867* (Toronto 1980), 32–7.

21 D.C. Masters, *Protestant Church Colleges in Canada: A History* (Toronto 1966), 30–1; C.B. Sissons, *A History of Victoria University* (Toronto 1952), 22–37.

22 C.B. Sissons, *Egerton Ryerson: His Life and Letters* I (Toronto 1937), 122.

23 Ibid., 274–311.

24 Sissons, *Victoria,* 33–5.

25 Quoted in Sissons, *Ryerson* 2 (Toronto 1947), 11, 17.

26 This was curious logic, since the charter granted by the Legislature of Upper Canada had necessarily received royal assent. According to Hilda Neatby, the rationale of the legal authorities of the Crown was: "First, the colonial legislature could not... incorporate a university, that being a prerogative of the Crown. Second, this irregular act having received royal assent through the governor general, the Crown could not gainsay itself by issuing a charter to amend its own act" (Hilda Neatby, *Queen's University,* vol. I, *1841–1917: And Not to Yield,* ed. Frederick W. Gibson and Roger Graham [Montreal/Kingston 1978], 27).

27 Masters, *Protestant Colleges,* 44–5; Neatby, *Queen's,* 43–8.

28 On the university reform issue see John S. Moir, *Church and State in Canada West: Three Studies in* *the Relation of Denominationalism and Nationalism, 1841–1867* (Toronto 1959), 85–98.

29 Macdonald to Ogle Gowan (30 Apr. 1847), in Frederick H. Armstrong, "The Macdonald-Gowan Letters, 1847," *OH* 63 (Mar. 1971), 6, emphasis in original.

30 Armstrong, "Letters," 92.

31 Metcalf, "Draper," 57–9; Moir, *Church and State,* 93–5.

32 Quoted in Moir, *Church and State,* 96; see also Macdonald to Gowan (3 Nov. 1847), in Armstrong, "Letters," 12.

33 Moir, *Church and State,* 97.

34 Brown and Baldwin quoted in ibid., 97–8.

35 Oliver Mowat to John Mowat (8 Dec. 1843), in Peter Neary, ed., " 'Neither Radical Nor Tory Nor Whig': Letters by Oliver Mowat to John Mowat, 1843–1846," *OH* 71 (June 1979), 100.

36 See Richard Sennett, *Authority* (New York 1980), 43–4; Reg Whitaker, "Images of the State," in Leo Panitch, ed., *The Canadian State: Political Economy and Political Power* (Toronto 1977), 34–43.

37 Hodgins, *Documents* I, 254.

38 Ibid., 253–61.

39 Quoted in R.M. and Janet Baldwin, *The Baldwins and the Great Experiment* (Don Mills 1969), 188.

40 Quoted in Goldwin S. French, *Parsons and Politics: The Role of the Wesleyan Methodists in Upper Canada and the Maritimes from 1850 to 1855* (Toronto 1962), 260.

41 Ibid., 267.

42 Quoted in Nathanael Burwash, *The History of Victoria College* (Toronto 1927), 516.

43 Sissons, *Victoria,* 93.

44 Quoted in William Ormsby, "Sir Francis Hincks," in Careless, ed., *Pre-Confederation Premiers,* 175.

45 Quoted in Stewart, "Provincial Government," 123.

46 See the text of the 1853 act in Hodgins, *Documents* I, 300–14.

47 John Langton, *Early Days in Upper Canada: Letters of John Langton from the Backwoods of Upper Canada and the Audit Office of the Province of Canada,* ed. W.A. Langton (Toronto 1926), 281–2.

Dimensions of Paternalism

Discipline and Culture in Canadian Railway Operations in the 1850s*

PAUL CRAVEN AND TOM TRAVES

Canada's economic historians have said a good deal about the rapid expansion of the colony's railway system in the 1850s—the mere 66 miles of track at the beginning of the decade grew to more than 2,000 by its close—but they have virtually ignored the corresponding growth of the railway workforce.[1] Yet this was the decade in which the railways became the country's first large-scale integrated industry and the giants among them became the country's greatest employers of labour. By the middle of the decade, the Grand Trunk, with its 2,600 workers on trains, in yards, shops, offices, warehouses and stations, and along the line of railway, was Canada's largest employer with a monthly payroll of $110,000. In second place was the Great Western (GWR), with a payroll about one-quarter the size of the Grand Trunk's (GTR).[2]

Railway work comprised many types of jobs. Train crews consisted of enginemen, firemen, conductors, and brakemen, with one or more baggagemen as well in the passenger service.[3] Cleaners, pumpers, woodmen, yardmen, and switchmen were involved in servicing and fuelling the locomotive, making up the train, and switching onto sidings to permit two-way traffic on the single-track railways of the time. Gangs of labourers worked under the direction of the engineering staff to maintain the track and roadbed and to clear ice and snow in the wintertime. Labour was required at stations for baggage and freight handling under the supervision of the stationmaster, who sold tickets, made out way-bills and receipts, and operated the telegraph at the smaller depots; at the bigger ones he would be assisted by clerks and operators. Passengers and employees alike passed under the watchful eye of the railway police force, whose members worked undercover on occasion to trip up defaulting agents or dishonest conductors.

Company headquarters boasted large central office staffs organized in various departments, overseeing operations and maintaining accounts. By 1861, the Grand Trunk's 223 locomotives travelled a third of a million miles each month; the smaller Great Western used 94 locomotives to travel 1.8 million miles in 1861, transporting half a million tons of freight and more than half a million passengers. This required a large amount of clerical labour, not only because of the sheer volume of business that had to be recorded, checked, and cross-referenced, but also because of the primitive techniques available for the purpose.[4]

Paul Craven and Tom Traves, "Dimensions of Paternalism: Discipline and Culture in Canadian Railway Operations in the 1850s," in Craig Heron and Robert Storey, eds., *On the Job: Confronting the Labour Process in Canada* (Montreal: McGill-Queen's University Press, 1986), 47–74.

*Research for this paper, and for the larger Canadian Railways Industrial Relations History Project of which it forms a part, has had the generous support of the Social Sciences and Humanities Research Council of Canada. At various times this project has benefited from the research assistance of Rose Hutchens, David Sobel, Lynne Brenegan, and Robert Nahuet.

But the railway companies were more than high-volume transportation companies. They also operated the country's largest and most complex manufacturing facilities. By 1857, the Grand Trunk and the Great Western, along with some of the smaller railways, possessed the capacity to build as well as repair their thousands of cars. By the end of the decade, they had upgraded their engine-repair facilities so that they could build locomotives as well. The same shops produced much of the hardware and machinery required for other aspects of the railway's operations: castings for bridges, say, or machinery for grain elevators. A large and diversely skilled work force was necessary for the shops. Thus by 1857, the Great Western's locomotive and car shops at Hamilton, Ontario, employed about 600 tradesmen and labourers, along with about 125 more in London, Ontario.[5]

Managerial control of the work process in this new industry was, from the start, a prime objective of the investors and officers who directed the companies. Complex organizational structures were established almost from the outset of rail operations. While these were intended in the first instance to co-ordinate multifarious operations and help control costs, they inevitably involved the institution of fairly sophisticated supervisory techniques. The general principles underlying railway organization included a careful division of responsibilities and the distribution of authority along with complex reporting procedures and swift discipline for all derelictions of duty.[6] Railway companies required much of their workers by way of loyalty, obedience, and care. Generally speaking, discipline—the habituation of the worker to the new mode of production—is a pervasive problem of industrialization. But for at least three related reasons, the problem of discipline assumed a special urgency on the railways.

First was safety, an anxious concern not only because of the inexperience or recklessness of workers, but also because of the inadequacies of the companies' equipment. Accidents caused injuries, deaths, lawsuits, and unplanned capital expenditure, so the railway companies, as well as the government, were keen to reduce their frequency. Second was the special significance of the clock in railway operations, where effective scheduling was necessary not only to avoid accidents but to meet the competition of other lines, make the necessary connections in a proliferating network of traffic and timetable agreements, and reduce the impact of heavy, fixed expenses by operating the company's equipment at optimal levels of efficiency. Finally, the problem of discipline was exacerbated by the spatial dispersion of the work force and by the fact that many of those whose work it was most crucial to regulate closely were beyond the reach of direct supervision.

Structural factors and self-conscious managerial policies conditioned the railway companies' attempts to regulate and discipline their employees. At its most immediate and overt level, discipline amounted to the enforcement of company rules, backed up by the authority of the state. But punitive measures must be placed in the broader context of a second level of discipline inherent in the conditions of working life—job hierarchies, pay structures, opportunities for advancement—that played their part in regulating workers' behaviour, and on labour-market conditions that placed structural limits on managerial autocracy as well. Finally a third, still broader, context of discipline requires discussion: the emergent culture of the railways' skilled workers, who reacted to managerial paternalism with a complex blend of deference and resistance.

Punitive Discipline

> The driver is, in fact, while his train is in motion, the sole, and almost the irresponsible Arbiter of the fate of all those entrusted to his care. It is most important...to teach this class of men, that they cannot always elude responsibility and punishment.[7]

The most explicit manifestations of management's effort to discipline the work force were the elaborate rule books that employees were required to carry with them at all times, on pain of a fine to be deducted from their wages. These rules were something more than the mere domestic regulations of private companies: they could be enforced judicially by the state. By their private acts of incorporation (and, after 1851, by the Railway Clauses Consolidation Act[8]), railway companies, like other corporations, were empowered to make regulations for the appointment and direction of their employees. Unlike most other corporations, however, they could look to the public courts to have these rules enforced. For example, the Great Western's revised Act of 1853 provided that fines levied by the company in accordance with its by-laws could be collected, "upon proof of the offence," by process before a justice of the peace, with the power to seize and sell property, or, failing sufficient goods to pay the penalty and expenses, by imprisonment not exceeding one month.[9] The Act for the Punishment of the Officers and Servants of Railway Companies, passed in 1856 following the report of a legislative inquiry into Great Western accidents, empowered magistrates to fine employees up to $100, and to imprison them for up to five years if, by their breach of company rules, they had put persons or property at risk. Otherwise, they could be fined one month's pay by the court, and the employer could dock a second month's pay.[10]

Indeed, not satisfied with these methods of publicly enforcing private laws, the legislature also supplied rules and regulations of its own making. The Railway Clauses Consolidation Act required, among other things, that railway servants wear badges indicating their office, made it a misdemeanour for conductors or enginemen to be drunk on duty, and provided penalties for conductors who permitted freight cars to be coupled in rear of passenger coaches, and for enginemen who failed to ring a bell or sound a whistle at level crossings.[11] The rule books themselves varied in length, from the Montreal & Champlain Railroad's two printed columns to the forty-four-page version published by the Great Western in 1854; but whatever the peculiarities of procedures on the various roads, they all prescribed much the same set of general regulations. The Grand Trunk's version is typical:

> Each person is to devote himself exclusively to the Company's service, attending during the regulated hours of the day and residing wherever he may be required. He is to obey promptly all instructions he may receive from persons placed in authority over him and conform to all regulations of the Company. He will be liable to criminal punishment for disobediences or negligence of an order, and dismissal for misconduct, incompetency, using improper language, cursing or swearing while on duty. He is not on any occasion to receive a fee or reward from any person without the sanction of the Company. No instance of intoxication will be overlooked; and besides dismissal, the offender shall be deemed guilty of a misdemeanor. Any case of rudeness or incivility to passengers will meet with instant dismissal. Every person must appear on duty clean and neat. No person is allowed under any circumstances to absent himself from duty, without the permission of his superior officer, except in case of illness, and then notice is to be immediately sent to his immediate superior officer. No person is to quit the Company's service without fourteen days previous notice; and in case he leaves without such notice, all pay then due will be forfeited. The Company reserves the right to deduct from the pay such sums as may be awarded for neglect of duty as fines and for rent due to the Company. Should any person think himself aggrieved he may memorialize the Board, but the memorial must be sent through the head of his department.[12]

These general rules were followed by descriptions of signals and other operating features of the line, and then by detailed regulations for different groups of workers. In 1854, for example, the Great Western listed 38 rules for enginemen, 22 for conductors, 27 for track-repair crews, 20 for stationmasters, and shorter codes for baggagemen, brakemen, porters, gravel-train conductors, drawbridge tenders, switchmen, and signalmen. Clerks were covered by a separate code in 1854, and telegraph operators got a rule book of their own in 1857.[13]

Of course, it is one thing to publish rules, and quite another to enforce them. There is some evidence that rules were not always routinely applied. Punishment seemed, at least on occasion, to vary less with the responsibility of the transgressor than with the difficulty of replacing him were he to be dismissed. In one instance, when an accident was blamed on the combined negligence of a conductor, a stationmaster and a porter, the conductor was suspended for ten days, the stationmaster fined a week's pay, and the porter fired. "The punishments and penalties employed on a railroad should, as for the discipline of all other large bodies of men, be clearly defined and invariable," the commissioners on GWR accidents urged. "As the matter now stands, they are arbitrary, uncertain, partial and ineffective. The man who is suspended for a fortnight or mulcted of a week's pay, may, if he is a favourite at head quarters, have all his arrears made good at the end of the month. The dismissed man is the only man who is really punished."[14]

However unevenly, though, discipline *was* enforced. Intoxication or negligence resulting in accidents usually led to dismissal, even in the face of petitions for mercy signed by fellow workers or local residents. [15] Dismissal was also meted out for "repeated absence and other irregularities," and, in another instance, for "grossly offensive language...addressed to the Vice President."[16] The threat of dismissal was also employed frequently, as when the Great Western's Finance Committee warned a clerk that it "would insist at all times on obedience to its orders, unless the parties disobeying were prepared to back up their disobedience...by the resignation of their situation."[17] Nor were the railway companies reluctant to go to the public authorities to have their rules enforced. To take a single example among several to be found in the police-court columns of local newspapers, the Great Western brought a complaint against the engineman on one of its gravel trains for disobeying orders and running his locomotive on the main line when a freight train was due. The magistrates sentenced him to pay a £4 fine or spend a month in jail.[18]

But using the courts to enforce discipline was not without its difficulties. Jurors were often unwilling to convict workers, who may have been their neighbours, and they exhibited an unfortunate tendency to blame the company itself when accidents could be traced to defective equipment. Great Western managing director Brydges complained to the accident commission about what transpired when he laid manslaughter charges against a section-gang foreman to whose alleged carelessness and disobedience an accident had been attributed: "He was tried and acquitted [by the jury] in the face of a very strong charge against him by Chief Justice Robinson." The commissioners subsequently recommended that "all cases affecting such Companies...should be removed to the jurisdiction of tribunals remote from the operation of local or personal influences."[19] But perhaps the greatest difficulty in prosecuting serious charges was simply laying hands on the miscreants. Switchmen in particular learned early to head for the hills—or the United States—whenever anything untoward happened in their bailiwicks.[20] In at least one such case, the Great Western offered a thousand-dollar reward for the apprehension of a conductor who had taken flight following a serious accident. The directors' zeal may have been especially aroused, though, by the fact that warrants had been sworn against each of them charging personal criminal responsibility for the accident.[21]

Needless to say, lesser penalties than dismissal and the laying of criminal charges were commonplace. The Great Western's outside locomotive paysheets show, for example, that three of the company's forty-eight enginemen were stopped fines ranging from 10*s.* to 12*s.* 6*d.* ($2–2.50) in October 1855.[22] The rule books made extensive provisions for the levying of fines. A Great Western engineman could lose a day's pay for failing to arrive at work at least one hour before his starting time, was subject to a "heavy" fine or dismissal for permitting unauthorized persons to ride on the engine, and could be docked one dollar for "getting off his Engine when alone to hold the Switches." Besides these strictures, peculiar to his occupation, he was also subject to the general rule that punishment could be expected for disobedience, neglect of duties, incompetence, negligence, misconduct, intoxication, swearing, smoking, incivility, rudeness, absence, and failure to keep a copy of the timetable and the rule book on his person.[23]

Hierarchy and Mobility

It would be a mistake to conclude that such overt instruments of discipline as rules and punishments were the only, or even the most important, mechanisms for optimizing the loyalty, obedience, and care of the railway work force. Disciplinary consequences could also flow from the conditions of railway employment itself. Railway workers were relatively well paid by mid-nineteenth-century standards. More important, theirs were steady, year-round jobs in what was very much a seasonal economy. While skilled railway workers in the shops and running trades were more likely to keep their jobs in periods of declining revenues or seasonal slumps in traffic than less-skilled labourers in station service and maintenance of way, railway workers in general enjoyed substantially greater regularity of employment than workers with similar levels of skill in the larger economy.[24] Some of the dimensions of and reasons for this distinction will be explored in the next section; here it is enough to note that for many railway workers the prospect of regular employment must have supplied a powerful incentive to good behaviour.

Indeed, many of the conditions of railway employment could be seen in a double light, as meeting some impersonal objective need, and as contributing toward employee discipline. This was true, for example, of company housing, for as a Great Western foreman put it, workers "should be provided with comfortable dwellings so as to keep a man near his work; and to make him feel that he has something to lose if he does wrong."[25] Railway managers' efforts to promote a sense of corporate identification included the provision of uniforms and the promotion or support of such early industrial welfare initiatives as insurance plans and company social gatherings. But the disciplinary core of the railways' paternalistic labour practices was the detailed reproduction of job hierarchies and the promise of career mobility. Workers were expected to be loyal, not merely to avoid discipline, or to keep good jobs, or even to show themselves deserving of promotion to better ones. Workers were expected to be loyal because it was in the nature of the hierarchical relations they and their employers took for granted; and workers could expect to be rewarded for their loyalty for the same reason.

In fact, there was not a single job hierarchy on the railways, but several. One reasonable indicator of a job's relative ranking is pay. While really adequate longitudinal data are lacking, good information on particular groups of workers at various moments in the decade is available. It points up the great diversity of railway work and the coexistence of various pay structures:

piecework, trip rates, day rates, and weekly, monthly, and yearly salaries. In terms of pay at least, this diversity is reducible to a series of distinct hierarchies existing roughly in parallel, representing occupational grades through which mobility occurred. The pay structure shows railway work to have been organized as a series of discrete ladders, each with a relatively small number of rungs. In the minds of those involved, however, the ranking scheme may have been far more finely detailed, so that the number of rungs increased manyfold: was it a step up to go from cleaning a freight locomotive to a passenger engine, even with no change in pay? Whose heart sank and whose spirits rose when, in December 1857, the Great Western moved agent Shaw from Waterdown to Wellington Square, and agent Parsons from Wellington Square to Waterdown? Whatever the specific answers to these questions might be, there seems little doubt that railway workers possessed an elaborate conceptual map of job strata that is only crudely represented in the pay figures.

There is a rich source of information about the Great Western shopcrafts in a series of manuscript paysheets covering most of 1854 and 1855, and comparable data for the Grand Trunk shops in 1859.[26] [...] With the exception of some of the Great Western bolt makers, who were on piecework, all the shop workers were paid by the day. Two features of the Great Western paysheets suggest that the organization of work more closely resembled the industrial than the artisanal model. First, the car-shop work force included a large and undifferentiated group of workers, the car builders, who accounted for almost half the total employment in the shop. While their pay varied, more than half received a single rate, $1.75 a day. Second, the range of pay *within* occupational groups may indicate something about the organization of work. In most categories of employment, the majority of workers received similar rates of pay, with one or two being paid at noticeably higher rates, and perhaps a few at significantly lower ones. This seems to suggest organization on a "lead hand" basis, as much in the traditional crafts (blacksmiths, for example) as in the relatively unskilled occupations (examiner, labourer). Nonetheless, these data quite clearly indicate the existence of a hierarchy of craft in the shops, and the insertion of new occupations into the pay structure.

Similar information is available for the Great Western's "outside locomotive" work force, comprising enginemen, firemen, engine turners (hostlers), and labourers engaged to clean locomotives, cut and store wood, and pump water. With some minor exceptions, outside labourers received $1 a day in 1854–5. A few enginemen were paid monthly ($50–$60), but the majority were paid by a combination of trip and day rates. In June 1854, enginemen received $2.25 or $2.50 per trip (amounting to a day's work), and 33 or 38 cents for every additional hour they were detained on the line. Their standard day rate for work in the engine sheds was $2. Firemen received half the enginemen's rate, but without the detention allowance: a few were paid by the month at $30. Firemen could consider themselves enginemen in training, and when they were called upon to drive, they received the engineman's trip rate. Both groups were reimbursed for the cost of lodgings. Finally, engine turners were paid by the month, $45 at Hamilton and $40 at the other depots. The railway's managing director estimated that enginemen averaged $70 "more or less" a month, and firemen $30–$40, but the paysheet evidence suggests this estimate was high.[27]

Conductors, baggagemen, and brakemen, employed by the railways' traffic departments, constituted a separate occupational hierarchy in their own right. In December 1856, the Grand Trunk employed 49 conductors at monthly salaries ranging between $40 and $60, 20 baggagemen at $30–35, and 78 brakemen at $30–32. The Great Western paid similar rates.[28] The traffic departments also included employees at stations. In December 1856, the Grand Trunk's 112 station and freight agents received yearly salaries ranging from £25 to £350. The Great Western's 39 stationmasters made between £90 and £200. Salaries varied with the importance of the station; the men in charge of the terminal depots earned the most. Agents at the larger stations were assisted by additional clerical workers, who possessed numerous special titles—first clerk, ticket clerk, lost-baggage clerk, freight clerk—and who in some cases supplemented their incomes by serving as telegraph operators as well. Clerks made between £50 and £150, so that their earnings were in many cases greater than those of agents at the smaller stations.[29]

Clerical salaries in the railways' head offices were similar to those on the line. For example, in 1857 the Grand Trunk's audit department employed an inspector and chief clerk at £200 each, two freight officers at £175 each, a ticket printer at £160, six passenger clerks with salaries ranging between £50 and £150, three freight clerks at £50, £70, and £100, and an assistant printer and a boy, each making £30.[30] [...]

Occupational mobility often required *geographic* mobility as well. As one GTR manager reminisced, railway officers were like Methodist preachers—they were movers.[31] Railway records are filled with instances of job transfers, especially in the salaried occupations. In many cases, though, it is impossible to know whether people were being moved up, down, or sideways.[32] All the same, many employees moved with a purpose: consider the case of John Porteous, who "in all his movements had one object in view, and that was to make a *step higher*!"

> In October, 1854, he joined the Great Western Railway at Hamilton, Ont., as billing and corresponding clerk in the freight department; six months afterwards he was doing the same kind of duty at Suspension Bridge. In 1855 he was corresponding clerk at Windsor, then promoted to the position of freight cashier and accountant at the same station. In November, 1857, his health giving way, he resigned and left for Scotland, but returned to Canada in July, the following year, when Mr. Brydges appointed him cashier and accountant of the Detroit, Grand Haven & Milwaukee Railroad at Milwaukee, Wis. In 1863 he removed to Portland, Me., to hold a similar office on the Grand Trunk Railway there. On the death of Mr. Graham, the Portland agent, in November of that year, Mr. Porteous succeeded him as freight agent at that important depot. In this position he remained until April, 1876, when Mr. (now Sir Joseph) Hickson sent him to England to establish the Grand Trunk agency at Liverpool. On Mr. Porteous' return to Montreal he was appointed assistant general freight agent of the G.T.R. on January 1st, 1877, and when the late Mr. P.S. Stevenson resigned the general freight agency, on account of sickness, Mr. Porteous succeeded him on July 1st, 1878, being the fourth G.F.A. since the opening of the line. This position he held until December, 1886, when he resigned to accept that of general manager of the through freight department of the Central Vermont Railroad, with headquarters at Boston... On the first of February, 1892, Mr. Porteous was again further promoted to the general managership of the National Despatch Freight Line, with office at Boston, which position he still retains.[33]

Mr Porteous's brilliant career is interesting for several reasons. We pass no comment on the happy accidents of sickness and death that made for its advancement at crucial stages. But note how narrowly constricted was the chain of opportunity that took him so far. Porteous's career path barely took him out of the freight office. And this, it seems, was typical of railway careers: firemen might become enginemen, brakemen could become conductors; junior clerks aspired to become station agents or better; and shop workers might become lead hands, foremen, or, albeit rarely, locomotive or car superintendents, but the lines *between* the occupational grades were infrequently crossed.[34]

Recruitment and Retention

The material basis for railway company paternalism was the scarcity of skilled labour and the companies' urgent desire to protect their heavy investment in recruitment and training. Particularly (although by no means exclusively) in the 1850s, with the start-up of operations on an unprecedented scale, railway companies were faced with the task of recruiting large numbers of specialized personnel whose required skills were usually scarce to the point of non-existence in the local labour market.

The Grand Trunk addressed this problem by hiring the bulk of its original work force in Britain, through the agency of its contractors, Messrs Peto, Brassey, Betts, and Jackson. It is not known just how many of the 4,000 masons, carpenters, quarrymen, enginemen, fitters, and other skilled tradesmen (as well as "large drafts" of navvies, or unskilled construction labourers) who contracted to come to Canada on five-year engagements in the spring of 1854 actually arrived and set to work in building the line. Nor is it certain how many of them remained to operate the road once construction was complete; the likelihood is that many did. The Grand Trunk also recruited all its senior operating officials in Britain, initially on five-year contracts.[35]

The recruitment practices of the Great Western are obscured slightly by the company's defensive reaction to contemporary criticisms that it had too many Englishmen and Scots on its line. Of its 36 enginemen in November 1854, however, 23 had British experience and only 7 American. Of the enginemen, 8 came from a single English line, the London and North Western, which had also provided the company's managing director, C.J. Brydges. Indeed, all the GWR's senior officers were recruited in Britain, as were at least a dozen station employees. Brydges reported in 1854 that of 77 stationmasters and other station employees who had been in Canada less than three years, "some came out from Railways in the old country, without knowledge of the Company or its officers, and upon making application for employment, were, upon being found suitable, taken on."

The Great Western reported 212 station employees in all, of whom only 13 had been born in Canada. Similarly, while Brydges claimed that the company had not "brought out" any conductors or baggagemen, only 13 per cent of them were Canadian born, and another 25 per cent American. Finally, of the "large staff of mechanics employed at the different workshops...a different class of men to any previously in the country," Brydges reported that "about twenty-five have been brought out by the Company, and most of the remainder have been men who have been taken on as ordinary workmen and gradually trained for the duties they now fulfill."[36] The local labour market presumably furnished the bulk of the company's demand for unskilled labourers and "ordinary workmen." Nonetheless, it appears from statements made by the shop workers themselves that the majority were first-generation immigrants from Britain, whether or not the company had directly recruited them there.

The railway companies' investment in recruiting and training skilled and specialized workers had direct implications for discipline. Good pay, welfare schemes of one sort and another, and a host of measures intended to build up loyalty to the company served to protect the proprietors' investment in manpower. At the same time, of course, the magnitude of that investment materially limited managerial autocracy. We have already suggested that scarce workers might only receive a reprimand in circumstances where unskilled labour would be fired. Beyond this, the railway companies strove to protect their investments by restructuring operations to provide work for engine crews and shop workers during slack times. Both the Grand Trunk and the Great Western began to manufacture their own cars in the mid 1850s, and their own locomotives by the end of the decade, in large part because it was better business to keep their shops working in slack periods than to lay off workers whom it could be difficult to replace when time improved.[37]

This policy is illustrated by the Great Western's aggregate payrolls, reported half-yearly from July 1854 on. These accounts report the wage-bill for five groups of occupations: enginemen and firemen; conductors, baggagemen, and brakemen; porters, policemen, and switchmen; locomotive-shop workers; and car-shop workers. Our preliminary analysis of these figures suggests that less-skilled workers, particularly those not involved in shop work or locomotive running, were far more susceptible to displacement in periods of economic downturn than were their scarcer co-workers.[38]

Following several years of rapid growth, the Canadian (as indeed the whole North Atlantic) economy suffered a sharp recession in the latter part of 1857. However, the Great Western's traffic receipts and net revenue had already begun to fall off quite steeply the previous year and only recovered with the general strengthening of the economy in 1859. Overall, the railway's payroll components follow this trend. A period of rapid growth, associated with the economic boom and the beginning of railway operations, is followed by a period of decline and, by the end of the decade, recovery. While this cycle can be identified to some extent for each of the components, the extent of its influence differs markedly among the different categories of employment. At one extreme, the payroll for porters, switchmen, and policemen soars dramatically in the earlier period and plummets in the later one. These workers were particularly vulnerable to market fluctuations because they were unskilled, paid at day rates, and the company had a minimal investment in their recruitment and training. Porters in particular were vulnerable to lay-off as the volume of passengers and freight declined between 1856 and 1858.

At the other extreme, the curve for car-shop payrolls is practically flat throughout the period. The locomotive-shop payroll climbed rapidly to mid 1857 and then levelled off. The payrolls of the remaining two occupational groups—engineers and firemen, and conductors, baggagemen, and brakemen—responded more moderately to the business cycle. While the more skilled of these employees represented a substantial investment in recruitment and training, they could not be fully employed in a period of declining train mileage. These data suggest that unskilled railway workers were exposed to a classical labour market during the decade; that the shop workers were protected by inelastic demand; and that the skilled workers in the running trades were cushioned by relatively inelastic supply.

In the Great Western's locomotive department, for example, outside labourers, the lowest-paid workers on the line, were the chief target of early cost-cutting efforts. The men who worked the GWR's water pumps were the first victims: when steam pumping engines (which could also be used to saw wood) were introduced between July and December 1854, sixty jobs were eliminated.[39] By contrast, the scarcity of qualified enginemen and firemen, and the substantial investment the railway had incurred in recruiting and training them, meant that they must be retained at almost any cost:

> The running of engines for gravel and wood trains whilst the line was being completed and ballasted, were of great benefit to this department, inasmuch as they found profitable employment during the summer months for a large number of engineers and firemen which it was absolutely necessary to retain on the staff

> for working the heavy traffic during the fall and winter, but as this opportune employment is now at an end, the Locomotive Department labours under a very great disadvantage because we cannot possibly discharge our steady and experienced men at each recurrence of slackness in traffic.[40]

This labour-market dualism was not purely a function of skill level, however, but depended on occupational grade as well. So long as the railway companies were committed to making work in the shops so as to retain skilled workers, there would be work for unskilled shop workers as well. This apparent dualism was undermined in several of the grades by the structures of occupational mobility. The line was drawn not so much between the skilled and the unskilled, but between the unskilled in outside labouring jobs (who lacked access to a mobility ladder) and the remainder of the work force.

Deference and Resistance

Railway managers liked to talk about "the existence between all classes of the Company's servants, of that spirit of unanimity and cordiality which is so indispensible to railway working."[41] There is evidence that sentiments like these were more than mere anodynes. During this decade in which the railways were a new industry just beginning operations, managers and skilled workers (at least) in each of the companies considered themselves members of a single community, although by no means a community of equals. This community was structured on paternalistic lines, but the paternalism was moderated—again, in the case of the skilled workers at least—by a good deal of pride and self-respect. This pride in craft and occupational solidarity could prompt Grand Trunk shop workers to hold an indignation meeting in support of their employer, and against newspaper charges that the company's cars were of shoddy construction.[42] It could equally prompt organized resistance when management overstepped itself. If we are to understand the two principal occasions of industrial conflict in railway operations during the 1850s, we have first to examine the strands that defined and knit together this railway community.

It was a paternalistic community, in which "every man should be taught to feel that he is cared for by his superior and that his good conduct will be noticed and rewarded."[43] The material basis for paternalism has already been described: it consisted in the imperfections of the labour market for the key shopcrafts and running-trades workers, in the companies' heavy investment in recruiting and retaining these scarce workers, and in the imperative of maintaining discipline in far-flung enterprises where direct supervision was impossible. This structural imperative to paternalism was expressed in the provision of company housing, the uneven enforcement of company rules, the relatively high rates of pay enjoyed by skilled workers, and their substantial job security. It was reflected, too, in the silver medals distributed by the Grand Trunk's directors to the "best men for economy, regular running, care and freedom from accidents," in the various incentive schemes whereby workers took a share of savings earned through greater productivity, and in the schools and churches erected by the companies for their workers' families.[44]

There were cultural links to knit the community together as well. Perhaps most significant was the fact that many managers and skilled workers were recent immigrants from Britain (and from England in particular) and may indeed have worked together on British railways. Certainly there was no end to the protestations of loyalty at the various festivals and dinners where the community congregated. Many a toast was drunk to the army and navy, the fatherland, the queen and royal family—and on at least one occasion during the Crimean war, to the emperor and empress of France as well.[45] A substantial proof of allegiance came in 1855, when the Great Western's employees subscribed more than £800 to a Patriotic Fund to support the war in the Crimea.[46] Another tie binding railway workers and managers together was common defence against often-hostile public and press. Just as general manager Brydges defended the character, sobriety, and competence of Great Western employees before the Accident Commission, so the workers did their part by rallying behind the company, telling the directors that "in all their trials they could count upon the united support of the employees, whenever anything was wanted from them, to maintain the high character of the road."[47]

Labour/management reciprocity extended to community affairs quite removed from the workplace. In Hamilton, for example, the Great Western's management could count on worker support at the polls for its electoral interests; the workers could similarly count on the managers to intervene on their behalf when they became embroiled in a dispute with the directors of the local Mechanics Institute.

In the 1857 election, both the Grand Trunk and the Great Western urged their employees to support candidates sympathetic to company interests. The Great Western posted notices in the shops that managing director Brydges would speak on behalf of a local candidate, and the men were invited to "volunteer" to come hear him. Election day was declared a holiday in the shops, where the men were marshalled and marched to the polls. Great Western workers also intervened in the elections in Galt and Essex. The politics of paternalism though, were not entirely dissociated from the coercion of property. After the election, a disgruntled partisan alleged that "McGregor the artisan" had been fired, despite four years' service, simply for refusing to vote for the company's candidate.[48] Such charges were a common theme in the abuse heaped upon the railway and its employees by newspapers on the other side of the political divide. The Great Western mechanics' answer came at their annual festival in 1857, where a locomotive-department worker insisted before the whole assembly that "the Great Western mechanics could compare favourably with those who aspersed them... He thought it right that the mechanics should do their duty to the Company, and then they would earn the respect of all."[49]

The dispute at the Hamilton and Gore Mechanics Institute arose when the Great Western workers attempted to transform the middle-class library and social club into an institution that would be more responsive to their needs. In 1854, the railway's board of directors had agreed to contribute £100 to the institute on condition that membership privileges be extended to its employees. By December of the following year, the railway workers had accumulated so long a list of grievances about the institute's management that they met to consider establishing an alternative institution of their own. They complained about high dues, the irrelevance of most of the literature stocked by the institute to the mechanics' concern with "scientific" matters, the speakers who were being brought in, and the complete absence of classes in mechanical principles and applications for workmen and their sons. The institute's president attended the meeting to defend his policies, but Brydges spoke up for the workers, urging the institute to recognize the validity of the grievances and to compromise. The meeting closed with "three hearty cheers" for Brydges, "the workmen's real friend." Two months later, the institute amended its bylaws, reduced its fees, and elected Brydges to its board. By 1857, classes were being held in Mechanical and Architectural Drawing (23 participants), Mathematics, Writing and Arithmetic (30 participants), French, and "Mutual Improvement, or Debating Class." All were taught by Great Western employees, and many of the students came from the local railway shops. The Great Western directors continued their annual grant in support of membership fees until 1866, when the company's mechanics built their own reading room.[50]

Democracy, progress through science, and education as the means to self-improvement were recurrent themes in the culture of the railway community. All these were celebrated regularly at the annual mechanics' festivals and at the numerous testimonial dinners mounted to honour the companies' officers. These gatherings, where elaborate speeches and toasts accompanied dinner, and music and dancing followed, were organized by workers' committees with the active support and participation of management. Typically, the hall would be decorated with portraits of managers, banners inscribed with the names of such "mechanical heroes" as Watt, Arkwright, and Fulton, slogans proclaiming "Success to Canadian Enterprise," pictures of locomotives, and the insignia of various fraternal organizations.[51]

These dinners both expressed and fostered the solidarity and values of the railway community. Managers would often use these occasions to advance corporate welfare proposals, as in 1857, when Brydges promised company support for an employees' sick fund, or 1858, when he urged the creation of a mutual benefit society and made another proposal that spoke to a key artisanal value: "A great many of the youths employed at the shops were destitute of the benefit of having received instruction in the first rudiments of a common education; and it was proposed to establish a School at the Works, for the purpose of instructing those youths; and it would give him and the Directors the greatest possible pleasure to aid and carry this suggestion into execution."[52]

The testimonial dinners honoured upward mobility and workplace harmony. When the Great Western's locomotive superintendent left the company to join the Buffalo and Lake Huron Railway (incidentally taking a number of fitters with him), 150 subscribers presented him with a silver tea service and a ring, as well as a dinner in his honour. "Mr. Yates is one of our own class," announced the evening's master of ceremonies, "having graduated amongst us, and we are now about to award him a diploma and spend a pleasant evening." On another occasion, 200 workers presented a retiring shop foreman with a purse of $200, "as a mark of our respect and esteem, and in acknowledging the power that was vested in you we all believe you used that power with mildness and affability." The community sometimes assembled on more solemn occasions. Following the Desjardins Bridge disaster of 1857, which claimed fifty-nine lives, the Great Western workers subscribed for a monument to the engineman and fireman, "a marble column upon the top of which stands a very pretty model of a locomotive," suitably inscribed:

> Life's railway o'er, each station past,
> In death we're stopped and cease at last
> Farewell dear friends, and cease to weep
> In Christ we're safe, in him we sleep.[53]

The paternalistic solidarity of the railway community was threatened by strikes only twice during the decade. This was in marked contrast to the railways' experience during their construction phase, which had seen an almost unbroken succession of strikes, riots, and other "ructions" by navvies and labourers, usually in response to wage reductions, changes in working hours, defaults by contractors, or frustration at the unavailability of work.[54] It was this pattern of construction-labour relations that led Pentland to classify the railways as "modern" market-oriented employers.[55] The experience of operations, as we have already suggested, was markedly different. What is particularly interesting about the two upheavals of the 1850s is that the paternalistic railway community seems to have survived them intact.

The strike on the Great Western began in November 1856, when a new locomotive superintendent, Alexander Braid, dismissed a popular shop foreman named Stephenson, apparently in order to replace him with a personal favourite. When Braid told the shop workers, who had convened to demand an explanation, that Stephenson "was in the habit of being drunk in his shop," the men denounced this as a "monstrous fabrication" and struck work, vowing not to return until Braid himself had been dismissed. The enginemen and tiremen threatened to strike in sympathy with their fellows in the shops. Brydges received the shop workers' grievance committee "in the courteous manner which characterizes that gentleman," expressed his regret at the strike, and agreed to reinstate Stephenson, although not to dismiss Braid. He also promised that no one would be discharged on account of the strike, reassured the deputation that a rumoured wage cut would not take place, and reaffirmed the practice of paying men who arrived at the shops a little late on Saturday for three-quarters of a day's work, rather than just half. Finally, he compromised the men's demand for free passes by agreeing to let them ride at half fare.[56] Once again, Brydges was hailed as the workmen's friend. Subsequently the mood was one of forgiveness. Braid was eventually welcomed back at the Mechanics Institute, and when he left the company in 1858, he was treated to a testimonial dinner where the men presented him with a $500 silver tea service.[57]

There are several versions of the 1859 conflict on the Grand Trunk. George Reith, the railway's new general manager, was on a tour of western U.S. railroads when he learned that wages elsewhere were lower than on the Grand Trunk. Without consultation, he apparently wired Montreal that all wages and salaries were to be reduced 10 per cent forthwith. The Toronto *Leader* claimed that Reith expected to earn a bonus by his cost-cutting measure; in any event, the Grand Trunk's employees got wind of the order and threatened to resign en masse. Their strike threat worked. The Grand Trunk's president convened the board of directors, announced that neither he nor the vice-president had been consulted about the cut, and reported that GTR wages were in fact lower than those paid on the Great Western or the Northern. The board rescinded Reith's order, effectively dismissing him. Reith managed to arrange a £4,000 settlement from the English directors of the Grand Trunk, a rather less-appropriate testimonial than the one sent him by a group of American railway executives—a large tray and goblets, made of tin. The Grand Trunk workers memorialized the event in a song that denounced Reith's attempted "piracy" while reaffirming their affection for other Grand Trunk officers:

> When rose-lipped June, enraptured, bent
> To sip the falling dew,
> A Reith conceived the foul intent
> To clap on us the screw
> Of ten per cent. But where's the man
> Who speeds the rail along
> But will take up, with heart in hand,
> The chorus of my song?
> May he who dares, with pirate hand,
> Our "little all" assail
> Storm-tost, behold no more the land,
> But perish in the gale.
> When honest bluntness is our theme,
> To Bidder we recur;
> For manliness, the very *name*
> Of Shanley we revere;
> But when we think of every ill
> That pirates can bequeath,
> Each object serves our minds to fill
> With reveries of Reith.[58]

How are these events to be interpreted? Some might see in these conflicts the early stirrings of class consciousness among the railway workers. There is some authority for this view: one of the Hamilton strikers declared "that it was all very well to say that they were independent of the Great Western Railway, but they should reflect that capital always tyrannized over labour." His view did not go unchallenged, though, for another rose to say that he "had had much to do with strikes in the Old Country, and had come to the knowledge of the fact that tyranny of the employee over the employer was as possible and hateful as that of the employer over the employee." Still others were content to urge their fellows to act "like men," to avoid "sacrificing their dignity."[59] Taking it all together, it seems a more convincing view that these events arose not out of class consciousness, but out of something antecedent, albeit related to it: an artisanal ideology compounded of pride in craft, personal dignity, and democratic aspiration, but shaded for all that by a sense of rank and mutual obligation. This was an artisanal view that did not look to petty proprietorship as the ultimate expression of success in work, but rather accepted the critical features of paternalistic employment relations in the large corporation, combining independence and deference to find its place in the railway community.

Dimensions of Paternalism

As H.C. Pentland has argued, the persistence of the "traditional" personal relation of worker and employer into the industrial age was a function of the underdevelopment of the labour market. It was a strategy whereby employers confronted the material reality of labour shortage and the seasonality of labour requirements in an attempt to ensure that workers would be available when required. In strictly economic terms, Pentland's personal labour relation amounted to the employer's assumption of some significant portion of the cost of supporting the worker and his family in periods of underemployment—a cost that is assumed wholly by the worker in the fully-formed classical labour market, and is partially socialized (with the burden falling on workers generally) in the welfare state.

But the personal labour relation clearly carried implications beyond the narrowly economic. The assumption of the worker's overhead costs rarely (if ever) took the indirect form of simple cash transfers. Instead, the employer effectively substituted his own decisions about consumption for those of the worker. Where few employees were involved, they might be taken into the employer's household, eat at his table, wear his family's cast-off clothing. Where the work force was larger, the employer might choose for and on behalf of his employees by supplying company housing, subsidizing prices in a company store, and arranging for the provision of doctors or schools. Apprenticeship, with its requirements of maintenance and training, placed the employer formally in loco parentis; so, too, may the general employment relationship justifiably be characterized as paternalistic to the extent that the employer undertakes to supply the material, political, cultural, or moral-cum-spiritual maintenance of the work force. In this more general sense, then, paternalism may flow not only from a rational calculation that market forces are inadequate or unreliable guarantors of employee loyalty or efficiency, but from ideological and broadly cultural wellsprings too. And in this more general sense, paternalism may persist and develop even after the demise of its original progenitor, the personal labour relation.

Employment in railway operations in the 1850s was clearly transitional with respect to both the personal employment relation and paternalism. More precisely, it can be located on the boundary between the paternalism of the personal labour relation and the newly emerging corporate paternalism of what would be known a half-century later as business's "welfare work."[60] Railway workers were bound by ties of personal loyalty, dependence or deference to particular foremen, supervisors, or managers, depending upon their position in the hierarchy. Such ties counted for much in an employment structure geared to personal mobility. But at the same time these personal relations were located in an increasingly impersonal corporate structure that centralized authority and operated according to imperatives quite independent of personality, for all that the "railway service" claimed the personal loyalties of its servants. This could lead to conflict, as the Braid and Reith affairs showed, but the relative decline of the personal labour relation did not mean an end to paternalism.

The crucial feature of paternalism in the 1850s was the railway companies' commitment to providing slack-time employment for the shopcraft and running-trades workers. Rapid growth associated with start-up combined with the scarcity of experienced workers in these trades to strengthen their position and provide them a base from which to proclaim their artisanal pride and independence, and to join with management in designing the institutions of community—all this, of course, shaded by deference and an acknowledgment of hierarchy, but not determined by it. By the mid 1870s, however, the underlying structure of paternalism would change markedly. Pressed by financial crises and conscious of the development of a better-stocked labour market, a new generation of corporate managers would abandon the old commitment to slack-time employment and embark on a policy of lay-off and retrenchment. The paternalism of the later 1870s would have two faces: first, the moral regeneration of railway labour through company-sponsored temperance and bible movements and the organization of the Railway YMCAs, and second, superannuation and accident insurance schemes intended, at least in part, to offset more directly the successes of the Railway Brotherhoods in unionizing important segments of the work force. While its form and content varied with the relative strengths of employers and particular groups of workers, and with the nature of the institutions they created, paternalism was to persist as a characteristic feature of railway labour relations well into the twentieth century.

Notes

1 For example, W.T. Easterbrook and Hugh G.J. Aitken, *Canadian Economic History* (Toronto 1963), ch. 14, "The Coming of the Railway."

2 Arthur Lower states that John Egan, "King of the Ottawa," employed 3500 men in timber making in 1854. They were distributed among a hundred establishments, however, with little imperative to close co-ordination, and can hardly be considered a single work force. *Great Britain's Woodyard: British America and the Timber Trade* (Montreal 1973), 166.

3 Occupational terminology varied, with the English terms gradually giving way to American ones over the period. For clarity's sake, we have adopted the better known terms: engineman instead of enginedriver; brakeman instead of brakesman or breaksman; conductor instead of guard; cleaner instead of wiper.

4 J.M. Trout and E. Trout, *The Railways of Canada* (Toronto 1871), 83, 100.

5 Public Archives of Canada, RG 30, *Canadian National Railways* (henceforth CNR) contains papers of most of the railways that eventually became part of the CNR system. CNR 2, 606 (2 March 1855) and 2, 635 (30 March 1855); Hamilton *Spectator,* 15 September 1855. For a detailed account of this aspect of railway operations, see Paul Craven and Tom Traves, "Canadian Railways as Manufacturers 1850–80," Canadian Historical Association, *Historical Papers* (1983), 254–81.

6 For studies of the development of railway management in the United States and Britain, see Alfred D. Chandler, Jr, *The Railroads* (New York 1965), and *The Visible Hand* (Cambridge, Mass. 1977); T.R. Gourvish, *Mark Huish and the London and North Western Railway: A Study of Management* (Leicester 1972). The "general principles" of management were set out by Daniel C. McCallurn, superintendent of the

New York and Erie Railroad, in that company's annual report for 1855 (see Chandler, *The Railroads,* 102).

7 The commissioners appointed to inquire into a series of accidents and detentions on the Great Western Railway, *Report,* Journals of the Legislative Assembly of United Canada, 18 Vict. App. YY, 1855 (henceforth *Accident Commission*). The Accident Commission report is imperfectly paginated.

8 14 & 15 Vict., c. 51.

9 16 Vict., c. 99, sect. XI.

10 19 Vict., c. 136.

11 An amending Act of 1853 (16 Vict., c. 169) made it a misdemeanour punishable by up to a year's imprisonment at hard labour to tamper maliciously with or damage railway property or cause any stoppage of operations. If damage to property carried on the road, or injury to persons, ensued, the offence became a felony punishable by not less than one and not more than two years in the penitentiary; while if loss of life was involved, the offence became manslaughter and the offender liable to from four to ten years in the penitentiary.

12 CNR 1000, 570f (1857).

13 Great Western Railway, *Rule Book,* 1854; CNR 2, 103 (June 1854); CNR 2, 1201 (1857). In the absence of other detailed information, these codes of rules are frequently the best available approximations to a description of the work process for various occupations in this period.

14 *Accident Commission.*

15 CNR 6, 768 (1857); CNR 6, 758 (1857); CNR 1000, 129 (1857).

16 CNR 6, 813f (1858).

17 CNR 5 (5 June 1855).

18 Hamilton *Spectator,* 11 November 1854.

19 *Accident Commission.*

20 Toronto *Globe,* 18 October 1853.

21 CNR 2, 445f (1854).

22 CNR 6394 (1854–5).

23 Great Western Railway, *Rule Book,* 1854.

24 This is admittedly impressionistic for the 1850s, since too little detailed quantitative work has been done on real incomes and regularity of work in a broad cross-section of occupations in the period to substantiate the information. By the late 1880s, we find explicit acknowledgments of the greater regularity of work on the railways (although many of the other working conditions characteristic of the 1850s no longer obtained), for example, in the testimony of David Cashion, a moulder in the Grand Trunk's Hamilton works, before the Royal Commission on the Relations of Labour and Capital (Ontario evidence, pp. 784–6).

25 *Accident Commission,* 119.

26 The 1854–5 Great Western paysheets are in CNR 6394. The Grand Trunk figures are reported in its locomotive superintendent's report, appended to the railway's *Annual Report* for 1859.

27 *Accident Commission.*

28 Special Committee appointed to inquire and report about the condition, management, and prospects of the Grand Trunk Railway Company, *Report,* Journal of the Legislative Assembly of Canada, 20 Vic., App. 6, 1857 (hereafter GTR *Report*); *Accident Commission.*

29 GTR *Report;* CNR 6, 795 (1857).

30 These are yearly salaries in Halifax currency, GTR *Report;* CNR 5, Finance Committee, 7 December 1854; 5 and 10 October 1854.

31 Myles Pennington, *Railways and Other Ways* (Toronto 1894), 186.

32 CNR 6, 791 (1857); 6, 796 (1857). Railway company rules typically required that employees reside wherever they were ordered.

33 Pennington, *Railways,* 186f. Porteous seems to have followed Brydges from the Great Western to the Grand Trunk; this was not an uncommon route for career moves in an industry where paternalism was accompanied by patronage.

34 One of the methods used to supply work in slack periods was to send enginemen and firemen into the shops for part of their working time; this meant that there was more interchange between the shopcrafts and the footplate trades than might otherwise have occurred. One machinist who became a fireman in the late 1850s transferred back again when his fiancee said she would not marry him unless he quit the road and went back to his trade (University of Western Ontario, Spriggs Collection, box 4312, W.K. Baines to Spriggs, 13 Feb 1934).

35 Toronto *Leader,* 30 March, 26 May, and 13 July 1854; GTR *Report,* 218; Pennington (the Grand Trunk's first goods manager) reports that James Hardman, John Roberts, S.P. Bidder, and he all came to Canada on five year contracts (*Railways, 81*).

36 *Accident Commission;* A.W. Currie, *The Grand Trunk Railway of Canada* (Toronto 1957), 163.

37 For details, see Craven and Traves, "Canadian Railways as Manufacturers."

38 This analysis is described in detail in our working paper, "Labour and management in Canadian railway operations: the first decade," presented to the Commonwealth Labour History Conference, Coventry, England, in September 1981. It remains tentative, however, until data covering a substantially longer time series are analysed.

39 CNR 1, 58 (26 September 1854), report of R.W. Harris to shareholders; CNR 1, n.p. (24 August 1854), report of G.L. Reid, chief engineer, to shareholders.

40 CNR 1, n.p. (17 August 1860).

41 The words are Walter Shanly's, quoted by Pennington, *Railways,* 124.

42 Montreal *Gazette,* 10 May 1856.

43 Quoted by Pennington, *Railways,* 87.

44 Grand Trunk, *Annual Report* (1859), 26; Montreal *Gazette,* 10 August 1853.

45 Montreal *Gazette,* 8 January 1855.

46 Hamilton *Spectator,* 23 May 1855.

47 *Accident Commission;* Hamilton *Spectator,* 23 January 1860, copying the London *Prototype.*

48 Hamilton *Spectator,* 12 December 1857, 13 January 1858, 4 January 1858; Toronto *Globe,* 8 January 1858.

49 Hamilton *Spectator,* 1 January 1858.

50 CNR 2, 59 (1854). Hamilton *Spectator,* 7 December 1855; 4 and 5 February, and 3 March 1856; 28 February 1857. CNR 6, 891 (1858); Bryan Palmer, *A Culture in Conflict* (Montreal 1979), 51. Workers on the Grand Trunk met at the Montreal Mechanics Institute in 1856 to plan their involvement in the upcoming festivities to celebrate the opening of the line. In 1857 they established the Grand Trunk Literary and Scientific Institution, and by 1859 it had opened a reading room at Point St Charles (Montreal *Gazette,* 22 October 1856; Montreal *Pilot,* 16 June 1857; Toronto *Globe,* 17 May 1859).

51 One of the Great Western workers' grievances against the Mechanics Institute was that in 1854 its directors refused to rent them the hall for the first festival on the pretext that there would be dancing (Hamilton *Spectator,* 7 December 1855). For accounts of various festivals, excursions, and other celebrations, see, for example, Toronto *Globe,* 11 February 1860; Hamilton *Spectator,* 7 January 1857, 23 January 1860; Montreal *Pilot,* 22 August 1859.

52 Hamilton *Spectator,* 25 February 1857; Hamilton *Times,* 9 January 1858.

53 Hamilton *Spectator,* 13 March and 5 October 1854, 27 September 1856, 21 February and 9 September 1857; Montreal *Pilot,* 29 December 1856, 22 July 1856; Hamilton *Evening Times,* 17 May 1861; Pennington, *Railways,* 126n.

54 These strikes took the typical form of "collective bargaining by riot," and represented the continuation of the labour struggles of the 1840s in canal building onto the railways in the 1850s. For a discussion of the canal navvies' battles, see Ruth Bleasdale, "Class Conflict on the Canals of Upper Canada in the 1840s," *Labour/Le Travailleur* VII (1981): 9–39.

55 This analysis suggests that the labour-market situation on the railways corresponded in many respects to what Pentland described as "personal labour relationships," particularly for those workers whose skills were relatively scarce. Pentland looked at labour relations in railway *construction* and concluded that the railway companies were modern, capitalistic employers; that is, that they took advantage of the evolving classical labour market to depersonalize employment relations. However true this may have been of relations with navvies in construction (and with unskilled outdoor labour like the porters discussed above), it would seem that personal labour relationships characterized the railways' relations with the majority of their operating personnel. We return to the question of paternalism in the concluding section of this essay. H.C. Pentland, *Labour and Capital in Canada 1650–1850,* ed. Paul Phillips (Toronto, 1981).

56 Hamilton *Spectator,* 7 and 8 November 1856.

57 Hamilton *Spectator,* 25 February 1857, 21 April 1858.

58 Pennington, *Railways,* 151; Toronto *Leader,* 29 November 1860; CNR 1000, 193f (1859); CNR 1003, 50–3 (1859); Pennington, 357: the song is signed "Philip Dormer, Fireman," and Pennington ascribes it, somewhat uncertainly, to a "rhymster of Maine." Bidder and Shanley preceded Reith as GTR general managers.

59 Hamilton *Spectator,* 8 November 1856.

60 These considerations apply to all groups of workers, with the partial but significant exception of outdoor labour. See Canadian Pacific Railway Company, *Welfare Work* (n.p.; n.d.: circa 1909), and more generally, Paul Craven, *"An Impartial Umpire": Industrial Relations and the Canadian State 1900–11* (Toronto 1980), 100–5; and Tom Traves, *The State and Enterprise: Canadian Manufacturers and the Federal Government, 1917–31* (Toronto 1979), chapter 5.

"French Canada Awakens" and "Patriotism and Sackcloth" (excerpts)

Jan Noel

French Canada Awakens

[...]

III

During the 1840s, when the impetus for change passed from the laity to the clergy, the torch passed to the cluster of ultramontane clergy identified with Ignace Bourget, who became Bishop of Montreal in 1840. For many, the name calls up unpleasant associations. Was it not Bourget who for years tried to suppress the intellectual freedom of the Institut canadien, an attempt that culminated in the notorious Guibord affair of the 1870s, when the bishop would not even let a liberal lie in peace in a Catholic cemetery? Then, too, there were the anachronistic Zouaves, young French-Canadian men whom Bourget decked out in exotic garb and sent off to Europe in the 1860s to defend ancient and crumbling claims of temporal papal power. Bishop Bourget's Catholicism conjured up a very literal spirituality, a constant mixing of God in everything. It seems a latter-day transfer from pre-literate societies in which the world was alive with spirits—convenient spirits used to explain everything that was not readily explainable. In Bourget's *mandements,* one encounters this very immanent God, who ruins the harvest to punish the people for drunkenness, and stems a typhus epidemic to reward them for their good behaviour.[1]

Moreover, the basic issue on which ultramontanes came together was opposition to liberal ideas, known in the bishop's terminology as "the forces of evil." His ultramontanes were counter-revolutionaries who stressed obedience to established authority. The bishop had an explicit counter-revolutionary aim in promoting temperance societies; he hoped that besides improving morality, they would substitute for the political clubs of the Rebellion years.[2] In this respect, he seconded the views of some English-Canadian magistrates (and the *Canada Temperance Advocate*) who asserted that the Lower Canada rebellions had been fomented in taverns.[3] Bourget and his followers also took an uncompromising stance towards other religions. The bishop asserted that "no one is permitted to be free in his religious and political opinions, for it was the prerogative of the church to teach sovereigns to govern with wisdom and subjects to obey in gladness."[4] This principle, in Phillipe Sylvain's opinion, "led directly to theocracy."[5] Bourget's church was colourful, intolerant, and profoundly out of step with many of the more progressive currents of the nineteenth century.

All this may sound sufficiently unpalatable to raise the question of why so many French

---

Jan Noel "French Canada Awakens" and "Patriotism and Sackcloth" from *Canada Dry: Temperance Crusades before Confederation* (Toronto: University of Toronto Press, 1995) 153–182. Reprinted by permission of the publisher.

Canadians adhered so ardently to this extreme form of Catholicism. Why was there so much support for Bourget's program that he became, as even a critic admits, "one of the great architects of the Province of Quebec"?[6] In fact, many of his enthusiasms cast him with the moderns rather than the ancients, and the image of a reactionary autocrat does not do justice to the dynamic bishop. His ultramontane state was sustained, not by martial or state power (still in 1840 in British hands), but by a strong body of public opinion. This support was won in the decades after the Rebellion—and particularly during the 1840s, the time which most concerns us here, because that is the period when French-Canadian temperance sentiment would peak.

During the 1840s ultramontanism had not yet clearly assumed its conservative, or *bleu,* coloration. Indeed, many of Bourget's early actions seemed quite progressive. In a society recently humiliated and demoralized by the Rebellions, Bourget was building anew. He promoted the alliance with the Baldwin-LaFontaine Reformers. He recruited the numerous religious orders who established the elementary schools for which progressives had long campaigned. To address growing urban poverty, he helped set up a network of new and timely parish organizations, such as the St Vincent de Paul Society, to administer poor relief, and the Ladies of Charity to look after country girls who migrated to town. When concern arose that too many French Canadians were emigrating, the clergy helped direct settlers towards the Eastern Townships and other regions where farmland was available. During the Irish famine immigration, Bourget led a contingent of nuns and priests who worked among the victims with a heroism that won praise from Catholics and Protestants alike. Such efforts were partially funded by wealthy laymen, particularly by one who has been labelled the bishop's "minister of finance," businessman Antoine-Olivier Berthelet—a philanthropist whose commitment to temperance and other social concerns paralleled that of English Montrealers such as Joseph MacKay and John Redpath.[7] Berthelet's bounty and Bourget's clergy created a whole range of new Catholic social welfare institutions, magdalens and orphanages, hospitals and asylums, and a school for the deaf founded on the most up-to-date principles. The church was the institution which most visibly addressed the social dilemmas of the day.

In many ways a modern man, Bourget even accepted innovations which came from Protestant quarters. An early riser and a tireless worker, he seemed to find the nostrums of Samuel Smiles congenial; like Protestant reformers, the bishop tried to encourage prudence and thrift. He declared idleness the mother of all vice. He encouraged practical education,[8] workers' savings banks, and insurance schemes.

Another modernizing feature of the bishop's program was temperance. Bourget did not dismiss temperance as a Protestant movement the way his predecessor, Bishop Lartigue, had done. Indeed, he became convinced that drunkenness was the "mal capital de ce pays,"[9] that drinking on saints' days was a prime cause of sexual immorality and domestic discord.[10] By 1845, the bishop concurred with another conclusion that Protestant temperance leaders had reached: that total abstinence was the only way to prevent backsliding in a world where there was such constant temptation to over-indulge in drink. Like the Protestants, Bishop Bourget upheld total abstinence as a form of charity that the strong should undertake in order to save the weak.[11] Bourget was a key figure in all three major mid-century temperance efforts in French Canada; in the *réveil religieux,* and also in the Chiniquy crusade and the Société de la Croix.

Another aspect of Bourget's Catholicism which might be considered progressive was its commitment to the masses rather than to the elite. The Montreal ecclesiastic built popular religious fervour by introducing large, impressive ceremonies which brought the warming influence of Mediterranean Catholicism to Canada. Thousands of people thronged to open-air masses, processions, and pilgrimages, which were said to produce a feeling of ecstacy not unlike intoxication.[12] Indeed, such ceremonies embodied the collective ideal of the ultramontanes. Religion, in Bishop Bourget's view, could correct a fault with which French Canadians were sometimes charged: that they were disunited, and too lacking in public spirit to be able to cooperate for the common good.[13] Ultramontane pageants which gathered thousands together symbolized a newfound unity. By contrast, the individualism which the liberals acclaimed could seem selfish and paltry. Mother Church instead called the people to a higher, collective destiny.

The flock was also attracted by popular preachers analogous to Protestant religious revivalists; and it was through this means that many French Canadians first heard about temperance. Although isolated parish temperance societies appeared in the 1830s, Catholic temperance really got under way when Bishop Bourget invited a hellfire-and-damnation preacher from France to preach at a series of parish religious services during 1840–1. The visit of Monseigneur Charles Forbin-Janson, bishop of the diocese of Nancy, to Canada East initiated a *réveil religieux,* or religious awakening. The French bishop used tactics such as darkening the church and recreating the sounds of hell so vividly that the worried organizers warned women and children to stay away. Forbin-Janson visited some sixty parishes from Gaspé to Bytown. Everywhere he was greeted with tremendous enthusiasm. Many lapsed Catholics used the occasion to return to the sacraments.[14] Often at the close of one of these revivals, the people would march in procession to erect a large public cross as a symbol of their renewed Catholic faith.

In order to reinforce resolutions to abandon immoral ways, Forbin-Janson founded temperance societies at the close of his services. After the revival in September 1840 at the parish of Notre-Dame in Quebec, a great crowd of men and women applied to join. The town's leading citizens provided enthusiastic leadership, and several thousand people of the neighbouring parishes of St Roch and St Patrick also enrolled.[15] At Trois-Rivières, six thousand similarly became members.[16] But Montreallers, who were not noted for obedience to the clergy, and whose town was a distilling centre, were not so enthusiastic. The city's elite had some hesitation about joining, and the women did not come forward; also, unlike some Quebeckers, the Montreallers showed no interest in pledging total abstinence. Nevertheless, several thousand men did pledge to restrict themselves to moderate drinking.[17] Montreal's *L'Aurore* called upon the principal citizens to support the society, urging that it was not, as many supposed, only for drunkards. Nonetheless, most of the early members were drawn from the lower classes.[18]

Meanwhile Bishop Forbin-Janson continued his circuit of the province. Returning to Quebec, he presided over a magnificent ceremony held in Beauport in the fall of 1841. This pageant, like many others of the 1840s, celebrated sobriety. Twenty-two ecclesiastics marched from the Quebec seminary to Beauport to erect a column in honour of temperance. Following the prelates were two white-robed girls carrying a snowy banner; then more banners, seven choirs of women, twenty-two cavaliers, each leading a contingent of men; a large group of priests (who were in town for a clerical retreat); and finally, a crowd of ten thousand people from the surrounding parishes who prayed, chanted, and cried out, "Vive la croix!" and "Vive Jésus!" *Le Canadien* could not find enough superlatives to report the experience:

> We have never seen such an immense multitude gathered in one place with such a noble aim. Man, no matter what the strayings of his heart and the impious revolts of his spirit, in the presence of so much majesty feels small... feels magnetised with respect and fear, possessed by the vast idea of his destiny...[19]

Not all were awestruck; some doubtless came for entertainment, and needy citizens found parish alms more forthcoming if they supported temperance.[20] For those who shared the reflective cast of mind of *Le Canadien*'s editor, though, here indeed was balm to heal the defeats and dissensions of the Rebellion years, and hope that French Canada would see glory once again.

Although Bishop Forbin-Janson presided over the Beauport ceremony, the affair had been arranged by the young curé of Beauport parish, Father Charles Chiniquy. The son of a Kamouraska notary, Chiniquy had been orphaned early in life. He had been encouraged by a friendly local priest to enter the seminary. After ordination, he began his priestly career as a chaplain at the Quebec Marine Hospital. After some exposure to British temperance literature, Chiniquy had become convinced that many of the ills he saw at the hospital could be traced to drink. He and several other priests had begun preaching temperance in parishes near Quebec City some months before the *réveil* got under way in 1840. They had been inspired by the temperance campaign Father Theobald Mathew was conducting in Ireland, which was said to be creating a moral revolution among the people there. After founding a temperance society in his own Beauport parish in 1840, Father Chiniquy perceived a dramatic new commitment both to morality and to schooling.[21] When Bishop Forbin-Janson arrived, Chiniquy had invited the visiting prelate to erect a temperance column, which would record for future generations the transformation of the people of Beauport.

After the French bishop departed for home, French Canada's Catholic churchmen worked to keep the spirit of the *réveil* alive. Reports from curés suggested that people tended to persevere in their new moral resolves in parishes where temperance societies had been founded. Bishop Bourget and Archbishop Joseph Signay of the Quebec diocese both promoted the spread of these societies.[22] Bourget invited the Oblate Fathers, a French order dedicated to preaching to the poor, to establish themselves in his diocese, and temperance work became a standard feature of their missions to the settlers, Indians, and lumbermen. The timber camps, in particular, were affected. In the spring of 1845, the residents of Point Gatineau were astounded to see usually riotous lumberjacks praying and singing hymns as they rode their rafts down the river to Quebec.[23] While the Oblates penetrated north and west into the Shield country, Father Chiniquy and several other priests also continued to preach temperance in various parishes east of Trois-Rivières.

The first wave of temperance lasted from 1840 until about 1845. In February 1842, Archbishop Signay was able to report that temperance societies had been established in every parish in the Quebec diocese. For two years thereafter, the movement continued to flourish. Father Chiniquy's temperance manual, published in 1844, reported 75,000 Catholic temperance society members in Canada East,[24] and Archbishop Signay congratulated his people on a marked increase in sobriety.[25] Declining liquor imports and merchants' records do suggest, besides, that the people (who in those years generally pledged moderation rather than abstinence) had in fact reduced their consumption of alcohol. A new brewery was established in Quebec City in 1844, supplying those who had taken the "moderation pledge" with a milder substance than spirits.[26] The *réveil,* in sum, had reawakened Catholic spirituality; the temperance movement which accompanied it in the early 1840s was an attempt to curb drunkenness because it corrupted that spirituality. Typically, though, the enthusiasm generated by religious revivals cannot be sustained; and by the mid-1840s, observers were noting that temperance fervour was on the wane.

IV

When French-Canadian temperance re-emerged in the second half of the 1840s, it focused more on social reform than on salvation. Sobriety began to appear less as a path to personal holiness, more as a solution to worldly woes. Some of the most glaring of these were the dislocation and crime associated with the growth of towns and the influx of impoverished immigrants. It was in the second half of the decade that Charles Mondelet, the Montreal circuit court judge, would issue to Montreal grand juries his series of well-publicized addresses singling out intemperance as the major cause of crime. Another grave concern in the late 1840s was the migration of French Canadians in swelling numbers to the United States. Some lay leaders began to relate the problem of drink to the question of French Canada's ability to survive in the midst of rapidly advancing anglophone communities in North America.[27]

This second wave of temperance sentiment in French Canada had some radical associations. Judge Mondelet, the most prominent of the lay temperance reformers, was a man of independent mind who has been called a follower of Voltaire.[28] No party man, Mondelet had broken with the *patriotes* in the 1830s over what he considered their extremism; but he acted as defence counsel for those same *patriotes* when they were imprisoned in 1837; in 1838 he too suffered arrest. Like some of the other progressives of his generation, he became interested in the questions Lord Durham had raised about what degree of anglicization was necessary to modernize French Canada. Mondelet dealt with the issue in his *Lettres sur l'éducation élémentaire et pratique.* On good terms with the city's young liberals, the judge was invited to address the Institut canadien on a variety of subjects during its peak of popularity in the late 1840s. There he dispensed modernizing advice: to rise early, eat and drink moderately, and keep busy; to educate women, that they might raise the moral tone of the whole household; to make tomorrow's society a rational one by keeping the young away from superstitious nursemaids.[29] Such ideas found favour with the young intelligentsia. The journal of the left-wing intellectuals, Montreal's *L'Avenir,* exhorted its readers to pass the long winter evenings in study and other forms of self-improvement.[30] Young French-Canadian leaders, the influential journalist Etienne Parent noted in 1848, no longer fell prey to the dissipated habits that had claimed so many of their elders.[31] This wing of the movement had not taken the clerical path to temperance beliefs; Mondelet's conversion was probably a result, not of the *réveil,* but of the influence of his father, a coroner who had long maintained that drink was largely responsible for crime.[32] Accordingly, when the free-thinking judge became a temperance activist around 1845, he introduced a secular and *rouge* strain into what had hitherto been a religious movement among French Canadians.

Judge Mondelet claimed that drink was a contributing factor in seven-eighths of the crimes annually committed.[33] He released to the press examples gathered during his years on the bench, and claimed that case after case had shown that excessive use of drink occasioned violence, arson, and theft. The Montreal jail-keeper as well as Mondelet's colleague on the bench, J.S. McCord, also declared that they had found a strong correlation between drunkenness and crime.[34] Mondelet further insisted that young criminals were learning their skills in taverns—veritable academies of crime, which also drained off the money which should have been used to send children to school.[35]

Temperance was presented as the most basic of all social reforms. Excessive drinking was a prime cause of human suffering which society could, and should, begin to eliminate. It led to the abuse of innocent wives, children, and parents. The wealthy, as well as the poor, were guilty—a point Mondelet supported by publicizing the drunken misconduct of seigneurs' sons, including the death by *delirium tremens* of a young gentleman at Longueuil.[36] Other observers seconded the judge's assertions that drink took a heavy toll. A writer who claimed to be familiar with rural inheritance practices said that liquor payments in the annuities that children promised to their aging parents added significantly to the burden of debt in assuming a farm.[37] Another writer calculated that drunkenness had led to the break-up of nearly seven hundred French-Canadian families, leaving about 3,800 children to beg for their bread.[38] When these claims were considered, it began to seem that curbing drink might be a forward step. Arson, suicide, and drunken accidents would decline; public health and manners would improve. The desire for education and self-improvement would spread, leading Canada at last to prosperity.[39] In Judge Mondelet's view, the drinking problem was so extensive, and current practices so injurious to society, that temperance would bring about "a complete revolution in human affairs."[40]

A growing chorus of reformers endorsed temperance reform. The editor of the *Lower Canada Agricultural Journal* said sobriety would improve farming in the most basic way, by making the farmer more vigorous.[41] School Superintendent J.B. Meilleur, who had long advocated levying higher liquor taxes as a source of school funding,[42] endorsed Chiniquy's temperance manual and recommended its use in the schools.[43] Political radicals such as T.S. Brown and Wolfred Nelson also endorsed the campaign against drink. Brown, who had led *patriote* forces at St Charles, became a platform speaker on temperance, presenting "King Alcohol" as the great oppressor of the poor.[44]

Mondelet, as has been noted, carried his convictions to what he saw as their logical conclusion. He urged the community to unite and take whatever steps were needed to see that the taverns closed down.[45] The judge lashed out at the provincial government's disregard for its citizens in granting licences upon appeal to people rejected by local authorities.[46] The priests had relied on individual conviction to curtail drinking; but Mondelet wanted civic action, and he recruited prestigious members of the grand juries to the cause. He predicted that temperance reform would be a rallying point which would unite laymen and priests, and people of various classes and groups.[47]

By the late 1840s, when Mondelet called for the abolition of taverns, others were sufficiently alarmed about Montreal's growing crime and misery to agree. The journal *La Revue canadienne* argued that for *les grands maux* one needed *les grands remèdes.* Since it was intemperance that filled the streets with ragged beggars and the jails with criminals, then "*à bas les licenses d'auberges,* qui sont la plupart d'infâmes repaires de brigands...à bas ces lieux inutiles remplis d'oisifs et de fainéants, qui sont la terreur et l'effroi, la honte et le désespoir, des villes et villages."[48]

Another cause of concern was the growing number of French Canadians who were emigrating to the United States. Could drink again be the culprit? A legislative committee appointed to enquire into French-Canadian migration found that lumberjacks who frittered away their wages on wild living had no savings to fall back upon when periodic slumps hit the timber trade. Thus, unemployed lumbermen were forced to emigrate. The committee also heard evidence of farmers drinking themselves into such heavy debt that they, too, had to sell out and leave.[49]

As such testimony mounted, those who worried about French Canada's future began to see drink as a menace. The Quebec Committee on Reform and Progress passed temperance resolutions, and the Montreal Institut canadien chose a temperance lecturer to address them on the subject of "National Industry and Economy."[50] Hector Langevin, then at the beginning of his long political career, declared that drunkenness had become so serious that it had replaced assimilation as the great national peril:

> ... ce petit peuple a grandi...sa langue et ses moeurs ne périront pas. Mais un danger plus grand le menace; cette fois, il ne s'agit plus de l'anglification; c'est le chancre de l'intempérance qui le dévore...ravissant la dignité de l'homme raisonnable...[51]

Other temperance campaigners were drawn from a group of devout entrepreneurs similar to those who supported the movement in English Canada, though priestly predominance and the relative scarcity of French-Canadian entrepreneurs kept this group small. One example, though, was Charles Seraphim Rodier, a representative of the new French-Canadian bourgeoisie whom *La Presse* would one day eulogize as having "proved the aptitude of our race for business."[52] Rodier had much in common with English-Canadian temperance supporters such as John Redpath and Joseph MacKay. He too was a self-made man, one who rose from carpentry to contracting to the manufacture of agricultural implements. "By energy and perseverance" he acquired an immense fortune; when he died in 1890, he was reputed to be the richest French-Canadian of his day.[53] Rodier contributed to various philanthropic causes. Although some would define a philanthropist as one who gives away what he should give back, Rodier seems to have been an exemplary employer, paying Montreal's highest wages.[54] Like some of his Protestant counterparts in Montreal, he was an active churchman, serving as president of the St Vincent de Paul and St Jean-Baptiste Societies. Another self-made man who actively endorsed temperance was Louis Renaud, who started out as a carter and ended up as Canada East's leading grain dealer.[55] Hubert Paré was another temperance supporter from the business community who combined an innovative career in banking, insurance, and railways with philanthropy and religious activism.[56]

By the second half of the 1840s, with *canadiens* such as Mondelet, Meilleur, Rodier, and Paré speaking out in favour of temperance, the movement was expanding beyond the devout group that had been converted during the *réveil.* Having drawn prominent supporters from the business and professional classes, it now had sufficiently strong endorsement to become a French-Canadian national crusade. It was at this point that Charles Chiniquy, who during several years of study in an Oblate monastery had been out of the public eye, came again to prominence, to lead a temperance campaign that would astonish the whole Province of Canada.

Patriotism and Sackcloth

Surprisingly, Judge Mondelet and Bishop Bourget were able to bring their reform hopes to fruition. Although Father Chiniquy's oratory was the catalyst, the groundwork had been laid before he began his tour across Canada East in 1847. By that time there were many parish temperance societies promising salvation to good Catholics, as well as a platform promising reform to good *rouges*. Embodying this new alliance of cleansing Catholicism and reforming nationalism, Chiniquy was able to satisfy groups that in other periods might be more clearly distinguished as the religious right and the secular left. In his day, the categories were not so clear, and he was widely seen as the way ahead.

Like other clergymen, Chiniquy, during the *réveil,* had regarded temperance primarily as a religious matter.[57] When he returned to campaigning in the late 1840s, he came back with a somewhat more worldly message: national survival depended on temperance. If French Canadians sobered up, they would become as productive and progressive as other North Americans. If they kept on drinking, they were committing collective suicide. When he linked temperance to *survivance,* Chiniquy was able to unite religious and secular temperance supporters, to create mass fervour which had no parallel elsewhere in British North America. Downplaying the polarizing political issues of the Rebellion era by focusing on social and economic modernization, this new nationalism appealed to *rouges* and ultramontanes, gentry and common folk. Leading this broad segment of the laity in a national campaign, Chiniquy was exercising the expanded priestly leadership which lay at the heart of the ultramontane program. Like other aspects of that agenda, temperance would tend to shed its progressive side after mid-century. Visions of social and economic development would yield in the 1850s to a much more conservative view of temperance—and life itself—as a form of religious asceticism.

I

Although well regarded by liberal nationalists, Father Chiniquy was an ultramontane Catholic who championed an extension of church authority. He publicly proclaimed the rights of the church and the duty to submit to the pope. With the ultramontane's disregard for the dividing line between religion and politics, he pronounced in favour of Reform politician L.-H. LaFontaine's party in a way LaFontaine himself considered improper.[58] When the developing rift between Bishop Bourget and some of the more anti-clerical *rouges* forced Chiniquy to take sides late in his campaign, he was to declare that "tout ce qui tient à la vertu, à l'ordre, à la justice, au droit, est du domain du prêtre, sachez le bien."[59] Reinforcing ultramontanism on the local level were Chiniquy's visits to hundreds of parishes. When he was taking his leave, a delegation of the local notables frequently came to thank him for changing their lives. He would give a clear directive as to where the people were to turn for future counsel. They must, as he told the people of St Geneviève in the spring of 1849, "suivez les sages avis du bon curé."[60]

The story of the Chiniquy crusade of 1848–51 has been told elsewhere.[61] Here a brief summary will suffice. He began visiting parishes in the Montreal diocese to preach temperance in the early months of 1848. After hearing him speak, hundreds, and sometimes thousands, of people in parish after parish stepped forward and pledged never to drink again. In the first eighteen months of campaigning, he visited 110 localities and persuaded 200,000 people to take the pledge.[62] Chiniquy generated much excitement because, to a considerably greater extent than during earlier campaigns, there clearly was a mass renunciation of alcohol. Believing, as nineteenth-century temperance converts tended to do, that a dry world would be dramatically better, the people became increasingly hopeful when they saw people all around them taking the pledge. They said Chiniquy reminded them of the *patriotes,* and they called him the new Papineau, for he raised their hopes in the same way the rebel hero had done.[63] As the crusade progressed along the dusty backroads of Canada East, it swelled to a triumphal march. Whole parishes turned out to greet the temperance priest with flags and marching bands, militia musters and cannonades. They quickly bought up ten thousand copies of his temperance writings, and they proudly hung his picture on their walls.[64]

Chiniquy continued to campaign through 1850 and most of 1851, going towards the end to preach in the Quebec diocese as well. Largely because of the excitement he generated, even parishes he did not visit hastened to take the pledge from other, lesser-known preachers who were also circulating. In 1850 the count mounted to 400,000 teetotallers.[65] That was nearly half the population of Canada East, and a clear majority of its francophone population.

Chiniquy's success was largely a result of his exceptional platform talent. In the ultramontane camp, he supplied a quality which his superior, Bishop Bourget, probably lacked: charisma. Bourget, we are told, was humble, grave, and dignified. He had the high forehead and mild eye of a philosopher. Meticulous in the smallest details of religious observance, he was a meditative man "with a spirit of true detachment." Despite his resolute spirit, he seemed, in fact, a somewhat timid person.[66] But turn the coin over, and there is Chiniquy: a flamboyant character with "blazing eyes" and "a brilliant imagination."[67] Unlike the retiring Bourget, he had the "orator's instinct" to proclaim his truth from the rooftops. Far from being detached, he was an emotional soul who enjoyed "a warm empathy with his audience." Taken together, these qualities gave him "the truly magical influence he exerted over the masses."[68] However, unlike Bourget, Chiniquy lacked judgment;[69] even his friends and allies worried about his stability. If Bourget was Cavour, Charles Chiniquy was his Garibaldi. Bourget, a stern man, was a careful strategist and administrator; Chiniquy was a hero. While the bishop was laying the solid foundations for a Catholic state, the priest went out onto the highways and byways to win recruits for it. He persuaded people to sign up for what was to be the first of a long series of clerical strategies for *survivance.*

Chiniquy was a skilled performer. He had to be seen in person to be appreciated; indeed, editors seldom reprinted his speeches, and they did so with apologies, complaining that they were unable to capture his effect.[70] Part of this sprang from the suspense he built up by using stage effects: his sudden, unexpected appearances prompted rumours that he had arrived by miracle.[71] When he strode out to face his audience, Chiniquy used his small frame to maximum effect. When people first saw him, they sometimes felt that he was overrated. He had the sad, sheepish look of a loser. But he approached the altar so solemnly that the crowd suddenly sensed a greater force than his own slight person at work. One observer reported that during the course of his sermons he seemed to transform himself from a lamb into a lion. At the climax, he would raise aloft the large golden crucifix the pope had given him and ask various groups in the audience to strike down the Goliath of drink. He would end on an exultant note, urging mothers to dry up their tears, children and pastors to rejoice; together the parish was going to strike a blow on their behalf. Chiniquy's performances moved people to tears.[72]

Apart from the theatrics, Chiniquy knew how to strike the right chords. A critic has described his technique as honeyed flattery.[73] An admirer called it "an orator's instinct which divined the composition of his audiences."[74] Thus, out in the country parishes, Chiniquy spoke in a direct way about daily concerns, departing from the usual formal sermon style.[75] Farm families, shaken by several decades of agrarian crisis, were worried about competition from British and American immigrants who seemed to till the soil so successfully.[76] "How you complain," he told the people who packed into the village churches, "of the newcomers who seem to be invading our land, of the contemptuous way they treat you." Immigrants had already acquired the best town properties, and ancient families were being driven from their seigneuries by the creditor's whip. "Your turn is coming," Chiniquy warned his audiences: "Yes, it is with a heart full of inexpressible sorrow that we declare to you: before many years, unless a prompt and universal change takes place among you, you will be driven from your homes, and your children will stay there in the capacity of servants and slaves."[77] God had deliberately sent the English, Scots, Irish, and Americans to punish Canada. The immigrants were not to blame, for their methods were entirely honourable; frugality, hard work, and a commitment to educating their children. It was almost a foregone conclusion that the habitants would lose their lands to these more disciplined people—unless the French Canadians were willing to give up the ruinous addiction that left them sluggish and disorganized.

Chiniquy also mastered town audiences, such as the one gathered in Bishop Bourget's cathedral in June 1849. By that time, the orator was already famous, and his temperance converts were being hailed as the long-awaited force for economic improvement. At the cathedral, a coterie of *rouge* members of the Société Mercantile de l'Economie sat amid the clerics and parishioners. Chiniquy pitched part of the address to them, praising the love of learning among the younger generation of Canadians. He called for a liberalization of ideas—another notion more likely to please the *rouges* than the bishop. Mindful of the latter as well, Chiniquy added that if the ideas of universal fraternity and equality were too liberal to suit everyone, they must at least exist as ideas in the hearts of ministers of the Gospel, for whom all souls were of equal value—a sentiment which Bourget, deeply committed to popular religion, no doubt appreciated.

Rouges and ultramontanes could both applaud Chiniquy's other theme, the call for development of native industry:

> We ought not to bring from Europe what we can get at home. We have been upwards of two hundred years in Canada and we manufacture nothing, not even a pin or a button. I have been ashamed while travelling in the United States, and seeing their extensive manufactures, to think that we are yet in our cradles. Last year I heard a party of gentlemen on board a steamboat conversing about some *great progress,* which turned out to be the establishment of a manufactory of *tobacco pipes*! We suffer from a want of nationality, a want of union, a want of energy.[78]

If French Canadians would only transfer their time and savings from drinking to schooling, they would, the preacher promised, soon be able to compete with other, more advanced countries.

By means of such presentations in town and country, Chiniquy swayed the group it was hardest for the clergy to sway: Papineau's followers. The priest was able to combine his reputation as a liberal with his role as Bishop Bourget's agent because, in that spring of 1848 when Chiniquy began his campaign, ultramontanes and *rouges* had not yet crossed swords. In those days, at the Montreal Institut canadien, the "ayes" were in fact carrying the debate on the question of whether large numbers of religious communities contributed to a country's advancement. A year later, they broke into repeated applause during Etienne Parent's prophetic address calling for an expanded social and national role for the clergy. Chiniquy was the very image of the new, activist priest of whom Parent spoke, and Parent commended his work.[79] The *rouge* journal *L'Avenir* singled out Chiniquy as a strong and eloquent voice, a priest moved by reason and love of country. He was characterized as a philanthropist who would relieve the people's distress by making them thrifty and sober.

Indeed, he aroused all sorts of passions and hopes among those who had demonstrated discontent with British rule. During his visit to Ste Anne Yamachiche, after the local militia fired off a cannonade, a Dr Desaulniers appeared at the head of a delegation and thanked Chiniquy for putting to flight the destroyer of their happiness and prosperity, one of the most powerful obstacles to their advancement. The preacher had, he said, "effacé la tâche qui souillait notre caractère national, et vous avez puissamment demontré à nos calomniateurs que le Canadien n'est pas sans qualité, mais qu'il est un peuple grand, un peuple noble, un peuple genéréux."[80] A convert in the parish of St Caesar combined *rouge* anti-Union sentiment with utopianism, hoping that "l'union détruite avec le temps, et l'ivrognerie disparu, le Bas-Canada sera à la porte du bonheur tel que nous pouvons le désirer ici-bas."[81] In March 1849 Chiniquy reached St Eustache, which had been a centre of rebellion in 1837 despite the church's condemnation of the uprising. No rebels now, the people lined up to take the pledge. Thanking their visitor afterwards, the villagers compared themselves to the ancient Israelites. In what was perhaps an allusion to the Rebellion or to Governor Colborne's repression afterwards, they lamented that "the walls of the temple had risen up against them."[82] They blamed it on their worship of a false god, the golden calf of drink. Now "Moses"—Chiniquy—had come to lead them into the promised land. There, with God's help and their curé's approval, they would find a new life. In closing, they declared "Peace on earth to all men!"[83] The sheep may have converted to temperance during the *réveil.* Chiniquy was performing the harder task of bringing in the goats.

Not only were priests and *patriotes* reconciled; class distinctions, too, were temporarily downplayed. Earlier temperance campaigns in French Canada had tended to appeal to the unsophisticated; but at Chiniquy's call, educated and influential people came into the fold as well. By autumn of 1848, *rouge* and ultramontane newspapers agreed that he had won over "all the most respectable inhabitants of the country" and "all of French Canada's most eminent people."[84] Mayors and other local notables came out to greet him. They chaired meetings at which resolutions were passed calling for regulations that would ensure their parishes stayed dry.[85]

Protestants and Catholics alike recognized this campaign as an unprecedented success. The Reverend William Taylor, a long-time Montreal Temperance Society activist, said so at a huge meeting held in Montreal to congratulate Chiniquy and pass temperance resolutions. Judge Mondelet and a crowd of some ten thousand admirers presented a medal to the hero-priest at a ceremony at Longueuil.[86] Also impressed was the parliament of the Province of Canada, which awarded Chiniquy an honorarium of £500 for outstanding service to the country and passed restrictive tavern legislation which he had helped to draft.[87] His sweep through the countryside was hailed as a moral revolution.

The fact was that French Canada had become quite startlingly dry. The 400,000 pledge-takers of 1848–50 had stopped, or greatly reduced, their drinking. Taverns, which often shut when Chiniquy came to town, stayed shut after he left. By the autumn of 1848, forty parishes and townships in the Montreal district had closed their drinking places. By the next summer, it was reported that seventy-five of the parishes across Canada East were dry.[88] By June 1849, nearly all the distilleries in Canada East had suspended operations,[89] and scores of puncheons had been returned by country merchants who had no buyers. Molson's, the largest distillery in the province, which had weathered earlier temperance campaigns without any serious inconvenience, reported a loss of £15,000 in 1849.[90] When the Chiniquy crusade got under way, imports of alcohol sank to the lowest point in decades.[91] Domestic production also hit bottom as the campaign crested during 1849–50.

By 1850, Chiniquy had apparently succeeded in turning a society long known for its *joie-de-vivre* into the most bone-dry temperance stronghold in North America.

CANADA EAST DISTILLERIES, GALLONS PRODUCED

1847	645,386
1848	317,840
1849	246,920
1850	79,914

Source: F. Ouellet, Histoire économique et sociale du Québec, 2:617

Trouble was stirring, though. By September 1851, Bishop Bourget had received so much disturbing information about his prize preacher that he could delay action no longer. He had just received a woman's testimony (later affirmed under oath) that Chiniquy had attempted to seduce her. This was all the more worrisome because there was solid evidence that Chiniquy had done the same thing several years earlier. He had made overtures to a woman in the parish of St Pascal during a week of temperance preaching there in 1846, only to be thwarted by the local curé, who, notified by the woman, had appeared in her stead at the appointed place of rendezvous. This incident, never publicized, had been whitewashed; Father Brassard, a long-time friend of Chiniquy's, had convinced Bourget that the conduct ascribed had not been serious enough to warrant taking action against the promising young preacher. However, evidence continued to mount that Chiniquy was making advances to women he met in the course of his travels. By 28 September 1851, Bourget had heard enough. He wrote a letter ordering his troublesome hero to henceforth cease all pastoral work in the Montreal diocese.[92]

Thus it was that in October 1851 Chiniquy boarded a westbound train and went off to work as a missionary to French-Canadian settlers in Illinois. Within five years, he would incur the wrath of the bishop of the Chicago diocese, becoming the subject of allegations of sexual misconduct and disobedience to superiors. Excommunicated from the Catholic Church in 1856, he would convert to Presbyterianism, marry, and return to the Canadas. He would carve out a second career for himself, becoming a world-renowned writer and lecturer *against* the Catholic Church. To the end, he retained a fiery tongue which he used to set hearts afire.

The most dramatic effects of the Chiniquy crusade did not last. While the orator's disgrace was not generally known, his absence was sufficient cause for a rapid plunge in enthusiasm. Tavern-keepers began setting up shop again when Chiniquy's campaign ground to a halt in the autumn of 1851. By 1852, Bishop Bourget was lamenting that enemies of temperance were attacking "de tous côtés, et avec fureur."[93] Liquor consumption began to climb again.[94] In 1853, a relieved Thomas Molson wrote to a friend that the temperance movement had relaxed and plans were under way for expansion of his Montreal distilling operation. It is true that many of Chiniquy's rural converts continued to shun alcohol, and one found pockets of teetotal farmers in Quebec for decades afterwards. But in the towns particularly, many people returned to their old ways.[95]

Chiniquy's more significant contribution was probably that which charismatic figures often make, that of mediating between old and new authority.[96] Canadians of the 1830s witnessed the failure of the radical and often anticlerical *patriotes.* In the following decade the people responded by turning their backs on radical politics, and finding their hero in a temperance priest who championed the authority of the church. Although his devoutly Catholic phase did not last very long, it came at a crucial time to usher in a changing of the guard. Chiniquy was part of the much broader process in which a whole people took a turn to the right, rejecting the radical politicians who had led them to defeat, shuffling into humbler procession behind their priests. With Father Chiniquy at the head, it did not *seem* humble; it seemed a triumphal march.

Notes

1 Ignace Bourget, "Mandement, 6 janvier 1850," in *Mandements, lettres pastorales, circulaires et autres documents publiés dans le diocèse de Montréal depuis son éréction jusqu' à l'année 1869* (Montréal, 1887), 80, 94–5.

2 J.-P. Bernard, *Idéologies québécoises au 19e siècle* (Montréal, 1973), 92.

3 See Archives Nationales du Québec, Ministère de la Justice, "Evénements de 1837–1838," particularly the August 1839 letters of W.F. Coffin to Major Goldie (no. 3575), and Charles Wethrall to Major Goldie (no. 3726). I am grateful to Professor Allan Greer of the University of Toronto for drawing my attention to this material. Given the small size of habitant houses and the unsympathetic attitude of the churches (and perhaps "the missus"), it seems plausible that radical meetings probably often did occur in taverns.

4 "Ignace Bourget," *Dictionary of Canadian Biography* (*DCB*), 11:101.

5 Ibid., 11:101.

6 Ibid., 11:105.

7 "Antoine-Olivier Berthelet," *DCB,* 10:53; J.I. Cooper, "The Social Structure of Montreal in the 1850s," *Canadian Historical Association: Historical Papers* (1956), 66–7. Berthelet is also discussed in H. Lapointe-Roy, *Charité bien ordonée: le premier réseau de lutte contre la pauvreté à Montréal au 19e siècle* (Montréal, 1987).

8 J. Grise, *Les Conciles provinciaux de Québec et l'Eglise canadienne (1851–1886)* (Montréal, 1979), 52; see also *Mandements et Circulaires* (1851), 194.

9 G. Lesage in P. Hurtubise, Le Laïc dans l'Eglise canadienne-francaise de 1830 à nos jours (Montréal 1972), 33–4.

10 Bourget, "Mandement, janvier 1849," 188.

11 Bourget, "Mandement, janvier 1842," 197.

12 *Mélanges religieux* (*MR*), 28 mars 1848.

13 This according to an 1842 *Mandement* by Bishop Bourget (*Mandements, lettres pastorales,* 197).

14 R. Hardy, "Aperçu du rôle social et religieux du curé de Notre-Dame de Québec (1840–1860)" (Thèse, D.E.S., Laval, 1968).

15 For reports of the rapid growth of temperance societies in Quebec after the bishop's visit, see *Le Canadien,* 20 déc. 1840 and 15 jan. 1841; Buckingham, *Canada, Nova Scotia, New Brunswick,* 261; Hardy, "Aperçu," 91; N.-E. Dionne, *Monseigneur de Forbin-Janson: sa vie, son oeuvre en Canada* (Québec, 1895), 67. See also C. Galarneau, "Mgr. de Forbin-Janson au Québec en 1840–41," in N. Voisine and J. Hamelin, dir., *Les Ultramontains canadiens-français* (Montréal, 1985), 121–42.

16 *MR*, 30 mars 1841. By April, 10,000 people in the Trois-Rivières district had joined (*Le Canadien,* 9 avril 1841).

17 *MR*, 19 and 22 jan. 1841; Wadsworth, 23.

18 *L'Aurore,* 8 jan. 1841; *MR*, 18 juillet 1843.

19 V. Levy-Beaulieu, *Manuel de la petite littérature du Québec* (Montréal, 1974), 103.

20 That this was the policy of the curé of Notre Dame parish in Quebec City is shown in Hardy, "Aperçu du rôle social et religieux du curé de Notre-Dame de Québec (1840–1860)."

21 *MR*, 19 nov. 1841; Trudel, *Chiniquy,* 41.

22 L. Pouliot, *Mgr. Bourget et son temps,* (Montréal, 1955–72), 2:158–9; *MR*, 11 fév. 1842. See also Bourget's *Mandement* of 25 jan. 1842.

23 *MR*, 21 oct. 1845.

24 C. Chiniquy, *Manuel ou reglément de la Société de Tempérance* (Québec, 1844), 125.

25 Lemay, 22; Hardy, "Aperçu," 45–6, 93; Chiniquy, *Manuel,* 125.

26 Cf. Ouellet, *Histoire,* 2:617; and National Archives of Canada, Robin, Jones and Whitman Company Correspondence, 1841–3, MG 28, III, 18, vol. 239, letter of clerk Elias de la Parelle from Caraquet, 24 August 1841: "A number of the folks here have joined the Temperance Society and the remainder will do so very shortly; so that we will not require Rum next season." See also N. Dorion, "L'Industrie de la bière: le cas de la Brasserie Boswell," *Material History Review* 33, (1991), 1–9. Later renamed Dow, the Boswell Brewery's success was such that it expanded into modern factory quarters around 1852 on the site of Talon's ancient brewery. By 1870 it was Quebec's largest brewery with some seventy-five employees.

27 *MR*, 3 avril 1846, 19 jan. 1847, 2 mai 1848; Hardy, "Aperçu," 45–6, 93.

28 M. Trudel, *L'Influence de Voltaire au Canada* (Montréal, 1945), 159.

29 *L'Avenir,* 31 déc. 1847, 12 fév. 1848.

30 Ibid., 16 oct. 1847.

31 J. Huston, ed., *Le Répertoire national* (Montréal, 1893), 4:81.

32 *CTA,* July 1836.

33 *MR,* 22 oct. 1847.

34 *JLAC,* 1849, Appendix ZZZ; *CTA,* 1 Feb. 1845.

35 *MR,* 22 oct. 1847.

36 Ibid.

37 Ibid., 7 juillet 1848.

38 Ibid., 10 oct. 1848.

39 Ibid., 22 oct. 1847.

40 Ibid, 24 oct. 1848.

41 *Lower Canada Agricultural Journal,* Sept. 1848.

42 "J-B Meilleur," *DCB,* 10:506.

43 *MR,* 3 mai 1849; Chiniquy, *Manuel* (1847), preface.

44 Brown, *Speech of T.S. Brown,* 3–5. Chiniquy, *Manuel,* (1849), 85.

45 *MR,* 22 oct. 1847.

46 Ibid.

47 Ibid., 22 oct. 1847, 24 oct. 1848.

48 Quoted in ibid., 2 nov. 1847.

49 Ibid., 4 dec. 1849.

50 Trudel, 100.

51 Chiniquy, *Manuel* (1849), 8.

52 Quoted in "C.S. Rodier," *DCB,* 11:763.

53 M. Bibaud, *Le Panthéon canadien,* (Montreal, 1891), 249; *DCB* 11:763.

54 Cooper, "Social Structure...," 68.

55 *DCB,* 10:613–14, discusses Renaud's career.

56 "Hubert Paré," *DCB,* 9:616–17. See also J.l. Cooper, "The Origins and Early History of the Montreal City and District Savings Bank," *Canadian Historical Association: Historical Papers* (1945–6), 15–25.

57 See Trudel, *Chiniquy,* 55, for Chiniquy's assessment that unless temperance increased piety, it was of little value.

58 P. Sylvain, "Quelques Aspects de l'antagonisme liberal-ultramontain," in Bernard, *Idéologies,* 135; Trudel, *Chiniquy,* 301.

59 *La Minerve,* 21 juin 1849.

60 Ibid., 7 mai 1849.

61 Trudel, *Chiniquy;* Berton, *My Country,* chapter 8.

62 Trudel, 96.

63 *Canada Temperance Advocate (CTA),* 1 May 1848; see also Chiniquy, *Manuel* (1849), 157.

64 Chiniquy's 1849 temperance manual containing his picture was so popular that even country grocers stocked it. A print of the Chiniquy portrait by Hamel was also available separately. (*Les Mélanges religieux* [*MR*], 31 oct. 1848, 8 jan. 1850); C. Chiniquy, *Mes Combats* (Montréal, 1946), noted that 4,000 copies of the 1844 manual were sold; then 6,000 of the 1847 edition were sold within eighteen months of publication. A third edition would be issued in 1849.

65 *MR,* 6 sept. 1850; G. "Carrière, 'L'Eglise canadienne vers 1841," *Revue de l'Université d'Ottawa* 24 (1954), 72.

66 E.J. Auclair, *Figures canadiennes* (Montréal, 1933), 18; L.O. David, *Mgr. Bourget and Mgr. Taché* (Montreal, 1912), 11–13.

67 See the funeral orations in Chiniquy, *Mes Combats* 682ff.

68 From the 1899 funeral oration by the Reverend R. Duclos, in Chiniquy, *Mes Combats,* 682.

69 *Montreal Daily Star,* 16 Jan. 1899; Monet, *The Last Cannon Shot,* 373.

70 *MR,* 10 oct. 1848.

71 Ibid., 30 mars 1849.

72 This description is drawn from *MR,* 30 mars 1849; *CTA* 1 May 1849; and Trudel, 94.

73 Trudel, 47.

74 Duclos, "Funeral Oration," in Chiniquy, *Mes Combats,* 682.

75 Ibid.; and *CTA,* 1 May 1849.

76 See Ouellet, *Eléments d'histoire sociale du le Bas-Canada,* 153–173.

77 Chiniquy, *Manuel* (1849), 143–4.

78 *CTA,* 1 May 1849.

79 Huston, 4:116; *L'Avenir,* 20 nov. 1847, 6 sept. 1848, 20 dec. 1848.

80 *La Minerve,* 16 juillet 1849.

81 *MR,* 2 juin 1848.

82 Ibid., 30 mars 1849.

83 Ibid.

84 Ibid., 8 sept. 1848; *L'Avenir,* 6 sept. 1848.

85 As elsewhere in British North America, there was a strain of rural populism. *L'Echo des campagnes* remarked on the novelty of this "réunion d'hommes de tous les rangs de la société, capables de peser et

juger les affairs de leur pays, sans le secours de jeunes *citadins* qui s'imposent à quelques comtes, comme seuls en état d'entendre les affaires publiques" (quoted in *MR,* 2 fev. 1849).

86 *MR,* 6 oct. 1848, 17 juillet 1849; Trudel, 98; *La Minerve,* 16 juillet 1849.

87 Trudel, 108–11.

88 *MR,* 19 sept. 1848, 26 sept. 1848, 1 juin 1848.

89 *CTA,* 1 Jan. 1849; *Journal of the Legislative Assembly of Canada (JLAC),* 1849, Appendix ZZZ.

90 Denison, *The Barley and the Stream: The Molson Story,* 119, 195, 207.

91 See the figures in Ouellet, *Histoire économique et sociale du Québec,* 617.

92 Trudel, 126–30.

93 Bourget, "Circulaire," 19 mars 1852, 293.

94 Ouellet, *Histoire,* 492.

95 *JLAC* 17.5 (1859), Appendix 43; *JLAC* 14.6 (1856), Appendix 62; J. Douglas, *Journals and Reminiscences of James Douglas, M.D., Edited by His Son* (New York, 1910), 211; Denison, 234. *Annales de la Temperance,* 8 fev. 1854; S. Gagnon, in Hurtubise, *Le Laïc,* 118.

96 For this idea, I am indebted to a discussion of this function in contemporary politics by C. Taylor in T. Hockin, ed., *Apex of Power: The Prime Minister and Political Leadership in Canada* (Scarborough, Ont., 1971), 112.

The Case Against Canadian Confederation

GED MARTIN

[...] A "high politics" view of Confederation would lead us to question the value of the actual arguments put forward against Confederation, since the root reason for opposition in many cases could be suspected to be resentment at not being taken aboard. At the very least, the prospect of loaves and fishes could soften the opposition of some critics of Confederation. Members of Albert J. Smith's New Brunswick ministry were prepared to take up the question in 1866, despite having been elected in 1865 to oppose it.[1] In Nova Scotia, the spectacular bolt to change sides in April 1866 was alleged to have been touched off by the suspicious decision of two anti-Confederates that others would rat first, and "we...had better get into line or we should be left out in the cold and lose all chance of obtaining good positions."[2]

The two major sources on which this paper is based are the *Confederation Debates* of 1865 in the province of Canada, and the Nova Scotia petitions of 1866 in the *British Parliamentary Papers.* The Canadian parliament had not previously printed its debates, and we may echo the lament of Dr. Joseph Blanchet, four weeks and 545 pages after discussion began on 3 February 1865, that the decision "to have the speeches of this House printed in official form certainly did no good service to the country." Yet vast as was the eventual volume, it does not necessarily do justice to the opposition case. In the early phases of the debate, there was a tendency to demand further information, for the Quebec plan required much fleshing-out of practical details on which the ministers were unforthcoming—and it was tempting to debunk the visionary orations of Macdonald and McGee by trumpeting that there was no case to answer. Luther Holton replied to the first great onslaught of explanations with the flourish that if the government's speeches "contain all that can be said in favour of this scheme, we have no fear of letting them go unanswered." As the Canadian debate was getting into its stride, so news arrived of Tilley's defeat in New Brunswick which, A-A. Dorion claimed, caused the issue "to lose much of its interest."[3] Much of the debate was taken up with members taunting each other with inconsistency, which often provoked elaborate apologetics. Some speeches were intended to drag matters out while petitions were circulated:[4] Cartier embarrassed Eric Dorion, by reading into the record a circular letter he had sent to supporters requesting them to have anti-Confederation petitions "signed as soon as possible by men, women and children."[5] Similar devices were used to produce petitions in Nova Scotia, as the governor-general, Lord Monck, and a former lieutenant-governor, the Marquess of Normanby, assured the House of Lords in 1867.[6] It is certainly hard to believe that the 210 inhabitants of the district of Port Medway who signed their names to a massive, two thousand word petition against Confederation were entire-

Ged Martin, "The Case Against Canadian Confederation, 1864–1867," in Ged Martin, ed., *The Causes of Canadian Confederation* (Fredericton: Acadiensis Press, 1990), 19–49.

ly unprompted,[7] and it may be doubted if any of the petitions emerged from the sober atmosphere of a political science seminar. At Yarmouth, Joseph Howe preceded a two hour assault on Confederation with "an eloquent eulogy on the character of Her Majesty Queen Victoria, as a child, a wife and mother, a queen and a widow" which was much cheered.[8] It is not surprising that in Nova Scotia opposition to Confederation became what modern American politics would term a "motherhood" issue.

There are other difficulties in accommodating the available material to the logical approach of the historian. A sound historical analysis would seek to balance arguments for and arguments against, coming to a fair and reasonable conclusion. The arguments *for* Confederation, which we normally equate with the reasons for its adoption, are clear enough and capable of neat presentation. The arguments *against* offend our sense of order. Cartier was able to have fun playing off opposites: the Montreal *Witness* warned that Protestantism in Lower Canada would be doomed by Confederation, while its deadly rival, the *True Witness,* saw it as leading to the destruction of French Canada.[9] The easy but fallacious assumption behind such debating devices is that the two strands of argument cancel each other out, whereas in reality one or the other—perhaps even both, but for different reasons—might well be entirely valid. Perhaps the real task of explanation is not to explain *why* Confederation was accepted, but *how* it managed to seize the central ground and divide the opposition to right and left.

"I do not know of any one opposed to union in the abstract," said New Brunswick's Timothy Warren Anglin. "But my impression is that the time has not arrived for any kind of union, and I will oppose it to the last."[10] This was a common theme among the critics: intercolonial union in principle, union one day, but not this union, not now.[11] As Edward Whelan put it, the critics accepted the principle of ploughing the field, but objected to destroying the daisies and field mice.[12] How sincere were these protestations—by some, but by no means all the critics of Confederation—in favour of an eventual British North American union? Perhaps they were gestures of open-mindedness merely to win over waverers. David Reesor found it "extraordinary" that so many members of the Canadian Legislative Council spoke "strongly and emphatically against many of the resolutions" while declaring their reluctant intention to vote for the package.[13] Yet even A-A. Dorion, who went to some lengths to clear his name of the slander of having ever spoken favourably of the idea, could leave open a faint and distant possibility: "Population may extend over the wilderness that now lies between the Maritime Provinces and ourselves, and commercial intercourse may increase sufficiently to render Confederation desirable."[14] As late as August 1864, admittedly at a social occasion, Joseph Howe proclaimed: "I have always been in favour of uniting any two, three, four, or the whole five of the provinces."[15] It is not necessary to follow McGee in the full flight of his oratory, but he may have been right in thinking of the idea of Confederation as an autonomous cause of its own happening. "If we have dreamed a dream of union...it is at least worth while remarking that a dream which has been dreamed by such wise and good men, may, for aught we know or you know, have been a sort of vision—a vision foreshadowing forthcoming natural events in a clear intelligence."[16]

If some of the opponents subscribed to the idea of an eventual intercolonial union, most of the critics in the province of Canada argued that Confederation was not a solution to present difficulties, and it would itself require a far greater degree of political wisdom than was necessary to rescue the existing system. Henri Joly felt that the various provinces would meet in a confederated parliament "as on a field of battle." Christopher Dunkin referred to the airy dismissals of such warnings by ministerial supporters: "Oh! there won't be any trouble; men are in the main sensible, and won't try to make trouble." If public men were so reasonable as to be able to work the new system, why then had the province of Canada had "four crises in two years"? In any case, even if it were accepted that Upper and Lower Canada were not living together in harmony, the answer was surely for them to work out a new system of government and not to claim that only through a wider union could they get along. Dunkin noted that in the five years between the lapsing of Galt's federation initiative in 1859 and the formation of the Grand Coalition of June 1864, "we quarrelled and fought about almost everything, but did not waste a thought or a word upon this gigantic question of the Confederation of these provinces." "Surely," Thomas Scatcherd argued, "if parties could unite as they did in June last, they could have united to prevent the difficulty complained of...without entering upon a scheme to subvert the Constitution."[17]

While some critics of Confederation admitted that the Canadian Union had its problems, others felt them to have been exaggerated. Henri Joly contrasted Taché's claim that "the country was bordering on civil strife" with the ministry's throne speech, which thanked "a beneficent Providence for the general contentment of the people of this province."[18] Joseph Perrault asked, "have we not reason to be proud of our growth since 1840, and of the fact that within the past twenty-five years, our progress, both social and material, has kept pace with that of the first nations in the world?"[19] For French Canadians, a crucial issue was whether they could indeed maintain the equal representation which the two sections of the province of Canada had in the Assembly. In 1858, Joseph Cauchon had believed that Lower Canada had enough allies in the upper province to stand firmly on its rights. By 1865, those allies were becoming fewer; the minority English-speaking representatives from Lower Canada now held the balance of power between French Canadians and an upper province increasingly united in its demand for representation by population. The entrenchment of equal representation in the imperial act of 1840, which required a two-thirds vote to change the balance of representation, had been repealed in 1854—and replaced by a simple majority, thus opening the way to the carrying of "rep. by pop." through the sudden defection of the Lower Canadian English. From that perspective, Confederation—a negotiated scheme which gave French Canadians their own legislature—was preferable to swamping within the existing structure.[20] However, other French Canadian politicians took the threat of "rep. by pop." less seriously, dismissing it—in Joly's words—as "one of those political clap-traps which ambitious men, who can catch them no other way, set to catch the heedless multitude." Joly argued that hypocrisy was proved by the alacrity with which Upper Canada Reformers had entered the Macdonald-Sicotte administration of 1862, which agreed not to press the issue—proof that "Upper Canada is much more indifferent, and its leaders much less sincere touching this question of the representation, than they would have us believe."

Perrault went much further. In a speech presumably aimed at stoking every French Canadian fear of assimilation—it ranged from the Acadian deportation, via the history of Mauritius, to the francophobia of Lord Durham's Report—Perrault denied that Upper Canada had more people than Lower Canada at all. The "true total" of the population of Upper Canada had been "greatly exaggerated" in the census of 1861, a fraud revealed by the fact that the census figure for population under the age of one year exceeded the live births of the previous twelve months by eight thousand. Perrault also claimed that the census had under-counted the population of Lower Canada, for "our farmers have always stood in dread of the census, because they have a suspicion that it is taken with the sole object of imposing some tax, or of making some draft of men for the defence of the country." Yet, confusingly, he contended that even if Upper Canada's population did exceed that of Lower Canada, it was no more than a temporary blip, caused by Irish famine migration, which had now ceased. So too had the outward flow of French Canadians to New England, with the result that within ten years, the higher birth rate of Lower Canada would bring the two provinces back to equality of population.[21]

The core of the case against Confederation was that there was no crisis sufficient to justify so large a change. Consequently, critics largely refused to enter the trap of offering alternative solutions. "We are asked, 'what are you going to do? You must do something. Are you going to fall back to our old state of dead-lock?'" Dunkin reported, adding that whenever he heard the argument "that something must be done, I suspect that there is a plan on foot to get something very bad done." Henri Joly took the same line. "I am asked: 'If you have nothing to do with Confederation, what will you have?' I answer, we would remain as we are."[22] "Now my proposition is very simple," Joseph Howe told the people of Nova Scotia. "It is to let well enough alone."[23] Not surprisingly, the opponents of Confederation indignantly rejected the argument that they were—wittingly or otherwise—working for annexation to the United States. They replied that the campaign for Confederation itself contained the germ of an annexationist threat. Matthew Cameron, one of the few prominent Upper Canada Conservatives to oppose the scheme, warned that the delusive arguments of material gain from Confederation with the tiny Maritimes "are arguments ten-fold stronger in favour of union with the United States."[24] Nor did the danger lie simply in encouraging hopes of greater prosperity, as was shown when a moderate Lower Canadian journal could proclaim "qu'à tous les points de vue, nos institutions, notre langue, et nos lois seront mieux protégés avec la confédération américaine qu'avec le projet de confédération de l'Amérique Britannique du Nord."[25] "Once destroy public confidence in our institutions," warned T.C. Wallbridge, "and it is impossible to predict what extremes may be resorted to."[26] Joseph Howe similarly predicted that the imposition of Confederation on unwilling provinces would lead to "undying hatreds and ultimate annexation."[27]

At first sight, it might seem surprising that the opponents of Confederation were able to escape the tactical trap of offering alternative solutions to intercolonial problems. Christopher Dunkin and Joseph Howe were on insecure ground in putting forward the far more ambitious idea of imperial federation,[28] while Tupper found that Maritime Union had no friends at all when he attempted the ploy of reviving it in 1865.[29] In the province of Canada, the demand for an alternative would have been dangerous for the cause of Confederation after its defeat in the New Brunswick election of 1865. The teleological and celebratory accounts of the textbooks stress that the Great Coalition of June 1864 was pledged "in the most earnest manner, to the negotiation for a confederation of all the British North American provinces." Less noticed is the fact that the agreement contained a fall-back position, that "failing a successful issue to such negotiations, they are prepared to pledge themselves to legislation during the next session of Parliament for the purpose of remedying existing difficulties by introducing the federal principle for Canada alone," with provision for future expansion. Minutes before the celebrated coalition deal was struck at the St Louis Hotel, Brown had still been insisting that "the Canadian federation should be constituted first." In March 1865, after the setback in New Brunswick, the coalition came close to breaking up over Brown's insistence on invoking the fall-back position. Brown pressed the issue again in the negotiations for the succession to Taché in August 1865, and forced John A. Macdonald to give formal endorsement, in the name of the new premier, Sir Narcisse Belleau, to his interpretation of the coalition deal. Brown, leader of the majority party in the majority section, could afford to be philosophical about the defeat of Confederation after the New Brunswick election: "If it fails after all legitimate means have been used, we will go on with our scheme for Canada alone."[30] For John A. Macdonald, such a solution could offer little comfort: as a Conservative, he had been dependent since 1857 upon Bleu support for his periods of office. Anything which strengthened Upper Canada and its Reform party against Lower Canada was likely to mean problems for the Conservative party. Once it seemed that New Brunswick had dropped out, Brown and his Upper Canada Reform colleagues were under pressure to deliver the small print of the coalition bargain. "The Administration could not give a pledge that they would carry the Confederation of all the provinces," A-A. Dorion reminded his former allies, "but they could pledge and did pledge themselves to bring in, in the event of the failure of that scheme, a measure for the federation of Upper and Lower Canada."[31] Far from heading a triumphant march to nationhood, Macdonald and his allies were walking a desperately narrow tightrope.

Consequently, supporters of Confederation could not afford to admit that rival schemes might be possible. Rather they were obliged to present the Quebec scheme as an immutable package, a balanced intercolonial treaty—thus denying themselves any room for manoeuvre to win over those Maritimers who objected to the terms rather than the aim of Confederation. Critics objected to being faced with the resolutions as a package. "What is the use of considering them if we cannot come to our conclusions and give them effect in the shape of amendments?" asked one Upper Canadian critic. At Quebec, Dunkin pointed out, twenty three men had sat for seventeen working days to produce "a scheme of a Constitution which they vaunt as being altogether better than that of the model republic of the United States, and even than that of the model kingdom of Great Britain."[32] William Annand of Nova Scotia thought that a scheme "matured in a few weeks, amid exhaustive festivities" could not be the best constitution possible.[33] Joseph Howe noted that the inflexibility of the Quebec scheme would be carried forward to the future: "No means are provided by which the people, should it be found defective, can improve it from time to time. Whenever a change is required they must come back to the Imperial Parliament."[34] Indeed, the Canadian people were to continue coming back to Westminster until 1982.

Coupled with resentment at the rejection of any possibility of amendment was anger at the total refusal of a popular vote on so major a constitutional change. An exasperated Hamilton paper exclaimed that if there was to be no general election on Confederation, the polling booths "may as well be turned into pig-pens, and the voters lists cut up into pipe-lighters."[35] In Nova Scotia, where petition after petition dwelt on the province's long tradition of representative and responsible government, the people of Shelburne put the issue in more fundamental and sober terms: "whilst Your Majesty's petitioners freely admit the right of their representatives in Provincial Parliament to legislate for them within reasonable limits, they cannot admit the right of such representatives to effect sudden changes, amounting to an entire subversion of the constitution, without the deliberate sanction of the people expressed at the polls." As Joseph Howe put it in more succinct and homely terms, the local legislature had "no right to violate a trust only reposed in them for four years, or in fact to sell the fee simple of a mansion of which they have but a limited lease." Even if the scheme were beneficial, which the people of Queen's County flatly doubted, "the means employed to force it upon the country without an appeal to the people, and with full knowledge of their intense dislike of the measure" were enough to discredit it.[36]

Both in Canada and the Atlantic provinces, opponents of Confederation attacked the scheme as "very costly, for the money is scattered on all sides in handfuls."[37] Simply listing the promised commitments left critics breathless with horror. Joseph Howe recounted that with a debt of $75 million, "the public men of Canada propose to purchase the territories of the Hudson's Bay Company, larger than half Europe," take over British Columbia and Vancouver Island, "provinces divided from them by an interminable wilderness," as well as absorb the Atlantic provinces, "countries severally as large as Switzerland, Sardinia, Greece, and Great Britain."[38] Dunkin similarly warned that with "a promise of everything for everybody," the scheme could only "be ambiguous, unsubstantial and unreal."[39] Others feared not disappointment but jobbery. "The proposed Constitution framed by arch jobbers is so devised as to provide for the very maximum of jobbing and corruption," Arthur Gordon assured Gladstone.[40] Unfortunately, responses to the threat of corruption depended on assessments by individuals of whether they would be victims or gainers from it. "Are the people of Nova Scotia prepared to yield up their flourishing customs revenue to a federal treasury in Canada, there to be squandered in jobbery and corruption?" asked the Yarmouth *Tribune*.[41] The people might indeed balk at the idea, but their elected representatives were perhaps open to persuasion: as Joseph Howe lamented, when John A. Macdonald "opened his confederation mousetrap he did not bait it with toasted cheese."[42] A scheme of government launched in this way could hardly bode well for the future. Christopher Dunkin warned that the representatives of each province would seek popularity back home by inching up federal subsidies or by taking special arrangements for one province as a benchmark and precedent for comparable concessions. They would prove to be "pretty good daughters of the horse-leech, and their cry will be found to be pretty often and pretty successfully—'Give, give give!' "[43] His warning can hardly be dismissed as inaccurate.

Related to the general question of cost were various predictions about the effect of Confederation on tariffs. James Currie predicted that Canada's tariff would have to rise by fifty percent to produce the necessary revenue to pay for Confederation. Other Canadian critics recognised that the province's existing tariff, which leaned towards protectionism, would have to be cut in order to meet the free-trading Maritimers half-way. This would reduce revenue at a time when more, not less, money was needed to meet increased costs. Letellier de St. Just predicted that "the deficit which that reduction of our revenue will produce will have to be filled up by the agriculture and industry of Canada" and Dunkin thought it "rather strange" that a government should propose to cut its tariff income and "at the same time, so to change our whole system as to involve ourselves in the enormous extravagances here contemplated." Dunkin felt that no plan of direct taxation could possibly meet the cost, and that the only alternative was a reckless policy of borrowing, except that "we cannot even borrow to any large amount unless under false pretences."[44] The argument that Confederation would create a larger credit base and make it easier to attract investment evidently did not convince everybody.

If Canadian critics feared the consequences of lowering the tariff at the dictation of the lower provinces, Maritimers feared even the compromise increase that Confederation seemed to imply. "Unless Canada consents to economize and curtail its expenses to a very considerable degree, which is not likely to happen," explained the Fredericton *Headquarters*, "the Lower provinces will have to raise their tariffs to that standard, as they will require a greater revenue to meet the expenses of government under the new confederation."[45] Whereas the Canadian tariff was intended to protect industry, Nova Scotia's commercial policy was aimed at fostering the province's worldwide carrying trade.[46] Thus raising the tariff would destroy trade rather than increase revenue—pointing to direct taxation which, Ambrose Shea warned, was "a point on which it is easy to alarm the masses everywhere." It certainly had that effect on Prince Edward Island, where the despairing Edward Whelan reported that it scared "the asses of country people, who can't see an inch beyond their noses."[47] A British journalist who visited Charlottetown in 1865 reported that taxation was regarded as "an evil which not only the Prince Edward Islanders, but the British colonies generally throughout North America, seem to consider as the greatest which can befall a community."[48] Historians have not been notably more sympathetic. When George Coles stated at Quebec that if Prince Edward Island surrendered control over customs and excise "she would have no revenues left with which to carry on the business of the Province," he was surely not adopting "the obstructionist tactics which were destined to characterize the Island's attitude" at the conference, but rather stating a simple fact. The province of Canada derived one third of its revenue from customs and would dominate the new political structure. Prince Edward Island raised three-quarters of its income from customs duties, and the Islanders would be a tiny minority in a British American union.[49]

Textbook explanations of the coming of Confederation assume that it was necessary for the construction of the Intercolonial Railway, and that the Intercolonial was necessary both for defence and to give Canada a winter outlet, freeing its trade from the twin strangleholds of a frozen St Lawrence and a capriciously hostile United States. Opponents accepted neither argument and indeed found much to object to in the whole scheme. First, to reassure Maritimers who had not forgotten the Canadian bad faith of 1862, the railway project was actually written into the Quebec Resolutions, and would thus form part of the British legislation and the constitution of the Confederation—"a novelty, perhaps, that might not be found in the constitution of any country."[50] It certainly gave an unusual status to a mere railway line, the more so as its route had yet to be agreed. Arthur Gordon argued forcefully that to include such a provision in an Act of the British parliament would "be either unnecessary or unjust"—unnecessary if, as everyone assumed, the federal legislature proceeded with the scheme and "unjust if it were to have the effect of forcing on the people of British America the execution of a work which their representatives in Parliament may consider it inexpedient to undertake." In any case, such a provision "would be impossible to enforce, as no penalty could be inflicted after the passage of the Act, in the event of the subsequent neglect of its provisions by the Federal Government and Legislature."[51]

Canadian critics were less concerned by the constitutional impropriety of giving a railway the same status as peace, order and good government as by the fact that the Intercolonial would gain an advantage over their own preferred projects, especially hopes for improved communications to the Red River.[52] Suspicions were further fuelled by ministerial reluctance to say where the Intercolonial would run or how much it would cost, thus prompting the prediction that "it will be a piece of corruption from the time of the turning of the first shovelful of earth."[53] It was widely appreciated that the reason for vagueness lay in the local politics of New Brunswick, where military security pointed to a route along the thinly populated North Shore, but political expediency required a vote-pulling line up the Saint John valley, never far from the American border. Tilley attempted to offer all routes to all men, prompting the only durable piece of doggerel from the Confederation controversy: "Mr. Tilley, will you stop your puffing and blowing / And tell us which way the railway is going?"[54] The question of the cost of the Intercolonial was a sore point to Upper Canada critics of Confederation. In 1862, the Sandfield Macdonald-Sicotte ministry had withdrawn, abruptly and in an unedifying manner, from an interprovincial agreement backed by an imperial loan guarantee, by which the province of Canada undertook to pay five-twelfths of the cost of the line—which, as Henri Joly pointed out, meant that the railway could be built if required without an accompanying political union. Now Canada, with three-quarters of the population, was accepting a *pro rata* obligation to shoulder double the share envisaged in 1862. "This will involve five to seven millions of dollars of an expense more than we had any occasion for incurring," complained David Reesor, "for the other provinces were all [sic] willing to have been responsible for the rest, and there is very good reason why they should."[55] Indeed, Galt had assured Maritimers at a banquet in Halifax in September 1864, "you will get the best of the bargain." Yet, ironically, Canada's sudden outburst of generosity aroused counter-suspicions. In New Brunswick, Albert J. Smith hinted darkly that Canada must have some hidden motive for increasing the very offer it had so recently dishonoured.[56]

Fundamentally, opponents argued that the Intercolonial was no more attractive a project in 1865 than it had been when rejected in 1862. "I have not heard any reason why we should pledge our credit and resources to the construction of the Intercolonial Railway, even previous to any estimate of its cost being made, that was not urged in 1862 when the question was before the country," A-A. Dorion asserted. William McMaster, a leading Toronto merchant, challenged the argument that the Intercolonial was "an indispensable necessity in order to secure an independent outlet to the seaboard." Rather than use the existing railways to American ports, Upper Canada merchants and millers preferred to pay warehousing, insurance and interest charges to keep wheat and flour in store through the winter months, "until the opening of the navigation." They were even less likely to use a railway to Halifax, which would be double the distance to the American winter ports. Henri Joly also doubted whether the Intercolonial could be used to send flour to the Maritimes, for "the cost of transport over five hundred miles of railway would be too great."[57]

The critics did not simply doubt whether trade could profitably flow along the Intercolonial; they also wondered whether Canada and the Maritimes were likely to have any trade at all. "Let us not...be lulled with fallacies of the great commercial advantages we shall derive from a Confederation of these provinces," intoned Eric Dorion. "We have wood, they produce it; we produce potash, and so do they."[58] "With regard to timber," said Henri Joly, "the Gulf Provinces have no more need of ours than we of theirs." Canada imported its coal direct from Britain, as ballast on returning timber ships. If that supply should ever fail, "Upper Canada will probably get its coal from the Pennsylvania mines, which are in direct communication with Lake Erie."[59] Yet, at the same time, Canadian critics could argue that free trade with the Maritimes could be achieved without "this mock Federal union," just as the provinces had enjoyed a decade of closer economic relations with the United States through the Reciprocity Treaty.[60] Not everyone shared these doubts: it was alleged that some Halifax merchants opposed Confederation precisely because they feared the competition it would bring, and it has indeed been contended that by 1874 "Central Canadian business owed its prosperity to its successful conquest of the market in the Maritimes."[61] Nonetheless, the belief that there was a prospect of major trading gains and the assumption that these would be dependent upon a political union were not held by everyone.

The critics were no more convinced by the argument that the Intercolonial was necessary for the defence of the provinces. A-A. Dorion argued that "a railway lying in some places not more than fifteen or twenty miles from the frontier, will be of no use whatever.... An enemy could destroy miles of it before it would be possible to resist him, and in time of difficulty it would be a mere trap for the troops passing along it, unless we had almost an army to keep it open." However far the Intercolonial snaked away from the American border, there was an existing stretch of the Grand Trunk "at places within twenty-six miles of the boundary of Maine," and thus easily vulnerable to American attack. Far from transporting large numbers of troops, the Intercolonial would need large forces simply to guard it. "Unless with a strong force to defend it, in a military point of view, it would be of just no use at all." In summary, the Intercolonial, centrepiece of so many textbook explanations of the causes of Confederation, was comprehensively dismissed by James L. Biggar: "Looking at it from a military point of view, it is well known that part of the proposed line would run within twenty-six miles of the American frontier, and that communication could be cut off at any moment by an American army; and that as a commercial undertaking it could never compete with the water route during the season of navigation; and in winter it would be comparatively useless on account of the depth of snow."[62]

The opponents of Confederation were unconvinced that the political union of the provinces would strengthen their defences in any way. "We do not need Confederation to give us that unity which is indispensable in all military operations—unity of headship. A commander-in-chief will direct the defence of all our provinces," argued Henri Joly. Defence had remained outside the orbit of colonial self-government until very recent times, and Canada's record on militia reform was hardly impressive. Consequently, the argument that unity meant strength is one which appeals more to the twentieth century observer than it did to contemporaries, especially when the unity proposed involved such tiny provinces. John S. Sanborn was simply bewildered. "How the people of New Brunswick could be expected to come up to Canada to defend us, and leave their own frontier unprotected," he could not comprehend. Conversely, Matthew Cameron asked why Canada should be taxed to build fortifications in the Maritimes: "Fortifications in St. John, New Brunswick, would not protect us from the foe, if the foe were to come here." Sanborn argued that if there were indeed a war with the United States, each province would be attacked from a neighboring state. "Under these circumstances, each section of the Confederation would have enough to do to attend to its own affairs." Except, contended A-A. Dorion, that New Brunswick could not defend itself, since the province's population of a quarter of a million was only one-third that of the adjoining state of Maine: "Those 250,000 Canada will have to defend, and it will have to pledge its resources for the purpose of providing means of defence along that extended line."[63]

In the Atlantic colonies, the arguments were inverted. Petitioners from Nova Scotia's Digby County were ready to rally to "the defence of their country and their flag" but were "not disposed to adopt, as a means of ensuring their more efficient defence, a union with a Province which in 1862 refused to sanction a measure involving increased outlay for the better and more elaborate organisation of their militia."[64] Joseph Howe deftly alluded to Canadian complicity in border raids by Southern sympathizers, and the resulting threats of Northern retaliation, proclaiming: "let those who provoke these controversies fight them out."[65] He objected to a system under which Nova Scotia's militia "may be ordered away to any point of the Canadian frontier."[66] Prince Edward Islanders feared that they would be "marched away to the frontiers of Upper Canada" or, as John Hamilton Gray put it with vivid bitterness, "drafted for slaughter."[67] In Newfoundland, the outspoken Charles Fox Bennett spoke of the island's young men "leaving their bones to bleach in a foreign land," a phrase which he was to refine in the 1869 election into the celebrated references to "the desert sands of Canada."[68]

In three of the four Atlantic provinces, insularity was a physical as well as a mental factor. "We are surrounded by the sea," proclaimed Joseph Howe and—what was more to the point—"within ten days' sail of the fleets and armies of England."[69] J.C. Pope of Prince Edward Island echoed Canadian critics in predicting that an American attack would make it "necessary to retain all available strength in each of the provinces for the defence of their respective territories." His emphasis differed in his confidence that local efforts would be powerfully seconded by the British navy and army.[70] Many critics argued that Confederation would actually make the defence of British North America more difficult. Henri Joly argued that there was "no need" of political union to warn "our neighbours" not to pick on a single province. The Americans were "sufficiently sharp-witted to discover, without being told it, that if they content themselves with attacking us at a single point at a time, of course they will have to meet all our strength." Perhaps, he added sarcastically, they could be persuaded to "enter into a contract, binding them to attack us at a single point only at one time—say Quebec." More seriously, L.A. Olivier warned that if Confederation was thrust upon an unwilling population, they could not be expected to rally to the defence of their homeland with the full enthusiasm shown in earlier conflicts. Joseph Howe similarly warned that if the rights of Nova Scotians were "overridden by an arbitrary Act of Parliament, very few of them will march to defend Canada."[71]

"With Confederation, neither the number of men in the several provinces, nor the pecuniary resources now at their disposal, will be increased." The kernel of the Canadian opposition case on defence was that Confederation involved too much territory and no additional manpower. "Can you alter the geographical position of the country?," asked Benjamin Symour. "Will you have any more people or means?" "If nature were to make the necessary effort and move their territory up alongside of us, and thus make a compact mass of people, I would at once agree that it would strengthen us in a military point of view," Philip Moore ironically conceded. In reality, however, Confederation "will weaken instead of strengthen us," since "the union will give an extension of territory far greater in proportion to the number of the population than [sic] now exists in Canada." The planned massive extension into empty and inaccessible territory westward to the Pacific struck A-A. Dorion as "a burlesque" in terms of defence. In short, critics found the defence argument literally laughable: "If we could attach the territory possessed by the moon to these provinces, and obtain the assistance for our joint defence of the man who is popularly supposed to inhabit that luminary, we might derive strength from Confederation."[72]

Critics were equally unimpressed by ringing talk of a "new nationality" in British North America. "I cannot see that the Federation of these provinces has anything of a national phase in it," commented Thomas Scatcherd. "When you speak of national existence, you speak of independence; and so long as we are colonists of Great Britain we can have no national existence."[73] Some Nova Scotian petitions protested that British North America was "incapable of forming a new nationality,"[74] but the loyal people of Barrington township had an each-way bet in wanting no part of "new nationalities too feeble to stand alone, yet difficult to be controlled."[75] Their governor, Sir Richard MacDonnell,

> was unable to see in what way England would be less vulnerable through Canada or Canada less vulnerable through England when a confederated Parliament meets at Ottawa than now. There is not a foot of territory in all these hundreds of thousands of square miles which would thereby become less English than now, so long as the Queen's Representative is head of the Federation; nor is there any obligation in regard to these Provinces which now devolves upon Britain that would be diminished by their being thus huddled into one heterogeneous assemblage.[76]

In fact, critics feared that Confederation would actually provoke Americans into hostilities. Howe warned: "let this guy of 'near nationality' be set up...and every young fellow who has had a taste of the license of camp life in the United States will be tempted to have a fling at it."[77] Christopher Dunkin even expressed alarm at the tone of the Confederation debates, asking "how is the temper of the United States going to be affected...by the policy here urged on us, of what I may call hostile independent effort—effort made on our part, with the avowed object of setting ourselves up as a formidable power against them[?]" The Northern States, A-A. Dorion pointed out, had put into the field an army of 2,300,000, "as many armed men as we have men, women and children in the two Canadas." Military expenditure on any large scale would be useless and "we are not bound to ruin ourselves in anticipation of a supposed invasion which we could not repel." Public opinion should force the Canadian press to cease its anti-American outbursts: "The best thing that Canada can do is to keep quiet, and to give no cause for war."[78] Joseph Howe agreed that British North America could never stand alone militarily against the United States, but he took the argument a stage further. "Inevitably it must succumb to the growing power of the republic. A treaty offensive and defensive with the United States, involving ultimate participation in a war with England, would be the hard terms of its recognition as a separate but not independent state."[79]

Given their overwhelming rejection of the case for Confederation as a defence measure, it is hardly surprising that this aspect of the scheme produced some of the most colourful imagery among critics. Joining with the Maritimes, said James Currie, "was like tying a small twine at the end of a long rope and saying it strengthened the whole line." Incorporating the vast Hudson's Bay Territories, said Henri Joly, would create "the outward form of a giant, but with the strength of a child."[80] John Macdonald, member for Toronto West, thought "the casting of the burden of defence upon this country is like investing a sovereign with all the outward semblance of royalty, and giving him a dollar per day to keep up the dignity of his court." Macdonald has been overshadowed by his namesake to the point of invisibility, but he had a homely touch in his comments, telling the legislators as they met for the last year in Quebec City that Confederation was like taking the engine from the Lévis ferry and using it "to propel the *Great Eastern* across the Atlantic."[81] In a far smaller town, an angry young Rouge editor denounced Confederation in less whimsical imagery. As a defence against the United States it was like being "armed with an egg-shell to stop a bullet...a wisp of straw in the way of a giant."[82] The writer's name was Wilfrid Laurier.

Studies of the opposition to Confederation within the individual provinces have tended to concentrate on the risks and disadvantages of Confederation to each community—an approach which by its nature portrays the critics as "parochial."[83] However, while the objections made on behalf of each province were naturally contradictory, they fell into a common pattern.

John Simpson denied that seventeen additional MPs would be of any use to Upper Canada, while Matthew Cameron argued that if the eighty-two Upper Canadians proposed to develop the North-West, they would be outvoted by "sixty-five members from Lower Canada and forty-seven from the Lower Provinces, whose interests will be united against US."[84] By contrast, Joseph Howe warned that New Brunswick and Nova Scotia "must be a prey to the spoiler" for "having but forty-seven representatives, all told, it is apparent that the Government of the confederacy will always rest upon the overwhelming majority of 147, and that, even when close divisions and ministerial crises occur, the minority can easily be split up and played off against each other for purely Canadian purposes."[85] French Canadians challenged that assumption of a unity of purpose, doubting that "all the members from Lower Canada would make common cause on any question." Although the province was guaranteed sixty-five MPs in perpetuity, they would not all be francophones: "we shall have forty-eight members in the Federal Parliament against one hundred and forty of English origin; in other words, we shall be in a proportion of one to four. What could so weak a minority do to obtain justice?"[86] Joseph Howe evidently felt that French Canadians possessed a greater measure of political skill than Maritimers, for he warned that "as the English will split and divide, as they always do, the French members will in nine cases out of ten, be masters of the situation."[87] A-A. Dorion agreed that they "would go as a body to the Legislature, voting as one man, and caring for nothing else but the protection of their beloved institutions and law, and making government all but impossible," but he felt this a "deplorable state of things."[88]

There was little direct contact between Canada and Maritimes prior to Confederation: during a visit to Montreal in 1860, T. Heath Haviland of Prince Edward Island had encountered "the utmost difficulty" in finding "so much as a newspaper from the Lower Provinces."[89] It is therefore surprising to discover the extent of their mutual antipathy. The "plain meaning" of the Canadian ministry's desire to force through the Quebec Resolutions without amendment was "that the Lower Provinces have made out a Constitution for us and we are to adopt it," said A-A. Dorion. Voting at the Quebec Conference had been by provinces, which "made Prince Edward Island equal to Upper Canada." Dorion complained of "the humiliation of seeing the Government going on its knees and begging the little island of Prince Edward to come into this union."[90] Only by appreciating the existence of this sentiment of disdain for the Maritimes among Canadian critics can we understand why Macdonald and his colleagues had no alternative but to outface and outmanoeuvre opposition in Nova Scotia and New Brunswick. Maritimers returned the hostility. James Dingwell of Prince Edward Island thought "Canadians had not been able to manage the business of their country as we have been to manage ours; and why should we trust the management of our own affairs to people who have never been able to manage their own with satisfaction?"[91] With colourful exaggeration, Joseph Howe claimed that Canadians were "always in trouble of some sort, and two or three times in open rebellion."[92]

Despite Howe's suspicions that Lower Canadian solidarity in the federal parliament would entrench French power, hostility to Confederation in the Atlantic colonies seems to have been directed against the whole of what later became the monster of "central Canada" and was relatively free of explicit francophobia. There was a hint of it in an open letter to the British Colonial Secretary in January 1867, when a recitation of Nova Scotia's loyal service to the Empire in wars against France was followed by the waspish comment: "We are now asked to surrender it to Monsieur Cartier."[93] Although francophobia was so endemic that it was not necessary to articulate it, inter-communal flashpoints in the mid-nineteenth century were more likely to concern sectarian schooling than the politics of language. Memories of their homeland's forced unification with Britain led many Irish Catholics to oppose Confederation. If anti-Confederates had warned of the danger of French power, Irish Catholics might have concluded that Confederation could bring benefits for their Church. In any case, Acadians were as suspicious of Confederation as their anglophone neighbours, and it suited Howe to portray them as one of the contented minorities—along with Micmacs and Blacks—who had flourished under the benign institutions of an autonomous Nova Scotia.[94]

In each province, critics argued that their constituents had got the worst of the bargain. That their arguments were contradictory did not much matter, since by definition they were intended for purely local consumption, directed at those whose "mental vision"—as an impatient Halifax newspaper put it—"is bounded by Dartmouth on the one side, and Citadel Hill on the other."[95] However, claims in each province of a bad deal provoked supporters of Confederation into refutations which were seized upon by critics elsewhere as confirmation of their fears. One of the earliest public expositions of the Quebec scheme came in a major speech by Galt at Sherbrooke in November 1864. Tupper admired it, but mildly complained that it was "a little too much from the Canadian point of view to suit this meridian." From Prince Edward Island, Edward Whelan similarly warned that "in the Lower Provinces a view of the Confederation question with a very decided Canadian colouring is apt to lessen confidence in it as we barbarians down in these lower regions are terribly doubtful and suspicious of Canadian intentions."[96] Within a few months, hard-pressed Confederates in the Maritimes had given similar hostages to the scheme's critics in the province of Canada. David Reesor read into the record extracts from Tilley's election speeches to show that politicians in the Maritimes "see the great advantage they have gained over Canada, and are not slow to set them [sic] before the people." Dorion similarly quoted Tilley and Whelan, and pictured them "chuckling over the good bargains they have made at the expense of Canada."[97]

Behind these mutual suspicions, there surely lay something deeper than the cussedness which we normally dismiss as parochialism. Even in the superheated provincial politics of the mid-nineteenth century it seems exaggerated that Cartier could have been accused of "la lâchéte la plus insigne dans la trahison la plus noire," merely for forming a coalition with George Brown, or that Prince Edward Island representatives at the Charlottetown conference were pointed out in the street as "the men who would sell their country."[98] The fact that such remarks were made suggests that the different provinces felt themselves to possess distinct social and political cultures. This was most obvious in predominantly French-speaking and Catholic Lower Canada: "Confederation is in fact a Legislative union, because upon the Federal Government is conferred the right of legislating upon those subjects which Lower Canada holds most dear."[99] The complication in Lower Canada was the existence of a minority-within-a-minority, equally suspicious of those aspects of the new constitution which guaranteed provincial autonomy under a local francophone majority. Principal Dawson of McGill thought that "scarcely anyone among the English of Lower Canada desires Confederation, except perhaps as an alternative to simple dissolution of the Union."[100] This was a case where clashing objections had a reinforcing effect, for every reassurance offered to the Lower Canada English was a confirmation of French Canadian fears.[101]

The separate identity of French Canadian society on an Anglo-Saxon continent was obvious enough. What may be less obvious is that in the Maritimes—and especially in Nova Scotia—there was as great a sense of being different from the province of Canada as modern Canadians would today feel separates themselves from their neighbours in the United States. True, Joseph Howe could welcome a party of Canadian visitors to Halifax in August 1864 with the sentiment: "I am not one of those who thank God that I am a Nova Scotian merely, for I am a Canadian as well."[102] Yet the picture which emerges from his subsequent anti-Confederation campaign is of a province not simply resentful of losing its autonomy, but fearful of being subordinated to the capricious and unattractive values of "those who live above the tide," "the administration of strangers."[103] A recurrent theme of Nova Scotian opposition was loss of its historic self-government. Behind the issue of high principle, there lay practical and local fears. The petitioners of Digby County pointed out that "while that portion of this county which borders on the sea is thickly inhabited and rapidly increasing in population and wealth, there are still considerable districts but lately reclaimed from the primaeval forest," which required grants of public money for the development of roads and bridges. They regarded "with dismay" the transfer of control over public expenditure "to a Government by which they would necessarily all be expended for widely different purposes."[104] Canada was associated with inflationary paper money and high interest rates. "Every post-master and every way office keeper is to be appointed and controlled by the Canadians."[105] Canada was as distant from Nova Scotia as Austria from Britain.[106] "You cannot... invest a village on the Ottawa with the historic interest and associations that cluster around London," wrote Joseph Howe—and he emphatically preferred "London under the dominion of John Bull to Ottawa under the dominion of Jack Frost."[107] To the modern mind, Joseph Howe was descending to the darkest depths of petty parochialism when he proclaimed that travellers "can scarcely ride five miles in Upper Canada without being stopped by a toll bar or a toll bridge. There are but two toll-bridges in Nova Scotia and all the roads are free."[108] Yet Howe's complaint was really little different in spirit from modern Canadian concern to defend welfare and regional programmes against American allegations of unfair wage subsidies.[109]

Another theme common to the critics, whatever their regional loyalty, was rejection of both the proposed provincial governments and the confederate upper house as safeguards for their rights. "Ce n'est donc pas une confédération qui nous est proposée, mais tout simplement une Union Législative déguisée sous le nom de confédération," argued A-A. Dorion.[110] George Coles predicted that under Confederation, the legislature of Prince Edward Island "would be the laughing stock of the world," left "to legislate about dog taxes, and the running at large of swine."[111] While some critics concluded that the whole plan of union should be abandoned, others argued from similar premises that the union should be strengthened. The Halifax *Citizen* agreed that the Quebec scheme "has given these local legislatures very little to do," and predicted that they would occupy themselves in mischief, preserving local loyalties which would prevent "the fusion of the British American population in one actual indivisible nationality."[112] "One of the worst features of the Union plan proposed by Canada is, that it will leave our local legislature still in existence," lamented the Saint John *Globe,* which would have preferred to see outright unification.[113] Even the fervent anti-Confederate, T.W. Anglin, writing in the rival *Freeman,* agreed that if they had to have Confederation, "it would be better to abolish the local Legislatures at once in appearance as well as in reality."[114]

The critics were not reassured by the fact that both lieutenant-governors and members of the upper house were to be appointed by the central government. The prospect of lieutenant-governors drawn from provincial politics aroused little enthusiasm. "Let any one of our dozen or twenty most prominent Canadian politicians be named Lieutenant-Governor of Upper or of Lower Canada, would not a large and powerful class of the community...be very likely to resent the nomination as an insult?," asked Christopher Dunkin.[115] In Canada, where the legislative Council had become elective in 1856—with life members retaining their seats—there was resentment at the reintroduction of nomination, "because the Maritime Provinces are opposed to an elective Chamber, and hence we in Canada—the largest community and the most influential—must give way to them."[116] There was also resentment at the provision in the Quebec Resolutions by which the first Confederate legislative councillors would be appointed from the existing Legislative Councils (except in Prince Edward Island)—a transparent bribe to curb the opposition in the upper houses. Worse still, the first Confederate upper house was to be appointed for life, on the nomination of the existing provincial governments—with the central government not even possessing a veto. A-A. Dorion's objection was not to the principle but to the unlucky fact that most British North American governments were Conservative. "For all time to come, as far as this generation and the next are concerned, you will find the Legislative Council controlled by the influence of the present government."[117] Future appointment by the central government aroused no more enthusiasm, since as Dunkin suggested, a government might be formed in which an entire province "either is not represented, or is represented otherwise than it would wish to be." How would such a province, "out in the cold," be served when vacancies in the upper house came to be filled?[118] Macdonald and McGee may strike posterity as the visionaries of the time, but it was the dry-as-dust Dunkin who foresaw the position of Alberta in the later Trudeau years, or Quebec under Joe Clark.

The arguments of the critics of Confederation must be conceded to have been at least plausible. Why then did they fail to prevent the passage of the British North America Act in 1867? First, of course, their arguments did not pass unchallenged. Just as conventional studies of the causes of Confederation tend to underplay the opposition case, so a study of the critics necessarily distorts the debate in their favour. Indeed, arguments which high-minded posterity may find irrefutable could perhaps have produced diametrically opposite responses among contemporaries: Upper Canadian critics, in damning the Intercolonial as an irresponsible waste of money, might have convinced some Lower Canadians of its pork-barrel value.[119] Even if the opposition case against the Intercolonial Railway had been overwhelming, Confederation might still have been supported on general grounds as the most practicable solution to a range of problems. The Confederation package mattered more than the interlocking detail, and not everybody bothered with those details. Bishop Laflèche did not allow ignorance of the latter to inhibit him from pronouncing on the former: "Le projet de Conféderation est tellement vaste et complexe en lui-même et dans ses détails qu'il est bien difficile de l'aborder sans en avoir auparavant faire une étude spéciale; et c'est que je n'ai point fait." What Laflèche saw was a province in which the legislative process was paralysed, where political opponents confronted each other almost like enemy camps, a state of affairs which could only end disastrously for Lower Canadians—either in "la guerre civile ou la domination du Haut-Canada dans l'Union Législative."[120] The bishop was probably wrong—at least in his fears of civil war—but could anyone be sure? In any case, even if the argument were won inside the provinces, there remained that "atmosphere of crisis" over the North American continent. "Look around you to the valley of Virginia," McGee challenged those who wanted to know why Confederation was necessary, "look around you to the mountains of Georgia, and you will find reasons as thick as blackberries."[121] Perhaps the fundamental mistake of the opponents of Confederation was to ask people to react logically to the activities of Macdonald and Cartier in the conference chamber rather than to the operations of Grant and Sherman on the battlefield. The question for explanation then becomes why it should have been intercolonial union—rather than, say, neutrality or annexation—which met the psychological need for a dramatic response to continental crisis. One explanation may be that the idea had been around for a long time, answer looking for a question. "Everybody admits that Union must take place sometime," said John A. Macdonald, "I say now is the time."[122] In seeking to account for the adoption of so vast a scheme as Canadian Confederation, historians have naturally turned to the arguments of its supporters, and have been tempted to conclude that the arguments put forward *for* Canadian Confederation equal the reasons *why* Canadian Confederation came about. Certainly hindsight finds it easy to draw neat lines of causation linking argument to outcome: the lines may be straight, but the process itself is circular, since it identifies the winners of history as—in Morton's terms—those who sensed the currents of events. Yet we should not forget that the case against Confederation was argued as tenaciously, as eloquently and—we must assume—as sincerely as the arguments in its favour. However much historians may admire the "Fathers of Confederation," only by recognising not just the strength of opposition to Confederation but also the plausibility of some of the arguments put forward, can we begin to see that the outcome was by no means inevitable. Of course, some historians believe that posterity is not entitled to second-guess past controversies, that a century later we cannot award points to individual arguments, for or against, since we cannot make ourselves fully part of the atmosphere of the time. Yet such an attitude is tantamount to an uncritical abdication of our own judgement to each and every claim made by those who were on the winning side perhaps for reasons other than the simply intellectual. "La raison du plus fort, c'est toujours la meuilleure," is not the most appropriate explanatory strategy for the historian to adopt. Hindsight may yet conclude that while the Antis lost the battle, they won at least some of the arguments.

Notes

1 Cf. A. G. Bailey, "The Basis and Persistence of Opposition to Confederation in New Brunswick," *Canadian Historical Review,* XXIII (1942), pp. 367–83 and Carl Wallace. "Albert Smith, Confederation and Reaction in New Brunswick, 1852–1882," *ibid..* XLIV (1963), pp. 285–312.

2 G. Patterson, "An Unexplained Incident of Confederation in Nova Scotia," *Dalhousie Review,* VII (1927), pp. 442–46.

3 *CD,* pp. 545 (Blanchet); 147 (Holton); 682 (Dorion).

4 *Life and Times,* p. 154.

5 Not reported in *CD,* but see Waite, ed., *Confederation Debates,* pp. xv–xvi.

6 *Hansard's Parliamentary Debates* (3rd series), CLXXXV, 19 February 1867, cols. 579–80, 577.

7 *British Parliamentary Papers* [cited as *BPP*], 1867, XLVIII, *Correspondence Respecting the Proposed Union of the British North American Provinces,* pp. 75–77.

8 *Ibid.,* p. 68. Howe's tour is described in J. M. Beck, *Joseph Howe: II, The Briton Becomes Canadian 1848–1873* (Kingston, 1983), p. 201.

9 *CD,* p. 61.

10 Speech of 7 April 1866, quoted in William M. Baker, *Timothy Warren Anglin 1822–1896: Irish Catholic Canadian* (Toronto, 1977), p. 103, and see also p. 58. Anglin was editor of the Saint John *Morning Freeman.* According to Creighton, Anglin was "an unsubdued ex-rebel" who "flung the full force of his abusive and mendacious journalism against Confederation" (*Road to Confederation,* p. 251, and see also p. 247). It is unlikely that Anglin took part in the Irish rising of 1848 and there is no reason to think that his journalism was unusually abusive or mendacious by contemporary standards, which were admittedly low. Thus have critics of Confederation been dismissed.

11 Similar views were expressed in the Canadian Legislative Council by James G. Currie, Bill Flint and David Reesor and in the Assembly by Christopher Dunkin, Joseph Perrault, Thomas Scatcherd and T. C. Wallbridge. *CD,* pp. 46, 164, 319, 483, 585, 749, 660.

12 Charlottetown *Examiner,* 30 January 1865, quoted in *Life and Times,* p. 186.

13 *CD,* p. 328.

14 *CD,* p. 248. In May 1860, Dorion had said that he regarded a federation of the two Canadas as "le noyau de la grande confédération des provinces de l'Amérique du nord que j'appelle de mes voeux." Quoted by Joseph Cauchon, *L'Union des Provinces de l'Amérique Britannique du Nord* (Quebec, 1865), p. 7.

15 Speech in Halifax, 13 August 1864, in J. A. Chisholm, ed., *The Speeches and Public Letters of Joseph Howe* (2 vols, Halifax, 1909), II, p. 433.

16 *CD,* p. 126.

17 *CD,* pp. 352 (Joly); 508, 485 (Dunkin); 747 (Scatcherd).

18 *CD,* p. 357.

19 *CD,* p. 586.

20 *CD,* p. 357 (Joly) and cf p. 591 (Perrault).

21 *CD,* pp. 593–95, 625–26.

22 *CD,* pp. 543 (Dunkin); 356–57 (Joly).

23 Open letter, 10 April 1866, in Chisholm, ed., *Speeches and Public Letters of Joseph Howe,* II, p. 463.

24 *CD,* p. 456.

25 *L'Ordre,* 7 June 1865, quoted in *Life and Times,* p. 147.

26 *CD,* p. 659.

27 Howe to Isaac Buchanan, 20 June 1866, in Chisholm, ed., *op. cit.,* II, p. 464. In his 1866 pamplet, *Confederation Considered in Relation to the Interests of the Empire,* Howe complained that in the New Brunswick election that year, "one half of an entirely loyal population were taught to brand the other half as disloyal." Quoted in *ibid.,* II, p. 484.

28 Dunkin spoke about imperial federation in *CD,* p. 545, and was criticised by Frederick Haultain, MPP for Peterborough, p. 646. Howe's long-standing enthusiasm culminated in his 1866 pamphlet, *The Organisation of the Empire,* quoted in Chisholm, ed., *op. cit.,* II, pp. 492–506. Tupper savagely exploited the logical contradictions in Howe's position: within an imperial federation, Nova Scotians would be in a far more insignificant minority than within Confederation, liable to fight in bloody wars in all corners of the world, a scheme "as useless as it would be unjust and repressive." Letter in Halifax *British Colonist,* 13 December 1866, in E. M. Saunders, ed., *Life and Letters of Sir Charles Tupper* (2 vols, London, 1916), I, pp. 139–40.

29 Creighton, *Road to Confederation,* pp. 266–67.

30 Pope, ed., *op. cit.,* p. 684, and quoted by Dorion, *CD,* p. 654. See also *CD,* p. 248 (and cf. p. 657) for the negotiations after the death of Taché, Pope, ed., *op. cit.,* pp. 700–706. George Brown's letter to his wife of 8 March 1865 is quoted in Careless, *op. cit.,* II, p. 190.

31 *CD,* p. 657.

32 *CD,* pp. 155, 158 (James Aikens, MLC); 487 (Dunkin).

33 Halifax *Morning Chronicle,* 24 January 1866, quoted in *Life and Times,* p. 221. Annand used the argument, not to reject Confederation, but as a device to suggest an alternative approach. The allusion to "festivities" may have been a coded reference to a campaign of denigration directed against John A. Macdonald's intermittent bouts of drunkenness.

34 *BPP,* 1867, XLVIII, Howe, Annand and McDonald to Carnarvon, 19 January 1867, p. 13.

35 Hamilton *Times,* November 1864, quoted in *Life and Times,* p. 122. See also Bruce W. Hodgins, "Democracy and the Ontario Fathers of Confederation," in Bruce Hodgins and Robert Page, eds, *Canadian History Since Confederation: Essays and Interpretations* (2nd ed., Georgetown, Ontario, 1979), pp. 19–28.

36 *BPP,* 1867, XLVIII, *Correspondence,* pp. 70, 75; Howe *et al.* to Carnarvon, 19 January 1867, p. 18.

37 *CD,* p. 179 (L. A. Olivier, MLC for the Lanaudière).

38 Quoted in Chisholm, ed., *op. cit.,* II, p. 473.

39 *CD,* p. 490.

40 Gordon to Gladstone, private, 27 February 1865, in Paul Knaplund, ed., *Gladstone-Gordon Correspondence, 1851–1896* (Transactions of the American Philosophical Society, n.s., Ll, pt 4, 1961), p. 46.

41 Yarmouth *Tribune,* 9 November 1864, quoted in *Life and Times,* p. 202.

42 Speech at Dartmouth, NS, 22 May 1867, quoted in Chisholm, ed., *op. cit.*, II, p. 514.

43 *CD*, p. 520.

44 *CD*, pp. 50 (Currie); 188 (Letellier); 524 (Dunkin).

45 Fredericton *Headquarters*, 19 October 1864, quoted in Bailey, "Basis and Persistence," p. 375.

46 "We have the trade of the world now open to us on nearly equal terms, and why should we allow Canada to hamper us?," Yarmouth *Herald*, 15 December 1864, quoted in *Life and Times*, p. 202.

47 Shea to Galt, 15 December 1864 and Whelan to Galt, 17 December 1864, in Ormsby, "Letters to Galt," pp. 167, 168.

48 Charles Mackay, "A Week in Prince Edward Island." *Fortnightly Review*, V (1865), p. 147.

49 Bolger, *Prince Edward Island and Confederation*, p. 68. In 1863, while the province of Canada derived 35.95 percent of its revenue from customs, New Brunswick derived 66.12 percent, Nova Scotia 81.09 percent, Prince Edward Island 74.66 percent and Newfoundland 86.08 percent. However, in per capita yield, Canadians paid roughly double Maritimers. The figures for 1863 customs revenues (with year of population in parentheses) were: Canada (1865) £1.04; New Brunswick (1861) £0.36; Nova Scotia (1861) £0.52; Prince Edward Island (1863) £0.36; Newfoundland (1857) £0.79. (Calculated from *BPP*, 1866, LXXIII, Colonial Trade Statistics, pp. 126, 148–49. 160–61, 168, 174.) Estimated wages rates (*ibid.*, pp. 159, 173, 181) for tradesmen in 1863 were between £0.3 and £0.4 per diem in Newfoundland, and £0.25 and £0.4 in New Brunswick, but the Prince Edward Island figure (£40 per annum) suggests that tradesmen were employed for only 100 to 160 days each year. Thus for a tradesman on Prince Edward Island supporting a wife and four children, a rise in per capita tariff yield to Canadian levels would have cost over £4 a year, or about five weeks' wages.

50 *CD*, p. 17 (Holton).

51 PRO, CO 188/143, Gordon to Cardwell, no. 23, 27 February 1865, fos 181–85, printed in *BPP*, 1867, XLVIII, *Correspondence*, pp. 88–89.

52 Article 69 of the Quebec Resolutions offered only that improved communications to the Red River "shall be prosecuted at the earliest possible period that the state of the Finances will permit." According to T. C. Wallbridge, this meant "that the North-West is hermetically sealed." *CD*, p. 453 and cf. Matthew Cameron, pp. 452–53.

53 *CD*, p. 759 (Scatcherd).

54 Fredericton *Headquarters*, 1 February 1865, quoted in Bailey, "Basis and Persistence," p. 379.

55 *CD*, pp. 356 (Joly); 164 (Reesor). The 1862 agreement involved only the two provinces of New Brunswick and Nova Scotia.

56 Wallace, "Albert Smith," p. 289. The Nova Scotian deputation to London in 1867 could "scarcely bring themselves to discuss" the Intercolonial, "so selfish and unfair at all times has been the conduct of the public men of Canada in regard to it." *BPP*, 1867, XLVIII, Howe *et al.* to Carnarvon, 19 January 1867, p. 8. For Galt's Halifax speech, see Edward Whelan, comp., *The Union of the British Provinces* (Charlottetown, 1865), p. 48.

57 *CD*, pp. 263 (Dorion); 230 (McMaster); 356 (Joly).

58 *CD*, p. 863, Canada took 1.11 percent of its imports from the other British North American territories, and sent them 2.2 percent of its exports. New Brunswick took 2.3 percent of its imports from Canada, to which it sent 0.87 percent of its exports. Prince Edward Island took 2.1 percent of its imports from Canada, to which it sent 0.6 percent of its exports. Newfoundland took 3.9 percent of its imports from Canada, to which it sent 0.68 percent of its exports. (Calculated from *BPP*, 1866. LXIII, *Colonial Trade Statistics*, pp. 132, 152, 170, 177.) Nova Scotia figures are less helpful, but in 1866 the province took 5.5 percent of its imports from Canada, and sent 7.15 percent of its exports (1865 figures being 3.5 percent and 4.96 percent). (Calculated from *BPP*, 1867–68, LXXI, *Colonial Trade Statistics*, p. 144.)

59 *CD*, p. 355.

60 *CD*, pp. 356 (Joly) and 528 (Dorion).

61 Halifax *Evening Reporter*, 10 December 1864, quoted in *Life and Times*, p. 208; Peter B. Waite, *Canada 1874–1896: Arduous Destiny* (Toronto, 1971), p. 76. This "conquest" of Maritime markets could not have been the result of the Intercolonial, which was not completed until 1876. In 1875, Senator A. W. McLelan of Nova Scotia described Canadian goods and produce arriving "by steamer and sail on the Gulf and by the Grand Trunk via Portland," *ibid.*, pp. 76–77.

62 *CD*, pp. 257 (Dorion); 750 (Scatcherd): 521 (Dorion); 883 (Biggar).

63 *CD*, pp. 355 (Joly); 123 (Sanborn); 456 (Cameron); 124 (Sanborn): 256 (Dorion).

64 *BPP*, 1867, XLVIII, *Correspondence*, pp. 69–70.

65 Halifax *Morning Chronicle,* 11 January 1865, quoted in Chisholm, ed., *op. cit.,* II, p. 435 (the first of the celebrated "Botheration Scheme" letters).

66 Speech at Dartmouth, 22 May 1867, quoted in *ibid.,* II, p. 512.

67 *Islander,* 6 January 1865 and J. H. Gray to Tupper, 7 January 1865, quoted in *Life and Times,* pp. 186, 183.

68 *Newfoundlander,* 12 January 1865, quoted in *Life and Times,* p. 167. It was alleged that in the 1869 election, Newfoundlanders were told "that their young children would be rammed into guns" by Canadians. James Hiller, "Confederation Defeated: The Newfoundland Election of 1869" in J. Hiller and P. Neary, eds, *Newfoundland in the Nineteenth and Twentieth Centuries: Essays in Reinterpretation* (Toronto, 1980), p. 83.

69 Quoted in Chisholm, ed., *op. cit.,* II, pp. 435–36.

70 Quoted in Bolger, ed., *Canada's Smallest Province,* pp. 175–76.

71 *CD,* pp. 354 (Joly); 180 (Olivier); *BPP,* 1867, XLVIII, Howe *et al.* to Carnarvon, 19 January 1867, p. 7.

72 *CD,* pp. 176 (Olivier); 203 (Seymour); 229 (Moore); 263 (Dorion); 234 (John Simpson, MLC for Queen's). The Halifax *Citizen* alleged that Tupper was perfectly capable of campaigning for federation with the Moon if he thought it would divert public attention. Quoted in *Life and Times,* p. 200.

73 *CD,* p. 748. Critics dismissed appeals to Italian and German unity as proving that the spirit of the times pointed to wider unions. Henri Joly gave a list of federations which had failed *(CD,* pp. 346–48), while the imperially minded Howe likened Confederation to a handful of small states withdrawing from the North German Confederation, or "a few offshoots from Italian unity" attempting to form "an inferior confederation." *BPP,* 1867, XLVIII, Howe *et al.* to Carnarvon, 19 January 1867, p. 21.

74 E.g. Petition from King's, *BPP,* 1867, XLVIII, *Correspondence,* p. 67.

75 *Ibid.,* p. 71.

76 PRO, CO 217/235, MacDonnell to Cardwell, 22 November 1865, fos 187–212.

77 Quoted in Chisholm, ed., *op. cit.,* II, p. 487.

78 *CD,* pp. 529 (Dunkin); 257 (Brome).

79 Quoted in Chisholm, ed., *op. cit.,* II, p. 489.

80 *CD,* pp. 46 (Currie); 353 (Joly). Henri Joly doubted comparisons between the Hudson's Bay Territories and European Russia, doubting that the West could ever support a large population. It may be noted that he ended his public career by serving as lieutenant-governor of British Columbia, 1900–1906. John A. Macdonald believed in 1865 that the prairies were "of no present value to Canada" which had "unoccupied land enough to absorb the immigration for many years." To open Saskatchewan would be to "drain away our youth and strength." Macdonald to E. W. Watkin, 27 March 1865, in Pope, *Memoirs,* pp. 397–98.

81 *CD,* p. 753.

82 Quoted in J. Schull, *Laurier: The First Canadian* (Toronto, 1966), p. 57.

83 Localism could also be harnessed to Confederation, influencing the kind of scheme which emerged. Elwood H. Jones, "Localism and Federalism in Upper Canada in 1865," in Bruce W. Hodgins, D. Wright and W. H. Heick, eds, *Federalism in Canada and Australia: The Early Years* (Waterloo, Ont., 1978), pp. 19–41.

84 *CD,* pp. 232 (Simpson); 452–53 (Cameron).

85 Quoted in Chisholm, ed., *op. cit.,* II, p. 490.

86 *CD,* pp. 191 (J. O. Bureau, Rouge MLC for De Lorimier); 624 (Perrault). McGee argued that in addition up to seven members from the Lower Provinces would represent largely francophone ridings. *CD,* p. 137.

87 Halifax *Morning Chronicle.* 13 January 1865, quoted in *Life and Times,* p. 212.

88 *CD,* p. 264.

89 Speech at Montreal, 28 October 1864, in Whelan, comp., *Union,* p. 115.

90 *CD,* pp. 252, 47, 656.

91 Quoted in Bolger, ed., *Canada's Smallest Province,* II, p. 177.

92 Howe to Earl Russell, 19 January 1865, quoted in Chisholm, ed., *op. cit.,* II, p. 437.

93 *BPP,* 1867, XLVIII, Howe *et al.* to Carnarvon, 19 January 1867, p. 16. See also *ibid.,* p. 12 for an unsubtle reference to the Hundred Years War.

94 *Ibid.,* p. 17. Cf. Leon Thériault, "L'Acadie, 1763–1978: Synthèse Historique" in Jean Daigle, éd., *Les Acadiens des Maritimes: Etudes Thématiques* (Moncton, 1980), pp. 63–68.

95 *Morning Chronicle,* 23 December 1864, quoted in *Life and Times,* p. 208.

96 Tupper to Galt, 13 December 1864, and Whelan to Galt, 17 December 1864, in Ormsby, "Letters," pp. 166, 168.

97 *CD,* pp. 329 (Reesor): 261 (Dorion).

98 *Le Pays,* 27 June 1864, quoted in Creighton, *Road to Confederation,* p. 78, and *ibid.,* p. 122.

99 *CD,* p. 174, and cf. pp. 192 (Bureau) and 350 (Joly). An emotive example cited was central control of divorce proceedings.

100 Dawson to Howe, 15 November 1866, quoted in *Life and Times,* p. 135.

101 *CD,* p. 351 (Joly).\

102 Speech, 13 August 1864, in Chisholm, ed., *op. cit.,* II, p. 433. Howe rose to speak at ten minutes to midnight. "Who ever heard of a public man being bound by a speech on such an occasion as that?," he asked three years later. Beck, *op. cit.,* II, p. 182. In fact, Howe spoke before the Charlottetown conference.

103 Speech at Dartmouth, 22 May 1867, in Chisholm, ed., *op. cit.,* II, p. 511.

104 *BPP,* 1867, XLVIII, *Correspondence,* pp. 69–70.

105 Dartmouth speech, Chisholm, ed., *op. cit.,* II, pp. 512, 511.

106 Port Medway petition, *BPP,* 1867, XLVIII, *Correspondence,* p. 76; Howe *et al.* to Carnarvon, 19 January 1867, p. 7.

107 *BPP,* 1867, XLVIII, Howe *et al.* to Carnarvon, 19 January 1867, p. 15. J. W. Longley, *Joseph Howe* (Toronto, 1906), p. 202, and cf. Beck, *op. cit.,* II, p. 202. The reference to "a village" was, of course, unfair, but Dunkin was concerned that the federal capital was to remain "within the jurisdiction of a subordinate province." *CD,* p. 507.

108 *BPP,* 1867, XLVIII, Howe *et al.* to Carnarvon, 19 January 1867, p. 17 and cf. Dartmouth speech, 22 May 1867, in Chisholm, ed., *op. cit.,* II, p. 517.

109 The Nova Scotia press, it was alleged, emphasised the less attractive aspects of Canadian life, just as modern Canadians often reflect a cataclysmic view of the United States. "Not a fight occurs, not a train runs off the track and kills one or two persons in that Province but it is blazoned forth in that press." Speech by Dr. Hamilton, *Debates and Proceedings of the House of Assembly of Nova Scotia 1865,* pp. 264–65. I am grateful to Dr. James Sturgis for this reference.

110 Dorion's anti-Confederation manifesto was widely published in 1864. Quoted in *Life and Times,* p. 142. His objection may partly have originated in an element of mistranslation: "Confederation" in English had come to be a shorthand term for a reasonably centralised form of intercolonial union, while its French equivalent continued to mean a loose alliance.

111 Quoted in Bolger, ed., *op. cit.,* p. 174.

112 Halifax *Citizen,* 19 November 1864, quoted in *Life and Times,* p. 203. The lieutenant-governor, Sir Richard MacDonnell, used the same argument a few days later in a despatch: "I do not believe that so long as the boundaries of the different Provinces are maintained and Local Legislatures and petty politics fostered, the Confederation can rise to that status, and that dignity of national feeling, which creates and maintains a national military spirit and self-reliance." PRO, CO 217/235, MacDonnell to Cardwell, 22 November 1864, fos 187–212.

113 Saint John *Daily Evening Globe,* 17 October 1864, quoted in *Life and Times,* p. 136.

114 Saint John *Freeman,* 3 November 1864, quoted in Baker, *Anglin,* p. 65. Joseph Howe also condemned the duplication of legislatures as "cumbrous and expensive." Howe to Earl Russell, 19 January 1865, in Chisholm, ed., *op. cit.,* II, p. 437.

115 *CD,* p. 504. Perrault alleged that some politicians were influenced by hopes of "being governor of one of the Federated Provinces," as did Letellier, who subsequently became a lieutenant-governor himself. *CD,* pp. 626, 188.

116 *CD,* p. 157 (James Aikins).

117 *CD,* p. 253. Dorion chose to overlook the provision in Article 14 of the Quebec Resolutions that "in such nomination due regard shall be had to the claims of the Members of Legislative Council in Opposition in each Province, so that all political parties may as nearly as possible be fairly represented."

118 *CD,* pp. 494–95. The fear was a real one for French Canadians. Cf. *CD,* p. 174 (Olivier).

119 Support for the Intercolonial might not translate into support for Confederation, as in the case of J. B. Pouliot, MPP for Témiscouata.

120 Laflèche to Boucher de Niverville, 2 March 1864, quoted in Walter Ullman, "The Quebec Bishops and Confederation," *Canadian Historical Review,* XLIII (1963), p. 218.

121 Speech at Montreal, 29 October 1864, in Whelan, comp., *op. cit.,* pp. 122–23.

122 Speech at Halifax, 12 September 1864, in *ibid.,* p. 46.

The British North America Act, 1867

An Act for the Union of Canada, Nova Scotia, and New Brunswick, and the Government thereof; and for Purposes connected therewith

Whereas the Provinces of Canada, Nova Scotia, and New Brunswick have expressed their Desire to be federally united into One Dominion under the Crown of the United Kingdom of Great Britain and Ireland, with a Constitution similar in Principle to that of the United Kingdom:

And Whereas such a Union would conduce to the Welfare of the Provinces and promote the Interests of the British Empire:...

Be it therefore enacted and declared by the Queen's Most Excellent Majesty, by and with the advice and Consent of the Lords Spiritual and Temporal, and Commons, in this present Parliament assembled, and by the Authority of the same, as follows:

I. Preliminary

1. This Act may be cited as the British North America Act, 1867.

II. Union

3. It shall be lawful for the Queen, by and with the Advice of Her Majesty's Most Honourable Privy Council, to declare by Proclamation that, on and after a Day therein appointed, not being more than Six Months after the passing of this Act, the Provinces of Canada, of Nova Scotia, and New Brunswick shall form and be One Dominion under the name of Canada; and on and after that Day those Three Provinces shall form and be One Dominion under that Name accordingly.
5. Canada shall be divided into Four Provinces, named Ontario, Quebec, Nova Scotia, and New Brunswick.
6. The Parts of the Province of Canada (as it exists at the passing of this Act) which formerly constituted respectively the Provinces of Upper Canada and Lower Canada shall be deemed to be severed, and shall form two separate Provinces. The Part which formerly constituted the Province of Upper Canada shall constitute the Province of Ontario; and the Part which formerly constituted the Province of Lower Canada shall constitute the Province of Quebec.
7. The Provinces of Nova Scotia and New Brunswick shall have the same Limits as at the passing of this Act.

The British North America Act, 1967, Public Domain, http://canada.justice.gc.ca/loireg/rapport/en/p1t1-1.html

III. Executive Power

9. The Executive Government and authority of and over Canada is hereby declared to continue and be vested in the Queen.

11. There shall be a Council to aid and advise in the Government of Canada, to be styled the Queen's Privy Council for Canada; and the Persons who are to be Members of that Council shall be from time to time chosen and summoned by the Governor General and sworn in as Privy Councillors, and Members thereof may be from time to time removed by the Governor General.

16. Until the Queen otherwise directs the Seat of Government of Canada shall be Ottawa.

IV. Legislative Power

17. There shall be One Parliament for Canada, consisting of the Queen, an Upper House styled the Senate, and the House of Commons.

THE SENATE

21. The Senate shall, subject to the Provisions of this Act, consist of Seventy-two Members, who shall be styled Senators.

22. In relation to the Constitution of the Senate, Canada shall be deemed to consist of Three Divisions:

1. Ontario;
2. Quebec;
3. The Maritime Provinces, Nova Scotia and New Brunswick; which Three Divisions shall (subject to the Provisions of this Act) be equally represented in the Senate as follows: Ontario by Twenty-four Senators; Quebec by Twenty-four Senators; and the Maritime Provinces by Twenty-four Senators, Twelve thereof representing Nova Scotia, and Twelve thereof representing New Brunswick....

24. The Governor General shall from time to time, in the Queen's Name, by instrument under the Great Seal of Canada, summon qualified Persons to the Senate; and, subject to the Provisions of this Act, every Person so summoned shall become and be a Member of the Senate and a Senator.

26. If at any time, on the Recommendation of the Governor General, the Queen thinks fit to direct that Three or Six Members be added to the Senate, the Governor General may by Summons to Three or Six qualified Persons (as the Case may be), representing equally the Three Divisions of Canada, add to the Senate accordingly.

29. A Senator shall, subject to the Provisions of this Act, hold his Place in the Senate for Life.

THE HOUSE OF COMMONS

37. The House of Commons shall, subject to the Provisions of this Act, consist of One hundred and eighty-one Members, of whom Eighty-two shall be elected for Ontario, Sixty-five for Quebec, Nineteen for Nova Scotia, and Fifteen for New Brunswick.

50. Every House of Commons shall continue for Five Years from the Day of the Return of the Writs for choosing the House (subject to be sooner dissolved by the Governor General), and no longer.

52. The Number of Members of the House of Commons may be from time to time increased by the Parliament of Canada, provided the proportionate Representation of the Provinces prescribed by this Act is not thereby disturbed.

MONEY VOTES; ROYAL ASSENT

53. Bills for appropriating any Part of the Public Revenue, or for imposing any Tax or Impost, shall originate in the House of Commons.

55. Where a Bill passed by the Houses of Parliament is presented to the Governor General for the Queen's Assent, he shall declare, according to his Discretion, but subject to the Provisions of this Act and to Her Majesty's Instructions, either that he assents thereto in the Queen's Name, or that he withholds the Queen's Assent, or that he reserves the Bill for the Signification of the Queen's Pleasure.

LEGISLATIVE POWER

90. The following Provisions of this Act respecting the Parliament of Canada, namely, — the Provisions relating to Appropriation and Tax Bills, the Recommendation of Money Votes, the Assent to Bills, the Disallowance of Acts, and Signification of Pleasure on Bills reserved, — shall extend and apply to the Legislatures of the several Provinces....

VI. Distribution of Legislative Powers

POWERS OF THE PARLIAMENT

91. It shall be lawful for the Queen, by and with the Advice and Consent of the Senate and House of Commons, to make Laws for the Peace, Order, and good Government of Canada, in relation to all Matters not coming within the Classes of Subjects by this Act assigned exclusively to the Legislatures of the Provinces; and for greater Certainty, but not so as to restrict the Generality of the foregoing Terms of this Section, it is hereby declared that (notwithstanding anything in this Act) the exclusive Legislative Authority of the Parliament of Canada extends to all Matters coming within the Classes of Subjects next hereinafter enumerated; that is to say,—

1. The Public Debt and Property.
2. The Regulation of Trade and Commerce.
3. The raising of Money by any Mode or System of Taxation.
4. The borrowing of Money on the Public Credit.
5. Postal Service.
6. The Census and Statistics.
7. Militia, Military and Naval Service, and Defence.
8. The fixing of and providing for the Salaries and Allowances of Civil and other Officers of the Government of Canada.
9. Beacons, Buoys, Lighthouses, and Sable Island.
10. Navigation and Shipping.
11. Quarantine and the Establishment and Maintenance of Marine Hospitals.
12. Sea Coast and Inland Fisheries.
13. Ferries between a Province and any British or Foreign Country or between Two Provinces.
14. Currency and Coinage.
15. Banking, Incorporation of Banks, and the Issue of Paper Money.
16. Savings Banks.
17. Weights and Measures.
18. Bills of Exchange and Promissory Notes.
19. Interest.
20. Legal Tender.
21. Bankruptcy and Insolvency.
22. Patents of Invention and Discovery.
23. Copyrights.

24. Indians and Lands reserved for the Indians.
25. Naturalization and Aliens.
26. Marriage and Divorce.
27. The Criminal Law, except the Constitution of Courts of Criminal Jurisdiction, but including the Procedure in Criminal Matters.
28. The Establishment, Maintenance, and Management of Penitentiaries.
29. Such Classes of Subjects as are expressly excepted in the Enumeration of the Classes of Subjects by this Act assigned exclusively to the Legislatures of the Provinces.

And any Matter coming within any of the Classes of Subjects enumerated in this Section shall not be deemed to come within the Class of Matters of a local or private Nature comprised in the Enumeration of the Classes of Subjects by this Act assigned exclusively to the Legislatures of the Provinces.

EXCLUSIVE POWERS OF PROVINCIAL LEGISLATURES

92. In each Province the Legislature may exclusively make Laws in relation to Matters coming within the Classes of Subjects next hereinafter enumerated; that is to say,—

1. The Amendment from time to time, notwithstanding anything in this Act, of the Constitution of the Province, except as regards the Office of Lieutenant-Governor.
2. Direct Taxation within the Province in order to the Raising of a Revenue for Provincial Purposes.
3. The borrowing of Money on the sole Credit of the Province.
4. The Establishment and Tenure of Provincial Offices and the Appointment and Payment of Provincial Officers.
5. The Management and Sale of the Public Lands belonging to the Province and of the Timber and Wood thereon.
6. The Establishment, Maintenance, and Management of Public and Reformatory Prisons in and for the Province.
7. The Establishment, Maintenance, and Management of Hospitals, Asylums, Charities, and Eleemosynary Institutions in and for the Province, other than Marine Hospitals.
8. Municipal Institutions in the Province.
9. Shop, Saloon, Tavern, Auctioneer, and other Licences in order to the raising of a Revenue for Provincial, Local, or Municipal Purposes.
10. Local Works and Undertakings other than such as are of the following Classes:—
    (a) Lines of Steam and other Ships, Railways, Canals, Telegraphs, and other Works and Undertakings connecting the Province with any other or others of the Provinces, or extending beyond the Limits of the Province:
    (b) Lines of Steam Ships between the Province and any British or Foreign Country:
    (c) Such Works as, although wholly situate within the Province, are before or after their Execution declared by the Parliament of Canada to be for the general Advantage of Canada or for the Advantage of Two or more of the Provinces.
11. The Incorporation of Companies with Provincial Objects.
12. The Solemnization of Marriage in the Province.
13. Property and Civil Rights in the Province.
14. The Administration of Justice in the Province, including the Constitution, Maintenance, and Organization of Provincial Courts, both of Civil and of Criminal Jurisdiction, and including Procedure in Civil Matters in those Courts.

15. The Imposition of Punishment by Fine, Penalty, or Imprisonment for enforcing any Law of the Province made in relation to any Matter coming within any of the Classes of Subjects enumerated in this Section.

16. Generally all Matters of a merely local or private Nature in the Province.

EDUCATION

93. In and for each Province the Legislature may exclusively make Laws in relation to Education, subject and according to the following Provisions:—

(1) Nothing in any such Law shall prejudicially affect any Right or Privilege with respect to Denominational Schools which any Class of Persons have by Law in the Province at the Union:

(2) All the Powers, Privileges, and Duties at the Union by Law conferred and imposed in Upper Canada on the Separate Schools and School Trustees of the Queen's Roman Catholic Subjects shall be and the same are hereby extended to the Dissentient Schools of the Queen's Protestant and Roman Catholic Subjects in Quebec:

(3) Where in any Province a System of Separate or Dissentient Schools exists by Law at the Union or is thereafter established by the Legislature of the Province, an Appeal shall lie to the Governor General in Council from any Act or Decision of any Provincial Authority affecting any Right or Privilege of the Protestant or Roman Catholic Minority of the Queen's Subjects in relation to Education:

(4) In case any such Provincial Law as from time to time seems to the Governor General in Council requisite for the due Execution of the Provisions of this Section is not made, or in case any Decision of the Governor General in Council on any Appeal under this Section is not duly executed by the proper Provincial Authority in that Behalf, then and in every such Case, and as far only as the Circumstances of each Case require, the Parliament of Canada may make remedial Laws for the due Execution of the Provisions of this Section and of any Decision of the Governor General in Council under this Section.

AGRICULTURE AND IMMIGRATION

95. In each Province the Legislature may make Laws in relation to Agriculture in the Province, and to Immigration into the Province; and it is hereby declared that the Parliament of Canada may from time to time make Laws in relation to Agriculture in all or any of the Provinces, and to Immigration into all or any of the Provinces; and any Law of the Legislature of a Province relative to Agriculture or to Immigration shall have effect in and for the Province as long and as far only as it is not repugnant to any Act of the Parliament of Canada.

VIII. Revenues; Debts; Assets; Taxation

111. Canada shall be liable for the Debts and Liabilities of each Province existing at the Union.

118. The following Sums shall be paid yearly by Canada to the several Provinces for the Support of their Governments and Legislatures:

	Dollars
Ontario	Eighty thousand.
Quebec	Seventy thousand.
Nova Scotia	Sixty thousand.
New Brunswick	Fifty thousand.
	Two hundred and sixty thousand;

and an annual Grant in aid to each Province shall be made, equal to Eighty Cents per Head of the Population as ascertained by the Census of One thousand eight hundred and sixty-one, and in the Case of Nova Scotia and New Brunswick, by each subsequent Decennial Census until the Population of each of those two Provinces amounts to Four hundred thousand Souls, at which Rate such Grant shall thereafter remain. Such Grants shall be in full Settlement of all future Demands on Canada, and shall be paid half-yearly in advance to each Province; but the Government of Canada shall deduct from such Grants, as against any Province, all Sums chargeable as Interest on the Public Debt of that Province in excess of the several Amounts stipulated in this Act.

119. New Brunswick shall receive by half-yearly Payments in advance from Canada for the period of Ten years from the Union an additional Allowance of Sixty-three thousand Dollars per Annum; but as long as the Public Debt of that Province remains under Seven million Dollars, a Deduction equal to the interest of Five per Centum per Annum on such Deficiency shall be made from that Allowance of Sixty-three thousand Dollars.

121. All articles of the Growth, Produce, or Manufacture of any one of the Provinces shall, from and after the Union, be admitted free into each of the other Provinces.

IX. Miscellaneous Provisions

133. Either the English or the French Language may be used by any Person in the Debates of the House of the Parliament of Canada and of the Houses of the Legislature of Quebec; and both those Languages shall be used in the respective Records and Journals of those Houses; and either of those Languages may be used by any Person or in any Pleading or Process in or issuing from any Court of Canada established under this Act, and in or from all or any of the Courts of Quebec.

The Acts of the Parliament of Canada and of the Legislature of Quebec shall be printed and published in both those Languages.

X. Intercolonial Railway

145. Inasmuch as the Provinces of Canada, Nova Scotia, and New Brunswick have joined in a Declaration that the Construction of the Intercolonial Railway is essential to the Consolidation of the Union of British North America, and to the Assent thereto of Nova Scotia and New Brunswick, and have consequently agreed that Provision should be made for its immediate Construction by the Government of Canada: Therefore, in order to give effect to that Agreement, it shall be the Duty of the Government and Parliament of Canada to provide for the Commencement within Six Months after the Union, of a Railway connecting the River St. Lawrence with the City of Halifax in Nova Scotia, and for the Construction thereof without Intermission, and the Completion thereof with all practicable Speed.

XI. Admission of Other Colonies

146. It shall be lawful for the Queen, by and with the Advice of Her Majesty's Most Honourable Privy Council, on Addresses from the Houses of the Parliament of Canada, and from the Houses of the respective Legislatures of the Colonies or Provinces of Newfoundland, Prince Edward Island, and British Columbia, to admit those Colonies or Provinces, or any of them, into the Union, and on Address from the Houses of the Parliament of Canada to admit Rupert's Land and the North-western Territory, or either of them, into the Union, on such Terms and Conditions in each Case as are in the Addresses expressed and as the Queen thinks fit to approve, subject to the Provisions of this Act; and the Provisions of any Order in Council in that Behalf shall have effect as if they had been enacted by the Parliament of the United Kingdom of Great Britain and Ireland....

Index

C

D

E

F

M

N

O

P

Q

T

U

X

Y